New Horizons for Human Factors in Design

McGraw-Hill Series in Industrial Engineering and Management Science

CONSULTING EDITOR

James L. Riggs, *Department of Industrial Engineering, Oregon State University*

New Horizons for Human Factors in Design

R. Dale Huchingson
Professor of Human Factors
Texas A&M University

McGraw-Hill Publishing Company

New York   St. Louis   San Francisco   Auckland   Bogotá   Caracas
Hamburg   Lisbon   London   Madrid   Mexico   Milan
Montreal   New Delhi   Oklahoma City   Paris   San Juan
São Paulo   Singapore   Sydney   Tokyo   Toronto

To Becky, Greg, and Chris
and to my colleagues in the trenches

This book was set in Times Roman by The Total Book (ECU/BD).
The editor was Julienne V. Brown; the production supervisor was Donna Piligra.
Fairfield Graphics was printer and binder.

NEW HORIZONS FOR HUMAN FACTORS IN DESIGN

5 6 7 8 9 0 HAL HAL 9987654320

Library of Congress Cataloging in Publication Data

Huchingson, R   Dale.
    New horizons for human factors in design.

    (McGraw-Hill series in industrial engineering and
management science)
      Includes index.
      1. Human engineering.   2.   Engineering design.
I.   Title.
TA166.H75   620.8′2   80-14356
ISBN 0-07-030815-2

Contents

1

THE HUMAN AS A SYSTEMS RESOURCE

2

AEROSPACE SYSTEMS

3

INDUSTRIAL SYSTEMS AND ENVIRONMENT

4

SURFACE TRANSPORTATION SYSTEMS

5

COMMUNICATIONS AND DATA PROCESSING SYSTEMS

Appendix: Additional Tables

Preface

Human factors is a comparatively new discipline concerned with designing manufactured objects so that people can use them more effectively and creating environments that are better suited for human living and work. The early investigators in human factors were concerned, of necessity, with the design of military products, especially the crew compartment of aircraft.

Over the past two decades there has been a dramatic change in the state of the art of technology. Human factors specialists have kept pace by becoming involved in the design of a variety of new systems. Their success has led to their being invited to contribute design information to still other systems, some new and others old, that previously were designed without adequate support from human factors personnel.

Technology encompasses many products and systems. In addition to aerospace vehicles and electronic products of interest to the military, there are also industrial systems, private ground vehicles, public transportation systems, traffic control devices such as the changeable message sign, a variety of both public and private buildings, consumer products, communication systems, computer terminals and innovative data entry devices, design aids for the handicapped, and so forth.

The world of human factors has a subject matter as broad as the equipment and products with which human beings interact.

In organizing the material for this book, I decided to take a somewhat different approach from that taken in previous textbooks on human factors. I felt that the scope of human factors could be better illustrated by dividing the chapters into areas of application.

This approach involved some risk of redundancy since it is possible that the same human factors information might be applicable to more than one area, thereby requiring cross-referencing. However, this risk was more than offset by the advantage of finding in one chapter all the information pertinent to an application area. Thus, the reader interested in design criteria for a sign that might be installed on a highway would not be obliged to rummage through a chapter on displays, most of which might deal with the design of aircraft instruments. (Traditional textbooks in human factors were modeled around devices such as controls, displays, workspace design, and so forth, and chapters included all information on that device regardless of the systems application.)

Thus, the chapter format of this textbook is based on the recognition that there are design problems unique to each application area. This approach necessitated presenting a somewhat more concise treatment of some application areas in order to devote sufficient space to the various new application areas. However, the final product is more representative of the types of areas to which human factors specialists are contributing in the 1980s. Older literature was carefully screened for relevance while new literature from a variety of journals and documents has been reviewed and included.

No introductory text in human factors can be expected to serve as a reference design guide in the various application areas simply because there are length limitations. The reader interested in a more comprehensive treatment will be referred to appropriate source documents. *New Horizons For Human Factors in Design* is recommended as the principal text in undergraduate or graduate level introductory courses.

A general-purpose text in human factors engineering is doomed to the error of omission. Researchers will comment: "Why didn't Huchingson say anything about my area of research endeavor?" To the slighted, the author can only plead ignorance and page limitations, hopefully correcting the injustice in the revision of the text.

This book is dedicated to the many researchers who are and were responsible for expanding the horizons of human factors and whose names are referenced throughout the text. I assume responsibility for any possible misinterpretation of their data. Appreciation is also extended to the many publishers who granted permission to reproduce or to adapt tables and figures.

I would like to express my appreciation to many colleagues and students who reviewed portions of the manuscript, to Bruce Pace for administrative assistance, and to Mrs. Carolyn Vajdak, Mrs. Linda Hatcher, and Miss Denise Clugey for typing the manuscript.

R. Dale Huchingson

List of Abbreviations

a,g	unit of acceleration in vibration
AFSC-DH	Air Force Systems Command Design Handbook (USA)
A I	articulation index in speech intelligibility
b	bit, binary digit
°C	temperature in degrees centigrade
cd	candela
C/D	control/display
c.g.	center of gravity
cm	centimeter
CMS	changeable message sign
cp	candle power
CRT	cathode ray tube (video)
dB	decibel
dBA	decibel on the A scale
DGR	discomfort glare rating
DVA	dynamic visual acuity
EL	electroluminescent
EMG	electromyographic
ET	effective temperature scale
EVA	extra-vehicular activity in space

°F	temperature in degrees Fahrenheit
fc	footcandle
fL	foot lambert
ft	foot
G	unit of acceleration
GL	glance legibility
H	unit of information
h	hour
HUD	head-up display
hz	hertz
in	inch
JND	just-noticeable difference
K	gain
kcal	kilocalorie
km	kilometer
L	lambert
lb	pound
LCD	liquid crystal display
LED	light emitting diode
lm	lumen
LOS	line of sight
lx	lux
m	meter
mi	mile
MIL-STD	military standard (USA)
min	minute
mL	millilambert
ms	millisecond
MT	movement time
MTFA	modulation transfer function area
MTM	methods time measurement
N	noise rating value
NC	noise criteria
nm	nanometer (millimicron)
NRC	noise reduction coefficients
o/s	degree per second (angular velocity)
oz	ounce
p	page
PB	pushbutton
PPR	persons per room
rad	radians
RH	relative humidity
RMS	root-mean-square
RT	reaction time
s, sec	second

SFPP	square feet per person
SIL	speech interference level
S/N	signal-to-noise ratio
SPL	sound pressure level
SRL	seat reference level
SRP	seat reference point
TL	transmission loss
USAF	United States Air Force
VL	visibility level
x, y, z	coordinates for direction (subscript)
WBGT	wet-bulb globe temperature
yr	year

Part One

The Human as a Systems Resource

Chapter 1

Introduction

While flying a new jet aircraft at low altitude, a young pilot pulled his throttle lever back and, in so doing, inadvertently pushed it slightly outboard. The lever moves in a slot and there was a detent, or jut, in the slot that was supposed to prevent moving the lever to full reverse except when the pilot wanted to cut off the engine. But this time the lever did go all the way back; the engine flamed out, and, due to the low altitude, there was not time to relight the engine.

The accident report might well have recorded the fatal crash as simply due to pilot error. The pilot was supposed to have been trained to be cautious and attentive to proper procedure. He should have known better. There was one fallacy in this logic. During a period of less than 2 weeks, there were two other instances of low-altitude flameouts and fatal crashes in the same aircraft model, which had only recently been accepted by the military service!

When the facts became known, the aircraft was grounded until the detents on the throttle slots were changed on every aircraft so that a more positive outboard force had to be applied before the throttle lever would go "around the horn." No further accidents were reported after the changes had been made.

A human error that results from a design deficiency is sometimes called a design-related error or, more emphatically, a design-induced error. Many pilots prefer to call the design a built-in booby trap. There are many examples of pilot errors that could be charged to questionable design—confusion of two identical controls located side by side, but controlling different functions; confusion due to unstandardized control locations between aircraft models; accidently bumping a control while reaching for another control; misreading a flight instrument that has three pointers.

The Services have long been interested in having their pilots anonymously report these types of near-accident errors they have made while flying. As useful as this approach may be in screening instances of hazardous or confusing designs, one might ask why many of these problems could not be anticipated in advance while the aircraft is being designed. The answer is that they could be anticipated and, in a majority of instances, have been anticipated through the concerted efforts of pilots, safety engineers, and human factors engineers.

The subject of this textbook is the comparatively new and important technology known as "human factors" or "ergonomics." Born in the battlefields during World War II, today it has diversified its areas of application to many commercial and nonmilitary products. But human factors is not limited to the design of products and large systems. It recognizes that the industrial worker requires a more efficient and safer working environment designed to reduce strains and localized muscle fatigue. Human factors is continuously seeking new horizons as modern technology changes and enlightened management recognizes the vital role of human factors in the design of new systems.

WHAT IS HUMAN FACTORS?

The expression "human factors" appears in works of both fiction and nonfiction, often implying little more than the human element or aspect of a particular situation. The indiscriminate use of the words human factors has led to some confusion even among professionals as to exactly what is implied. Therefore, it may be helpful, even at the risk of semantic arguments, to attempt to clarify what human factors is and to distinguish this endeavor from other related disciplines.

The terms "human factors," "human factors engineering," "human engineering" and "ergonomics" have appeared interchangeably in the literature. The United States Air Force Systems Command (AFSC) is one of the major organizations responsible for seeing that new systems are planned to take advantage of known human capabilities. In the introduction to one of their handbooks, AFSC distinguishes the terms:

> As used in this textbook the term "human engineering" is not synonymous with human factors. The term "human factors" is more comprehensive, covering all biomedical and psychosocial considerations applying to man in the system. It includes not only human engineering, but also life support, personnel selection and training, training equipment, job performance aids, and performance measurement and evaluation. [1]*

---

*The numbers in brackets refer to references that are listed at the end of each chapter.

When the focus is on this broader interpretation, it is common to speak of the development of a human factors subsystem or a personnel subsystem. In this broad sense, human factors is concerned with virtually every consideration of the human in the system, for example, reasons for being in the system; functions and tasks, the design of jobs for various personnel, training and evaluation.

In this broad focus, human engineering (or human factors engineering) is only one of several endeavors, the one concerned with the design and layout of equipment, facilities, and environment. A very simple definition of human engineering is "a discipline concerned with designing man-made objects (equipment) so that people can use them effectively and safely and creating environments suitable for human living and work."

If equipment is poorly designed or arranged so that it requires capabilities the human does not have, then the human either cannot perform required tasks on schedule or will make errors in attempting to do so. Errors may degrade the operation of the system and may compromise users' safety and even the success of the mission itself.

The environments referred to in the definition may be extreme or unusual environments required by the particular mission of the system, such as high atmosphere, loud noises, high accelerations, or unfavorable lighting. If the individual is to be subjected to such stresses it is important to insure that the environment does not exceed the human's minimum bodily needs and performance requirements. The particular environment could be one of high altitude or outer space, underwater, the roadway of a surface vehicle, or a factory or industrial plant.

The people referred to in the definition are typically those who operate, maintain, or service the system. Human engineering is concerned with human-machine interface. The people are those who will interact with the system's design, for example, pilots of aircraft, factory workers, drivers of automobiles, and users of computers or household appliances. The term "human-machine" is used in this text to avoid specific sexual reference. The "user," "operator," or "person" has been employed in most instances.

Human engineering has its roots in the behavioral and life sciences. Engineering psychologists have been one of the major contributors to data on human capabilities and limitations as they relate to equipment and systems design. This data base is applied to planning, designing, and testing the human-machine systems to obtain improved reliability, efficiency, and safety.

Human engineering, then, had its origins in the design of human-machine equipment such as displays and controls used in aircraft and other military products. However, there are other manufactured objects about which one could argue as to whether or not they were equipment. Is a technical publication equipment? Is a static road sign equipment? Equipment refers to the things we furnish a user. They need not have mechanical or electronic components.

Human engineering also has its origins in disciplines concerned with design of the workplace. Ergonomists, anthropologists, and biomechanic specialists have focused on the human as a physical being occupying space, constrained in movement and strength, and subject to muscle fatigue and physiological stresses imposed by the workplace design and the ambient environment.

Finally, a question of jurisdiction must be raised. No single professional group is responsible for research in human engineering or for the application of human engineering to the design of systems. Psychologists, physiologists, anthropologists, physicians, and various engineering professions are among the contributors. Recently, there has been a movement to require that only certified professional engineers be allowed to use a job title that includes the word "engineer." Thus, those who are not professional engineers have tended to use the title "human factors specialist," and to refer to human factors in design of a particular system. This practice will be followed in this book to avoid any possible connotation that only professional engineers were contributors to the data.

SCOPE AND OBJECTIVES OF HUMAN FACTORS

Within the broad scope of human factors, human engineering is only one of several so-called milestones in the development of a personnel subsystem. In Chapter 2, the steps in planning the development of such a subsystem are discussed in various phases or stages of systems design. The major point here is that a systems approach involves planning from the conception of a particular system (such as an aircraft system), the important functions which will be under human control. The discipline of human factors would be remiss if it waited until others had made the important decisions and then entered the design loop to answer only detailed questions regarding design of particular displays, controls, and workplace environment.

What are some of these important questions that must be decided upon from the beginning [Gustafson and Rockway, 6]?

1   Do we *need* the human at all? Can the human, as a systems component, contribute something to the functioning of the system that is going to be designed and built?

2   If needed, what *functions* should the human perform as the primary controller; which functions should be automated; which functions should one only monitor and serve as a backup element to override automatic control in the event this system should fail?

3   Accomplishment of each human function requires a series of tasks. How should these tasks be *organized into jobs* so that the task demands are not too great for any single operator? Who does what and how?

4   What human-machine equipment is required? How should it be *designed* and *arranged* to facilitate performance?

5   How can the operator be best *protected* from the ambient environment during the operational mission? What is required to sustain the operator in terms of air pressure and oxygen, food and water, and other life-support provisions.

6   What *kind* of person is needed for the various jobs? The tasks defined earlier must be broken down into the *skills* and *knowledge* required to effectively perform each task.

7 After selection of personnel, the practical problem remains: How can we best *teach* the system user? Where and how should this teaching be accomplished? Again, the task descriptions may serve as the groundwork for a training syllabus. But the user will need also special training equipment, job aids, technical manuals, and checklists.

8 Finally, throughout the development of a personnel subsystem, it is important to know *how valid* were the decisions that were made to each of the above questions. The questions imply a *test program* to evaluate the system under development.

Engineering is said to be an iterative process. Seldom can an exact answer be given the first time a question is asked, hence, these questions are posed again and again as the system reaches various stages of development.

The objectives of an effective human factors program may be summarized as follows: (1) improved human performance as shown by increased speed, accuracy, and safety, and less energy expenditure and fatigue; (2) less training and reduced training costs; (3) improved use of manpower through minimizing the need for special skills and aptitudes; (4) reduced loss of time and equipment as accidents due to human errors are minimized; and (5) improved comfort and acceptance by the user/operator. Human factors is concerned with improving the productivity of the operator by taking into account human characteristics in designing systems.

Because the responsibilities of human factors, in addition to equipment design, are so immense, it becomes necessary to have specialists on the human factors team. No one person is likely to have the time to provide all the answers in the development of a major system. In the next section, we shall examine the types of skills required by the human factors team members.

WHO ARE THE HUMAN FACTORS SPECIALISTS?

Human factors is said to be multidisciplinary. Education in no single academic specialty such as psychology, industrial engineering, or work physiology is likely to prepare the practitioner for the range of problems that will be encountered. Traditionally, therefore, human factors teams located in engineering organizations of contractors were comprised of specialists from several academic disciplines.

For example, experimental psychologists were often assigned responsibility for applied research in the human performance area; personnel psychologists and industrial engineers became involved in developing the task and job analysis portions of the personnel subsystem; work physiologists or flight surgeons were responsible for life support and medical aspects of protection and sustenance; physical anthropologists were responsible for studies of workspace involving body dimensions, reach profiles, and dynamic movement; ergonomists were responsible for industrial workplace design; learning psychologists and educators were involved in training systems.

In addition, the human factors team often had several members who were users or operators of the particular system (for example, jet pilots or ground control operators). Often senior drafters and industrial designers were assigned to the group to develop conceptual designs and mockups of the workplace. When applicable, specialists in personal protective equipment, escape systems, and display technology were also assigned to human factors groups in engineering organizations.

The trend in recent years has been to educate and train human factors specialists who are knowledgeable in several of the areas of responsibility. Smaller industries may be able to afford only a generalist knowledgeable in the classical industrial engineering sciences, but with special training in human factors. Today, several universities have human factors graduate programs that are typically located in the departments of industrial engineering or psychology [Pearson, 10].

Research and Implementation Specialists

Human factors specialists may be classified into two broad categories: those primarily concerned with research to generate human factors data (such as the data reported in this text) and those concerned with the implementation of human factors data into systems and workplace design.

The research specialists may work in government laboratories. Some examples are the U.S. Air Force (USAF) Aerospace Medical Research Laboratories, the U.S. Army Human Engineering Laboratories, the U.S. Naval Personnel Research and Development Center; or the NASA Ames Research Center. Each branch of the service has many research centers. Much of the research is contracted competitively to other organizations—private consultants, universities, and industrial human factors organizations. Many industrial organizations conduct their own company-sponsored research and development. The Federal Highway Administration and the National Highway Traffic Safety divisions of the Department of Transportation contract much of their research to other organizations.

The implementation specialists are those working primarily in industry. A military document, MIL-H-46855, entitled "Human Engineering Requirements for Military Systems, Equipment, and Facilities," [9] specifies requirements and procedures for documenting the human factors effort on any military system that has been awarded to a contractor to design. There are other documents, among them MIL-STD-1472 and AFSC DH-1-3, that provide detailed design information for military equipment design. The implementation specialists work directly with the designers who are drafting drawings involving the human-machine interfaces. They provide human capability and design information and often develop design standards that will be followed in the design of human factors interfaces.

Many human factors specialists work as consultants or in private industries that are not bound by government design requirements except in regard to safety. Examples are the automotive industry, computer and communications systems, and consumer products. Other specialists work in industrial plants and are concerned with improving the workplace design.

The name of the organization may be human factors, but it may also be given other names (personnel subsystem, life sciences, bioastronautics, biotechnology) or it may be a group within another department (systems effectiveness, aerospace medicine, systems reliability, maintainability, or safety). In Europe and in certain engineering societies the term "ergonomics" is employed for human factors.

BRIEF HISTORY OF HUMAN FACTORS

The current formalized interest in human factors stems from technological advances in the development of elaborate military, space, and electronic systems. By the early 1940s, these systems had become so complex that it became mandatory that human factors be taken into account. By 1960 the military had assigned responsibility for human factors in design, analysis, and evaluation to the manufacturer awarded the contract to design and develop the new system. As a result, human factors groups were founded in the engineering departments of most government contractors.

To provide some perspective for the current position of human factors in the design of equipment, let's go back to the beginning and briefly trace the origins of human factors.

Origin of Human Factors Thinking

In one sense, human factors in design is an outlook toward life in which one is looking for better ways of designing equipment and environment for human use. Even without specialized training in human factors, a person may be aware of problems he or she has personally encountered in the use of tools, controls, displays, or workspace. He notices that he has difficulty in locating a control on his television set; she notices that her first response in activating a control is in the wrong direction; he notices that in using a torquing tool he tires readily; she notices that her workspace is laid out in a manner that results in wasted motion or eye scanning.

Using oneself as a sample of one, a person is aware of problems encountered and may wonder if the problem is unique to himself or herself or if perhaps others are having the same types of problems.

The distinguishing characteristics of human factors thinking is that the person first determines that other people are making the same mistakes (suggesting that poor design rather than training may be the issue) and, second, he or she looks for alternate ways of designing the equipment. Design approaches are then tested to determine which is the better design solution.

The prehistoric man who first employed an implement (a club, stick, or stone) in his protection or service was, in this sense, the founder of human factors thinking. The principle of the lever was basic to developing the club, oar, ax, and hoe. Prehistoric man eventually discovered that the size and shapes of handles increased his skill. The invention of the bow and arrow extended his range of hunting and defense and helped compensate for his inferior speed in comparison with many animals.

Without tracing the history of technological changes in the development of tools and equipment, we are aware that there has been a progressive trend toward adapting equipment as well as environments to human use [McCormick, 8]. Illustrations from our century are modifications in the traditional design of the automobile. There are obvious improvements in comfort and environmental control, reduction in noise and vibration, better handling and ignition mechanisms, to mention only a few. The improvements in design are evident in all types of equipment—aircraft, tools and machinery, design and layout of buildings and homes, and so forth.

Origin of the Specialty

As early as 1919, F. B. Gilbreth, an industrial engineer, published research in applied motion study. He believed that work methods provide the basis for differences in skill and effectiveness at various stages of training. These differences in work methods could be analyzed by slow-motion photography to find errors and to teach new workers the superior methods of the skilled worker [Barnes, 2].

Industrial engineers recognized that not only methods, but also equipment, facility, and tool design influenced the workers' efficiency, fatigue, and occupational diseases.

Early industrial psychologists such as Edward K. Strong, Jr., were interested in testing vocational interests; Hugo Munsterberg researched industrial accidents. The Hawthorne studies in the late twenties and early thirties originally focused on the effects of environment on worker output but, most significantly, led to a discovery of the importance of worker attitude and morale on output [Gilmer, 5]. Industrial hygienists and safety engineers identified hazardous working environments and developed design approaches for preventing inadvertent injury of the worker.

The history of industrial engineering, safety engineering, and industrial psychology is beyond the scope of human factors. Suffice it to note that these disciplines shared an interest in human performance and safety at the workplace, causes of errors and inefficiency, and methods of improving performance and reducing risks of injury.

Traditionally, engineers were responsible for design of new systems and equipment; psychologists were responsible for selection and training of men to use the equipment. However, during World War II, equipment (such as that in aircraft cockpits) seemed to become so complex that it exceeded the capabilities of men to operate it. Experimental psychologists were enlisted to collaborate with engineers in designing various military equipment—aircraft cockpits, radar consoles, binoculars, gunsight reticles and controls, combat information centers, and synthetic training devices [Fitts, 4].

The name "engineering psychology" was adopted by many working in this area of equipment-design research. Originally these researchers were interested almost exclusively in determining how best to display information to the senses, how to utilize human motor output, and how to secure good dynamic characteristics in controller systems. The results of their research on detailed design characteristics have been published in military specifications and design guides. Much of the data is still in use today.

In the USAF, the technology of human factors in equipment design reported to the Air Materiel Command. Meanwhile, the organizations responsible for personnel selection and training were located in a research center in a different command. When the USAF formalized the weapon system concept in the early 1950s, the Air Research and Development Command was formed and personnel selection, training, and equipment design were integrated at the research level.

The major influence of the personnel and training research specialists was to insist on the responsibility of weapon systems contractors in providing information about the tasks and functions of both operators and maintenance crews. This meant that contractors had to acquire personnel to prepare documents that would predict the crew requirements during the hardware design phase (tasks, skills, training, and training equipment). The human-machine systems concept was adopted by the various services as a requirement for contractors in MIL-H-46855 [9].

No discussion of the origins of human factors would be complete without mention of the influence of anthropometrists and flight surgeons. In 1954 Hertzberg and colleagues reported body dimension data on a large sample of USAF personnel [7]. This data, in conjunction with other smaller samples, provided a data base that was highly significant in defining bodily requirements for workspace, consoles, clothing, and personal equipment.

Paralleling the human factors movement was the movement in aerospace medicine to establish the effects of unusual environments on human tolerances, performance, and comfort. Elaborate moving-base simulators and centrifuges were employed in research. Impact research devices also explored the effects of deceleration. An outgrowth of aerospace research was development of antigravity suits (anti-g), partial-pressure suits, pressurized compartments, and escape devices. Safety centers were also established to monitor aircraft accidents and their causes. Aeromedical, human factors, and personal equipment functions were integrated in these centers. The manned space programs of the 1960s enlisted the services of hundreds of human factors specialists in industry and government.

Recent Applications of Human Factors

Human factors as a specialty originated in the military and manned space programs of the 1950s and 1960s, primarily because there was both a need and a requirement for this type of service. During the 1970s, a reduction in effort along these product lines was accompanied by an increase in effort along other product lines. The Federal Highway Administration was interested in driver communications and updating its *Manual on Uniform Traffic Control Devices* to include design recommendations based upon human factors research [Dudek, Huchingson, et al., 3]. Our legal system became cognizant that manufacturers of consumer products that were designed without consideration to human factors could be liable for accidents resulting from the design or instructions for use. Workers' claims of job-related injuries and disabilities focused attention on design of the workplace and the ambient environment.

Manufacturers of private vehicles, data processing, and communication devices became interested in improving the design of the human-machine interfaces. Organizations that lacked the resources to hire a full-time human factors specialist began to train their designers, to provide them with design guides containing human factors information, and to hire consultants to monitor their efforts. High-speed surface transportation systems were designed with guidelines provided by human factors specialists.

As we enter the 1980s, the data base of human factors information has difficulty keeping pace with our expanding technology. Specialists are in demand far in excess of the supply by academic institutions. The new horizons for human factors appear to be limited only by the systems developed in our modern technology and an enlightened management's providing the resources to improve their systems design. Human factors in design has now come of age.

QUESTIONS AND PROBLEMS

1   Define human engineering.
2   What are five topics with which human factors in its broader sense is concerned? These are milestones in personnel subsystem development.
3   What are three indicators of a successful human factors program?
4   Distinguish the two major types of human factors specialists.
5   What characterizes human factors thinking relative to design?
6   List five engineering or scientific groups that have contributed heavily to human factors data.
7   Other than military systems, list three product areas that have attracted human factors research in recent years.
8   Although there has been a trend toward adapting equipment to human usage, this is not always true (the better design being compromised for styling or economy). Give an example of what you feel is a step backwards in product design.

REFERENCES

1   Air Force Systems Command Design Handbook 1–3, *Human Factors Engineering*, 3d ed., Jan. 1, 1977, chap. 2.
2   Barnes, R. M.: *Motion and Time Study*, 6th ed., John Wiley, New York, 1968.
3   Dudek, C. L., R. D. Huchingson, et al.: *Human factors requirements for real-time motorist information displays*, FHWA–RD–78–5, September 1978.
4   Fitts, Paul M.: Engineering psychology and equipment design, in S. S. Stevens (ed.), *Handbook of Experimental Psychology*, Wiley, New York, 1951, chap. 35.
5   Gilmer, B. von Haller: *Industrial and Organizational Psychology*, McGraw-Hill, New York, 1971.
6   Gustafson, C. E. and M. R. Rockway: "The Air Force Personnel Subsystem

Concept," presented to Southwestern Psychological Association, Fort Worth, Texas, April 6, 1962.

7 Hertzberg, H. T. E., et al.: *Anthropometry of flying personnel—1950,* WADC-Technical Report 53–321, September 1954.

8 McCormick, E. J.: *Human Factors in Engineering and Design,* 4th ed., McGraw-Hill, New York, 1976.

9 Military specification, *Human engineering requirements for military systems, equipment, and facilities* (MIL-H-46855), May 2, 1972.

10 Pearson, R. G. (ed.): *International directory of educational programs in ergonomics/human factors,* sponsored by the International Ergonomics and Human Factors Society, August 1979.

Chapter 2

Development of
Human-Machine Systems

Human factors encompasses a number of activities other than human engineering in equipment design. In this chapter the concept of a human-machine system will be examined and the procedures for acquiring the necessary information about human activities in a human-machine system will be discussed.

WHAT IS A SYSTEM?

Prior to defining a human-machine system, we should consider what is meant by a system in its more general sense. Hall and Fagen [6] define a system as a "set of objects together with relationships between the objects and between their attributes." The objects are components of the system whether they be planets, arteries, or missiles. Systems occur within an environment and changes in the environment affect the system and its attributes. What are some of the attributes of a system?

Systems are hierarchical in nature. Table 2-1 illustrates the hierarchical nature of equipment and human activities. A system may be divided into subsystems, the subsystems divided into modules, and the modules divided into components and smaller elements. Similarly, human activities in a system may be divided into job operations, jobs (positions), duties, tasks, subtasks, and behavioral elements.

Table 2-1 Basic Terms in Systems Hierarchy

Subsystem

A module, or combination of modules plus components contributing to modular functions, all interconnected and performing a specific function.
Ex: Guidance and control subsystem

Module (sub-subsystem)

Combination of components in one package or arranged so they are common to one mounting and providing a complete function.
Ex: Guidance and control computer

Component

Combination of units or parts providing a self-contained capability necessary for operation of a module, subsystem, or system.
Ex: DC power supply, digital display readout

Unit

Combination of parts making up a component or a functional potential essential to component operation.
Ex: Chip

Part

Smallest practical subdivision of equipment of a system. The piece has inherent functional capability but cannot function without other parts or forces.
Ex: Resistor, diode, transistor

Job operation

Combination of duties and tasks essential to accomplish a system function. May involve one or more positions or career specialties.

Position (job)

Grouping of duties and responsibilities constituting the principal work assignments of one person (operator, maintainer, controller, etc.).

Duty

Set of operationally related tasks within a given position. Job descriptions are usually stated in terms of a set of duties.

Task

A composite of related activities performed by an individual, directed toward accomplishing a specific amount of work within a work context.

Subtask

Actions fulfilling a limited purpose within a task.
Ex: Making a series of related machine adjustments

Task element

The smallest logical definable set of perceptions, decisions, and responses required to complete a task or subtask.
Ex: Identify a specific signal or a specific display, decide on a single action, actuate a specific control, or note a feedback signal.

Source: DeGreene [3] and AFSC DH 1-3 [7].

Systems are assumed to exist for a purpose. In nature, most scientists subscribe to the viewpoint that systems serve a useful function, are goal-directed, and adapt themselves to the environment. Systems also change over time—they grow and differentiate, but later degenerate and decay. Manufactured systems become obsolete.

Real-world systems interact with their environment by exchanging information, energy, and materials with the environment. System scientists are interested in the study of transfer functions whereby various inputs are transferred into outputs. An important characteristic of closed-loop systems is that they regulate and control themselves to some degree by sampling their own outputs and feeding the information back as inputs. The thermostat is an example of a system that is self-regulatory. The feedback may either inhibit or enhance action of the system. There is also some degree of predetermined control built into the functioning of a system by its structure. The genes of the human body and the computer program in certain systems illustrate the predetermined control of a certain sequence of functional changes.

Although systems may function somewhat independently, they are still dependent upon other systems. For example, the human heart cannot exist for long outside the body. It is the interrelatedness of activities and properties of systems that has attracted systems scientists to look for a common systems theory for communicating across academic disciplines. Human factors has adopted much of this language in describing the role of the human in various systems.

WHAT IS A HUMAN-MACHINE SYSTEM?

A human-machine system is a particular type of system that is governed by the same characteristics described earlier for systems in general. It is defined as an operating combination of one or more persons with one or more equipment components; they interact to bring about some desired output from given inputs. And, of course, they interact within the constraints of a particular environment.

Figure 2-1 illustrates three types of human-machine systems—the manual, the mechanical (or semiautomatic), and the automatic. An example of a manual system would be a person operating a simple hand tool such as a hoe. The hoe extends the human's capability, but the human provides both the power and the control. Note that information is fed back visually which permits altering movements appropriately.

Following the industrial revolution, complex machinery came into being. Instead of operators' receiving environmental information directly through their senses, devices were developed to sense changes in the environment or the machinery. For example, in an automobile, an instrument or display panel showed the car's speed and indicated the amount of gas in the tank. Instead of controlling the power source directly, the operator was given a number of control devices for controlling machine output. Unlike the person with the hoe, the machine provided the power to make the system move. The operator then

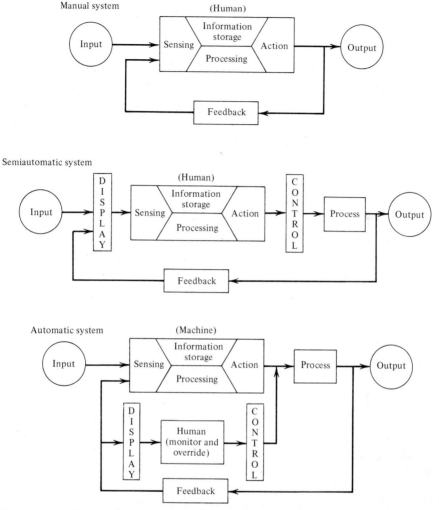

Figure 2-1 Schematic illustration of manual, semiautomatic, and automatic types of human-machine systems. *(Adaptation of McCormick, 3d ed., 1970.)*

exercised control by sensing inputs through displays (as well as by visual contact with the outside world through the automobile windows) and by output devices such as the steering wheel, brake, and accelerator. Systems where the machine provides the power and the human provides control are semiautomatic systems.

With automatic systems, the machine does both the sensing and the controlling as the normal operating procedure. The operator functions as a monitor entering the control loop to override the automatic system and enter new data when required. For example, pilots set and later unset their autopilots. At night we may change the thermostat setting in our homes.

The usefulness of a human has been demonstrated in many so-called automatic systems. The experiences of the United States space program during emergencies has provided a strong argument for continuing to have the human on board as a backup capability and for maintenance and repair. In Chapter 3, human capabilities are discussed and compared with machines. Such comparisons are used in making a decision on function assignments.

As systems grew larger and more complex, it became common practice to speak of both the operator and the machine as a part of some larger system. Instead of building a telephone, we speak of building a "communications system." Instead of building an aircraft, we speak of building an "interceptor system." This is more than a question of semantics. The system now refers not only to the primary machine, but also to the personnel who will use it. It refers also to operating and maintenance procedures, logistics, support facilities, communications, electronics, and management organizational structure. It refers to everything required for a system to perform its mission.

WHAT IS A SYSTEMS APPROACH?

In designing a new system, many factors must be considered in addition to the hardware item itself. The systems approach takes into consideration where the system will be used, how and by whom it will be used, and what it must accomplish given certain limitations.

A systems approach involves a *process of planning ahead* to anticipate problems. Prior to systems thinking, equipment was designed and built, and only then was consideration given to the tasks, skills, potential errors, and training of the operator. With military weapon systems, the contractor today must provide the support capability at the same time the first machine rolls off the assembly line. Thus, from the initial conception of a system, the contractor must begin planning for logistics, personnel requirements, job descriptions, training, and evaluation.

Systems Management

Systems design may involve very complex systems, such as air defense or sociotechnical systems. Sociotechnical systems may deal with the impact of technological change on society. Examples are a transportation system for a state, crime and delinquency, government information handling, energy conservation, and public health care. For complex systems there are high expenditures, numerous contractors, and numerous technical efforts that must be brought together and managed in some orderly manner. A definition of systems management, given by DeGreene [3], is as follows:

> Systems management is a time-phased, monitorial, evaluative, and integrative activity involving the recognition of technical (for example, analytic) criteria; the assignment of organizational and contractual responsibilities; the definition of milestones; the assignment of required documentation, hierarchies of contributing

organizations, and feedback responses to initial documentation. In parallel with, and utilizing, system analysis and engineering, it proceeds from the general to the specific, from the hypothetical to the real, and from the conceptual through research and development and production, to the operational. The systems concepts of interface, evolution, and integration are of paramount importance.

Consequences of Poor Planning

So we see that management of systems under design and development involves much planning, organizing, and coordinating the combined efforts of contractors and technical efforts to accomplish system program objectives. The penalties for not doing this may be underestimating costs, inefficient use of human resources, duplicated efforts, insufficient definition of requirements, unrealistic scheduling leading to slippages and late delivery of the end items. Most important is a failure to anticipate potential design problems, resulting in increased probability of accidents.

There is some indication that the Three Mile Island nuclear power plant incident involved lack of sufficient attention to human factors interfaces. A report of the Nuclear Regulatory Commission soon after the incident stated:

> Human factors engineering has not been sufficiently emphasized in the design and layout of the control rooms. The location of instruments and controls in many power plants often increases the likelihood of operator error or, at least, impedes the operator in efficiently carrying out the normal, abnormal, and emergency actions required of him [*The Houston Post,* 18].

Probably the most severe consequence of inadequate systems planning—short of a holocaust—is the weakening of the credibility of systems operation relative to community safety.

There are various ways in which we may study systems and their attributes. One of the major methods is analysis of the system into its constituent parts. Other methods involve: (1) developing flow charts depicting information transmission and interactions; and (2) modeling and simulating the operation of a system.

Characteristics of a Systems Approach

The systems approach, then, implies that analyses will be conducted to ensure that systems requirements are met in a logical and functional order according to a predetermined work plan. In addition to requirements, factors that limit the performance of the system must be identified. These so-called constraints could be limitation in hardware, personnel, information availability, scheduling, environment, and so forth. Human factors must ensure that the system makes the most effective and safe usage of the human operator in assignment of functions to him or her.

From earliest thinking, systems performance criteria need to be developed.

These criteria are like a master answer sheet for a test; they provide a standard for gauging the effectiveness of the system and will be used in both design and testing.

The systems approach is a functional approach. Each system, subsystem, and equipment item that is incorporated in the system design must be tailored to specific needs. One should not merely pattern a new system after an existing system if the requirements are different. Those subsystems and equipments that are necessary for the particular mission of the new system will be added; those in a previous model that are not essential must be deleted. Overall, the system must provide as much capability as required by the sponsoring organization, but no more than this capability. Drawing an analogy, if a compact car is ordered, do not design a full-sized limousine!

Although human factors is one of the important systems goals in developing a system, it is not the only goal. Oftentimes the ideal human factors system must be compromised against constraints of cost, delivery schedule, and so forth.

The systems approach involves a new way of looking at all the subsystems of a system. It is inappropriate to think only in terms of "fitting the person to the machine" (through training or selection) or "fitting the machine to the person" (through ideal human engineering). Rather, the best combination of both approaches is called for to meet systems goals within the practical constraints.

STEPS IN DEVELOPING A HUMAN-MACHINE SYSTEM

It was noted in Chapter 1 that a military specification abbreviated as MIL-H-46855 defines human engineering requirements on military systems. The emphasis in the document is more on general requirements than on procedures. The exact procedures, in terms of specific types and levels of analysis, are only partially defined. The Systems Project Office (contract manager) leaves the contractors some freedom for innovation in how they comply with the requirements.

Of course, civilian systems are not bound by this specific document, but the same systems analysis procedures could and should be applied to any system being designed.

Areas of Systems Development

The contractors' human factors effort must participate in three major areas of systems development:

1   Systems analysis to identify and define systems functions and to allocate these to the human, equipment, or human-equipment combinations
2   Design and development of equipment, procedures, work environments, and facilities used by the human in performing functions
3   Test and evaluation of equipment, procedures, work environment, and facilities to verify that human performance and life-support requirements are compatible with overall system requirements

In this section, the major steps in conducting systems analysis and test evaluation will be discussed. In the subsequent section, some procedures for incorporating design recommendations into systems will be given.

Documenting the Human Factors Effort

The human factors specialists on military systems are required to submit considerable documentation. Even before being awarded a contract, in the contractor's proposal there must be a "human engineering plan," which describes exactly how human factors specialists will participate in the program, the specific personnel available, and a schedule of beginning and end dates for accomplishing the activities. After award of the contract, there will be a conference between the company and military personnel, followed by a revised and more detailed human engineering plan. Any major deviations from this "blueprint" of human engineering effort must be reported. Throughout the design effort, periodic progress reports are required, which include such information as the results of trade-off studies and research studies. Memos and other documents issued by the human engineering effort are kept in a documentation file that may be inspected by the project officer.

Systems Analysis Overview

Systems analysis is the basic tool for systematically defining the equipment, personnel, facilities, and procedural data required to meet systems objectives. The analyses are repeatedly updated as new information comes in. For example, if a crew-loading analysis should determine that one crew member is over-worked, certain functions might be reassigned to another crew member. In general, these analyses are required in allocating systems functions to the human and equipment; in identifying equipment used by the human; in analyzing equipment-oriented tasks; and in preparing performance measures for testing.

Life-Cycle Phases Systems analysis activities continue throughout the development of a system. In the USAF, the so-called life cycle of a system is divided into four phases: (1) conceptual phase, (2) definition phase, (3) acquisition phase, and (4) operational phase. Other writers on systems analysis prefer to use different terms such as: (1) predesign or initiation phase, (2) preliminary design phase, (3) detailed design, production, and test phase, and (4) design verification in the field.

Activities in Each Phase The major activity of the conceptual or predesign phase is the development of a systems concept (a detailed description of a system) that will satisfy the mission requirements. The concept is one that is indicated by analyses to be suitable, feasible, and acceptable both in terms of performance and costs.

In the definition phase, the systems concept is defined in greater detail. This concept includes specification of personnel, equipment, facilities, costs, sched-ules, and other activities. The acquisition phase is the phase in which the final detail design is frozen and production begins. In-plant testing of subsystems and preliminary field testing is done during this phase.

Finally, during the operational phase, testing of the entire system under near-operational conditions is conducted, although product improvements and retrofitting are sometimes required even after the system is fully operational. Eventually all systems become obsolescent and go through a period of phasing out of the Services.

The trend has been for the government contracting agency to assign more responsibility for conceptual phase analyses to the company awarded the contract. It should be clear that human factors personnel alone cannot perform all these activities. Systems engineering specialists may perform many analyses with inputs from human factors groups. Most decisions involving the human's role in the system require an active input from the human factors specialty.

Steps in Systems Analysis

Although authorities disagree somewhat on procedures for conducting systems analysis, the overall approach seems to be generally accepted. Figure 2-2 presents a simplified schematic of the systems analysis activities in design and development of a human-machine system. The activities shown in the column on the right involve people problems while those on the left involve hardware problems. Development of the personnel subsystem should not be conceived, however, as a series of analyses conducted independently and in parallel with development of equipment. The important interface between human factors engineering and equipment design will be discussed later in this chapter.

Define System and Mission Requirements   Requirements are the objectives of the system—what it is supposed to be able to do. Obviously, new systems are required to do things that existing systems cannot do, which is the reason the system has been funded for development.

In addition to requirements, systems constraints must be known. Constraints include the operational environment, available funding, time limit for development, the state of the art in technology, and so forth.

Performance requirements are given both for operating and maintaining the operational capability. Examples of operational requirements for a naval aircraft are the range, altitude, and airspeed of an aircraft, the crew size, weapon delivery capability, and a capability for landing on an aircraft carrier.

Mission profile analysis is a technique of analyzing the mission into time-phased segments (such as launch, orbit, and reentry of a space vehicle), and then determining the critical environments during each phase, supporting systems needed, and constraints on equipment and the human.

Analyzing systems requirements and constraints provides a basis for identifying specific functions that must be performed. Many of the requirements and constraints are identified for contractors as guidelines for the system they are required to design and build.

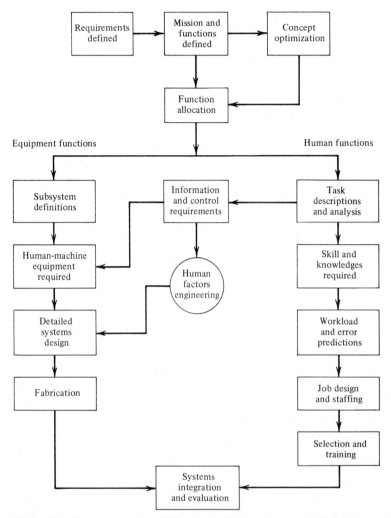

Figure 2-2 System analysis activities in developing a human-machine system.

Identify and Describe System Functions   The systems analyst must go through a logical exercise of reasoning from the general operational requirements to specific functions, tasks, and equipment requirements.

A system function is a broadly defined activity contributing to the systems goals. A statement of a function consists of a verb, a noun, and modifiers. For example, "Make a midcourse correction" is a function that satisfies some systems requirement for a manned space voyage. Note that functions do not necessarily imply that a human will be responsible for the action. Neither is there necessarily mention of specific equipment. These decisions have presumably not been made at this stage of development.

Conduct Optimization of Systems Concept   The contractor is responsible for developing a systems concept that describes the structure and function of the system and its capabilities and also describes the interrelationships of systems components (people, hardware, and so forth). A study of the types of analyses used in deciding among alternative conceptual systems is beyond the scope of this text, but several analyses will be mentioned.

- *Economic analyses* of alternative systems are conducted, such as cost/effectiveness studies and benefit/cost studies.
- Qualitative *trade-off studies* are used that simply list the pros and cons associated with various alternative systems approaches or conceptual designs.
- There are various types of *functional flow diagrams.* Figure 2-3 illustrates one type of flow diagram: On the second row is shown a first-level listing of the sequence of major phases of a space mission. The boost phase is then divided into second-level phases, and one phase is further analyzed into a third-level function flow. These charts may be broken down into more detailed functional levels. A systems engineering document, AFSCM 375-5, describes procedures for conducting such an analysis [8].
  Another diagramming method is the *information-decision-action diagram* (IDA), which codes each of the types of activities and depicts the flow of information through the system. Another more complex diagramming method is the *operational sequence diagram* (OSD), which has several uses including a comparison of a manual and a computer-aided system [Kurke, 11].
- *Operations research* methods such as linear programming and the queuing theory have also been used to determine optimum routing in transportation systems, manpower allocations to positions, and so forth [DeGreene, 3].
- Sometimes a decision must be based upon the opinion of experts in a specialty area. The *Delphi method* [Pill, 14] is one type of opinion-polling technique that seeks greater concensus among experts by providing feedback of how one's answer compared with that of other experts. Anonymity of response is an important feature that distinguishes the method from the conventional face-to-face committee decision making.

Allocate Functions   Once the systems functions are defined, a decision must be made as to whether the function can best be accomplished by human or instrumented capabilities or by a combination of the two. This process involves studying the alternative capabilities of the human and equipment and determining the best combination leading to successful mission completion with constraints. The operations sequence diagrams discussed above may be helpful in making such decisions. Information on human capabilities in comparison with instrumented capabilities in a systems context is discussed in Chapter 3.

Describe Tasks and Analyze Requirements   Having defined the human functions required in a system, the next step is to list in sequence the tasks necessary to carry out each function. Further analysis of tasks will depend upon

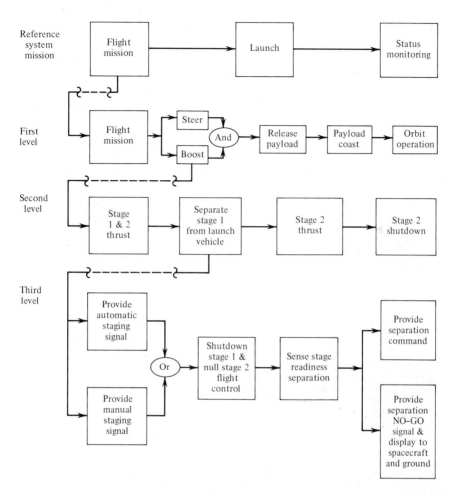

Figure 2-3 Example of functional flow block diagram. *(Modified from U.S. Air Force System Engineering Management Procedures, AFSCM 375-5, 1974, and appearing in DeGreene, 1970.)*

the objectives of the analysis. Task analyses may be used to determine information and control requirements prior to selecting equipment operated by the human; to determine skill and knowledge requirements for job specification purposes; to estimate errors associated with tasks; to predict workload and scheduling (by using a time base for the tasks), and so forth. A task analysis that gives time information is called a *time-line analysis.* Some task analyses are conducted in tabular format; others use flowcharts.

Developing task analyses can be very time-consuming. The military requirement is to conduct a gross task analysis. However, those tasks identified as requiring critical human performance or reflecting unsafe practices must be analyzed in greater detail.

Information and Control Requirements Analysis   By defining for each task the inputs needed and the outputs to be accomplished, the task analysis provides a technique for defining the types of human-machine equipment that must be provided. As an example, it may be determined that a pilot will be monitoring the aircraft's altitude. The range of significant values are 0 to 30,000 feet, and the accuracy required is $\pm$ 50 feet. This information alone would define the scale for an instrument and the number of graduation marks (tick marks) needed. Other information required in an aircraft may be merely qualitative feedback of whether or not a system is on or off or whether a warning or caution state exists. Only an indicator light may be needed. However, if very precise information is needed, a counter or digital readout may be required. On the control side of the problem, it is necessary to know how many positions are needed on a switch or how accurately a control knob must be tuned. The task analysis defines the range and accuracy limits for controls and displays.

Other equipment requirements may also be identified, such as tools, check lists, manuals, and job aids. Sometimes this analysis is discussed as an *equipment requirements analysis*.

Skill and Knowledge Requirements Analysis   One of the most common reasons for conducting a task analysis is to determine the level and type of skills and knowledge that will be required to perform the various tasks. This information will be used in preparing job specifications, selecting personnel to perform the tasks, and in training the personnel (see Job Design and Staffing). Task difficulty is also rated in terms of time required to learn a task; its priority or urgency may be rated as well.

Scheduling and Workload Analysis   Task analyses are usually conducted along a cumulative time base. An estimate is also made of the time required to perform each task. Often, time requirements are based upon actual performance studies in which measurements are taken. In some systems, stored data exists on task-time requirements. In industrial engineering, Methods Time Measurement handbooks [Maynard, 12] list stored data on time required to complete common worker tasks. In conducting a task analysis, the analyst often determines the task delay tolerance, that is, must the task be performed at the indicated time or could it be performed earlier or later?

From the standpoint of scheduling tasks, it is important to know that the operator is not assigned too many tasks to perform within a given time period. It may be necessary to reassign tasks to another time period if feasible; to assign motor tasks to the other hand or to a foot; to assign the tasks to another crew member or, perhaps, to automate a function. A crew workload analysis will establish the profile of work for each crew member with regard to both visual monitoring and control activities.

The goal of a crew-loading analysis is to predict the peaks in workload profiles prior to developing a firm crew-station design. While this may seem to be a formidable task, the analyst already knows approximately where the mission peaks will be. For a military aircraft, for example, they would likely be during landing and weapons delivery, and possibly be during takeoff. Given a script of tasks required by each crew member along an elapsed time base and, further, by estimating the approximate times to perform each sensory and control task, it is possible to estimate the degree to which each operator will be underloaded, fully loaded, or overloaded.

There are technical problems, of course, in estimating task times using stored data banks. In part, the times will be based upon distances traveled by the eyes and the hands based upon the layout of the cockpit displays and controls. Decision time is difficult to estimate. Whether visual and motor task times should be added or corrected by some other value is another technical issue in estimating the workload at a given time. The attention demands of tasks performed simultaneously are not necessarily equal to the sum of the component tasks.

Siegel and Wolf [16] have proposed the time-stress index as a unit of workload. Time stress is defined as the ratio of time required to perform remaining tasks to the time available. While a time stress of 1.0 would mean that the operator was fully occupied, research suggests that operators may compensate to some degree by working faster and that a state of overload or breakdown does not occur until a time stress of 2.0 or greater occurs.

Another approach to studying workload is by means of secondary loading tasks [Knowles, 10]. In assessing the workload required by a driving task, for example, the instructions are that the driver-subject is to perform this primary task and to devote any spare time to another artificial task, such as repeating numbers or centering a dot on a scope. The notion is that the more demanding the primary task, the less time the driver will have to spend on the secondary task. Hence, performance on the secondary task provides an indirect measure of the attention demands of the primary task. Other techniques used to measure mental workload include heart-rate variability, ratings on an opinionnaire, and performance on a primary driving task as measured by steering error and reversals [Williges and Wierwille, 19].

The discussion of workload has been limited to mental workload. (In Chapter 6, the energy costs of physical work will be discussed.) Mental workload depends not only on the number of tasks involved, but also upon the difficulty level of the tasks. In Chapter 3, the topic of information-processing time, based on number of possible choices, is discussed, and in Chapter 5, the difficulty of tracking-type control tasks will be elaborated.

Sometimes the interest is not so much in an exact assessment of time required to perform various tasks as it is on a relative assessment of the amount of time devoted to a series of tasks comprising a duty assignment. In this situation, estimates may be made of the percent of total duty time devoted to a task, or a rating is made on a scale of one to nine of the relative time spent (for example, much above average, very much below average). The USAF Comprehensive Occupational Data Analysis Program (CODAP) has employed the rating system in occupational research studies applied to currently existing, but not well-defined, jobs [Christal, 2].

Error Analysis Another variation of the task analysis is the error prediction analysis. For each task there are given errors that have been reported in similar systems in association with this task. The error analysis should estimate the probability of the error's occurring and the criticality or importance of the error in terms of its consequences on the accomplishment of the mission. Obviously, an undetected error is more serious than one caught in time and an irreversible error (for which nothing can be done to avert its full consequences) is one of the most serious errors of all. The low-altitude flameout of an aircraft (illustrated in Chapter 1) is an example of an irreversible error.

Classifications of Human Errors Error classifications are often based on the presumed cause of the error. Errors may be due to failure to perceive a stimulus, inability to discriminate among stimuli, misinterpretation of the meaning of stimuli, not knowing what response to make, responding out of sequence, or being physically unable to make the required response. The *error of omission,* often ascribed to forgetting, is illustrated by the wheels-up landing of aircraft. Two common control-activation errors reported in accident literature are the *confusion error* due to improper coding of control knobs to differentiate their function and the *psychomotor* or "bumping" error that is often due to improper guarding of a control or failure to design it to prevent accidental movement. Changing the location of controls on different models of a vehicle requires a relearning process, and errors may occur due to negative transfer of training or interference from previous habits. A movement to standardize control locations on aircraft has helped eliminate the latter type of error.

Human Reliability Systems reliability specialists have often sought to assign a reliability number to the operator's contribution to the system. They have failure rate data on the hardware but lack information on the human operator who is obviously a part of the total operating loop. Total systems reliability depends also upon whether the human operates in series or in parallel. Adding components (including human functions) increases reliability when they are in parallel, but adding components decreases reliability when they are in series.

In its simplest description, human reliability may be defined as "1 minus the probability of a human error." Thus, if a typist types a page consisting of 1000 characters and spaces and if he or she should make five typographical errors, the human reliability estimate would be 1 minus .005, or .995. Should a number of typists be evaluated and should they average five errors per page, the *error rate* would be .005 (probability of error per opportunity to make an error).

The human reliability movement has attempted to develop data banks of error rates and associated human reliabilities in a manner similar to the way that the time-study analysts have developed data banks of task times [Meister, 13; Swain, 17].

The Sandia Human Error Rate Bank (SHERB) is an example of a body of data consisting of human error rates for certain industrial tasks based on many observations. An example follows [Rook, 15]:

Type of error	Probability of error, P	Reliability $1-P$
Two wires which can be transposed are transposed	.0006	.9994
A component is omitted	.00003	.99997
A component is wired backward	.001	.999

The empirical determination of error rates is regarded as the preferred approach. Other researchers [Irving, Levitz, and Freed, 9] have attempted to have experts estimate human error rates by rating the probability of making an error on a 10-point scale and then mathematically deriving a reliability estimate. This approach has been less successful because it may call for knowledge beyond the capability of the expert. Error-rate data can be most useful only when used in conjunction with estimates of the severity or criticality of the error.

Error-rate data is useful not only in calculating systems reliability, but also in other human factors activities such as allocating functions (based upon errors with and without the human); quantifying the error consequences of human-engineered equipment; and estimating the success of training programs.

Job Design and Staffing   In theory, the various tasks identified in the previous step have not yet been assigned to a particular crew member. After work functions the human is to accomplish have been identified and analyzed into tasks, they must be grouped into jobs or positions in such a manner that the individual performing the job is not overloaded, inefficient, or error-likely from excessive task loading. In practice, the various duty positions may already be conceptualized. For example, the contracting agency may decide they want an aircraft developed that can be operated by two or perhaps three operators. Therefore, the decision on crew size may be preordained and the human factors task may be one of dividing the tasks between or among the crew members in an effective manner.

Job design must also consider job satisfaction. The trend in many industrial applications has been enlargement of the scope of activities performed by one person so he or she can identify with the output. Individual responsibility and greater freedom in methods often enhance job satisfaction.

Staffing refers to the steps in specifying and recruiting the numbers and types of operators needed to staff a system [Chapanis, 1]. In the USAF, for example, support specialties already exist and are identified by code number for various technicians and mechanics. Staffing studies involve identifying which of these personnel will be needed for a particular system. The skills and knowledge analysis discussed previously will identify the level and types of skilled personnel needed. Sometimes personnel are limited and training time is costly, so it is necessary to attempt to design hardware and operating procedures that can be used without highly specialized or highly trained technicians.

Staffing studies describe the various jobs or positions in detail. Such information is necessary to establish tables of organization. The studies provide a basis for forecasting use of the human resources available to an organization. Techniques for designing the job and workplace are elaborated in Chapter 6.

Selection, Placement, and Training   Having identified the various jobs necessary in support of a system, there still remains the task of locating people to fill the jobs. Personnel selection may involve looking at a large number of applicants and finding the few who most nearly meet the job requirements. In practice, there may be a number of jobs and certain applicants may be better qualified than others for more than one of the jobs. So the question of job placement is complicated.

Placement involves making decisions as to which person should be assigned to which job. The person best qualified for a given job (job A) may need to be assigned to another job (job B) for which he or she is also best qualified because there is another person nearly as skilled in job A, but no one available to perform job B. In short, placement decisions are made to maximize the performance of the system as a whole so as to get the highest-average aptitude scores across all people and jobs. There are various solutions to complex staffing problems, and an operations research technique called linear programming is sometimes used to solve the problems. The placement decision must also be consistent with the desires of the person involved. Many may resign (or fail to reenlist) if arbitrarily assigned to jobs not in their primary area of interest. Recent military recruitment policies have recognized this human relations principle.

Cost trade-offs must also be made between selection and training. Sometimes it is cheaper to select only a few carefully screened applicants and thus be able to retain a large percent of them after a training program. This strategy A may be less costly than strategy B—selecting half of the applicants and then sending them through a costly training program. After training, there is a rigid screening process and the same number of personnel are assigned to the job as in strategy A. Assuming that training is expensive, it may be more economical to place the emphasis on selection in achieving the same number of qualified personnel.

Procedures for selecting and training personnel are beyond the scope of this design-oriented textbook. Ordinarily, these functions are performed by specialists.

Systems Test and Evaluation   Most of us think of systems testing as an activity that comes at the end of a program, after a system has been developed. The USAF distinguishes three categories of testing [DeGreene, 3]. There are tests conducted in the factory, using company personnel. These may be to see if the various subsystems are working according to specified performance. Other tests are conducted on a prototype or finished product; these tests may be conducted in the real world, using both company and user personnel. Finally, tests may be conducted under near-operational conditions by user personnel only.

In each instance, systems performance is measured and any deficiency is reported to the appropriate organization for a decision on changes that need to be made. Sometimes these are design changes; sometimes they are necessary improvements in the quality of a product; sometimes they are due to training deficiencies. Human factors personnel monitor these evaluations for possible design changes at the human-machine interface.

Evaluation, in the broader definition of the term, is a continuing process that goes on throughout the development of a system. Paper-and-pencil trade-off studies of alternative designs and cost/benefit studies could be considered a form of evaluation. In fact, any activity designed to improve the quality of design decisions, to correct design deficiencies, and to achieve a better match between personnel and hardware could be considered as an evaluation.

To illustrate this point, human factors specialists may scrutinize a drawing of the design of equipment and compare it with design specifications or standards such as MIL-STD-1472 [5]. Does the equipment meet specifications? This is a form of evaluation. The specialists may also conduct studies in full-scale mockups or simulators. This activity also involves evaluation. In some instances they may need to conduct studies to compare the effectiveness of two or more items of equipment or to establish the error rate associated with use of certain equipment. These are all forms of evaluation.

Techniques of evaluation include expert or user opinion surveys, human engineering checklists, observation of operators performing activities in the field, examination of accident or failure reports, and simulation and modeling techniques, as well as the formal experimental methods of controlled evaluation in the laboratory.

IMPLEMENTING HUMAN FACTORS IN SYSTEMS DESIGN

Human factors engineering provides the interface between human factors activities and equipment development. In Chapter 1, implementation specialists were discussed as those human factors specialists who are primarily concerned with seeing that systems are designed according to human factors criteria. In subsequent chapters, extensive data will be presented on how equipment and facilities should be designed. However, an often neglected topic is a discussion of the process by which human factors personnel are successful in getting their recommendations incorporated in the design of human-machine systems. The focus of the following discussion relates to human factors organizations located in the engineering departments of large manufacturing companies, such as the aerospace or automotive industry.

Indicators of Management Support

The implementation specialist must have the confidence of the engineering management to be effective. The best indicator of this acceptance is the extent to which human factors specialists are granted the authority to influence design—for example, having signature approval on drawings involving human-machine interface design.

A strong management is willing to improve the design of a system even when the human factors design approach is more expensive than a less-effective approach. It recognizes that good human factors is worth the price in the long run. An example of this recognition would be a decision to use wraparound consoles in a missile-monitoring control center, as opposed to using a number of upright racks. The consoles provide for long-term operations by a seated operator who has better access to controls and displays.

The location of a human factors group in the engineering organization is another indicator of management acceptance. There should not be more than one level of management between the supervisor of the human factors group and the director or chief of the engineering department.

A human factors implementation group can be more effective in influencing design if it is located organizationally in the department responsible for preparing design drawings of the human-machine interfaces, for example, a crew station design group or a furnishings group. Recommendations from an insider are usually accepted more readily than those of an outsider. Also, both the design engineer and human factors engineer may report to the same department head and internal approval procedures may be easily developed by the supervisor's authorization.

Steps in an Effective Human Factors Design Effort

Human factors personnel must first acquaint themselves with systems specifications and performance specifications. They must understand fully what the system being designed is required to do and the conceptual thinking that may have gone on prior to their entering the organization.

Current Mockup Building a human factors mockup is a useful design aid for studying access, layout, and workspace problems. In the conceptual phase it will not be feasible to have moving displays and controls. The mockup may be made of flexible and inexpensive materials such as cardboard or foam core. Conceptual designs on blue line drawings of various panel fronts may be secured at the recommended locations in the mockup.

By then inviting knowledgeable systems designers to review the proposed layout, the human factors specialists will be kept abreast of current developments in systems design. Changes should be made as needed. Eventually the mockup may be shown by management to the customer as evidence of progress in conceptual design. By keeping abreast of the most recent designs, the human factors effort has an opportunity to influence design decisions in areas such as labeling, control selection, display design, and workspace layout.

Design Problems   Human factors implementation specialists should be more than librarians of human factors design guides or military specifications. Many senior designers may already have such documents among their reference books; however, they may have questions whose answers are not contained in the standard design guides. Also, they may wish assistance of human factors personnel in working out a solution to a design problem. Human factors personnel should issue by memorandum fully documented design recommendations. Usually, these should be issued after an informal discussion and acceptance of the design information by the requesting source.

Control of Design   An effective human factors program has control over human-machine interface drawings by signature approval of the drawings before release. In some organizations human factors specialists issue design directives that must be observed as well as issuing design information recommendations that are optional. An illustration of a situation calling for a design directive is when various panels are being designed independently by different design engineers, but the panels will all be monitored and operated by the same operator. In this situation, there may be a need to standardize sizes and shapes of control knobs and to standardize labeling conventions so that the operator is not confused by the differences.

It is also important that the human factors specialists be aware of all the various panels and subsystems being designed at any given time, because there will always be some designers who would prefer not to have others monitor their handiwork. Human factors specialists should have a logbook that lists the various drawings and their stage of development. They should follow nondirective counseling techniques to gain the cooperation of designers in following their suggestions. Again, they should always have the confidence and approval of the highest-level systems designers, who will support the design recommendations to subsystems designers.

Human factors personnel should always participate in design development review meetings to defend any proposed design and, at the same time, to be kept abreast of any changes in the required functions that affect the panel fronts.

Changing the Design   Occasionally, a request for engineering change (REC) may be necessary by a human factors specialist. Changes in design after the design has progressed are costly in time and money. Normally they are issued only when a design simply will not work, rather than as an improvement item. A REC should not be released unless it is believed that there is a good chance it will be approved. One technique is to conduct a test program that will demonstrate that the present design will not work and to use as subjects preferably those individuals who will ultimately be responsible for approval of the REC. The results of the test program will underscore the need for the change in design. Thus, the need for the REC will be evident prior to its being issued. The feasibility of the design solution should also be discussed and demonstrated in advance of submission of the REC.

Open-Minded Approach The implementation specialist must not be viewed by colleagues as one who is uncompromising in his or her design standards in the face of strong evidence that it is not practical to insist on an ideal solution. The effectiveness of a human factors effort in selling recommendations rests largely on adopting a firm yet realistic attitude in dealing with design engineers.

QUESTIONS AND PROBLEMS

1   Think of an example of a system where the use of a computer might be more efficient than the use of a human.
2   Can you think of a system where the user or the public would resist automating the system even though the system might work as well or better with computer control as with human control?
3   Can you think of an example of an aircraft development program where inefficient systems planning led to late delivery or even cancellation of a production contract?
4   A manufacturer is going to build a power lawn mower on which the operator rides. You are asked to list a set of systems requirements that will serve as guidelines when the performance specifications are prepared later. Think of at least five requirements. They may involve performance or safety in the mowing operation.
5   In the definition of systems management, the statement is made that systems analysis and engineering "proceeds from the general to the specific, from the hypothetical to the real, and from the conceptual through research and development and production, to the operational." Having read the steps in systems analysis, can you explain what is meant by these procedures?
6   Is the following statement a function or a task—"release payload"?
7   Suppose you determine that the time required to accomplish a given task is 5 minutes and the time available to do it is 4 minutes. What is the time-stress ratio value? Does this mean that the operator is overworked? Discuss.
8   An inspector observes articles passing by him on an assembly line. It is known that 200 of these articles are defective, but the inspector catches and rejects only 195 of the defective articles. Calculate his human reliability.
9   How does building a human factors mockup permit human factors to influence design decisions?
10 Why should human factors be reluctant to issue an REC until strong evidence has been collected for a need for the change?

REFERENCES

1   Chapanis, A.: "Systems staffing," in K. B. DeGreene (ed.), *Systems Psychology*, McGraw-Hill, New York, 1970, chap. 12.
2   Christal, R. E.: The United States Air Force occupational research project, Air Force Human Resources Laboratory, Air Force Systems Command. Paper presented at Symposium, The State of the Art in Occupational Research and Development, Naval Personnel Research and Development Center, July 1973.
3   DeGreene, K. B. (ed.): *Systems Psychology*, McGraw-Hill, New York, 1970.
4   Department of Defense, Military specification: *Human engineering requirements for military systems, equipment, and facilities* (MIL-H-46855A), May 2, 1972.

5 Department of Defense, Military specification: *Human engineering design criteria for military systems, equipment, and facilities,* MIL-STD-1472B, May 15, 1970.
6 Hall, A. D. and R. E. Fagen: Definition of system, *General Systems Yearbook of the Society for the Advancement of General Systems Theory, I* (L. von Bertalanffy and A. Rappaport, eds.), 1956, pp. 18–28.
7 Headquarters, Air Force Systems Command: *Personnel Subsystem* (AFSC DH 1-3), Washington, D.C., 1969.
8 Headquarters, Air Force Systems Command: *Systems engineering management procedures,* Andrews Air Force Base, Wash., D.C., AFSCM 375-5, February 1964.
9 Irwin, I. A., J. J. Levitz, and A. M. Freed: Human Reliability in the performance of maintenance, *Proceedings, Symposium on the Quantification of Human Performance,* Albuquerque, New Mexico, Aug. 17–19, 1964.
10 Knowles, W. B.: Operator loading tasks, *Human Factors,* 1963, vol. 5, no. 2, pp. 155–161.
11 Kurke, M. I.: Operational sequence diagrams in systems design, *Human Factors,* vol. 1, no. 1, March 1961, pp. 66–73.
12 Maynard, H. B.: *Industrial engineering handbook,* 2d ed., McGraw-Hill, New York, 1963.
13 Meister, D.: Methods of predicting human reliability and man-machine systems, *Human Factors,* vol. 6, no. 6, December 1964, pp. 621–646.
14 Pill, J.: The Delphi method: substance, context, a critique and an annotated bibliography, *Socio-Economic Planning Sciences,* vol. 5, 1971, pp. 57–71.
15 Rook, L. W., Jr.: *Reduction of Human Error in Industrial Production,* Sandia Corporation, Albuquerque, New Mexico, SCTM 93-62, vol. 14, 1962.
16 Siegel, A. I. and Wolf, J. J.: *Man-machine simulation models,* Wiley, New York, 1969.
17 Swain, A. D.: Some problems in the measurement of human performance in man-machine systems, *Human Factors,* vol. 6, no. 6, December 1964, pp. 687–700.
18 The Houston Post: "Human error worsened mishap, NRC staff says," Associated Press article, May 12, 1979.
19 Williges, R. C. and W. W. Wierwille: Behavioral measures of aircrew mental workload, *Human Factors,* vol. 21, no. 5, October 1979.
20 Meister, D.: *Human Factors: Theory and Practice,* Wiley-Interscience, a division of John Wiley & Sons, New York, 1971.

Chapter 3

Human Capabilities and Limitations

The human is a remarkable creature. Although slow and weak in comparison with many animals, the human is endowed with a superior brain and delicately coordinated movements of its forward limbs and digits. A baseball hitter swinging a bat at a curving ball traveling at 80 mi/h (128 km/h) or more requires superior vision, near-perfect timing of the swing, and coordinated movement of the limbs and torso to meet the ball squarely at an exact instant.

The human senses and appendages could be viewed as implements for reception and expression of the handiwork of a superior brain. Historically, the human brain provided the capability for inductive reasoning and creativity necessary for the development of technology. The simultaneous control of vocal chords, lips, tongue, palate, and breathing gave the human the unique skill of speech and the ability to communicate ideas among the species. Through speech, writing, and drawing, the inventions of humanity were transmitted and modified by successive generations. The human alone has extended its capabilities by developing protective clothing, sophisticated weapons, vehicles, and advanced technology.

The ability to discover the laws of nature and to harness the forces of nature for the advancement of its well-being has given the human a position of dominance over other species. The human recognized its own inferiority in certain areas and exploited domesticated animals for transportation, communications (the pigeon), advanced warning, and enforcement. Dogs can be trained to sniff for hidden drugs, and pigeons can be trained to detect orange objects on the ocean from an aircraft.

The objective of this chapter is not to extol the talents of Homo sapiens nor to trace the history of the human's achievement. Rather it is to discuss the human as a component in complex systems of the human's own creation and to note the functional advantages and limitations of the human in relation to automated system components. As noted in Chapter 2, the function allocation process is an important one early in the conceptual design of any system. A requirement for the human in a system where he or she is at a disadvantage can be a design error as great as failure to employ human capabilities where they could contribute to effective performance of the system. The study of human capabilities and limitations also permits the designer to create an environment that allows for human limitations functionally and physically.

Beginning with Chapter 4, the remainder of this book is oriented toward the design of specific facilities, systems, subsystems, and components. In subsequent chapters human capabilities will be introduced only as a relevant measure for development of design criteria or selection between two or more alternative approaches to system design. Human factors, the science, is distinguished from the behavioral and life sciences principally by its focus, which is the implications of human capabilities and limitations for systems design (rather than the processes of sensing, thinking, behaving, or adapting physiologically and psychologically as objectives, regardless of the particular application of such knowledge). This approach has led to a pragmatic way of viewing human processes and attributes as human capabilities and limitations.

Many users of human factors data have only a fragmentary knowledge of human performance and lack the background in the behavioral, biological, and social sciences to properly interpret human factors data. Therefore, a brief introduction to the subject is warranted. Those who wish to pursue the technology of human factors engineering in greater depth should pursue advanced study of how the human being functions and behaves and the conditions influencing the humans' capabilities and limitations. The science of human factors has sometimes been referred to as the parent discipline for advanced study in the technology of human factors engineering.

HUMAN-MACHINE COMPARISON

Rather than beginning with an academic discussion of various sense organs, behavioral principles, biological processes, or biomechanical models, a more enlightening approach may be to compare the human's. capabilities and limitations with those of a machine, computer, or instrumented capability. The systems designer is most interested in the bottom line as a basis for decision making.

Table 3-1 presents one such comparison that is organized around four major

Table 3-1 Functional Advantages and Disadvantages of the Human and the Machine

Functional area	Man	Machine
Data sensing	• Can monitor low-probability events not feasible for automatic systems because of number of events possible	• Limited program complexity and alternatives; unexpected events cannot be handled adequately
	• Absolute thresholds of sensitivity are very low under favorable conditions	• Generally not as low as human thresholds
	• Can detect masked signals effectively in overlapping noise spectra	• Poor signal detection when noise spectra overlap
	• Able to acquire and report information incidental to primary activity	• Discovery and selection of incidental intelligence not feasible in present designs
	• Not subject to jamming by ordinary methods	• Subject to disruption by interference and noise
Data Processing	• Able to recognize and use information, redundancy (pattern) of real world to simplify complex situations	• Little or no perceptual constancy or ability to recognize similarity of pattern in spatial or temporal domain
	• Reasonable reliability in which the same purpose can be accomplished by different approach (corollary of reprogramming ability)	• High reliability may increase cost and complexity; particularly reliable for routine repetitive functioning
	• Can make *inductive* decisions in new situations; can generalize from few data	• Virtually no capacity for creative or inductive functions
	• Computation weak and relatively inaccurate; optimal game theory strategy cannot be routinely expected	• Can be programmed to use optimum strategy for high-probability situations
	• Channel capacity limited to relatively small information throughput rates	• Channel capacity can be enlarged as necessary for task
	• Can handle variety of transient and some permanent overloads without disruption	• Transient and permanent overloads may lead to disruption of system
	• Short-term memory relatively poor	• Short-term memory and access times excellent

functional areas—data sensing, data processing, data transmitting, and so-called economic properties [Lyman and Fogel, 45]. Other authors [Chapanis, 13; Fitts, 24; and Meister, 50] have similar listings, but the organization in terms of functional areas corresponds somewhat with the outline of this chapter.

Constraints to Comparison Tables

There are several limitations to the use of such listings as a basis for function allocation. First, the state of the art in technology is changing at a rapid pace. What was technically unfeasible for automated systems at the time of this writing may be feasible and practical in a few years.

Second, an allocation decision is based upon criteria other than the functional superiority of one subsystem to another. Criteria include cost of

Table 3-1 *(Continued)*

Functional area	Man	Machine
Data transmitting	• Can tolerate only relatively low imposed forces and generate relatively low forces for short periods	• Can withstand very large forces and generate them for prolonged periods
	• Generally poor at tracking though satisfactory where frequent reprogramming required; can change to meet situation. Is best at position tracking where changes are under 3 radians per second	• Good tracking characteristics over limited requirements
	• Performance may deteriorate with time, because of boredom, fatigue, or distraction; usually recovers with rest	• Behavior decrement relatively small with time; wear maintenance and product quality control necessary
	• Relatively high response latency	• Arbitrarily low response latencies possible
Economic properties	• Relatively inexpensive for available complexity and in good supply; must be trained	• Complexity and supply limited by cost and time; performance built in
	• Light in weight, small in size for function achieved; power requirement less than 100 watts	• Equivalent complexity and function would require radically heavier elements, enormous power and cooling resources
	• Maintenance may require life support system	• Maintenance problem increases disproportionately with complexity
	• Nonexpendable; interested in personal survival; emotional	• Expendable; nonpersonal; will perform without distraction

Source: Bekey in DeGreene [18] as modified from Lyman and Fogel [45].

development and maintenance, weight, power, reliability, and availability by a certain date. Sometimes the second-best capability may still be satisfactory and substantially more cost effective.

In addition, the value system of the public must be taken into account. An automated rail system between airport terminals may be technically feasible, functional, and provide the best benefit/cost ratio, yet some passengers may refuse to board it. The public may need to be educated to accept a completely automated transportation system.

Other value systems must be considered. The buying public may prefer to control or steer their own vehicle even when advanced transportation concepts that would make individual steering unnecessary are practical. Organized labor may be concerned with the loss of jobs when a person is replaced with a machine. The federal government may decide that it is in the national interest to demonstrate a capability for landing a human on the moon irrespective of whether an automated system could be made to perform the same functions. (This is not to say that such a capability should have been pursued but to illustrate that factors other than functional requirements may dictate the decision to automate or make manual a given system.)

Most important is recognition that seldom is the applied question one of *either* the human *or* the machine in control of a system. The human and the machine complement one another in achieving systems performance. The human may not be required as a primary controller but may be necessary as a programmer, as a backup system (when a computer fails), and as a maintenance source. Increasingly, the human's role is becoming one of making decisions and performing in contingency situations that occur infrequently. Human intervention is, nevertheless, essential to the success of the mission when these contingencies do occur. The dimension of automation-manual control has many levels or degrees. The direction of future research will be toward assessing the reliability of a system with the human as a system component at various levels of participation.

Data Sensing

The summary statements in Table 3-1 suggest that the human has something to contribute in the area of data sensing. Note the capability to sense unusual or low-probability events in the environment, a capability for which it would be difficult to program an automated system. Sometimes these events are unexpected and incidental to the primary activity. An automated system can be programmed to detect a certain class of stimuli (for example, a smoke detector), but it must be preprogrammed to respond to any specific event.

The human can also sense very low levels of energy. For example, the eyes have an absolute threshold for detecting electromagnetic waves as small as 10^{-4} millilamberts (mL); a match lit miles away in total darkness is visible. The ears are sensitive to 0.0002 dyne per square centimeter in sound intensity. Absolute thresholds (smallest and largest) for various senses are available in Van Cott and Warrick [71].

Although the human is excellent at detecting low stimulus levels, he or she is sensitive to only a narrow bandwidth of electromagnetic energy. The visible spectrum is approximately 380 to 760 nanometers (nm) (formerly millimicrons). The radiant energy spectrum includes a much wider spectrum. Radar, infrared, ultraviolet, and X-rays are beyond the visible spectrum limits and could be sensed only by appropriate instrumentation. The same restrictions apply to the other senses; for example, the audible range is at most 20 to 20,000 hertz (Hz).

The human is also fairly effective at detecting signals masked or partially obscured by an ambient noise field. These signals may be blips on a cathode-ray tube or tones heard over a headset. However, monitoring or vigilance tasks are generally boring when prespecified events occur very infrequently. Techniques must be developed to maintain the human's attention. There are differences in people's willingness to report a given stimulus as a signal when it is nearly masked in noise. Some consider the more serious error to be missing a signal while others are more concerned with reporting a signal's presence when they are not sure the stimulus is a signal (a false alarm).

Communications engineers have made advances in techniques for improving the detection of signals in noise (including more automatic methods). AFSC DH 1-3 [1] assigns primary responsibility for vigilance and detection following periods of inaction to automated systems. However, a role for the human in certain kinds of watchkeeping and inspection activities, where errors occur more often, appears to be secure.

Van Cott and Warrick [71] conclude that the human sensing system is reliable, consistent, precise, and fails less often than most electromechanical systems. Inconsistencies attributed to the human are often due to equipment design failures, such as blurring or flickering display tubes, rather than human errors.

Data Processing

Data of all sorts may be processed either by the human or by automated methods. For certain functions the human is ideally suited; for many functions, the human is inadequate. Data processing includes recognizing and interpreting complex patterns of stimuli, reprogramming based on related experience, reasoning both inductively and deductively, adaptive functions (learning), retrieving information from both short-term and long-term storage, and considerations of the effects of overload on decision making.

Perceptual psychologists have noted the phenomenon of perceptual constancy. It is an asset to be able to recognize visual objects as being the same when viewed from different vantage points, at different distances, and in different degrees of lightness. Automatic scanners can sometimes be confused by changing situations. In Chapter 12, the problem of developing machines that can recognize words in natural speech is discussed. The human can understand the spoken language in a variety of voices and dialect, and secretaries can translate from handwriting in a variety of styles. Technically, machines require a more standardized vocal and printed input for recognition.

The human has the ability to store and later recall a fairly large amount of information over a long duration (particularly principles and strategies rather than masses of details). Pertinent information may be retrieved with fair reliability. Unlike the computer the human does not require previous programming for all situations but, instead, makes a decision by drawing upon a variety of experiences in similar situations. This ability to adapt previous decisions to a new and different situation and to reprogram (or reason) is especially useful in emergency situations. The human is said to provide flexibility by rapid shifts in attention and by pursuing alternate modes of operation. A machine capable of doing these things would be complex, requiring extensive programming.

One should not expect computers to invent new principles or discover unknown relationships. The computer responds only to the operations fed into it. The intelligent human is capable of inductive reasoning (generalizing from the particular to the general situation).

The human may act on hunches and test their validity by controlled experimentation. However, the human's capability for deductive reasoning, as in math or logic, is sometimes limited and inaccurate. It is in this area that electronic data processors are rapidly phasing out the human. Even at a fast-food restaurant, the attendant selects the order and the machine seeks the prices, totals, adds tax, and computes the correct change.

The computer is supplanting the human not only for bookkeeping and other business functions, but also for scientific data processing. Advanced operations research techniques permit optimum decisions quickly and accurately, provided constraints can be defined.

Modern computers can perform 100 million operations per second (compared to about 40 bits/second for the human) and can store more than a million words [Baker, 6]. The human has limited memory for detailed information. We must practice and rehearse to be able to reproduce adequately on the day of the exam. Computers can store, retrieve, analyze, and communicate detailed data much more quickly and accurately.

On the other hand, when the human is overloaded, the breakdown is more often in stages. The highly motivated human may compensate by working harder under adversity and improving performance up to some point. The human may also adopt strategies such as concentrating on the more important activities. When overloaded or malfunctioning, computers more often fail completely and give absurd answers.

Data Transmission

It is in the area of data transmission (output) that the human has some severe limitations, yet due to preferences and value systems (discussed earlier) the choice of a human is dictated in certain situations for which he or she has less capability.

The human is physically weak, in comparison to machinery, and fatigues rapidly, necessitating frequent rest pauses. Machines can both withstand and impose larger forces. A hydraulic lift can manage 50 tons, 1000 times the weight an average human can handle [Baker, 6]. Machines don't exhibit the gradual fatigue cycle of the human. The human is more willing to surrender the role as a source of power than the role as a controller. The human enjoys driving and directing vehicles. Current system changes have been in the direction of simplifying the human's task in tracking so that the higher, quasi-mathematical functions are managed by the system (Chapter 5); consequently, control activities are physically easier as well.

The human has a slow reaction time (high response latency) and is generally slow and variable in executing activities. Aircraft can reach speeds of 2000 mi/h (3200 km/h), some 500 times the human walking pace [Baker, 6].

The human performs not only with the limbs, but also with the voice.

Prerecorded voice tracks are becoming commonplace for routine answering and communications (in Chapters 12 and 13 the development of automated speech synthesis and recognition devices is discussed). However, as a live communication source in systems, the human may transmit complex information that could not be anticipated in the initial design and programming of an automated system.

In general, machinery is excellent for routine, repetitive activities such as counting, performing several activities simultaneously, or making very precise movements consistently and rapidly. In data transmission the human provides for flexibility (reprogramming) but often lacks consistency of performance.

Economic Properties

In the final section of Table 3-1, the authors dealt with an economic comparison of the human and the machine. Whenever questions of comparative costs are raised, the systems designer must consider the total cost of the two systems based upon current market conditions and must weigh the benefits for the specific application and its functional requirements. Granted, it would be expensive to build a computer that could perform all the many things the human can do. However, many human capabilities may not be required for the particular operation. In conducting a trade-off study one must analyze the functional requirements satisfied by the human capability for the particular mission.

Some readers would argue with the statement that humans are in good supply when the requirement is for a highly skilled and educated specialist rather than for manual laborers. The cost of recruitment, training, and fringe benefits may be the major deterrent to including the human in a system unless essential.

Life support on long missions, particularly space missions, is a major constraint to having the human aboard. On air and sea voyages the vehicle may need to land and resupply at intervals. A trade-off may be needed between the cost of increased reliability and an on-board maintenance capability.

Finally, the high value placed on human life and safety increases the cost of any system where the safety of the on-board operator is risked. Weight is added by protective provisions and escape systems. The human is an emotional being subject to shifts in motivation and morale over the long term. Obviously, an inanimate system has no such constraint and performance is more consistent. The highly motivated and mature astronauts selected for our space program have not degraded systems performance through excessive concern for their own well-being. Still, when the risks are very high, humanitarian values certainly indicate increased consideration of automated systems.

THE HUMAN AS A DATA SENSOR

The previous section presented an overview of human capabilities and limitations in relation to machine capabilities. This section will provide more specific information on the human as a data sensor, processor, and transmitter.

Eighty percent of human knowledge is acquired visually, according to one estimate [AFSC, 1]. Hence, this discussion will be limited principally to the visual sense. Audition is discussed in Chapter 4 with interfaces in Chapters 7, 9, 12, and 13. There are many excellent references on sensation and perception [Geldard, 28; Kaufman, 38] for those interested in an in-depth discussion. Chapters 4, 8, and 10 also stress visual problems.

Intensity Detection

The minimum amount of electromagnetic energy necessary for human detection of light is termed the absolute threshold. As previously noted, the average value is about 10^{-10} lambert (L). Light sensitivity is influenced by many factors, such as individual characteristics (age, physiological, and psychological condition); duration of exposure (short flashes require more intense light); the contrast of light with the background (brighter backgrounds require a more intense light source for visibility) and, certainly, the region of the retina stimulated.

The retina on the back of the eyeball consists of rods and cones. Cones are located near the fovea; rods are more prolific on the periphery. Cones are used in daytime and permit color vision. Rods take over at night, which explains why the greatest sensitivity at night is about 40 degrees from the fovea on the nasal side and 20 degrees from the fovea on the temporal side.

Frequency Detection

The human is sensitive to wavelengths between about 380 and 760 nm. The shorter wavelengths are perceived as violet, the intermediate wavelengths, blue, green, and yellow, and the longest wavelengths, orange and red. In daylight the eye is most sensitive at 555 nm (yellow-green) while the dark-adapted eye is most sensitive at 507 nm (green). This shift from photopic (cone) vision to scotopic (rod) vision at approaching darkness helps explain why red loses its color more so than the shorter wavelengths.

It takes about 30 minutes (min) for the eyes to completely adapt from daytime to nighttime vision.

About 8 percent of the male population and .05 percent of the female population have difficulty in discriminating certain colors, but only .003 percent of the population is completely color-blind.

Discrimination

There are two ways of discriminating—relatively and absolutely. With relative discrimination two stimuli are present and the person reports a detectable difference. With absolute discrimination the person is given the stimuli one at a time and rates or classifies the stimulus attribute. Judgments are based upon recall with no standards other than past experience as a guide to estimation. Absolute discrimination or identification is in the domain of information processing discussed subsequently.

Relative discrimination involves comparative judgments with sensed physical standards. Many more relative discriminations are possible, for example, 570 differences in brightness of a white light, but only 3 to 5 brightnesses are discriminable on an absolute basis.

Relative discrimination sensitivity (difference threshold) is the least change in a stimulus, or least difference between two stimuli, which is "just noticably different" (JND). Weber [28], a sensory physiologist, discovered in the early nineteenth century that over a typically useful range of some stimulus dimensions, $\Delta I / I = K$, that is, the increment in intensity in proportion to the intensity itself is a constant. For example, to detect the addition of a weight to a heavy base weight requires substantially more pounds than to detect a weight added to a light weight. However, the increment to either base weight that would be detectable is about the same (1/40). The Weber fraction (2 to 5 percent) applies to the midrange in visual intensity discrimination and to loudness and several other sensory dimensions [28].

Acuity

Visual acuity is the ability to resolve details. The lens of the eye normally changes shape or accommodates to focus images on the retina. Near-sighted people (with bulging lens) cannot focus on far objects without glasses because the image focuses in front of the retina. Far-sighted people (with flat lens) cannot focus on near objects without corrective lens because the object focuses behind the retina (Figure 3-1). Astigmatism and presbyopia (an age-related hardening of the lens impairing close focusing) are other anomalies of the lens.

The six major types of visual acuity are separable, perceptible, visible, vernier, stereoscopic, and dynamic visual acuity. *Minimum separable acuity* is the smallest gap or space between parts of a target (or letter) that the eye can detect. Standard optometric techniques such as letter charts and checkerboard patterns are employed to calculate the resolution capability. Technically, it is the reciprocal of the visual angle subtended at the eye by the smallest detail. In common usage, the acuity value is referenced to what a person with normal eyesight can resolve at 20 ft (6m).

Detection of black letters on a white background improves with increased background luminance up to about 1 or 2 mL. However, white letters on a black background tend to blur above about 10 mL due to irradiation or spread of the light. Blackwell [9] found a 50 percent detection probability when the gap subtended 0.8 minutes* of visual arc and a 95 percent detection probability at 1.4 minutes. In general, the normal eye can detect 1 minute of visual angle indoors using targets of high luminance contrast [Grether and Baker, 29].

Minimum perceptible acuity is the smallest dot that can be detected against a background. Light dots on a dark background are detected at a smaller visual angle than dark dots on a white background. Detection improves with percent contrast with the background and with increases in background luminance. See Chapters 4 and 8 for extended discussion.

Minimum visible acuity is the minimum width of a line that can be detected.

*1 minute = 1/60 degree.

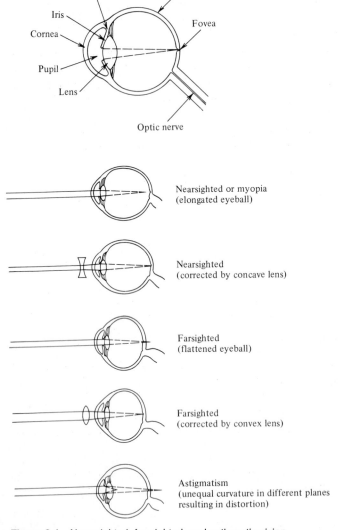

Figure 3-1   Near-sighted, far-sighted, and astigmatic vision.

Minimum vernier acuity is the minimum detectable lateral displacement of one line with respect to another parallel line (as a pointer tip and tick mark on a dial).

Stereoscopic acuity is depth detection. Picture two targets at slightly different distances in front of the eyes. The two eyes must converge on each target with the images from each eye fusing into a single image. The parallactic visual angle is the angle from a target to the two eyes. Stereoscopic acuity, then, is the minimum detectable difference in the visual angle of two targets.

Perception of depth and distance is not dependent solely on binocular disparity or convergence of two eyes. There are many monocular cues, such as linear perspective, interposition of objects, and texture gradients. Distance judgment is also aided by objects of known size in the vicinity.

Dynamic visual acuity (DVA) is the smallest detail that can be detected when the target is moving. At low rates the detail is easy to detect. DVA is quickly lost when the rate of movement exceeds 60 degrees per second [Burg, 12]. At 150 °/s angular velocity, DVA is only 19 percent of normal detectable acuity [AFSC, 1].

Field of View

The binocular visual field is about 130 degrees vertically and 208 degrees horizontally, assuming the neck to be stationary and the eyes to be fixated straight ahead. The vertical field extends from 60 degrees above horizontal to 70 degrees below. The horizontal field extends 104 degrees laterally (left and right). Each eye has a horizontal field of about 166 degrees. With the head and eyes fixated straight ahead, color vision will necessarily be restricted. The range of color vision is 30 degrees above, 40 degrees below a horizontal plane, and 62 degrees to either side of the vertical plane [AFSC, 1]. Neck and eye movement increase the visual field. Visual discomfort occurs when glare sources are within 60 degrees of the line of sight (see Chapter 8).

Visual Search

A target sighted with peripheral vision must be several times larger than one sighted with foveal vision. The eye successively fixates on different points in an area at a rate of three points per second [White and Ford, 77]. Fixation time is a useful measure for establishing the conspicuity of targets, and eye dwell durations have been used to infer reading, interpreting, and interest.

Bright orange and fluorescent materials enhance luminance contrast and provide the necessary visibility against all types of terrains and backgrounds. Signing research has established recommended color combinations for reading messages (see Chapter 10). Discrimination of color depends upon light intensity and is inversely proportional to the square of the distance to the target. Since greater acuity is generally required for identification than detection or recognition, more intense illumination is also required.

Target visibility or message legibility depends on the visual angle subtended at the eye by the viewed object rather than absolute target size. Given target diameter or character height *(L)* and distance to the target *(D)*, it is a simple matter to compute the visual angle in minutes from the following ratio [Grether and Baker, 29]:

$$\text{Visual angle (min)} = \frac{(57.3)\ (60)L}{D}$$

The constant value applies only for angles less than 10 degrees (600 min).

Distance, Speed, and Acceleration Estimation

The human is notoriously poor in estimating distance, speed, or acceleration in absolute terms [Grether and Baker, 29]. Most of us are not accustomed to performing such tasks. An unfamiliar target viewed at a distance, without familiar objects in between, will typically be overestimated in distance. The moon on the horizon behind reference cues appears much larger than in the open sky.

Estimates of speed and acceleration also depend upon knowledge of object size. An insect flying by may appear faster than a high-flying aircraft.

Although humans are poor at absolute assignment of values to parameters, by some mechanism the human develops skill in estimating relative speeds. The skilled baseball hitter knows approximately when to swing the bat although he or she would be hard-pressed to estimate the exact speed of the ball. Skeet and game shooters and race drivers are adept at estimating rates and distances in a relative sense. In general, the human is better at estimating velocities of inputs than at estimating accelerations and should not be required to estimate higher derivatives of inputs in operational situations. Judging a baseball that changes its velocity in route is extremely difficult. Chapter 5 includes a discussion of pursuit tracking and ways to enhance it.

THE HUMAN AS A DATA PROCESSOR

From the standpoint of the human, data processing involves perception, thinking and reasoning, and learning and recalling information. The human has a temporary buffer store that holds the physical characteristics of an image for a few seconds, after which the image rapidly decays. Information in the buffer is encoded by contact with semantic, pictorial, and other imagery in long-term memory. For example, by use of mnemonic techniques, we are able to associate names and faces, and by certain alphanumeric codes, we are better able to recall a long license-plate number.

Much of the information in short-term sensory store does not get processed. By a selective attention mechanism, some information is filtered out, some gets categorized in broader categories, and some is encoded verbatim by rote learning.

Long-term storage suffers from interference from other conflicting data, as we shall discuss in relation to population stereotypes in later chapters. Highly practiced verbal and motor responses rely on these organized subroutines that are called up on command without relying on thinking about the steps in the activity.

There are many excellent textbooks in cognitive and perceptual psychology that discuss the situational factors which influence processing performance [Hochberg, 80; Kaufman, 38; Attneave, 4; Neisser, 52]. This section will provide a brief review of a few of the factors influencing human information processing, principally in the areas of perception, pattern recognition, information loading, and decision making.

Perception and Pattern Recognition

The human is capable of recognizing terrain features, photographic details, and so forth against a background of visual noise and is still superior to electrooptical scanners in this respect [Grether and Baker, 29]. The human recognizes targets more quickly and accurately when there are fewer distracting stimuli; when the target is symmetrical and the background objects asymetrical or otherwise heterogeneous; when there are redundant cues to a targets identity such as size, shape, color, and movement; and when there are familiar cues or landmarks in the area. Chapter 4 presents a further discussion of some of these factors.

Gestalt psychologists argued that human sensations could not be analyzed into elementary events because when we perceive, we are influenced by a combination of elements that interact and are qualitatively different in patterns from the individual sensations. Gestalt means form or configuration. The psychologists postulated a series of laws of perceptual organization that attempt to explain, for example, why we group dot images into patterns (proximity, similarity, common fate or movement, and so forth). We are familiar with figure/ground phenomena in which we see different patterns in some pictures depending upon whether we fixate on one aspect or the other. Examples are the old woman or the young woman and a goblet or two faces (Figure 3-2).

Throughout the twentieth century people have pondered the reasons for such phenomena, but more recently perceptual psychologists have directed their attention to laboratory studies of the factors influencing perception and to theories that could account for perceptual phenomena, including illusions. A recent text on perception [Kaufman, 38] includes topics such as perception of constancies in contrasting degrees of lightness, perception of color, depth, size and distance, real and apparent movement, and perceptual rearrangements from viewing objects in mirrors.

Social psychologists have been impressed with the effects of need, values, and group opinion on perception. Poor children tend to overestimate the sizes of coins. A classic study [Sherif, 67] involved judgment of the extent of movement of a dot of light in total darkness. In fact the dot was stationary, but without reference cues it appeared to move (autokinetic effect). Sherif found that the opinions of others regarding the extent and direction of movement influenced the viewer's report and apparent perception of movement.

More recently, information theory (discussed in the next section) has been applied to perceptual phenomena. Complex shapes are more difficult to process because they are asymmetrical and require transmission of information at each change in direction of the figure, while symmetrical figures or forms are highly redundant and hence predictable (seeing part of the form may help one anticipate the remainder). In one study [Alluisi, 2], patterns or "histoforms" were created by randomly blocking in adjacent cells of a matrix. These were compared with constrained, or redundant, histoforms. Identification performance was found to decrease as the complexity of the histoforms increased. Although the findings might have been predictable without the research being coined in informational theory terms, by doing so it is feasible to express

Figure 3-2   Perceptual illusions related to figure/ground.

quantitatively phenomena that heretofore were discussed and investigated on a qualitative phenomenological basis.

Measurement of Information

Information is that which reduces uncertainty or enhances one's probability of being correct. Inputs that tell us what we already know are not information. In solving problems, we must employ certain optimum strategies in selecting information so as to solve it in the most efficient way.

The human operator is sometimes thought of as a communication channel into which information is fed via the senses and out of which information is transmitted via control responses. The human's limitations in both amount and speed of information transmission constitute major constraints on the maximum speed and effectiveness of operator decision making. Chapter 4 presents a discussion of the effects of these limitations on the number and types of codes that may be displayed within a stimulus dimension. For example, size, shape, and color coding are affected by our ability to discriminate on an absolute basis various categories of each type of information.

Information theorists have conducted research to determine the maximum amount of information a human can transmit. This is important because when an operator is overloaded by information presented, his or her performance and the system's performance degrade.

Amount of information is expressed in terms of binary digits or bits. A bit is the logarithm to the base 2 of the number of two-choice discriminations required to specify a particular event from alternative ones.

Attneave [4] presents a simple illustration of the concept. By asking a series of questions each answerable only by "yes" or "no," what is the minimum number of questions required to locate in Figure 3-3 the checkerboard square marked with an "X"?

The optimum strategy is one of successively dividing regions of the checkerboard into halves and asking: "Is it in the right half"? (no); "Is it in the upper 16 squares of the left half"? (no); "Is it in the 8 squares in the right half of the 16 squares remaining"? (yes), and so forth. By successively halving, the square marked "X" or any square may be located with a minimum of six questions. Hence, six bits of information are required to locate a square when the events are equiprobable. H, the amount of information, equals the logarithm

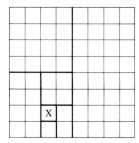

Figure 3-3 Uncertainty regarding the location of a square as defined by $H = \log m$. (*From* Applications of Information Theory to Psychology, *Fred Attneave.* © 1959 Henry Holt Co., Inc. Reprinted by permission of Holt, Rinehart and Winston, Inc.)

to the base 2 of the number of alternatives. For an 8 × 8 checkerboard, $H = \log_2$ alternatives (64) = 6. Similarly, the amount of information in the throw of a die is log 6 = 2.58 bits (b) and for the draw of a playing card is log 52 = 5.70.

Since most events are not equiprobable, the more general form of the Shannon-Wiener [64] information measure, H, is:

$$H = \overset{i}{\Sigma}\, p_i \log 1/p_i \text{ or } H = -\overset{i}{\Sigma}\, p_i \log p_i$$

Each alternative is weighted by the particular probability of its occurence, log $1/p_i$, and alternative probabilities are summated.

Information Transmission

Our primary objective is not to determine simply information presented per stimulus exposure (H_x), but to determine how much of the information is transmitted to the person ($\hat{T}$, x; y) and how much is lost. The concept of information transmission through a human channel involves multivariate informational analysis. Table 3-2 presents hypothetical data in a two-way data matrix consisting of stimulus and response categories and cells that show the frequency with which a particular stimulus produced a particular response. After summing rows and columns the probability of occurence of each stimulus, X, and each response, Y, may be computed.

The Shannon-Wiener formula above* is used to compute $H(x)$ and $H(y)$, the information per stimuli and information per response, respectively. The

*In the example, $\hat{H}(x)$ = log 5 since stimuli are equiprobable.

Table 3-2   Problem Illustrating Information Transmission Concepts

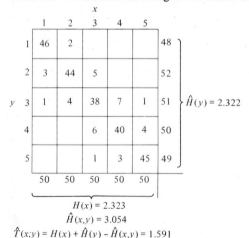

	x					
	1	2	3	4	5	
1	46	2				48
2	3	44	5			52
y 3	1	4	38	7	1	51
4			6	40	4	50
5			1	3	45	49
	50	50	50	50	50	

$\hat{H}(y) = 2.322$

$H(x) = 2.323$
$\hat{H}(x,y) = 3.054$
$\hat{T}(x;y) = H(x) + \hat{H}(y) - \hat{H}(x,y) = 1.591$

following formuli are needed to compute $\hat{T}$ *(x; y)*, the information transmitted: (1) $\hat{H}(x; y)$, the estimated information in the joint occurrence of a particular stimulus and response; (2) $\hat{H}$ *y(x)*, the conditional probability of a response given a particular stimulus; (3) $\hat{H}$ *x(y)*, the conditional probability of a stimulus given a response.

$$\hat{H}(x;y) = \overset{ij}{\Sigma} \ \hat{p}_{ij} \log 1/\hat{p}_{ij} \ (\hat{p} \log \hat{p} \text{ values summed for all cells})$$
$$\hat{T}(x;y) = \hat{H}(x) + \hat{H}(y) - \hat{H}(x;y)$$
$$\hat{H} \ y(x) = \hat{H}(x;y) - \hat{H}(y) = \hat{H}(x) - \hat{T}(x;y)$$
$$\hat{H} \ x(y) = \hat{H}(x;y) - \hat{H}(x) = \hat{H}(y) - \hat{T}(x;y)$$

Figure 3-4 may be helpful in conceptualizing the relationships between the components. In verbal terms, $\hat{T}(x; y)$ is the information transmitted from stimulus *X* to response *Y*. *H y(x)* is the uncertainty of the stimulus when the response is known and *H x(y)* is the uncertainty of the response given the stimulus. The last two terms may be thought of as "noise" or ambiguity.

Note in Figure 3-4 that the information transmitted is actually the overlap of the *H(x)* and *H(y)* distributions and may be calculated either by summing *H(x)* and *H(y)* and subtracting *H(x; y)* or by subtracting the two noise terms from *H(x; y)*. With no transmission, $\hat{T}(x; y) = 0$; *H(x) + H(y) = H(x; y)*; *H(x) = H y(x)* and *H(y) = H x(y)*. With perfect transmission, $\hat{T}(x; y) = H(x) = H(y) = H(x; y)$ and *H y(x)* and *H x(y) = 0*.

Channel Capacity

This brief introduction to information theory may provide a better appreciation of findings of studies conducted to determine human channel capacity for processing information for various sensory dimensions. Table 3-3 summarizes a few of the findings. Note that our channel capacity for vision is slightly higher than for other senses.

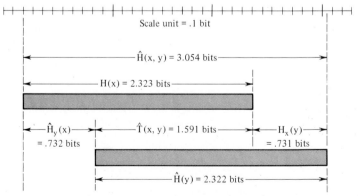

Figure 3-4 Relationship between informational components. *(Attneave, 1959.)*

Table 3-3 Channel Capacity of Senses for Different Unidimensional Stimuli

Sense	Stimulus dimension	Channel capacity (bits)	Discriminable categories	Investigator
Vision	Dot position (in space)	3.25	10	Hake & Garner (1951)
	Dot position (in space)	3.2	10	Coonan & Klemmer (in Miller, 1956)
	Size of squares	2.2	5	Eriksen & Hake (1955)
	Dominant wavelength	3.1	9	Eriksen & Hake (1955)
	Luminance	2.3	5	Eriksen & Hake (1955)
	Area	2.6	6	Pollack (in Miller, 1956)
	Line length	2.6–3.0	7–8	Pollack (in Miller, 1956)
	Direction of line inclination	2.8–3.3	7–11	Pollack (in Miller, 1956)
	Line curvature	1.6–2.2	4–5	Pollack (in Miller, 1956)
Taste	Salt concentrations	1.9	4	Beebe-Center et al. (1955)
Audition	Intensity	2.3	5	Garner (1953)
	Pitch	2.5	7	Pollack (1952, 1953)
Vibration (on chest)	Intensity	2.0	4	Geldard (in Miller, 1956)
	Duration	2.3	5	Geldard (in Miller, 1956)
	Location	2.8	7	Geldard (in Miller, 1956)
Electrical shock (skin)	Intensity	1.7	3	Hawker (1960)
	Durations	1.8	3	Hawker & Warn (1961)

Source: Van Cott and Warrick [71].

Note also that most of the studies report that there are between 4 and 10 categories that are discriminable on an absolute basis. In a classic article, Miller [51] spoke of a "magic number seven" (2.8 b) as a nominal limit value for processing information in one stimulus dimension, recognizing that some dimensions have slightly more and others slightly fewer categories that are discriminable.

Again note that the data are for absolute discriminations or identifications only. Pollack [55], for example, found that listeners could only sort pitch tones into about seven different "pigeonholes," regardless of the number of different tones given or where they appeared on a frequency scale. Obviously, the number of relative discriminations (JNDs) would be much greater.

Increasing Information Processing: Redundancy and Chunking

The user of data from information theory research is entitled to know that such unidimensional studies, although valid for their objective, do not fully represent human channel capacity for many situations of interest. Most objects in everyday life differ from one another in many different ways. Whether we are referring to a human face or to technology such as an automobile exterior, there are differences in size, shape, color, and so forth. Each dimension conveys some information not conveyed by another dimension. Studies of multidimensional stimuli have found a substantial increase in discriminable categories and channel capacity (see Table 3-4).

Buckner and McGrath [11] have shown that using vision and audition in a redundant fashion can increase the percentage of signals detected. By increasing simultaneously both brightness and loudness of an intermittent signal, more signals were detected than by increasing either brightness or loudness of the signals individually.

Studies of redundancy in the printed language have also led to some fascinating findings regarding the human's ability to process such information. Dividing a long string of binary digits into groupings or chunks substantially increases our short-term memory. For example, the sequence, 1010111101110, would be fairly difficult to memorize. However, by regrouping it as 1 010 111 101 110 sets of three binary digits in octal coding is read as 12753. Thus, by patterning or recoding the 13 elements into 5 chunks, the information may be read quickly and recalled. Telegraphers and speed readers also assimilate information in large chunks.

Table 3-4 Channel Capacity of Senses for Multidimensional Stimuli

Stimulus dimension	Channel capacity (bits)	Discriminable categories	Investigator
Size, brightness, and hue (varied together)	4.1*	18	Eriksen (1954)
Frequency, intensity, rate of interruption, on-time fraction, total duration, and spatial location	7.2	150	Pollack & Ficks (1954)
Colors of equal luminance	3.6	13	Halsey & Chapanis (1954)
Loudness and pitch	3.1	9	Pollack (1953)
Position of points in a square (no grid)	4.6	24	Klemmer & Frick (1953)

Note: The capacity of each dimension separately was approximately 2.7 bits.
Source: Van Cott and Warrick [71].

Another way we extend our processing limits is by using redundancy inherent in the language itself. The language consists of a sequence of symbols in particular patterns. There are "sequential dependencies" such that by seeing one letter, one has a fair degree of confidence as to the subsequent letter (or the limited few it is likely to be). For example, we know that a word will have a vowel; the length of the word limits the possible letters, and the parts of speech follow in a somewhat predictable order in sentence structure.

Shannon [63] gave subjects passages of printed material and had them guess the identity of each successive letter (much like deciphering cryptograms). If incorrect they continued to guess. The following is a sentence given; below each letter or space is the trial on which the subjects typically guessed the correct letter or space:

T H E R E   I S   N O   R E V E R S E   O N   A   M O T O R C Y C L E .
1 1 1 5 1 1 2 1 1 2 1 1 (15) 1 (17) 1 1 1 2 1 3 2 1 2 2 7 1 1 1 1 4 1 1 1 1 1

Note that 24 of the 35 letters and spaces were guessed correctly on the first trial. Shannon has estimated that the English language is 50 percent redundant over distances of about eight letters. Redundancy is an important safeguard against errors and misunderstandings. It permits proofreading without the original text, although it sometimes results in our overlooking typographical errors.

Lists of numbers often lack sequential dependencies and hence are very difficult to repeat. Recall of numbers is aided by dividing them into groups of three or four and by employing letters in combination with numbers.

Decision Making

Decisions are characterized by risks or uncertainty. In testing an hypothesis by a statistical test, one must state in advance the percent of the time one is willing to be incorrect. Decisions under risk occur when there are several known alternatives, each leading to a set of possible outcomes, and each outcome has a known probability of occurrence. Decisions under uncertainty occur when the probability of particular outcomes or possible outcomes are unknown, as may be true under tactical or strategic decision-making situations.

Although some decisions may be made without risk, most decisions do involve risks. It has been theorized that the human behaves in a manner that will maximize utility. This assumes that the various alternatives may be ranked in order of desirability. In engineering and economic trade-off studies, this is what is done. However, in many real-world situations people do not necessarily act in accord with objective probabilities. There is no simple relationship between the real odds and the odds perceived by the person making the decision.

The subjective expected utility (SEU) for a situation is obtained by multiplying the person's estimate of success probability by the payoff or gain anticipated. In general, risks will not be taken unless the payoff is high. In simple situations, such as throwing a fair die, the probability of each outcome is known (or knowable) so one could easily calculate what would be a profitable wager and an irrational wager. Life insurance companies use actuarial data on life expectancy to determine objectively wagers that maximize making a profit. However, in many real-life situations probabilities are not well defined and payoffs are sometimes vague, so behavioral guidelines for decision making are based upon incomplete information. We may seek expert judgment in situations where time and funding do not permit subjecting the problem to empirical testing.

As noted by Van Cott and Warrick [71], many decisions occur in sequence and the information available for later decisions depends upon the nature and consequences of earlier decisions. In command and administrative situations one is concerned with the outcome of a series of events (the bottom line) rather than the consequences and payoff of any single event in the series. They propose that in such situations the human acts as an intuitive statistician who estimates the mean of a series of numbers from small samples and attaches confidence to this judgment.

Speed and Load Stress

It is no great surprise to learn that accuracy in decision performance will decrease when the operator is required to respond more rapidly than he or she is capable of responding or when required to respond at the same rate but to a greater number of stimuli. Thus, the decision task may be made difficult by having too many channels to monitor (load stress) or by having to monitor a given channel at a rapid rate (speed stress).

Mackworth and Mackworth [46] employed a complex visual search task to study the effects of load and speed stress. The details of the clock-watching study are complex, but essentially task load was increased by requiring the subject to scan frequently changing numbers on as many as three clocks, compare the numbers read with numbers printed in various columns, and report the column with the number most nearly matching the clock reading. Speed was increased by varying the rate at which the information on the clocks changed. They found that errors increased linearly as load increased, and errors were uniformly greater for 6 decisions per minute than for 3 decisions per minute.

Time sharing may involve shifting attention between two or more sensory channels, performing multiple activities, or both. Weisz and McElroy [75] conducted a study in which the subject's task involved several activities such as detection, identification, remembering locations, and searching for extreme variations. Each activity was related to variations in four geometric shapes presented simultaneously by frames with a CRT. With increasing speed stress it was found that tasks requiring the subject to make a response for each frame yielded the smallest increase in errors. Greater increases in errors with speed stress occurred for tasks that required sensing for events that did not appear in every frame (low-probability events), especially those requiring short-term memory from one frame to the next.

Most of the literature in this area deals with variables that affect the capacity to process information and with techniques that have been successful in improving processing capabilities. Few of the studies addressed the issue of human transmission rates for various presentation rates. Obviously, the transmission rate will be improved by decreasing the rate of stimulus presentation, but expressing human transmission rates quantitatively is a sticky business and may be somewhat unique to the situation. AFSC DH-1-3, DN 2B9 [1] reports that 1 to 3 b per stimulus may be transmitted at a rate of 1 to 3 stimuli/second. However, such findings may be more applicable to visual search tasks than to reading verbal material or responding to more complex informational sources.

Table 3-5 summarizes several techniques for improving human processing. The context is for decision making principally in the area of enhancing human processing for signals received over scopes or headsets [AFSC, 1].

Time-Stress Limits

It was noted in Chapter 2 that one measure of the time constraint imposed by a system operation is the time-stress index [Siegel and Wolf, 62]. This was defined as the ratio of time required to perform the remaining tasks in a series to the time available to do so. Although time required is sometimes based on an average response time across subjects, Huchingson [34] has noted that, due to subject variability, it is preferable to base time required on each subject's pretest

---

Table 3-5   Techniques for Improving Human Processing in Time-Sharing Tasks

- Minimize the number of potential competing informational sources.
- Provide priorities for attention. Weight signals by importance and relative probability of occurrence and inform operators of the weights.*
- Minimize a requirement for short-term memory or for dealing with low-probability events.
- Physically arrange signals to take advantage of weightings and sequential effects that might reduce uncertainty.
- Reduce to a minimum the number of signals that occur at intervals less than 0.25 seconds apart.
- Allow operators to control the pace of inputs, if feasible.
- Display only signals that are to be responded to immediately or in the near-future (where precisely timed outputs are required to continuous inputs).
- Use auditory signals where considerable visual time sharing would be required.
- Direct attention to most important sources by advanced cues (light, sounds).
- When listening to several channels at once, make the relevant auditory message different from the irrelevant messages by increasing the intensity of the relevant message (making it louder), giving it distinct spectral characteristics, selectively filtering irrelevant messages, and otherwise adding redundancy to the signal to distinguish it from noise.
- When coding information, it is better to increase the number of input dimensions than to add new steps along a single dimension.

---

*(See Chapter 4 for discussion of signal-enhancing techniques.)
Source: Adapted from AFSC DH-1-3 [1].

asymptotic performance level at the end of task training (otherwise, time stress may not be experienced by many in relation to a time limit).

Time-stress levels could then be studied by introducing proportional reductions in time available. For example, if it took 1 min for subject A to accomplish a task sequence at the end of training, a time stress of 2.0 could be programmed by giving the subject 30 seconds on a time-remaining clock to accomplish the same task. Thus, each subject, regardless of skill at task, would be required to work twice as fast as previously to finish on time. By having them watch the seconds tick off, presumably an equivalent degree of subjective stress would occur at 2.0 for each subject.

Vroom [73] and several motivational theorists have noted that increasing one's motivation in pressure situations initially results in an improvement in performance, but further increases in motivation result in reduced performance. Typically, the subject increases speed but decision making is progressively impaired as motivation increases.

Siegel and Wolf [62] have noted such a curvilinear relationship with respect to increasing time-stress levels. They reported a study where the peak performance in the negatively accelerated curve came at about 2.3, after which performance deteriorated. Little research is known of the effects of systematically increasing levels of time constraint. However, it would appear that the so-called breaking point or critical time-stress value would depend heavily on the consequences of failure to finish in time (death, injury, embarrassment, or simply loss of reward would be expected to have different critical values).

Research has found that subjects worked the hardest to do well when the probability of success or failure was 50:50. Huchingson [34] studied tracking performance and "locking on" to a criterion number of targets under various

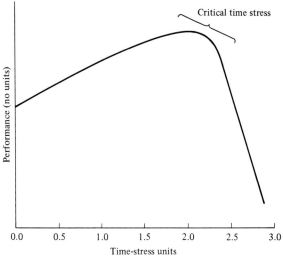

Figure 3-5 Curvilinear relationship between time stress and performance. The critical time stress region and shape of function varies with motive-incentives and subjective likelihood of success.

time-stress levels. As predicted, performance degraded with increasing time constraint. However, it was found that heart rate increased significantly in situations where the success/failure outcome was in doubt until the end (such as eventual near-misses or finishing in the nick of time), but it remained unchanged when the task was either too easy or hopelessly difficult (ample time to finish or much too little time to finish). This effect was observed in relation to a monetary-reward/competition-type incentive system.

Other Processing Capabilities

There are other processing capabilities which merit discussion but which are beyond the scope of this text. The human learns and recalls certain information from long-term memory but forgets other information. Many excellent sources exist regarding conditions that contribute to learning, transfer of training, forgetting, and so forth [Tarpy, 81; Underwood, 82].

The concept of population stereotype as a learned characteristic influencing perception and behavior in relation to equipment is discussed at length in subsequent chapters. Many of the topics that other authors have discussed in terms of stimulus/response compatibility are discussed in Chapter 5 in relation to control/display relationships. Obviously, the relationships are mediated by interpretive processes learned in the course of experience with equipment. Decision reaction time will be discussed in the next section on data transmission capabilities, along with other temporal response measures.

THE HUMAN AS A DATA TRANSMITTER

In this section the human will be considered as an output source. The human introduces a lag in the transmission of data, and we are interested in the factors affecting reaction time, decision-making time, and movement time. In performing various types of movements the human anatomy affects both speed and accuracy. Human joints are limited in range of movement and, in conjunction with limb length, they limit the maximum reach capability.

The human has limited strength and endurance. Localized muscles fatigue quickly when required to lift objects from an awkward position. In Chapter 6 some of the factors affecting and enhancing these capabilities will be examined. The physical dimensions of the body are critical to defining workspace requirements and sizing clothing and equipment. In this section and the final section, each of these factors will be examined briefly. The human as a physiological being and as a social being will be deferred to Chapters 6, 7, 8, and 9.

Reaction and Decision-Making Time

Total response time is comprised of three sequential components: reaction time (RT), movement time (MT), and systems response time (SRT). Simple RT, as studied in the laboratory, is the time required to initiate a specific preplanned response to a specific, unambiguous stimulus. The subject generally knows the approximate time at which the stimulus will appear; the task will be to detect its onset only. The finger is resting on a reaction-time key or button and the person is set to respond. Under such ideal conditions, RT typically ranges from 0.15 to 0.20 s (150 to 200 ms).

Several variables that influence simple RT have been identified:

1 There are slight differences between sense modalities. Auditory and touch RTs are approximately 0.15 s; vision and temperature RTs are 0.2 s; smell, 0.5 s; pain and taste, 1.0 s. Peripheral vision takes slightly longer than foveal vision, as one might expect.

2 Line of sight (foveal vision) and time sharing are more important in the applied setting than sensory differences. Sharp [65] has shown that RT to warning lights takes much longer when they appear approximately 57 to 96° to the left of the center plane and when the person is busy tracking. Reaction time was variable, but up to 2.5 s were required without a warning tone.

3 Visual conspicuity factors affecting reaction time include signal size, intensity, contrast, duration, and intermittency. Flashing lights are more important in attracting attention when brightness is low than when it is high. RT is slightly faster to green than to red or blue. Once signals are above a critical signal/noise ratio, no briefer RT is likely.

4 RT increases with age and men have slightly shorter and more consistent RTs than do females [AFSC, 1].

5 Temporal uncertainty or the degree to which one is prepared to respond is a major variable. Alerting signals can reduce RT as well as variability. Warrick et al. [74] studied secretaries who were asked to press a button 9.5 in to the left of their typewriters in response to a buzzer that came on only once or twice a week. In a second study the same subjects were alerted verbally 2.5 s prior to the buzzer. The median response time, including RT, to the unexpected signals after 4 weeks was 610 ms, whereas with the alerting signal it was 510 ms. Johansson and Rumar [36] found a slightly greater difference in RT for braking an automobile to anticipated and unanticipated auditory signals. These times were 540 and 730 ms, respectively. They recommended a 1.35 correction factor for estimating RT under surprise conditions from a known anticipated RT value. During the first week of testing, Warrick et al. found median RTs of approximately 600 and 800 ms, respectively, which is consistent with the correction factor ($1.35 \times 600 = 810$).

6 RT with the hand is 20 percent faster than with the foot. The preferred hand (usually the right hand) is 3 percent faster than the unpreferred hand.

7 Motivation, feedback of success, fatigue, and environment all affect reaction time in predictable directions (Chapters 6, 8, and 9).

Decision reaction time (sometimes termed choice, complex, disjunctive, or processing reaction time) refers to reaction time in situations where judgment is involved. The subject may be required to respond only to a certain class of stimulus (for example, a red light), ignoring all others, or may be required to select one of several response keys appropriate for a particular class of stimulus.

Information transmission properties such as number of alternatives, their relative probability of occurrence, and sequential dependencies affect processing time. Decision RT is a direct function of the number of choices available and seems to be related to the number of bits of information involved ($\log_2$ of alternatives available). Damon et al. [17] reported the following data:

Number of choices:	1	2	3	4	5	6	7	8	9	10
Approximate RTs:	.20	.35	.40	.45	.50	.55	.60	.60	.65	.65

These data would apply when the probability of occurrence of each choice was the same. If one's prior information should bias the odds in favor of particular alternatives as in the case of sequential dependencies, obviously the reaction time for these alternatives would be briefer.

Pew [54] has noted that average processing time is influenced by the amount of information in the input primarily with simple *information-conservation* tasks. An example is typing, where the information in the input signal is retained in the output response. One simply locates a key corresponding to the next character to be typed. This situation may be contrasted with one involving *information filtering*. Examples of the latter are proofreading or monitoring the state of several instruments. One does not respond except when the value of a variable is in a critical state. Processing time depends on the rate of presentation of stimuli and the difference between the critical signal and the other signals. If the presentation rate is slow and the critical signals are very different, then processing time varies with information in the input, as with the typing task. However, if the critical signals are similar to the irrelevant ones, processing time will be increased.

Neisser [53] surprisingly found that processing time per signal did not increase from 1 to 10 signals, provided that the operator made a single response to all critical signals. In other words, multiple signals require no additional time unless the operator must classify each signal and respond to it differently.

Information condensing is a third situation in which the amount of information in the output is less than in the input signals. Imagine a radar operator classifying every signal as friendly, enemy, or noise. The greater the information reduction (difference in bits between input and output), the longer the processing time required [Posner, 56]. Extra time is needed when much information must be condensed into a small set of output classes.

Predicting exact processing times in the applied situation without prior testing is a challenging task, although several investigators have attempted to do so by making certain assumptions, developing a model, and then testing the model in simulator studies.

The factors enhancing simple RT also enhance decision RT. Moreover, coding techniques that increase the discriminability of stimulus classes will reduce decision time, especially for search tasks.

Movement Time

Movement time (MT) refers to the time required to execute a response following a signal. Some RT studies also include elements of movement time, but reaction time is supposed to include only the time from stimulus onset to the initiation of a response, while MT begins at this instant and continues until the human response is completed.

Variables affecting MT are the device used and its manner of activation (Chapter 5), the distance traveled, the direction and type of movement, and the load being moved. In developing the Methods Time Measurement System (MTM), Maynard [47] and others have documented specific time values for elemental motions. These values are well known to time-study engineers.

AFSC DH 1-3 [1] summarizes a few findings: horizontal hand movements are faster than vertical movements; continuous curved motions are faster than abrupt direction changes; the time taken to start or stop a movement remains nearly the same regardless of movement length; time required to reach maximum velocity varies directly with load. In numerous studies discussed subsequently, MT will be the dependent variable measured.

Fitts and Peterson [26] attempted to quantify the difficulty of a motor task following a choice. Operators responded to a binary signal (two directional lights), after which they moved a stylus either left or right various distances or amplitudes *(A)* to a target area of experimentally controlled widths *(W)*. They proposed that the index of task difficulty *(ID)* equalled $\log_2 2A/W$ and demonstrated that MT increased linearly with increases in task difficulty levels (Figure 3-6).

Systems Response Time

In evaluating systems performance it is impossible to isolate the role of the human from that of the machine. The measurements may be systems measures such as time to track and lock-on to another aircraft, or accuracy in maintaining a heading, altitude, or airspeed. The human and systems components complement one another so it is difficult to establish to what degree the driver or the race car won the race.

Similarly, total systems response time consists of operator reaction and response time followed by and confounded with vehicular performance characteristics. An example would be the time required for a car to move three lanes on a busy expressway and be in position to exit from the right-hand lane. Total time is affected by traffic volume, rear-view vision capability, vehicle maneuverability, and a host of other factors. No amount of knowledge of the human in isolation can be substituted for evaluations or models that include the many relevant factors affecting systems performance.

Types of Movements

As was noted in Chapter 2, movements may be studied at a macrolevel (functions, tasks, and subtasks) or at a microlevel (specific behavioral responses to accomplish the tasks). The focus here is at the microlevel.

Movements discussed in this section are classified as positioning (discrete action) movements, continuous or tracking (continuous adjustive) movements, repetitive movements, manipulative movements, and static (holding) reactions.

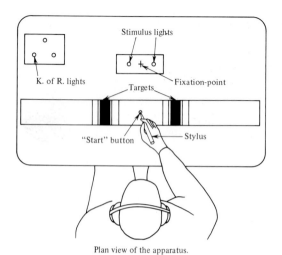

Plan view of the apparatus.

Target characteristics employed in the series of experiments

Target	Movement amplitude (A. In.)	Target width (W. In.)	Index of difficulty (ID. Bits)
A	3	1.0	2.58
B	3	0.5	3.58
C	3	0.25	4.58
D	3	0.125	5.58
E	6	1.0	3.58
F	6	0.5	4.58
G	6	0.25	5.58
H	6	0.125	6.58
I	12	1.0	4.58
J	12	0.5	5.58
K	12	0.25	6.58
L	12	0.125	7.58

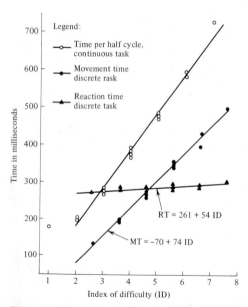

Figure 3-6   Relation of reaction time and movement time to task difficulty. Upper left figure depicts apparatus. Upper right table presents experimental task requirements. Bottom figure presents data. Solid data points depict reaction time and movement time in relation to an index of difficulty with ID = $\log_2 2A/W$. Open circles show mean response times per movement for a serial tapping task. (*Fitts and Peterson, 1964*).

Measures of speed, accuracy, or both are generally taken. Discrete movements may be random or sequential in their order of accomplishment.

Movement performance varies with work posture, the particular limbs employed, and the interface between anatomical structure and workspace. In the next section limits to movement and reach imposed by our anatomy and body dimensions will be presented. Movements in relation to work and equipment are discussed in Chapters 5 and 6.

Other investigators have focused on the psychomotor skills associated with types of movements and their task organization (for example, manual dexterity, steadiness, eye-hand coordination). Measurable levels of psychomotor skill are required for certain tasks and individuals differ markedly in their psychomotor abilities.

Still other investigators have evaluated movements and associated work in terms of the physiological energy costs (fatigue), subjective evaluations, and the consequences of poor performance in terms of errors and accidents. These topics and factors affecting them are discussed in subsequent chapters.

Positioning Movements

Positioning movements are illustrated by reaching for something or moving an object to another location. They consist of a gross, primary movement and a final, corrective movement. Positional movements have an MT that is proportional to but not linearly related to the distance traveled. Much of the total MT is associated with the final corrective movement of bringing the hand precisely to a position; this time is independent of distance.

Terminal reach time is also longer when one is not sure of the location of the object being reached for, or when it is necessary to reach for an object among other objects. These are processing factors manifested in the movement time measure.

Positioning accuracy depends upon the extent, direction, and plane of movement. Briggs [10] studied subjects' ability to successively punch a hand-held stylus or dart within a series of small circular holes of various diameters (punctate steadiness). Measures were taken of the frequency of hits within a period of 20 s. The holes varied in both distance away and angular displacements from 0 to 90°. The greatest accuracy was found to be at 60° to the right and away from the body (away was 14 in or 37 cm from a central point with measures in a horizontal plane). Schmidtke and Stier [61] studied positioning times and accuracy in a horizontal plane and found that average times were shorter from lower-left to upper-right (much like a right-handed person writing at a table). Best performance was achieved when only the elbow pivoted. Upper-left and lower-right positioning took longer because shoulder and upper-arm movements were involved in extended or retracted positioning movements.

In Fitts' classic study of blind reaching [25], it was found that blindfolded subjects with hand-held styluses were more accurate in hitting bull's-eye targets when the targets were located directly ahead. Accuracy was poorest for targets 135° to the left and right and for targets in the tier above the head. When reaching with kinesthetic feedback (no vision), greater accuracy can be expected when the hand is within 8 in (20 cm) above or below the heart level and straight ahead.

Continuous Movement

Continuous adjustment movements are involved in tracking a continuously moving target (see Chapter 5). Errors in tracking a rotating disc on a turntable will obviously increase with the revolutions per minute and with an irregular velocity. In a study with the target moving at constant velocity, Corrigan and Brogden [15] also confirmed the positioning study finding cited earlier that fewest errors occur at near-left (7:30 o'clock) and far-right (1:30 o'clock). Hence, errors in extent and direction of reach for right-handed subjects is again related to a requirement for only elbow-pivoting. More errors occurred with extended reach and extreme retraction.

Dynamic arm steadiness is also measured by moving a stylus with a right-angle tip down a narrow groove. Wall contacts are recorded as discrete errors. Mead and Sampson [49] found that arm tremor is greatest when the plane of movement is in-out (away from or toward the body) as opposed to left-right or up-down. Over 200 contacts occurred when the movement was away or toward the body and the groove was mounted on either a vertical or horizontal surface. Only 32 errors occurred when the arm movement was right-left on a horizontal surface, and 45 errors occurred when arm movement was up-down with the groove on a vertical surface, sagittal plane (perpendicular to the body). Once again, greatest arm steadiness occurs with left-right or lower-left to upper-right movements with only elbow pivoting.

Repetitive Movements

Cranking and tapping are repetitive movements. A drummer may tap with the entire arm or a typist may tap with individual fingers. Dvorak et al. [22] found that the right-hand digits move at a slightly faster rate than those on the left hand when moved individually. (Presumably, most subjects were right-handed.) The index and big fingers moved faster than the ring and little fingers on either hand. Reading left to right from the little finger, left hand to little finger, right hand, the taps per second were: 3.2, 3.8, 4.2, 4.4 / 4.7, 4.6, 4.1, 3.7.

AFSC DH 1-3 [1] recommended that if the responses are to be made to individual signals, the signals should appear at intervals greater than 0.5 s. If greater speed than this is needed, one cue should serve as a stimulus for a series of responses.

Other Movements

Manipulative movements involve a combination of the other types of elemental movements with emphasis on finger and manual dexterity. Consider the tasks of a watch repairer: positioning accuracy in picking up tiny parts, steadiness in the use of small tools, rapid and precise movements over very short ranges. The control tasks of operators also involve a high degree of manual and finger dexterity skill.

Static reactions involve holding a fixed posture unsupported or supporting a weight. Holding a weight is three to six times more fatiguing than lifting the same weight up and down [AFSC, 1]. Such tasks are being designed out at the workplace.

Page limitations do not permit a discussion of specialized types of movements. Sports and physical conditioning involve whole body coordination of movement and speed, strength, and endurance. Speech is a specialized type of movement discussed in Chapter 12. Of practical interest also is reading time and comprehension, which obviously involves eye movements but also is dependent upon a host of sensory and processing variables such as legibility, and message content and format (see Chapters 4 and 10).

THE HUMAN BODY: DIMENSIONAL AND ANATOMICAL CONSTRAINTS

The human is limited in its flexibility of movement and posture by the particular manner in which the bones are connected at the joints. For example, the fingers are hinged at the knuckles, the elbow pivots, the shoulder and hips are ball-in-socket joints capable of rotational movements. The human anatomy thus constrains our angular movements and reach capability.

Anatomical Limits to Movement

Joint movement is measured at the angle formed by the long axis of two adjacent body segments or at the angle formed by a body segment and a vertical or horizontal plane. Range of joint movement is measured between the two extreme positions and is expressed in total angular degrees or angular degrees from a null position before forming the angle. If the data were given in linear measures rather than in degrees, subject variations in trunk and limb length would affect the maximum capabilities.

Prior to presenting research findings, it is first necessary to define a few terms commonly used in describing types of movements. *Flexion* refers to bending or decreasing the angle between parts of the body. *Extension* is the opposite—straightening or increasing the angle. *Hyperextension* occurs when the member is moved beyond its normal limits as whiplash of the neck, hyperextension of the knee when bent forward, or the spine when bent backward too far.

Adduction and abduction are also opposites. *Adduction* is moving toward the midline of the body; *abduction* is moving away from the midline. Shoulder adduction occurs when the arm is moved horizontally in front of the body, and abduction occurs when the arm is swung back in a horizontal plane.

Lateral rotation is turning away from the body's midplane; *medial rotation* is turning toward the midplane. The hips permit flexion, adduction, abduction, and rotation. Sitting on a table without moving the knee position, we may rotate the lower leg outward (lateral) or inward (medial). Pronation and supination are also opposites. *Forearm pronation* is illustrated by rotating a hand-held cylinder from a vertical position to palms down with the elbow stationary; *forearm supination* would be rotating the cylinder backward to a palms-up position.

Some writers use slightly different terms. Figure 3-7 may help conceptualize the types of movements as applied to limbs.

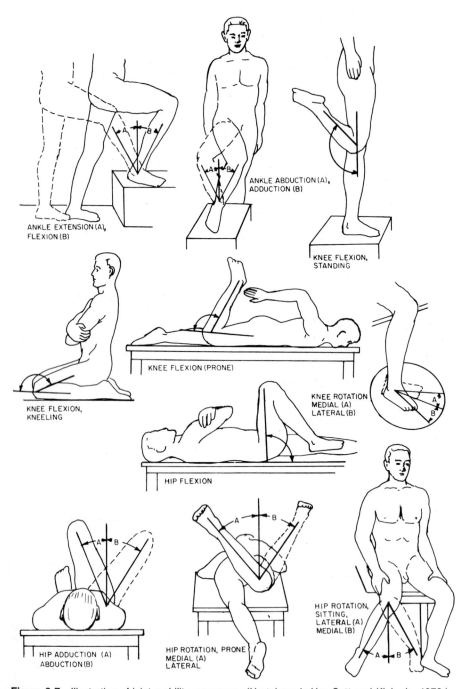

Figure 3-7 Illustration of joint mobility measures. *(Hertzberg in Van Cott and Kinkade, 1972.)*

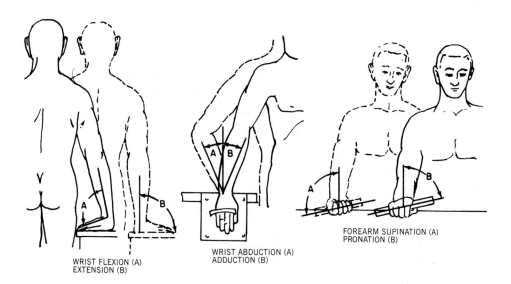

WRIST FLEXION (A)
EXTENSION (B)

WRIST ABDUCTION (A)
ADDUCTION (B)

FOREARM SUPINATION (A)
PRONATION (B)

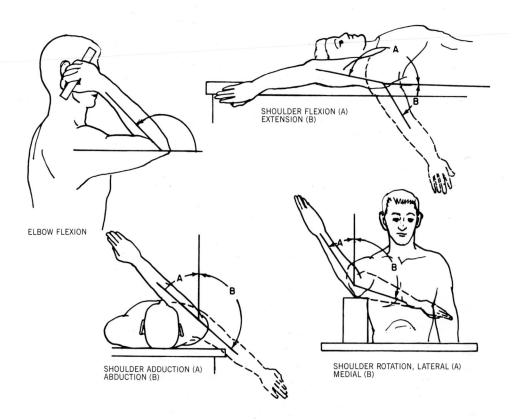

ELBOW FLEXION

SHOULDER FLEXION (A)
EXTENSION (B)

SHOULDER ADDUCTION (A)
ABDUCTION (B)

SHOULDER ROTATION, LATERAL (A)
MEDIAL (B)

Table 3-6 Range of Joint Movement (angular degrees)

Joint	Movement	Male			Female		
		5th	50th	95th	5th	50th	95th
Ankle	Flexion	23	35	47	8.6	18.8	29.0
	Extension	18	38	58	35.5	49.7	63.9
	Adduction	9	24	39	19.8	37.6	55.4
	Abduction	11	23	35	14.3	30.0	45.7
Knee	Flexion (stand)	92	113	134	120.9	133.8	146.7
	Flexion (kneel)	129	144	159		(posture unknown)	
	Flexion (prone)	109	125	142			
	Medial rotation	15	35	55	24.7	43.8	62.9
	Lateral rotation	23	43	63	40.1	55.8	71.5
Hip	Flexion (supine)	92	113	134	55.7	79.6	103.5
	Adduction (supine)	33	53	73 }	52.7	71.8	90.9
	Abduction (supine)	11	31	51 }			
	Medial rotation (sit)	16	31	46	24.7	43.8	62.9
	Lateral rotation (sit)	15	30	45	40.1	55.8	71.5
	Medial rotation (prone)	23	39	56		(posture unknown)	
	Lateral rotation (prone)	18	34	51			
Wrist	Flexion	70	90	110	54.8	79.7	104.6
	Extension	78	95	120	43.3	60.6	77.6
	Adduction	12	27	42	32.6	50.4	68.2
	Abduction	35	47	59	14.7	29.7	44.7

Table 3-6 *(Continued)*

Joint	Movement	Male			Female		
		5th	50th	95th	5th	50th	95th
Forearm	Supination	77	113	149	60.7	88.9	117.1
	Pronation	37	77	117	76.8	101.9	127.0
Elbow	Flexion	126	142	159	139.7	151.4	163.1
Shoulder	Flexion	168	188	208	151.4	167.9	184.4
	Extension	38	61	84	25.0	41.5	58.0
	Adduction	33	48	63	151.0	169.5	188.0
	Abduction	106	134	162			
	Medial rotation	61	97	133	139.4	160.0	180.6
	Lateral rotation	13	34	55	15.3	33.6	51.9
Neck	Flexion	–	–	–	41.7	58.7	75.9
	Extension	–	–	–	73.0	89.3	105.6
Spine	Flexion	–	–	–	43.3	61.9	80.5
	Extension	–	–	–	8.7	29.3	49.9

*Differences between sexes are due in part to different measurement techniques. Male data used photography; female data, a flexometer. Postures are unknown in Harris and Harris study.

Source: Male data from Barter et al. [7]; female data from Harris and Harris [31].

71

Table 3-6 summarizes the range of movement data for certain joints. Note that the voluntary limits are slightly less than forced limits. For example, when one is lying prone the knee may be flexed only about 125°, but when one is kneeling it may flex 144°.

Most of the data on range of movement is based on college-aged males [Barter, Emanuel, and Truett, 7] and females [Harris and Harris, 31]. From ages 20 to 60, the decline in range is only about 10 percent [West, 76]. However, it is not known if this population included arthritic or other handicapped. The brackets in Table 3-6 imply that the female data combined adduction and abduction measures. Holland is abstracted by Laubach in the *Anthropometric Source Book* [43] as concluding that range of joint movement is a highly specific factor and that measurement of one or several body parts cannot be used to predict range of movement in other body parts.

Anatomical Limits to Reach

From the standpoint of workspace design, one of the most important measures is functional reach, more often referred to as thumb-forefinger grasping reach. Kennedy [40] devised a technique for measuring functional arm reach envelopes from a constant seat reference point (SRP) or seat reference level (SRL). See Figure 3-8.

The device employed a series of staves 15° apart and mounted on an arclike supporting structure. The seated subject grasped a knob on the end of a stave and pushed it until the arm was fully extended without moving the shoulders away from the seat back. Each stave pointed toward the approximate center of the right shoulder joint. As shown in Figure 3-8, measures were taken in a horizontal plane from 5 in below to 55 in above the seat reference line.

Table 3-7 presents the results of a study of right-arm reach distances taken at various angles from the vertical midplane through the SRP. As expected, the reach envelope was greatest when the arm was 15 to 35 in above the SRL. Smaller arcs were formed both above and below. The data shown is for a fifth percentile male, so reaches above 45 in above SRL were not to be expected. Missing values in the upper left may be accounted for by the body's occluding right-hand measurements, which were low and to the left. In 1976, Kennedy [39], reported comparable data for female subjects. Complete data for both men and women are summarized by Stoudt [68].

Kennedy and Filler [41] have also taken measures of how far one can reach through an opening of various breadths, heights, and distances above the floor. Measures were taken as a function of body position (sitting or standing, reaching forward or laterally), with one or two hands, and in shirt-sleeves and pressure suits.

Another technique used to measure three-dimensional reach envelopes involved photographic methods (either a single camera or two cameras about 5 ft apart and 12 ft from the subject). The subject sat in front of a grid, and flash exposures were taken with the arm in various positions. Dempster [19] analyzed these photographic tracings of contours of the hand in various positions and

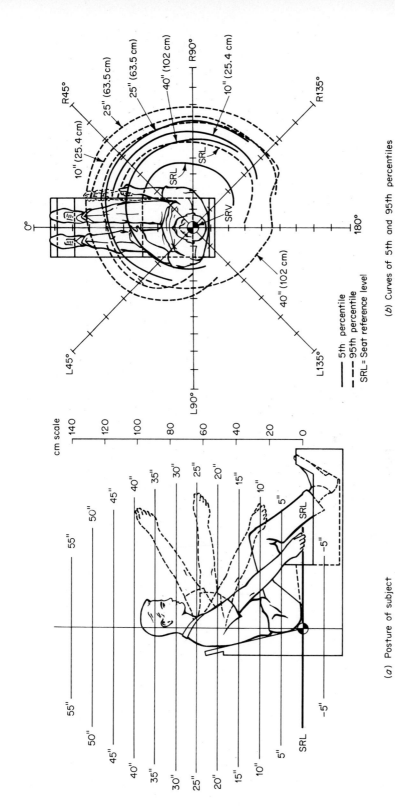

cm scale

140

120

100

80

60

40

20

0

55"

50"

45"

40"

35"

30"

25"

20"

15"

10"

5"

SRL

-5"

R45°

25" (63.5 cm)

25" (63.5 cm)

40" (102 cm)

R90°

10" (25.4 cm)

10" (25.4 cm)

SRL

SRL

R135°

0°

SRV

180°

40" (102 cm)

L45°

L90°

L135°

——— 5th percentile
– – – 95th percentile
SRL = Seat reference level

(b) Curves of 5th and 95th percentiles

(a) Posture of subject

Figure 3-8 Subject postures and tasks in measuring functional reach envelopes. *(Kennedy, 1964, as adapted by McCormick, 1976.)*

Table 3-7 Right-Hand Grasp Reach from Seat Reference Vertical for Fifth Percentile Male

Horizontal plane measured from seat reference point (m/in)

Angle from midplane	−5	SRL	5	10	15	20	25	30	35	40	45	50	55
L 165°											266.70 (10.50)		
150°											222.25 (8.75)		
135°											196.85 (7.75)		
120°									273.05 (10.75)	285.75 (11.25)	190.50 (7.50)		
105°									311.15 (12.25)	298.45 (11.75)	184.15 (7.25)		
90°									349.25 (13.75)	311.15 (12.25)	184.15 (7.25)		
75°									381.00 (15.00)	317.50 (12.50)	190.50 (7.50)		
60°								438.15 (17.25)	406.40 (16.00)	336.55 (13.25)	196.85 (7.75)		
45°					482.60 (19.00)	495.30 (19.50)	508.00 (20.00)	482.60 (19.00)	438.15 (17.25)	355.60 (14.00)	215.90 (8.50)		
30°					552.45 (21.75)	546.10 (21.50)	571.50 (22.50)	546.10 (21.50)	488.95 (19.25)	393.70 (15.50)	241.30 (9.50)		
L 15°					590.55 (23.25)	596.90 (23.50)	609.60 (24.00)	603.25 (23.75)	533.40 (21.00)	431.80 (17.00)	279.40 (11.00)		
0°					628.65 (24.75)	647.70 (25.50)	666.75 (26.25)	647.70 (25.50)	565.15 (22.25)	482.60 (19.00)	323.85 (12.75)		

Table 3-7 (Continued)

Horizontal plane measured from seat reference point (m/in)

Angle from midplane	-5	SRL	5	10	15	20	25	30	35	40	45	50	55
R 15°					673.10 (26.50)	711.20 (28.00)	717.55 (28.25)	692.15 (27.25)	628.65 (24.75)	533.40 (21.00)	393.70 (15.50)		
30°		444.50 (17.50)	603.25 (23.75)	685.80 (27.00)	723.90 (28.50)	762.00 (30.00)	768.35 (30.25)	736.60 (29.00)	679.45 (26.75)	577.85 (22.75)	444.50 (17.50)		
45°		495.30 (19.50)	641.35 (25.25)	717.55 (28.25)	762.00 (30.00)	787.40 (31.00)	787.40 (31.00)	768.35 (30.25)	717.55 (28.25)	628.65 (24.75)	482.60 (19.00)		
60°		520.70 (20.50)	654.05 (25.75)	736.60 (29.00)	787.40 (31.00)	812.80 (32.00)	800.10 (31.50)	787.40 (31.00)	736.60 (29.00)	647.70 (25.50)	520.70 (20.50)		
75°		508.00 (20.00)	654.05 (25.75)	742.95 (29.25)	800.10 (31.50)	819.15 (32.25)	812.80 (32.00)	793.75 (31.25)	749.30 (29.50)	660.40 (26.00)	520.70 (20.50)		
90°		495.30 (19.50)	654.05 (25.75)	742.95 (29.25)	787.40 (31.00)	819.15 (32.25)	819.15 (32.25)	793.75 (31.25)	755.65 (29.75)	666.75 (26.25)	533.40 (21.00)		
105°		476.25 (18.75)	641.35 (25.25)	730.25 (28.75)	781.05 (30.75)	806.45 (31.75)	800.10 (31.50)	787.40 (31.00)	755.65 (29.75)	679.45 (26.75)	546.10 (21.50)		
120°		463.55 (18.25)	622.30 (24.50)	704.85 (27.75)	749.30 (29.50)	774.70 (30.50)	774.70 (30.50)	768.35 (30.25)	736.60 (29.00)	666.75 (26.25)	539.75 (21.25)		
135°		419.10 (16.50)	577.85 (22.75)	666.75 (26.25)							508.00 (20.00)		
150°		355.60 (14.00)									393.70 (15.50)		
165°											374.65 (14.75)		
180°											323.85 (12.75)		

Source: Adapted from Kennedy [40].

75

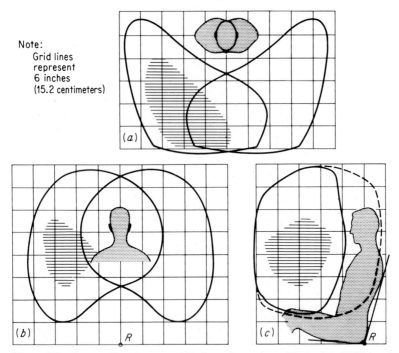

Note:
  Grid lines
  represent
  6 inches
  (15.2 centimeters)

Figure 3-9   Range of hand movement in three dimensions. *(Dempster, 1955, as adapted by McCormick, 1976.)*

developed functional reach envelopes in three planes. The tracings when combined were termed *strophospheres* (Figure 3-9).

Static Body Dimensions

Engineering anthropometrists have compiled not only data on mobility and reach, but also data on the physical dimensions of the body. Collectively, this data is basic to defining workspace dimensions, sizing clothing, and tailoring equipment operated and maintained by the human. Before making a set of binoculars we would need to know the range of interpupillary distances.

   Sources of Variability   Human body dimensions vary with age, sex, race or ethnic group, and occupation, so it is essential that the design population be defined before referring to tables of data. Since there are also changes from generation to generation, it is important to know the publication date of the body measurements.

   Generation Variability   From military clothing and armor, we have a fairly accurate record of long-term changes in stature and other body dimensions of the military population. Annis [3] has graphed the growth in stature of various ethnic groups since 1840. He noted that there was little change in stature of young, American males between 1863 and 1919, possibly due to the large immigration of shorter southern Europeans. Since 1920 there has been a growth in stature of 0.4 in (1.00 cm) per decade. Between World Wars I and II, stature increased 0.7 in (1.8 cm), and from 1952 to 1967 another 0.7 in. Improved nutrition, life style, and heterosis (cultural inbreeding) are given as reasons for the phenomenal growth.

Using the 0.4 in/decade as a model, McConville and Laubach [48] forecasted the various body dimensions in 1985. For example, they projected the mean male stature in 1985 as 70.2 in (178.4 cm). However, Hamill et al. [30] of the National Center for Health Statistics concluded from measuring 20,000 children from 1965 to 1977 that the trend toward increasing size is leveling off, and that we may have reached the limits of our genetic potential for growth. Significant increases beyond the present 69.6 in- (176.8 cm) male and the 64.0 in- (162.6 cm) female should not be expected.

Age Variability   Horizontal studies (taken on approximately the same date) have compared the stature of samples at each year of age. The data indicate that stature increases to about age 25 and decreases after age 30 at a progressively increasing rate each decade. These changes, particularly the pronounced drop after age 70, are based largely on differences in the sample characteristics that are confounded with generation variability. Longitudinal measures taken over a lifetime have not noted substantial shrinkage in individuals. Unlike stature, weight and chest circumference increases through age 60 before declining.

Sex Variability   The maximum growth rate in girls is from ages 10 to 12 (about 2.5 in/yr), after which the rate tapers off gradually until age 17. The maximum growth rate in boys is from ages 13 to 15 (about 2.7 in/yr), and growth increases decelerate until age 20 [69]. Twelve-year-old girls are 1.3 inches taller and 6 pounds heavier than their male counterparts. As adults, female dimensions average about 92 percent of the comparable male values [Annis, 3], although there are variations in certain dimensions as described subsequently in Tables 3-8 to 3-10.

Racial and Ethnic Variability   In 1965, Long and Churchill [44] compared black and caucasian males in the United States Air Force. They found that blacks tended to have longer arms, legs, hands, and feet, but a shorter torso. The mean height (approximately 69 in, 175 cm) was identical. In 1972, Yokohori collected comparable data for the Japanese Air Force [79]. The Japanese were shorter (65.31 in, 166 cm), had shorter arms and legs, but their torsos and mean sitting height did not differ much from the caucasian males.

Annis [3] compared mean stature and weight for inhabitants of many countries around the world. The mean Oriental statures ranged from 62.5 (158.7 cm) to 66.1 in (168.0 cm). The Northern Europeans (Finland, Iceland, and France) were almost as tall and heavy as the Americans. The blacks encompassed the extremes: The Batutsi tribe was the tallest of all (69.3 in, 176.0 cm), and the Pygmies the shortest (56.0 in, 142.2 cm). Hertzberg [33] has reported many other ethnic group statistics.

Other sources of Variability Body dimensions vary also with body build and occupational group. Sheldon et al. [66], attempted to describe human body builds in terms of the degree to which people could be classified into each of three categories: ectomorphy (thinness), endomorphy (obesity), and mesomorphy (muscularity). Also, skinfold thicknesses at certain locations may be used to estimate percentage of body that is water, fat, protein, or mineral.

To the extent that people with certain body builds gravitate to certain occupations, differences should be expected between occupational groups in weight and body dimensions. Policemen are larger than average, and airline stewardesses are taller and thinner than other females. As discussed subsequently, samples from the population that exclude extreme dimensions will be biased for design purposes wherever the extremes are required to use the equipment.

Dimensional data is typically shown in percentiles, the percentage of the population with a body dimension of a certain size or smaller. If one were to measure each of one's own body dimensions, convert them to percentile values, and depict the various measures in a histogram, one might be surprised to note the variability in various dimensions. It is often stated that there is no such thing as an average person, meaning that being average in stature, for example, does not necessarily imply that one is at the 50th percentile in other dimensions.

Correction Factors in Using Anthropometric Data Most anthropometric measures are taken with subjects standing erect or sitting erect. Most of us do not assume such a body posture for long. The slump-posture eye height is about 0.75 in (2 cm) lower when standing and 1.75 in (4.5 cm) lower when seated than the corresponding erect posture eye heights [Hertzberg, 33]. These conversions should be considered in workspace design.

Linear distances change over the body surfaces when various joints are moved. When arm muscles are flexed their circumferences are greater. Emanuel and Barter [23] measured these increases in bicep, elbow, and forearm circumference. For clothing design purposes the flexed muscle dimensions are relevant, and measures were so taken. They also found that full flexion of the elbow increased arm length by 3.34 in (8.48 cm) for a male sample. This helps explain why long-sleeve shirts that are a comfortable length with arms extended may feel tight when the arms assume functional positions. The distance from arm pit (scye) to arm pit across the back increases some 4.5 in (11.4 cm) when the shoulders are moved forward. This explains, for example, why pajama tops may be uncomfortable when lying on one's side.

An increment for the bulk of clothing must be added to the static dimensions when establishing clearance requirements for workspace. The military and NASA have developed numerous tables of increments to be added to the nude dimensions to allow for bulky winter clothing, flight gear, astronaut pressure suits, helmets, and so forth.

Steps in applying anthropometric data are as follows [Hertzberg, 33]:

1 Determine the relevant dimension for the problem.
2 Define the user population.
3 Select the range of users to be accommodated (for example, 5th percentile female to 95th percentile male).
4 Extract percentile data from an appropriate table.
5 Add corrections for clothing and posture.

Some dimensional data is given only in terms of means and standard deviations. However, simple conversion factors exist for converting to percentile data [33].

Body Dimensions Percentile Data   For purposes of design of workspace, equipment, and clothing, a range of body dimensions from the 5th percentile female to the 95th percentile male is relevant. This design range provides for 90 percent of the user population and MIL-STD-1472B, Notice 2 [21] presents only these values. Tables 3-8 through 3-10 present selected body dimensions. Other dimensions and circumferences are given in the Appendix.

There are many sources of military percentile data [33, 20, 1], but the 1472B data are presented because they were collected by combining several sources. With the large sample size there is less likelihood of error in representing the military personnel dimensions. The ground troop data were based upon 6682 U.S. Army men and 2008 U.S. Marines in 1966 and 287 U.S. Army men in 1977. The data on aviators represents 1482 U.S. Army aviators (1970), 1549 U.S. Navy pilots (1964), and 2420 U.S. Air Force flying personnel (1967). Data on the USAF population have been widely circulated in Van Cott and Kinkade [33] and in the NASA *Anthropometric Source Book* [48].

The data on military women were based on statistics of 1330 U.S. Army WAC personnel and Army nurses (1977) and 1905 U.S. Air Force WAC and nurses (1968).

A variety of dimensions are shown, using wherever possible the layperson's terminology rather than anatomical descriptions. The reader is encouraged to study the dimensions carefully and try to conceive of workplace, equipment, and apparel requirements that would depend upon knowing these dimensional values. In subsequent chapters these dimensions will be applied to practical problems.

Civilian Data Needed   One may ask why data is presented for military personnel when the system to be designed may be used by a cross section of civilians. Admittedly, the military data present a somewhat biased sample. Initial screening by age, health, and compatibility with military equipment has already excluded large segments of the population.

The answer is that military equipment operation is critical, and the military

Table 3-8 Standing Body Dimensions

	Percentile values in centimeters					
	5th Percentile			95th Percentile		
	Ground troops	Aviators	Women	Ground troops	Aviators	Women
Weight (kg)	55.5	60.4	46.4	91.6	96.0	74.5
Standing body dimensions						
1. Stature	162.8	164.2	152.4	185.6	187.7	174.1
2. Eye height (standing)	151.1	152.1	140.9	173.3	175.2	162.2
3. Shoulder (acromiale) height	133.6	133.3	123.0	154.2	154.8	143.7
4. Chest (nipple) height*	117.9	120.8	109.3	136.5	138.5	127.8
5. Elbow (radiale) height	101.0	104.8	94.9	117.8	120.0	110.7
6. Fingertip (dactylion) height		61.5			73.2	
7. Waist height	96.6	97.6	93.1	115.2	115.1	110.3
8. Crotch height	76.3	74.7	68.1	91.8	92.0	83.9
9. Gluteal furrow height	73.3	74.6	66.4	87.7	88.1	81.0
10. Kneecap height	47.5	46.8	43.8	58.6	57.8	52.5
11. Calf height	31.1	30.9	29.0	40.6	39.3	36.6
12. Functional reach	72.6	73.1	64.0	90.9	87.0	80.4
13. Functional reach, extended	84.2	82.3	73.5	101.2	97.3	92.7

Table 3-8 *(Continued)*

	Percentile values in inches					
Weight (lb)	122.4	133.1	102.3	201.9	211.6	164.3
Standing body dimensions						
1 Stature	64.1	64.6	60.0	73.1	73.9	68.5
2 Eye height (standing)	59.5	59.9	55.5	68.2	69.0	63.9
3 Shoulder (acromiale) height	52.6	52.5	48.4	60.7	60.9	56.6
4 Chest (nipple) height*	46.4	47.5	43.0	53.7	54.5	50.3
5 Elbow (radiale) height	39.8	41.3	37.4	46.4	47.2	43.6
6 Fingertip (dactylion) height		24.2			28.8	
7 Waist height	38.0	38.4	36.6	45.3	45.3	43.4
8 Crotch height	30.0	29.4	26.8	36.1	36.2	33.0
9 Gluteal furrow height	28.8	29.4	26.2	34.5	34.7	31.9
10 Kneecap height	18.7	18.4	17.2	23.1	22.8	20.7
11 Calf height	12.2	12.2	11.4	16.0	15.5	14.4
12 Functional reach	28.6	28.8	25.2	35.8	34.3	31.7
13 Functional reach, extended	33.2	32.4	28.9	39.8	38.3	36.5

*Bustpoint height for women.
Source: MIL–STD–1472B [21].

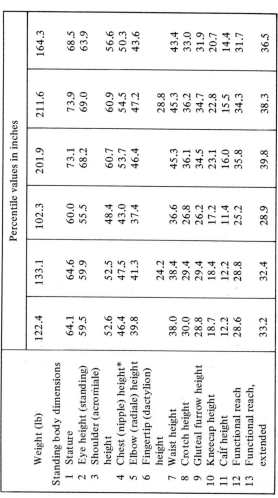

12
13*

*Same as 12, however, right shoulder is extended as far forward as possible while keeping the back of the left shoulder firmly against the back wall.

Table 3-9 Seated Body Dimensions

	Percentile values in centimeters					
	5th Percentile			95th Percentile		
Seated body dimensions	Ground troops	Aviators	Women	Ground troops	Aviators	Women
14 Vertical arm reach, sitting	128.6	134.0	117.4	147.8	153.2	139.4
15 Sitting height, erect	83.5	85.7	79.0	96.9	98.6	90.9
16 Sitting height, relaxed	81.5	83.6	77.5	94.8	96.5	89.7
17 Eye height, sitting erect	72.0	73.6	67.7	84.6	86.1	79.1
18 Eye height, sitting relaxed	70.0	71.6	66.2	82.5	84.0	77.9
19 Mid-shoulder height	56.6	58.3	53.7	67.7	69.2	62.5
20 Shoulder height, sitting	54.2	54.6	49.9	65.4	65.9	60.3
21 Shoulder–elbow length	33.3	33.2	30.8	40.2	39.7	36.6
22 Elbow–grip length	31.7	32.6	29.6	38.3	37.9	35.4
23 Elbow–fingertip length	43.8	44.7	40.0	52.0	51.7	47.5
24 Elbow rest height	17.5	18.7	16.1	28.0	29.5	26.9
25 Thigh clearance height		12.4	10.4		18.8	17.5
26 Knee height, sitting	49.7	48.9	46.9	60.2	59.9	55.5
27 Popliteal height	39.7	38.4	38.0	50.0	47.7	45.7
28 Buttock–knee length	54.9	55.9	53.1	65.8	65.5	63.2
29 Buttock–popliteal length	45.8	44.9	43.4	54.5	54.6	52.6
30 Buttock–heel length		46.7			56.4	
31 Functional leg length	110.6	103.9	99.6	127.7	120.4	118.6

Table 3-9 *(Continued)*

Seated body dimensions	Percentile values in inches					
14 Vertical arm reach, sitting	50.6	52.8	46.2	58.2	60.3	54.9
15 Sitting height, erect	32.9	33.7	31.1	38.2	38.8	35.8
16 Sitting height, relaxed	32.1	32.9	30.5	37.3	38.0	35.3
17 Eye height, sitting erect	28.3	30.0	26.6	33.3	33.9	31.2
18 Eye height, sitting relaxed	27.6	28.2	26.1	32.5	33.1	30.7
19 Mid-shoulder height	22.3	23.0	21.2	26.7	27.3	24.6
20 Shoulder height, sitting	21.3	21.5	19.6	25.7	25.9	23.7
21 Shoulder–elbow length	13.1	13.1	12.1	15.8	15.6	14.4
22 Elbow–grip length	12.5	12.8	11.6	15.1	14.9	14.0
23 Elbow–fingertip length	17.3	17.6	15.7	20.5	20.4	18.7
24 Elbow rest height	6.9	7.4	6.4	11.0	11.6	10.6
25 Thigh clearance height		4.9	4.1		7.4	6.9
26 Knee height, sitting	19.6	19.3	18.5	23.7	23.6	21.8
27 Popliteal height	15.6	15.1	15.0	19.7	18.8	18.0
28 Buttock–knee length	21.6	22.0	20.9	25.9	25.8	24.9
29 Buttock–popliteal length	17.9	17.7	17.1	21.5	21.5	20.7
30 Buttock–heel length		18.4			22.2	
31 Functional leg length	43.5	40.9	39.2	50.3	47.4	46.7

Source: MIL–STD–1472B [21].

83

Table 3-10 Depth and Breadth Dimensions

	Percentile values in centimeters					
	5th Percentile			95th Percentile		
	Ground troops	Aviators	Women	Ground troops	Aviators	Women
Depth and breadth dimensions						
32 Chest depth*	18.9	20.4	19.6	26.7	27.8	27.2
33 Buttock depth		20.7	18.4		27.4	24.3
34 Chest breadth	27.3	29.5	25.1	34.4	38.5	31.4
35 Hip breadth, standing	30.2	31.7	31.5	36.7	38.8	39.5
36 Shoulder (bideltoid) breadth	41.5	43.2	38.2	49.8	52.6	45.8
37 Forearm–forearm breadth	39.8	43.2	33.0	53.6	60.7	44.9
38 Hip breadth, sitting	30.7	33.3	33.0	38.4	42.4	43.9
39 Knee-to-knee breadth		19.1			25.5	
	Percentile values in inches					
Depth and breadth dimensions						
32 Chest depth*	7.5	8.0	7.7	10.5	11.0	10.7
33 Buttock depth		8.2	7.2		10.8	9.6
34 Chest breadth	10.8	11.6	9.9	13.5	15.1	12.4
35 Hip breadth, standing	11.9	12.5	12.4	14.5	15.3	15.6
36 Shoulder (bideltoid) breadth	16.3	17.0	15.0	19.6	20.7	18.0
37 Forearm–forearm breadth	15.7	17.0	13.0	21.1	23.9	17.7
38 Hip breadth, sitting	12.1	13.1	13.0	15.1	16.7	17.3
39 Knee-to-knee breadth		7.5			10.0	

provided a "captive audience" for taking large samples. Until very recently large-scale civilian studies were nonexistent because there was no appointed central agency with the funding to collect such data. There have been civilian studies with limited sample size for specialized occupational groups such as bus and truck drivers, flight attendants, air traffic control trainees, and law enforcement officers [Van Cott et al., 72]. In 1960 to 1962, the National Center for Health Statistics took approximately 14 dimensions of 1165 civilians [Stoudt et al., 70]. However, it is difficult to generalize from these small specialized samples and older studies to the current U.S. population. Also, the number of dimensions taken was usually limited.

In recognition of the needs of industry and commerce for reliable

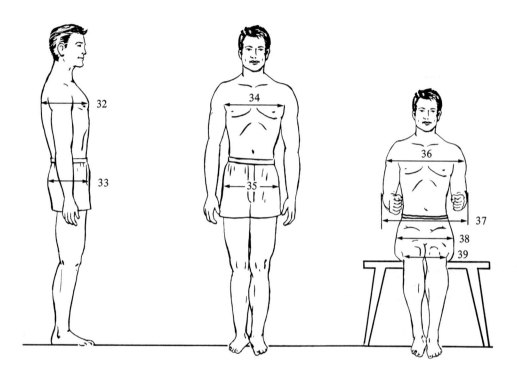

*Bust depth for women.
Source: MIL–STD–1472B [21].

anthropometric data, the National Bureau of Standards is currently developing a Standard Ergonomics Reference Data System (SERDS) and is planning for the early 1980s a national survey that will include initially anthropometric data and later human response data representative of the U.S. population [72]. Planning is required to decide on the list of measurements required by potential users, the most effective and standardized measurement techniques, and a multistage, stratified sampling plan that will include age, race, occupational, and income groups from major geographical areas among other strata. Most important will be to develop techniques to insure that the physically deviant and partially handicapped are included. Body stockings may be worn by persons participating in the survey.

Static Force Application

The human as a generator of forces is discussed with respect to controls in Chapter 5 and with respect to industrial work in Chapter 6. Important situational factors influencing the maximum static arm force that may be applied is the plane in which the force is exerted relative to the body, the direction of force, and the degree of arm extension.

Note in Table 3-11 that push/pull strength is much greater than in other directions, especially when the arm is fully extended. Other important factors influencing force application are posture (seated is better than prone), bracing of the back and feet, seat back angle, distance from the midsagittal plane (8 in to the right is best for right-handed people).

Weight lifting studies (Chapter 6) indicate that important variables are the

Table 3-11   Design Values for Maximum Force

Arm strength*

Seated (in pounds)

Elbow flexion	Push		Pull		Up		Down		In		Out	
	R	L	R	L	R	L	R	L	R	L	R	L
180°	50	42	52	50	14	9	17	13	20	13	14	8
150°	42	30	56	42	18	15	20	18	20	15	15	8
120°	36	26	42	34	24	17	26	21	22	20	15	10
90°	36	22	37	32	20	17	26	21	18	16	16	10
60°	34	22	24	26	20	15	20	18	20	17	17	12

Prone (in pounds)

Elbow flexion	Push		Pull		Up		Down		In		Out	
180°	31	26	31	18	8	5	13	7	12	10	9	4
150°	29	24	29	21	13	7	15	10	15	8	12	5
120°	29	21	31	22	13	11	15	11	15	9	11	6
90°	26	18	24	23	15	15	16	12	16	13	13	6
60°	24	17	21	17	13	13	13	10	16	11	12	8

Note: R = right hand, L = left hand.

distance from the floor of the weight (hips to shoulder height is best), the dimensions of the container (compact is best), and the distance of the moment from the center of gravity of the body (close to the body is best).

Endurance

Static strength is the maximum force that muscles can exert isometrically (statically) in a single voluntary effort. However, many operational tasks involve maintaining a force over a prolonged duration. Rhomert [58] found that the maximum time that a force could be held bears a nonlinear relationship to the maximum static force the person can apply. The relationship is as follows:

$$T_s = -90 + \frac{126}{P} - \frac{36}{P^2} + \frac{6}{P^3}$$

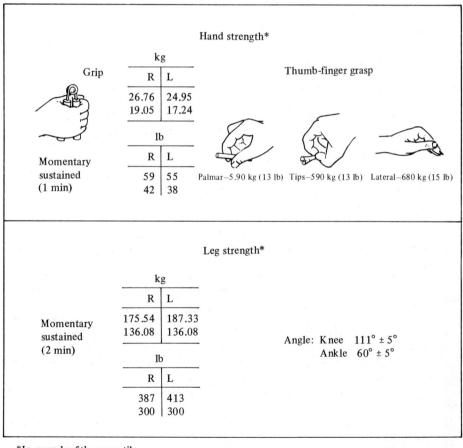

Hand strength*

Grip	kg		Thumb-finger grasp		
	R	L			
	26.76	24.95			
	19.05	17.24			
	lb				
	R	L			
Momentary					
sustained	59	55	Palmar–5.90 kg (13 lb)	Tips–590 kg (13 lb)	Lateral–680 kg (15 lb)
(1 min)	42	38			

Leg strength*

	kg		
	R	L	
Momentary	175.54	187.33	
sustained	136.08	136.08	
(2 min)	lb		Angle: Knee 111° ± 5°
	R	L	Ankle 60° ± 5°
	387	413	
	300	300	

*In pounds; 5th percentile.
Source: AFSC DH 1-3 [1].

where P = the decimal fraction of maximum force held (strength)

T_s = the predicted maximum time in seconds that the subject can hold this percentage of maximum force (endurance)

To illustrate, if an operator's maximum static force was 36 lbs and he or she were required to lift 21.6 lbs (60 percent of maximum), the predicted maximum duration or endurance would be:

$$T_s = -90 + 210 - 100 + 28 = 48 \text{ sec}$$

Functional Workspace Dimensions

The early studies of body dimensions were carried out to provide data applicable to sizing clothing and wearing apparel. Many human factors and biomechanics specialists were interested in three-dimensional spatial relationships, such as reach envelopes while sitting or standing.

Work situations also call for other postures such as lying prone, kneeling, crawling, and squatting. The following table summarizes the height and length of the workspace required for the 5th and 95th percentile male worker, based upon a U.S. Air Force study [Hertzberg, 32].

	5th		95th	
	in	cm	in	cm
Kneeling (knuckles on floor)				
Height	29.7	75.4	35.5	90.2
Length	37.6	95.4	48.1	122.2
Crawling				
Height	26.2	66.5	30.5	77.5
Length	49.3	125.1	58.2	147.8
Prone				
Height	12.3	31.2	16.4	41.7
Length	84.7	215.1	95.8	243.3
Squatting height	40.8	103.6	47.0	119.4

Functional workspace dimensions, like reach envelopes, are based on but not limited to static body dimension measures. The designer may not find the type of information needed except when the body assumes certain functional postures. In Chapters 5, 6, and 7, other particular workspace dimensions based upon the body at work are given.

Other Physical Properties

The designer of an aircraft ejection seat would be interested in properties of the human body other than linear dimensions or self-generated forces. Studies have been conducted [Santschi et al., 60; Chandler et al., 14] to determine shifts in the center of gravity and mass moment of inertia of the body as a function of posture (for example, standing versus sitting with thighs elevated). The values are expressed in terms of an X, Y, Z coordinate system. Inertial properties and estimated weights of body segments are also available [Reynolds, 57].

Body volume, specific density, and surface area are also sometimes required by environmental designers. Katch and Weltman [37] found that for males the volume of body segments were: 46.2 percent torso, 16.9 percent each leg, 6.3 percent each arm, and 7.4 percent head and neck. Kjeldsen [42] found the comparable percentages for females were: 50.7 percent torso, 15.6 percent each leg, 4.7 percent each arm, and 8.8 percent head and neck.

Mean specific density of the body varies from 1.0975 to 1.0260 depending upon the obesity of the person [Roebuck et al., 59]. Specific densities of body segments range from 0.85 for neck and torso to 1.08 for the hands [NASA, 8]. According to Reynolds [57] segment weights may be calculated from body segment volume and mean specific densities.

A nomograph exists for estimating body surface area given an individual's height and weight [8]. In short, almost any physical property measurable for inanimate objects has been tabled for the human body as well.

Modeling the Human

The approach taken in this chapter was to describe the human as a system component and to spotlight the limit values that will be useful in later designing the environment to complement such limitations. Other scientists have taken quite different approaches.

For centuries people have been interested in building automata, sometimes in their own likenesses, which possess skills that transcend their own: the fictional Frankenstein monster and, more recently, robots that can think and perform beyond our abilities yet hopefully remain under human control.

Many of the concepts introduced in this and the previous chapter were employed by Wiener [78] in his classic document *Cybernetics:* concepts such as information flow, feedback, and control. Practical spinoffs have been teaching machines, synthetic speaking machines, pattern recognition devices, and powered prosthetics. Bioengineering has also been interested in *bionics,* the study of living systems to identify concepts applicable to the design of artificial systems (for example, the bat and the dolphin gave us important concepts applicable to radar and sonar). Recently, there has been interest in modeling neurons in the hope of constructing smaller and more flexible computers and simulating electronically neuron behavior.

Remote handling devices have been developed not only to complement the human's weaknesses in lifting, but also to permit the human to handle hazardous radioactive material. The control systems for remote control of manipulator arms or roving unmanned vehicles have been termed "teleoperators". An example of human factors research in this area comes from Crawford [16], who found that a single joy stick was superior to individual levers for controlling remote manipulator arms in a task of placing discs in holes. A single control operated six different movements of the manipulator arms at the shoulder, elbow, hips, and grip.

Badler and Smoliar [5] have recently summarized various approaches to using a digital computer to record information describing the movements of the human body. Movements could be filmed and digitized for processing for any conceivable application. The problem is that the scenario (for example, movements of a ballet dancer) involves an immense amount of data. Exact positions of the body must be symbolically represented from analysis of successive frames to accurately describe movements. Laban [Hutchinson, 35] developed a system that records translation direction, rotational movements, orientation of some point of the body, contact points with surfaces, and path of certain body parts—all concurrently or in sequence.

In computer animation, the body may be represented by stick figures, surface point models, or volume models (cylinders, ellipsoids, or cartoon-like characterizations). By using some 300 spheres a high-fidelity likeness of the human body moving in silhouette may be generated on vector or raster displays.

Modeling and simulation of human functions (perceptual, processing, or movements) is an extremely difficult and perplexing task. The models are still primitive and deal more with general processes than with limit values. However, the test of our knowledge in any area must come from our ability to describe the system well enough to simulate its operation. Although this is not critical to improving the human's environmental design, human modeling has application to refinement of operating techniques and ultimately to replacement of certain functions or extension of human capabilities.

QUESTIONS AND PROBLEMS

1 A word message on a sign 1000 ft away has letters that are 18 in high. What would be the visual angle (in minutes) at the eye?

2 Suppose the word message in question 1 were to appear at a distance of 100 ft. To keep the same visual angle as that of question 1, what should the letter height be?

3 Given a matrix of 16×8 categories. How many bits of information are required to locate any given cell in this matrix?

4 Given $H(x;y)$, the information in the joint occurrence of S and R is 5.0 b and the noise or uncertainty in stimulus, $H\, y(x)$, and response, $H\, x(y)$, is collectively 2.0 b. How much information is transmitted in bits?

5 Administer the following cryptogram to three friends:

   XXX   XXXXX   XX   XXXXXXX   XXXX   XXXXX

Ask them to begin with the first X and attempt to guess the letters one by one. You will tell them when they are correct. Record the number of the trial (guess) on which they are correct. Tally the frequency of letters guessed correctly on each trial, and plot the frequency distribution for each friend and for their composite scores (divided by 3). The correct answer is: THE GRASS IS GREENER OVER THERE.

6 Suppose an individual decides to reject making a $1 wager with a friend on a closer estimate of a final score of a game, but decides to make the same wager in a pool with 10,000 participants and a single winner taking $5,000. Is the person more likely to win in the second situation? Why do you think the person made the wager? Do you think the average pool wagerer has sufficient information to assess objective probabilities?

7 An investigator wishes to establish a subjective time stress equivalent to 2.5 in three subjects. At the end of a training session, subject A completes the task in 150 s; subject B takes 125 s; subject C requires only 100 s. In the time-stress experiment how much "time remaining" should be given on a countdown clock for each subject so that the time-stress level for each would be 2.5?

8 In the Warrick et al. study of alerted RT, approximately how much of the total time was due to moving the hand from the typewriter to the RT key?

9 In what plane of movement do you erase a blackboard and why?

10 Are typewriter keyboards laid out to take into consideration differences in movement rates of various fingers? Why or why not?

11 What is one practical application of data on range of joint movement?

12 Using a tape measure for circumferences and a commercial or homemade caliper for linear dimensions, have someone take at least ten of your own measurements. Determine the difference between your measures and the 5th and 95th values given in the text tables. What can you conclude?

13 What is the relevant static dimension for the following?
   a the depth of a seat
   b the minimum height of the underside of a work surface (measured from a seat surface)
   c minimum bench seat width
   d minimum height of a doorway
   Indicate if the 5th or 95th percentile is relevant.

14 A worker's maximum static lifting capability is 50 lb. How long would the worker be able to lift 15 lb using Rhomert's formula?

REFERENCES

1 AFSC DH 1–3, sec. 2B, *Human Performance Capabilities and Limitations*, Jan. 1, 1977.
2 Alluisi, E. A.: Information and uncertainty: the metrics of communications, in K. B. DeGreene (ed.), *Systems Psychology*, McGraw-Hill, New York, 1970, chap. 6.
3 Annis, J. F.: "Variability in human body size", in *Anthropometric Source Book*, vol. 1, chap. 2, NASA Reference Publication 1025, NASA Scientific and Technical Office, 1978.
4 Attneave, F.: *Applications of Information Theory to Psychology*, Holt-Dryden, New York, 1959.
5 Badler, N. I. and S. W. Smoliar: Digital representation of human movement, *Computing Surveys*, vol. 11, no. 1, March 1979.
6 Baker, W. O.: Man and machines, *The Random House Encyclopedia*, Random

House, New York, 1977.

7 Barter, J. T., I. Emanuel, and B. Truett: *A statistical evaluation of joint range data,* Report No. WADC-TN-57-311, Wright Air Development Center, WPAFB, Ohio, 1957.

8 *Bioastronautics Data Book,* 2d ed., NASA SP-3006, U.S. Government Printing Office, Washington, D.C., 1973.

9 Blackwell, H. R.: Contrast thresholds of the human eye, *Journal of the Optical Society of America,* vol. 36, 1946, p. 624.

10 Briggs, S. J.: A study of design of work areas, unpublished doctoral dissertation, Purdue University, 1955.

11 Buckner, D. N. and J. J. McGrath: A comparison of performance on single and dual sensory mode vigilance tasks, Human Factors Research, Inc., Los Angeles, California, TR 8, ONR Contract Nonr 2649(00), NR 153-199, February 1961.

12 Burg, A., Visual acuity as measured by static and dynamic tests: A comparative evaluation, *Journal of Applied Psychology,* vol. 50, no. 6, 1966, pp. 460–466.

13 Chapanis, A.: "Human Engineering," in C. D. Flagle, W. H. Huggins, and R. H. Roy (eds.), *Operations Research and Systems Engineering,* John Hopkins Press, Baltimore, 1960, chap. 19.

14 Chandler, R. F., C. E. Clauser, J. P. McConville, H. M. Reynolds, and J. W. Young, *Investigation of Inertial Properties of the Human Body,* AMRL-TR-74-137, Aeromedical Research Laboratories, WPAFB, Ohio, 1975.

15 Corrigan, R. E. and W. J. Brogden: The trigonometric relationship of precision and angle of linear pursuit-movements, *American Journal of Psychology,* vol. 62, 1949, pp. 90–98.

16 Crawford, B. M.: Joy stick vs. multiple levers for remote manipulator control, *Human Factors,* vol. 6, no. 1, 1964, pp. 39–48.

17 Damon, A., H. W. Stoudt, and R. A. McFarland: *The Human Body in Equipment Design,* Harvard University Press, Cambridge, Mass., 1966.

18 DeGreene, K. B. (ed): *Systems Psychology,* McGraw-Hill, New York, 1970.

19 Dempster, W. T.: *Space requirements of the seated operator,* USAF, WADC, TR 55-159, July 1955.

20 Department of Defense, *Human Factors Engineering Design for Army Material,* Mil-HDBK-759, March 12, 1975.

21 Department of Defense, *Military Standard 1472B, Notice 2,* May 10, 1978.

22 Dvorak, A., N. I. Merrick, W. L. Dealey, and G. C. Ford: *Typewriting Behavior,* American Book Co., New York, 1936.

23 Emanuel, I. and U. T. Barter: *Linear Distance Changes Over Body Joints,* WADC-TR-56-364, WADC, WPAFB, Ohio, 1957.

24 Fitts, P. M.: Functions of men in complex systems, *Aerospace Engineering,* vol. 21, no. 1, 1962, pp. 34–39.

25 Fitts, P. M.: "A study of location discrimination ability" in P. M. Fitts (ed.), *Psychological Research in Equipment Design,* Army Air Force, Aviation Psychology Program, Research Report 19, 1947.

26 Fitts, P. M. and J. R. Peterson: Information capacity of discrete motor responses, *Journal of Experimental Psychology,* vol. 67, no. 2, 1964, pp. 103–112.

27 Frost, G.: "Man-machine Dynamics," in H. P. Van Cott and R. G. Kinkade (eds.), *Human Engineering Guide to Equipment Design,* rev. ed, Washington, D. C., U.S. Government Printing Office, 1972, chap. 6.

28 Geldard, F. A.: *The Human Senses,* Wiley, New York, 1965.
29 Grether, W. F. and C. A. Baker, "Visual presentation of information," in H. P. Van Cott and R. G. Kinkade (eds.), *Human Engineering Guide to Equipment Design,* rev. ed., Washington D.C.: U.S. Government Printing Office, 1972, chap. 3.
30 Hamill, P., T. Drizo, C. Johnson, R. Reed, A. Roche, *NCHS Growth Charts, 1976,* Monthly Vital Statistics Report, Health Examination Survey Data, HRA 76-1120, vol. 25, no. 3, supplement, June 22, 1976; National Center for Health Statistics, HEW, Public Health Resources Administration, Rockville, Maryland, 1976.
31 Harris, M. L. and C. W. Harris: *A Factor Analytic Study of Flexibility,* paper presented at the National Convention of American Association of Health, Physical Education, and Recreation Research Section, St. Louis, Mo., 1968.
32 Hertzberg, H. T. E.: Dynamic anthropometry of working positions, *Human Factors,* vol. 2, no. 3, 1960.
33 Hertzberg, H. T. E.: "Engineering Anthropometry," in H. P. Van Cott and R. G. Kinkade (eds.), *Human Engineering Guide to Equipment Design,* rev. ed., Washington, D.C., U.S. Government Printing Office, 1972, chap. 11.
34 Huchingson, R. D.: The effects of time constraint on closed-loop tracking performance and change in heart rate, *Perceptual and Motor Skills,* vol. 36, 1973, pp. 1195–1198.
35 Hutchinson, A.: *Labanotation,* Theatre Arts Books, New York, 1970.
36 Johansson, G. and K. Rumar: Drivers' braking reaction times, *Human Factors,* vol. 13, no. 1, 1971, pp. 23–27.
37 Katch, V. and A. Weltman: Predictability of body segment volumes in living subjects, *Human Biology,* vol. 47, no. 2, pp. 203–208.
38 Kaufman, L.: *Sight and Mind: An Introduction to Visual Perception,* Oxford University Press, New York, 1974.
39 Kennedy, K. W.: *Reach capabilities of men and women,* doctoral dissertation, Union Graduate College, Yellow Springs, Ohio, 1976.
40 Kennedy, K. W.: *Reach capabilities of the USAF population:* Phase I. The outer boundaries of grasping reach envelopes for the shirt-sleeved operator, USAF, AMRL, TDR 64-59, 1964.
41 Kennedy, K. W. and B. E. Filler: *Aperture size and depth of reach for one- and two-handed tasks,* Report No. AMRL-TR-27, 1966, AMRL, WPAFB, Ohio.
42 Kjeldsen, K.: Body segment weight, limb lengths, and location of center of gravity in college women, Master's thesis, University of Massachusetts, Amherst, Mass.,1972.
43 Laubach, L. L.: "Range of Joint Motion", in *Anthropometric Source Book,* vol. 1, NASA Reference Publication 1024, NASA Scientific and Technical Information Office, 1978, chap. 6.
44 Long, L. and E. Churchill, *Anthropometry of USAF Basic Trainees Contrasts of Several Subgroups.* 1965 Paper presented to the 1968 meeting of the American Association of Physical Anthropometrists and reported also in Annis [3].
45 Lyman, J. and L. J. Fogel: "The Human Component," in E. M. Grabbe et al. (eds.), *Handbook of Automation, Computation and Control,* volume 3, Wiley, New York, 1961, chap. 2.
46 Mackworth, N. H. and J. H. Mackworth: Visual search for successive decisions, *British Journal of Psychology,* vol. 49, 1958, pp. 210–231.
47 Maynard, H. B.: *Industrial Engineering Handbook,* 2d ed., McGraw-Hill, New York, 1963.

48 McConville, J. T. and L. L. Laubach: "Anthropometry," in *Anthropometric Source Book,* vol. 1, NASA Reference Publication 1024, NASA Scientific and Technical Office, 1978, chap. 3, Appendix B.

49 Mead, P. G. and P. B. Sampson: Hand steadiness during unrestricted linear arm movements, *Human Factors,* vol. 14, no. 1, 1972, pp. 45–50.

50 Meister, D.: Methods of predicting human reliability in man-machine systems, *Human Factors,* vol. 6, no. 6, 1964, pp. 621–646.

51 Miller, G. A.: The magical number seven, plus or minus two: Some limits on our capacity for processing information, *Psychological Review,* vol. 63, 1956, pp. 81–97.

52 Neisser, U.: *Cognitive Psychology,* Appleton-Century-Crofts, New York, 1967.

53 Neisser, U.: Decision time without reaction time: Experiments in visual scanning, *American Journal of Psychology,* vol. 76, 1963, pp. 376–385.

54 Pew, R. W.: Recent psychological research relevant to the human factors engineering of man-machine systems, *Proceedings—National Electronics Conference,* vol. 21, October 1965.

55 Pollack, I.: The information of elementary auditory displays II, *Journal of the Acoustical Society of America,* vol. 25, 1953, pp. 765–769.

56 Posner, M. I.: Information reduction in the analysis of sequential tasks, *Psychological Review,* vol. 71, 1965, pp. 491–504.

57 Reynolds, H. M.: "The Inertial Properties of the Body and its Segments," in *Anthropometric Source Book,* vol. 1, NASA Reference Publication 1024, NASA Scientific and Technical Office, 1978, chap. 4.

58 Rhomert, W.: Ermittlung vonErholungspausen fuer statische arbeit des Menschen, *Internationale Zeitschrift Angewandte Physiologic,* 1960, pp. 123–164.

59 Roebuck, J. A. Jr., K. H. E. Kroemer, and W. G. Thomson: *Engineering Anthropometry Methods,* Wiley, New York, 1975.

60 Santschi, W. R., J. Dubois, and C. Omoto, *Moments of Inertia and Centers of Gravity of the Living Human Body,* AMRL-TDR-63-36, Aeromedical Research Laboratory, WPAFB, Ohio, 1963.

61 Schmidtke, H. and F. Stier: Der aufbau komplexer bewegung sablaufe aus elementtarbewegungen, *Forschungberichte des landes Nordrhain-Westfalen,* no. 822, 1960, pp. 13–32.

62 Siegel, A. I. and J. J. Wolf: *Man-machine Simulation Models,* Wiley, New York, 1969.

63 Shannon, C. E.: Prediction and entrophy of printed English, *Bell Systems Technical Journal,* vol. 30, 1951, pp. 50–64.

64 Shannon, C. E. and W. Weaver, *The Mathematical Theory of Communications,* Urbana, University of Illinois Press, 1949.

65 Sharp, E. D.: Effects of primary task performance on response time to toggle switches in a workspace configuration. Report No AMRL-TR-190, Aerospace Medical Research Labs, Wright Patterson Air Force Base, Ohio, April 1967.

66 Sheldon, W., S. Stevens, and W. Tucker: *The Varieties of Human Physique,* Harper, New York, 1940.

67 Sherif, M.: *An Outline of Social Psychology,* Harper, New York, 1948.

68 Stoudt, H. W.: "Arm-leg reach and workspace layout," chap. 5, in *Anthropometric Source Book,* vol. 1, NASA Reference Publication 1024, NASA Scientific and Technical Information Office, 1978.

69 Stoudt, H. M., A. Damon, R. A. McFarland, and J. Roberts: Heights and weights of white Americans, *Human Biology,* vol. 32, 1960, p. 331.

70 Stoudt, H. W., A. Damon, R. A. McFarland, and J. Roberts: *Weight, Height, and Selected Body Dimensions for Adults,* Washington, D.C., National Center for Health Statistics, series 11, no. 8, U.S. Department of Health, Education, and Welfare, 1965.

71 Van Cott, H. P. and M. J. Warrick: "Man as a system component," in H. P. Van Cott and R. G. Kinkade (eds.), *Human Engineering Guide to Equipment Design,* rev. ed., Washington, D.C., U.S. Government Printing Office, 1972, chap. 2.

72 Van Cott, H. P. et al.: *A Standard Ergonomics Reference Data System: The Concept and Its Assessment,* NBSIR 77-1403, Institute of Applied Technology, National Bureau of Standards, Department of Commerce, June 1978.

73 Vroom, V. H.: *Work and Motivation,* Wiley, New York, 1964.

74 Warrick, M. J., A. W. Kibler, and D. A. Topmiller: Response time to unexpected stimuli, *Human Factors,* vol. 7, no. 1, 1965, pp. 81–86.

75 Weisz, A. Z. and L. S. McElroy: Information processing in a complex task under speed stress, Decision Sciences Laboratory, Electronic Systems Division, AFSC, USAF, Report EDS-TDR 64-391, May 1964.

76 West, C. C.: "Measurement of Joint Motion", *Archives of Physical Medicine,* vol. 26, 1945, pp. 414–425.

77 White, C. T. and A. Ford: Eye movement during simulated radar search, *Journal of the Optical Society of America,* vol. 50, no. 9, 1960, pp. 909–912.

78 Wiener, N., *Cybernetics or Control and Communications in the Animal and the Machine,* Wiley, New York, 1948.

79 Yokohori, E., *Anthropometry of JASDF Personnel and Its Application For Human Engineering,* Aeromedical Laboratory, Japanese Air Self Defense Force, Tachikawa Air Force Base, Tokyo, 1972.

80 Hochberg, J. E.: *Perception,* Prentice-Hall, Englewood Cliffs, N.J., 1965.

81 Tarpy, R. M.: *Basic Principles of Learning,* Scott-Foresman and Co., Glenview, Ill., 1975.

82 Underwood, B. J.: *Experimental Psychology,* rev. ed., Appleton-Century-Crofts, New York, 1966.

Part Two

Aerospace Systems

Chapter 4

Design of Aerospace and Electronic Displays

A display is any device that presents information to the human senses. Typically, the reference is to visual and auditory displays, although tactual feedback in control systems or Braille for the blind are examples of the use of the sense of touch for communicating information.

For purpose of discussion, displays and controls (Chapter 5) will be treated separately. However, in Chapter 2 we saw that closed-loop systems involve an input (sensed information), human information processing and storage, and output (control devices), all interacting to provide systems control. A control is also a display whenever it has information displayed on it. Therefore, it is difficult to discuss displays without also considering controls and the intervening human information processing.

This chapter is entitled "Design of Aerospace and Electronic Displays" because, historically, one of the major areas of human factors research was in the design of controls and displays for military aircraft and military electronic products. Much of the research data have led to human engineering design criteria documented in design guides [Van Cott and Kinkade, 48; AFSC, 1; MIL-HDBK-759, 36] and Military Standard 1472 [12], which are primarily applicable to aerospace and military products. However, controls and displays exist about us in consumer products (Chapter 14), surface transportation (Chapter 11), industrial systems (Chapter 6), the roadway environment (Chapter 10), and, in fact, in almost every system application. The design information presented in Chapters 4 and 5 is generally applicable, but the emphasis will be on aerospace and electronic products.

There have been two major areas of research directed at design criteria for displays. The first deals with the information itself and techniques for formating, coding, or organizing the displayed information to minimize the probability of human error in reading and interpreting it. The second deals with ways of ensuring that the displayed information, visual or auditory, is, in fact, seen or heard against a background of noise or interference. Detection, recognition, and interpretation are all essential to effective action.

VISUAL DISPLAYS

For visual displays to be useful they must be conspicuous and legible, and they must display the type of information the operator needs to know in a way he or she can understand it.

General Guidelines

MIL-STD-1472B [12] lists a number of design guidelines applicable to visual displays. The *content* of the information displayed should be limited to what is necessary to perform specific actions or make decisions. Information should be displayed only to the *precision* necessary. The *format* should be in a directly usable form so the operator does not need to transpose, compute, interpolate, or translate into other units of measurement. *Redundancy* in displayed information should be avoided unless necessary for reliability. Combining information on a single display that is used for different purposes (operation, troubleshooting, and so forth) is normally discouraged. *Failure* of a display or display circuit should be immediately apparent. *Unrelated* information (for example, trademarks) should not be displayed on a panel face.

The above criteria imply that a display should be uncluttered and easy to interpret. One should be able to read it quickly and accurately to the degree necessary. If the need is for only a "yes" or "no" indication the display must so provide. If the need is for exact quantitative information, a different type of display is necessary. Rules for visual display selection are given subsequently.

Gross reading errors may be brought about by a requirement to read a particular number that is shown in a typeface that is difficult to read or is shown on a poorly designed scale. Errors may occur also when movement relationships are ambiguous or misleading, or the display is viewed under conditions of poor contrast or illumination. These are examples of detailed design mistakes. (Similar errors in the design of a roadway display are discussed in Chapter 10.)

Types of Visual Displays

Dynamic and Static Displays   An example of a *dynamic* display is a moving instrument dial such as a speedometer. The information varies over time and is fed back from some system parameter such as vehicle velocity. *Static* displays are stationary over time and are not connected to system output. Examples are graphic and tabular material in a book, labels and placards engraved on instrument panels, and conventional road signs.

Some dynamic displays that change their message may update the information so infrequently that they may appear static or, worse, appear to be inoperable. A digital watch may have a pulsating colon between the hours and minutes, which reassures that the watch is running. A rotating drum road sign may at any given time appear static to a driver, and, hence, may detract from its credibility as a source of real-time information. Conversely, commercial signs may employ techniques of apparent movement, yet the information may not vary with time. Thus, movement typically defines dynamic displays, but a connection to system output is the critical criterion.

Pictorial and Symbolic Displays   A display may be *symbolic, pictorial,* or a *combination* of symbolic and pictorial information. Conventional dials such as a clock or engine instrument are symbolic. Numbers and tick (graduation) marks indicate particular parameter values. Word messages are technically symbolic also, but they are often discussed as a separate type of display.

Pictorial displays include photographs of terrain, TV pictures, road signs with silhouettes of objects, and so forth. One of the advanced aircraft instrument programs depicts the real world on a dynamic display as a pilot would view it through the windscreen. This type of pictorial display is termed a *contact analog* display.

Combined pictorial/symbolic displays are simplified pictures with symbols. Illustrations are maps, PPI radar scopes such as those seen on TV weather reports, wiring schematics and flow charts, and the conventional gyro-horizon aircraft attitude indicator. Certain display elements have *geographical* or *functional* analogies to the real world environment (hence, they are pictorial in this sense), while other display elements are numbers, names, or other symbols.

Combined and Integrated Display   A display may present only one type of information or may combine two or several types of information. Figure 4-1 illustrates a combined display, the radio magnetic indicator. Displayed are both the aircraft's current heading and its bearing with respect to two radio stations.

Combined displays should be used only when the information is related. In the illustration, one parameter is a first derivative of the other parameter. Combining information saves panel space, reduces eye scan time, and may simplify interpretation. *Integrated* displays treat the entire panel as a display. The contact analog display, mentioned earlier, is an advanced integrated display of many parameters such as altitude, airspeed, attitude, and flight path.

Other types of displays, such as quickened and predictor displays, will be presented in Chapter 5.

Other Display Classifications

Electronic displays may be classified in terms of their size, resolution capability, and whether or not there is a computer-interface requirement. Nolan [29] has

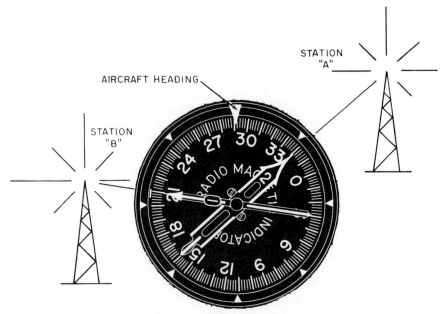

Figure 4-1 Combined display using superimposed needles. *(AFSC DH 1–3, 1977.)*

also classified displays as active or passive, that is, whether they actively emit light such as a light-emitting diode display, or whether they passively modulate or reflect ambient light as with liquid crystal displays. Recent electronic technology will be discussed later in this chapter.

Displays can vary in size from small, hand-held devices like calculators and wristwatches; to medium-sized displays like computer terminal displays (Chapter 14); to large-scale TV projection systems seen simultaneously by a group of operators.

In terms of resolution, raster-scan displays are now being employed to display not only continuous video pictures, but also discrete alphanumeric data. They vary in screen size, raster lines per picture, spot size, color capability, brightness contrast ratio, and so forth.

Functions of Displays

Grether and Baker [53] have identified five common functions of displays:

1 continuous system control (tracking or steering a vehicle)
2 monitoring systems status (warning light for engine parameters)
3 briefings (flight plans, maintenance checkout sequence)
4 search and identification (pattern recognition in recognizing targets on photographic or radar displays)
5 decision making (trouble shooting malfunctioning equipment or deciding on the presence or absence of a target on a sonar display)

In addition to these, static displays may be used as labels or markings to identify equipment functions, units of measurement, and so forth.

Population Stereotypes

The most important single concept in the interpretation of displayed information is the concept of population stereotype. Researchers in the area of aircraft symbology and movement relationships have long sought information as to which movement relationships are most natural. An example of a stereotype is as follows. A clockwise, upward, forward, or right control movement implies an increasing function to most of us. We also expect the direction of control and display movement to be compatible. These stereotyped interpretations are learned in the course of our exposure to technology. Whenever a design practice conflicts with such ingrained responses, the possibility of human error exists. If a control is designed to move left to increase a display function value, we may learn this but under stress we may forget and move the control in the opposite direction. This type of error is a *reversal error.*

Population stereotypes are not limited to bimodal situations such as the control movement problem. They could occur whenever there is a strongly preferred response regardless of the number of potential erroneous responses. This concept will be encountered frequently throughout this text.

Guidelines for Selecting Displays

There are a variety of potential displays that a designer could select. One of his or her primary responsibilities is to select the type of display most appropriate for the particular situation. Table 4-1 provides some general guidelines for selection of displays. This listing is not comprehensive.

Sometimes considerations other than human factors may dictate the display choice, for example, limited display space may lead to the choice of a moving tape display even though a moving pointer display is preferable.

A moving pointer against a fixed scale provides qualitative or approximate quantitative information, qualitative trend, and rate information. Consider the conventional dial watch. Accuracy may be very slightly less and reading time slightly longer than a digital watch, but one is less likely to make a major error such as misreading the hour as 6 instead of 8. Indeed, one could remove all numbers from a dial and still read it fairly accurately because *pointer positions have unique meanings.* Moving pointer aircraft instruments also permit the detection of relative rates of movement and direction of change. The moving pointer is also superior for setting in numbers, check reading, and for tracking.

Counters are excellent for exact quantitative readings. Elkin [15] found only 3 errors in 1440 readings. Reading time was also faster than that of moving pointer scales for exact readings. But when the task was to classify numerical readings into "high," "OK," and "low" categories, reading time was slower than moving pointer scales.

The subject of moving pointers, moving scales, and display of spatial information will be discussed subsequently in relation to whole panel displays.

Table 4-1 Guidelines for Display Selection

Display requirement	Examples	Select	Reason
Two-valued information Discrete indication of a continuous variable Warning/caution	Go-no go Start-stop Safe-unsafe state	Light Backlighted legend Flashing light	Easy to tell if on or off No greater precision required Attracts attention
Quantitative information	Any exact numerical quantity	Digital counter Printer readout	Only one number is visible reducing chance of error Quicker & more accurate than scales, but must be read Subject to gross reading errors
Approximate quantity Qualitative information Check reading	Rate of change Trends Direction of movement	Moving pointer against fixed scale	General position of pointer gives rapid clue to quantity plus relative rate of change
Set-in quantity	Selector knob set at a particular value	Moving pointer, fixed scale	Simple and direct relation between pointer motion and control motion
Set-in qualitative mode	Touch-tone channel selector display	Array of backlighted pushbutton displays	Better visibility and quieter than selector switch Quicker to activate
Tracking (compensatory)		Single pointer Cross-pointer	Provides error information only for quick correction Simple relation to manual control motion See Chapter 5
Spatial information	Vehicle attitude Geographical position Command guidance	Controversial area	See discussion of principles of motion
Equipment performance Analysis of parameters		Meter CRT wave form Pen recording	Meter—simple to interpret Waveform shows multiparameter relations Pen gives permanent record
Verbal instructions	RELEASE EJECT	Backlighted enunciator lights	Simple action instructions reduce response time

Source: Based on Woodson and Conover [52] with modifications.

Detail design criteria for many of the displays mentioned in Table 4-1 will be given also.

Location and Arrangement

Ideally, displays should be located on a plane perpendicular to the operator's line-of-sight (LOS) to avoid distortion. Displays should be very close to the LOS angle for foveal vision without excessive eye movement. When there are numerous instruments, as in a cockpit, this may not be feasible for all displays. MIL-STD-1472B [12] sets certain limits for display placement.

Visual Angles   Figure 4-2 (a) indicates that the instrument face should form an angle not less than 45° from the LOS. Acute angles result in visual distortion and parallax. A familiar illustration of horizontal parallax is the passenger of an automobile reading the fuel gage as empty when, in fact, the driver can see there is still a quarter of a tank of fuel remaining. Peripheral vision is also inferior to foveal vision for most tasks, as noted in Chapter 3.

Instruments used most frequently should be grouped together and located in the optimal visual zone. As shown in Figure 4.2 (b and c) this zone is bounded by 15° vertically and horizontally from the normal LOS (sometimes referred to as the 30° cone of vision). The maximum viewing angles shown assume eye

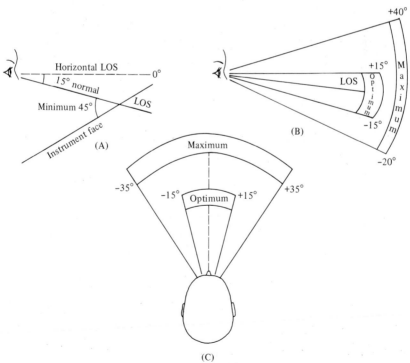

Figure 4-2   Optimum and maximum visual fields for display placement. *(MIL-STD-1472B, 1974.)*

Table 4-2 Recommended Heights of Displays

Operator	Height of normal display*	Height of special display†	Height of warning display
Seated‡	6–46 in 150 mm–1.17 m	14–35 in 360 mm–890 mm	22.5–in 570 mm
Standing	41–70 in 1.04–1.78 m	50–65 in 1.27–1.65 m	

*Normal refers to use in normal equipment operation.
†Special refers to frequently used displays requiring precise readings.
‡Seated heights are referenced to the sitting surface.
Source: Adapted from MIL-STD-1472B, Notice 1[12].

rotation but stationary neck. With neck movement the maximum range is 90°
above LOS and ± 95° horizontally from LOS. Table 4-2 expresses locations in
terms of display height above the seat surface level or above the floor for
standing operations. Note that "special" or frequently used displays must be
located within a more restricted range corresponding to the 15° visual angle.

Space-Shared Displays   Crew stations are expanding beyond the feasibility
of locating individual data sources within a favorable viewing angle. There are
simply more types of information needed than space available. Since certain
items are required only occasionally, there is no reason why they should be
displayed continuously or occupy panel space reserved for the information only.

Interactive display technology permits the sharing of information on a
cathode-ray tube (computer terminal display). The system may be commanded
to display certain information via a keyboard, joy stick, or other control device.
Parameters of information (for example, radio communications information) are
stored until the operator requires the specific information. "Menu-type" data
entry systems are discussed in Chapter 14.

Consistency   For fixed-position instruments, a consistent location and
arrangement of displays is required from application to application, for example,
from model A to model B of an aircraft. (This is location coding.) The
consequences of inconsistency are time wasted searching or, worse, reading the
wrong instrument. In recent years, aircraft instrument panels have become more
standardized in display location and arrangement. Techniques for determining
optimal arrangement are discussed in Chapter 6. Although displays must be
consistent in location and manner of presentation, they must also be distinguishable or coded in other ways.

Some panels have a series of instruments that are always scanned in a fixed
sequence. The instruments should be arranged left to right and top to bottom in
the same format in which we read printed material. Other panels are arranged

by frequency of use, importance, or logical functional groupings. See Chapters 5, 6, and 7 for examples of usage.

Viewing Distances   Instrument panels are typically located at a viewing distance of 28 in (710 mm), which is also a convenient arm reach for control adjustments. Standards for the sizes of numbers, letters, and markings are based on this assumed viewing distance. Should special circumstances require viewing a display at a greater or closer distance, the required character height may be ascertained by multiplying the recommended character height (for 28 in) by $X/28$ in ($X/710$ mm). In the formula, X equals the required viewing distance in inches.

$$H \text{ at } X \text{ in} = (H \text{ at } 28 \text{ in}) \left(\frac{X \text{ in}}{28}\right)$$

Example: A counter must be read at 56 in. The recommended (28 in) numeral height at low luminance is 0.25 in. The required height is $0.25 \times 2.0 = 0.50$ in.

MIL-STD-1472B [12] also states that the effective viewing distance should never be less than 13 in (330 mm) and preferably not less than 20 in (508 mm). An exception is the cathode-ray tube (CRT), which may present dim signals. The CRT viewing distance should be 16 in (406 mm) and never less than 10 in (254 mm).

These criteria are for typical operational situations. Obviously, the critical factor is visual angle. A distant sign or aircraft identification symbol must be much larger, while a numismatist studying old coins must be much closer and must use magnification aids to read critical dates and markings.

Visual Coding

In Chapter 3 it was noted that identification of a stimulus or its magnitude was a question of absolute judgment rather than relative judgment and that the human is limited in ability to make absolute judgments. Interpreting coded information is limited by the number of distinct steps or levels that can be discriminated on an absolute basis. Information theory studies have determined for vision as well as other senses the number of steps or categories which may be discriminated or the information which may be transmitted in bits. For a single dimension, the categories typically vary from 4 to 11 and the associated bits from 1.6 to 3.3.

Tables 4-3 and 4-5 depict the maximum and recommended number of steps to employ for various coding systems again based on human limitations to discriminate on an absolute basis. Also, there are given advantages and constraints to use of the codes.

Color Coding   Chapanis and Halsey [8] found 10 specific spectral colors or hues that subjects could reliably identify (with less than 2 percent error) after a brief training period. Considerably more (20 to 60) may be discriminated using combinations of hue, saturation, and lightness from black to white. However, only 3 or 4 color-coded lights are recommended for high accuracy.

Table 4-3 Color- and Shape-Coding Methods

	Number of code steps		Constraints	Uses and advantages
	Maximum	Recommended		
Colors				
Lights	10*	3 or 4	Must select for color-weak persons	Quick search time
				Little space required
			Yellow/white confused at low background luminance; blue requires high intensity for equal visibility	Ambient illumination less critical inside vehicle
				Standardized meaning
Surfaces	50	9	Illumination must be controlled	Same as for lights except illumination
Shapes				
Alpha-numerics	Unlimited		Good resolution required	Good for identification
			Some symbols confused in matrix dots and segmented numerals	Little space required
				Meaning of numbers understood without training except when used for qualitative coding
			Search time longer than color, pictures	
Geometrics	15	5**	Memory required	Use for symbolic representations not amenable to pictures (on CRTs)
			Some shapes have misleading meanings	
			Inferior to color for search tasks	
Pictorial silhouettes (pictographs)	30	10	Inferior to color for search tasks	Easily learned if meaning is not obvious

*Up to 60 combinations of hue, saturation, and lightness distinguished by trained subjects.
**More codes with training.

Meaning of Colors In military systems there are already standardized meanings for certain colors (see Table 4-4.). We shall see in Chapter 10 that many of these same color conventions also apply to roadway color coding. Whenever colored lights or surfaces are used to connote meaning, it is important that such codes not be violated.

Color Coding Zones on Dials Operating ranges are often color-coded on moving pointer instruments. For example, lines around the edge of the dial may be coded red for dangerous ranges of values, green for normal ranges, and

Table 4-4 Color-Coding Conventions for Lights and Surfaces

Light color	Meaning
Red*	Malfunction, action stopped, failure, stop action, error
Flashing red	Emergency condition (immediate action to avert disaster)
Yellow	Caution, delay, check/recheck, condition marginal
Green	Go-ahead, in-tolerance, acceptable, ready, power-on
White	Status indication (no right or wrong), action in progress
Blue	Advisory or alternative status (generally avoid using)

Paint color	Meaning
Red	Fire (alarm boxes, extinguishers), stop, hazard, emergency
Yellow	Caution, physical hazards (yellow/black stripes)
Green	Safety, first-aid equipment
Orange	Dangerous conditions (hazardous moving parts)
Blue	Caution against starting equipment under repair
Purple	Radiation hazard, radioactive material

*MIL-STD-1472B permits the use of red LED alphanumeric displays (with approval) in violation of this coding system because of their better visibility in ambient lighting or direct sunlight. They may not be used in proximity of red lights used for coded purposes. Green and yellow LEDs may not be used without approval.

Sources: Transilluminated LED and Incandescent Displays [MIL-C-25050A, 13]; Surface Color Coding [AFSC DH 1-3, DN2C4, Section 3, 1].

yellow for marginal or caution zones. Under red lighting, where color coding would not be feasible, distinctive shapes such as parallel diagonal or barber-pole lines may be used. Color coding display zones aids in seeing trends, direction, and rate of changes and provides an aid for decision making without memorizing the critical ranges.

Color Coding in Search Tasks   Color coding is superior to shape coding and most other techniques for search, scan, and location tasks such as map reading, wire selection, and card filing [Konz and Koe, 22]. Shontz et al. [39] found that a larger percentage of color-coded dots could be located in a briefer time than could gray dots or printed labels.

With surface colors (pigments), Conover [10] found nine colors that can be reliably discriminated. Haines and Rhoades [20] found 50 combinations of hue, saturation, and lightness from black to white. However, these studies were based on people with considerable training. In application to a population with unknown training, it is better to limit the number of colors to nine (see p. 164).

Eight percent of adult males are partially color-blind. It may be easier to carefully select the colors than to exclude this population from using the system. Federal Standard 595 lists nine surface colors that are discriminable by color-weak individuals: red, orange, yellow, blue, purple, grey, buff, white, and black as specified by numbers designating the exact colors. In lights AFSC DH 1-3 [1] recommends aviation red, green, and blue for color-weak viewers. Yellow and white were excluded because red is confused with yellow and green is confused with white.

Color codes employed on objects to be viewed at a distance, such as road signs, ground targets, and aircraft, must consider the color of the background and brightness of the color. Military aircraft fuselages are sometimes painted a bright fluorescent orange primarily for greater visibility at a distance. Blue lights require much greater intensity to be as visible as other lights.

Shape Coding Shape coding includes not only geometric and pictorial shapes, but also numbers and letters (alphanumerics).

Alphanumerics There are an unlimited number of combinations of letters and numbers. When three-digit numbers are used there is a danger of a *transposition* error, particularly, reversing the sequence of the last two digits. A letter between two numbers is recommended. Long lists of numbers and similar numbers should be avoided if possible. Grouping 7-digit numbers into sets of three and four aids in recall.

In search tasks it takes longer to locate a given number if all numbers are not oriented upright [Green et al., 19]. Although numbers have a learned meaning when used in a quantitative sense, numbers and letters employed in coding systems must *be* learned. For example, few highway drivers are aware of the meaning of interstate highway numbers for geographical reference.

Geometric shapes Sleight [42] found 15 geometric shapes that are highly discriminable if their apparent size is at least 12 minutes of visual angle and there is high contrast with the background. These included common shapes such as the triangle, circle, star, square, and pentagon. These shapes may be used in coding, but their meanings must be taught. Other shapes among the 15 such as the swastika, heart, half-moon, or aircraft silhouette have certain conventional meanings that could detract from their usage in other applications.

Pictographs Pictorial silhouettes or pictographs are intended to have obvious meanings and hence would not need to be learned. Whether or not the intended meaning is, in fact, apparent to nearly all viewers should be tested (see Chapter 10). Examples of military pictographs are aircraft, ships, missiles, and antiaircraft guns. Pictographs such as these are located more quickly and with fewer errors than geometric shapes because they are very distinctive. However, pictographs take longer to locate and have more errors than geometric shapes if they are very similar, such as a variety of aircraft models [Smith and Thomas, 45].

Magnitude Coding Magnitude coding refers to coding systems that employ size, length, frequency, or intensity differences. There are a variety of magnitude coding systems but only two to four categories are recommended for most of them (see Table 4-5). *Area* or size coding is illustrated by a series of solid circles of graduated size. Five areas comprising 5, 7, 12, 21, and 30 minutes of

Table 4-5 Magnitude and Angular Coding Methods

Code	Number of code steps		Constraints	Uses and advantages
	Maximum	Recommended		
Area (size)	6	3	Large symbol space required	Search time quick Character size graduation used for labeling
Visual number	6	4	Large symbol space required	Limited use
Flash frequency	4	2	Distracting	Use for attention-getting to specific areas Distant communications application
Brightness	4	2	Controlled illumination required	Limited use
Stereo-depth	4	2	Requires a stereoscope Individual differences in depth	Limited use
Length of line	6	3	Large symbol space required	Limited use (target speed)*
Inclination angle	24	12	Must learn scale values	Quantitative coding (approximations) Use for target course*

visual arc may be discriminated with 5 percent error. Four areas may be distinguished with 2 percent error and three areas with 1 percent error [Muller et al., 27].

Number of dots   have been studied by tachistoscopic presentations of about 1/10 s exposure time. Oberly [30] found that codes employing five dots or less could be identified accurately, but when the observer had to estimate (without time to count) a larger number of dots, error scores rose sharply. Patterning dots as on dominoes or playing cards should increase the coding capacity by visual number.

Flash rates   have been used on lighthouses, ship navigation aids, and for coding target parameters such as speed. Cohen and Dinnerstein [9] found that only four rates could be accurately distinguished by trained subjects. Flashing is annoying in continuous usage and should be used mainly to attract attention. Since ambient lighting influences discrimination, only two rates are recommended for coding. Also, only two *brightness* levels should be used—bright and dim. Brightness is obviously affected by ambient lighting and contrasts.

Stereodepth   By taking two slightly different pictures of an object, depth may be created synthetically when the images are superimposed (as with the stereoscope of bygone days). Only two categories of *stereodepth* are recommended because there are large individual differences in binocular disparity.

Line Length and Inclination Coding   The length of a line as a coding technique has been researched in conjunction with another coding method, angle-of-line inclination. We have developed skills in judging inclination angles by reading watches and other circular dials. Alluisi [2] found that 24 angles of inclination could be identified by trained subjects with less than 5 percent error. However, only 12 angles, as illustrated by the hours on a clock, are recommended for coding.

Lines could be as short as 0.1 in, but better performance is achieved with longer lines. No more than three different lengths is recommended for coding. Symbolic information, such as target speed on a CRT, sometimes employs line length while target course is shown by inclination angle.

Location Coding   Location coding applies to both controls and displays. In fact, it applies to any object which is assigned a given location and which we have experienced to be in that position many times. An office worker may learn the location of his or her mail cubicle as "top row, second from the left." The nameplate may be referred to only during initial learning. Should cubicles be reassigned without notice, there is a risk of error. With practice we learn location cues and, whether we are sighted or blind, these cues are one of if not the primary source for locating objects.

Multiple Coding   In practice, designers may use a combination of coding techniques. Complex systems may require limiting the use of coding to one code for each type of information and, thereby, increasing the number of parameters that may be displayed. However, when there are only a few categories there is merit to using two or three codes to convey the same types of information. For example, road signs may be coded by shape, color, and alphanumeric message—all designating an interstate highway. Redundancy in this sense increases the likelihood of recognition and comprehension.

Warning and Caution Lights

Backlighted (transilluminated) legend lights may be designed to turn on to indicate various conditions. They may be appropriately color-coded, as shown earlier in Table 4-4, and they may be engraved with words or numbers. The lights should attract attention without preventing the operator from continuing to attend to other duties. They should be used sparingly for situations requiring immediate action or important systems status. Routine usage reduces their novelty and attention-getting value. Too many lights also compromise the dark adaptation required for reconnaissance flight missions or CRT scope tasks.

Simple indicator lights have limited application because the legend must be given on the panel nearby, and it is difficult to read the legend under some lighting conditions. Their main usage is for power on for a single unit.

Flashing red lights denoting emergency situations are most effective at a rate of 3 to 5 flashes/s. Master warning and caution lights are located near the line-of-sight to attract attention to a subsystem failure, after which the pilot directs his or her attention to a subsystem component.

Table 4-6 presents design criteria for warning and other legend lights. In addition to consideration of location, usage, and legibility, the designer must also be concerned with lamp failure. When a redundant (dual) filament bulb fails, there is a drop in intensity rather than a total loss of information. Lamp-testing provisions must also be provided by testing all at once or by individual bulb press-to-test techniques. Lamps should be removable from the panel front without tools.

Table 4-6 Design Criteria for Warning Lights and Other Legend Lights

Usage

Use sparingly to display necessary information only. Use master caution, warning, advisory, and summation lights to indicate condition of an entire subsystem. Subsystem component status is shown on another panel.

Use flashing lights only to call attention to situations requiring immediate action. Flash rates of 3–5/ s with equal ON and OFF time.

A light going off should never be used to indicate either GREEN or RED light functions. Must have positive feedback to attract attention.

Location

Master warning or caution lights are within ±15 degrees of LOS. Often arrayed across the cowl in military aircraft. Signal or status lights are often grouped in a single panel that is located lower on the instrument panel.

An exception to this grouping is backlighted displays that are associated with particular controls. They should be located adjacent to or as an integral part of the control. The association must be unambiguous and the light must be visible during control usage.

Legibility

Lights must be at least 10% brighter than surrounding luminance. Provide a dimming switch when used under varied ambient illumination.

Lettering on the legend must be visible whether or not the light is ON.

Use black characters on white background when ambient illumination is greater than 1 fc (11 lx). Brighter background will get attention quicker. White characters on black are OK for status information.

Blacklighted characters should be 0.2 to 0.3 in high for legibility at low-light levels.

Table 4-7 Design Criteria for Scale Indicators

Layout of fixed scales

Numbers increase clockwise, left to right, bottom to top, depending on the display design and orientation.

With one revolution of circular scales, zero is usually at 7 o'clock and the maximum value is at 5 o'clock, with a 10 degree break in the arc. This format prevents increasing values to the left.

When check-reading positive and negative values, the zero or null position is at 12 o'clock or 9 o'clock. With a matrix of circular displays, deviations from a 9 o'clock null position are easily detected in check reading. Zero is at 12 on multirevolution dials.

All numbers should be oriented upright. They should be outside the tick (graduation) marks unless doing so would constrict the scale. (While this is desirable for preventing pointer head obstruction of numbers, the crowding of markings on small dials has resulted in most numbers being inside the marks.)

Layout of moving scales

Numbers on moving scales progress in magnitude like fixed scales, but the numbers increase in value by counter-clockwise dial movement.

Numbers are read at 12 o'clock for right-left directional information and at 9 o'clock for up-down information.

The window should be large enough to permit seeing one numbered graduation on each side of the indexed number whenever the display is used to set in values. For tracking, the whole dial face is exposed.

Detail design of fixed scales

The pointer should extend from the right of vertical scales and from the bottom of horizontal scales.

The pointer should extend to but not obscure the shortest graduation marks.

Graduation interval values should be 1, 2, 5, or decimal multiples thereof. Numbering by 1, 10, or 100 is recommended for progressions.

Nine is the maximum number of tick marks between numbers.

Tick marks should be separated at least 0.07 in for 28 in (710 mm) viewing under low illumination (0.03–1.0 fL).

Dials must not be cluttered with more marks than necessary for precision.

Zones may be color-coded by edge lines or wedges. (Zones indicate operating ranges, dangerous levels, and so on.) Use red, yellow, and green.

Shape coding or striping is necessary when red lighting or blackout station conditions prevail.

Information should be in a directly usable form (for example, percent RPM).

See Table 4-9, Design criteria for panel labeling, for character dimensions.

Scale Indicators

Table 4-7 presents design criteria for scale indicators. Mechanical or scale indicators may be found in various shapes: circular, curved (arced), horizontal straight, or vertical straight. Figure 4-3 illustrates shapes in combination with

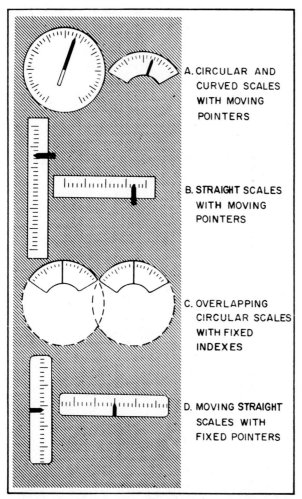

Figure 4-3 Variations of moving-pointer and moving-scale indicators. *(AFSC DH 1-3, 1977.)*

A. CIRCULAR AND CURVED SCALES WITH MOVING POINTERS

B. STRAIGHT SCALES WITH MOVING POINTERS

C. OVERLAPPING CIRCULAR SCALES WITH FIXED INDEXES

D. MOVING STRAIGHT SCALES WITH FIXED POINTERS

moving scales or pointers. As noted previously, the moving pointer on fixed scale is recommended for qualitative information, for check reading, for setting in numbers, and for tracking. It requires more panel space than either the moving tape (scale) or the counter. The moving tape, however, requires more space behind the panel for feeding and collecting the tape.

Long-Range, Precise Reading Displays

Given a range of relevant values and a required reading accuracy, the display designer must select an appropriate display. Suppose the display calls for a range from 0 to 70,000 ft (0-213.6 m) in altitude and an accuracy to 20 ft (6.046 m). To display this much information on a fixed scale would require a scale of 245 in (6.2 m)! It is not feasible to compress the information on a single scale since the

graduation marks would be too close together to be discernible, and interpolation between marks would not provide the needed precision.

Use of multiple pointers is one solution to reading to greater precision over
a wide range. The conventional clock does just that. However, combining three
or more different pointers results in an increased likelihood of gross reading
errors. An example from the accident literature is the three-pointer altimeter.
Two is the maximum number of pointers recommended to avoid confusion
errors [Department of Defense, 12].

Grether and Baker [53] recommend the use of vernier subcounters or
subdials for gross readings, but they discourage the use of subtapes (moving
scales) in combination with the moving pointer (see Figure 4-4).

Counters or moving tapes could also be used to display a wide range of
values to great precision. However, as noted previously, they are poor for
qualitative information. Direction and magnitude of deviation are more difficult
to detect. Counters or tapes are difficult to read during periods of rapid change.

Moving scale numbers must increase *in magnitude* in a clockwise, right, or
upward direction (as do numbers on the moving pointer, fixed-scale display). As
scale values increase, the tape itself must actually move counter-clockwise,
right-to-left, or downward. It is confusing to some people to be turning a control
clockwise and see the tape drive moving in the opposite direction! Moving
pointer displays do not have this incompatibility of control and display direction
of movement.

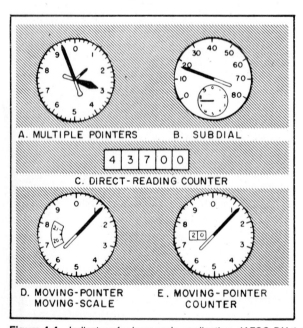

Figure 4-4 Indicators for long-scale application. *(AFSC DH 1–3, 1977.)*

Principles of Movement in Whole-Panel Displays

The issue of moving pointer versus moving scale has been a major one in two whole-panel display programs. Williams et al. [51] proposed and developed an advanced instrument system which followed a design philosophy that all instruments should employ the moving pointer, fixed-scale design. This included not only the altitude, airspeed, rate of climb, and so forth, but also the attitude instrument and the navigation or heading instrument.

Inside-Out Versus Outside-In   Traditionally, attitude indicators consist of a stationary aircraft symbol and a horizon line that "tips" to indicate banking movements. This approach is termed the "inside-out" approach since the aircraft's attitude was shown as it would appear to a pilot inside an aircraft looking at the horizon (Figure 4-5).

While training new pilots in simulators, it was found that reversal errors in banking were quite common, that is, the control stick was moved laterally in the opposite direction from required. Williams et al. took the position that the moving horizon, like the moving tape, was an unnatural situation. They designed an attitude indicator in which the aircraft symbol banked against a stationary horizon. This approach was termed "outside-in" since the motion of the aircraft was viewed as it would appear from outside, looking at the aircraft from the front or rear against the horizon.

The concept was extended to the navigation/heading display. A tiny aircraft symbol was shown moving across a stationary map. This was in contrast to the inside-out approach where the map moved under a stationary aircraft symbol. Other flight instruments on vertical scales also employed moving indices against fixed scales (Figure 4-6, right).

Air Force Integrated Instrument Panel   In contrast with the moving-index display panel was the Air Force Integrated Flight Instrument Panel developed by

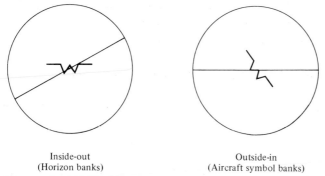

Inside-out
(Horizon banks)

Outside-in
(Aircraft symbol banks)

Figure 4-5 Aircraft attitude indicators depicting the aircraft banking to the right with an inside-out and outside-in display.

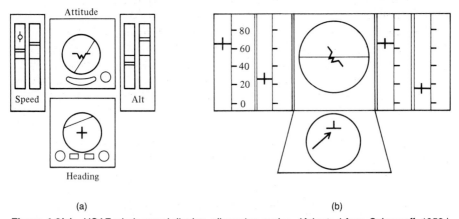

(a)   (b)

Figure 4-6(a)   USAF whole-panel display, all moving scales. *(Adapted from Svimonoff, 1958.)*
Figure 4-6(b)   Whole-panel display, (all moving indices.) *(Adapted from Williams et al., 1956.)*

the USAF Flight Dynamics Laboratory [Svimonoff, 47]. Like the other system, airspeed and altitude were shown on vertical scales on either side of the attitude indicator (see Figure 4-6, left). However, the scales were all moving tapes. Each tape was read from a central lubber line that extended horizontally on a line coinciding with the stationary aircraft symbol on the attitude display. Quantitative values could be read from this reference line with a minimum of eye scan.

In both systems the vertical scales depicted both actual performance and desired (command) performance for a particular parameter. In the USAF system two parallel lines on a tape gave command performance. The relative position of the command index to the reference line indicated the extent of error. The pilot's task was one of compensatory tracking or nulling error as the command index moved to the central reference line. Since the range of visible numbers was restricted (and the command index might not be visible), there was a counter readout of the command value at the bottom of each scale. Maximum safe limits were shown also on the tapes by barber-pole lines.

The Williams et al. system employed a fixed scale with shape-coded symbols. A cross resembling an aircraft gave the present performance value, a diamond displayed the command value, and a solid dot, the predicted value in one minute. Roscoe [37] demonstrated that an integrated altimeter, showing the three values on one vertical scale, resulted in superior performance to displaying the same information on three separate circular scales, three counters, or an integrated circular scale. The vertical scale provided a spatial analog to the parameter—altitude. Roscoe has also maintained that a pursuit tracking task, where actual and desired performance indices each move, results in better performance than a compensatory tracking task where only the command index moves (see Chapter 5).

Both systems encountered some problems. As already noted, moving tapes sacrifice position cues and trend information with possible gross reading error.

The outside-in approach encountered technical problems with the moving index navigation display (the aircraft would eventually reach the side of the map). The USAF integrated panel encountered no such problem since it employed a moving map and fixed aircraft symbol. There was also resistance to the Williams et al. system from experienced pilots. Changing the moving element on the attitude indicator required relearning since they were trained with a moving horizon line.

The question remained: How serious is the potential for reversal errors with the inside-out attitude indicator? There is some evidence that by adding more detail, color, and so forth to the attitude indicator, there is less likelihood of confusion in using the inside-out attitude indicator.

More recently Beringer, Roscoe, and Williges [4] investigated an attitude indicator that is a hybrid of the moving-aircraft and moving-horizon displays. This frequency-separated display permitted both symbols to move—the horizon in its conventional manner and the aircraft symbol in immediate and direct response to aileron control inputs. Simulator research found little evidence of reversal errors among nonpilots while experienced pilots adapted to it as a moving-horizon display to which roll-rate prediction had been added. Tracking error, both in simulators and in flight, was reported to be less than with the moving-aircraft or moving-horizon displays. The *Kinalog attitude concept,* proposed by Fogel [17] and illustrated in Figure 4-7, also addressed the problem by having the aircraft symbol bank first. Then the horizon banks in the opposite direction while the aircraft symbol gradually returns to a straight-and-level position.

Army-Navy Instrument Program   The Army-Navy Instrument Program (abbreviated ANIP and later JANAIR) was a unique approach to developing a whole-panel display [34]. Basically, it attempted to free the pilot of the task of reading many separate instruments and comparing and combining numbers to understand the flight situation. A computer could do the calculating by evaluating sensor data. During instrument flight the pilot would monitor a forward-and-downward-looking display showing synthetic pictures of the situation in geometric perspective. This contact analog display did not attempt to provide a complete TV-type picture of the visual field ahead. Rather it presented only the basic elements required for perception of the aircraft's position and movement in space.

The contact analog integrated display illustrated in Figure 4-8 was believed to be applicable to helicopters [Dougherty et al., 14], space vehicles [Burke and Huchingson, 5], submarines, and other vehicles. Research studies were sponsored in each area. Geometric perspective was provided by reference lines radiating from a point on the horizon and horizontal lines crisscrossing. Only selected "corn fields" or squares needed to be displayed to create the sensation of perspective. The size of the squares provided a qualitative cue to altitude; the rate of movement of the squares toward the viewer provided airspeed; and conventional displacement of the horizon provided attitude cues. Localizer and

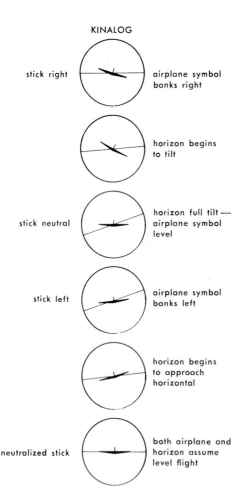

KINALOG

stick right — airplane symbol banks right

horizon begins to tilt

stick neutral — horizon full tilt — airplane symbol level

stick left — airplane symbol banks left

horizon begins to approach horizontal

neutralized stick — both airplane and horizon assume level flight

Figure 4-7 The Kinalog display concept *(Fogel, 1959, from* Human Factors, *vol I, no. 2, 1959. Copyright 1959 by The Human Factors Society, Inc. and reproduced by permission.)*

glide slope path were shown by means of a "highway in the sky" extending to the horizon. If the aircraft was to the right, the highway appeared to the left (as shown in Figure 4-8). If the aircraft sunk below the glide slope, the highway appeared in the sky above the viewer instead of below it. (The Kaiser Flight Path System employed a different technique: the apex of the highway, or commanded flight path, extended above the horizon line to indicate that the vehicle was too high.)

Dougherty et al. [14] tested the helicopter version and found there was less mean absolute error with the contact analog than with conventional displays. The pictorial displays were found to be easy to assimilate and, in addition, provided during nighttime or adverse weather the visual cues that would be available during a clear, daytime flight.

Conventional instruments were retained for backup and for reporting exact

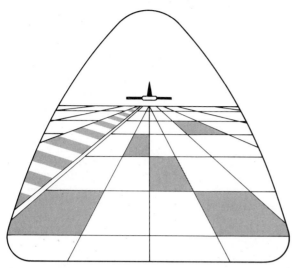

Figure 4-8   Contact analog display.

values. Early contact analog concepts involved an optical projection technique whereby the display was on the windscreen. The pilot could continue seeing outside without lowering the eyes to scan instruments. This type of head-up display (HUD) will be discussed subsequently; however, the basic contact analog concepts can be and currently are employed in military aircraft as separate instruments and need not be projected on the windscreen.

Head-Up Displays

It is sometimes desirable to give a pilot information on altitude, airspeed, and heading on the windscreen during certain mission phases such as an instrument landing. The pilot would not need to take his or her eyes off the visual world to read cockpit instruments. The collimated or head-up display provided such a capability.

The basic optics of the HUD consist of collimated images that are reflected to a transparent mirror or prism and then reflected off the windscreen. The image brightness may need to be adjusted to anticipated visual backgrounds.

One combined display system in operation on naval aircraft displayed weapon delivery information in the center of the display. Airspeed and altitude were shown on vertical scales on the left and right, respectively. Heading was shown on a horizontal scale across the top. The altitude and airspeed displays employed thermometer-type indicators that are easier to see peripherally than are moving dots or arrows. Counters at the top of vertical scales provided major units of airspeed and altitude while the scales provided the more precise units.

Another display system under development [Watler and Hoover, 50] employs the highway-in-the-sky flight path system discussed previously. So-called moving tar strips display the required flight path. A series of moving dots adjacent to the path display speed qualitatively. Firing command point and location of the target aircraft are also displayed along the flight path.

The head-up display concept has been adapted to helmet visors [Monroney and Barnette, 26]. This innovation was necessary because in some systems, for example, a helicopter, the pilot was shifting his or her vision a great deal to the side windows, and the display needed to move with head movement. One prototype helmet-mounted system displays red light-emitting diode arrays (dot-matrix characters) and patterns of dots for energy management [26].

Another innovative display technique is the laser-generated, *holographic* display [Benton, 3] in which a highly realistic virtual image of an object appears in space in the proper location, that is, three-dimensional depth cues are provided. Further technical advances are necessary before the technique may be applied to aircraft display systems.

Recent Electronic Display Technology

As recently as 1970 numeric readouts for desk calculators employed either electromechanical displays or NIXIE tubes (a trademark of the Burroughs Corporation). Today, multidigit electronic displays are employed on miniaturized calculators and are being considered for automotive dashboard applications [Nolan, 29].

In addition to the digital-address, flat cathode-ray tubes, a few of the other electrically excited, flat-panel display systems in use are light-emitting diodes (LED), the liquid crystal display (LCD), a-c and d-c plasma panels, and electroluminescent films (ELF).

The LED are employed for numeric readout in push-to-display wrist watches, in many hand calculators, and as aircraft backup displays. Numbers usually appear in red or green in heights from 0.1 to 0.5 in. Recent watches and calculators employ the LCD, a reflective system not dependent upon light-emitting elements. The LCD may be viewed in direct sunlight or in changing ambient illumination. However, it presents a problem in total darkness, and many watches have an auxiliary light source that is turned on in low light levels.

Plasma panels are being developed for video displays and alphanumeric message boards. The a-c plasma panel provides an orange-red emission and the d-c panel, a neon emission. Electroluminescent displays are discussed in instrument lighting. Other display technology is being studied in the laboratory and will soon be available in the commercial area. Among these are electrochromatic, electrophoretic, and the fluid dipole displays.

Cathode-Ray Tubes and Image Recognition

Table 4-8 presents techniques for increasing the probability of target recognition on CRT displays. Criteria for large screen displays, counters, and flags are also given. In the following sections, variables influencing target recognition are presented.

Table 4-8　Design Criteria for CRT Displays and Other Displays

<u>CRT</u>

Target size. Complex shapes should subtend a visual angle of 20 minutes or more.

Displays at a viewing distance of greater than 16 in (410 mm) will require increased display and symbol size, brightness, line-pair spacing, and resolution.

Ambient illumination should contribute no more than 25% of screen brightness through diffuse reflection or phosphor excitation.

Scopes must be hooded, shielded, recessed, or filtered when faint signals must be detected and ambient illumination exceeds 0.25 fc (2.7 lx).

Surfaces adjacent to a scope should have a dull matte finish and a brightness of 10–100% of screen luminance. Only emergency lights should be brighter than the scope.

Ambient illumination suitable for visual functions should not interfere with signal visibility.

<u>Large-screen displays</u>

Characters should be visible at the maximum visual angle and distance with a minimum of 15 minutes of visual arc (see Chapter 10). Labeling criteria (Table 4-9) give height-to-width ratios, stroke width, size, and spacing of display symbols.

<u>Counters</u>

Use for quantitative data only.

Mount counters close to panel front to minimize shadows and parallax and maximize viewing angle without occlusion.

Movement: snap action, maximum rate of 2 per second for consecutive readings. Automatic reset capability upon completion of a sequence.

Numerals: height-to-width ratio of 1:1; spacing: $\frac{1}{4}$ to $\frac{1}{2}$ numeral width.

Illumination: high contrast between numeral and background; self-illuminated where display luminance is below 1 fL (3.4 cd/m^2); dull finish on bezel to minimize glare.

<u>Flags</u>

Use for qualitative, nonemergency conditions only.

Mount close to panel surface, snap action, minimum of 50% contrast with background.

Target Recognition in Imaging Displays　Reconnaisance missions sometimes involve observing radar or infrared displays and searching for targets in the terrain picture. The pictures may be displayed as photos, transparencies, projected images, CRT or telescopic images.

Visually, the problem is one of recognizing distinctive target patterns or reference landmarks against patterned backgrounds. Detection and recognition are aided by the following: increased target size, reduced background clutter (that is, fewer irrelevant targets), high contrast, color, larger display area, magnification, viewing time up to two minutes, restriction of search area from prior knowledge of approximate location, and use of two or more observers. Range markers and illuminated reticles also aid in reporting target positions once located. The human is poor at absolute estimation of brightness and is also poor at estimating size, distance, speed, and acceleration in absolute, numerical terms.

Image Size   Steedman and Baker [46] found that for target images, search time and errors decreased markedly if the visual angle of the largest target dimension was greater than 12 minutes of arc. Although 12 minutes is acceptable for recognition, 20 minutes subtense is recommended for critical targets viewed under operational conditions [Grether and Baker, 53]. Magnification improves resolution of details but this is sometimes offset by less viewing time and reduced area of ground coverage. Radar images typically show reflective targets as bright areas and low-return surfaces as dark areas.

Display Size   Visual image size typically increases with display size. A 1000-raster line display, 5-in (12.7 cm) square, can resolve a gap or detail of 0.005 in. This is too small for the average observer to resolve. For example, at 30 in (76 cm) viewing distance it would subtend only 0.6 minutes of arc. However, the same display when 10-in (25.4 cm) square can resolve a gap of 1.1 minutes at the observer's eye, which has a 75 percent probability of detection.

The minimum display size for target identification may be calculated by the following formula [Davis and Shaw, 11]:

Display size = 0.0058 V (R/T)

Where V = viewing distance from scope
$\quad\quad\quad R$ = range on the ground being displayed
$\quad\quad\quad T$ = smallest target's dimension

To illustrate, let us assume a scope viewing distance of 12 in. The smallest target to be recognized is 1000 ft and the range on the ground shown on the display is 243,040 ft (40 nautical miles). For these conditions the display must have one dimension of 16.9 in.

Image Quality Index

Snyder [43, 44] and others have engaged in research to determine the effects of CRT display variables on performance measures associated with image quality. Among the variables studied were size and shape of the dot elements, spacing between them, viewing distance and angle to the display, matrix size (number of rows and column of dots), and luminance contrast.

Snyder studied the ability to recognize human faces on TV displays as a function of the "modulation transfer function area" (MTFA), an index developed to evaluate image quality in photography. He discovered that image quality in terms of spatial frequency and contrast was inversely related to observer response time and directly related to percent of correct matches of TV facial images to facial photographs. The research suggested the MTFA metric may be used to predict observer performance in extracting details from displays. By calculating the MTFA value for the display, one may determine in the design stage the observer's recognition performance. A practical application would be specifiying for TV bank monitors the face image quality needed for identifying a robber.

Character Design

In a subsequent section on labeling panel fronts, certain dimensional data for characters are presented. These dimensions were based on research that employed standard stroke characters such as the Leroy, Mackworth, or AMEL (Naval Aeromedical Electronics Laboratory) stroke fonts. There are two quite different types of alphanumeric characters in use on computer-generated display devices, electroluminescent displays, and light emitting diodes. The *segmented numeral,* formed by lighting appropriate segments of a matrix, is found on digital watches, hand calculators, and many types of electronic displays. The *dot-matrix* character, formed by lighting appropriate diodes, is used on the common computer terminal CRT, television graphics, and so forth. Due to limitations in the equipment, that is, the number of rows and columns of dots and the number of strokes in segmented numerals, compromises must be made in generating classic Arabic letters and numerals. (The state of the art in technology permits higher resolution displays, for example, 10×15 dot-matrix and 39 segment numerals, but less information could be displayed at once.)

Segmented Numerals   Plath [32] studied segmented numerals consisting of only seven segments, as illustrated by the numeral 8. Note that all numerals may be composed from a minimum of seven segments (Figure 4-9). Five-digit numbers were presented at exposure times of .02, .1, and .5 s. Subjects attempted to read the numbers. Plath found that over twice as many errors were made for segmented numerals as for the conventional AMEL font. There were more errors at briefer exposure times.

Gibney [18], in reviewing the literature on segmented numeral legibility, concluded that the legibility decrement of segmented numerals (in comparison with standard designs) was not significant when the task was more complex or when it involved using the information read.

With practice most of us have learned to read our digital watches and calculators with a fair degree of accuracy. Ellis and Hill [16] found that training was effective in overcoming reading difficulties with segmented numerals, but that periodic retraining was necessary. They also found that the numbers 3, 6, and 8 had the highest probability of being confused in seven-segment numerics.

Construction of letters is another issue. Letters require a minimum of 14 segments because of the many diagonal lines required. There are more opportunities for error with 36 alphanumerics than with 10 numerals.

ABCDEFGHIJKLM
NOPQRSTUVWXYZ
0123456789

Figure 4-9 Examples of character font styles for conventional, segmented, and dot-matrix characters—conventional *(MIL-STD, MS 33558* [ASG], 1959) segmented numerals, *(Grether and Baker, 1972);* dot-matrix characters, *(Huchingson et al., 1979.)*

Dot-Matrix Displays There has been a continuing research effort to develop an optimum font for dot-matrix displays and to determine the effects of various factors on legibility. Many dot-matrix characters (and scoreboards with bulbs) are formed by 5 × 7 or 4 × 7 arrays. Errors generally vary inversely with matrix size, but no compelling evidence has established that 5 × 7 is significantly superior to 4 × 7 arrays. Vartabedian [49] found that characters formed by a 7 × 9 dot pattern were as readable as conventional stroke characters made with a Leroy lettering set. He also found that words in upper case were searched faster than those in lower case.

A comparison of eight different font styles [Huchingson et al., 21] found there was general agreement on how to form simple characters such as the E, F, H, L, and T. However, there was considerable difference among the font styles in forming characters involving arcs and diagonals.

Without taking sides as to which font style is most legible, it should be mentioned that the fonts were developed according to different design criteria. Some fonts attempted to develop unique characters that would not likely be confused with one another by the experienced user. Others tried to use a maximum number of dots [Maddox et al., 23] to increase the legibility at a distance; others attempted to develop characters that more exactly resembled the conventional stroke font. In a series of studies, Shurtleff [41] has investigated parameters affecting the legibility of the Lincoln-Mitre font.

Recent advances in display technology for scoreboards, television graphics, and changeable message road signs have raised a host of other issues that are only beginning to be studied [Huchingson et al., 21]. Among the issues are dynamic modes of movement, presentation rates, use of color, unique modes of character formation such as double-size or thick/thin stroke, the effects of the shape of the dots (square or round), and alternating figure-background flash modes. While many of these variables may not be applicable to aerospace products in the near future, their potential needs to be explored (see Chapter 10, Character Factors).

Printed Material

Design criteria have been developed for labeling panels and for graphic and tabular representation of information.

Labeling Panel Fronts   Table 4-9 presents design criteria for labeling panels. Some of these criteria are also applicable to other printed material such as checklists and decals.

The words selected should be concise, familiar, unambiguous, and legible in the ambient lighting. Each subpanel should be delineated by lines. Labels should be readily associated with controls and displays to which they relate.

Character heights required vary with distance, luminance, and criticality of material. Peters and Adams [31] developed a formula for ascertaining required character height *(H)*:

$$H = 0.0022D + K_1 + K_2$$

where D = viewing distance
K_1 = correction factor for illumination and viewing conditions
K_2 = correction factor for importance

Table 4-10 may be used in determining values for K_1 and K_2 for four specified viewing distances.

Graphic and Tabular Representations   At oral presentations speakers often employ pictorial methods of displaying quantitative information such as pie charts, bar charts or histograms, and line graphs on the assumption that trends can be grasped more quickly than from tabular data. Although there has been limited research, Shutz [38] compared vertical bar graphs, horizontal bar graphs, and conventional line graphs with six data points each. Subjects were scored on both time to estimate trends and on accuracy. The line graph was read slightly quicker and with greater accuracy. The horizontal bar chart gave poorest performance.

However, it should be noted that graphs are appropriate for continuous (interval scale) parameters and not for discrete categories (nominal scale data). No more than three functions are recommended on a single line graph. If additional parameters must be shown, additional graphs should be used. Numbered grids should be bolder than unnumbered grid lines. Logarithmic scales are recommended for long ranges of information. Curve fitting simplifies the presentation.

If interpolation will be required, graphs or scales are preferable to tables

Table 4-9 Design Criteria for Panel Labeling

Label controls, displays, and other equipment (except where the identity is obvious).

Where frequent changes are anticipated, provide for ease of alteration. Pull-offs and engraving are the extremes.

Location

Orient labels horizontally, left to right. Vertical labels, when required, should be read top to bottom (N/A to graphs).

Locate labels above controls and displays that they identify (when the panel is above the eye level, they may be labeled below).

Abbreviated units of measurement are typically below the readout window.

Consistent labeling locations throughout a system are most important.

Use enclosure lines around a panel (or "dog ears") as appropriate (see Chapter 5).

Content

Describe the function of equipment, not engineering nomenclature (for example, "altitude" not "altimeter").

Use standard abbreviations, according to military specifications. Omit periods. Use same abbreviation for singular, plural, all tenses.

Messages should be brief, unambiguous, and familiar to operators. Avoid redundant words, for example, control, display.

Use size graduation to distinguish group labels (panel titles) from control/display labels and control positions/units. The three letter heights should differ by 25%.

Legibility

Lettering is black on gray panels (USAF). Army/Navy have own standards.

Black is required above 1 fc (11 lx). Use white on black for night vision.

Font style: Futura demi-bold or Futura medium (typically).* Use all capital letters except extended copy (instructions), which are lower case.

Letter widths: Width is $\frac{3}{5}$ height except "I" and "l" ($\frac{1}{5}$) and "M," "W," and "4" ($\frac{4}{5}$). If a reduced character width is required, stroke width must also be reduced. On curved surfaces, use 1:1 ratio.

Stroke width: $\frac{1}{6}$ of height; $\frac{1}{7}$ or $\frac{1}{8}$ when white on black.

Minimum letter spacing: One stroke width within words; one character width between words. Line spacing: $\frac{1}{2}$ character height.

Character height: Dim lighting at 28 in, 0.2–0.3 in (5–7.5 mm) for critical information. Above 1 fL (3.4 cd/m²), 0.12 in is minimum. (See Peters and Adams formula for a more exact criterion.)

*See MIL-STD-33558 for military systems.

[AFSC, 1]. If interpolation is not required and exact numbers are more important than trends, a table should be employed.

A problem often encountered in the use of some tables is scanning across the page from the cell value to the row title. (Tables of contents often use a series

Table 4-10 Table of Heights of Letters and Numerals Recommended for Panels for Varying Distances and Conditions

Formula H (in) $= 0.0022D + K_1{}^* + K_2$

Viewing distance, in	0.0022D value	Nonimportant markings, $K_2 = .0$			Important markings, $K_2 = .075$		
		$K_1 = .06$	$K_1 = .16$	$K_1 = .26$	$K_1 = .06$	$K_1 = .16$	$K_1 = .26$
14	0.0308	0.09	0.19	0.29	0.17	0.27	0.37
28	0.0616	0.12	0.22	0.32	0.20	0.30	0.40
42	0.0926	0.15	0.25	0.35	0.23	0.33	0.43
56	0.1232	0.18	0.28	0.38	0.25	0.35	0.45

*Applicability of K_1 values:

$K_1 = .06$ (above 1.0 fc, favorable reading conditions)
$K_1 = .16$ (above 1.0 fc, unfavorable reading conditions)
$K_1 = .16$ (below 1.0 fc, favorable reading conditions)
$K_1 = .26$ (below 1.0 fc, unfavorable reading conditions)

Source: Based on formula by Peters and Adams [31] as given in McCormick [24].

of dots called leaders.) The use of bold lines or spacings after every five vertical listings is one solution. Columns should be separated by at least 0.166 in (.42 cm) unless vertical lines are used. The most important information may be located in the first column after row titles (exam marks are more important than attendance records in grade books). By convention, row totals are given in the extreme right column.

Tables are sometimes used to display temporal information. Television program listings on various channels is an example of the use of tables to show concurrent information. The reader is interested in the beginning time, total program time, and other programs shown at the same time that conflict with or overlap a given program in time. A program table which lists time on the vertical axis and stations on the horizontal axis is preferable to listing all programs which begin at a given time (with program duration in the text), because the latter does not depict concurrency of programming.

Listings should be organized in tabular format. For example, in listing the draft of amateur athletes into the professional ranks, the columns should be (a) professional team; (b) player names in order of draft for each team; (c) colleges, positions, and so forth. Listing in text format the names and other information in the order of draft, as received from the teletype, makes it very difficult to locate specific players or other information.

Display Illumination

General workspace illumination is presented in Chapter 8. The following deals with specialized techniques for illuminating instruments, panels, and CRT scopes.

Red Lighting and Dark Adaptation Dark adaptation refers to the increased sensitivity of the eye to dimly illuminated objects after prolonged periods in darkness or near-darkness. If a pilot is preexposed to a less bright area, vision will already be dark-adapted before entering the cockpit. Preexposure to a 1.1-mL light of various colors has shown that red is the color which provides dark adaptation in the briefest duration. The brightness threshold is illustrated by ability to see tiny spots of light in darkness. The threshold is lower for red than for other colors after 5 min of preexposure. Pilots often wear red goggles in the ready room before a night flight to preadapt their eyes.

To maintain maximum dark adaptation, a low-brightness red lighting system is recommended [AFSC, 1]. A constraint on the use of red lighting is that color discrimination for pigments is lost. Color-coded maps, for example, would be ineffective. However, colored warning lights are not affected by ambient red lighting.

Burke and Huchingson [5] found that panel lights such as those employed in weapon delivery sequences and other panel lights reduced the probability of detection of pinpoint light sources viewed through the pilot's windshield in otherwise total darkness. The 50th percentile* for source light detection was 18×10^{-7} candela (cd) for total darkness, 22×10^{-7} cd for night flight with weapon delivery configuration, and 28×10^{-7} cd for the above, plus projected map display (unfiltered) at bright intensity.

In addition to panel and scope lighting, there are outside light sources such as moonlight and thunderstorm lighting that may compromise dark adaptation. The latter may also cause flash blindness for a second or so.

Reflections and Distribution Reflections from the windshield reduce the operator's ability to see through it. Reflection hazards are minimized by a glare shield above the instrument panel, by directing flood lights downward, and by the use of dark, matte surfaces.

The lighting system in an aircraft must permit adequate indicator reading. Chambers et al. [7] found that gross reading errors increased rapidly when the indicator luminance was less than 0.02 footlamberts (fl). The instrument face must also have a fairly uniform light distribution. While this is difficult to do technically, the brightest and dimmest portions of the indicator must not exceed a 7:1 ratio.

Techniques of Lighting Instruments There are at least five methods of instrument and panel lighting: flood, indirect, edge, rear lighting, and electroluminescent lighting. Electroluminescent lighting is applicable to panel legend lighting.

Flood Lighting As shown in Figure 4-10, flood lights are usually above the indicator, providing a fairly uniform distribution of light for decals, knobs, and

*1 to 99th percentile values were calculated for the S-shaped distribution. Values quoted are for a mean of upper- and lower-threshold readings according to the method of limits.

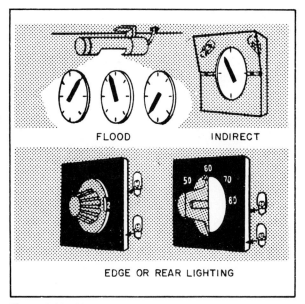

FLOOD   INDIRECT

EDGE OR REAR LIGHTING

Figure 4-10   Methods of indicator and panel lighting. *(AFSC DH 1–3, 1977.)*

switches. Few luminaries are needed. However, considerable light is scattered and bezels cast shadows on the indicator faces at acute angles of incidence.

Indirect Lighting   Indirect, edge, and rear lighting are forms of integral lighting (lighting built into the individual instrument). Indirect lighting provides light around the rims of the indicator by reflection from a light shield or transmission through plastic. Minimum light is scattered. The light can be tailored to the individual instrument. However, it is difficult to obtain a uniform light distribution. Instrument faces may appear to float because of contrast with the nonilluminated panel.

Edge Lighting   Edge lighting is better suited for control knobs and labels than for instruments. Light from the edges comes through transparent plastic and escapes through markings in an otherwise opaque or black covering over the plastic. There is a minimum of light scattering, but it is difficult to provide a uniform distribution.

Rear Lighting   Rear lighting, like edge lighting, involves transmitting light through translucent markings in an otherwise opaque covering over transparent plastic. Light distribution is more uniform, but access to the luminaires for replacement is more difficult. It also requires a packaging design with unobstructed space behind the lighted surface.

Electroluminescent (EL) Lighting   This is a relatively new type of integral lighting in which a laminated conducting plate glows when an electrical potential is applied. This solid-state display technique is excellent for panel legend lighting. It permits uniform brightness and color coding.

Radar Room Lighting   There are four techniques for lighting radar rooms. Each has certain advantages and disadvantages see [AFSC DH 1-3, 1]. The light sources are sodium, mercury, fluorescent, and incandescent. Three of the techniques require the operator to wear goggles and all require filters over the scope.

AUDITORY DISPLAYS

Under certain conditions the use of auditory signals is preferable to visual displays. Speech communications (Chapter 12) is one of the primary forms of auditory communications. This section will deal primarily with alarm systems used to attract our attention and with tones or signals heard over a headset. Techniques are given for enhancing signal detection, discrimination, and identification, particularly in a noise field.

Visual and Auditory Displays

Table 4-11 compares auditory and visual displays in terms of conditions of recommended usage. Auditory presentations are effective as warning signals, especially in situations where vision is already overburdened or degraded or where the task calls for moving the head or body. Since the ears are omnidirectional, attention is attracted quicker than through the eyes.

Table 4-11 Guide to Use of Auditory and Visual Display

Use auditory displays when . . .

the message is simple and short
the message calls for immediate action
the message will not be referred to later
the message deals with events in time
the operator's visual system is already overloaded
the illumination limits vision
the job requires moving about frequently
the stimulus is acoustical in nature

Use visual display when . . .

the message is long and complex
the message does not necessarily require immediate action
the message will be referred to later
the message deals with locations in space
the operator's auditory system is overloaded
the location is too noisy
the job permits the operator to remain in one position
the stimulus is visual in nature

Although rapid detection of sounds make it adaptable to events in time, this does not rule out its application to events in space. The display of steering error by auditory reference is an application to orientation in space. Verbal instructions from a service station attendant regarding directions to a location in a city may be learned, although reference to a map is easier for many and permits later reference if necessary. In general, retention of long, complex auditory messages are difficult unless the message is repeated several times.

Auditory displays have also been used for sonar and radar range signals, the range to the target being given by the time it takes for the signal to reach the target and return. Auditory displays permit operators to detect the presence or absence of a signal or an alarm state, to discriminate two or more signals, or to identify the class of a particular signal.

Rules for Selecting Alarms

Table 4-12 presents the major types of alarms, their intensity and frequency characteristics, and their relative ability to attract attention and to penetrate noise. Certain alarms are of high intensity and applicable to outdoor use or transmission through barriers. Other alarms are intended for indoor use or conditions where background noise is minimal. One does not enjoy being startled by an overdesigned alarm, so chimes and buzzers are supplanting bells. Clock radios employ music or voice to awaken us. New technology offers voice warning systems on aircraft to identify both a problem and the nature of the problem.

The choice of alarms depends upon the nature of the background noise and its masking effects. The signal should be selected in a frequency range to contrast with the background noise. Fog horns on ships are good for penetrating noise except when the background noise is also low frequency. High-frequency sounds are absorbed and do not carry a long distance, but horns, whistles, and sirens, although high intensity, may not be very high frequency. For a sound to carry over 1000 ft, a frequency below 1000 Hz is recommended. For a sound to pass through partitions or bend around barriers, frequencies below 500 Hz are recommended.

Modulating a sound also improves its ability to get attention. Modern sirens have increased the rise and fall of the pitch to a rate of 1 to 3 hertz. A method of acknowledging the alarm is also a way of assuring attention in some applications, such as an alarm clock.

Range Signals and Spatial Orientation

Auditory signals have been used to display "yes/no" information such as deviation from a course, speed, attitude, or other normal conditions. The signal should be confined to only one dimension such as course. A tone presented continuously and automatically usually can be heard over speech. For guidance, the operator compares the tone with a normal or standard tone and effectively, nulls error. A change in intensity rather than frequency is recommended for this application.

A multidimensional system that was quickly learned by pilots employed

Table 4-12 Types of Auditory Alarms and Their Characteristics

Alarm	Intensity	Frequency	Attention-getting ability	Noise penetration ability	Special features
Foghorn	Very high	Very low	Good	Poor in low-frequency noise	
Horn	High	Low to high	Good	Good	Can be designed to beam sound directionally and rotate
Whistle	High	Low to high	Good if intermittent	Good if proper frequency is used	Can be made directional by reflectors
Siren	High	Low to high	Very good if pitch modulates	Very good with rising and falling frequency	Can be coupled to horn for directional transmission
Bell	Medium	Medium to high	Good	Good in low-frequency noise	Manual shutoff insures alarm until action taken
Buzzer, chimes, or gong	Low to medium	Low to medium	Good to fair	Fair if spectrum is suited to background noise	Same as bell
Music	Low to medium	Low to medium	Fair	Same	Application principally to awakening the listener
Voice	Low to medium	Low to medium	Fair	Same	Provides message as well as alarm capability

Source: Deatherage, chap. 4 in Van Cott and Kinkade [48] with modifications.

binaural intensity differences to localize the sounds direction, pitch differences to indicate climbing or descending, and a slow interruption rate (putt-putt sound) to indicate changes in speed.

Sound Characteristics

The major characteristics of sound are amplitude (intensity), frequency, periodicity (waveform), and phase differences. Amplitude or sound pressure level is measured in watts or dynes per square centimeter. Amplitude pressure levels correspond to sensations of loudness. Measures are in decibels (dB), a logarithmic scale referenced to 0.0002 microbar (the human's absolute threshold for a 1000-Hz tone). Frequency is measured in hertz and corresponds to a sensation of pitch. Frequency may be in pure tones (simple sinusoidal waveforms) or complex tones made up of a set of sinusoids (timbre quality). Complex sounds may be periodic or may be aperiodic, for example, clicks, hisses, booms, and roars. Phase difference refers to the arrival time of a sound to the respective ears.

Sound Localization

The techniques of stereophonic sound production involve two or more separate sound tracts synchronized so that the sound may appear to come from one direction or the other, or it may appear localized in the center of the head when it comes from the left and right simultaneously. People are able to tell the direction of a sound from two binaural techniques: (1) differences in interaural phase. The sound arrives at the near ear a fraction of a second earlier than at the farther ear; (2) amplitude differences. The sound in the nearer ear appears to be slightly louder than in the farther ear.

A *dichotic* sound stimulation refers to presenting different signals to the two ears by employing the techniques of amplitude differences and interaural phase differences. *Diotic* sound stimulation refers to presenting exactly the same sound in each ear, the sound then being localized in the center of the head. (See Chapter 12 for applications to speech localization.)

In theory, at least, the detection of signals in a noise field could be enhanced if the signal and noise could be separated with the signal appearing in one apparent azimuthal location and the noise in another or in the center of the head. Unfortunately, it is difficult to independently manipulate signal and noise since the noise is not under direct control.

Inverting the connection on one earphone to put that signal 180° out of phase with the signal in the other ear has been found to enhance the signal gain while leaving the ambient noise essentially unchanged. Reversing the signal phase at one ear applies mainly to low-frequency, high-intensity noises such as those from a propeller aircraft.

Masking Effects

The absolute auditory threshold is defined as the minimum sound level of a signal or tone necessary for detection 50 percent of the time when no noise is present. A profile of thresholds at selected frequencies yields an audiogram such as illustrated in Figure 4-11. The ear is most sensitive (detects the lowest-intensity sounds) in the 2000 to 5000 Hz range. Age, training, where the measures are taken, and the quietness of the room affect the exact values of this threshold.

The *masked* threshold refers to the minimum sound pressure level of a signal necessary for 50 percent detection when the signal is masked in a noise field. *Masking* refers to the difference between the absolute and masked threshold at any given frequency. Sometimes it is called a "threshold shift" since the threshold is raised in the presence of a noise field. The masking effect is the extent of the threshold shift. Oftentimes the degree of masking is stated in terms

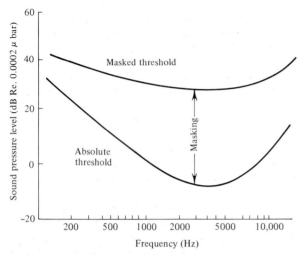

Figure 4-11   Illustration of absolute threshold, masked threshold, and masking.

of a *signal-to-noise ratio* (S/N ratio). This is simply the algebraic difference in the signal intensity and noise intensity at threshold.

Communications engineers are concerned with conditions and techniques that will permit hearing signals at lower S/N ratios. A negative value means the noise level exceeds the signal level. It is possible to hear signals as low as −25 dB but we would not want to assign an operator to a communication system which required doing this.

Figure 4-12 illustrates three principles of masking. Note that the masking effect of a 60-dB tone on the signal (blip) is greater than that of the 40-dB tone.

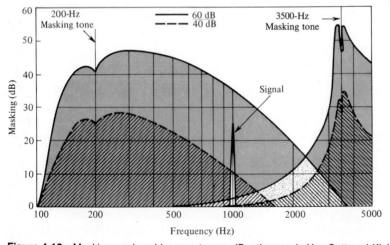

Figure 4-12   Masking produced by pure tones. *(Deatherage in Van Cott and Kinkade, 1972.)*

Hence, the intensity of the masking tone influences the degree of masking. Also, note that the low-frequency tone (200 Hz) masks the 1000 Hz signal much more than the high-frequency tone (3500 Hz). Masking does not tend to spread downward. Other things equal, the closer the masking tone to the signal the greater the masking.

More often signals are masked by wideband noise than by pure tones. The various effects of masking are out of scope here. However, it may be noted that with each increase in wideband noise, the tone must be increased an equal number of decibels to be detected. This linear increase in masking applies to frequencies above about 20 Hz.

Signal Detection, Discrimination, and Identification

Signal detection may be enhanced by reducing the noise level or by selecting signals that are audible in the noise field. Obviously, reducing the noise level without reducing the signal level would be one technique for enhancing signal detection. The use of low-pass filters in the frequency range immediately above the signal will permit increasing the intensity of the signal without also increasing the overall noise level.

Setting the frequency and intensity ranges for signals depends very much upon the nature of the task. If the task involves detection of changes in intensity the signal level should be at least 60 dB above the absolute threshold. To detect changes in frequency, the signal should be at least 30 dB above threshold. Forty to 50 dB above the threshold is the most comfortable range. However, a rule-of-thumb for the optimum signal intensity at the entrance to the ear is that it should be midway between the masked threshold and 110 dB.

Dynamic range is the intensity range between absolute or masked threshold and the threshold of discomfort due to intense volume. Signals must always be kept within the dynamic range of the system. Radio broadcast announcers control their voices by monitoring a volume meter. The signal can be controlled by the listener or by a compressor or an automatic volume control (AVC) circuit. Peak-clipping is an electronic technique for passing the center of sounds while discarding the peaks or extreme amplitudes and, thereby, restricting the intensity range. In voice communications excess power in the vowels, rather than the consonants, are primarily affected by peak-clipping so that understanding speech is not affected very much. See Chapter 12 for electronic techniques for improving speech intelligibility.

Signal Characteristics for Discrimination

Discrimination involves hearing just noticeable differences between signals. Shower and Biddulph [40] found that it was slightly easier to discriminate the frequencies of pure tones when they were below 1000 Hz. Deatherage [Van Cott and Kinkade, 48] recommended a 500- to 1000-Hz range for frequency discrimination. The duration of a signal should be at least 200 to 300 ms [Munson, 28]. If it must be of shorter duration, signal intensity should be increased.

Riesz [35] and Miller [25] found that for best discrimination of pure tone of various frequencies, the intensity of the tones should be at least 60 dB above absolute threshold. For best detection of small changes in intensity, signal frequencies should be from 1000 to 4000 Hz.

Absolute Identification in Auditory Coding

Sometimes an operator must identify a stimulus (for example, a channel frequency) on an absolute basis. Deatherage [48] recommended that a maximum of four intensities and a maximum of five frequencies be used in auditory coding. With a combination of intensity and frequency, eight steps or channels could be identified correctly.

In real-life situations we employ many different facets or dimensions to identify the voice of an individual or particular sounds. With respect to such multidimensional coding, Pollack and Ficks [33] found that it is better to use more dimensions with fewer steps per dimension rather than a few dimensions and more steps each. For example, one could use eight dimensions (direction, tone frequency and level, noise frequency and level, repetition rate, on-off fraction, and duration) and select two or three widely discriminable steps within each of these dimensions.

Principles of Auditory Display Selection

McCormick [24] has abstracted a set of auditory display principles that summarize and extend the design recommendation above. *Compatibility* refers here to encoding signals so as to exploit population stereotypes such as increasing pitch suggests higher altitude, a wailing sound suggests emergencies, and so forth. Newly installed signals should not conflict in meaning with previously learned signals. *Approximation* refers to first using a signal to attract attention, then employing another signal for more precise information. *Dissociability* refers to the use of signals that are highly discernable from ongoing audio input. Do not use bells when other bells are ringing often. *Parsimony* again admonishes one to limit input signals to those necessary. *Invariance* refers to standardization of signal meaning.

In selecting auditory alarms or signals, one should avoid extremes of auditory dimensions. The designer should base signal intensity on background noise levels, should use interrupted or variable signals rather than steady-state ones for important ones, should test initially for detectability, and should train users to the meaning of new signals prior to removing previous (visual) displays.

When several signals come in on two or more channels at approximately the same time, it is best to have separate operators for each channel. Nonurgent messages should be taped, stored, and played back on demand when time permits. This assures greater accuracy than direct listening.

TACTUAL AND OTHER DISPLAYS

Tactual verification of stimuli are probably employed much more than we recognize; however, formalized tactual coding systems have limited application to aerospace systems. Extensive research has been done on shape-coding, texture-coding, and size-coding of control knobs. However, the use of gloves while piloting greatly reduces tactual sensitivity. Braille print for the blind and other tactual design aids are discussed in Chapter 13. Rumble strips are used on highways and some parking lots to alert drivers to the need for reduced speed. Pressures on the body (particularly the buttocks) during high acceleration provide qualitative feedback.

The sense of touch along with pain and temperature are termed "somesthetic" senses. Heat and pain are a natural coding method for avoidance of certain hazards, but they have not been employed much in the design of systems. Similarly, the sense of olfaction (smell) has a limited application in detection of hazardous chemicals, smoke, and so forth.

The kinesthetic and vestibular senses are obviously involved in motion sensing in aerospace systems. In Chapter 9 we shall study vibration, acceleration, and weightlessness and their effects on these senses. The design implication is one of avoidance of excessive rotation and oscillation.

The application of forces on controls and tools involves kinesthetic feedback through mediating devices. Sometimes controls must be located and positioned without the aid of visual cues. Lever detents, snap action switches, and resistances are subtle cues to system activation. The elimination, by design, of all resistance or control feedback may handicap the pilot or the driver. See Chapter 5 for resistance criteria for controls and a discussion of handling qualities.

QUESTIONS AND PROBLEMS

1 For particular conditions of use, it was determined that character heights on a vehicle panel should be 0.25 in. At a distance of 50 feet, under the same conditions of use, how high would the characters need to be?

2 Table 4-2 lists recommended heights for various displays for seated and standing operators. What are two variables that would influence the accuracy of these values with respect to complying with visual angle standards shown in Figure 4-2?

3 Which of the types of coding discussed are employed on a standard road map? List at least five types and cite examples.

4 Design standards for characters list a stroke width of 1/6 of the character's height for black characters on a white background and 1/7 to 1/8 for white characters on black. How would you account for the difference?

5 Determine the minimum dimension of a CRT for the following conditions: viewing distance from scope, 12 in; smallest target's dimension, 300 ft; range on ground which is displayed, 10 nautical miles (60,760 ft).

6 A panel label is viewed under unfavorable conditions in an illumination of 3 fc. It is important that the markings be seen, and the viewing distance is 28 in. Using the Peters and Adams formula, determine the minimum character height.

7 Critique the circular dial on the following page using the criteria given in Table 4-7. List at least five violations of design criteria. Do not include size of dial or esthetics of the drawing. Dial is located at eye level.

8   Critique the following labeling using the criteria given in Table 4-9. List at least five violations of design criteria. Do not critique control or indicator design. The functions of the equipment are immaterial in this context.

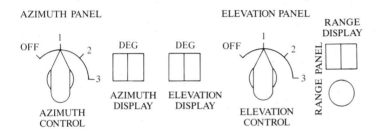

9   Why are shrill, high-frequency alarms not employed more often in the outdoors?
10 How much more intense than the absolute threshold do a series of tones need to be for a listener to discriminate between their frequencies?
11 Suppose each frequency had a unique meaning for coding purposes. What is the maximum number of different frequencies that should be used?

REFERENCES

1   AFSC DH 1–3, sec. 2C, Design of Displays, *Human Factors Engineering,* 3d ed., January 1, 1977.
2   Alluisi, E. A., Linear inclination in encoding information symbolically on cathode ray tubes and similar displays, USAF, Aeronautical Systems Division, ASD TR-61-741, Wright Air Development Center, WPAFB, Ohio, 1961.
3   Benton, S. A., Holographic Displays—A Review, *Proceedings of the Third Advanced Aircrew Display Symposium,* May 1976.
4   Beringer, D. B., S. N. Roscoe, and R. C. Williges, The transition of pilots to a frequency-separated aircraft attitude display, *Human Factors,* vol. 17, no. 4, 1975.
5   Burke, J. E., R. D. Huchingson, The effects of cockpit lighting variables on target detection thresholds, LTV Aeronautics Report No. 2-56620/2R-3027, 1971.
6   Burke, J. E., R. D. Huchingson, R. J. Koppa, and H. E. Sewell, Jr., *First and Second Simulator Evaluations of Advanced Integrated Display and Control Systems,* National Aeronautics and Space Administration Report NASA CR-762, June 1967.
7   Chambers, E. L., M. Goldstein, and W. E. Kappauf, The effects of illumination on dial reading, USAF Aeromedical Medical Laboratory Report No. AF-TR-6021, 1950, WPAFB, Ohio.

8 Chapanis, A. and R. Halsey, Absolute judgment of spectral colors, *Journal of Psychology,* vol. 42, 1956, p. 99.

9 Cohen, J. and A. J. Dinnerstein, Flash rate as a visual coding dimension for information, USAF, WADC TR 57-64, Wright Air Development Center, WPAFB, Ohio, 1958.

10 Conover, D. W., The amount of information in the absolute judgment of Munsell hues. WADC-TN58-262, Wright Air Development Center, WPAFB, Ohio, 1959.

11 Davis, G. and E. Shaw, Human engineering design criteria for controls and displays, Vought Aeronautics Division, LTV Aerospace Corporation Specification No. 209-16-108, February 1971, p. 27.

12 Department of Defense, MIL-STD-1472B, *Military Standard, Human Engineering Design Criteria for Military Systems, Equipment, and Facilities,* Dec. 31, 1974. Notice-1, May 10, 1976.

13 Department of Defense, MIL-C-25050A, General requirements for colors, aeronautical lights, and lighting equipment, 1963.

14 Dougherty, D. J., J. H. Emory, D. C. Curtin, Comparison of perceptual work load in flying standard instrumentation and the contact analog vertical display. Bell Helicopter Co., Fort Worth, TR D 228-421-019, 1964, Contract NONR 1670 (00).

15 Elkin, E. H., Effect of scale shape, exposure time, and display complexity on scale reading efficiency, USAF, WADC TR 58-472, February 1959.

16 Ellis, N. C. and S. E. Hill, A comparative study of seven segment numerics, *Human Factors,* vol. 20, no. 6, 1978, pp. 655–660.

17 Fogel, L. J., A new concept: The Kinalog Display System, *Human Factors,* vol. 1, no. 2, 1959, pp. 30–37.

18 Gibney, T. K., Legibility of segmented versus standard numerals: A review. Aeromedical Research Laboratories Report No. AMRL-TR-67-116, WPAFB, Ohio, June 1967.

19 Green, B. F., W. J. McGill, H. M. Jenkins, The time required to search for numbers on large visual displays, Massachusetts Institute of Technology Lincoln Laboratory, TR No. 36, 1953.

20 Hanes, R. M. and M. V. Rhoades, Color identification as a function of extended practice, *Journal of the Optical Society of America,* vol. 49, 1960.

21 Huchingson, R. D., C. L. Dudek, R. J. Koppa, R. Q. Brackett, and R. D. Williams, A review of literature, design of dynamic displays, *Human factors design of dynamic visual and auditory displays for metropolitan traffic management,* DOT-FH-11-9459, Volume 1 (Interim Report), Texas Transportation Institute, College Station, Texas, 1979.

22 Konz, S. A. and B. A. Koe, The effect of color coding on performance of an alphabetic filing task, *Human Factors,* vol. 11, no. 3, 1969, pp. 207–212.

23 Maddox, M. E., J. T. Burnette, and J. C. Gutmann, Font comparison for 5 × 7 dot matrix characters, *Human Factors,* vol. 9, no. 1, 1977.

24 McCormick, E. J., *Human Factors in Engineering and Design,* 4th ed., McGraw-Hill New York, 1976, p. 128.

25 Miller, G. A., Sensitivity to changes in intensity of white noise and its relation to masking and loudness, *Journal of the Acoustical Society of America,* vol. 19, 1947a, p. 609.

26 Monroney, W. F. and J. F. Barnette, Human factors considerations in the design and evaluation of a helmet mounted display using a light emitting diode matrix, *Proceeding of the Human Factors Society,* 22nd Annual Meeting, 1978.

27 Muller, P. F., R. C. Sidorsky, A. J. Slivinske, E. A. Alluisi, and P. M. Fitts, The symbolic coding of information on cathode-ray tubes and similar displays, USAF, WADC-TR-55-375, Wright Air Development Center, WPAFB, Ohio, 1955.

28 Munson, W. A.: The growth of auditory sensation, *Journal of the Acoustical Society of America,* vol. 13, 1947, p. 584.

29 Nolan, J. F.: Survey of electronic displays, paper #750364 presented to the Society of Automotive Engineers, February 1975., and in *Automotive Electronics II,* SAE Publication No. SP-393.

30 Oberly, H. S., The range of attention, cognition, and apprehension, *American Journal of Psychology,* vol. 35, 1924, p. 332.

31 Peters, G. A. and B. B. Adams, Three criteria for readable panel markings, *Product Engineering,* vol. 30, no. 21, May 25, 1959, pp. 55–57.

32 Plath, D. W., The readability of segmented and conventional numerals, *Human Factors,* vol. 12, no. 5, 1970, pp. 493–497.

33 Pollack, I. and L. Ficks, Information of elementary multi-dimensional auditory displays. *Journal of the Acoustical Society of America,* vol. 25, 1952, pp. 765–769.

34 Progress Report Symposium, Army-Navy Integrated Instrument Program, sponsored by U.S. Army Signal Corps, Office of Naval Research, and Bureau of Aeronautics, Dallas, Texas, Aug. 31–Sep. 1, 1959.

35 Riesz, R. R., Differential intensity sensitivity of the ear for pure tones, *Physiological Review,* vol. 31, 1928, p. 867.

36 Department of Defense, MIL-HDBK-759, Military Standardization Handbook, Human Factors Engineering Design for Army Materiel, March 12, 1975.

37 Roscoe, S. N., Airborne displays for flight and navigation, *Human Factors,* vol. 10, no. 4, 1968, pp. 321–332.

38 Schutz, H. G., An evaluation of format for graphic trend displays-Experiment II, *Human Factors,* vol. 3, 1961, pp. 99–107.

39 Shontz, W. D., G. A. Trumm, and L. G. Williams: Color coding for information location, *Human Factors,* vol. 11, no. 3, 1971, pp. 237–246.

40 Shower, E. G. and R. Biddulph, Differential pitch sensitivity of the ear, *Journal of the Acoustical Society of America,* vol. 3, 1931, p. 275.

41 Shurtleff, D. A., Studies in display symbol legibility: XXI. The relative legibility of symbols formed from matrices of dots, USAF Electronics Systems Division, ESD-TA-69-432, MTR-798, February 1970.

42 Sleight, R. S., The relative discriminability of several geometric forms. *Journal of Experimental Psychology,* vol. 43, 1952, pp. 424.

43 Snyder, H. L.: Image quality and face recognition on a television display, *Human Factors,* vol. 16, no. 3, 1974, pp. 300–307.

44 Snyder, H. L., R. L. Keese, W. S. Beamon, and J. R. Aschenbach: *Visual search and image quality,* USAF Technical Report AMRL-TR-73-114, 1974.

45 Smith, S. L. and D. W. Thomas, Color versus shape coding in information displays, *Journal of Applied Psychology,* vol. 48, 1964, p. 137.

46 Steedman, W. C. and C. A. Baker, Target size and visual recognition, *Human Factors,* vol. 2, no. 3, 1960, pp. 120–127.

47 Svimonoff, C., The Air Force Integrated Flight Instrument Program USAF Flight Control Laboratory, WADC TR 58-431, Wright Air Development Center, WPAFB, Ohio, 1958.

48 Van Cott, H. P. and R. C. Kinkade (eds.), *Human Engineering Guide to Equipment Design,* U.S. Government Printing Office, Washington, D.C., 1972, chap. 4.

49 Vartabedian, A. G. Developing a graphic set for developing cathode-ray tube displays using a 7 × 9 dot matrix. *Applied Ergonomics,* vol. 4, no. 1, 1973, pp. 11–76.

50 Watler, J. F., Jr., and G. W. Hoover: The maneuvering flight path display, Proceedings of the Third Advanced Aircrew Display Symposium, May 1976.

51 Williams, A. C., Jr., M. Adelson, and M. L. Ritchie: A program of human engineering research on the design of aircraft instrument control and displays, USAF, WADC-TR-56-526, December 1956.

52 Woodson, W. E. and D. W. Conover: *Human engineering guide for equipment designers,* 2d ed., University of California Press, Berkeley, 1970.

53 Grether, W. F. and C. A. Baker, Visual Presentation of Information, in H. P. Van Cott and R. C. Kinkade (eds.), *Human Engineering Guide to Equipment Design,* U.S. Government Printing Office, Washington, D.C., 1972, chap. 4.

Chapter 5

Design of Aerospace Controls and Control Systems

CONTROLS

If one would itemize the number of objects he or she manipulates each day (objects that control processes), one might be surprised at the number and variety of controls. There are alarm clocks, lavatory and bath controls, kitchen appliances, automobile controls, keys, light switches, radio, television, and telephone controls, to mention only a few. In this chapter only a limited number of these controls will be presented, principally the ones in common use on aerospace and electronic products and military/NASA systems. In subsequent chapters other controls unique to other applications will be introduced. As with displays, the principles and criteria presented are generally applicable. From our experiences in manipulating controls, we have developed certain population stereotypes that carry over to our expectations of how electronic and mechanical equipment should move and be arranged. These stereotypes apply to new as well as familiar controls.

As with display systems, the human factors specialist may have the task of selecting a control appropriate for the required output function and optimizing the detail design of the control, its position, and arrangement with respect to displays, the operator, and the workplace.

Guidelines for Control Selection

The following six questions must be answered prior to control selection. First, what type of change needs to be accomplished? Does it concern discrete states or values as inputs to the system or is there a continuous range of values? Second, if the input is discrete how many states will there be? If continuous, what is the range of values and what is the precision, force, and speed of movement required by the control task? A control requirements analysis (discussed in Chapter 2) will aid in identifying this type of planning information.

Third, is there a danger of confusing one control with others and activating the incorrect control? How can controls be coded, labeled, or positioned to distinguish them and reduce the likelihood of this type of error? Fourth, what feedback is there that the system has accepted the control input?

The fifth question is: How can the designer reduce the probability of control error that originates from unintentionally bumping and activating a control? An ideal solution might be to provide sufficient space between controls so that the possibility of error is unlikely. However, panel or console space is usually a constraint to the designer. Sometimes the availability of space on a compact panel may dictate not only the size but also the choice of controls. Some controls require little panel space while others require sufficient space to grasp and rotate a control. Some may combine functions; others control only a single function. In this chapter techniques for reducing bumping errors will be described.

Control movement must be considered in relation to display movement, the equipment component controlled, and the vehicle function affected. Therefore, the sixth question is: what are the population stereotypes relative to control movements that are "natural" and compatible with the movement of these other components of the system? There are also design criteria in regard to spatial relationships and rates of movement between the control and its associated display.

It is also important that workload be distributed among the limbs to prevent overburdening at critical times and to insure that the assignments of control functions are compatible with speed, precision, and force requirements of the control task. Controls should be located and arranged within the workspace in a functional manner based upon conditions of use, a system of priorities, and physical limitations of the operator. Each of these topics will be discussed in this chapter.

Types of Controls

Before discussing further the factors influencing control selection, it is necessary to consider the variety of controls available. According to MIL-STD-1472B [25] controls are classified by (1) discrete selection or continuous adjustment, and (2)

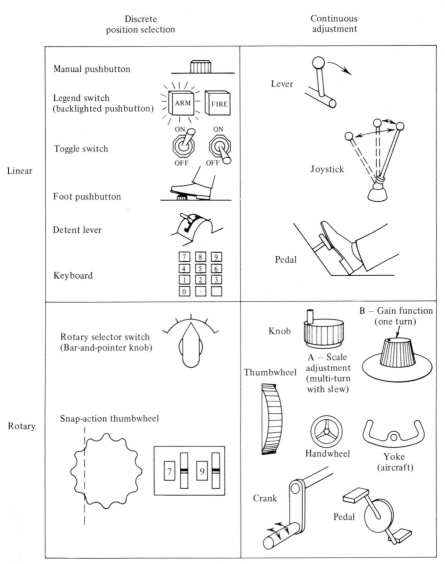

Figure 5-1 Classification and illustration of controls.

rotary or linear movement. Figure 5-1 illustrates some common controls classified into combinations of these four categories.

Tables 5-1 and 5-2 provide general guidelines for control selection. Discrete controls are typically classified in terms of the number of control positions or settings that they may display. There are controls suitable for selecting only two settings, those suitable for only three settings, and those that may be used for substantially more discrete states.

Continuous controls are often classified by their range of adjustment, by the

Table 5-1 Guide to Discrete Control Selection

Control requirement	Select	Examples
• Select two discrete settings or states: stop-start on-off insert momentary signal	Manual push button	Keyboards Elevator button Doorbell, horn (auto) Cruise control (auto)
	Toggle switch*	Wall lights
	Rocker switch	Hard-copy word processor
	Foot-actuated PB	Headlight dimmer (older auto)
	Slide switch	Flashlight Calculator–ON/OFF
	Cords and variations	House lamps
	Key operated switch	Ignition (auto)
	Knob (volume/on combo)	Radio
	Push/pull switch	Headlights–ON/OFF (auto) TV–ON/OFF
• Two settings-larger force	Detent lever	Landing gear (aircraft)
	T-handle or stirrup	Hand brake (auto)
• Select three settings	Three-position toggle	Emergency fuel selector switch (aircraft)
	Rotary selector	Channel selector
• Select three or more settings	Legend switches or backlighted PB	Car radio Keyboards (TV channels; dialing)
	Rotary selectors	Black boxes (alternate modes of operation)
	Detent lever	Throttle (aircraft) Gear shift (auto)
	Circular dial (poor)	Conventional telephone
• Setting-in numbers	Detent thumbwheel and digital readout	Radio frequency selector (4 digits) on aircraft

*Small levers are used in many applications like toggles, for example, on auto for wiper/washer, temperature control mode selection, seat position, steering wheel position.
  Source: Based on Woodson and Conover [29] with modifications.

speed with which the range may be transitioned, and by the force required of the operator. Handwheels, pedals, large cranks, and levers are applicable to situations calling for large forces whereas push buttons, knobs, toggle switches, rotary switches, small levers, small cranks, and thumbwheels are devices found often in aircraft and on electronic "black boxes," which require only small finger

Table 5-2 Guide to Continuous Control Selection

Control requirement	Select	Examples
• Precise adjustment small range, little force	Knob	Volume controls
	Continuous lever	Joy stick (aircraft)
	Continuous thumbwheel	Attitude trim (aircraft)
• Rapid adjustment large range, small force	Spinner on multirotational knob	Movie camera windup
	Small crank	Paper dispenser Manual windows (auto)
Slewing electronic displays	Toggle or bat-handle	Slew command marker (USAF aircraft)
	Electric keyboard	Electric typewriter
	Guarded momentary PB	Minute clock on electric scoreboard
• Gross adjustment large force, small range	Handwheels	Steering wheel (auto) Artillery Valves
	Translatory pedal	Brake (auto) Accelerator (auto)
	Reciprocating pedal	Rudder (aircraft yaw)
	Rotary pedal	Bicycle
	Continuous lever	Lawnmower throttle
large force, large range	Large crank	Artillery
• Multiple continuous positioning	Joy stick	Attitude (aircraft)
	Wheel/yoke and joy stick combo	Attitude (aircraft)
	Pantograph	Remote manipulators

Source: Based on Woodson and Conover [29] with modifications.

or hand forces. Cranks, handwheels, and multirotation knobs are among controls suited for a large range of continuous settings.

Discrete Selector Controls A common type of push button is the legend switch with the function labeled on the surface. Another advancement is the backlighted push button that illuminates when pressed and turns off when pressed again. The manual push button (in any of its varieties) and the toggle switch are controls commonly used for selecting between two settings such as "ON" or "OFF." The toggle may also be used for three positions, with the center position "OFF," provided there are at least 18° between the positions. A push button (PB) or toggle permits a very quick control setting and requires less control space than many rotary controls and levers. Arrays of *backlighted* PBs and toggles are also effective for quickly identifying control states or positions, that is, one may check-read a row of toggles or lighted PBs and tell which is "ON" and which is "OFF." Several toggles or several PBs may also be actuated simultaneously.

Foot-actuated PBs are sometimes used for noncritical operations when the hands are occupied. However, they require more space between them, are easily actuated accidentally, and have poor visual access. Recent model automobiles have moved the headlight beam control from the floor to the steering column. No more than two foot controls per foot is recommended.

There are numerous variations of the push button. The *latching* type involves push-on/lock-in and is accompanied by a clicking sound or integral light activation. This type is common for channel selection. They may be interlocking (when one PB is pressed the other snaps back up) or they may permit simultaneous activation.

The *alternate action* PB operates on the principle of push-on/push-off, for example, the headlight beam control. The *momentary contact* PB is illustrated by doorbells, buzzers, or lamp testing PBs. The PB returns to null position upon release of pressure. There are also large *heavy-duty* PBs for hand, thumb, or heel use.

The click sound is desirable when there is no other positive feedback of activation. However, for room light switches the click is unnecessary and possibly annoying. Hence, silent-contact wall switches are becoming common. *Touch-sensitive* PBs, which are not recessed on activation, are coming into use. Examples are the keyboards on microwave ovens, cash registers at quick-service restaurants, and pocket calculators.

As shown in Table 5-1, there are many other two-position switches in everyday usage. When the situation calls for selection among three or more discrete settings, the interlocking PB with backlighted legends is desirable. The *rotary selector switch* has been widely used for military equipment. One switch takes less space than an array of pushbuttons and is generally less expensive. However, we know from touch-tone TV channel selectors that PBs are quicker in selecting channels, less noisy, and do not display intermediate channels (that others in the household might prefer watching!). They are also adaptable to remote control. Keyboards are discussed in Chapter 14.

Detent thumbwheels are mounted perpendicular to the panel surface and are recessed for finger or thumb use. They have application to a control/display digital readout. The numbers may be either on the thumbwheel or on a readout adjacent to it (as shown in Figure 5-1). Thumbwheels save panel space but are slower to operate than many other selector controls.

Continuous Adjustment Controls   The *knob* is the most common continuous adjustment control for use on aerospace electronic panels. It requires little force and permits a precise adjustment, such as in frequency tuning. Moving pointer knobs are recommended to moving scale knobs for most applications (the combination lock is a notable exception).

The USAF AFSC DH 1-3 [23] distinguishes between a class A knob and a class B knob. The class A knob is used to make scale adjustments that involve multirevolution turns. For rapid spinning it may be equipped with a lift-up spinner handle; for fine adjustments the handle folds into a recess. The class B knob is used for turns less than one complete rotation, such as a gain function. It has a pointer or dot to distinguish positions. Knobs with a pointer should have a skirt for the fingertips.

Continuous thumbwheels are used for fine adjustments in gain or in vehicle attitude (pitch, roll, and yaw). They must have built-in resistance so they are not subject to accidental activation.

Handwheels are illustrated by the conventional steering wheel, the yoke steering control, the valve wheel, and artillery or naval applications of the handwheel. They require more space and are selected primarily for two-handed operations requiring larger forces.

Cranks are used primarily for multirevolution turns at high rates. Large cranks also permit the application of large forces. They permit a wide range of settings and may be used with knobs or handwheels for rapid slewing.

Levers may be used either for continuous adjustment or for discrete selection. The automobile gear shift and the aircraft throttle have a discrete selection capability. Long-handled levers may be used when larger forces must be overcome. However, smaller levers are used in many applications, such as temperature selection on some automobiles and as a slewing control for electronic equipment. As a slew control, the lever is held while a parameter rapidly changes on a display, for example, slewing numbers on a counter or electronic scoreboard. When several levers are arrayed together and each controls a different function, coding techniques must be used.

The aircraft joy stick is a lever for multiposition, continuous positioning. In theory, such a control could be free-moving with the only feedback coming from distance moved. This is termed a position or *isotonic* control. A control could also remain stationary with pressure feedback varying with the force applied. This is termed a pressure or *isometric* control. Conventional joy sticks employ both displacement and pressure feedback.

Pedals may be linear (translatory), reciprocating, or rotary. Rotary pedals, such as those used on a bicycle, have limited aerospace application. Translatory pedals are used for large displacement or force, for example, the foot brake and accelerator on a ground vehicle. Reciprocating pedals are illustrated by the bobsled and by the yaw control on aircraft.

Push-pull controls, such as those used for automobile handbrakes, also permit the application of great forces. They may be employed for continuous adjustment or to select one of two positions. Studies of maximum force capability have found that for greatest force, push-pull controls should be located above the waist near the chest. Handle rotation produces the next highest force, followed in order by up-down and right-left movements.

In the Appendix, additional detailed design criteria are presented for various discrete and continuous controls. The reader should study these criteria critically. Other specific design criteria exist for military systems. In general, these criteria indicate the maximum and minimum values for control size, displacement, resistance, and separation. Table 5-4, shown later in this chapter, gives the separation between various controls recommended for military systems.

Location and Arrangement of Controls

Guidelines for placement of controls within a workspace are in some respects similar to placement of displays, for example, functional considerations such as importance and frequency of use may dictate location priorities. In other respects controls differ from displays. They may or may not be used by visual reference; they must be within functional reach; they must have adequate clearances to minimize accidentally bumping other controls during activation.

Control placement is also dictated by limb assignment and by positioning to achieve maximum efficiency. In general, rapid, precise settings are assigned to the right hand and large, continuous forces to the feet. Foot controls are sometimes assigned to prevent manual overloading as well.

Spatial Relationship to Functions Controlled   The location and direction of movement of controls must bear a natural relationship to functions affected by control movement. The issue of movement compatibility is discussed in the next section. However, it may be noted here that a requirement for logical spatial relationships will dictate the orientation of the operator who is controlling the direction of vehicle movement. The operator controlling direction of movement should face in that direction whether or not outside vision is possible. Consider a set of controls for four aircraft engines. The controls must be arranged consistent with the spatial arrangement of the engines, that is, the extreme left control affects the extreme left engine, and so forth. While this logical spatial relationship may enhance association of control and engine for an operator facing in a forward direction, an operator facing the back of the vehicle might be somewhat confused as to which control affects which engine.

In addition, whenever a control affecting forward movement is different from a control affecting backward movement, the forward control should be located above or in front of the control affecting backward movement—again, a logical, spatial relationship.

Priorities in Placement   The placement of controls within the operators' workspace should be based on a priority system. Primary controls, which are used frequently, precisely, or in emergency conditions, should be assigned the most accessible locations. Figure 5-2 identifies with respect to the seat reference

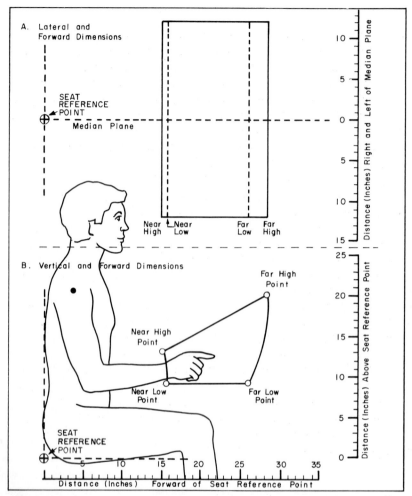

Figure 5-2 Plot of optimum manual space for seated operator. *(AFSC DH 1–3, 1977, with operator added.)*

point the dimensions of the optimal manual space. In general, this area falls between shoulder and elbow height for most operators. The near points are restricted to a smaller area because it is difficult to work at shoulder height and apply forces at close range.

Secondary controls (temperature, lighting, communications management, and so forth) may be assigned to less accessible or lower priority locations. These may be above, but not directly overhead, or they may be to the right or left as long as they are within 95° of a median plane through the vertical axis of the operator. Figure 5-3 indicates recommended regions for primary and secondary controls.

Duplicate primary controls are recommended for operators seated side-by-

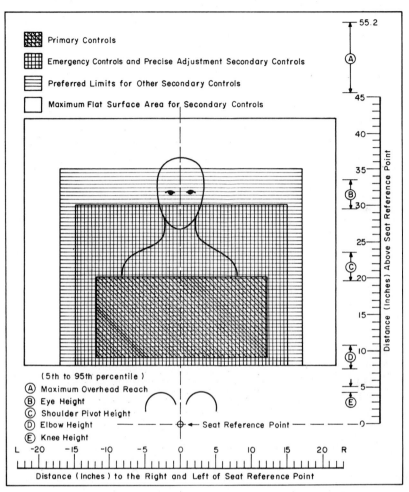

Figure 5-3 Preferred surface areas and limits for manual control. *(AFSC DH 1–3, 1977, with operator added.)*

side, such as the pilot and copilot. However, when primary or secondary controls must be shared they should be located between the operators and should be highly accessible to both operators.

Chapanis [Van Cott and Kinkade, 4] recommended the following priorities in the assignment of controls and displays to the workspace. First priority should go to primary visual tasks and second priority to controls used with the primary displays. Third priority should be that controls are located near the displays they affect.

In Chapter 4 other criteria for placement and arrangement were mentioned that are also applicable to controls. Chapanis [4] lists the fourth, fifth, and sixth priorities, respectively, as sequence of use, frequence of use, and consistency of layout within the same or similar systems. Fowler et al. [9] compared mean task time to carry out tasks on panels laid out by different arrangement criteria and found a different order for maximum efficiency than the order by Chapanis. In order of increasing task time, Fowler found sequence of use, functional groupings, importance, and frequency of use. It would be convenient to assign a priority to an arrangement criteria when they are in conflict. However, in practice the weight assigned will depend upon the particular operational requirements of the task in question. In Chapter 6 techniques for optimizing the arrangement of equipment are given. In the present context frequency of use and importance are inherent in the concept of primary controls.

Functional Groupings   Controls serving a common function, such as the throttles on a multiengine aircraft, should be located adjacent to one another. Controls that are all associated with a particular subsystem such as lighting, communications, or temperature control should be grouped into separate functional entities.

The same relative location of similar controls should be used on all similar models of equipment. For example, a gain control on each panel might be consistently located in the lower-right corner, the on-off control always in the upper-left corner, and so on. This reduces search time and memory load and should aid in reducing error. This issue is discussed under "Location Coding" and applies to all components.

A functional group on a panel must be clearly identifiable. It was noted in Chapter 4 that panels should be delineated by dog ears or a border. Other techniques for accentuating panels are the use of contrasting colors or shading of the panel, extra spacing between panels, recessing or protruding the entire panel from the surrounding surface (a form of panel relief that exaggerates the panel's border). Panels may also be accentuated by appearing on a separate slanted surface or on a separate module.

Sequential Arrangement   On a particular panel or console certain controls must always be activated in a fixed sequence. They should be laid out in the manner in which we read, that is, left to right and in a sequence of rows. Ganged concentric knobs (two or more knobs graduated in size mounted on a single shaft) must always be connected electronically so that the large knob (high gain) is the one to be activated first, and the small knob (low gain) is last (AFSC DH 1-3, 23).

Body Limitations   The optimum and marginal locations of controls are also based upon anthropometric data such as body dimensions, body part dimensions (hands, feet), and functional reach envelopes of the limbs. The larger operator (95th percentile) will dictate clearance requirements between controls and the smaller operator (5th percentile) will dictate requirements for reach and operation. Sometimes the compromise solution in workspace layout is to provide an adjustable device that accommodates both extremes.

The human body also constrains the designer in both dimensions and force requirements. People can apply heavier forces and incur less fatigue when controls are located in certain positions and operate in certain planes, as noted in the Appendix with regard to the crank, pedal, and lever (see also Chapters 3 and 6).

Posture also affects spatial locations. Standing operations are sometimes required for increased mobility where precise movements are not critical. Reach envelopes are also affected by the degree to which the operator is reclining in the seat.

Other Workspace Arrangement Considerations   There are quite a number of factors influencing the layout not only of controls but also of other equipment and facilities used by personnel. Techniques for optimizing workspace arrangement for specific systems and facilities are discussed at length in Chapters 6 and 7.

In addition to those factors mentioned above, consideration should be given to anticipated safety hazards to operational and maintenance personnel; to visibility requirements both for instruments and for outside the aircraft; to procedural efficiency, that is, a layout based upon method-study analysis; to fatigue and psychological factors which limit the efficiency and the acceptability of the arrangement; to environmental factors such as glare and noise which limit the location of personnel in workspace, and vehicle acceleration which limits the forces which can be applied to controls at certain locations (see Chapter 9). Protective clothing and footgear also increase clearance requirements.

A Systems Approach   It was noted earlier that selection of equipment is based upon functional requirements derived from systems analysis. The layout and arrangement of controls must also be viewed in a systems context since an effective design involves the proper marriage of controls, displays, workspace, and the operator.

The systems analyst must first define what the operator must see (outside, displays, controls, other operators, and so forth); what must be heard and what must be manipulated (controls, tools, telephones, and so forth). Beginning with an ideal workspace design, the designer must be prepared to make compromises based on a system of priorities that he or she has developed. From a knowledge of what is essential, what is desirable, and what would be preferable in the design and layout of controls (or other equipment), the designer must be prepared to bargain for the optimal design possible within constraints. A scale mockup and drawings with movable components are important tools for designing, testing, and optimizing the location of controls at a workstation.

Control/Display Integration

Most of the systems of interest in aerospace and electronics involve closed-loop systems where controls are used in relationship with certain displays. The two system components must be planned concurrently. The topics in this section include control/display movement relationships and positional relationships.

Control/Display Movement Relationships   As a part of growing up in our society, we have learned certain population stereotypes regarding both display and control movement. As noted in the previous chapter, movements of display elements that are clockwise, forward, up, or to the right are expected to result in increasing the function, whereas the reverse of each of these results in a decrease in the function.

These same function stereotypes apply in most instances to control movements as well. For example, a clockwise movement of a volume knob is expected to increase loudness. In addition, activation by pressing or squeezing certain controls should result in an increasing function.

The control movement must be designed for compatibility with the display movement. If a circular scale pointer moves clockwise to increase values, it is essential that the associated control also move clockwise (if a rotary control) or forward, up, or to the right (if a linear control). Moreover, the planes of movement should also be compatible. For a vertical linear scale, the associated linear control should be directly to the right of it. Increasing scale values should result from control movements up or forward. Similarly, the control for a horizontal linear scale should be directly below it with display values increasing during right-control movements.

AFSC DH 1-3 (23) recommends the use of a rotary control if the display indicator moves through an arc of over 180°. If the indicator moves through less than 180° and if the path of the control and indicator parallel one another, a linear control may be used. Although levers may be used to control pointer movement of displays when they travel through parallel arcs, knobs are usually selected for display pointer settings.

Controls in Violation of Movement Relationships   The preferred control/ display movement relationship is the natural relationship of compatible directions of movement. Control/display relationships in conflict with the preferred relationship are generally unacceptable. However, a third category, acceptable, is reserved for certain relationships that violate in part the preferred relationship. Consider again the moving tape display where the designer is faced with the dilemma of either having the scale values in inverted sequence or having the tape drive move in the opposite direction from control movement. The control for a home thermostat is often a thumbwheel with the temperature scale values increasing from bottom to top. However, the wheel is moved *downward* to increase the desired temperature. This liberty is permissible when the control and display are adjacent and when the display values increase clockwise, right, up, or forward with control movement [23].

By tradition, the aircraft joy stick was designed so that moving it forward caused the aircraft to pitch down or dive and pulling back caused it to pitch up.

Obviously, the altitude display and other flight displays will operate in compatibility with the joy stick movement rather than with the preferred control/display relationship. Continuous thumbwheels used for pitch trim will move like the joy stick also.

Another control that violates the expected relationship by force of tradition is the valve. Water faucets and oil field valves typically turn on by counterclockwise rotation. Push-pull controls also violate the expected control movement stereotype. Chapanis [4] discourages the use of such controls on the front panel because pulling conflicts with the forward-to-increase stereotype. However, the manual choke, hand brake, and pull-to-activate light switch are still in common use in surface vehicle transportation.

Adhering to the population stereotypes generally will reduce reaction time, reduce the frequency of reversal errors, and improve the speed and precision of adjustments. Parenthetically, horizontal control movements are generally faster than vertical ones and fore-and-aft movements are generally faster than lateral ones.

Control/Vehicle Movement Relationships   It has been noted that the direction of control movement should be compatible with certain functional stereotypes for increasing and decreasing parameters and, in addition, should be compatible with movement of the associated display. Two other areas of compatibility are desirable. The changes resulting from control movement should be compatible with movement of the vehicle (increasing speed, turning right, and so forth) and with movement of the equipment component that intervenes in effecting the change (gun turret, landing gear, and so forth). Most of us would expect that moving a landing gear lever downward would result in the aircraft wheels being lowered. For this reason it is essential that this control be oriented in a vertical plane.

A common misconception is that operators always think in terms of the purpose or function of a control rather than the intervening part used to accomplish the function. When the direction of a control dictated by purpose and by part are in conflict, the purpose is recommended to take priority [Chapanis, 4]. For example, a control movement to increase automobile temperature should be up, forward, right, or clockwise regardless of how the air vent opens. This recommendation has numerous exceptions and extreme caution should be taken in following it without testing.

Two examples will illustrate this point. Some jet aircraft have the capability of "sweeping" their wings. The wings pivot back toward the fuselage, reducing wind resistance and permitting the aircraft to increase airspeed. The wing-sweep control is typically a lever mounted on the left wall of the cockpit. Since sweeping the wings has the effect of increasing airspeed, the designer reasoned that a forward movement should sweep the wings. It was found in flight testing that pilots tended to think in terms of movement of the wings (the intervening part) and attempted to pull back to sweep the wings. Retrofit was required.

One model of a station wagon has the control lever for the rear window mounted on the air-conditioning panel. As a compromise for a compact panel, the lever was mounted horizontally. The circuit design provided that a right movement opened the rear window, that is, let in air. However, a pilot study made with the window halfway down found that 90 percent of the subjects moved the control left to move the window downward and right to move it upward. Apparently, they were thinking in terms of the part controlled rather than the ultimate purpose of the control act [Huchingson, 11].

Population stereotypes governing control movements for functions not displayed are complex and should be empirically tested rather than relying on rules of thumb.

Controls affecting the direction of a vehicle's movement will normally move in the corresponding planes, for example, a forward throttle movement would increase the velocity vector in a forward direction. Visualize a single operator controlling three handwheels, each mounted on a vertical plane. The wheel on the left is on the left wall and the one on the right is mounted on the right wall. Each control affects direction of movement of the vehicle. In this instance, the handwheel on the right wall should increase in a *counterclockwise* direction. This apparent stereotype violation is necessitated by a need to rotate both the left and right control forward (perhaps simultaneously) to increase a vehicle function parameter.

Control/Display Ratio   The control/display ratio (C/D ratio) is the ratio of the distance of movement of the control relative to that of the moving element of the display in continuous control tasks. The C/D ratio is the reciprocal of gain or sensitivity (D/C). For linear controls that affect linear displays the C/D ratio is based on the controls' displacement and the displays' displacement. When rotary controls are used with linear displays the C/D ratio is

$$C/D = (\frac{a}{360} \times 2\pi L)/\text{display movement.}$$

where a = the angular movement of the control
  and L = the length of the lever arm

The C/D ratio may be applied also to situations where there is no actual instrument but instead a measure of system response, such as the angle of turn of an automobile.

Figure 5-4 illustrates high and low C/D ratios. Note that a low C/D ratio implies high sensitivity while a high C/D ratio means low sensitivity.

If a marked change in the display element (five units) was brought about by only one unit of movement of the control, then the C/D ratio would be 1/5 or 0.20, a very sensitive system. If a paper dispensing machine allowed only five pieces of paper for 20 turns of the crank, this would be a very high C/D ratio, but low sensitivity.

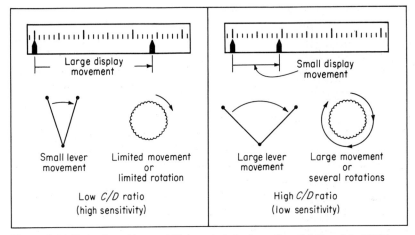

Figure 5-4   Illustration of low and high control-display ratios. *(McCormick, 1976.)*

In positioning a continuous adjustment control there are two types of movement involved: an initial gross adjustment movement in which the operator slews the control to the approximate desired position, followed by a fine adjustment movement in which the operator brings the control element to the exact desired position, as in radio tuning.

Jenkins and Connor [12] studied slewing time and fine adjustment time in knob setting for C/D ratios from 4.55 to 0.03. Their findings are shown in Figure 5-5. Note that slewing time is very long with high C/D ratios but drops almost to an asymptotic level in the midrange of ratios. Conversely, fine adjustment time

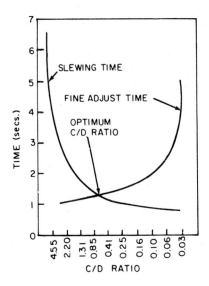

Figure 5-5 Slewing time and fine-adjustment time for knob settings with various control-display ratios *(Jenkins and Connor, 1949.)*

is lengthy with low C/D ratios but reaches an asymptote in the midrange of values. With such a high-sensitivity system, the operator tends to overshoot the desired setting. If one were interested in minimizing the total time (slewing plus fine adjustment), the optimum C/D ratio would be in the midrange (0.2 to 0.8), including the point where the two curves cross (0.5).

These findings apply to knobs of the type investigated. Chapanis [4] recommended empirically determining the optimum C/D ratios for particular conditions. Operators should be timed in a task of moving a display element to a series of specified scale positions under a set of C/D ratios.

C/D ratios are sometimes expressed in unreduced ratio format (X:1). For levers the optimum C/D ratio is in the range of 2.5:1 to 4:1 [4]. For counters controlled by knobs, 50 display counts (five rotations) are recommended for one knob rotation [AFSC, DH 1-3, 23].

The precision of tolerances acceptable, that is, the courseness or fineness, will affect the optimum C/D ratio (more precise adjustments require a less sensitive, higher C/D ratio). Therefore, the tolerance should always be specified. Other factors affecting the C/D ratio are the display size and lag time between control movement and a response of the display. An enlarged display will decrease adjustment time. A system with a long exponential lag will require a smaller optimum C/D ratio than will one with a very brief delay.

Control/Display Arrangements   Earlier it was noted that there is a conflict of movement relationships when an operator is seated facing the side or rear when controlling the vehicle's direction of movement. Although control movements normally operate with respect to the direction one faces, the arrangement of controls and displays should be as though one were facing in the direction the vehicle is traveling, for example, engine controls should be laid out in the same left-to-right arrangement as they would appear to the pilot (Figure 5-6A).

As previously noted, controls should be located near the displays they affect (either below or to one side). The preferred lateral location is on the right so that right-handed operators will not block the view of the display while operating the control (Figure 5-6B).

When there are a large number of controls, each controlling a single display, a consistent and logical relationship should be maintained. The best arrangement is with each control directly beneath its associated display (Figure 5-6C). If there are spatial limitations on the panel or an accessibility problem with respect to reaching the controls, the displays may be grouped into matrices and the controls may be located on a more compact console. Figure 5-6D shows an analogue arrangement where there is no question as to which control is associated with which display.

Figure 5-6E is a compromise solution with the controls in a single row. Dividing the controls into sets of three in correspondence with the rows and numbering controls and displays reduces the chance of confusion. Vertically arrayed controls associated with horizontally arrayed displays (or vice versa) are

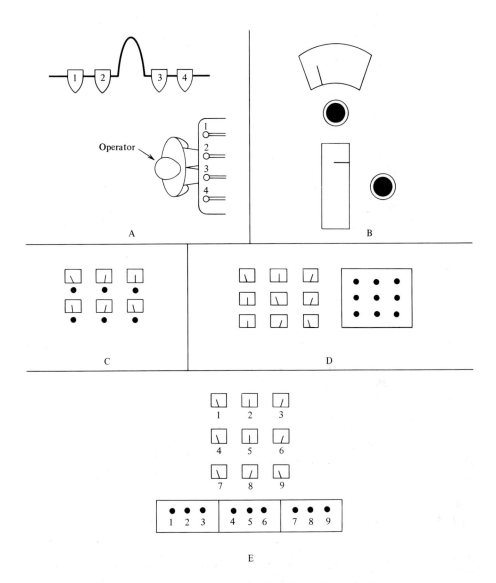

Figure 5-6 Recommended arrangement of controls and associated displays.

permitted, but not recommended.

Chapanis and Lindenbaum [30] studied the arrangements of controls of household ranges with respect to the burners the controls affect. The findings are applicable to any system when the controls are horizontally arrayed and the displays are in a four-cell matrix. In the following summary the circled letters were burners and the bottom letters were controls on the front of the range:

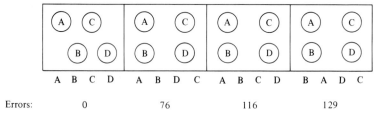

Errors: 0   76   116   129

In 1200 attempts to turn on designated burners, the data indicate that staggering the burners (far left) eliminated all errors in control/display association. Many present-day countertop ranges have the burners arrayed in an arc with the controls similarly arrayed under them, thus eliminating confusion.

In a later study, Chapanis and Mankin [31] studied 10 different configurations of displays, each with the associated controls arrayed vertically on the right (far left figure). Data shown are errors (in 768 attempts) and mean reaction time for the five best configurations.

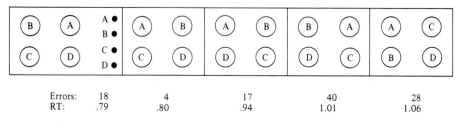

	Errors:	18	4	17	40	28
	RT:	.79	.80	.94	1.01	1.06

The second configuration, with displays arrayed in an apparent Z-shaped pattern, was superior. Again, this is the manner in which we were taught to read. The authors report that all 40 errors in the fourth configuration were reversals of A with B and reversals of C with D, again implying that the Z-shaped pattern was anticipated. In Chapter 14 expected patterns on keyboards are given.

Coding of Controls

The aircraft accident literature includes many examples of pilot error that are due to confusion in the identification of controls. Controls similar in knob design and method of activation are often located near one another, but each controls different functions. Examples from the literature include the landing gears being activated instead of the flaps lever, canopy jettison T handle activated instead of the hydraulic system T handle, propeller A feathered accidentally instead of propeller B, and a rocket pickle-shaped control activated instead of a bomb pickle-shaped control. Control-coding techniques improve the operator's ability to discriminate between control functions visually and/or tactually.

Six common methods for coding controls are labeling, color, shape, size, mode of operation, and location coding. Each method has certain advantages and disadvantages depending upon conditions of use. Several methods may be combined to achieve maximum identification and differentiation of control function.

The choice of coding method depends upon the total demands on the operator at the time of use, the speed and accuracy with which the control must be used, the training the operator has had in its use, the extent to which the code has already been employed for coding other controls, the panel space available, and the number of controls to be coded.

Labeling Techniques for labeling controls and displays on a panel were discussed in Chapter 4. In general, labels should be located horizontally above the control, should be brief, should give the function in terms familiar to the operator, should be readable while the operator is activating them, and should use standardized, highly legible letter and numeral styles.

Advantages of labels are that they require less training than other codes and that a very large number of different labels may be employed. Disadvantages are that there must be adequate visibility or lighting and that they take extra panel space. Labels typically are used in the initial learning of functions.

Color Coding The standardized meanings of surface colors were discussed in Chapter 4. The conventions also apply to coding controls. AFSC DH-1-3 [23] recommends the use of a maximum of eight categories when rapid, unaided, absolute discrimination is required. Table 5-3 identifies the specific colors by numbers from Federal Standard 595 [24], which should be used for codes employing three or four hues, five or six hues, eight or nine hues, and for color-deficient individuals. First consideration should be given to red, orange, yellow, green, and blue. For maintenance tasks where there is ample time to refer to a code chart, more than eight categories may be used for comparative discrimination. Patterns, such as red and black stripes, may also be employed.

Color is excellent for search tasks and permits excellent discrimination, particularly as a supplement to other coding techniques. As noted for displays, the use of surface colors requires adequate white illumination and is discouraged for highly variable illumination. Certain color codes must be learned and the colored control must be visible, of course, for identification.

Shape and Texture Coding Considerable research has gone into the development of controls, particularly knobs, that are readily distinguishable both visually and tactually. Jenkins [13] had blindfolded subjects feel knobs one at a time and tell if other knobs were the same as or different from the first one. From this type of research a set of tactually discriminable shapes for lever handles was developed (Figure 5-7).

A set of class A knobs were developed that may be used in situations where more than one turn is required (Figure 5-8). Class B knobs are recommended for coding single-turn functions where knob position is not critical (Figure 5-8). If five or fewer categories are to be used, A-1 should not be used with A-2, A-3

Table 5-3 Preferred Color Combinations for Control Coding

FED STD 595 Color	Number	A Normal applications requiring 3-4 hues	B Normal applications requiring 5-6 hues	C Normal applications requiring 8-9 hues	D For use by color-deficient personnel	E Order of preference when contrast is critical 1	2	3	4
Red	11105	X	X	X			X		
Orange	12246		X	X					
Yellow	13538	X		X					
Yellow	13655		X		X			X	X
Green	14187	X							
Green	14260		X						
Blue	15102		X	X	X				X
Blue	15123	X							
Magenta (purple)	17142			X					
Gray	16251			X					
Black	17038			X	X	X		X	
White	17875		X	X	X	X	X		
Buff	13594			X					

Source: AFSC DH 1-3, DN 2D4 [23].

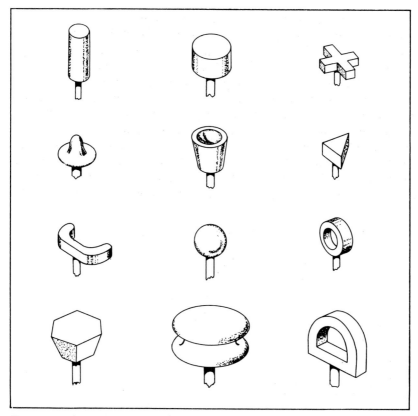

Figure 5-7 Tactually discriminable shapes for lever handles. *(AFSC DH 1–3, 1977.)*

with A-4, nor A-6 with A-7. Within the class B set, do not use B-1 nor B-2 with either B-4 or B-5. No more than 2 or 3 class B knobs should be used on a single panel.

Military electronic equipment currently employs nine distinctive shapes paired with nine distinctive colors and shades to distinguish functions such as intensity, focus, tune, and range [26]. There are also sets of distinctive shapes for rotary selector switches (Figure 5-9). In coding lever knobs for aircraft a set of standard shapes has been developed that bears a relationship to the function controlled, for example, a wheel for a landing gear knob and a wing-shaped knob for the flaps. Figure 5-10 presents these standard shapes.

In general, shape coding is a useful technique for identifying a relatively large number of categories. It has the potential for both visual and tactual coding, thus permitting correct identification without focusing on the control. However, tactual identification is slower than visual coding and the hand must be bare or lightly gloved for feedback.

Texture coding also is heavily dependent upon adequate tactual feedback. Continuous thumbwheels are controls amenable to tactual discrimination by

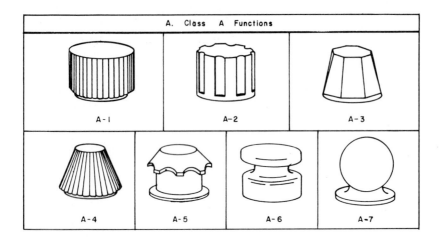

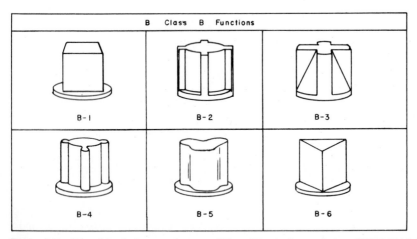

Figure 5-8 Class A knob shapes, above, and Class B knob shapes, below. *(AFSC DH 1–3, 1977.)*

differences in texture of the rims. Bradley [2] found that surfaces which had smooth, serrated, or fluted edges could be discriminated from each other. Higher denomination coins are notched or serrated. Fluted refers to concave grooves with pointed surfaces. Knurling, a form of rough texture, is also employed for texture coding. Shape and texture codes, like most coding systems, must be learned.

Size Coding Size coding may be used to depict the relative importance of a control. Another application is to easily identify controls performing the same function on different panels. Those performing a different function could be a different size.

Size coding has application both to situations where the control can and

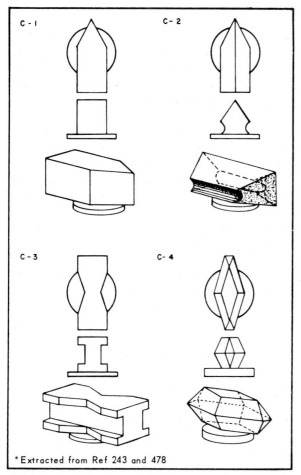

Figure 5-9 Preferred coding shapes for Class C discrete adjustment knobs. *(AFSC DH 1–3, 1977.)*

cannot be seen. Disadvantages are that it is limited to three or four categories and requires more panel space than other methods; in addition, the association of size and function must be learned. Some controls must employ varying sizes for mechanical advantage.

Large knobs should control major functions or high gain. Smaller knobs should control minor functions or low gain as noted earlier. On ganged concentric knobs the larger knob should be at least 20 percent larger than the smaller knob for relative discrimination, but should be considerably larger for absolute discrimination (see Knobs in Table F in the Appendix).

Mode-of-Operation Coding Each control has its own unique mode of activation—push/pull, turn, slide, press, snap-action, and so forth. Only by

Figure 5-10 Standard aircraft control shapes. *(AFSC DH 1–3, 1977.)*

activation in the manner required will the control perform its function. This method of using feedback from the mechanics and dynamics of the control operation as a basis for identification is termed mode-of-operation coding. Its advantages are that it does not require vision and is compatible with other coding methods. However, since operation or attempted operation is required, the method necessarily delays response time and should not be used in situations where faulty selection would be a serious matter. In general, it is a backup coding method to confirm initial control selection.

Location Coding Location coding refers to identifying controls by their position on a panel or console. As discussed earlier, it is a basic method of coding both individual controls and groups of controls. Consistent control locations permit one to operate by means of blind reach, thus limiting search time. Sequences of controls also may be arranged to minimize response time. Although location coding is basic to layout and arrangement of components, this method should be combined with other coding methods. Variations in panel sizes and shapes may make it difficult to maintain a consistent spatial arrangement on every panel.

Preventing Inadvertent Actuation

Coding techniques, including standardized locations, are effective methods for dealing with errors of identification. But what about errors that are due to accidentally bumping a control with the foot, hand, sleeve cuff, or clipboard? This type of unintended activation is sometimes difficult to detect and aircraft accident literature includes many instances where the pilot could not discern the cause of the problem, never suspecting it was of his or her own doing.

Techniques to Reduce Bumping Errors   There are at least seven methods for preventing the unintentional or inadvertent-activation error. Push-buttons and toggles are sometimes *recessed* so as not to protrude above the panel surface. Another technique is to *physically prevent accessibility* either by the use of raised barriers (as recommended between pushbuttons that are very close together) or by placing a protective cover or hinged transparent guard over a seldom-used control that must not be activated.

Horizontal-axis linear controls such as levers and toggles may be more easily bumped in the course of moving the hand horizontally or walking in some applications. A third technique is *orienting* the control (usually vertically) so that accidental bumping is less likely to occur in the direction the control will move.

A fourth technique is *locking* the control into position. This technique is illustrated by a lever that moves fore and aft in a slot with short perpendicular slots or detents for each discrete position. To release the control it must be moved laterally first. Locking refers here to the requirement of moving the control sequentially in at least two directions before it will move to another position.

A fifth technique is an extension of the locking concept to a series of *interlocks*. Each of a series of steps must be performed before the final and critical step can take place. A "busy box" of various types of controls to be operated in a sequence was once proposed for automobiles to prevent intoxicated drivers from turning on the ignition. There are two variations of the interlock. With the busy box, the steps prior to the last step may have no direct effect on system output other than enabling the next step to occur. In another variation, the steps may have a direct effect on output, for example, an arming switch that is activated before a bomb-release control.

A sixth technique is simply *isolating* one control from the others. Again, this would be more applicable to a seldom-used control that must not be activated. A related spatial technique is the use of recommended *clearances* between controls to reduce the likelihood of inadvertent activation of frequently used controls in their normal operation. The variables influencing recommended control spacing are discussed subsequently.

Finally, the proper amount and kind of *resistance* should be used to prevent inadvertent actuation. There are maximum and minimum amounts of resistance recommended for each type of control. Continuous thumbwheels, for example, require a breakout force of 3 to 4 ounces and an operating torque of between 0.021 and 0.045 N m (3 and 6 in -oz) depending upon thumbwheel diameter [AFSC, DH 1-3, 23]. Optimum resistance for operation should not be exceeded, however, in attempting to design for inadvertent actuation. There are alternative solutions, such as a disengage switch that enables each thumbwheel or other control to be activated.

Resistance The major types of resistance are elastic, static, viscous-damping, and inertial. Elastic resistance means that the control is spring-loaded. The greater the displacement the greater the resistance. The pilot's joy stick is an example of elastic resistance. The pilot feels a pressure proportional to the distance of the control stick from center. When the stick is released it returns to a neutral position. Pressure cues improve tracking in higher-order control systems. Elastic resistance is also involved in the snap action of toggle switches. Resistance first builds up and then decreases as the position is reached.

Static or sliding resistance is illustrated by pressing on a pencil eraser while moving it across a table top. It resists initial movement, causing a slight delay. When reversing a control movement there is another delay in trying to overcome the friction. Once the friction threshold is exceeded a little force moves the control rapidly. Cheaper smoking pipes employ friction in the connecting piece between the bowl and stem. After a period of use the friction is reduced. It is difficult to design a constant amount of static friction since it is not related to displacement, velocity, or acceleration. Also, overcoming friction in heavy controls can be fatiguing, resulting in a slower rate.

A common type of resistance used with controls is viscous-damping. Imagine moving a spoon through thick syrup, or recall trying to run in a swimming pool. This type of resistance is used in hydraulic door control systems to prevent slamming and yet assure that the door closes. A force operates opposite to output, but proportional to output velocity. (It is not related to displacement or acceleration.) The effect is one of resisting quick movements and assuring a smooth control movement. Gain control thumbwheels incorporate viscous damping and minimize static and inertial resistance.

Inertial resistance is a resistance caused by the mass (weight) of the mechanism involved. It is related only to acceleration, not to velocity or displacement. An example is a large handwheel that stops spinning because of inertial resistance. Larger forces are required both to start and to stop the control. Precise adjustments are more difficult.

Elastic and viscous-damping methods are involved in the design of many controls to prevent inadvertent activation. Inertial resistance is inherent in many larger controls.

Clearances between Controls Adequate spacing must be provided between the same type of controls used to control different functions. Keys on a typewriter keyboard, for example, are separated an exact distance based on key surface area, finger size, and conditions of use. Table 5-4 presents the recommended minimum and preferred separations between controls for several conditions of use.

The recommended spacing between controls depends upon at least eight design considerations: (1) the size of the control and its extent of displacement. Some controls require additional panel space around them for grasping. As noted earlier, the push button requires limited space for actuation by a single finger; (2) the body member used. Foot actuation requires wider separation than hand actuation; (3) two-hand or one-hand actuation; (4) a requirement for sequential or simultaneous activation. For example, whenever two levers are activated at once by one hand they should be closer together than when each lever is actuated in sequence; (5) whether the control is actuated randomly or in

Table 5-4 Control Separation Criteria

		Separation*			
Control	Condition	Minimum		Preferred	
		mm	in	mm	in
Push button	One finger – random order	12.7	1/2	50.8	2
	– sequential order	6.4	1/4	25.4	1
	Different fingers – random or sequential order	12.7	1/2	12.7	1/2
Toggle switch	One finger – random order	19.1	3/4	50.8	2
	– sequential order	12.7	1/2	25.4	1
	Different fingers – random or sequential order	15.9	5/8	19.1	3/4
Rotary selector	One hand – random order	25.4	1	50.8	2
	Two hands – simultaneous	76.2	3	127.0	5
Continuous adjustment knob	One hand – random order	25.4	1	50.8	2
	Two hands – simultaneous	76.2	3	127.0	5
Crank	One hand – random order	50.8	2	101.6	4
	Two hands – simultaneous	76.2	3	127.0	5
Handwheel	Two hands – simultaneous	76.2	3	127.0	5
Thumbwheel		6.35	1/4	–	–
Lever handle	One hand – random order	50.8	2	101.6	4
	Two hands – simultaneous	76.2	3	127.0	5
	Maximum simultaneous operation, one hand span	–	–	152.4	6
Pedal	One foot – random order	101.6	4	152.4	6
	One foot – sequential order	50.8	2	101.6	4

*Edge-to-edge measurement.
Source: AFSC DH 1-3, DN2D9 [23].

a sequence. Push buttons operated in random order must be at least one-half inch apart while those pressed in sequence need only be one-quarter inch apart. Similar differences in separation apply to other controls; (6) reaching for controls without visual feedback (blind reach) necessitates that there be more spacing between them; (7) large boots and pressure-suit gloves require more spacing between controls; (8) critical controls that must not be inadvertently actuated must be separated a greater distance.

Constraints to optimum spacing and control locations include restrictions in panel size, standardization requirements (such as the standard typewriter keyboard), internal packaging requirements, and the use of off-the-shelf assemblies, already designed and inserted as a unit, which may be less than optimum in control spacing.

CONTROL SYSTEMS

To this point controls have been discussed for the most part independently of the system being controlled. In a dynamic system, the reaction of the entire system to control inputs tends to influence performance. The pilot of an aircraft and the driver of an automobile are very much concerned with vehicle stability and handling qualities. In this section some basic concepts and relationships will be defined. These include types of tracking displays, types of system input and how the operator adapts to them, types of control order and their tracking requirements, operator describing functions, several modifications to simplify human tracking, and the effects of handling qualities on performance.

Criteria for a Useful Control System

Five criteria for a useful and acceptable control system are that it should not be too expensive; it should be reliable or consistent in its performance; it should respond quickly to a control input; it should permit accurate following of a desired course or target (minimizing tracking error); and it should provide system stability.

Some control systems are inherently unstable. On some vehicles if a steering wheel is suddenly jerked in one direction, any attempt to compensate for the movement may result in worsening the situation so that the vehicle oscillates back and forth and eventually goes out of control. The same thing has occasionally occurred in an aircraft. Control systems should be designed so that when an input is removed, the system stabilizes.

In Chapter 2 the closed-loop system was introduced and distinguished from the open-loop system by feedback of the system output. The operator senses the error signal either from a display or from observing through the windshield the behavior of the vehicle relative to its course or a target. The environment is also a part of this control loop in the sense that turbulence or wind gusts may influence the error signal.

Since the human operator is a primary component in the control loop, the success of effecting an accurate, stable, quick-reacting system will depend upon the operators' performance. The design of the control system must complement his or her capabilities. For example, the control dynamics and associated displays, if properly designed, may take over the more difficult, mathematical operations in higher-order control systems, leaving the human to perform control tasks that are within his or her capability.

Types of Tracking Displays

Tracking is an adaptive process of adjusting responses to a given set of conditions and to a controlled element. For continuous control systems, the input to the system defines the system goal or output. The input may be a constant value such as flying at a fixed heading or altitude, or it may be a variable value such as flying or driving a course that changes often or tracking a moving target. The variety of system inputs will be discussed subsequently, but for the moment the focus is on tracking displays.

At least two types of information must be displayed: an index of one's present performance and an index of desired performance. The index of present performance reflects the vehicle's position as a result of control actions or other factors. The index of desired performance reflects where the vehicle should be. The present-performance index is variously termed a controlled element, a follower, a cursor, or a chaser. The desired-performance index is termed a command index, a target, or a bogie. The difference between the two indices is termed *tracking error*.

There are numerous measures of tracking error: average error with sign of error ignored (average absolute error); root-mean-square error (square root of squared errors), constant position error (average error taking into account the sign). These are discussed subsequently.

Figure 5-11 illustrates two types of tracking displays—pursuit and compensatory. With pursuit tracking there are two moving elements (target and follower) and one fixed element. The fixed element may be explicit, for example, a reference line or reticle mark on a CRT, or it may be implicit, such as a textured display background [Frost, 10]. The distance between the target and the reference line represents systems input or forcing function. The distance between the follower and reference line represents systems output. Hence, a pursuit display permits seeing both input and output as well as tracking error.

Compensatory displays have only two elements—one fixed and one moving. As with pursuit tracking, a moving element is the follower. However, the reference line and target are now one and the same. All the operator sees is the difference between systems input and output. One has no way of telling how much of the error displayed is due to inaccurate tracking and how much is due to the target's changing course. One might ask: Is this important? Does the operator need to see the true state of affairs or is it sufficient that one see the direction and extent of error? As noted in Chapter 4, the glideslope indicator is a compensatory display. The pilot simply nulls error and in so doing guides the aircraft to a safe landing. Other parameters such as altitude require that the pilot be able to distinguish one's own systems output regardless of target altitude. So

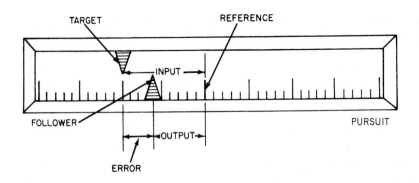

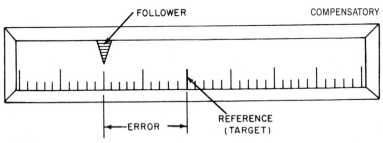

Figure 5-11 Information displayed on pursuit and compensatory displays. *(Frost, in Van Cott and Kinkade, 1972.)*

whether or not it is important depends on the application. Poulton [18], however, following an extensive review of research comparing the two displays, concluded that whenever there is a choice between true motion display and relative motion display, true motion display (pursuit tracking) should be used.

It was noted in Chapter 4 that the outside-in display was a pursuit display and the inside-out display was a compensatory display. There are certain problems in display-control movement compatibility with the inside-out display. An advantage of the compensatory display is that it permits the magnification of tracking error (much like a moving tape display) since it need not show the total range of system input. The pursuit display is handicapped in this regard since it must either be sufficiently large to show the total range of possible target and follower positions or else it must sacrifice scale resolution and, hence, risk the discriminability of target and follower parameters.

On the other hand, pursuit displays tell the operator whether the error is induced by the target or by the system. By showing the actual locations of both target and follower in space and their courses and velocities, the pilot may anticipate future conditions and plan actions such as short cuts based on where and when the two might intersect. Pursuit displays are useful when the output is complex and there is high rate of movement.

System Input

The system input displayed to the operator may come from several different sources and may exhibit combinations of characteristics as illustrated in Figure 5-12. The signal may come from the system as a command signal or from the environment of a moving vehicle. It may occur infrequently or continuously and it may occur in a predictable, periodic fashion or at unscheduled (aperiodic) times.

Figure 5-13 illustrates six common types of input and their correspondence to the various categories in Figure 5-12. In general, the usefulness of these inputs depends upon where they came from, what the operator did with the control, what the machine did upon being controlled, and what happened in the environment.

Types of Control Order

The various types of inputs specify desired system output. Before discussing how an operator would track such inputs, it is necessary to introduce the concept of control order because this specifies the nature of the response required.

Table 5-5 defines four types of control order by name and by number. It illustrates that the higher the order of a control system, the more difficult are the associated mathematical operations required for tracking the input. For example, to anticipate velocity, the first derivative of phase angle, requires a differentiation of phase angle. Higher-order control functions require the operator to perform several mathematical operations to determine what to do with the control device and when to do it. Kelley [14] showed that the higher the control order the more control movements necessary to track successfully.

Obermayer, Swartz, and Muckler [17] studied tracking performance with position, rate, and acceleration control systems and found that performance (as measured by three different types of error) degraded with increasing control order.

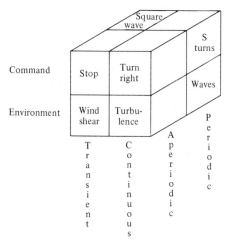

Figure 5-12 Three classes of inputs to control systems.

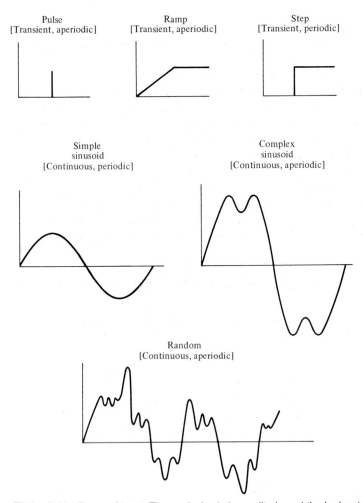

Figure 5-13   Types of input. The vertical axis is amplitude and the horizontal axis is time.

A zero-order system requires only the adjustment of gain, that is, multiplying the ratio of input signal to desired output response by some constant value. The gain operation is relatively simple. However, McCormick [15] has noted that estimating velocity requires a mental operation analogous to differentiation and estimating acceleration requires double differentiation. Moreover, estimating future positions at specified times from velocity estimates requires integration and estimating future position from acceleration estimates requires double integration and algebraic addition. Without detailing the various operations, it is clear that the operator is being required to perform combinations of mathematical operations that are difficult and sometimes impossible. Hence, control systems designers are devising system modifications that relieve the operator of some of these tasks, as discussed subsequently.

Table 5-5   Control Orders and Required Operator Responses

Type	Order	Control output determines	Operator response	Example
Position	Zero	Machine output—lever displacement produces a corresponding output displacement	Amplification (gain adjustment)	Gun pointer
Rate (velocity)	First	Rate of change of machine output	Amplification, differentiation, integration, and algebraic addition (velocity estimation)	Auto accelerator
Acceleration	Second	Rate of change of velocity of output	Amplification, differentiation, two integrations, and addition (acceleration estimation)	Rudder and flaps on an aircraft
Jerk	Third	Rate of change of acceleration of output	Amplification, differentiation, two integrations, and addition	Submarine depth control

Required Tracking Responses

The complexity of higher-order control responses is illustrated by the rudder control on a ship, a second-order control system. The position of the rudder control produces a rate of movement of the rudder and also results in angular acceleration of the ship. This produces a velocity vector that controls the rate of change of lateral position relative to the desired course. It can be seen that an initial operator movement may set off a chain reaction effect in higher-order control systems. A position change in one variable changes the velocity of the next variable and the acceleration of still another variable.

Figure 5-14 illustrates three types of input (ramp, step, and sine wave). For each type of input a different type of tracking response is required with position, rate, and acceleration control systems. The dashed lines indicate the desired operator output to track a particular input with a particular control order. Note that with a zero-order control system and sine wave input, the gain control should be moved in a manner to correspond to changes in the input pattern.

With a first-order control system, unless the operator can anticipate the sine wave pattern, the tracking line will lag behind it in a mimicking fashion. This is shown by the human tracking response lying to the right of the input track line. With simple, symmetrical patterns, *leading* the input is desirable, that is, by knowing the input will come at a predictable time, the control movement may be initiated slightly before the input signal occurs. This is shown by the tracking response to the left of the input line. If the input is complex and aperiodic, the best solution is to ignore random variations and instead seek a pattern that moves through the average error (as in mathematical curve fitting).

The desired tracking response for a step input (shown in Figure 5-14) would be appropriate only for a very slow response. The typical pattern is to slightly

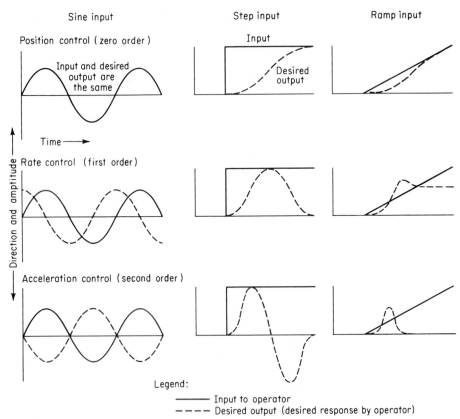

Figure 5-14 Tracking responses to sine, step, and ramp inputs for satisfactory tracking and position, rate, and acceleration control. *(McCormick, 1976.)*

overshoot (go above the horizontal line), then to slightly undershoot and gradually approximate the line. If the gain applied by the operator is too great, the overshooting and undershooting may continue for some time, indicating marginal dynamic stability. If the system is unstable, the pattern of amplitude variation may increase rather than decrease with time.

Operator Describing Functions

A professional movement has attempted to develop models for describing human performance in essentially engineering terms [McRuer and Krendel, 16]. The human is much like an electromechanical adaptive control system used in high-performance jet aircraft. If one could accurately describe the operator's contribution to the system, one could predict the stability and accuracy of any proposed control system in the design stage. The human transfer function could be inserted in the control loop and standard analysis techniques could then be used to evaluate total system stability.

A transfer function is basically a ratio of output to input. The human transfer function, $G_H(s)$, is the ratio of the response from the human to the controlled element divided by the sensory input to the human. It is sometimes expressed as $C_H(s)/E(s)$, where $C_H(s)$ is the output from the human and $E(s)$ is the input from the display.

In a simple quasilinear form, the operator describing function may be given* by the following formula [D'Azzo and Houpis, 6]:

$$G_H(s) = \left[\frac{K_H(T_L s + 1) \, e^{-ts}}{(T_I s + 1)} \right] \left[\frac{1}{T_N s + 1} \right] + R$$

where K_H = gain
$T_L s + 1$ = lead time constant
$T_I s + 1$ = lag time constant
e^{-ts} = transport delay (reaction time)
$T_N s + 1$ = neuromuscular lag
R = remnant or residual term accounting for nonlinearity

The first expression (in brackets) is the most important part since it is the adaptive portion of the formula. The second expression, neuromuscular lag, is fairly constant at 0.1 to 0.2 s, and the last expression, the remnant, simply includes those factors not specified that if included would increase the predictive strength of the model. It may be due to variation in phase lag, nonlinear strategies, or variations in steadiness while tracking.

Under certain conditions the remnant term can be a major factor. Elkind [8] found the remnant accounted for over 70 percent of the operator's total mean square output when the input was high frequency (144 Hz) and a nonlinear strategy (unrelated to the track frequency) was adopted. However, it was only 5 percent of output when tracking a low frequency in a position control system. McRuer and Krendel [16] found a remnant of 65 percent with a higher-order aircraft control system. Poulton [18] concluded that about 35 percent of the operator's mean square output may not be fitted by a describing function.

The remnant term recognizes the quasilinear nature of human response over time and individual. To the degree that the operator can predict the track and preprogram his or her responses, the remnant term may become quite small.

Another term, e^{-ts}, is human reaction time (discussed in Chapter 3). Although varying slightly with conditions of use, it may be taken as between 0.12 to 2.0 s in most applications.

The variables adjusted by the human operator are gain, lead time, and lag time. To optimize systems performance in a closed-loop system the adaptive terms must be multiplied by the machine transfer function, $G_1(s)^*$. Suppose $G_1(s) = K_M(T_x s + 1)/s(T_y s + 1)$ represents a machine with gain K_M,

---

*The operating function changes with time and could be shown by a differential equation, d/dt; however, it is usually transformed to an equation involving s (Laplace transform), which is easier to manipulate mathematically.

lead $T_x s + 1$, and a second-order lag $s(T_y s + 1)$ [D'Azzo and Houpis, 6]. If we assume unity feedback ($H_{(s)} = 1$) and multiply the machine transfer function by the human transfer function, rearranging products will yield the following forward-transfer function [Sheridan and Ferrell, 22]:

$$\frac{K_H K_M (T_L s + 1)(T_x s + 1)e^{-ts}}{(T_I s + 1)(T_y s + 1)(T_N s + 1)}$$

The human operator changes K_H such that the product of $K_H K_M$ establishes a gain that provides acceptable stability and control. In similar fashion the lag and lead time constants may be changed to improve handling qualities. For a specific task and controlled element, these terms become fairly constant once the operator becomes proficient in the task. A maximum lag time constant is about 10 s and a maximum lead time constant is approximately 1 s [Woodson and Conover, 29].

Human transfer functions describing human tracking behavior in compensatory tracking systems have been developed and work is in progress adapting functions to pursuit tracking systems [Frost, 10].

Modifications to Improve Tracking Performance

There are at least four techniques for modifying a system to make it easier for an operator to track a target: aiding, quickening, unburdening, and predictor displays.

Aiding   Aiding involves modifying the output of a control so that it is easier to track. According to McCormick [15], aiding was originally developed for gunnery tracking sytems. Suppose the task is tracking a high-flying target with a high-powered telescope in a rate-aided system. Whenever the operator begins to lag behind, the control mechanism will automatically speed up the rate and make a position adjustment to correct for it. Conversely, if the telescope should begin to lead the target, a position corrective motion will automatically slow the telescope's rate of movement. Hence, the position of the telescope at any instant will more nearly match the position of the target. Comparisons of unaided and aided systems (both rate- and acceleration-aided) have demonstrated that aiding does substantially reduce tracking error [15].

The top diagram of Figure 5-15 illustrates an original, uncompensated system that required three integrations ($1/s$) and a gain (a_1). The middle figure illustrates an aided system. The feedforward loops around the integrators imply that the output has been modified for a given display error, providing a stable system and relieving the operator of this responsibility.

In general, an aided system manages complex functions like differentiation and integration, reducing the operator's task to one of amplification or gain (K) control. A simple operator control response controls a more complex machine output.

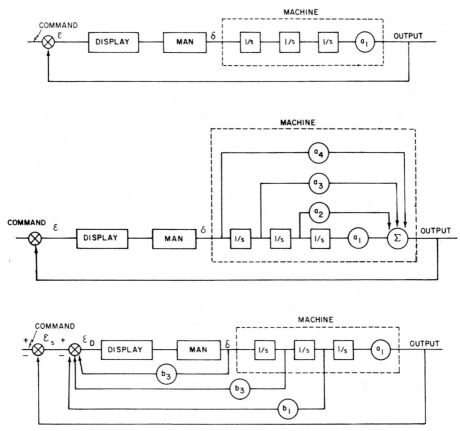

Figure 5-15 Diagram of an uncompensated, aided, and quickened control system. *(Frost, in Van Cott and Kinkade, 1972.)*

Quickening Quickening is a form of display augmentation applicable to second-, third-, and higher-order systems. Unlike aiding, the output is not modified; only the displayed information is changed. As shown in Figure 5-15 (bottom figure), quickening a display takes the signals and feeds them back to the display, leaving the machine transfer function unchanged. Rate and acceleration terms are now added to the display. The operator need not perform analogue differentiations or sense derivative information.

A quickened display has application primarily to systems where the control dynamics are very slow such that there appears to be a delay in the systems response to a control action. A quickened display tells the operator by an error signal the control action to take to achieve a particular control output. Again, the operator is relieved of the more difficult mathematical operations necessary to determine the correct control movement. Birmingham, Kahn, and Taylor [1] demonstrated that a quickened display resulted in more time on target than an unquickened display.

Quickening applies mainly to compensatory displays and to systems where there is delayed feedback. As discussed in the comparison of compensatory and pursuit displays, the operator using a compensatory display cannot see the actual state of affairs. In Figure 5-15, the operator receives ϵ_D, which is not the same as ϵ_s, the actual system error. Aiding, on the other hand, may apply to pursuit tracking and the operator can see the current state of affairs. *Unburdening* is a general term for relieving the operator by raising the order of the control system, that is, the burden of performing as an integrator or differentiator is removed from the operator. Aiding is a form of unburdening. Providing an electric motor as an integrator also unburdens the operator.

Predictor Displays The predictor display is another modification to enhance pursuit tracking performance with higher-order control systems. The display is designed to provide advanced knowledge of required control movements. This is accomplished by showing future responses of the system, given that the operator moved the control in various directions. The system uses a model of the system operating over an accelerated time frame, that is, the model repeatedly computes future system output based on assumptions about what the operator will do with the control device—return it to neutral, hold it where it is, move it to the extreme left or right, and so forth. A predictor display then shows the error at future times. For example, if a submarine depth control were immediately returned to neutral, a plot of future depth might show that 10 seconds later the submarine would have changed from a 15° dive to a 5° rise.

The technique is still largely experimental, but it offers the promise of telling us what will happen if we do or do not change our response. Kelley [14] and others have shown its application to situations where there is delayed feedback or where visual contact is not possible, such as submarine depth

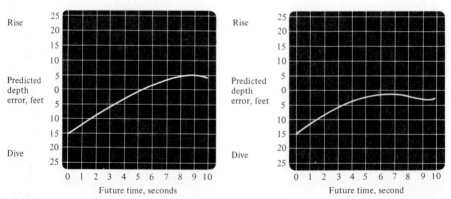

Figure 5-16 Examples of predicator displays for two submarines of different dynamic control characteristics. The displays show predicted depth error in feet extrapolated to 10 sec, assuming that controls were immediately returned to a neutral position. *(Kelley, 1968.)*

control, spaceship rendezvous [14], ship navigation in fog [Brigham, 3] or guidance of a vertical takeoff and landing (VTOL) aircraft [Dey, 7].

Handling Qualities

It was noted earlier that one of the primary criteria for a useful control system is that it should have good handling qualities, notably tracking accuracy, stability, and quick response.

Accuracy   There are several measures of tracking error: integrated absolute error, steady-state error (for positioning accuracy), root-mean-square (RMS) error (a measure of amplitude variation in each track frequency used for regulating systems with external disturbances), time on target (for gunnery accuracy), and so on. Hence, the appropriate metric depends somewhat upon the tracking problem. Poulton [18] noted that time on target is a less sensitive measure since small errors from the target are weighted as heavily as large errors.

Obermayer, Swartz, and Muckler [17] found that average absolute error and average RMS error correlate very highly when using the same experienced subjects. However, they do not correlate so highly when subjects are less skilled. Constant (unidirectional) position errors also correlate about $+.50$ with variability in error.

It was noted earlier that overshooting and undershooting are common errors in position occurring at points of reversal in the track. There is a tendency to undershoot reversals of the track when they are located far out on either side (since the operator knows the track will return to center after approaching the edge of the display). Moreover, the operator will overshoot reversals occurring near the center of the display (perhaps in anticipation of further movement to the outside). This phenomenon is termed a *range effect,* a tendency to make responses that deviate in the direction of the average of the series. This central tendency of judgment is also shown by naive subjects tending to overshoot small step inputs and to undershoot large step inputs.

Stability   The study of factors influencing stability of a control system is a complex area beyond the scope of this text. However, it may be instructive to look once more at instability. A single integrator element in the model is stable but two or more cascaded integrators are unstable elements, as noted in the discussion of the uncompensated system diagram (Figure 5-15). The output of an integrator may be fed back, adding to the input and causing it to grow after the original input is removed. When the sign of the output and input is the same, there is a positive feedback, leading to instability of the system. If the sign of the integrator is opposite to the input sign, the output will rise to the level of the input and then decay to zero when the input is removed, thereby leading to a stable system.

Output may be related to input by gain (K), but there is also usually a lag between input and output, depending upon the order of the control system. In some systems the lag is so long that the operator, in an attempt to control the system, increases gain, causing instability. When the operator attempts tighter control (closer tracking) by increasing gain, system output starts oscillating and the oscillations increase until gain is reduced or until the system becomes unstable and destroys itself. Hence, the operator induced the oscillations but the poor system design allowed the possibility of their occurring.

System transfer functions are typically plotted in polar form (Nyquist plots) or logarithmic form (Bode plots). An unstable system shown on a Nyquist plot will encircle the center point (actually, −1 point) in a clockwise direction, whereas a stable system will not.

A source of information on aerodynamic handling qualities of systems is often pilot opinion or ratings. A popular, standardized system of ratings is the Cooper Ratings Scale [5]. Although the categories employed are subjective, the ratings requested may be very specific, such as for various combinations of frequency of oscillation (H_z) and time in seconds required to damp them. The ratings may then be plotted to show regions of equally good handling qualities [5] or regions that are satisfactory, unsatisfactory, or totally unacceptable.

Systems Response Lag   It was noted above that system lag interacting with increased gain may induce instability. Lag may also influence accuracy in tracking. A delay between input and output may be a constant interval or it may follow an exponential function following a step input. Lag degrades performance only under certain conditions. For example, compensatory tracking performance is degraded by lag when there is a high control/display ratio (1:6 to 1:3) but not when there is a low C/D ratio [Rockway, 21].

Backlash and deadspace may also degrade performance under certain circumstances. *Backlash* is sometimes termed "displacement-displacement hysteresis" caused by looseness in the mechanical linkage [Frost, 10]. Imagine a joy stick operating inside a hollow cylinder. The cylinder may be moved in several directions, but its movement is not sensed until it makes contact with the joy stick. Without contact, control movements have no effect on the control system. Even .01 inch of backlash increases the mean error of pilot accuracy in tracking [Poulton, 18]. Rockway and Franks [19] found that with a higher gain (D/C ratio), performance in a system with backlash is degraded more than with a lower gain. Display gain should be reduced when backlash is a problem.

Deadspace is a form of backlash around the central position of a control. It could be thought of as the amount of control movement that results in no movement of the device being controlled. A deadspace of only 6 percent of the maximum, required control movement is found to degrade time-on-target scores, especially when the control system gain is high [Poulton, 18]. Rockway [20] found that time-on-target performance was degraded as the degrees of free movement of the control stick increased from 0 to 3°.

QUESTIONS AND PROBLEMS

1 Why is the detent thumbwheel located on the right of the display readout in Figure 5-1?

2 The common house lamp or desk lamp employs a variety of ON/OFF switches. Browse around your home and note at least three different types of switches on lamps. Describe them and comment on the comparative ease of activation of each switch.

3 In your opinion is the absence of tactual feedback from touch-sensitive push buttons an asset or a liability to efficiency of operation?

4 Two common principles of arrangement are sequence of use and functional grouping. With respect to plant layout techniques, what are the corresponding names for the principles?

5 Is there a population stereotype with respect to door knobs,
  a in their direction of turning movement for opening?
  b in their location on the door itself?

6 Assume an exponential lag between a control movement and the response of the display element. Would tracking improve if there were a higher or lower C/D ratio? Explain why.

7 **a** Which of the coding methods is dependent upon seeing the control?
  b Which method(s) require tactual feedback?
  c Which method(s) may employ visual, tactual, or both forms of feedback?

8 Discuss an operational problem in requiring that automobiles have a busy box of sequentially activated controls as a means of preventing intoxicated drivers from starting their engines.

9 Why is it important to design controls for both maximum and minimum resistance to movement?

10 Why is there an interest in developing operator describing functions?

11 What is the major similarity and the major difference in the techniques of aiding and quickening?

12 Read off from the SRP in Figure 5-3, the corner point locations (in inches) of the three surface areas (excluding the maximum area surface). Then calculate the dimensions of each area.

REFERENCES

1 Birmingham, H. P., A. Kahn, and F. V. Taylor: *A demonstration of the effect of quickening in multiple-coordinate control tasks,* USN, NRL Report 4380, June 23, 1954.

2 Bradley, J. V.: Tactual coding of cylindrical knobs, *Human Factors,* vol. 9, no. 3, 1967, pp. 213–226.

3 Brigham, R. R.: Ergonomic problems in ship control, *Applied Ergonomics,* vol. 3, no. 1, 1972, pp. 14–19.

4 Chapanis, A., "Design of Controls," in H. P. Van Cott and R. G. Kinkade, (eds.), *Human Engineering Guide to Equipment Design,* rev. ed., U.S. Government Printing Office, Washington, D.C., 1972, chap. 8.

5 Cooper, G. E.: Understanding and interpreting pilot opinion. *Aeronautical Engineering Review,* vol. 16, 1957, pp. 47–52.

  6 D'Azzo, J. J. and C. H. Houpis: *Feedback Control System Analysis and Synthesis,* McGraw-Hill, New York, 1966.
  7 Dey, D.: The influence of a predictor display on a quasi-linear describing function and remnant measured with an adaptive analogue-pilot in a control loop, in *Proceedings of 7th Annual Conference of Manual Control,* NASA SP-281, National Aeronautics and Space Administration, Washington, D.C., 1972.
  8 Elkind, J. I.: Characteristics of simple manual control systems. MIT Lincoln Laboratory Technical Report 111, Lexington, Mass., 1956.
  9 Fowler, R. L., W. E. Williams, M. G. Fowler, and D. D. Young: An investigation of the relationship between operator performance and operator panel layout for continuous tasks, USAF AMRL-TR-68-170, December 1968 (AD-692 126).
  10 Frost, G.: "Man-machine Dynamics," in H. P. Van Cott and R. G. Kinkade (eds.), *Human Engineering Guide to Equipment Design,* rev. ed., U.S. Government Printing Office, Washington, D.C., 1972, chap. 6.
  11 Huchingson, R. D.: Population stereotypes regarding rear window control movement in station wagons, Industrial Engineering memorandum, Texas A&M University, 1979.
  12 Jenkins, W. L. and M. B. Connor: Some design factors in making settings on a linear scale, *Journal of Applied Psychology,* vol. 33, 1949, p. 395.
  13 Jenkins, W. O.: "The tactual discrimination of shapes for coding aircraft-type controls" in P. M. Fitts (ed.), *Psychological research in equipment design,* Army Air Force, Aviation Psychology Program, Research Report 19, 1947.
  14 Kelley, C. R.: *Manual and automatic controls,* Wiley, New York, 1968.
  15 McCormick, E. C.: *Human Factors in Engineering and Design,* 4th ed., McGraw-Hill, New York, 1976.
  16 McRuer, D. T. and E. S. Krendel: Dynamic response of human operators, USAF Wright Air Development Center (WADC), Technical Report 56-524, Wright Patterson Air Force Base, Ohio, 1957.
  17 Obermayer, R. W., W. F. Swartz, and F. A. Muckler: The interaction of information displays with control system dynamics in continuous tracking, *Journal of Applied Psychology,* vol. 45, 1961, pp. 369–375.
  18 Poulton, E. C.: *Tracking skill and manual control* Academic Press, New York, 1974, p. 138.
  19 Rockway, M. R. and P. E. Franks: Effect of variation in control backlash and gain on tracking performance, USAF, WADC TR 58-553, January 1959.
  20 Rockway, M. R.: Effect of variation in control deadspace and gain on tracking performance, USAF, WADC TR 57-362, September 1957.
  21 Rockway, M. R., The effect of variations in control-display ratio and exponential time delay on tracking performance, USAF, WADC TR 54-618, December 1954.
  22 Sheridan, T. B. and W. R. Ferrell: *Man-Machine Systems,* MIT Press, Cambridge, Mass., 1974.
  23 United States Air Force, Air Force Systems Command, AFSC DH 1-3, DN2D, Design of Controls, January, 1977.
  24 U.S. Department of Defense, Federal Standard 595, Colors (no date).
  25 U.S. Department of Defense, Military Standard 1472B, *Human Engineering Design Criteria for Military Systems, Equipment, and Facilities,* December 1974.
  26 U.S. Department of Defense, Military Standard 91528 (no date).

27 U.S. Department of Defense, Military Standardization Handbook 759, *Human Factors Engineering Design for Army Materiel,* March 12, 1975.

28 U.S. Department of Defense, Military Standard 1280 (no date).

29 Woodson, W. E. and D. W. Conover: *Human engineering guide for equipment designers,* 2d ed., University of California Press, Berkeley, 1970, pp. 6–32.

30 Chapanis, A. and L. Lindenbaum: A reaction time study of four control-display linkages, *Human Factors,* vol. 1, no. 4, 1959, pp. 1–7.

31 Chapanis, A. and D. A. Mankin: Test of ten control-display linkages, *Human Factors,* vol. 9, no. 2, 1967, pp. 119–126.

Part Three

Industrial Systems and Environment

Chapter 6

Design of the Industrial Workplace

The design of the industrial workplace has long been the focus of attention of many specialists, each viewing the problem from a slightly different vantage point. The human factors specialist working in this area must be a generalist who is acquainted with data and techniques employed in these diverse areas and who must be able to apply the data to the design of particular workplaces.

In this chapter the work of some of these specialists will be reviewed, with examples of how the human factors generalist or ergonomist may apply the information. The subject of facility layout and design will be discussed in Chapter 7. The industrial workplace also involves considerations of lighting, temperature and atmospheric control, noise, and vibration. These issues will be discussed in Chapters 8 and 9.

WHO ARE THE WORKPLACE DESIGN SPECIALISTS?

From the inception of industrial engineering the *methods study* engineers were concerned with workplace design and positioning of fixtures as an adjunct to improving work methods for increased productivity.

The *physical anthropologists* are providing data on the worker's body dimensions, reach profiles, and viewing angles and limits that have implications for establishing dimensions of the workplace, for example, work surface height, knee clearances, and seat design. This body of data (introduced in Chapter 3) is illustrated in its application to workplace design.

Plant layout specialists are also concerned with an overall functional layout of the facility as well as the arrangement of workers within an area and the layout of individual equipment at the work station. Certain techniques directly relevant to layout of the work station will be discussed in this chapter.

Specialists in *work physiology and biomechanics* are concerned with the energy costs of work as measured by physiological parameters and the muscular effort and fatigue associated with dynamic and static loads. These data have implications for workplace and tool design as well as for methods study, scheduling rest breaks, and eliminating stress hazards.

The *occupational safety and hygiene engineers,* under the impetus of the Occupational Safety and Health Act [34], are examining the workplace and the industrial environment for potential hazards to the worker. This effort involves both research to establish standards as well as inspection of workplaces and development of predictor methods. Controlling losses by reducing accidents and long-term disabilities is an asset to both management and the worker. *Environmental equipment specialists,* such as illumination engineers, heating and air-conditioning engineers, and noise control engineers, are also directly involved with implementing environmental design.

Behavioral scientists, human relations, and labor relation specialists are all concerned with job design for improved motivation. There are many socio-technical issues, for example, management's attitudes as reflected in the organization of work and, indirectly, in the workspace design and layout itself.

This list is by no means exhaustive. *Industrial psychologists* are concerned with many of the above issues as well as training and selection. *Time study specialists, job analysts, occupational research specialists, personnel specialists, maintainability engineers, and management consultants* are all concerned with the measurement and improvement of worker performance. To the degree that the workplace design influences performance, these specialists are also concerned with the quality of its design. Figure 6-1 illustrates the variety of specialties which impact on workplace design.

With the diversity of industrial specialists and interests and with the many types of industrial tasks that have been investigated, a comprehensive treatment of the industrial workplace is beyond the scope of this chapter. However, examples of the types of work being done in several of these areas are presented. Although the technical interests of some specialists may be principally in the organization of work and job design, the emphasis here is on the design of the workplace itself as the framework for design of the job.

METHODS STUDY AND WORKPLACE DESIGN

Methods study or work simplification goes beyond simply studying human motions to make them more efficient. Methods study involves various methods

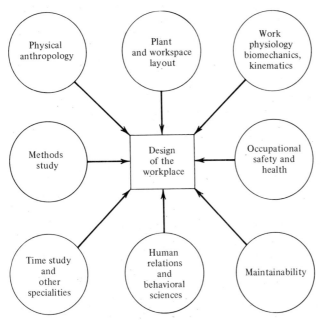

Figure 6-1 Industrial specialties providing data to workplace design.

of cutting production costs by improving the design of the job. Improved work practices can be achieved only through an appropriate workplace design. The early industrial engineers recognized that improvements in work behaviors required a workplace laid out in a functional manner and that equipment, tools, and materials needed to be provided in such a way as to reduce movement and effort, improve efficiency, and reduce costs. Hence, we shall see that the principles of motion economy are much more than directions on how to move the arms and other parts of the body to be more efficient. The principles encompass workplace design, fatigue reduction, safety engineering practices, and workplace ergonomics.

Historical Note on Work Improvement

Motion economy study was originated by Frank Gilbreth in 1910 and greatly expanded by Barnes [6] and other industrial engineers in the 1930s. Greater efficiency increases productivity or output per unit time, and reduces the cost of production. From the workers' standpoint, it means reduced effort in performing tasks, comfort, and less likelihood of injury.

Antagonists have viewed the efficiency expert as someone who requires working in a more exacting way and who cuts out part of the work. They were concerned that their job would become more boring and repetitive and that some jobs could be eliminated. In recent years, there has been a movement toward trying to make industrial tasks more inherently interesting, diversified, and challenging through employee participation in job design, job enrichment programs, and job enlargement, to include more activities. The idea of greater challenge, work pride, and variety of work appeals to many workers, while other workers still prefer performing easy, repetitive work.

Regardless of the type of activity performed, the notion of work improvement is a viable concept that even office workers and professional people can employ in their daily activities. Methods study, then, involves finding better ways to do the job by getting rid of unnecessary movements, by shortening movements that cannot be eliminated, and by making movements less tiring.

Motion Economy Principles

The following are some examples of principles of motion economy [Barnes, 6; Niebel, 32; AFSC DH 1-3, 44]:

1 Use two-hand operations that are symmetrical and simultaneously away from or toward the body. Both hands should begin and complete their motions at the same time.

2 Continuous, curved motions are preferred to straight-line motions with abrupt changes in direction. Use a motion sequence that employs few stops. Ballistic movements are faster and easier than controlled ones.

3 Keep the elbows close to the body as much as feasible. Finger motion conserves energy more than arm and body motion. Use the limbs and digits that are most appropriate for the task. Relieve the hands of work that could be performed by the feet or another part of the body.

4 Arrange the work to permit an easy and natural rhythm. Successive movements should be planned so that one movement passes easily into the next movement.

5 Provide fixtures to hold parts so the hands are not wasted as a holding device. Avoid static work.

6 Eliminate unnecessary movements by providing drop delivery of work items, gravity feed chutes or bins for parts, belt conveyors, and so on. Tapered channels can make it easier to assemble two mated parts without unnecessary positioning.

7 Arrange workspace so that a movement does not have to be made against the force of gravity.

8 Arrange parts for easy access without long arm reaches or movement. Short-armed workers should be able to reach everything. Use recent functional arm-reach data. Older and weaker employees may require even shorter reaches [Tichauer, 42].

9 Tools and materials should be prepositioned (standardized locations) to eliminate searching and selecting.

10 Alternate sitting and standing is desirable for some work tasks.

11 Arrange the height of the workplace and seat to provide for the comfort of the worker, including provisions for adjustments in height.

12 Arrange the workplace so the visual work items are close and frequently used controls are accessible (between elbow and shoulder height). Controls should be located to provide the best mechanical advantage for the strongest muscle groups. Controls and tools should be designed according to force requirements, hand dimensions, and other ergonomic and biomechanical principles.

> **13** Provide power tools and materials handling devices.
> **14** Provide for safety and comfort in the environment.
> **15** Schedule work pauses to reduce fatigue and eliminate boredom.
> **16** Promote orderliness, cleanliness, and good housekeeping.

This list is far from complete, but it is illustrative. Like many human factors checklists, it suggests goals that must be reached, but the user must then refer to other data sources for more specific information on how these principles may be accomplished. Before studying some of the other specialty areas, it may be helpful to review some specific examples of workplace design studies.

WORKPLACE DESIGN STUDIES: SOME EXAMPLES

The human factors implementation specialist, discussed in Chapters 1 and 2, is assigned the task in an industrial engineering organization of translating design information, specifications, and standards into design of products. Similarly, the implementation or ergonomics specialist who is assigned to the solution of manufacturing problems is vested with responsibility for applying human factors data (anthropometric, ergonomic, biomechanic, methods study guidelines, and so forth) to the design of industrial workstation problems.

To some readers, mention of an industrial workstation may solicit the image of a man working on an automobile assembly line, riveting on an aircraft fuselage, working in a foundry or at a loading dock. In a later discussion of the work physiologist's job and biomechanical research, the moderate-to-heavy-load workstation will be considered. Today, however, many female workers are employed in electronic assembly work. They perform relatively light physical work that is taxing in terms of its visual demands and the tedious nature of the tasks. Janousek [24] and Rosenthal [36] have recommended ways of modifying the workstation of women engaged in electronic panel assembly and micro-welding, respectively. These examples may clarify the role of human factors in a particular type of manufacturing activity.

Case Study 1—Electronic Manufacturing

Janousek [24] was assigned to design and develop a workspace layout for an electronic manufacturing area to improve efficiency and to reduce fatigue and hazards. The existing workplace design required women to work at a high work bench with blueprints spread out over the work surface. Tools cluttered the surface, and the panel assembly had to be propped up. The result was poor posture and wasted motion searching for blueprints and tools, bending over, reaching, and so forth. Janousek recommended several changes in the design (Figure 6-2).

1 A print holder, which also served as a workspace dividing wall. The holder was 20 in above the surface and at an angle of from 0 to 15° from vertical. It was constructed of sheet metal so that magnets could hold prints of various sizes. As a divider it prevented eye contact with a facing worker and, hopefully,

Figure 6-2 Soft mockup of human factors engineering recommended workstation. *(Janousek, 1969. From* Human Factors, *1969, vol. 11, no. 2. Copyright 1969 by The Human Factors Society, Inc. and reproduced by permission.)*

reduced conversations as well. A drafter's lamp was mounted on the holder, thus uncluttering the work surface.

    2 A tool caddy. This was a tool drawer below the surface. An orderly arrangement made the tools accessible without searching. Certain tools like the soldering iron and wire stripper were stored in a special holder or hung from a hook in front of the bench (thus preventing damage). The electric plug was on the front of the work bench, eliminating tangled wires on the surface.

    3 The size of the workbench surface was reduced to 30 × 60 in (76 × 152 cm). This recommendation was based upon data regarding the 5th percentile female forward and lateral reach limits. The reduction was also to discourage storage of bins of material on the surface and to avoid the worker's stretching and leaning to reach objects beyond her reach. The work surface was also lowered to 29 in (74 cm) for seated operations and was covered with a plastic material for ease of cleaning.

    4 A panel holder was installed on the surface (see Figure 6-2). The holder was inclined at a 15° angle and was large enough to hold the largest panel assembly securely (20 × 25 in or 51 × 63 cm).

    These workstation recommendations were based upon physical limitations of the personnel, requirements of the task, physical dimension of articles worked upon, and principles to reduce posture-induced fatigue. Soft and hard mockups were later fabricated and tested. Finally, management requested funds to purchase workstations for the entire organization of assembly workers.

Case Study 2—Microwelding in a Machine Shop

Rosenthal [36] was concerned with the design of a microwelding workstation in the machine shop of an aircraft manufacturer. The operation involved as many as 60 welds of grid wires on a single grid to be worked on by women workers peering through power microscopes. After locating the joint to be welded between two electrodes, a foot pedal caused the electrodes to close; upon contact with the joints, a weld was effected. Grid wires were then trimmed. Missing a single weld or trim caused an electrical failure of the module.

The workstations consisted of standard Flow-Tron tables with microscopes, weld units, and Dazor drafting lamps. The first human factors task was to identify problems. The techniques involved observing individual differences in work habits, reviewing human engineering data, and interviewing workers regarding problems at the workstation (which was part of a worker motivation program).

A drawing was then made of the female worker relative to her workstation (Figure 6-3). Note the requirement for a 7-in (18 cm) table height adjustment range and a 5-in (13 cm) adjustment range in seat height. These requirements were to accommodate the range of operators and were based upon female anthropometric data [Dreyfuss, 16]. A plan view drawing was also made showing maximum reach distances of 20 to 25 in (51 to 63 cm), and the most effective work area for a seated operator. Rosenthal recommended an area of 24 × 14 in (61 × 36 cm), beginning about 7.75 in (20 cm) in front of the shoulder joint.

The scope viewing task involved long periods of leaning on the elbows. Operators reported the perforated rubber pad was irritating. A design solution was an elbow rest on the table made of foam rubber and covered with Naugahyde.

Operators also complained of foot cramps from keeping the foot raised without support as they actuated the pedal. Human engineering data confirmed a design deficiency—a heel support is needed wherever the pedal angle exceeds 20°. Other problems identified were the need for an improved layout to reduce wasted motion and better illumination of the work task (which was only 50 to 100 fc).

The human engineering specialist, with the assistance of industrial design, developed some conceptual drawings aimed at resolving the problems. An island station was proposed, consisting of four workstations in a circular arrangement, with each workstation occupying a quadrant. Each table had a continuous, vertical adjustment capability to accommodate the range of operators.

Initially, a foamcore mockup was developed and after design verification, a prototype mockup was fabricated. Welding workers evaluated the prototype and any additional deficiencies were identified. Figure 6-4 is a photograph of the prototype workstation.

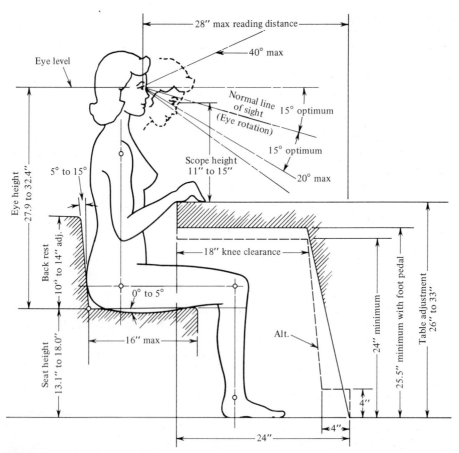

Figure 6-3 Anthropometric and workstation dimensions. *(Rosenthal, 1973. From* Human Factors, *1973, vol. 15, no. 2. Copyright 1973 by The Human Factors Society, Inc. and reproduced by permission.)*

Note the contoured table with the smooth plastic top. Push button controls for adjustment of height and a wasted-clipping container are shown. Curtains separated workstations. Instructional material is shown hanging on a rod. An adjustable heel rest for the footpedal was one of the design improvements in that area.

An illumination intensity of 150 fc was required, but there were individual differences in the surface lighting desired. Therefore, in addition to the indirect, fluorescent lighting system, each worker was given a high-intensity light with a gooseneck for focusing.

To improve the brightness contrast between wires and the background, several colored backgrounds were studied and a medium-blue background was selected. The tip of the electrode was also modified to eliminate a parallax problem. Finally, each workstation was given a storage cabinet adjacent to the

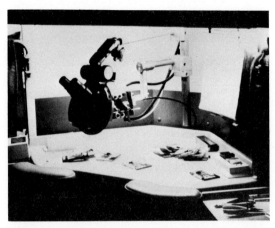

Figure 6-4 Close-up of new welding workstation. *(Rosenthal, 1973. From* Human Factors, *1973, vol. 15, no. 2. Copyright 1973 by the Human Factors Society, Inc. and reproduced by permission.)*

workstation. The top of the cabinet was adaptable as an additional work surface for placing parts and tools.

After the 48 workstations (12 islands) had been in operation for a year, it was found that there was a steady decrease in the percent failures of the welded items because of workmanship. The degree to which this was due to the new stations or to other factors, such as variety of work, could not be isolated, but operators were reported to take considerable pride in their individual stations.

DIMENSIONING AND ARRANGING THE WORKSPACE

These two examples of human factors activities in manufacturing workplace design would indicate that the dimensions of the workplace and the arrangement of equipment around the worker are two important considerations. Recommended dimensions for the female worker were given in Figure 6-3. Figure 6-5 presents similar dimensional requirements for the seated male operator at a workbench or console.

Since this figure is rather saturated, it may be helpful to extract some of the major workplace dimensions.

Seat Dimensions

The science of seating design in various applications is given in Chapter 7. However, it should be noted here that for the male operator the seat height should be adjustable within a 15 to 18 in (38 to 46 cm) range. The seat depth should be no more than 15 in (presuming an open base). The backrest should be at least 6 in (15 cm) high and no wider than 13 in (33 cm) for elbow clearances. It should permit reclining 5 to 15°. Elbow rests should be 7 to 9 in (18 to 23 cm) above the seat surface. A desirable length is 9 to 12 in (23 to 30 cm), as measured

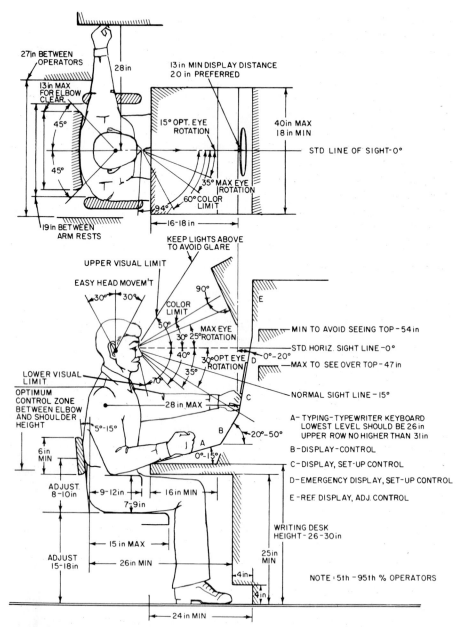

Figure 6-5 Suggested parameters for mockup of a seated operator console. *(Van Cott and Kinkade, 1972.)*

from the seat reference point (SRP). The SRP is where the seat surface and seat back intersect. There should be about 19 in (48 cm) between the two arm rests.

Workbench Dimensions

The height of a work surface should be between 26 to 30 in (66 to 76 cm) for chair-seat operations. (The standard table height is 29 in or 73.7 cm.) As shown in Figure 6-5, the work surface may be slanted up to 15°.

The undersurface height should be a minimum of 25 in (63.5 cm) for thigh and knee clearances. If there is a vertical surface under the work surface (as with a console or counter), the minimum depth of the undersurface for knee clearance should be 18 in or 45.7 cm [Dreyfuss, 16]. Ayoub [5] reports that a reduced knee room of 12 in (30.5 cm) could be tolerable. The minimum depth at the floor should be 24 in (61 cm) to allow room for the feet. Measured from the SRP, the minimum distance is 26 in (66 cm), as shown.

The back of the console should be 28 in (71 cm) horizontally from the shoulder joint. This standard is for young, healthy males. Console panel fronts may be angled as shown to provide a perpendicular line of sight and easier reach. The most important displays should be in areas D and C near the normal line of sight. Note also that if you do not want the operator to see over the back, the height should be at least 54 in (137 cm); if seeing over is necessary, the height should not exceed 47 in (119 cm).

Elevated Work Surfaces

Ayoub [5] has documented some recommendations for work surfaces based principally upon the visual demands of the task. For close visual work, a portion of the work surface on which the workpiece rests should be elevated above the bench-top level. The following are recommendations for both seated and standing operators:

| | Recommended work surface height (in) | | | |
| | Seated | | Standing | |
Task	Male	Female	Male	Female
Fine assembly work	39–41.4	35–37.5	–	–
Precision work (mechanical assembly)	35–37	32.5–34.5	43–47†	40–44.5†
Light assembly work or writing*	29–31	27.5–29.5	39–43	34.5–38.5
Coarse or medium manual work	27–28.5	26–27.5	33.5–39.5‡	31–37‡

*Typing 2 to 3 in lower.
†With supported elbows.
‡Heavy work.

Sometimes the nature of the task requires standing. For manual work (unspecified) the operator's hands should be 2 to 4 in (5 to 10 cm) below the elbows. Elbow height is currently about 45 in (114 cm) for the average male and 42.5 in (108 cm) for the average female. Thus, the average working height would be 41 to 43 in (104 to 108 cm) for men and 38.5 to 40.5 in (98 to 103 cm) for women. The above recommendations are modifications to improve visual acuity for fine component work. Adjustments must be made to accommodate extreme statures.

Other recommendations [Ayoub, 5] are to use foot controls for seated operations only. If a standing operation is required, the control should be operable by either foot. Locate the controls for best mechanical advantage. Required forces should be less than 30 percent of maximum for a muscle group when used frequently, and less than 50 percent for occasional use (5 min or less). (See Chapter 3.)

Also, use adjustable footrests and chairs to maintain a posture that is comfortable. Provide for alternate sitting and standing, if possible. For standing operations, design for the tall operator who would be uncomfortable stooping. The shorter operator could be given a platform. For reaching tasks, the layout should be designed for the shorter operator.

Techniques for Planning Equipment Arrangement

Procedures for layout of facilities have been studied by plant layout specialists. However, there are three techniques that are directly applicable to layout of equipment at the workplace, whether the equipment be controls and displays, machinery, tools, pallets of work items, or whatever. One technique is *link analysis* [Van Cott and Kinkade, 45; Chapanis, 10]. The others are the *association chart* and the *activity relationship chart*. The last two will be discussed first because they provide information required in doing a link analysis.

Activity Relationship Chart and Association Chart   The activity relationship chart [Apple, 3], sometimes used in plant layout studies, is shown at the top of Figure 6-6.

This chart documents ratings of *how important* it is for a particular function or activity area to be located next to any other activity area. One of six letters is used to code the closeness. Also, a reason is given for the rating by a number code. The example is obviously for rooms within a manufacturing facility; however, the activity areas or functional elements could have as well been several machines, pallets, workers, or supervisors.

The association chart [Whitehead and Eldars, 47] shown at the bottom of Figure 6-6 also appears to be like a mileage chart on a road map. But instead of giving mileage or estimates of the importance of areas being close together, it records the *frequency* of movements between any two work areas. The example is for the number of times nurses went from one room to another. The two techniques provide basic data for step 6 of the link analysis.

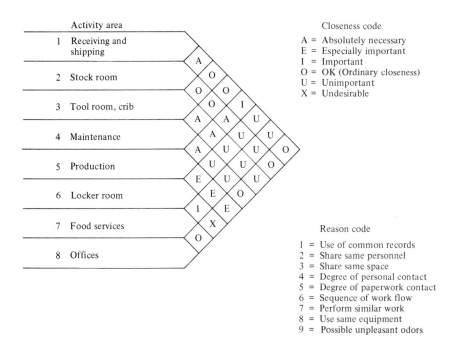

Activity area

1 Receiving and shipping
2 Stock room
3 Tool room, crib
4 Maintenance
5 Production
6 Locker room
7 Food services
8 Offices

Closeness code

A = Absolutely necessary
E = Especially important
I = Important
O = OK (Ordinary closeness)
U = Unimportant
X = Undesirable

Reason code

1 = Use of common records
2 = Share same personnel
3 = Share same space
4 = Degree of personal contact
5 = Degree of paperwork contact
6 = Sequence of work flow
7 = Perform similar work
8 = Use same equipment
9 = Possible unpleasant odors

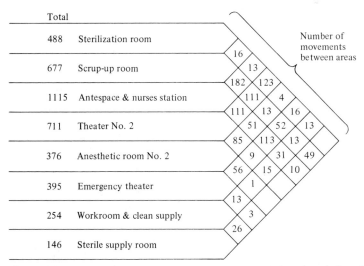

Total

488   Sterilization room
677   Scrup-up room
1115 Antespace & nurses station
711   Theater No. 2
376   Anesthetic room No. 2
395   Emergency theater
254   Workroom & clean supply
146   Sterile supply room

Number of movements between areas

Figure 6-6 Activity relationship chart, above, and association chart, below. *(Adapted from Apple, 1963; and Whitehead and Eldars, 1964. Association chart adapted by McCormick, 1976.)*

Link Analysis A link is a connection between (a) an operator and a machine; (b) two operators; (c) two parts of a machine. An operator-machine link is illustrated by an operator using a device such as a control or tool. An operator-operator link is illustrated by communications between two operators. A machine-machine link could refer to operating switch A and then switch B. A linkage may be visual (as in a sequence of instrument scans) or it may be an action (talking to someone, working on an item, walking from one place to another).

Link values may represent either *frequency* with which a link occurs or *importance* of a connection between two components. The frequency of usage may be obtained by observing an existing system in operation, simulating the operation in a mockup, or, if neither is feasible, rating the frequency of use by asking an experienced operator of a similar system. One could photograph an operation and analyze the film to see how often a particular linkage occurred. An occulometer or eye-marker camera is sometimes used to study visual scan patterns and see how many times instrument A is used in conjunction with instrument B. Frequencies may later be grouped into categories in developing link values.

Thomson [49] has listed a series of steps in conducting a link analysis, which are summarized as follows:

Step 1 Draw a circle for each person in a system and label it with a code *number*.

Step 2 Draw a square for each equipment item used by an operator and label it with a code *letter*.

Step 3 Draw connecting lines (links) between each person and any other person or persons known to have a direct interaction in operating the system.

Step 4 Draw connecting lines between each person and any machines with which he or she interacts.

It should be noted that operators and equipment are shown in their correct spatial relationship according to some existing or conceptual layout. Therefore, inefficient arrangements are shown by comparatively *long* linkage lines and by paths *that cross* one another. These linkages are especially poor when the linkages have either high usage or high importance ratings.

Step 5 Redraw the diagram reducing to a *minimum the number of crossing lines* to obtain the simplest possible arrangement. Obviously, this is achieved by moving certain components (operators or machines) closer together on the workspace drawing.

Step 6 Calculate the frequency of use (using an association chart) and the importance of each linkage (using an activity relationship chart or similar technique). Then assign an appropriate weight to each factor to obtain a composite value for each link. For example, a link value may equal 2 × frequency plus 1 × importance. The composite value is sometimes called the "use-importance" link value.

Step 7 Again, redraw the diagram so that the linkages having higher values are shorter than those having lower values. Thus, an optimum link diagram is one where *distances are minimized* when the activity (linkage) occurs frequently or is very important. Computer-aided link analyses have been conducted [Haygood et al, 22].

Step 8 Sometimes the workspace available and its dimensions are fixed so it may be necessary to redraw the link diagram to fit into this available space. Ideally, the workspace should be modified to fit the link diagram.

Step 9 Confirm the final link analysis on a scale drawing of actual positions to visualize the physical dimensions of all equipment, operators, chairs, and so forth, and to check for unidentified problems.

Chapanis [10] presents a schematic link diagram of a combat information center aboard the U.S.S. Louisville during an air attack. Officers move about in carrying out their duties while plotters, radar operators, and radio operators stay in one location at consoles. Figure 6-7 shows the initial layout and also the revised layout after link analysis.

The revised layout eliminated all crossing lines between operators or between operators and machines, thus eliminating bumping into one another. By rearranging consoles, long walks were eliminated and total lengths of paths were substantially reduced.

The use-importance links in the combat center were graded from 1 to 9 and were shown by the number of lines between operators and consoles or between two operators. Thus, the number of lines as well as the superimposed number provide an indication of the value of the linkage.

Again, the illustration is for rearranging a room for greater efficiency, but the link analysis technique has application to any workspace problem, for example, arranging tools or work items at a workstation or instruments and controls in a vehicle.

ENERGY COSTS OF WORK

Work physiology is a specialized application of physiological data to the workplace. Physiology deals with neuromuscular, cardiovascular, and metabolic measures. Unlike the medical physiologist who focuses on pathology or the sports physiologist who is concerned with maximum human effort, the work physiologist is concerned with the energistic effects of typical work, whether it be extremely heavy or moderate in its demands on the worker.

Davis et al. [15] point out that no single measurement technique can measure the effects of all types of loads on the individual. In some cases, measures of physiological response (for example, heart rate, oxygen consumption, or blood pressure) may be appropriate. In other instances, a secondary loading task (see Chapter 2) or a visual acuity test (see Chapter 3) may be more appropriate. In producing photographic products like cameras, the tasks may be highly skilled and the loads extremely light. However, Davis et al. found that 32 percent of the production jobs studied in this type of plant were amenable to investigation with physiological measurement techniques.

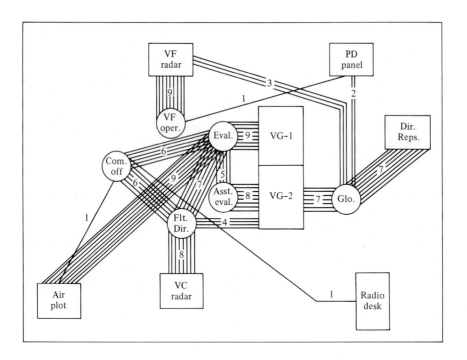

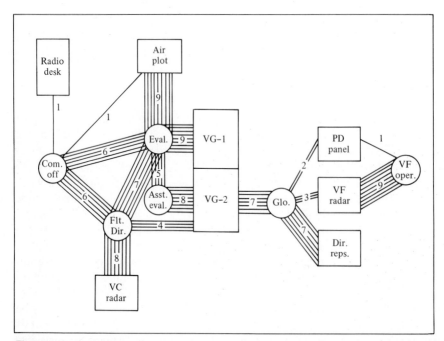

Figure 6-7 Comparison of room arrangements before and after link analysis. *(Chapanis, 1959. © Johns Hopkins University Press, 1959.)*

Why Take Physiological Measures?

The reasons a work physiologist might be called in to measure the physiological demands of a job are several:

- Safety—It may be suspected that the job, as presently designed, is beyond the capabilities of the people in terms of physiological demands such as heart rate and oxygen consumption.
- Methods evaluation—Physiological measures may be used to decide which of several proposed ways of doing a job is easier, for example, use of two arms only or the arms and legs combined.
- Scheduling breaks—The measures may be used to determine the frequency and duration of rest pauses for physically taxing work. In some instances, periodic rotation of personnel may be recommended, as in sporting events such as basketball.
- Job specifications and selection—Sometimes a particular worker may not be capable of performing a particular job because of age, the effects of illness, attitudes, and so on. Yoder et al. [48] discuss a freight elevator worker whose job involved loading and unloading materials using a pallet jack. He had a poor attendance record, reportedly poor motivation and attitude, and nonspecific health problems. The 144-lb worker complained the work was too heavy and wanted a job change. Following a physiological field study using two other workers, it was recommended that the job specification be changed to require "heavier and more robust" individuals and that the individual be transferred to a job more suited to his capabilities.
- Job evaluation—Physical effort or difficulty is one of the factors used by wage and salary analysts in determining pay scale for each job. The work physiologist may be asked to rank jobs according to physical difficulty.
- Environmental stress—The atmospheric, temperature, and mechanical environment (noise/vibration) may also be associated with physiological changes (as may psychological stress and sleep loss).

Techniques for Measuring Physiological Strain

Table 6-1 summarizes and defines some of the common chemical, electrical, and physical measures that have been taken as indicators of strain or the effects of stresses on the individual [Singleton, 38]. Electromyographic recordings (EMG) are inked tracings of electrical impulses occurring in various muscles while constant forces of so many foot-pounds are applied. We shall have more to say about them when the biomechanics of work is discussed later. Irregularities in heart-rate patterns (sinus arrhythmia) have been shown to be associated with mental loads as expressed in terms of binary choices per minute.

Although many physiological responses may be measured in the laboratory, Davis et al. [15] used only heart rate and oxygen consumption to estimate the load of physically demanding tasks in the actual work situation. Ricca [35] has shown that heart rate, instead of very precise cardiac output measures, is a sufficiently accurate measure for most industrial jobs. Heart rate is sensitive to temperature and to emotional stress, whereas oxygen consumption is less

Table 6-1 Physiological and Psychological Measures of Strain

Physiological

Chemical	Electrical	Physical
Blood content	EEG (electroencephalogram)	Heart rate
Urine content	EKG (electrocardiogram)	Heart-rate recovery
Oxygen consumption	EMG (electromyograph)	Sinus arrhythmia
Oxygen deficit	EOG (electrooculogram)	Pulse volume
		Pulse deficit
Oxygen recovery curves	GSR (galvanic skin response)	Body temperature
Calories		Respiratory rate

Psychological

Work-rate decrement	Eye-blink rate
Errors	Boredom and other attitudinal factors

Source: Adapted from Singleton [38].

influenced by individual differences and, hence, is the more stable of the two measures for measuring the loads imposed by a particular work task. Both measures are needed, according to Davis et al.

In measurement of heart rate, Davis et al. fastened two Beckman biopotential electrodes to the skin on either side of the chest. The electrodes were connected to a Biocom FM telemetry system. Heart rate was measured at rest before a given work cycle, during each minute of the work cycle, and continuously for 3 min during the recovery period. Measurements were taken throughout the work day.

Oxygen consumption measurements consisted of determining the minute volume of expired air and its concentration in oxygen. Analysis of the carbon dioxide was not considered to be necessary. Oxygen consumption, in kilocalories per minute, was taken during the last 5 min of the work cycle using a Max Planck respirometer and a Beckman C_2 oxygen analyzer. Measurements were made at hourly intervals throughout the work day.

Figure 6-8 shows a worker being measured while performing his normal job. A backpack respirometer and mask are shown. The experimenter is monitoring heart rate over his headphones.

Standards for Energy Output

Lehmann [27] calculated that 5 kilocalories (kcal)/min is the maximum energetic output a normal male worker can afford. This is based upon a 4800 kcal/day of which 2500 kcal/day is for basal metabolism and leisure activities and 2300 kcal/day is for an 8-hour working day. Thus, the maximum kcal/min would be approximately 5; a normal load was estimated at 4.2 kcal/min.

According to Davis et al. [15], a load of 5 kcal/min at standard conditions

Figure 6-8 Heart rate and oxygen consumption being studied on an industrial task. (*Davis et al., 1969.*)

should not produce a heart rate of more than 120 beats min. Therefore, these values may be used as standards.

Christiansen [11] has provided a table for grading work in terms of energy expenditures (kcal) and oxygen consumption (liters/min).

	Energy expenditure		Approximate oxygen consumption liters/min
Grade of work	Kcal/min	Kcal/8 h	
Unduly heavy	over 12.5	over 6000	over 2.5
Very heavy	10.0–12.5	4800–6000	2.0–2.5
Heavy	7.5–10.0	3600–4800	1.5–2.0
Moderate	5.0–7.5	2400–3600	1.0–1.5
Light	2.5–5.0	1200–2400	0.5–1.0
Very light	under 2.5	under 1200	under 0.5

Figure 6-9 illustrates the energy costs of work in kcal/min for some common work tasks.

Scheduling Rest Breaks for Heavy Jobs

Higher caloric expenditures or unusually stressful environments will produce higher heart rates and, more significantly, the heart rate may increase throughout the working day, exceeding the maximum long-term limit. Figure 6-10 illustrates this effect for a laboratory task of lifting a 40-lb case from the floor to 20 in above the floor at a rate of 6 lifts/min [Lehmann, 27]. This task requires 6.7 calories per minute. The data shown is with a 2 min rest break after each 10 min of work. Obviously, these breaks are not of sufficient duration to prevent the climbing heart rate. A 7 min break after 10 min of work was found to be sufficient for this task with little increase in heart rate over a 60 min period.

The following are examples from Davis et al. [15] of workload measures for

Figure 6-9 Examples of energy costs of various types of human activities. *(Gordon, 1957. Copyright 1957, American Medical Association. Reprinted by permission.)*

a variety of industrial jobs using the techniques described previously. These data do not take rest breaks into consideration and are to illustrate comparatively the different energy costs for different jobs.

	Weighted working average	
Job	Energy expenditure (Kcal/min)	Heart rate (beats/min)
Unload coal cars in power plants	8.0	150
Handling 38-lb cans of chemicals	6.5	123
Stitch and dispose cases of 8-mm movie film	6.1	147
Tending cartoning machine no. 1	5.2	112
Cleaning floors and tables	4.5	112
Packing on conveyor	3.7	113
Bagging and packing paper rolls	2.5	113

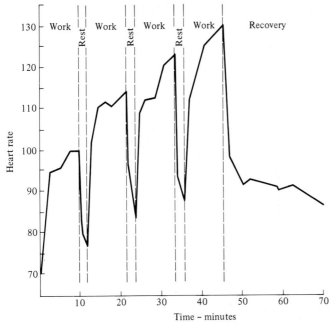

Figure 6-10　Heart-rate pattern for a lifting task with 2-minute rest breaks. *(Lehmann, 1958, in Davis et al., 1969. From* Human Factors, *1969, vol. 11, no. 2. Copyright 1969 by The Human Factors Society, Inc. and reproduced by permission.)*

It is apparent that "Unloading coal cars" requires a much longer rest period than would "Tending cartoning machine no. 1." Murrell [31] presents a formula for estimating the total amount of rest (scheduled or not scheduled) required for any given work activity.

$$R = \frac{T(K - S)}{K - 1.5} = \frac{60(6 - 4)}{6 - 1.5} = 27$$

where R is the rest required in minutes; T is the total working time; K is the average kcal/min of work; and S is the calories/min adopted as a standard (for example, 4 kcal/min). The constant, 1.5, is the approximate resting level in kcal/min. To illustrate the use of the formula, a task of 6 kcal/min performed over a 60-minute period would require a rest period of 27 min/h.

Figure 6-11 [McCormick, 30] graphically illustrates the recommended duration of rest breaks per hour and per 8-hour day as a function of the energy requirements of the work and the particular standard adopted. For example, if the standard were 5 kcal/min instead of 4 kcal/min in the problem above, it can be seen that a total rest break of 13 min/h would be required.

The scheduling of rest breaks as discussed above is based strictly on the energy costs of work. For light and moderate work tasks, some investigators recommend a 10- or 15-minute break in the middle of the morning and afternoon

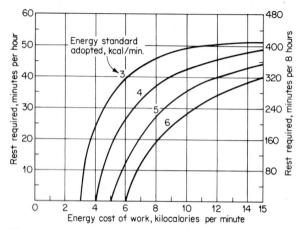

Figure 6-11   Total rest requirements per hour (left scale) and per 8 hours (right scale) for work activities of varying energy costs, kcal/min. *(Murrell's formulation, 1965, as developed by McCormick, 1976.)*

for daywork employees. Professional people prefer to take unscheduled breaks. Those working at continuous watch-keeping tasks involving much responsibility, such as air traffic controllers, require more frequent work breaks. The technology of scheduling rest pauses is a complex sociotechnical issue beyond the scope of this design-oriented text.

Heart Rate Recovery

Rate of body movement, as in jogging or sprinting, has a pronounced effect on heart rate and the duration of time after stopping that is required to reduce the heart rate to its initial rate. To test an individual's cardiovascular capabilities, the physical exam sometimes includes a "step test" in which the patient runs in place on a step for a specified duration. Heart rate is measured immediately and then after a period of several minutes.

Figure 6-12 depicts increasing heart rates of men while marching for 1600 m (1 mi). Note the increasing rates as the speed of marching increases above 8.1 km/h (5 mi/h). Also, note the differences in rate of recovery. At slower speeds recovery may be complete within three minutes for the young, male population, whereas for faster speeds it may take ten minutes or more for the heart rate to return to its resting level.

Methods Evaluation by Energy Measurements

Physiological measurements provide a basis for establishing which of several methods of performing an act requires the least energy. As examples, this section will present studies involving work postures, load carrying, and load lifting. In the next section, which deals with the biomechanics of work, other findings will be given in which muscular effort is measured by the electromyograph while the worker is performing various movements.

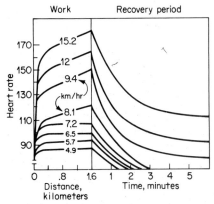

Figure 6-12 Heart rate during and after a march of 1 mile (1.6 km) at various speeds, km/hr (LeBlanc, 1957.)

Work Postures Vos [46] was interested in minimizing energy costs for agricultural tasks carried out on or near the ground. As one might expect, bending over with no arm support requires the most energy (3 kcal/min) while kneeling or squatting with the weight supported on one hand required less energy (2 kcal/min). Sitting on a low stool is better still, but not very practical if the task involves almost continuous movement, as in picking fruit or vegetables. A stool on wheels, as discussed in Chapter 13, might be applicable in flat terrain.

Load Carrying Datta and Ramanathan [13] found differences in load-carrying techniques as measured by oxygen expenditure. The double-pack method (one pack centered on the shoulders and the other on the chest) and the head method (pack on top of the head) resulted in the least oxygen consumption. Carrying two loads by the yoke method (on the ends of a bar) or in the two hands extended vertically to the sides (as we carry two suitcases) required more oxygen. Maintaining a postural balance that least affects the center of gravity is important to carry loads efficiently.

Load Lifting Tichauer [43] studied methods of lifting weights off the floor as measured by electromyograph recordings of muscles activity. He found less muscle activity involved when the load was close to the body while squatting and lifting with the legs.

Davies [14] reports research by Frederick [20] dealing with efficient methods of lifting boxes with two hands to various heights as measured by energy expended per foot pound. In general, lifting weights from 40 to 60 in requires less energy than lifting them from the floor to 20 in, from 20 in to 40 in, or overhead, 60 to 80 in. In work situations where workers must lift a number of heavy boxes, they should be located within this range of 40 to 60 in.

Table 6-2 provides maximum acceptable weights that can be lifted by male and female industrial workers in various height ranges.

Table 6-2 Distribution of the Maximum Acceptable Weights That Can Be Lifted by Male and Female Industrial Workers

	Percent of population				
	90	75	50	25	10
Lifts			(pounds)		
Floor to knuckle height					
Males	37	42	53	65	76
Females	19	21	33	39	46
Knuckle to shoulder height					
Males	40	47	55	62	69
Females	23	25	27	30	31
Shoulder to reach height					
Males	36	42	42	56	49
Females	18	22	27	31	35

Source: Chaffin and Ayoub [9].

Work Pace Frederick [20] has developed a formula for estimating the energy costs in kilocalories per hour for any number of lifts per hour, for any weight, and any lift range:

$$\text{Kcal}/h = \frac{f \times a \times w \times c}{1000}$$

where f = number of lifts/h
      a = lifting height in feet
      w = weight in lbs
      c = energy in gram calories per ft lb

Other values may be determined by manipulating the formula. For example, let us presume that 200 kcal/h were set as a limit for energy expenditure per hour. The question might be: What is the maximum number of lifts of a 40-lb weight that could be made to a height of 2 ft if it were determined that 4 gram calories per ft-lb was the estimated energy cost per lift? The formula would be:

$$f = \frac{200 \times 1000}{2 \times 40 \times 4} = 640 \text{ lifts per hour}$$

Frederick provides estimates of the energy consumption for lifting various weights in four height ranges (Figure 6-13).

Age and Sex Differences in Load-Lifting Job Standards The International Occupational Safety and Health Information Center [29] recommended maxi-

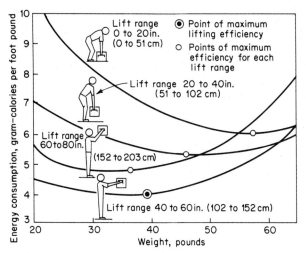

Figure 6-13 Energy consumption in lifting units of various weights and specified lift ranges. *(Frederick, 1959, as presented in Davies, 1972.)*

mum weights that may be lifted occasionally by males and females classified into six age groups (see Table 6-3).

Women craftworkers are increasing in numbers and legislation prohibits discrimination in job placement because of sex. Job descriptions and job designs may need to be altered to comply with this law. In general, female strength varies from 58 to 74 percent of male strength. Loads acceptable to 90 percent of the male population would be acceptable to only 50 percent of the industrial female population. Since women may be assigned to tasks formerly considered suitable for men only, the job may need to be redesigned in terms of maximum load lift and total work output. Also, work postures, based upon male body dimensions, may be unfavorable for women workers. Hand tools are often sized for the male hand [Ducharme, 18].

Two-Arm versus One-Arm Work Andrews [2] tested one of Gilbreth's canons of motion economy—two hands should work together. He compared

Table 6-3 Recommended Maximum Weights for Occasional Lifting by Any Method for Different Age Groups of Either Sex

	Age groups					
	14–16	16–18	18–20	20–35	35–50	Over 50
Male (lb)	33(15)*	42(19)	51(23)	55(25)	46(21)	36(16)
Female (lb)	22(10)	26(12)	31(14)	33(15)	29(13)	22(10)

*Values in parentheses are in kilograms.
Source: International Occupational Safety and Health Center [29] and as given in McCormick, 1976.

one-armed and two-armed tasks in terms of the increase in energy expenditure rates required to accomplish the same results. At higher levels of a dynamic task (cranking) with a load from 30 to 40 watts and at all levels of a static (pull) task of 10 to 30 watts, the increase in energy expenditure rate was, in fact, significantly lower for the two-armed method than for the one-armed method.

BIOMECHANICAL HAZARDS IN WORKPLACE DESIGN

The design of the workplace may subject the worker's anatomy and physiology to excessive and highly concentrated stresses and strains. Persistence of these stresses may lead to health disorders and deformities of the anatomy.

An awkward posture may be imposed by the equipment provided and the workplace arrangement. Examples are operators who stand on one leg while operating foot controls or bend, lean, and stretch to reach machinery in maintenance tasks. Static loads on the cervical vertebrae may lead to lesions of the spine. Improperly designed hand tools may inflame the wrist tendons, obstruct the flow of blood in the palm, or call for the use of weaker muscles. Aside from the hazards, a secure grasp and efficiency of work may be compromised. Postures, techniques for manually handling materials, hand-tool design, and seat design are four areas where the biomechanical specialist has been most concerned. Seat design will be discussed in Chapter 7.

Work Postures and Materials Handling

Pearson and Ayoub [33] mention a condition known as "lasters' back," which is a disability of shoemakers, who work in an unnatural posture with the head inclined to the right while standing on one leg. It is manifested in a projecting right-shoulder blade, a raised position of the right shoulder, and other backbone abberations. According to Brown [7], lifting injuries include lower-back sprain (32 percent), hernias (12 percent), and slipped discs (4 percent). He also noted that 60 percent of lifting injuries were due to lifting objects beyond the worker's physical capability. Material handling devices should be used wherever feasible.

Table 6-4 summarizes a few of the biomechanical recommendations in regard to postures for working, lifting, reaching, and applying forces [Tichauer, 41].

Factors Influencing Manual Materials Handling Chaffin and Ayoub [9] have discussed manual materials handling as comprising four components: the characteristics of the worker, the material container, the task, and the work practices. Singularly and collectively they pose hazards, but specific standards have not been developed for the variety of interactions. Worker characteristics include age, sex, body build, sensory motor skills, training, and health. Material container characteristics include its dimensions, location of the unit center of gravity with respect to the worker, grasping aids (handles), and stability of the load, for example, liquids. Task characteristics include the movement distance, frequency, duration and pace of movement, foot traction, and work environ-

Table 6-4   Materials Handling Postures and Workplace Design

Recommendation	Research finding
Keep elbows down while performing wrist movement tasks at a table.	If the height of the chair is 3 in too low relative to the work surface, this will introduce a 45° elbow angle stressing the shoulder and chest muscles (upper arm rotations is restricted).
Keep the object near the center of gravity in lifting; minimize loads on the vertebral column.	Lifting a 10 lb box that is 3 × 3 ft and 1-ft wide exerts the same bending moment as a compact 32 lb weight held close to the abdomen (Figure 6-14).
Consider sex differences and avoid "covert" lifting (lifting the weight of one's own head, trunk, or limbs; for example, in bending over).	When bending over to lift off of the floor, women have 15% greater stress on their backs. This is due to the socket of their hip joint being several inches in front of the center of gravity of the body. Lifting off a surface at least 12 in high minimizes sex differences.
Keep the forward reach short.	Frequent forward-reaching tasks performed by women should not be farther out than about 16 in. Age and health affect structure of the spine and minimize reach.
Make the movements slightly arced rather than straight-line fashion.	Hinged joints function better with arcing movements. Only one muscle is contracted while straight-line movements require coordination of two muscles.

Source: Adapted from Tichauer [41].

ment. Work practices include posture and lifting technique, administration and organization of safety/hygiene function.

Awkward Lifting   In general, deep containers tend to increase the horizontal distance between the person and the center of gravity (c.g.) of the object being lifted. Figure 6-14 provides a formula by Tichauer [42] for calculating the bending moments on a person's back (sacrolumbar joint) as a function of the object's weight and the distance to the box's c.g. Workers often stoop over to pick up large cardboard boxes stacked in columns some distance from the worker's c.g. If the weight is over 35 lbs, excessive stress is placed on the lower back. When lifting, a worker's hands should be no lower than 20 in from the floor nor should they be higher than the shoulders (also, this decreases the possibility of dropping the load). Lifting loads assymetrically from one side of the body should always be avoided. Two people should carry a load (with

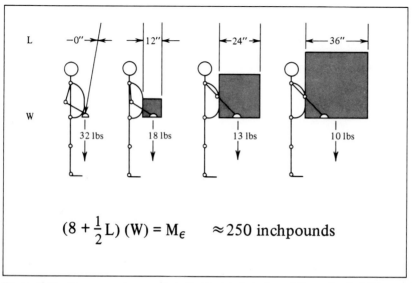

$$(8 + \frac{1}{2}L)\,(W) = M_\epsilon \quad \approx 250 \text{ inchpounds}$$

Figure 6-14 The moment concept applied to the derivation of biomechanical lifting equivalents. Examples show loads all producing approximately equal bending moments on the sacro-lumbar joint. *(Tichauer, 1978.)*

handles) if it is over 20 in (51 cm) in breadth or requires a single worker's hands to be extended more than 16 in (41 cm) in front of the hips.

Quick Lifting   We often lift quickly hoping to reduce the total time under stress. However, the increased accelerations may double the peak stresses on the musculoskeletal system. The implication is that one should always use a normal, smooth, well-controlled movement of loads. Muscle fatigue contributes to injuries, so rest allowances should be scheduled according to stress limits based on heart rate and energy expenditure rates, as discussed previously.

Sustained Muscular Exertion and Performance

One should not assume that because a job involves sedentary activities at a desk there is no local muscular fatigue. Sustained muscular exertion leads not only to complaints of discomfort, but also to decreases in performance. After sustained muscular exertion in supporting the forearm and hand in space, there is increased muscular tremor and greatly increased time is needed to perform tasks requiring precise positioning of the hands [Lance and Chaffin, 25]. Immediately after sustained exertion, one tends to overestimate light loads, producing more overshoots of targets when attempting fast, discrete hand movements [Sharum and Chaffin, 37]. When the muscles involved are fatigued, electromyogram (EMG) measures have shown a large shift in EMG power from about 40 Hz to below 30 Hz (60 percent of the total surface EMG power is then in the 4 to 30 Hz range) (see Figure 6-15). This shift is accompanied by reports of cramping with

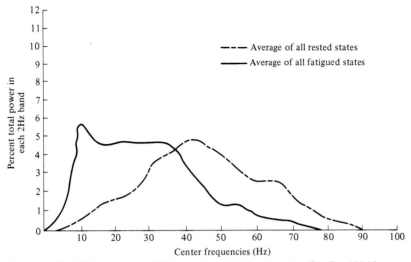

Figure 6-15 Shift in average EMG spectra with fatigued state. *(Chaffin, 1971.)*

deep, intermittent hot pains. Chaffin [8] has termed these symptoms as indicative of a Class II muscle fatigue. Table 6-5 indicates some of the other performance changes associated with various classifications of muscle fatigue.

Chaffin and colleagues have conducted a series of studies measuring the effects of various work postures upon localized muscle fatigue. The following are examples.

Shoulder Abduction Angle   If one holds the hands close together in front of the body and then lifts the elbows, one may visualize angles formed between the vertical axis and a line through the upper arm. The anatomy permits lifting the elbows above shoulder level up to as much as 120°. This is a very tiresome posture. However, some work tasks, such as operating a straight-angle soldering iron on a flat workbench, may require lifting the elbows high with the forearms angled down. Chaffin found that the higher one lifts the elbows above 30°, the less time the elbows need be held in that posture to achieve Class II muscle fatigue. Fatigue was measured both by discomfort ratings and surface EMG power spectral shifts toward the lower frequencies. Figure 6-16 presents the average fatigue time data, and Figure 6-17 illustrates a soldering iron that would permit performing the task without lifting the elbows very high.

Hand Positions   Employing similar methods, Chaffin found that the time to reach Class II fatigue decreased with hand reach heights and horizontal distances. For example, a person holding a 1 lb weight held only 12 inches (30.5 cm) from the seat reference point did not reach Class II fatigue for about 23 min, whereas the same weight held 20 in (51 cm) away fatigued the holder in about 5 min. (Vertical height was 12 in above a 30-in (76.2 cm) table top in both

Table 6-5   Effects of Muscle Fatigue States on Performance and Bicep EMG Condition

Definitions of muscle fatigue states

Performance conditions:	Muscle fatigue state classifications			
	I	II	III	IV
Muscle discomfort	Realization of "tightness" or "slight cramping"	"Cramping" continuous with deep, "hot" pain intermittent	"Hot" pain continuous with desire to abandon task	Unable to sustain activity
Increase in eye-hand coordination test times	105%	110%	116%	122%
Increase in hand tremor	138%	225%	300%	350%
Increase in hand precision positioning times	no data	no data	155%	230%
Increase in bias of light force sensing ability	no data	no data	140%	200%
Increase in vertical movement over-shoot	no data	no data	120%	150%
Corresponding biceps EMG conditions below:				
% Increase 4–30 Hz EMG power	19%	32%	42%	49%
% Decrease 40–70 Hz EMG power	5%	10%	15%	20%
% Decrease 60–100 Hz EMG power	9%	15%	17%	20%

Source: Chaffin [8].

instances.) These data support the recommendations in Table 6-4 with observable measures of fatigue correlated with the lifting postures.

Even when there is an elbow support, it was found for a series of weights from 5 to 20 lb that fatigue was much more rapid with a 140° elbow angle (entended arm) than with a 90 or 85° angle.

Head Tilt   Looking through a microscope or reading a book on a flat surface may involve a posture of leaning the head forward for long durations.

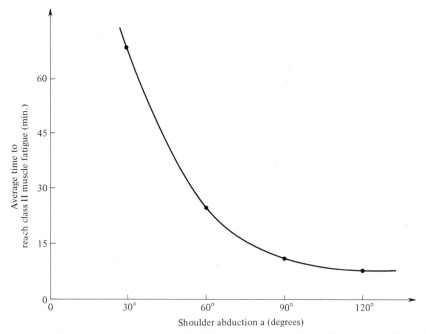

Figure 6-16 Average time to shoulder fatigue versus shoulder abduction angle for continuous holds. *(Chaffin, 1971.)*

This covert lifting of the head stresses the neck muscles. The greater the angle of head tilt (30, 45, 60°), the less time to reach Class II fatigue of the neck extensor muscles. However, 15° forward produced no discomfort or EMG change after 6 h. The obvious design solution is to provide for workpieces to be tilted up rather than to lie flat on a surface. Microscopes should not involve looking downward and reading material could be mounted on the wall or a sloping stand similar to those used by orchestra musicians.

Figure 6-17 Redesigned soldering irons to relieve shoulder fatigue. *(Chaffin, 1971.)*

Table 6-6   Hand-Tool Design Criteria Based upon Biomechanical Analysis

Design criteria	Effects of incorrect design
Use offset tool handles for pliers; keep wrists straight while rotating forearm and hand.	Radial deflection while rotating wrists leads to tennis elbow; deflection of wrist outward while rotating outward may inflame wrist tendons (tenosynovitis).
Size the handle to the user; avoid form-fitted grips that are incompatible with hand sizes.	If too large or too small, the metal ridges cause discomfort to joints of fingers and reduce the force that can be applied.
Use plastic grips on metal handles of pliers.	Gripping tightly with bare hand can cause stress concentration.
Redesign handles of tools such as paint scrapers so they do not press against the palms.	Obstruction of the blood flow to tissue (compression ischemia) may be due to the handle shape or how it is held in the palm.
Use handles that absorb vibration on pneumatic drills and other vibrating hand tools.	Vibrating power tools may cause "white finger syndrome." Parts of the body will react in resonance with certain critical frequencies, causing physical ailments (numbness, swelling of hand tissues).
Avoid use of rachet screwdrivers over long periods.	Outward rotation of the forearm uses strong biceps, but inward rotation uses weaker muscles that quickly fatigue.
Apply forces and torques with the elbow at 85°. Move close to the work object.	Torquing a screwdriver with extended arm resulted in sore arms for 23 of 35 female workers.
Provide for secure grasp of tools and objects.	If glove fingers are too thick, pressures between the fingers may result in an insecure grasp. Also, flexing the wrist (forward) reduces ability to hold a rod securely. Keep wrist straight.

Source: Adapted from Tichauer [41].

Hand-Tool Design

Table 6-6 summarizes some hand-tool design criteria again based upon a biomechanical analysis of the worker-tool system.

In addition to those mentioned in Table 6-6, a few other observations regarding tool design are as follows:

- Use power tools wherever feasible.
- Design gripping surfaces to prevent slipping.
- Provide a funnel to direct a screwdriver to a test point where there is a danger to adjacent structure and possible hazards.
- Modify the tips of tweezers and other pickup devices for compatibility with the shape and size of the components.

• In packaging units that require removal or adjustment of components, allow sufficient clearances between components and sufficient access space to operate the torquing tools. Tables have been developed giving the "swept profiles" or space envelopes for a variety of manual torquing tools [Huchingson and James, 23]. Long delays could occur if a limited arc of rotation is necessitated by an obstacle internally or if the access hole is too small for the worker to reach and torque.

Tichauer [41] has demonstrated that improperly designed hand tools can induce biomechanical stress. In a classic study by Western Electric [Damon, 12], it was found that standard straight-arm pliers induce biomechanic stress on the wrists, elbow and shoulder. The straight arms necessitated that the wrist be deflected or bent sideways. Even then the axis of rotation of the tool did not coincide completely with the axis of rotation of the forearm. From an anatomical standpoint the pliers should have the arms bent or offset so they may be grasped similar to a pistol handle. The modified handle in common use today does not require that the wrist be bent in an awkward and tiring posture.

Yoder et al. [48] reported a similar problem with standard diagonal cutting pliers in combination with an awkward work position. Workers complained of forearm and wrist fatigue because of repetitively closing the hand with the wrist at an awkward angle. Part of the problem was that the first and second fingers could not provide much contractive force in squeezing. Two modified tool designs that were believed to allow more work by the powerful muscles were evaluated. Electromyographic recordings were taken on the flexor digitorium muscles of 21 female employees. Results support the superiority of one modified plier design (Figure 6-18).

EMG energy levels increased for significantly more women with this design than with either the standard design or the other modified design. Hence, more muscles were being used in cutting. Changing the hand orientation relative to the work surface may also have helped alleviate the problem.

Techniques in Biomechanics

According to Tichauer [42] a biomechanical profile is the joint record of motion characteristics and muscular effort necessary to produce it. The devices used are: the *electrogoniometer* for measuring the angular displacement of limb segments about a joint, and the *electromyograph* for measuring muscle activity during a movement. Displacement, velocity, and acceleration of an anatomical reference point may be measured by *kinesiometers*. The *myograms* (ink tracings) indicate the sequencing and effectiveness of muscular activity. These are recorded simultaneously with the parameters of motion, thus providing a measure of the effort associated with making the motion.

An example of a biomechanical profile applied to a simple workplace problem is a worker throwing a finished article into a bin. The tossing motion may involve a hypertension of the wrist and muscular effort. According to

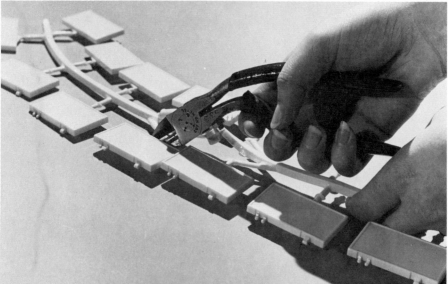

Figure 6-18 Standard diagonal cutting pliers in use, upper figure; modified tool and cutting position, lower figure. *(Yoder et al., 1973. From* Human Factors, *1973, vol. 15, no. 2. Copyright 1973 by The Human Factors Society, Inc. and reproduced by permission.)*

Tichauer, the act may not be possible by workers with a wrist disease or may be difficult for employees of a certain age. Changing the location of the bin so that disposal by tossing is unnecessary may be the design solution.

SAFETY ENGINEERING IN WORKPLACE DESIGN

As we have seen, the work physiologist is quantifying whole-body energy expenditure for a variety of industrial jobs and the biomechanics effort is examining work practices, workplace design, and tool designs for localized fatigue and potential safety hazards. Also, industrial engineers have long recognized that healthful work postures and rest pauses are needed for high productivity under heavy loads. Still another discipline—occupational safety engineering—has taken a systematic approach to recognizing, analyzing, and controlling hazards wherever they may occur within industry.

The Occupational Safety and Health Act (OSHA) of 1970 [34] assigned responsibility to the employer for reducing hazards and providing healthful working conditions at the place of employment. The law set safety and health standards, established an organization, National Institute of Occupational Safety and Health (NIOSH) for enforcing the standards, and authorized safety research and training of specialists to become familiar with the standards. Similarly, it would behoove industry to have persons knowledgeable in safety engineering and industrial hygiene.

Faulkner [19] noted that attitudes have polarized toward this movement for higher safety standards. Some were concerned that it would result in a suffocating mass of federal regulations, some of which were unnecessarily stringent and costly. However, he points out, OSHA-mandated changes in the manufacturing process may provide the industrial engineer an opportunity to introduce additional changes to improve efficiency at the same time. Also, the industrial engineer, who is involved in the initial phase of manufacturing system design, is in an excellent position to introduce safety in design right along with efficiency in design. He or she must insure that work practices reflected in job designs are compatible with OSHA standards [17]. Another legislation, the Equal Employment Opportunity Act (EEO), which forbids discrimination on the basis of age, sex, and marital status, also introduces a need to redesign workspace for slightly smaller and weaker bodies, as already noted in the biomechanics and work physiology sections.

Situational Approach to Hazard Reduction

Safety engineering typically takes the approach that potential hazards leading to accidents may be due to the interaction of the task, the human, and the environment. This situational approach is in contrast to older approaches such as the accident-prone individual. There is still an interest in identifying the characteristics of people who frequently have accidents and there is still interest in safety campaigns and improved methods for changing attitudes about safe practices. Pearson and Ayoub [33] have been highly critical of safety contests and zero defect approaches. Punitive measures may stifle the workers' reporting

Table 6-7 Safety Engineering Design Guidelines in Workplace Design

- Design equipment so that it is physically improbable that the worker would do something that would hurt herself or himself (it is fail-safe or impossible to be hurt unless a conscious effort is made to circumvent the design). Examples are:
  - ▲ A rotary blade that will not start unless a guard is in place.
  - ▲ Interlocks that prevent operation unless the worker's appendages are in a safe position.
    - ★ A classic illustration is a forming press for shaping metals, which requires two controls to start it so one hand cannot be inadvertently under the press.
  - ▲ One-way installations
    - ★ Connecting pins that are assymetrical so they will fit into a connector cable plug in only one way rather than 180° out of phase.
- Cover or guard all moving parts of machinery that could cut a worker or fly off.
- Use a hood over equipment giving off noxious fumes.
- Provide convenient fire extinguishers and an automatic sprinkling system.
- Use nonslip surfaces on floors and stairways. Eliminate steep ramps used with rolling devices.
- Use reliable equipment that will not fail at unscheduled times or explode.
- Eliminate design features associated with accidents; redesign workspace to eliminate awkward postures, to reduce fatigue, and to keep worker alert while performing repetitive tasks.
- Label hazards clearly and conspicuously.
- Provide protective equipment free or at costs (hard hats, unbreakable eyeglasses or goggles, safety shoes, ear muffs and plugs, aprons and gloves that will not conduct electricity).
- Provide warning devices and feedback in control devices and displays.

accidents, thinking they will be held at fault rather than design or work practices.

Although direct approaches at modifying human behavior are frequently useful, the emphasis in safety engineering is clearly on design changes. Table 6-7 illustrates some safety engineering measures in workplace design. As we shall see in Chapters 7, 8, and 9, safety engineering is an important criterion in facility design and environmental design.

Techniques for Hazard Analysis

Safety engineers analyze hazards in several ways: (1) assessment measures such as accident statistics; (2) activity evaluations; (3) predictive models. Statistics such as accident rates are viewed by Ayoub [4] as useful for assessing the overall performance of a safety program and setting target goals, but they offer less potential for understanding cause-and-effect relationships. Despite the limitations of abstracted statistics, fully documented accident investigations can be a useful source of information. Isolated accidents may be due to human error, but when several operators make the same mistake with respect to the same equipment, the error may well be in the design.

Activity evaluations involve safety inspections, job safety analysis, and critical incident reports of near-accidents. This approach attempts to identify hazardous features at the workplace before they are manifested in accidents.

Predictive models attempt to recognize and control hazards at the design stage by fault tree analysis, failure mode-and-effect analysis, and other techniques. Predictive models are sometimes very time-consuming and are still in their infancy.

Techniques for Hazard Control

Before specific measures of control are recommended, it is first necessary to identify how much hazard can be tolerated at the workplace. Every activity involves some small risks, but OSHA standards [17] define precisely safe exposure limits. (See Chapters 8 and 9 for environmental standards.)

Hazard control measures can be applied to the source, to the path, or to the receiver. They can be applied to various hazards such as mechanical energy [OSHA, 40], noise [National Safety Council, 1], electrical [1], chemical [Stellman and Daum, 39], and thermal stress [Leithead and Lind, 28]. Table 6-8 illustrates control techniques in these areas.

In general, it can be seen that source control is achieved through various techniques such as guarding, enclosing, insulating, or isolating the source. It is also achieved by reducing speed, forces, or physical demands.

Path control is achieved by increasing the distance between the source and the receiver and by applicable techniques such as muffling noises, grounding electricity, and ventilating the atmosphere.

Receiver control is accomplished by both engineering and work method changes. Providing protective equipment, pull-away devices, aids to placing, feeding, and ejecting work pieces are illustrative engineering changes. Method changes include acclimatization to heat, salt and water provisions, work-rest schedules, limiting exposure times, and so forth.

Safety Mangement

Although the hazard control activities could be accomplished by a generalist in a smaller plant, the diversity of responsibilities generally calls for a specialist in a large organization. Safety performance may be achieved by a management program to include assurance of acceptable exposure levels, identifying problem areas, defining safety goals, and providing methods for compliance with OSHA standards. Safety engineering may also recommend how to spend a safety budget to best achieve safety goals [Ayoub, 4].

Safety or loss control, like human factors in design, is embraced in an attitude toward all equipment and work practices. This outlook is shared by several disciplines, since reduction of accidents and long-term disabilities is a major goal of many industrial efforts, management, and certainly the workers themselves.

Maintainability in Design

Tool design, discussed previously, is only one facet of the problem of design for maintainability. Human factors engineering interfaces with maintainability in the design and packaging of prime equipment, design of test equipment and tools, and design of maintenance procedures and manuals.

Table 6-8   Examples of Control Techniques Currently Being Used to Combat Environmental and Machine Hazards

		Control measures	
Hazard	Source	Path	Receiver
Mechanical energy (40)	Enclosure guards (fixed or adjustable) Interlocking guards (mechanical or electrical) Reduction in speed Limitation of stroke	Guarding by location (rope off area, and so forth) Remote control	Education Rules and regulations regarding clothing Pull-away devices Aids for placement, feeding, ejecting of work pieces Two hand-trip switch buttons
Noise (1)	Enclosure Surface treatment Reduction of impact forces	Building layout Increase distance Channel away Acoustic filters Mufflers Path deflectors	Protective equipment Earmuffs Earplugs Limiting exposure time Education
Electrical (1)	Low voltage instrumentation Fuses, circuit Insulation Lock outs Labeling and test points	Grounding Use of ground fault detectors	Protective equipment Education
Thermal stress (28)	Shielding Insulation Painting Ventilation Limiting physical demands of the job	General ventilation	Selection and placement Acclimatization program Adequate supply of water and salt Special clothing (ventilated suits) Proper work-rest schedules Limiting exposure time
Chemical hazards (39)	Isolation Substitution Change in process	Ventilation	Protective equipment, respirators, and so on.

Source: Ayoub [4].

The five major considerations in human factors design for maintainability are: accessibility, standardization, modularization, identification, and safety considerations.

Accessibility refers to three aspects: (1) The arrangement of parts so that the most frequently replaced items can be reached first (without removal of other parts that seldom fail and, hence, are less frequently removed). In automobile maintenance it is sometimes necessary to perform several operations because the failed item was not easily accessible. (2) Visual accessibility means planning the package design so that the item can be viewed quickly. Sometimes the solution may be as simple as locating test points in one built-in unit or providing spring-loaded hinges or quick-opening fasteners so the person does not need to remove screws or bolts. At other times, windows, mirrors, or even fiber optics may be employed to enhance visibility of components. (3) Anthropometric accessibility may mean providing sufficient space around a component so that the person can grasp it or can work with torquing tools (as noted in tool design). The solution may imply also pullout drawers, rollout racks, or locating internal components for ease of access. Captive bolts without nuts make it easier to change a license plate.

Standardization was discussed in relation to controls and displays. Here it may refer to interchangeable parts throughout a model so that replacement is simplified. It may also refer to standardized locations of components under the hood of a vehicle or standardized tools and procedures.

Modularization or unitization refers to a design that permits removal and replacement of an entire unit so that it is not necessary to work in the field on a particular component. Identification refers to the coding or stamping of components so they are easily distinguishable. Color-coded electric wires reduce the likelihood of connections to the wrong terminals.

Safety considerations in maintainability include restrictions in locating internal controls in areas of high voltage, hot components, and so forth. Safety engineering with respect to consumer products is discussed in Chapter 14.

Many human errors are due to poorly designed maintenance manuals. They should be written for the user with clear schematics, simple language, and a minimum of referrals to other manuals.

QUESTIONS AND PROBLEMS

1 Each of us has a workstation, even if it be a desk and chair or, perhaps, a shop in our garage. Measure and record the dimensions of your workstation and chair. Compare the measures with the dimensional data given in this chapter and record any deviations and the extent and direction of deviations. Discuss your findings and make recommendations for an improved workstation layout.
2 An industrial employee performs three different jobs each hour with an equal time on each job. A work physiologist measured the kilocalories per minute for each job and found they were respectively: 5.5, 3.0, and 6.5 kcal/min. Using a standard of 4.5 kcal/min, determine the total rest period the worker should have each hour (according to Murrell's formula).
3 Using a modification of Frederick's formula, determine the maximum number of lifts per hour given a 30-lb weight lifted from the floor to a height of 2 feet and consuming 4 gram calories per foot-pound. Assume that 200 kcal/hour is the maximum safe energy expenditure.
4 Approximately what percentage of the female population could lift a weight of 30 lb from floor to knuckle height? Would OSHA recommend such a lift if the women were 55 years old?
5 Using Tichauer's formula, calculate the inch-pounds on a male dock loader's back when lifting a 40-lb box that is 40 in in depth (measured horizontally in front of him).

Next, recalculate the lifting equivalent value assuming the weight were housed in a box only 10 in in depth. What is the difference in pound-inches? What do you conclude was the cause of the difference in bending moments?

6   Offset tool handles have been shown to induce less stress on the wrist, elbow, and shoulders. Let us suppose that an inventor claims that a 19-in (14- to 24-in) bend at the ends of *any* manually handled object will make it a natural extension of the hand, wrist, and arm, thus allowing greater forces to be applied and reducing stress on the forearm. Examples of applications are tennis rackets, fishing rods, pool cues, hammers, writing pens, canes and crutches, wheelbarrows, handles, cooking pot handles, and door knobs. Comment on why you think that bends in these types of tool handles might or might not be successful.

7   Figure 6-19 presents the present layout of an office complex consisting of nine professionals, five secretaries, and a receptionist. In addition, there are frequent visitors and six work areas or rooms (conference, reproduction, laboratory, stores, coffee area, and mail area).

      Following complaints of long-distance walks and general inefficiency, the

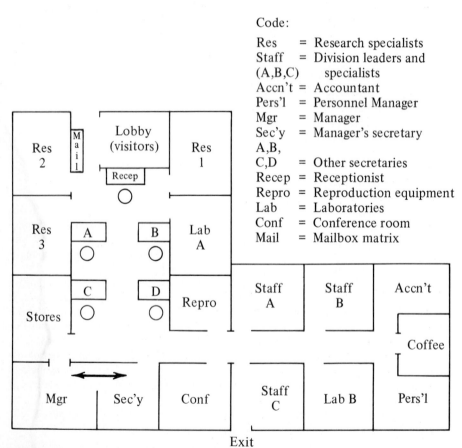

Code:

Res = Research specialists
Staff = Division leaders and
(A,B,C)   specialists
Accn't = Accountant
Pers'l = Personnel Manager
Mgr = Manager
Sec'y = Manager's secretary
A,B,
C,D = Other secretaries
Recep = Receptionist
Repro = Reproduction equipment
Lab = Laboratories
Conf = Conference room
Mail = Mailbox matrix

Figure 6-19   Current layout of office complex (problem).

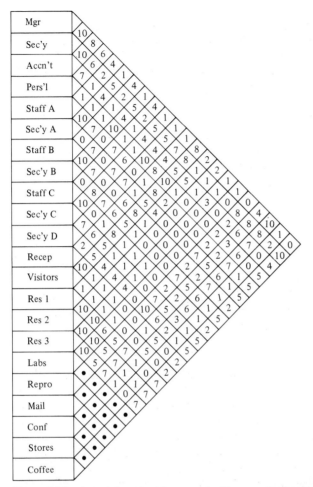

Figure 6-20 Association chart for current office complex (problem).

activities of each employee (the numbers of visits to other employees and to work areas) were recorded for 1 week. These frequencies were then classified into categories from 0 to 10 (10 means the most frequent contacts; 0, the fewest contacts). This information is summarized in an association chart, Figure 6-20.

Examine the association chart and then rearrange the assignments of personnel and work areas to offices. Redraw the floor plan given in Figure 6-19. Draw double-arrow linkage lines between all persons or work areas that had a use-frequency rating of 10 only (an example is given for the manager-secretary link). The analysis should include all use-frequency linkages, rather than 10 only, but doing so would clutter your drawing. Now compare these distances with those required by the original layout. Have you shortened at least 12 of the lines? Your answer should include a redrawing of the office complex with room assignments and 17 lines with arrows, all of short distance and with as few crossing as possible. Other link values should be considered in the layout but need not be shown.

REFERENCES

1   *Accident Prevention Manual for Industrial Operations,* National Safety Council, Chicago, 1969.
2   Andrews, R. B.: Estimating values of energy expenditure from observed values of heart rate, *Human Factors,* vol. 9, no. 6, December 1967.
3   Apple, J. M.: *Plant Layout and Materials Handling,* 2d ed., Ronald Press, New York, 1963.
4   Ayoub, M. A.: The problem of occupational safety, *Industrial Engineering,* vol. 7, no. 4, April 1975.
5   Ayoub, M. M.: Workplace design posture, *Human Factors,* vol. 15, no. 3, June 1973, pp. 265–268.
6   Barnes, R. M.: *Motion and Time Study,* 3d ed., Wiley, New York, 1949.
7   Brown, J. R.: *Manual Lifting and Related Fields; An Annotated Bibliography,* Labor Safety Council of Ontario, Ontario Ministry of Labor, Ontario, Canada, 1972.
8   Chaffin, D. B.: Localized muscular fatigue—definition and measurement, Paper presented to the 56th annual meeting of the Industrial Medical Association, Atlanta, Georgia, April 19–22, 1971.
9   Chaffin, D. B. and M. M. Ayoub: The problem of manual materials handling, *Industrial Engineer,* vol. 7, no. 7, July 1975, pp. 24–29.
10 Chapanis, A.: *Research Techniques in Human Engineering,* Johns Hopkins Press, Baltimore, 1959.
11 Christiansen, E. H.: Physiological evaluation of work in the Nykroppa iron works, in W. F. Floyd and A. T. Welford (eds.), *Ergonomics Society Symposium on Fatigue,* Lewis, London, 1953, pp. 93–108.
12 Damon, F. A.: The use of biomechanics in manufacturing operations, *The Western Electric Engineer,* vol. 9, 1965, pp. 11–20.
13 Datta, S. R. and N. L. Ramanathan: Ergonomics comparison of seven modes of carrying loads on the horizontal plane, *Ergonomics,* vol. 14, no. 2, 1971, pp. 269–278.
14 Davies, B. T.: Moving loads manually, *Applied Ergonomics,* vol. 3, no. 4, 1972, pp. 269–278.
15 Davis, H. L., W. T. Faulkner, and C. L. Miller: Work physiology, *Human Factors,* vol. 11, no. 2, April 1969.
16 Dreyfuss, H.: *The Measure of Man,* 2d ed., Whitney, New York, 1966.
17 Department of Labor, *Occupational Safety and Health Standards,* Federal Register, vol. 39, no. 125, Part II, June 27, 1974, pp. 23502–23828.
18 Ducharme, R. E.: Women workers rate "male" tools inadequate, *Human Factors Society Bulletin,* vol. 20, no. 4, April 1977.
19 Faulkner, T. W., The IE and OSHA, *Industrial Engineering,* vol. 7, no. 5, May 1975.
20 Frederick, S. W.: Human energy in manual lifting, *Modern Materials Handling,* vol. 14, no. 3, 1959, pp. 74–76.
21 Gordon, E. E.: The use of energy cost in regulating physical activity in chronic disease, *AMA Archives of Industrial Health,* vol. 16, November 1957, pp. 437–441.
22 Haygood, R. C., K. S. Teel, and C. P. Greening: Link analysis by computer, *Human Factors,* vol. 6, no. 1, February 1964.
23 Huchingson, R. D. and R. G. James: A preliminary design guide of human

engineering criteria for maintenance and repair of advanced space systems, LTV Astronautics Report No. 00.474, Contract NAS9-1670, June 1964, pp. 182–188.

24 Janousek, J. A.: Human factors engineering in manufacturing, *Human Factors,* vol. 11, no. 2, 1969, pp. 131–137.

25 Lance, B. M. and D. B. Chaffin: The effect of prior muscle exertions on simple movements, *Human Factors,* vol. 13, 1971, pp. 355–361.

26 LeBlanc, J. A.: Use of heart rate as an index of work output, *Journal of Applied Physiology,* vol. 10, 1957, pp. 275–280.

27 Lehmann, G.: Physiological measurements as a basis of work organization in industry, *Ergonomics,* vol. 1, 1958, pp. 328–344.

28 Leithead, C. S. and A. R. Lind: *Heat Stress and Heat Disorder,* Cassell, London, 1964.

29 *Manual Lifting and Carrying,* International Occupational Safety and Health Information Center, Geneva, CIS Information Sheet 3, 1962.

30 McCormick, E. J.: *Human Factors in Engineering and Design,* 4th ed., McGraw-Hill, New York, 1976.

31 Murrell, K. F. H.: *Human Performance in Industry,* Reinhold, New York, 1965.

32 Niebel, B. W.: *Motion and Time Study,* 5th ed., Richard D. Irwin, Inc., Homewood, Ill., 1972.

33 Pearson, R. G. and M. A. Ayoub: Ergonomics aids industrial accidents and injury control, *Industrial Engineering,* vol. 7, no. 6, June 1975, pp. 18–25.

34 Public Law 91-596, Occupational Safety and Health Act, Dec. 29, 1970.

35 Ricca, B.: *Physiological Basis of Human Performance,* Lea and Febiger, Philadelphia, 1967, pp. 105–106.

36 Rosenthal, M.: Application of human factors principles and techniques to the design of electronic production equipment, *Human Factors,* vol. 15, no. 2, 1973, pp. 137–148.

37 Sharum, J. and D. B. Chaffin: Force judgments decrements following muscular exertions, University of Michigan TR No. 13, 1970.

38 Singleton, W. T.: The measurement of man at work with particular reference to arrousal, in W. J. Singleton, J. G. Fox, and D. Whitfield (eds.), *Measurement of Man at Work,* Taylor and Francis, London, 1971, pp. 17–25.

39 Stellman, J. M. and S. M. Daum: *Work is Dangerous to Your Health,* Vintage Books, New York, 1973.

40 *The Principles and Techniques of Mechanical Grounding,* U.S. Department of Labor, OSHA 2057, August 1973.

41 Tichauer, E. R.: *Biomechanical Basis of Ergonomics,* Wiley Interscience, New York, 1978.

42 Tichauer, E. R.: Biomechanics sustains occupational safety and health, *Industrial Engineering,* vol. 8, no. 2, February 1976.

43 Tichauer, E. R.: A pilot study of the biomechanics of lifting in simulated industrial situations, *Journal of Safety Research,* vol. 3, no. 3, September 1971, pp. 98–115.

44 United States Air Force, Air Force Systems Command, AFSC DH 1-3, DN 2B12, January 1977, p. 4.

45 Van Cott, H. P. and R. G. Kinkade (eds.): *Human Engineering Guide to Equipment Design,* rev. ed., U.S. Government Printifg Office, Washington, D.C., 1972, pp. 392–393.

46 Vos, H. W.: Physical workload in different body postures while working near to or below ground level, *Ergonomics,* vol. 16, no. 6, 1973, pp. 817–828.

47 Whitehead, B. and M. Z. Eldars: An approach to the optimum layout of single-storey buildings, *The Architects Journal*, June 17, 1964, pp. 1373–1380.

48 Yoder, T. A., R. L. Lucas, and G. D. Botzum: The marriage of human factors and safety in industry, *Human Factors,* vol. 15, no. 3, June 1973, pp. 197–205.

49 Thomson, R. M.: "Design of Multi-Man Machine Work Area," in H. P. Van Cott and R. G. Kinkade (eds.), *Human Engineering Guide to Equipment Design,* rev. ed., U.S. Government Printing Office, Washington, D.C., 1972, chap. 10.

Chapter 7

Design of Buildings

In the previous chapter, the industrial workplace was spotlighted. In this chapter, design criteria are given for workspace in many different types of buildings, such as office buildings, family dwellings, and schools. Criteria are also presented for structures facilitating pedestrian movement therein (traffic spaces, doors, stairs) and for user habitation (seats, bathrooms, and so forth). Additional criteria applicable to the handicapped are discussed in Chapter 13.

The design recommendations are based largely upon human requirements: psychosocial needs, visual and auditory requirements, and anthropometric dimensions. Therefore, these design recommendations are generally applicable to any building. There are also functional requirements associated with the particular objectives of the facility and its plan for usage. A functional design and layout must be tailored to specific requirements determined by functional analysis.

The question of esthetic appeal has not been completely omitted. Psychosocial issues raise questions of acceptability, esthetic preferences, and meanings expressed by designs. These issues are discussed to the degree that studies have been conducted in which subjects rated various designs. However, innovation and creativity must remain the prerogative of the architect. The design information given is intended to supplement rather than to provide definitive guidelines for esthetic design of buildings.

The office population is growing at a rate of 1.3 million a year. Harris and Associates [Hodge, 21] surveyed 1047 office workers regarding their office environment in 200 statistical sampling areas across the United States. Seventy-four percent felt they could produce more in a day than they were presently producing if working conditions were changed. Deterrents to job output were lack of conversational privacy (ability to talk without being overheard), lack of visual privacy (the sense of being alone when necessary), and noise distraction. The survey also found that corporate heads and even office design professionals did not fully understand the sources of office worker satisfaction. Sixty percent of the designers emphasized remodeling, repainting, and refurnishing, whereas only 20 percent of the employees mentioned these as important. Employees wanted more personal space, more privacy, and a neater, better organized office appearance. They also believed that they should be consulted in planning their office and selecting equipment.

While even the optimum working environment cannot be a substitute for an interesting or satisfying job, the fact that management is sensitive to the employees needs may itself go a long way toward improving the worker's morale and possibly his or her productivity as well.

FUNCTIONAL AND PSYCHOSOCIAL CONSIDERATIONS

Table 7-1 itemizes certain functional and psychosocial considerations in building design with particular emphasis on room design and arrangement. Workspace must be tailored to the particular characteristics and activities of anticipated users.

Functional Usage

Facility layout specialists typically determine from analyses the rooms or work areas required. From the user's standpoint, one of the principal design considerations is providing a facility that includes the rooms and work areas necessary to perform essential tasks, but does not include unnecessary rooms. While this requirement may seem obvious, there is a continuing change in users' needs that must be reflected in the design. The middle-class American home provides an example. During the 1950s and 1960 single-family homes were constructed with both a living room (formerly called a parlor) and a family room, or den. As building costs per square foot skyrocketed, builders tended to build houses with a single, large living room. This decision was not to deny that families would like a formal living room, but rather that there were other rooms that took priority. Those with children recognized the need for a recreation room and sometimes converted two-car garages into such rooms. The separate dining room became a luxury in homes with few children where there was also a breakfast area or informal dining area near the kitchen. When such a special-occasion dining room existed, it could be used for other functions, such as a study or sewing room. The need for conveniently located additional bathrooms has taken higher priority in family homes.

Table 7-1   Functional and Psychosocial Considerations in Design of Building Interiors

Consideration	Design question	Measures and requirements
Functional usage	Are planned rooms really necessary? Are necessary rooms and areas provided?	Frequency and duration of room usage in similar usage facilities. Ratings of same
Functional layout	Are rooms and work areas arranged in a functional manner?	Frequency and importance of contacts between work areas. Sequence of use and functional groupings of activities.
Flexibility in room arrangements and furnishings within	Does design permit modification for changing needs? May furnishings be arranged in multiple ways?	Listing of planned future needs.
Minimum space requirements per person	Is sufficient space allotted per person to meet psychological and work needs?	Compare with criteria. Consider territoriality, personal space, and arrangements for defensible space.
Open and closed plans	Are worker needs better met by rooms, cubicles, or open work areas? How to design for noise?	Consider advantages of various plans. Measure preferences and efficiency.
Windows and no windows	Are worker needs better met by providing windows? How to select windows and building designs?	Consider advantages of work areas with and without windows. Planning for window design and location.
Room color	Should walls be painted various colors? Who should select colors?	Consider alternative color schemes; interview room users.
Background music	Should music be broadcast in work areas? If so what music and how to control it?	Consider nature of work tasks, user preferences; design for control.
Esthetics and meaning of visual forms	Do particular visual forms express the meaning planned by the architect?	Semantic differential scaling

Functional usage requirements could be assessed by asking dwellers to report the frequency of usage of various rooms and the purpose of such visits [Black, 6]. Another approach involves taking work-sample counts of the number of times per month that people enter a particular room and use furniture or equipment therein. One could determine the need for a piano room in a university student center by visiting a university of comparable size and composition and counting at randomly selected times the frequency of use of the piano and students present. The same approach could be applied to any facility where rooms were entered on a somewhat optional basis.

These approaches are applicable when buildings similar to the one being planned already exist and are in use. When no comparable facility exists it may be necessary to have potential users rate the importance of various rooms and the frequency and duration of contemplated usage. However, there is a danger of overestimation when asked what one would do in situations where there is no prior experience. The major point here is that simply patterning the design of a new facility after currently existing facilities may result in a mismatch with user needs when the current facilities are themselves deficient in some rooms and oversupplied in others.

Functional Layout

Functional layout refers to the arrangement of rooms and work areas by functional criteria. Facility layout specialists determine optimum arrangements based on analysis of functional requirements. In Chapter 6 the link analysis technique was introduced as a technique for locating functional-related activities next to one another. Efficient layouts may minimize the number of steps taken. In addition to *frequency* and *importance* as criteria for arrangement, other principles of arrangement include *functional groupings* (for example, all activities related to a particular industrial process located in one area) and *sequence of use* (for example, lining up work stations in the order of work flow).

McCormick [25] notes that frequency and importance are more important to *locating* components in a general area in a workplace and sequence of use and functional groupings are more applicable to *arranging* of components within a general area. The choice between functional groupings and sequence of use depends upon whether the activity is sequential in nature or if such a layout would necessitate a great deal of backtracking.

An effective layout must also consider environmental criteria such as noise, visual distractions, and, in some instances, odors. Becker [2] found in a survey of room arrangements for multifamily housing units that a majority of people did not like a combined living and dining room because of the odor of foods entering the living area. Environmental criteria are discussed in a subsequent section of this chapter.

Flexibility

A flexible arrangement is one that may be easily changed to accommodate changing functional needs. One argument for movable walls or partitions is ease of alteration with changing needs. Becker [2] found a preference for a partition between the dining room and living room, which could be removed depending upon the particular occupants' preference for an enclosed dining room or a common dining area/living area.

One viewpoint in the design of elementary schools subscribes to "creative space arrangements" and opposes the "egg-crate" school that divides classrooms permanently into equal-sized blocks [Erwin, 13]. Open plans that have no dividing walls between classes, or those that make use of bookshelves as dividers, permit the formation of large or small aggregations of students as needs change. The landscaped office or bank building also follows the open-plan concept using house plants, low screens, cabinets, and shelves as dividers. Open and closed plans are discussed subsequently.

Another approach to flexibility is the use of prefabricated, modular buildings or rooms where the entire room may be purchased and added to a facility almost overnight. Buildings may be constructed in such a way as to allow for planned expansion at a later date.

Periodically, users may want to rearrange furniture within a room. A room that is constrained by the placement of doorways and other permanent features so that no alternative arrangement of furnishings is feasible is objectionable to many occupants. Some homes have only one wall against which a long, four-cushion sofa may be placed. A room may also be constrained to a single furniture arrangement by the placement of electrical outlets (without use of extension cords), TV-cable outlets, and telephone connector cables. Planning for at least two furniture arrangements should be part of the initial room-design concept.

Minimum Space Requirements per Person

Later in this chapter physical space requirements to accommodate body movement, clearances, and visual needs are discussed. However, aside from these needs there has been considerable interest in the psychosocial needs of people in enclosed work spaces.

Territoriality   A characteristic of many types of communal animals and insects is a tendency to attack intruders that may enter their territory. Dogs may bark when a visitor comes to the door or even walks down the street. Newman [31] has defined territoriality as "the capacity of the physical environment to create zones of territorial influence." A single-family house is a territorial claim to land. Shrubs, fences, walls, and gates serve as symbolic indicators of this claim. One may also have an unspoken claim to a certain chair in the living room. A homemaker may resent others "taking over" the kitchen while she is preparing the meal.

Defensible Space   Newman also speaks of "defensible space" in relation to inhibiting crime. An area may have features which emphasize territoriality and a sense of community among the inhabitants which implies a safe, well-maintained living space. Newman found a higher crime rate when there were many apartment units opening into a common hallway. Also, high-rise apartment buildings and poor visual surveillance of people entering lobbies, entrances, and elevators are associated with crime. Smaller buildings with more entrances and good visual surveillance from L-shaped buildings provided defensible space.

Personal Space   While territoriality implies a more permanent claim to land, "personal space" is a portable, invisible boundary surrounding a person, within which an intruder is not welcome [Sommer, 33]. Fast [16] illustrated a similar concept with two men seated in a restaurant at a small table. One man placed his plate, silverware, and cigarette pack three-quarters of the way across the table in front of the other person's plate. The other person felt troubled or uneasy about the invasion of his half of the table.

Anecdotal examples of personal space and acceptable social distances are numerous. Unfortunately, it is difficult to provide a table of distances that have uniform meaning such as a distance for intimacy, a distance for confidential discussions, a distance for impersonal transactions with an individual, and a distance for public discussions. The problem is that there are cultural differences in acceptable distances and variations in distance with the nature of the social activity. For example, on a crowded bus or at a football game the permissible distance may shrink so that total strangers may be acceptable in very close proximity.

Despite the inability to prescribe design distances, by reducing the space allotted per person prolonged crowding does result in aggressive reactions in some people. Whether or not crowded homes can be designated as a prime contributor to crime, pathology, and maladjustment is still uncertain. McCormick [25] suggests that socially disorganized families may tend to migrate to crowded facilities so a positive correlation between density of people and pathology is not necessarily a cause-and-effect relation. In any event, there is a trend toward increasing the floor space per individual in work areas above the absolute minimum for physical movement.

Criteria for Space per Person   Two negatively correlated indices are often used to express the spatial adequacy of dwelling units: (1) Persons per room (PPR) is the total number of occupants divided by number of rooms. (2) SFPP (square feet per person) is the square feet allowed each occupant. Studies reported on space criteria are principally in the context of housing. Black [6] found that 0.69 PPR is the national average for housing and that acceptable limits are 1.00 to 1.20. Chombart de Lauwe [10] proposed the following criteria for categories of housing adequacy:

SFPP	Category	Percentage (121 houses)
Less than 130	Poor housing	2
131–215	Adequate	21
Over 215	Very good	77

The last column gives the percentage of houses meeting these criteria in a survey conducted in Salt Lake City [McCormick, 25]. Such criteria provide minimum guidelines, however; many middle-class families of four might feel a little cramped in a house with only 860 square feet of living space.

Woodson and Conover [42] provided recommended footage per person in a work area devoted to office space, engineering drafting, assembly, machine shops, and so forth. These recommendations were based on sound logical planning rather than experimentation. Sixty-five to 100 square feet per person was recommended, depending upon accessory equipment needed. They also recommended a maximum of two people to a 10 × 12 foot office and a maximum of one person to a 9 × 10 foot office. These recommendations would depend upon the amount of floor space occupied by equipment. Ideally, space should be specified in terms of useful space, exclusive of cabinets, machinery, and so forth. Some activities require private offices for confidential communications with clients, patients, or employees and for creative concentration. Shared offices or even open spaces are feasible for other activities involving little confidential conversation, activities which do not require unbroken concentration, and for which cooperation between workers is sometimes necessary.

Open Plan versus Closed Plan

The subject of open- and closed-plan offices is one of the more controversial issues in architectural design. There are at least two different types of closed-plan offices: (1) private offices for each individual worker with full-length, acoustically treated walls separating offices; (2) a small group of workers and their supervisor performing related activities in a single office (a total of two to five people). There are also at least two different open-plan offices: (1) large groups of people working in a single room with desks lined up in rows and columns in a maximum density plan (the number of persons per room may vary from six to hundreds); (2) large groups of people in a single carpeted room with desks staggered or nonparallel. Desks are generally more widely separated and divided by plants and file cabinets to symbolize separate work areas. This arrangement for clerical as well as managerial personnel is sometimes termed a "landscaped office" [Brookes, 8].

Between these extremes are semiclosed (or semiopen) plans where all or at least key personnel are housed in partitioned cubicles. The partitions serve as spatial delineators and have little or no acoustical function. The height of the partition is generally 7 to 8 ft. A cubicle is generally open in the front. A popular variation of the cubicle is an office with open doorway partitioned to a height of 40 inches with a transparent extension on top of the partition. Figure 7-1 illustrates two open plans and semiclosed office plans.

Unfortunately, limited research has been conducted comparing the various types of open and closed plans. Wells [40] conducted a study in Great Britain in which a group of office workers were asked their preferences for offices that varied from complete openness (one large room) to most closed (nine partitioned rooms). This was a comparison between what is defined here as the "type-2" closed office plan and the "type-1" open office plan. In addition, there were three divisions of the total room space—into two, four, and six smaller rooms. The study found that workers preferred the "most closed" office and disliked the others in direct relation to their degree of openness. Supervisors of small groups ranked the five layouts in exactly the same order as the workers. On

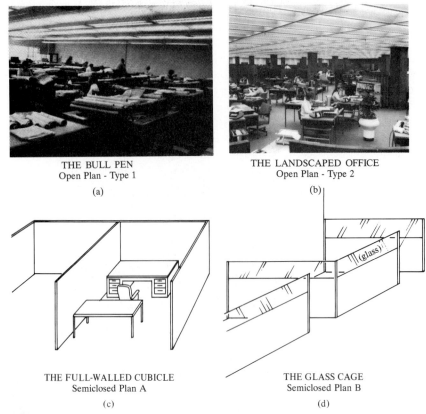

THE BULL PEN
Open Plan - Type 1

(a)

THE LANDSCAPED OFFICE
Open Plan - Type 2

(b)

THE FULL-WALLED CUBICLE
Semiclosed Plan A

(c)

THE GLASS CAGE
Semiclosed Plan B

(d)

Figure 7-1   Illustration of open and semiclosed office plans *(Landscaped office from McCormick, 1976.)*

the other hand, managers liked the four-room office the best, followed by the two and one-room offices, and they ranked the nine-room office the poorest. Presumably, they preferred visual surveillance over their workers.

Nemecek and Grandjean [30] studied open-space office workers in Switzerland and found somewhat conflicting results. Fifty-nine percent of workers stated they would accept another job in such an office whereas 37 percent stated they would not. Sixty-two percent of the latter eventually adjusted to open-space offices. No studies are known comparing type 1 (private) offices directly with various open plans except the Harris and Associates survey, discussed earlier, which emphasized a need for privacy.

Formerly, engineering personnel in large aerospace organizations worked in the type-1 open-space office (colloquially termed a "bull pen"). There were advantages to this arrangement, particularly for drafting personnel. One could see across the room whether or not a particular person was at his or her drafting board and, also, if other personnel were visiting. Some felt it expedited

Table 7-2 Advantages of Open and Closed Office Plans

For closed-plan offices (type 1)	For open-plan offices (type 1)
Preferred by most workers	Not objectionable to some workers [Nemecek and Grandjean, 30]
Better performance on certain tasks	
Less visual and auditory distraction; fewer unplanned social interruptions	Less costly for temperature control
Permanent walls mask noise better	Unrestricted communications (can talk across room or observe presence of others)
Requires less floor space for equal reduction of noise levels	Managerial control; can observe employees at work [Wells, 39]
Permits private communications	No wasted floor space for corridors and aisles, hence, maximum density of people per square foot
Protected floor space and freedom to re-arrange furniture	
Professional atmosphere	Easy to rearrange a room of desks or drafting boards
Private offices associated with status	

For closed-plan offices (type 2)	For open-plan offices (type 2)
Preferred by most workers to be open plans [39]	Not objectionable to many workers [30]
Group identity may improve morale	Same advantages as open plan type 1, but more expensive and wasteful of space
Less visual distraction than open plans	More widely separated desks than open plan type 1 permit less noise and better private communications
Unrestricted communications within work area	
Supervisory control of small group	Carpeting and greenery may improve morale over open plan type 1.
Less costly to control temperature than private offices	
Easy to rearrange within small room	

communications and allowed several people to assemble around a drafting board. Other advantages, shown in Table 7-2, include flexibility in rearrangement, maximum usage of floor space, and less costly temperature control (since ventilation of the room was not interrupted by walls).

Those who have worked under these conditions are aware of potential distractions. Social conversations unrelated to work develop easily between adjacent workers. Telephone conversations and conferences at adjacent desks can easily distract one from his or her work. Private communications are virtually impossible. The minimum floor space offers no freedom for rearrangement of desk, reference table, bookcases, and so forth. In fact, maximum density arrangements may result in a loss of some of one's territory overnight when new desks necessitate narrower aisles and smaller distances between desks.

Brookes and Kaplan [9] evaluated the type-2 open-plan, or landscaped office. They interviewed 120 workers before and after 9 months of working in such an office and found workers felt it was more esthetically pleasing (carpeting, plants, and so on), but less functionally efficient than conventional office plans. In particular, they complained of visual distractions, loss of privacy, and increased noise level.

A trend toward greater professionalism in the aerospace and electronics industry has resulted in modern individual cubicles separated by partitions. The modern cubicle provides some of the advantages of a private office while at the same time allowing for the ventilation and temperature control simplicity of the open plans.

Herman Miller, Inc. [45] offers a semiclosed office plan featuring portable, free-standing panels in heights ranging from 34 to 96 inches. The connecting panels, available in oak or walnut finishes, are in sections 1, 2, and 4 feet wide (30, 61, 122 cm) for flexibility in configuration. Curved panels for corners and glazed transparent panels are also available. Instead of conventional desks and drafting boards, the work surfaces, shelves, and cabinets are hung to the panels. The low-paneled fronts allow one to observe others and to be observed, while the high-paneled backs eliminate work distractions (Figure 7-2).

There are also acoustical panels with noise reduction coefficients of .95, a high sound-absorption rating. These panels may be interchanged with standard panels. For greater privacy, floor-to-ceiling acoustical panels are available. A 10 × 12 ft (305 to 366 cm) room may be assembled by two people in 3½ h, and the unit may be skidded to another location with little effort.

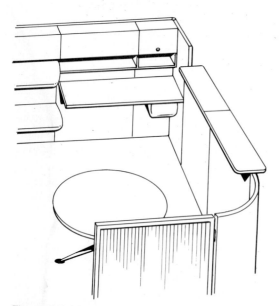

Figure 7-2 Modern engineers semiclosed office. *(Sketch based on a brochure from Herman Miller, New York, 1976.)*

Noise Control in Open-Plan Offices and Schools

Acoustics specialists Nebalek and Nebalek [28] have recommended two criteria for open-plan offices. They recommend an articulation index (see Chapter 12) of at least 0.5 for speech intelligibility in a noise field and an articulation index of *no more* than 0.2 for minimum privacy, that is, few spoken words are understood by adjacent personnel. Obviously, such criteria are contradictory for any fixed distance between speaker and listener. However, a conversation between a worker and a visitor may be face-to-face and at a distance of only 3 or 4 ft, whereas the adjacent worker may be at least twice this distance away. There is a 5-dB loss in voice intensity as distance is doubled [28], but this offers little hope of oral privacy unless desks are widely separated or unless there are acoustical barriers.

A continuous background sound such as electronic noise, air conditioning, or music will provide some masking for privacy. Herman Miller [45] offers an "acoustic conditioner," a portable one-piece unit designed to insure oral privacy in work stations only a few feet apart. The masking effect covers a 12-foot in diameter area and is produced by a nondirectional electronic sound. The sound automatically changes pitch slightly on a random basis so the background sound does not become monotonous. Volume is adjustable up to 50 dB. The conditioner is housed in a globe-shaped unit and comes in free-standing, ceiling-hung, and fixed-wall models.

The principal problem in open-plan schools is the annoyance and distraction of fluctuating high noise levels, rather than privacy of speech [28]. Walsch [38] measured noise levels in open-plan schools and found a 70 dBA level for kindergarten classes with a decreasing level at higher grade levels. The Japanese Ministry of Education has a maximum limit of 55 dBA for all schools. Nebalek and Nebalek recommend a limit of 65 dBA for U.S. schools.

Techniques for noise reduction in schools include the use of absorbent, abuse-resistant wall materials, carpeted floors, and full-length curtains. They also recommend allowing 50 to 60 ft^2 (4.6 to 5.6 m^2) per student, as opposed to the conventional room allowance of 25 to 35 ft^2 (2.3 to 3.2 m^2) per student, to reduce speech disturbances.

The visual distraction of movement by other students or classes may be a more severe problem in open-plan schools than the auditory distraction. The judicious use of bookcases and other partitions may help overcome this problem.

Windows and No Windows

Before the era of temperature-controlled buildings and fluorescent lighting, windows were a necessity. Students were taught to sleep always with their bedroom window open. When lighting was limited to the incandescent lamp or gaslight, homes and industrial plants were very dark and dingy without exterior illumination.

Today, the window is viewed by some as a luxury. Fluorescent lighting provides a more uniform lighting than sunlight. Heat lost or gained through windows increases the cost of energy. Open windows invite other environmental problems such as outside noises, odors, and dust. Windows in school buildings are thought by some to encourage daydreaming and distraction by playground activities. (Some managers also view windows as a source of distraction). The wall space occupied by windows could be used for other useful purposes (blackboards, displays). Windows may also provide an entry for burglars.

Despite these constraints and the lack of necessity of windows, Manning [24] found that 89 percent of workers surveyed preferred to have a work area with a window. Wells [40] found that employees whose work stations were a considerable distance from a window in the room tended to overestimate the percent of daylight falling on their station and to underestimate the illumination from artificial lighting. Such indirect evidence of awareness of daylight should not be construed as indicating a psychological need for contact with the outside world. However, there are many practical benefits from window lighting. Table 7-3 summarizes some of the benefits as well as the disadvantages. Windows and skylights save electricity on sunny days. Observation of weather changes can provide a guide to proper clothing before going outdoors. In the event of a fire, windows at ground level or near a balcony or fire escape may be broken and serve as an emergency exit. Windows that open are also useful when smoke or foul odors engulf a room, and at some times of the year they may provide temperature control.

Building Designs with Windows   Many modern buildings are designed so that not every office or work area has a window and, hence, windows may become a status symbol for the privileged. Woodson and Conover [42] proposed

Table 7-3   Advantages of Windows and No Windows

Windows	No windows
Strongly preferred	Sunlight not necessary with fluorescent lighting
Saves electricity on sunny days	
Information on outside weather conditions or happenings	May be a source of glare
Emergency exit in the event of fire	Temperature and noise control an added expense
Windows that open provide ventilation of smoke and odors	Open windows allow dust and odors to enter; higher noise level in some instances
Status symbol (when few other windows)	Outside visual distractions for full-length, ground-level windows
Landscaped exterior may improve morale of workers	Windows use wall space
Full-length windows symbolize friendliness	May compromise security against break-ins

a sort of E-shaped building design that has a series of parallel wings with courtyards between the wings. The narrow wings permit windows for all shop areas and offices.

Aircraft defense plants during World War II were usually designed without windows. At the time the government was conscious of the threat of nighttime air attacks and illumination through the windows of such a building could easily identify it as a target (unless there were blackout curtains). However, today many engineering buildings for military and space products are constructed with a continuous wall of windows that often overlook an attractive landscape, such as a courtyard with a pool and even a shooting-water display (Figure 7-3). The orientation of the building on the lot should be planned to minimize sunheat buildup through windows.

Window Materials   Glazed windows to reduce sun brightness are discussed in Chapter 8. Modern advances in the technology of materials for windows have helped overcome the problems of glare, noise transmission, and loss of heat or sunheat buildup [*Factory Management,* 41]. Many modern office buildings feature an entire exterior surface of windows with diffusers and "shading coefficients." Some of the current technology available includes fiberglass reinforced facesheets bonded to both sides of a structural aluminum grid; double-walled polycarbonate sheets, glass blocks with 40-dB noise attenuation,

Figure 7-3   Modern engineering building. *(Courtesy of IBM Corp., Boca Raton, Fla.)*

and double panes for home usage. The initial cost is obviously greater than a single-pane window, but over a period of 3 to 7 years such windows can pay for themselves in energy efficiency alone.

While the emphasis in development seems to be on windows that provide uniform lighting, noise reduction, and energy conservation, from the standpoint of human preferences windows should be transparent. Filtered windows, similar to those used in automobile windshields for glare reduction, are currently used in office and engineering buildings. Some also feature one-way vision, thus providing the privacy of a wall from pedestrian traffic, while also providing a glare-free view of the outside.

In summary, the window is not a necessity. Attacks of claustrophobia do not necessarily follow assignment of workers to the confines of four walls (although prisoners in small cells might argue the point). Evidence does support their preference. Be assured that the school principal in a building with only one window or the manager of a industrial plant with few windows will have, in each instance, an office with a window.

Room Color

Room color, including wood paneling, is discussed in terms of its effect on brightening a room in Chapter 8. In addition, interior decorators and industrial designers have long emphasized the esthetic effects of color in walls, furniture, drapery, and decor. Military facilities at one time employed a uniform color (pale green or blue, usually) on the walls throughout a building. Although unsupported by much empirical evidence, sameness of color, however attractive, is believed to have a depressing effect. Today, it is not uncommon to find a single wall or column painted a bright color and to find the use of a variety of colors. Machinery also is sometimes painted a bright color.

In 1941 Eysenck [14] obtained over 21,000 judgments of the order of preference for common hues. At that time the order was blue, red, green, violet, orange, and yellow. Such information is of little use today for several reasons: (1) Only six hues were studied whereas the Munsell Color System [27] and other color systems contain hundreds of combinations of hue, saturation, and lightness. (2) Color preferences are not necessarily consistent across context of usage even for an individual. We may prefer a certain color for an automobile exterior, another for clothing, and still another for walls or furniture. Moreover, if too many others select our favorite color we may select a different color. (3) There are differences in esthetic appeal across individuals and cultures as well as within an individual over a period of time.

In art courses we were taught that certain colors are "warm" and others are "cool." However, studies [Ittleson et al., 22; Manning, 23] have failed to find any evidence that wall colors actually change peoples' judgment of the perceived temperature or thermal comfort in a room. It is strictly an "intellectual effect" or belief that blue is cool and red is warm [22].

Acking and Kuller [1] report some physiological effects of color. Ertel [12] found an increase in intelligence quotients among children tested in rooms thought by them to be "beautiful." Srivastava and Peel [34] found that visitors' behavior differed when visiting a museum of art in which, under one condition, the walls and carpet were a light beige and, in another condition, the walls and carpet were a dark brown. The visitors took more steps and spent less time in the brown room. Thus, color can affect behavior in measurable ways.

In summary, people certainly prefer color to black and white, but it is difficult to specify particular colors. Walls should probably be selected principally for purposes of brightening a room. Some feel that greenery, pictures, drapes, and decor may be used to provide color without the use of bright colors on walls. Bright colored plaques, signs, and nameplates are commercially available. To the degree feasible, the employees should be allowed to select colors. A concern for their interests by management may improve morale and, indirectly, improve performance or other measures of effectiveness.

Background Music

We are familiar with professional offices and public places that have either continuous music or FM station broadcasts. Many industrial plants have also used background music in hallways, lobbies, restrooms, cafeterias, and even in work areas. The principal concern here is the effect of music upon persons at work. As we know, there are age and cultural differences in preferences for type of music. What is highly preferred for some may be objectionable to others.

Workers engaged in simple, repetitive, monotonous tasks seem to produce better with music, whereas those engaged in complex or creative work may do no better and, in some instances, do worse with music [Uhrbrook, 35]. Since the effect of music is an individual, subjective experience, it is important that each worker have some control over the choice of music. One solution for sedentary workers working in close proximity would be individual headsets with channel selection, such as that offered to commercial aircraft passengers. Another solution would be volume control at semiprivate work stations or offices so that music could be rejected. A compromise solution is to play soft orchestral music, which may not be highly preferred but which is less likely to be objectionable.

Esthetics and Meaning in Architectural Design

In previous sections discussions have been presented on preferences for personal space, open and closed work areas, windows, wall colors, and background music. Wools and Canter [43] were interested in the characteristics of an office that would be perceived as "most friendly" and "least friendly." Eight line drawings of rooms were presented, which had various combinations of windows, desk arrangement, and type of ceiling. Those judged to be most friendly had a sloping ceiling, floor-to-ceiling window, and a grouping of chairs without a table between two persons. The least friendly room had a flat ceiling, small window at the top of the wall, and a desk between the two persons.

There are many attributes of our perceptual environment: visual form, proportion, scale, line, light and shadow, texture, and so on. In addition, architects have long been interested in the meaning attached to perceptions. According to Hesselgren [20], the streamlined form of an automobile, for example, its long hood and flowing lines, expresses speed and efficiency; columns on a Greek temple express strength or support; certain uniquely shaped door handles imply functions of pulling or pushing, and so forth. Thus, visual forms may connote meanings as well as being emotionally loaded. When interpretations of meaning or aesthetic appeal are left strictly to the interpretation of a single artist or architect, the statement is in the domain of phenomenological analysis. However, when a large number of naive observers independently rate a visual object or its attributes in the same way, greater confidence can be given to the statement. In other words, the viewing public is also likely to attach such meanings to the visual forms.

Although there are simpler techniques for rating peoples' judgments, a technique developed by Osgood et al. [32] termed the "semantic differential" is commonly used. The technique involves psychological scaling data analyzed by a statistical technique known as *factor analysis*. Wools and Canter [43] used the technique to identify three attitudinal dimensions that they state are employed when people appraise their physical environment: *activity* (fast-slow), *harmony* (clear-obscure), and *friendly* (welcoming-unwelcoming).

The semantic differential scale involves subjects' rating an object in terms of many pairs of opposing adjectives, such as pleasant-unpleasant, depressing-elevating, heavy-light, radical-conservative, discouraging-stimulating. Given a stimulus object (visual form, word), the subject checks somewhere on a scale (usually 7-point) anchored by the opposing adjectives. In the Wools and Canter study there were 49 such pairs of adjectives considered relevant to describing rooms. The mean values may be plotted as a profile (see Figure 7-4 from Hesselgren [20]). Many of the adjectives may, in fact, be synonymous, but this is no real drawback. Factor analysis reduces the number of dimensions to a few groups that go together statistically, as discussed above.

Hesselgren, an architect, used the technique in his dissertation to determine preferences for various types of "townscapes." His subjects were given a series of perspective line drawings created in such a way that two drawings always showed the extremes of outdoor space. Each was rated according to the 34 dimensions shown in Figure 7-4. The profile shown is for "deep outdoor space" and "shallow outdoor space." Although there are dimensional differences, clearly the shallow attribute tends toward the positive end of the scale much more often.

Among his other findings were slight preferences (toward the positive end on nearly all dimensions) for a separate building landscape (open outdoor space) instead of a courtyard or closed outdoor space; two-story building courtyard in preference to a high-rise courtyard; curved outdoor space (looking down a street of buildings) in preference to straight outdoor space, and a leafy square to a barren, open square without trees.

In summary, the semantic differential is one of many rating techniques that

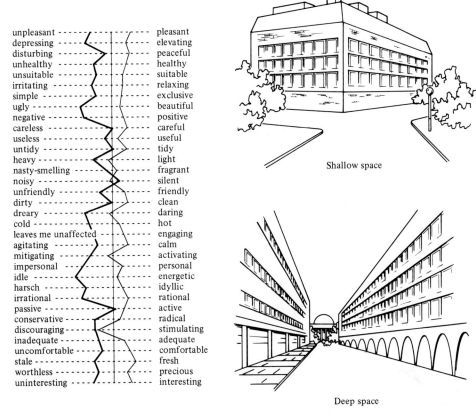

unpleasant	pleasant
depressing	elevating
disturbing	peaceful
unhealthy	healthy
unsuitable	suitable
irritating	relaxing
simple	exclusive
ugly	beautiful
negative	positive
careless	careful
useless	useful
untidy	tidy
heavy	light
nasty-smelling	fragrant
noisy	silent
unfriendly	friendly
dirty	clean
dreary	daring
cold	hot
leaves me unaffected	engaging
agitating	calm
mitigating	activating
impersonal	personal
idle	energetic
harsch	idyllic
irrational	rational
passive	active
conservative	radical
discouraging	stimulating
inadequate	adequate
uncomfortable	comfortable
stale	fresh
worthless	precious
uninteresting	interesting

Shallow space

Deep space

Figure 7-4 Semantic differential profile for shallow outdoor space (thin line) and deep outdoor space (thick line). *(Adapted from Hesselgren, 1975.)*

is also useful in further analysis in terms of attitudinal dimensions. Architectural judgments regarding the meaning expressed by visual forms should be subjected to testing by some type of rating or scaling technique to be confident that the public does share the meaning intended by the design.

ENVIRONMENT DESIGN FOR NOISE CONTROL

The topics of illumination, temperature control, and noise control are discussed at length in Chapters 8 and 9. With respect to noise control, the emphasis in Chapter 9 is on very high noise levels that risk impaired hearing and techniques for their reduction at the source, path, or receiver. In the present context, noise control will be limited to techniques applicable to building design.

Noise Transmission from Outside Sources

The U.S. Department of Housing and Urban Development (HUD) discourages the construction of dwelling units on sites that have, or are projected to have, unacceptable noise levels. A level of 65 dBA would be "normally acceptable," but exceeding this level for more than 8 hours daily is "normally unacceptable;" 45 dBA for no longer than 30 minutes each 24 hours is listed as "acceptable" [HUD, 36].

Noise Barriers   When new office buildings, apartments, or motels are to be located close to noise sources, such as interstate highways or freeways, natural or human-made barriers may be interposed. A rolling terrain (hill with trees and underbrush) or a roadway embankment may serve as barriers to traffic noises. Depression of the highway below ground level serves the same function. The building may also be located behind a larger, high-rise building, thus interrupting the direct pathway of sound. A high wall near the source will also be effective but a height of 20 ft (6 meters) is usually prohibitive [Nebalek and Nebalek, 28].

Building Orientation   Noise coming to a complex of buildings from a busy highway should not be trapped in an area, bouncing to and back from surrounding walls. Figure 7-5 illustrates arrangements of buildings that should be avoided because the parallel orientation permits repetitive sound reflections [Berendt et al., 5]. U-shaped courtyards facing the noise source also permit reflections. Designs that do not encourage noise reflections are also shown in Figure 7-5.

Building Exterior Wall   Rigid, nonporous partitions such as concrete blocks transmit little airborne sound, but considerable impact noise. Flexible materials such as windowpanes and porous materials allow transmission of acoustic waves. Acoustics specialists have calculated the transmission loss (TL) in decibels of various types of materials of various thicknesses. Transmission loss is simply the difference in sound intensity between the source side and the other side of the partition. Total noise reduction (NR) depends not only on the transmission loss, but also on the total absorption properties of walls in the receiving room (a) and the area of wall transmitting sound in ft^2 or m^2 (S) according to the following formula:

$$NR = TL + 10 \log a/S$$

Thus, one must know sound absorption coefficients of surface materials in a room and their surface area. Sound absorption coefficients have been calculated for common materials used on walls, floors, ceilings, chairs, and so on [Farrell, 15]. These coefficients vary somewhat with frequency, however; a single noise reduction coefficient *(NRC)* is often given for acoustic materials. The NRC is the mean of absorption coefficients for four frequencies (250, 500, 1000, and 2000 Hz).

Calculating the TL for a particular wall is complicated by the fact that it may be comprised of several diverse materials such as brick and glass. Hence, TL is

Poor Better

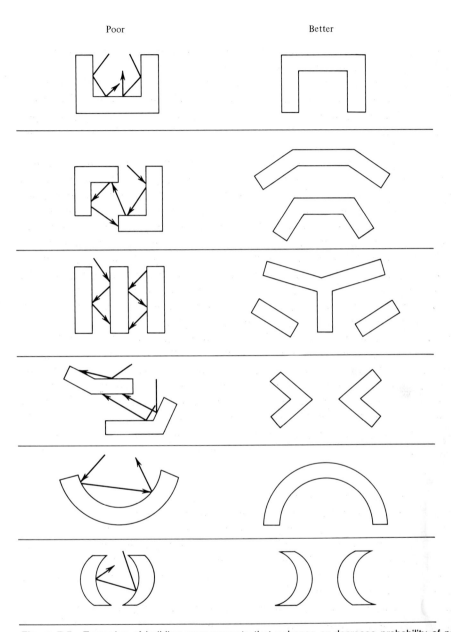

Figure 7-5 Examples of building arrangements that enhance or decrease probability of noise reflections. *(Adapted from Berendt et al., 1967, in Nebalek and Nebalek, 1978.)*

based upon the sum of the transmission coefficients (γ_n) of each material times its area (S_n):

$$TL = \frac{S}{(\gamma_1 S_1 + \gamma_2 S_2 + \gamma_n S_n)}$$

Obviously, the weight of a partition has an effect upon TL, however, doubling the weight does not double the transmission loss. There is also a considerable decrease in TL by leaks over and under some partitions, doors, electrical outlets, and air-conditioning ducts. Hence, knowing the above coefficients, one can predict to some degree the noise reduction, but it is still necessary to measure the internal noise level to determine the extent to which it meets acoustical comfort criteria.

Noise Transmission from Internal Sources

The following table depicts preferred noise criteria for various indoor spaces [Beranek et al., 4]. A noise reduction program should attempt to meet these criteria. Low levels of background noise do not disturb occupants nor interfere with speech communications.

Type of space	Noise level in dBA
Concert halls, opera houses	20–30
Large auditoriums	Max 30
Small auditoriums, churches, conference rooms	Max 42
Bedrooms, hospitals	34–47
Large offices, stores, cafeterias, restaurants	42–52
Lobbies, small shops, laboratories	47–56
Kitchens, laundries, computer rooms	52–61
Work spaces without risk of hearing damage	66–80*

*See Chapter 9 for specific damage risk criteria.

Floor/Ceiling Ratings A particularly disturbing type of noise that many apartment dwellers have experienced is the impact noise from walking, moving furniture, or dropping objects on the floor above. Such intermittent noises are more disturbing than continuous noises because of their intrusive nature.

Acoustics specialists measure the impact insulation class (IIC) rating of floor-ceilings by generating noise from a tapping machine on the floor and taking noise level measures at 16 test frequencies in the room below. The Federal Housing Administration recommends minimum IIC ratings of 48, 45, and 52 for interior noise levels of 45, 40, and 35 dBA, respectively [Nebalek and Nebalek, 28]. A few specific examples of IIC ratings are as follows: reinforced concrete slab alone, 25; with a layer of plaster, 31; with an additional layer of wood flooring, 47; with carpeting and pad, 80. Impact noise transmission may be reduced on floors by providing "floating floors" (a layer of concrete on a porous sound absorber).

Interior Planning for Noise Control   While most of us would likely call in an acoustics specialist for advice on materials selection, there are certain steps a facility designer may take to avert the probability of a noise problem. The simplest approach is to increase the distance between quiet areas and noisy areas. In a home this would mean the bedrooms and study should be at one end of the house and the garage, shop, laundry room, recreation room, and kitchen should be at the other end. Figure 7-6 presents the floor plans of well-planned apartments [Berendt et al., 5]. Note that the partitions between adjacent apartments separate similar functional spaces. (Kitchens for apartments C, D, E, and F are adjacent as are baths for apartments A, B, C, and D.) The hallways of the two parallel apartments, C and D, serve as a buffer area.

The townhouse or rowhouse concept, with bedrooms on the second floor of each unit, ameliorates the floor-ceiling problem of older apartment houses.

Absorption of Reflected Sounds   We are familiar with the reverberating voice of an announcer over a loudspeaker at a nearly empty football stadium. We have also noticed something akin to an echo when talking in a large, empty room with bare walls.

Both reverberation and echoes are caused by reflection of sound off walls, ceilings, floors, or other low-absorptive surfaces. The delayed sound is superimposed on the direct sound. With an echo the delay is long enough to distinguish two separate sounds; with reverberation the delay is briefer and the delayed sound fuses with the direct sound. Fletcher [17] has shown that the intelligibility

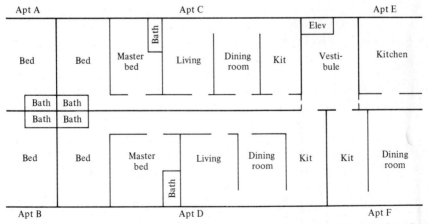

Figure 7-6   Example of well-planned apartments in terms of acoustics. *(Adapted from Berendt et al., 1967, in Nebalek and Nebalek, 1978.)*

of speech is inversely related to the reverberation time (longer delay interfering with understanding speech).

Some reverberation in a room is desirable to avoid the dead sound of a completely anechoic space. A live room, in contrast, is one in which the sounds do not cease when the source noise stops. Reverberation time (T) is the time in seconds between stopping the source and a decrease in sound pressure level by 60 dB from the level when the source was stopped.

$$T = 0.0049 \ V/a^*$$

where V = room volume in cubic feet
a = total room absorption in sabins

To calculate total room absorption, one would need to know the sound absorption coefficients of various room surfaces, multiply each by its square footage, and then summate. Although this may appear somewhat technical, it is clear that the absorptive characteristic of surfaces is inversely related to the reverberation time.

Absorptive materials such as carpeting, drapes, and ceilings are sufficient to reduce reverberation time in smaller enclosures. Farrell [15] reported the optimum reverberation time was 0.8 to 1.5 for an auditorium; 0.4 to 1.2 for a conference room or classroom, and 0.0 to 0.7 for a speech studio. MIL-STD-1472B [26] indicates that acceptable reverberation times increase linearly with the volume of the room and may be about 0.5 s greater for auditoriums than for conversational speech. Farrell's guidelines apply to rooms of less than 30,000 ft³, according to Figure 35 in MIL-STD-1472B.

Absorptive materials also reduce the noise level in a room. The ceiling is usually treated first because it is a large, usually untreated area. Ceiling treatment typically reduces the noise about 8 dB. Treating all walls in addition to the ceiling reduces it by 15 dB. This is about the maximum noise reduction by absorption [Nebalek and Nebalek, 28]. Carpeting is used mainly to reduce surface-generated noises rather than to absorb sound. Hence, carpeting thickness is not too important.

Long, narrow, high rooms or hallways have a problem called "flutter echo," which is sound reflecting back and forth between parallel surfaces. Treatment may be effectively applied to surfaces above ear height.

Reverberation and Speech Intelligibility   Noise reduction in buildings has been discussed with respect to reduction of external noise transmission, impact noise reduction, planning to increase noise distances, and absorptive techniques. Masking of noise or unwanted speech by playing music or steady, broadband noise was mentioned earlier.

---

*$T = 0.163 \ V/a$ when V and a are expressed in cubic meters and square meters, respectively.

Improved speech intelligibility in large enclosures may be achieved by lessening reverberation. Using several low-powered loudspeakers rather than a single speaker is recommended. The squealing of the public address system, which we have noted occasionally, is caused by acoustical feedback from the loudspeaker to the microphone in highly reverberant rooms. When the room acoustics cannot be altered, the speaker may talk closer to the microphone, reduce gain, use a directional microphone, or shield the microphone.

DESIGN OF GROUP FACILITIES FOR VISION AND MOVEMENT

The focus of this section will be on multioperator facilities such as conference rooms, auditoriums, and classrooms, particularly from the standpoint of viewing screens or other visual displays. Most buildings also have traffic spaces (hallways and aisles), a variety of doors, and elevating structures such as stairs and ramps. For certain equipment specific dimensional criteria have been developed, based principally on visual line of sight and anthropometric data. For other equipment the recommendations are limited to when and if they should be used, based on safety considerations.

Special design criteria have been developed for making buildings accessible to the physically and sensory-motor handicapped, especially the person in a wheelchair [General Service Administration, 11]. This topic will be discussed at length in Chapter 13.

Visual Requirements for Large Displays

Most modern motion picture theaters are designed rather narrowly so that patrons seated in the less advantageous positions, near the side walls, are still able to view the screen at an acceptable angle. Oblique viewing angles introduce distortion of perspective and visual parallax problems.

Thomson [47] recommends a line of sight to a display surface from 60 to 90° and never less than 45°. Figure 7-7 illustrates this point. To achieve the 60° minimum angle, the front row of operators should be seated no closer than the width of the screen and preferably at a distance of 1.5 times the display width.

Seated operations are standard in most viewing situations, however; in certain situations some may be sitting, others standing, or all standing. A technique has been developed to determine the required elevation of one viewer when standing directly behind another viewer who is either seated or standing. Figure 7-8 defines certain self-explanatory dimensions.

The following formula defines the extent to which the second operator must be elevated above floor level for a clear view of the entire screen:

$$\text{Elevation} = D - E + \frac{(D - A)C}{B}$$

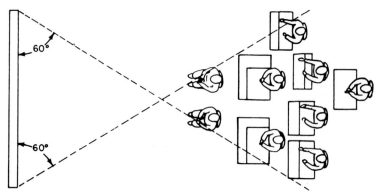

Figure 7-7   Areas within which operators can view a display. *(Thomson in Van Cott and Kinkade, 1972.)*

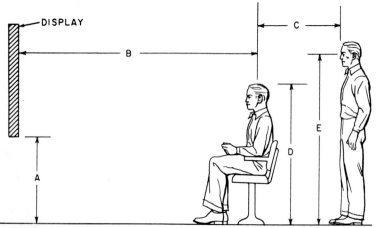

Figure 7-8   Dimensions used to compute positions of standing and seated operators. *(Thomson in Van Cott and Kinkade, 1972.)*

Let us suppose that the front person is standing and is 74.2 in (188 cm) in stature *(D)*. The shorter person behind has an eye height of 61.9 in (157 cm) *(E)*. To be able to see horizontally, the rear person must be elevated 12.3 in (31 cm). However, this would not allow her or him to see the bottom of the screen. To determine the total elevation required, it is necessary to know the values of *A, B,* and *C* as well. Suppose $A = 60$ in (152 cm), $B = 96$ in (244 cm), and $C = 48$ in (118 cm). The total elevation in inches would then be: $74.2 - 61.9 + (74.2 - 60.0)(48)/96 = 12.3 + 7.1 = 19.4$. The rear viewer would need to be elevated 19.4 in (49 cm).

The formula is applicable to a variety of situations where distances and heights are parameters. It may be noted that if the rear operator were closer to the front operator, he or she would not need to be elevated so much, but if the screen were closer he or she would need to be elevated much more. These relationships are also involved in auditorium design discussed subsequently.

Conference Rooms

Conference rooms pose few visual problems when only five persons are present, but pose difficulties in seeing a display when 25 or 30 persons are present. Thomson [47] illustrates the situation with 10 principals seated at a table and the others seated around the room (Figure 7-9).

The persons seated along the side of the table are perpendicular to the screen. The closer their lateral distance (distance between chairs), the more the person nearer the screen occludes the view of the person seated next to him or her. At a minimum each person should be allocated 30 in (76 cm) lateral distance at the table. In practice, we know that one person will shift backward and the other forward in order to see. However, a large group viewing a screen or blackboard presentation from a conference table is at a disadvantage compared to a group viewing from a room with narrow tables arranged similar to those shown previously in Figure 7-7. Another solution would be to elevate the screen in the conference room.

The minimum size of a conference room varies with the size of the table. However, there should be at least 4 ft (122 cm) and preferably 5 ft (152 cm) between the table and the wall as aisle space. The chair backs of many will be as much as 3 or 3½ ft (91 to 102 cm) from the table in order that the audience can view the speaker better and they can cross their legs.

Classrooms

Thomson [47] recommends a classroom arrangement consisting of four rows of tables with four adjacent tables in each row. With two students at each table a total of 32 students may be accommodated. A 3- × 6-ft (91 to 183 cm) table will allow 3 ft head-to-head lateral distances. A minimum of 30 in (76 cm) between rows is required; however, for ease of ingress and egress, 36 in (91 cm) is recommended. The back row, which will serve as a major aisle, should be 42 in (107 cm). Side aisles should be 36 in (91 cm) and there should be 8 ft (244 cm) from the front row of tables to the front wall. The shape of a classroom is not specified. Screen presentations dictate a narrow room; however, reading blackboard information requires that the distance not be too great.

Tables allow more work space than individual arm chairs, but at a sacrifice of a row of seats, which is important in maximum-density seating plans. Individual arm chairs should provide for book storage. Chairs that are bolted to the floor are to simplify room cleaning. Chair design for comfort will be discussed in a later section.

For graduate seminar courses, the emphasis should be on face-to-face communications. For small classes a slightly oblique table improves eye contact between students seated along one side. (Round tables are optimal from this standpoint, but they waste floor space.) A practical solution is four or more standard tables abutted to form a C-shaped pattern with the instructor's table in the center completing an O-shaped pattern.

Auditoriums

Arrangement of seating in an auditorium should be designed for near-perpendicular line of sight to a screen. Distortion due to visual angle is obviously

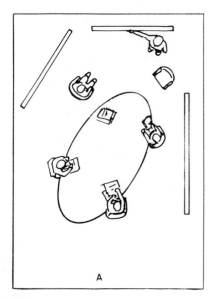

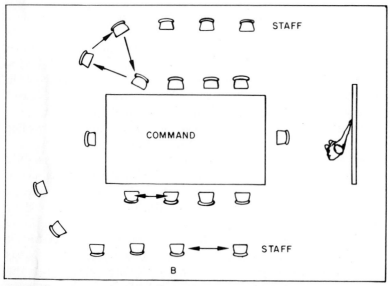

Figure 7-9 Conference room arrangements for five (above) and for 21 persons (below). *(Thomson in Van Cott and Kinkade, 1972.)*

more serious when alphanumeric and graphical information is shown (as in training films or technical society conventions) than it is for recreational movies or live entertainment.

The truncated wedge or fan-shaped arrangement of seats, as shown in Figure 7-10 (A), provides a viewing angle meeting the 60° criterion. The vertical viewing angle (up and down) should not exceed 10° from horizontal line of sight. Viewers should not be required to lean back or forward to achieve a normal (90°) line of sight (LOS).

There are several design techniques that can be used to achieve the desired

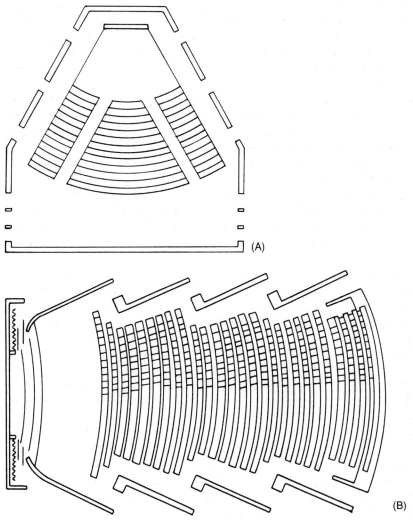

Figure 7-10 Auditorium seating arrangements—(A) truncated wedge with two aisles, (B) auditorium with side aisles for rapid egress. *(Thomson in Van Cott and Kinkade, 1972.)*

angle. The height of the screen bottom above the floor line may be elevated (the exact height varying, of course, with the depth of an auditorium having an inclined floor). An elevated screen is fine for the back rows but to accommodate the front-row viewers, the front row must be set back at least the width of the screen. Another solution is to tip the screen a few degrees forward. As shown in Figure 7-11, a bisecting angle to the center of the screen is more nearly within 10° vertical from the LOS of front-row viewers and is still acceptable from the balcony.

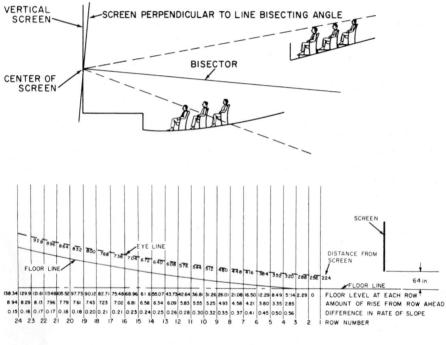

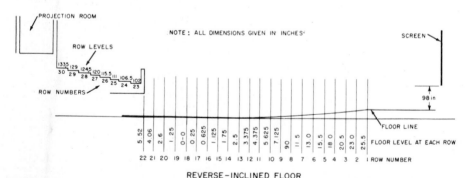

Figure 7-11 Screen positions approximating normal line of sight for all viewers, above; incline requirements for screen viewing, below. *(Thomson in Van Cott and Kinkade, 1972.)*

Another solution to the front-row, visual-angle problem is to provide reverse pitch or gradual incline for the first 10 or 11 rows. Not only does this lessen the viewing angle but also it lessens the total elevation of seats in a deep auditorium. The required ceiling height is thereby reduced. Also, a balcony can be lowered, thus improving the vertical visual angle for these viewers as well. Balconies for screen presentations must be set back to maintain the 10° visual angle, but for live entertainment the balcony should be moved forward for improved hearing and image size.

Another problem, mentioned previously, is seeing directly over the head of another viewer. One solution is to stagger the rows of seats so that a second-row viewer is looking directly over the arm rest of two seats in the row ahead. A gradual incline of 4 to 8° with a 36-in (91-cm) row separation will permit a short person to see over the shoulder of a tall person with a minimum of screen obstruction.

Auditorium seats should be at least 28 in (71 cm) wide with two arm rests for each seat and should be appropriately upholstered. Foldup writing tablets should be provided for auditoriums used for lectures and note taking.

Exiting Auditoriums   A major annoyance in many auditoriums is people arriving or exiting at unscheduled times. One solution is to provide a 40-in (102-cm) separation between adjacent rows. However, maximum density plans may require reducing this dimension to a 32-in (81-cm) separation. The use of spring-type seats, which spring up when not in use, converts a row of seats to a wider aisle.

Figure 7-10 (B) depicts a plan with the main aisles along the side of an auditorium and a series of exit doors on each side. This plan expedites exiting. Note also the absence of a center aisle. Center aisles add a visual distraction or obstruction when people enter late or leave at unscheduled times. However, with very wide auditoriums used for live entertainment, the absence of aisles would mean more people passing in the rows in front of a seated viewer. Unless the rows are widely separated, one or two center aisles are a necessity. Narrow movie auditoriums without side aisles necessarily have center aisles with emergency exits at the front and rear.

Corridors at the rear of an auditorium should be wide and arranged so that people exit by funneling outward in each direction rather than funneling into a single corridor (or into a right-angle corridor where people get jammed into a corner). Emergency and side exits make the egress of a crowd through a narrow lobby unnecessary. Safety laws require that exit doors be pushed open from the inside.

Traffic Spaces

There are obvious functional considerations in the planning of aisles, corridors, and hallways. Plant layout specialists consider such factors as type, amount and weight of materials, frequency and sequence of use, speed of travel required, and other planning considerations.

Aisles   For people wearing indoor clothing, an aisle or hallway 24 in (610 mm) wide is the minimum width to avoid brushing against structures or equipment. For two people to pass, 54 in (1372 mm) is recommended; 44 in (1118 mm) is minimum. If one person stands against the wall while the other passes, 36 in (914 mm) is sufficient, but such a design is limited to space-constrained systems such as ships or passenger aircraft.

A few recommendations for safety and efficiency are:

1   Locate aisles centrally within a building so as to minimize walking distances to them.

2   Locate aisles or paths for minimum distance between traffic-generating sources. (Sidewalks on public grounds are sometimes not used because they violate this simple principle.)

3   Provide traffic guidance markings on walls or floors (for example, directions to rooms).

4   Make intersecting aisles converge at 90°.

5   Avoid blind corners, if feasible.

6   Do not permit doors to open into narrow corridors. A door opened suddenly in front of a passerby could be hazardous. The exceptions, as noted, are auditoriums and similar traffic generators. Outward opening doors are sometimes recessed from the front wall of a building.

7   Keep aisles clear of equipment and supporting columns.

8   Avoid one-way aisles if feasible. They are inefficient and difficult to enforce.

Catwalks and Tunnels   Under special conditions, such as over high-bay assembly areas, workers may be required to walk on catwalks. The minimum width of the walkway is 12 in (305 mm), walking "cat-fashion." At the head and shoulders, 25 in (635 mm) is required. Although slight stooping is sometimes necessary, it is not recommended for any length of walk. To walk erect a clearance height of 77 in (1956 mm) is recommended. For safety, guard rails with protective wire mesh screening on the lower half should be provided. Fully enclosed tunnels are recommended where feasible.

The dimensions of tunnels depend upon the method of locomotion. The minimum dimension tunnel (such as between air-locked compartments) is one where the person lies supine and pulls himself or herself through on a movable platform or lies prone and is pulled through with a cable attached to the platform. The width of the tunnel must be at least 25 in (635 mm). If prone, the vertical distance between the platform surface and the top of the tunnel must be at least 16 in (410 mm); if supine, pulling oneself through with an overhead cable through the tunnel, a 25-in vertical distance is required including at least 2-in (5-cm) clearance between the cable and top of the tunnel.

Hatches   MIL-STD-1472B [26] recommends certain depth and width dimensions for hatches or emergency exits such as on aircraft. These are really minimum dimensions for structural integrity and were based upon body dimension data for young males. Larger exits would be needed if the persons were wearing parachutes or were civilian passengers. The following table provides minimum dimensions for both top and bottom accesses and side hatches. The bulky clothing data is recommended for civilian applications such as hatches in buildings for maintenance. Circular hatches, or manholes, must be at least 30 in (760 mm) in diameter.

Dimensions	Depth/Height		Width	
Clothing	Light	Bulky	Light	Bulky
Top and bottom hatches	13″ (330 mm)	16″ (410 mm)	23″ (580 mm)	27″ (690 mm)
Side hatches	26″ (660 mm)	29″ (740 mm)	30″ (760 mm)	34″ (860 mm)

There are also bulkhead-mounted side hatches such as on ships. The recommended dimensions are 20 to 24 in (508 to 609 mm) wide and 60 to 76 in (1524-1930 mm) from the floor to the top of the hatch. The bottom of the hatch (combing) may be 10 in (254 mm) from the floor. Ideally, wall hatches like doorways should be flush with the floor. However, for structural reasons, the hatch dimensions must be smaller than optimal for people. When the vertical dimension is limited there is less risk of muscular strain from stepping over a combing than from stooping excessively. For military personnel, the combing should not exceed 20 in (508 mm), which is 6 to 10 in (152 to 254 mm) below crotch height for a 5th percentile person.

Doorways Doorways will be used here to refer to common openings in buildings for personnel passage whether or not a door is fitted therein. The height of a doorway must accommodate 99 percent of the population without stooping and assuming no hats or other headwear. The standard height of doorways in most modern homes is about 79 in (2007 mm) allowing for the molding at the top. The width of doorways is usually based upon considerations other than body clearances. In homes, the outside doorway is the widest; bedroom doorways, intermediate width; bathroom and hinged-door closets, the most narrow.

A doorway without doors (archway) should be at least 54 in (1372 mm) wide to accommodate the passage of two people concurrently.

Doors Figure 7-12 illustrates a variety of doors. Within a building an open doorway is preferable to a closed doorway when there is heavy traffic and no requirement for a door. An example is the open doorway with an interior wall restricting vision into restrooms at airport terminals.

Hinged doors Unless otherwise specified, most of us think of a hinged door when a door is mentioned. In most enclosures, hinged doors are located in

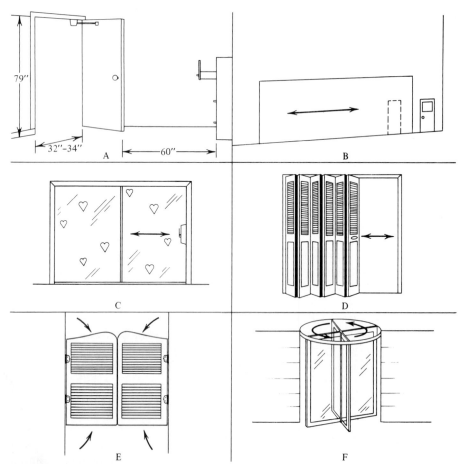

Figure 7-12 Types of doors (a) hinged door with automatic door close (b) sliding hangar door with adjacent hinged door (c) patio sliding door with decals (d) folding door (e) swinging "bar room" door (f) revolving door.

the corner of the room. This may be dictated by building layout, but it is also done to conserve wall space and to keep the open door out of the way. Where there is an option as to door location, as in a row of offices, all doorways are located in a corner nearest the exit, or in a consistent fashion. A door may be located in the center of the wall in a large room where there is considerable traffic passing through the doorway.

As mentioned previously, hinged doors usually open inward. Exceptions include small hat closets where this would not be feasible. Study desks, conference tables, and classroom chairs should face in the opposite direction from the doorway, if feasible, to avoid visual distractions. Cabinets and equipment in use should not be located closer than 5 ft (152 cm) from the open door. Doorsills on outside doors are not recommended because they may be a stumbling block. Weather stripping to the base of the door is preferable. (See Chapter 13 for other door interfaces.)

Sliding and Folding Doors   Sliding doors conserve wall space and are used where hinged doors would bump into things or block passageways. Sliding refers here more to the direction of movement than the type of movement. Some work on a friction principle, but most operate on small rollers on a track. Horizontal sliding doors are found on aircraft hangars and industrial assembly rooms where large finished products are transported outside. MIL-STD-1472B requires that there be an alternative personnel exit, such as a separate hinged door in or near the sliding door. Large sliding doors are easy to jam and are cumbersome and slow to move.

In dwellings, horizontal sliding doors are useful in clothes closets or small bathrooms where there is no room on either side for a hinged door to open. Glass sliding doors are also common on patios or living rooms. Bright decals are recommended for full-length transparent doors on patios to avoid confusion with an unobstructed opening.

Vertical sliding doors are employed on most garages to expedite opening. Radio-actuated doors are becoming common in homes to save time and energy and to avoid bad-weather exits from the car to open the door. Folding or accordion-type doors are also employed on closets and between certain rooms where a hinged door would not be feasible.

Swinging and Electronic-Actuated Doors   Hinged doors which are closed by spring actuation are somewhat hazardous, especially doors which swing open in either direction, such as the proverbial "barroom door." A single door that opens in either direction is not recommended for public places. However, a single door may be used decoratively in bathrooms to separate the bath and wash areas.

Spring-actuated doors that open in only one direction may be used in pairs with conspicuous IN and OUT signs on each side of each door.

We are all familiar with the outward swinging doors, at grocery markets and other stores, that are actuated by pressure-sensitive floor pads. The area in front of the swinging exit must be guarded by railings and must be conspicuously labeled as an exit. An improved design for such doors is one in which the door slides horizontally when one steps on a pad on either side of the door. A single wide door may be used for entry and exit without the hazard of a swinging door.

Revolving Doors   The revolving or rotary door was an early attempt to provide temperature control in department stores and hotels without depending upon people to close a door after entry or exit. A hazardous situation developed when a slow-moving person fell and was trapped on one side while a fast-moving person was pushing on the other side. With hydraulic-closing doors and electronic-actuated doors, the use of revolving doors is no longer necessary.

Stairs and Other Elevating Devices

MIL-STD-1472B [26] recognizes four types of elevating structures, each applicable to a certain range of angles of ascent. The following table lists both the recommended and maximum angles. Choice of structure should be based on the angle of slope required.

Structure	Maximum angle	Recommended angle
	(Degrees from horizontal)	
Stairs	20 – 50	30 – 35
Stair-ladders	50 – 75	50 – 60
Ladders	75 – 90	75 – 85
Ramps	0 – 20	7 – 15

Stairs   Figure 7-13 provides design criteria for stairs and associated banisters and handrails [1472B, 26]. While there is some leeway given in riser height (6.5 to 7.0 in; 165 to 178 mm), the most important consideration is exact consistency in height. Nelson [29] found that people lift their feet only as high as necessary to clear the next riser. A fall could occur from a riser even a quarter of an inch higher than previous ones.

The depth of the tread should be 11 to 12 in (279 to 305 mm) since the 95th percentile male foot is almost 12 inches in length. The dimension is particularly important on descent, where the ball of the foot must not extend beyond the front edge of the tread. Tread depth is a trade-off against angle of ascent; more building space is required with lower angles. However, a 1-in (25-mm) nosing (see Figure 7-13) permits the use of a slightly more shallow tread. At least the nosing and preferably the entire tread should be friction-coated to minimize skidding in wet weather.

Climbing stairs is physically taxing for elderly, handicapped, and heavy people. Landings should be provided every 11 or 12 treads. Handrail height at landings should be 36 in (914 mm) as opposed to 33 to 34 in (838 to 854 mm) from tread to top of the rail. Cylindrical handrails are easy to grasp. They should be provided on both sides whether the stair flight is open or between walls.

When two stair flights are at right angles separated by an open landing, a guard screen or other enclosure should be provided below the guard rail so that dropped objects cannot fall on persons below.

Ladders   Figure 7-14 provides design criteria for fixed ladders. Fixed ladders are usually vertical and without handrails. The more vertical the ladder, the less hatch space required for body clearance at the top (see dimension G, Figure 7-14). Vertical ladders are used between two or more decks in military

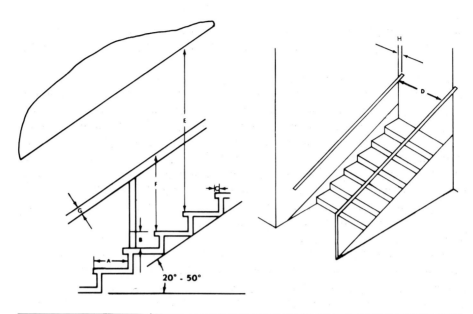

20° - 50°

	Dimension	Minimum	Maximum	Recommended
A	Tread depth (including nosing)	9.50" (240 mm)	12.00" (300 mm)	11–12" (280–300 mm)
B	Riser Height	5.00" (125 mm)	8.00" (200 mm)	6.5–7.0" (165–180 mm)
C	Depth of Nosing (where applicable)	0.75" (19 mm)	1.50" (38 mm)	1.00" (25 mm)
D	Width (handrail to handrail) one-way stairs two-way stairs	30.00" (760 mm)	---	36.00" (910 mm)
E	Overhead clearance	76.00" (1930 mm)	---	78.00" (1980 mm)
F	Height of handrail (from leading edge of tread)	30.00" (760 mm)	36.00" (910 mm)	33.00" (840 mm)
G	Handrail diameter	1.25" (32 mm)	3.00" (75 mm)	1.50" (38 mm)
H	Rail clearance from wall	1.75" (45 mm)	---	3.00" (75 mm)

Figure 7-13 Stair dimensions. *(MIL-STD-1472B, 1974.)*

systems and should be offset at each level so that users cannot fall more than one floor.

When used for climbing to roofs or towers, landings should be provided every 10th or 12th tread. Fixed ladders of more than 20 ft (6 m) should be provided a 27- × 28-in (68- × 71-cm) cage to preclude falling backward.

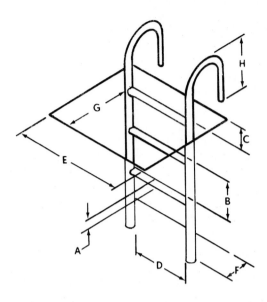

	Dimension	Minimum	Maximum	Recommended
A	Rung thickness	Wood−1.125" (32 mm) Protected metal −0.75" (19 mm) Corrosive metal −1.00" (25 mm)	1.50" (33 mm)	1.40" (35 mm)
B	Rung spacing	9.00" (230 mm)	15.00" (380 mm)	12.00" (300 mm)
C	Height, rung to landing	6.00" (150 mm)	Rung spacing	Rung spacing
D	Width between stringers	12.00" (300 mm)	---	18–21.00" (460–530 mm)
E	Opening (climbing clearance) width clearance depth	24.00" (610 mm)	--	30.00" (760 mm)
	F To wall	6.00" (150 mm)	---	8.00" 200 mm)
	G On climbing side	36.00" (910 mm)	for 75° to 30.00 (760 mm) for 90°	
H	Heights of stringer above landing	33.00" (840 mm)	--	36.00" (910 mm)

Figure 7-14   Fixed ladder dimensions. *(MIL-STD-1472B, 1974.)*

Rungs are cylindrical and approximately 1.4 in (35 cm) in diameter for ease of grasping while climbing. However, standing for extended durations on rungs places a painful pressure on the balls of the feet. Flat steps are recommended for painting, wallpapering, and so forth. The climber needs an extension of the vertical supports (stringers) above the landing so he or she is not required to crawl onto the landing. Portable extension ladders should be of light-weight metal and should have a positive friction base. Again, the stringers should extend at least 24 in (610 mm) above the top.

Stairladders, employed at intermediate slopes of 50 to 75°, more nearly resemble stairs than ladders since they have a flat tread and handrails. Loading docks at warehouses and fold-down attic ladders in many homes are familiar examples.

Ramps   The more gradual slope of ramps makes them less efficient than stairs in the use of space. Movement is also slower for healthy, young adults. However, the gradual slope is easier for the elderly or persons in poor physical condition. Switchback ramps are employed effectively in football stadiums and gymnasiums for egress of large numbers of people at approximately the same time. Ramps are also used in terminal buildings, the Pentagon in Washington, D.C., and other locations with high-density movement.

A requirement that public buildings be usable by a person in a wheelchair has led to the installation of many ramps in buildings and at the curb (Chapter 13). Ramps are used in industry by small motorized vehicles, but the dangers of uncontrolled push vehicles on ramps has discouraged their use for freight movement.

Cleats spaced every 14 in (360 mm) and extending at right angles to the line of traffic are recommended for pedestrian ramps at slopes of 15° or more [MIL STD 1472B, 26]. Nonskid materials should be applied to very gradual slopes.

Circular Staircases   Decorative staircases that gradually arc no more than 180°, have been employed in homes where space is not a constraint. However, spiral staircases such as those used in lighthouses and other tall, narrow structures, require special design for safety. The problem is that the depth dimension varies considerably from the interior to exterior portion of the tread. When the interior tread fails to meet tread-depth criteria in space-constrained, spiral staircases, the risk of falling during descent is increased. Where necessary, they should be descended backwards as with a ladder and holding a handrail.

Poles   Vertical poles for rapid descent have been employed in fire stations with multistory construction. The high accident frequency has led recent designers of fire stations to have the ready room on the same level as the fire engines [Thomson, 47].

Escalators and Moving Sidewalks   Escalators, like ramps, provide for movement of large numbers of people with a minimum of energy expenditure. The escalator or moving staircase typically has an ascent angle of 30 to 45°, with 30° recommended.

The recommended rate of movement is 120 to 138 ft/min (37). Although rates from 90 to 180 ft/min can be found, the slower rates may encourage some users to walk up the escalator and the faster rates may cause users to pause to judge their footing at entrance points. The pauses slow traffic to an extent that offsets the travel time gained by the faster rate.

Thomson [47] recommends the use of high-contrast bars or diamonds every 18 in (457 mm) on solid black handrails to make movement of the rails more apparent. Guard walls should extend 5 to 6 ft (1.52 to 1.83 m) beyond the upper and lower ends of the escalator to allow the user to become accustomed to walking again. The entryway should also be guarded to allow the person time to adjust to stepping onto the first step.

A 52-in (1.321-m) tread width allows two users to stand side by side. While this is desirable for parents with children and for conversation, it may also encourage passing.

Moving sidewalks, consisting principally of a moving belt, are becoming common in aircraft terminals and in business districts using newer concepts of transportation. Design criteria are similar to escalators. Historically, there have been accidents reported at the beginning and ends of escalators and moving sidewalks. Entries and exits should be appropriately illuminated and, if necessary, signed to promote safety in transition.

Elevators   Elevators permit the rapid movement of people with a minimum of energy expenditure. Elevators are usually faster than other means for moving a limited number of people over a distance of three or more levels. Obviously, the number of people moved depends upon the number of elevators available for simultaneous operation. However, even packed to capacity, they would hardly be suitable for evacuation of a football crowd!

Elevators are also a necessity for movement of the physically handicapped and freight. The reliability of elevators requires that buildings have staircases as an alternate mode of vertical transportation. Elevators have made high-rise buildings and skyscrapers a practical building concept, and express elevators have expedited movement.

Design requirements, in addition to appropriate environmental control and safety provisions, include interior and exterior controls and displays. The minimum exterior requirements are up and down selector buttons backlighted upon pressing, arrow-shaped lights indicating the current direction of travel, and appropriate lights to indicate "in use" and "out of order." A chime should also sound immediately before the doors open to expedite boarding. Interior controls should include floor selector buttons, also backlighted upon actuation and arrayed in a logical manner; a display over the door of the present location of the elevator cab and floor numbers on the side of the doorway when the door opens. A door-opening, override push button and an emergency telephone, buzzer, or speaker are also essential (see Chapter 13).

Movable Work Platforms   Movable platforms are elevators that are not fully enclosed for use by workmen, such as at construction sites or mines.

MIL-STD-1472B [26] requires that exterior personnel platforms have a top rail not less than 42 in (1.072 m), an intermediate rail, a toeboard, and a guard screen.

Freight elevators and hydraulic-operated work platforms must also have load-limit signs, guards on controls to prevent accidental operation, limit stops, and an automatic fail-safe brake or other self-locking device. Unlike elevators, the control system does not provide for automatic stopping at the level of a floor. Since a breakdown may occur between floors, it is desirable to have a method for manually lowering the platform.

Seat Design

In Chapter 6 certain dimensional data were given relative to seat design for operators. Seat design obviously varies with the particular usage. The secretary or typist requires a semierect, armless chair while the supervisor may require a more reclining, upholstered arm chair. Figure 7-15 illustrates recommended dimensions for two types of chairs.

Pan Dimensions The minimum height of the seat pan from the floor must be such as to be comfortable for the short person. (A seat too high would apply excessive pressure on the thighs.) A first to fifth percentile person has a popliteal height of 14.0 to 15.5 in (36 to 39 cm). On the other hand, a 95th percentile male has a popliteal height of 19.3 in (48 cm) plus shoe heel height. A 14-in pan height would provide little thigh support and possibly introduce a convex posture in the lumbar back area. Hence, an adjustable range from 15 to 19 in (39 to 48 cm) is recommended. The height of the underside of the work surface is obviously a major factor in pan height. For sit/stand applications there should be either a footrest or a metal ring around the base of the stool for latching the heels.

The maximum depth of the pan must also permit clearance of the calf of the short person's legs. The maximum depth recommended by Grandjean et al. [19] for multipurpose chairs was 16.8 in (43 cm). Although the buttock-to-popliteal length of a tall person is several inches longer, complete thigh support is not required for comfort.

The minimum seat width should be 15.7 in (40 cm). For a general population of users, broader hip breadths may be anticipated. Recommended dimensions are 18 in (46 cm) at the rear of the pan and 19 to 21 in (48 to 53 cm) at the front to allow for leg spread.

When seated side by side on bleachers, the critical dimension is not hip breadth but rather shoulder breadth or elbow-to-elbow breadth. The shoulder breadth of a 95th percentile male is 19 to 20 in (48 to 51 cm) not including an overcoat. Reserved seating for bleachers should never be less than 19 in (48 cm) per person.

Seat pans, whether upholstered or solid material, should be slightly contoured at front without seam or ridge.

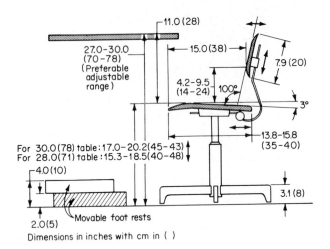

For 30.0 (78) table : 17.0–20.2 (45–43)
For 28.0 (71) table : 15.3–18.5 (40–48)

Dimensions in inches with cm in ( )

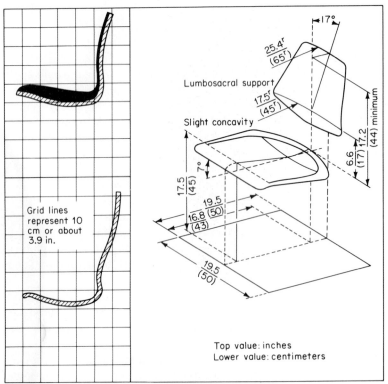

Grid lines represent 10 cm or about 3.9 in.

Lumbosacral support

Slight concavity

Top value: inches
Lower value: centimeters

Figure 7-15 Typical dimensions of secretary and multipurpose seats. *(Burandt and Grandjean, 1963, and Grandjean et al., 1973, as given in McCormick, 1976. From* Human Factors, 1973, vol. 15, no. 3. *Copyright 1973 by The Human Factors Society, Inc. and reproduced by permission.)*

Backrests The recline angle of the backrest depends upon the function of the seat. A typist's chair has an angle of only 100° between the pan and the backrest. (The front of the seat is elevated about 3°.) For reading, Grandjean et al. [18] found that people prefer a backrest angle of 101 to 104°, and for resting, 105 to 108°.

Modern office chairs are designed with an articulating back with the back reclining while the pan itself remains stationary. This permits a change of posture and negates thigh pressure while reclining.

The important consideration is support in the sacrolumbar region (small of the back), more so than in the shoulder or sacral regions. The required support is 4.2 to 9.5 in (11 to 24 cm) above the seat pan. Desk chair backs typically extend to 18 in above SRP. In multipurpose chairs and, in fact, in most chairs, the sacral region is open for protrusion of the buttocks. In continuous back chairs, the lumbar region is slightly concaved for this purpose. Typists' chairs have a small back support, slightly concaved horizontally and pivoting (back) for postural changes. Backrests should be no wider than 15 in (38 cm) for elbow clearance.

Armrest An armrest length should be 9 to 12 in (23 to 30 cm). Full-length arms, such as those found in easy chairs at home, are an obstacle to getting close to the work surface or in rotating for egress. The front supporting column should be curved inward so as not to press against the thighs. Some steel-armed chairs are cantilevered without a front armrest supporting column. Armrests are typically 8 or 9 in (20 to 23 cm) above the pan and there is a minimum of 19 in (48 cm) between armrests.

Movement In addition to reclining and articulating, most operator chairs also pivot and roll. Chairs used at work surfaces should pivot 360° for ease of ingress/egress and access to various surfaces. Hard rubber casters are quieter on hard surfaces. The casters may also be slanted sideways slightly for better movement over cracks or cables on the floor. Locks on casters are desirable when inadvertent movement is likely.

Cushioning People are more comfortable when the body weight is borne by the ishial tuberosities, bony structures of the buttocks. The distribution of weight should be greatest at these two loci and progressively less at more distant contours.

High-density urethane foam cushion is more comfortable over long durations than is the traditional soft seat with spring and upholstery [Branton and Grayson, 7]. Grandjean et al. [18] conducted a paired-comparison study of rated comfort of many different seat designs for multipurpose chairs. The recommended chair included 2 to 4 cm (about 0.75 to 1.5 in) of foam rubber. Another Grandjean et al. study [19] found 6 cm (2.5 in) of cushioning and upholstery was desirable for reading and resting. Seat design criteria for vehicles are discussed in Chapter 11, and seats for physically handicapped are a subject of Chapter 13.

Bathrooms

Provisions for personal hygiene in public buildings have undergone several functional improvements (including design for the physically handicapped, Chapter 13). Design of the home bathroom has had few major improvements since the 1920s, although there are more bathrooms per occupants of a dwelling.

Public Bathrooms   Larger buildings should have two or more sets of widely separated bathrooms on each floor. Locations at the end of a hall offer not only privacy, but also outward swinging doors do not obstruct traffic. An interior separating wall insures visual privacy.

Several techniques are employed for drying the hands. The single-tissue dispenser recessed in the wall with waste receptable immediately under it requires maintenance, but it is less objectionable than the continuous towel roller. Motorized blowers do not require maintenance, but they are slower, noisier, and less acceptable when face washing is required.

Lavatory controls should be spring-loaded to prevent leaving the water running. Flushing levers above urinals and stools are preferable to foot-actuated controls for flushing, although automation is recommended.

Toilet cubicles should have walls high enough for visual privacy. The open bottom part of the door allows one to tell if the cubicle is occupied; however, a more positive feedback is desirable. Spring-loaded doors are perhaps the cheapest solution.

For control in dispensing tissue, the paper should be installed to dispense over the top of the roll. The dispenser should be convenient and visible while seated.

Private Bathrooms   Full baths in living dwellings are becoming compartmentalized by function to permit simultaneous use of different units. The lavatory may be located in a dressing area with the toilet and bath behind another door. An extension of this concept not generally exploited is separate rooms for bath and toilet. Although requiring more space, the arrangement is less expensive than additional bathrooms, and may be a practical solution when three or more occupants share a common bathroom.

Separate hot and cold water controls for lavatories are being supplanted by a single lever. The feature has been recommended by arthritics and others who find grasping and twisting to be slightly painful. Home lavatories should provide sufficient surface on the counter for the myriad of containers and equipment used. Counter height should be tailored to user heights. (Some counters used by adults are so low that taller adults must stoop to reach the basin.) Full-length mirrors with diffuse overhead or side-mounted lighting fixtures are recommended. Lighting should emphasize visibility functions such as shaving. Where two occupants are likely to use the lavatory at the same time, two basins should be provided at least 5 ft (1.52 m) apart.

Minimum shower stall dimensions should be 36 × 42 in (91 × 107 cm). A separate bathtub and shower stall may be desirable, if economically feasible. However, when only one bathroom is permissible, the strong preference of some users for one or the other would dictate a combined functional capability (particularly for home resale value). Tub accessories for increased safety include handrails for grasping and friction strips on the bottom. Several improvements in the design of the shower head include a relaxing stream modulation and directional flexibility. A desirable innovation would be a head that returned to a neutral position when the shower was turned off so the water would not inadvertently spray out on the floor when activated by the next user. A single, programmable temperature control is desirable. Users of bath or tub should not be required to feel the water and adjust two valves to obtain a desirable mix of hot and cold. Scalding temperatures should be precluded by automation.

Few modifications have been made in the design of the tub itself for comfort in a supine position. The standard length of the bathtub is not compatible with 95th percentile male body dimensions with full-length extension. Also, studies of the shape of the "head" end of the tub have shown that it is not compatible with the shape of the back and neck for restful reclining [Kira, 44]. Three contours for reclining as developed by Kira are shown in Figure 7-16.

Little consideration has been given to ease and safety of ingress/egress

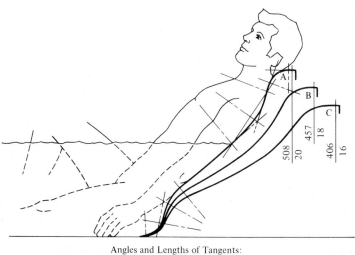

Angles and Lengths of Tangents:

A 102 (4) @ 80°   254 (10) @ 40°   178 (7) @ 55°   64 (2½) @ 70°
B 102 (4) @ 75°   229 (9) @ 32.5°   190 (7½) @ 45°   76 (3) @ 62.5°
C 102 (4) @ 70°   203 (8) @ 25°   203 (8) @ 35°   89 (3½) @ 55°

Figure 7-16 Proposed contours and angles of tub backrests. *(From* The Bathroom, Rev. Ed., *by Alexander Kira. © 1966, 1976 by Alexander Kira. Reprinted by permission of Bantam Books, Inc. All rights reserved.)*

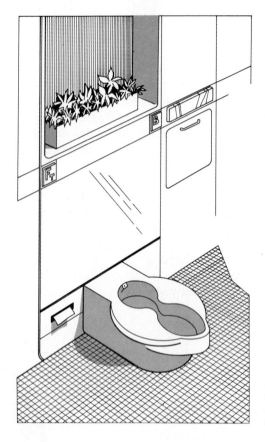

Figure 7-17 Modified water closet based upon support and functional requirements. *(From* The Bathroom, *Rev. Ed., by Alexander Kira. © 1966, 1976 by Alexander Kira. Reprinted by permission of Bantam Books, Inc. All rights reserved.)*

although falling in a tub is a common accident. Transition from a squatting to standing position is a difficult movement for older and heavier persons. When used as a tub only (not as a shower), an elevated bottom with a wide rim on the sides may be easier than a floor-level design. Few anthropometric studies are known relative to tub design and associated rim dimensions for ease of entry by these users, but handrails may not be the only solution.

Kira [44] proposed a design of a toilet seat pad (Figure 7-17) which incorporated a principle of seat design—that the weight should be supported by the ishial tuberosities (buttocks bones). He recommended a narrowing of the seat opening, noting that the present design transfers weight to the thighs. (It sometimes cuts off circulation as well.) The oblique shape in front also has an obvious functional advantage and has been incorporated in the better, modern toilet bowl and pad designs.

The act of defecation is improved physiologically by assuming a squatting posture. An anthropologist recommended a seat height of from 9 to 11 in (23 to 28 cm). The elderly, arthritic, and obese may have difficulty assuming such a posture. Handrails or "push-up" hand supports that transfer the weight may also presuppose considerable arm strength. An unexploited design is a footrest that may be pulled out or otherwise erected after the user has been seated on a pad of standard height. This design permits flexing the thighs to the abdomen without requiring body weight lifting imposed by a squatting posture.

The flushing lever at the back of the seat is an inconvenience long tolerated for the technical simplicity of the common toilet. A hand- or foot-operated control that is more accessible while seated would be a convenience long overdue.

QUESTIONS AND PROBLEMS

1 A family of six live in a townhouse with 1000 square feet. What is the SFPP? How would you classify the footage per person provided?
2 What are two things wrong with the following office design?

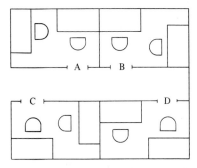

• Each office is 10 × 7 feet.

3 Person B is standing directly behind person A. The distance between A and B is 60 in. The distance from A to the screen is 60 in and the bottom of the screen is 60 inches from the floor. The height of A is 70 in and the standing eye height of B is 60 in. Determine how much person B must be elevated to see the entire screen. If the screen were 600 in away from person A, how much would B need to be elevated for unobstructed screen vision?
4 A seminar course with eight students is planned using 3 × 6 ft tables, with two students per table. The instructor also has a 3 × 6 table. The back of the table and the side of the nearest student tables are 5 ft from the front wall. Sketch a floor plan of five tables with the students arranged in a C-shaped pattern. With 4-ft aisles behind all students, calculate the minimum dimensions of the room.
5 What were the minimum dimensions of the classroom for 32 students discussed in the chapter [Thomson, 47]? Assume 36 in between rows of tables.
6 An acoustically treated room has a total absorption of 24.5 sabins. The room volume is 8000 cubic feet. Calculate the reverberation time. Indicate if the room would be acceptable as a conference room (according to Farrell).
7 a Which of the dimensions of stairs A on the following page are out of specification?
   b What are three things obviously incorrect with stairs B? (These are unrelated to the dimensions.)

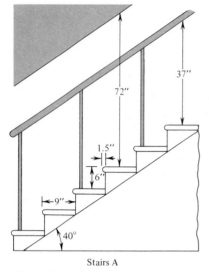

Stairs A   Stairs B

Figure 7-18   Stairs A and B.

REFERENCES

1   Acking, C. A. and R. Kuller: The perception of an interior as a function of its colour, *Ergonomics,* vol. 15, no. 6, 1972, pp. 645–654.

2   Becker, F. D.: *Design for living: The resident's view of multifamily living.* Center for Urban Development Research, Cornell University, Ithaca, N.Y., May 1974.

3   Bennett, C. A. and P. Rey: What's so hot about red? *Human Factors,* vol. 14, no. 2, 1972, pp. 149–154.

4   Beranek, L. L., W. E. Blazier, and J. J. Figwer: Preferred noise criterion (PNC) curves and their application to rooms, *Journal of the Acoustical Society of America,* vol. 50, 1971, pp. 1223–1228.

5   Berendt, R. D., G. E. Winzer, and C. Burroughs: A guide to airborne, impact, and structure borne noise-control in multifamily dwellings, U.S. Department of HUD, September 1967.

6   Black, J. C.: Uses of spaces in owner-occupied houses, Ph.D. dissertation, University of Utah, Salt Lake City, April 1968.

7   Branton, P. and G. Grayson: An evaluation of train seats by observation of sitting behavior, *Ergonomics,* vol. 10, no. 1, 1967, pp. 35–51.

8   Brookes, M. J.: Office landscape: Does it work? *Applied Ergonomics,* vol. 3, no. 4, 1972, pp. 224–236.

9   Brookes, M. J. and A. Kaplan: The office environment: Space planning and effective behavior, *Human Factors,* vol. 14, no. 5, 1972, October 1972.

10 Chombart de Lauwe, P.: The sociology of housing methods and prospects of research, *International Journal of Comparative Sociology,* vol. 2, no. 1, March 1961, pp. 23–41.

11 *Design Criteria for new public building accessibility,* General Service Administration, Public Building Service PBS(PCD) D G 5, May 1977.

12 Ertel, H.: *Blue is beautiful, Time,* September 1973.

13 Erwin, D.: Escape from the egg-crate school, *Southwest Scene,* Sunday Magazine, Dallas Morning News, March 28, 1971.

14 Eysenck, H. J.: A critical and experimental study of color preferences, *American Journal of Psychology,* vol. 54, 1941, pp. 385–394.

15 Farrell, W. R.: *Reverberation time criteria,* Bolt, Beranek, and Newman, Cambridge, Mass., 1958.

16 Fast, J.: *Body Language,* Pocket Books, New York, 1971.

17 Fletcher, H.: *Speech and hearing in communication,* Van Nostrand, New York, 1953.

18 Grandjean, E., A. Boni, and Krestzschmer: The development of a rest-chair profile for healthy and nostalgic people, *Ergonomics,* vol. 12, no. 2, 1969, pp. 307–315.

19 Grandjean, E., W. Hunting, G. Wotzka, and R. Sharer: An ergonomic investigation of multipurpose chairs, *Human Factors,* vol. 15, no. 3, 1973, pp. 247–255.

20 Hesselgren, Sven: *Man's perception of man-made environment, an architectural theory,* Dowden, Hutchinson, and Ross, Inc., Stroudsburg, Pa., 1975.

21 Hodge, S.: "Your Office Environment," a report of the Harris and Associate, Inc. survey of office personnel, *The Houston Post,* December 29, 1978, p. 1B.

22 Ittleson, W. H., H. M. Proshansky, L. G. Rivlin, and G. H. Winkel: *An introduction to environmental psychology,* Holt, Rinehart, and Winston, New York, 1974.

23 Manning, D. R.: "Thermal comfort during surgery," Master of Industrial Engineering thesis, Texas A&M University, 1978.

24 Manning, P.: Windows, environment and people, *Interbuild/Arena,* October 1967.

25 McCormick, E. J.: *Human Factors in Engineering and Design,* 4th ed., McGraw-Hill, New York, 1976, pp. 291–292.

26 Military Standard 1472B, Human Engineering Design Criteria for Military Systems, Equipment, and Facilities, Department of Defense, December 31, 1974.

27 *Munsell Book of Color,* Munsell Color Co., Baltimore, 1929.

28 Nebalek, A. K. and I. V. Nebalek: Noise control by acoustic treatment, in D. M. Lipscomb and A. C. Taylor, Jr. (eds.), *Noise Control Handbook of Principles and Practices,* Van Nostrand Reinhold Company, New York, 1978, chap. 6.

29 Nelson, G.: Engineering-Human Factors Interface in Stairway Tread-Riser Design, Master of Science thesis, Texas A&M University, 1973.

30 Nemecek, J. and E. Grandjean: Results of an ergonomics investigation of large space offices, *Human Factors,* vol. 15, no. 2, 1973, pp. 111–124.

31 Newman, O.: *Defensible Space,* Macmillan, New York, 1972.

32 Osgood, C. E., G. C. Suci, and P. H. Tannenbaum: *Measurement of Meaning,* The University of Illinois Press, Urbana, 1957.

33 Sommer, R.: *Personal space: The Behavioral Basis of Design,* Prentice-Hall, Englewood Cliffs, N.J., 1969.

34 Srivastava, R. K. and T. S. Peel: *Human movement as a function of stimulation,* Environmental Research Foundation, Topeka, Kansas, April 1968.

35 Uhrbrook, R. W.: Music on the job: Its influence on worker morale and production, *Journal of Applied Psychology,* vol. 14, 1961, pp. 9–38.

36 U.S. Department of HUD Transmittal Notice 1390.2, August 4, 1971.

37 Van Cott, M. P. and R. G. Kinkade (eds.): *Human Engineering Guide to Equipment Design,* U.S. Government Printing Office, Washington, D.C., 1972.

38 Walsch, D. P.: Noise levels and annoyance in open plan educational facilities, *Journal of Architectural Research,* vol. 4, 1975, pp. 5–16.

39 Wells, B. W. P.: The psycho-social influence of building environment: Sociometric

findings in large and small office spaces, *Building Science,* vol. 1, 1965, SfB(92): UDG 301.151, pp. 153–165.

40 Wells, B. W. P.: Subjective responses to lighting installation in a modern office building and their design implications, *Building Science,* vol. 1, 1965, SfB: Ab7:UCD 628.9777, pp. 57–68.

41 "The windowless look becomes passe," *Factory Management,* June 1977.

42 Woodson, W. E. and D. W. Conover: *Human engineering guide for equipment designers,* 2d ed., University of California Press, Berkeley, 1970, pp. 2–170.

43 Wools, R. and D. Canter: The effect of the meaning of buildings on behavior, *Applied Ergonomics,* vol. 1, no, 3, 1970, pp. 144–150.

44 Kira, A.: *The Bathroom* (rev. ed.), The Viking Press, New York, 1976.

45 Miller, Herman: Action Office by Herman Miller, a brochure by Herman Miller, Inc., Zeeland, Michigan, 1976.

46 Burandt V. and E. Grandjean: Sitting habits of office employees, *Ergonomics,* vol. 6, no. 2, 1963, pp. 217–228.

47 Thomson [See Ref. 49 for Ch. 6].

Design of the Environment: Lighting, Temperature, Atmosphere

In the last chapter the spatial environment of the worker was examined. In Chapters 8 and 9, criteria for the design of the ambient environment will be presented. Chapter 8 is concerned with techniques for assessing and providing adequate workplace illumination, control of temperature, and atmospheric content and pressure. In Chapter 9, similar techniques will be presented regarding the mechanical environment—noise, vibration, and acceleration.

The 1970s and early 1980s could be characterized as the era of energy conservation. Guidelines were sought to distinguish energy levels which are necessary for human functioning from those which would be wasteful consumption. Americans were cautioned to conserve electricity by turning off indoor lights not in use and by extinguishing ornamental outdoor lighting.

The president recommended room temperatures of 78°F minimum for the summer and 65°F maximum for winter months. Energy conservation checklists were widely distributed and federal income tax credits were an incentive to encourage home insulation, sealing, and weather stripping. Solar heating to capitalize on natural sunlight was incorporated into the design of many new homes.

In Chapter 11, the impact of fuel conservation for internal combustion engines will be presented in relation to human interfaces in automotive design.

LIGHTING

Visual tasks vary in difficulty from reading the scale on a micrometer or inspecting for flaws in dark clothing to stacking boxes in a warehouse. The lighting system provided must be compatible with these diverse seeing needs.

In addition to the quantity of illumination, there are qualitative factors that are also vital to a lighting system: control of glare and brightness contrast, control of direction, distribution, diffusion, and uniformity. While it is difficult to isolate the effects of inadequate lighting in industry from other factors, an improperly designed lighting system may contribute to eye fatigue, to increased errors and, in extreme instances, to an increased accident rate.

Principles and Concepts in Lighting

Prior to discussion of design techniques for providing workspace lighting, it is necessary to define some basic terms and units of measurement.

Illumination Illumination is used in a qualitative sense to refer to the act of illuminating or state of being illuminated. More technically, it refers to the density of luminous flux incident on a surface.

The intensity of a light source was traditionally expressed in terms of candlepower (cp). Today, however, instead of candles, the more precisely defined unit of illumination is the *candela* (cd).*

The *lumen* (lm) is the unit of flow of light. It is the light from a point source of 1 cd falling on an area of 1 ft^2, where every point on the surface is at a distance of 1 ft. A common unit of illuminance is the *footcandle* (fc). This is the density of light falling on the inner surface of a sphere of 1 ft radius when a point source of light with an intensity of 1 cd is placed at the center of the sphere. One fc incident to a surface equals 1 lm/ft^2.

The footcandle unit of illuminance is widely employed. However, current practice is to express distances and areas in metric units. Thus the illumination on a spherical surface 1 meter square at a radius of one meter has been defined as a 1 *lux* (lx). A lux is 1 lm/m^2; 1 fc = 10.76 lx; 1 lx = .0929 fc. Other units and conversion factors may be found in the *IES Lighting Handbook* [16].

Inverse Square Law The illuminance on any surface may be computed from the number of candelas emitted by a source and the distance to the surface.

$$\text{Illuminance (lux)} = \frac{\text{intensity of source (candela)}}{\text{distance (meters)}^2}$$

Thus, a 1 cd source would produce 1/4 lx at a distance of 2 meters; 1/9 lx at a distance of 3 meters, and so on.

*The candela is the luminous intensity of 1/600000 square meter of projected area of a blackbody radiator operating at the temperature of the solidification of platinum (2047 degrees K).

Luminance   Luminance is a measure of the amount of light reflected by a surface; it is independent of the distance to the object reflecting the light. Brightness is a sensation associated with luminance, but apparent brightness is influenced also by contrast, adaptation, and other factors besides the physical energy in the stimulus.

Luminance depends upon the intensity of its illumination and its reflectivity. If the surface on which the light were incident were a perfect reflector, then the surface would have a luminance of lx times $1/\pi$* or 1 nit. The *nit* is the metric unit of luminance. However, a widely used unit of luminance is the footlambert (fL). The *footlambert* is equivalent to $1/\pi$ cd/ft^2 (3.4246 nits) whereas the nit is equivalent to $1/\pi$ cd/meter^2 (0.292 fL). Other units of luminance are the *lambert* ($1/\pi$ cd per square centimeter) and the *millilambert* (mL) (1/1000 lambert), which is almost equal to a footlambert (1.076 fL = 1 mL).

Figure 8-1 illustrates the luminance levels of some common environments [Van Cott and Kinkade, 33]. Note that the human eye is sensitive to levels as low as 0.000001 fL, but that 100 to 1000 fL is typical of an outside environment.

Reflectance   Most of the light by which we see is reflected from one or more surfaces. Two surfaces, white paper and dark fabric, may have the same

---

*$1/\pi$ (.3183) is used to convert from a curved to a flat surface. *Lux* refers to a curved wave front whereas *nits* are on a flat surface.

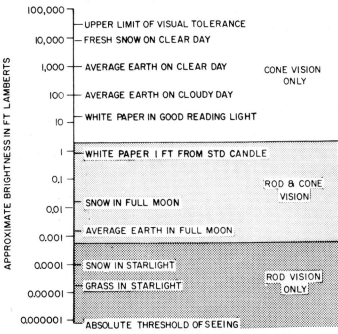

Figure 8-1   Examples of various levels of luminance. *(Van Cott and Kinkade, 1972.)*

illuminance on them, but their luminances may be quite different because their reflectances are different.

In real life even the most diffusing surface (mat white) has only about 95 percent reflectance. Reflectance percentage is defined by the formula:

$$\text{Reflectance percentage} = 100 \times \frac{\text{luminance}}{\text{illuminance}}$$

It follows that the average luminance of any surface may be calculated from the formula:

$$\text{Luminance} = \text{illuminance} \times \text{reflectance percentage}$$

As an example, the average reflectance of grass may be 3 to 5 percent, and sunlight may be 10,000 fc on a clear day. The brightness of the grass would thus be 300 to 500 fL. A metric example: 1000 lx and 9 percent reflectance would produce a surface brightness of $1000 \times 1/\pi$ (.3183) $\times$ .09 = 286.5 nits. (Note the $1/\pi$ to convert to a typically flat surface.)

Required Illumination The required illuminance for any task may be computed from the formula:

$$\text{Required illuminance} = \frac{\text{required luminance}}{\% \text{ reflectance}}$$

If an electronic assembly task has a 20 percent reflectance (1/5) and the desired brightness is 300 fL, the required illumination is 300/.2 or 5 $\times$ 300 or 1500 fc. In general, it can be seen that the smaller the reflectance, the higher the required illumination to achieve a given task brightness.

Luminance (brightness) Contrast The brightness contrast between an object and its background is one of the critical factors in detection of an object such as a road sign or an aircraft in the sky. The contrast in luminances is expressed as follows:

$$\text{Contrast percentage} = 100 \times \frac{\text{Lb} - \text{Ld}}{\text{Lb}}$$

where Lb equals the luminance of the brighter of two contrasting areas and Ld equals the darker area.

The formula is also applicable to reflectances. Thus, if paper has 80 percent reflectance and print has 10 percent reflectance, the brightness contrast would be (100) 70/80 or 88 percent [McCormick, 25].

By using the brighter of two areas as the denominator, contrast percentages are always positive values less than 100 percent. A variation of the above formula is as follows:

$$\text{Contrast percentage} = 100 \times \text{Lb} - \text{Lt/Lb}$$

where Lb = background luminance
Lt = target luminance

Note that when the target is brighter than the background, the contrast value will be a negative value from 0 to infinity [Van Cott and Kinkade, 33].

Luminance Ratio   The luminance ratio is simply the ratio of the work area luminance to the surrounding area luminance. The Illumination Engineering Society (IES) has recommended certain maximum luminance ratios as shown in Table 8-1 [16]. In general, a 3:1 ratio should not be exceeded between a task and an adjacent surface, or a 10:1 ratio between the task and more remote surfaces. Lower ratios are desirable.

Illumination Design Considerations

The design of workplace lighting involves consideration of sources of illumination, the technology of luminaire design and placement, reflection from surfaces, glare reduction methods, and the intensity of illumination required for particular tasks.

Day Lighting   Natural lighting should not be overlooked in the design of a lighting system. Rays may enter through windows or skylights and fall directly or indirectly on the task area. Placement, size, and glazing of windows must be

Table 8-1   Recommended Luminance Ratios for Offices and Industrial Situations

	Recommended maximum luminance ratio	
Areas	Office	Industrial
Task and adjacent surroundings	3:1	
Task and adjacent darker surroundings		3:1
Task and adjacent lighter surroundings		1:3
Task and remote darker surfaces	5:1	10:1
Task and remote lighter surfaces	1:5	1:10
Luminaires (or windows) and surfaces adjacent to them		20:1
Anywhere within normal field of view		40:1

Source: IES Lighting Handbook [16].

planned. The tops of windows should be high in a room to allow maximum utilization of light. To reduce the luminance ratio, the workers should not be facing the windows. Glazing with low-heat, low-light transmission glass will also decrease the brightness ratio. Outside louvers and diffusing glass will also reduce sky brightness.

Artificial Lighting Artificial lighting fixtures may vary from totally direct to totally indirect. Luminaires are classified by the International Commission on Illumination (CIE) in terms of the percentage of total luminaire output emitted above and below horizontal. If 10 percent or less of the output goes up and 90 to 100 percent goes down, the light is direct. The reverse (that is, 90 to 100 percent going up) is indirect lighting. General diffuse lighting is provided by enclosing a bulb in a translucent surface. The light is emitted over a large area with 40 to 60 percent of the light going up and a comparable percentage going down. There are also semidirect and semiindirect lighting systems where 10 to 40 percent of the light goes up or down respectively.

While direct lighting is most efficient in terms of output per electrical power (lumens/watt), it also has the problems of glare, contrast, and shadows. Indirect lighting provides for a more even distribution of illumination, but it requires more electric power for the same illumination.

Fluorescent lamps minimize shadows, particularly when they are arranged in continuous rows or checkerboard grid patterns. Diffuse lighting with fluorescent units and baffles or translucent surfaces is common both in industry and in offices. Lion et al. [19] have demonstrated visual and manipulative performance with fluorescent lighting to be superior to incandescent, tungsten-filament lighting. They attribute the superior performance to less glare and greater diffusion of light. Fluorescent lamps generally have longer life, control of color, and greater efficiency. A flickering effect, due to an alternating intensity, can be reduced by using multitube fixtures with adjusted phases.

Industrial fluorescent lighting typically employs *distributing*-type fixtures. These fixtures are spaced so that the distance between them is about equal to the mounting height above the floor [Schuman, 29]. In high bay areas, *concentrating* light units are typically employed. Units should be closely spaced not to exceed ⅗ of the mounting height. Incandescent or mercury vapor (long-life) bulbs are often used. *Semidirect* lighting has the advantage of reducing the luminance ratio between the fixture and its surroundings. Walls and ceilings should be a light color to increase brightness and reduce contrast.

Rather than discrete levels of illumination, variable intensity may be desirable by means of a rheostat. Auxiliary lighting, based on individual preference or unique task requirements, is discussed subsequently.

Explosion-proof ceiling fixtures are required in areas where a flammable atmosphere can occur. Dirty lamps and reflectors increase maintenance cost and can reduce output from 20 to 60 percent [Schuman, 29]. Open-bottomed or louvered-bottom designs minimize the collection of dust.

Figure 8-2 displays the recommended ranges of percentage reflection for

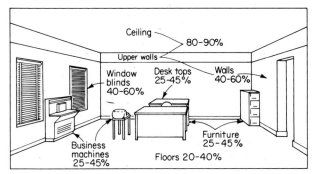

Figure 8-2 Reflectances recommended for room and furniture surfaces in an office. *(IES Journal, 1973.)*

walls, ceilings, floors, and furniture [*IES Journal,* 5]. The higher reflectance of the ceiling is especially important with indirect lighting systems.

The surface colors of walls should be pastels and light gray rather than darker shades. Walnut-finished walls in offices are attractive but may darken the room as compared with maple or lighter-colored wood.

Intensity of Illumination The *IES Lighting Handbook* [16] provides recommended illumination levels, both in footcandles and dekalux, for some common work-task situations. These may range from 5 to 20 fc for closets and hallways to 1000 fc or more for extrafine assembly tasks (Table 8-2).

The method for determining required illumination is somewhat involved. It is based on extensive research by Blackwell [8]. The original method involved first determining the most difficult visual task that will be required in any particular work area and measuring its average reflectance. Next, one selects from a long list of bench-mark tasks the one that is most nearly like the visual task in question. These tasks are classified in terms of five categories (easy, ordinary, difficult, very difficult, and most difficult). Each represents tasks for which Blackwell has calculated the required luminance. The required illumination is then calculated by dividing the required luminance by the reflectance percentage [*Illuminating Engineering,* 27]. As noted previously, required illumination increases as reflectance decreases or as task luminance increases.

The difficulty of a visual task depends upon the luminance contrast between the task detail and its background, the size or visual angle of the detailed features, and the time allowed to see it. If feasible the detail should be enlarged, for example, by using a large-sized print. Magnification aids should also be employed whenever this is a practical trade-off to increasing illumination levels.

Blackwell's Visual Performance Criteria The *IES Handbook* [16] has reprinted a visual performance criterion function and a visibility reference function. These curves (Figure 8-3) were derived from Blackwell's research. They show the luminance contrasts required for different levels of background

Table 8-2 Illumination Standards Recommended by the IES for Several Selected Types of Situations and Tasks

Situation or task	Recommended illumination	
	fc	Dekalux*
Assembly:		
Rough easy seeing	30	32
Rough difficult seeing	50	54
Medium	100	110
Fine	500	540
Extra-fine	1000	1080
Machine shops:		
Rough bench and machine work	50	54
Medium bench and machine work	100	110
Fine bench and machine work	500	540
Extra-fine bench and machine work; grinding	1000	1080
Storage rooms or warehouses; inactive	5	5.4
Offices:		
Cartography, designing, detail drafting	200	220
Accounting, bookkeeping	150	160
Mail sorting	100	110
Corridor, elevators, stairways	20	22
Residences:		
Kitchen, food preparation	150	160
Reading, writing	70	75

*1 dekalux = 10 lx or 1.076 fc.
Source: Examples selected from *IES Lighting Handbook* [16] pp. 9–81 to 9–95.

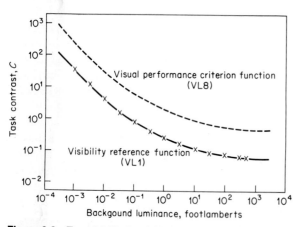

Figure 8-3 Two-visibility level (VL) curves *(IES Lighting Handbook, 5th ed., 1972.)*

luminance. Blackwell's research involved presenting tachistoscopically (1/5 sec) small luminance discs of 4 minute arc.* To determine the luminance required for threshold visibility, the subjects adjusted the contrast of the discs relative to the background until they were on the borderline of visibility. The lower function in Figure 8-2 defines threshold visibility, (VL_1). The upper function, (VL_8), provides additional contrast for three other situations: dynamic presentations (moving targets), uncertainty as to when or where the object will appear in the visual field, and 99 percent probability of detection. The upper curve requires multiplying the values in the bottom curve by 8.

The VL_8 function represents a trade-off between contrast and luminance required for equal visibility of a given target under the conditions of the three situations. Any given task may be compared to the standard task (VL_8) to determine the equivalent contrast. This value may be used to determine the required luminance of a given task.

Blackwell has also developed contrast multipliers for different age groups, for example, 1.17 for age 40; 1.58 for age 50, and 2.66 for age 65. Thus, the required luminance may be substantially higher when providing illumination for older workers.

Alternatives to Increased General Illumination   McCormick [25] surveyed the literature to determine if actual work performance was increased by improvements in illumination. While increases in output ranged from 4 to 35 percent, it was also noted that some of the original illumination levels were very low (1 to 5 fc). Thus, the performance benefits associated with increases at already high levels of illumination are not well documented.

There has been a tendency to set higher standards for illumination over a period of years. However, with the energy crisis a requirement for a demonstrated need for high illumination became more urgent.

For some tasks too much illumination can sometimes be worse than too little illumination. Faulkner & Murphy [12] found that loose threads of cloth could be made more visible by *surface grazing* illumination than by higher-intensity general illumination. Note in Figure 8-4 that the details of the blemish may appear washed out by the high-intensity illumination whereas surface grazing by angular illumination with low-intensity light will emphasize the density of surface patterns. Such directional lighting creates shadows and a three-dimensional effect.

There are individual differences in the lighting levels preferred for visual tasks, as well as differences in task requirements. For inspection tasks Faulkner and Murphy have recommended special-purpose lighting techniques: polarized light, spot lighting, edge lighting, stroboscopic lighting, and black lighting, as well as surface grazing.

Desk and table lamps are forms of auxiliary lighting. Their placement

---

*A minute of arc is the visual angle associated with 1/60 of a degree.

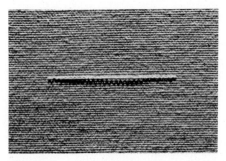 

Figure 8-4 Loose thread of cloth seen under 650 fc, general (diffuse) illumination and under 75 fc of surface-grazing illumination, left. *(Faulkner and Murphy, 1973. From* Human Factors, 1973, vol. 15, no. 2. *Copyright 1973 by The Human Factors Society, Inc. and reproduced by permission.)*

should be such as to enhance task visibility without introducing reflected or direct glare. The simplest controls work on either a push or pull principle rather than twisting a rotary switch. Controls should be at the base of the lamp, not near the bulb where either blind reaching or looking into the bulb is required.

Reduction of Glare   We are all familiar with the discomfort and annoyance of both direct and reflected glare. Luckiesh and Moss [23] systematically lowered the elevation of a 100-W frosted-inside, tungsten filament lamp from 40 to 5 degrees above the subject's line of sight. They reported a systematic reduction in visual effectiveness the more nearly the lamp was directly in line with the subject's line of sight. The *IES Lighting Handbook* [16] classifies glare in terms of *disability glare*, which interferes with visibility or visual performance and *discomfort glare,* which may be uncomfortable but does not affect performance directly.

Table 8-3 presents recommendations for reducing both direct and reflected glare. The *IES Handbook* has presented methods for calculating the discomfort glare rating (DGR) for any specific lighting layout that may be planned. DGR ratings are inversely related to visual comfort probability (VCP). The latter is the percentage of observers who would judge a light condition to be at or more comfortable than the borderline between comfort and discomfort.

In general, direct glare will not be a problem if (1) the VCP is 70 or more; (2) the ratio of the maximum-to-average luminance does not exceed 5:1 (preferably 3:1) at angular degrees of 45, 55, 65, 75, and 85 degrees from nadir both crosswise and lengthwise; (3) the maximum luminances do not exceed 2250, 1605, 1125, 750, and 496 fL, respectively, at the five angles [*IES,* 34].

Consult the *IES Handbook* [16] for a detailed discussion of techniques for estimating DGR. Situational factors include room size and shape, room surface reflectances, illumination level, type and size of luminaires and lighting distribution, numbers and locations of luminaires, luminance of the entire visual field, observer location and line of sight, and equipment and furniture in the room.

Reflections from bright surfaces on a tool, for example, a wood planer, can

Table 8-3   Techniques for Direct and Indirect Glare Reduction

Direct glare

- Position luminaires so they are not within 60 degrees of the center of the visual field.
- Avoid having workers look alternately from light to dark places.
- Select luminaires with low discomfort glare ratings.
- Use several low-intensity sources rather than one high-intensity source.
- Increase luminance of area around a glare source (reduce luminance ratio).
- Use shields, hoods, screens, and visors where glare cannot be reduced.
- Reduce glare from windows by shades, blinds, louvers, outdoor overhangs, and planned location of windows relative to work areas.

Reflected glare

- Use diffused, indirect lighting.
- Use dull, matte surfaces (flat paints, crinkled finish, desk blotters) rather than glossy polished surfaces or reflecting materials on machinery or other surfaces.
- Position light sources or work areas so that reflected light will not be directly in the eyes.
- Again, use many small light sources to provide a good general level of illumination while keeping low individual luminaire levels.
- Provide window shades and baffles that, when closed, allow no streams of sunlight at the extreme ends of vertical venetian blinds.

be a source of distraction. Changing the location of a luminaire can shift the attention of the worker away from the polished surface reflection and redirect it to the cutter itself [Hopkinson and Longmore, 14].

Illumination relevant to aircraft and space vehicle lighting was discussed in Chapter 4 and automobile lighting will be discussed in Chapter 10.

TEMPERATURE CONTROL

The human body has the capability to thermoregulate itself in different environments. The core-shell concept of thermal regulation [AFSC DH 1-3, 4] views the body core as producing heat that is lost to the environment through the shell or skin. Using the sensors in both the core and shell for information feedback, the body attempts to maintain core temperature (98.6°F; 37°C). The body has the capability of producing or losing extra heat and changing the conductivity of the shell.

Thermoregulation Process

In a hot environment, vasodilation causes the blood flow to the skin to increase, which, in turn, increases the conductivity of the skin and its temperature. This allows more rapid heat loss by convection and radiation. When the environmental temperature still exceeds the blood temperature, sweating occurs to maintain heat balance. Thus, sweating is a necessary process in maintaining core temperature. Resting and removal of insulation (clothing) are behavioral techniques to maintain thermal balance in a hot environment.

In a cold environment, vasoconstriction causes blood flow to the skin to reduce, increasing shell insulation and decreasing skin temperature and, thereby, reducing heat loss to the environment. Shivering and "goose flesh" are muscular activities to produce heat. Behavioral techniques to maintain balance are increased muscular activity and insulation.

Although the body can control its rate of heat exchange, the physical state of the environment also has an effect on transfer. Four major environmental factors affecting heat exchange are air temperature, humidity, air velocity, and radiation from the sun and other sources. These factors, individually and collectively, influence the heat transfer processes.

The human may be viewed as a heat exchanger who reacts with the environment via the processes of evaporation, convection, radiation, and, to a minor degree, conduction and ingestion of hot or cold fluids. The thermodynamic process for heat exchange between human beings and environment is often described by a *heat-balance equation:*

S (storage) = M (metabolism) − E (evaporation) ± R (radiation) ± C (convection) − W (work accomplished)

S refers to the amount of heat gained or lost and is zero when the body is in thermal balance. Figure 8-5 shows that these factors contribute in varying

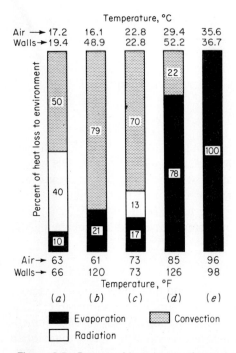

Figure 8-5 Percent of heat loss to the environment by evaporation, radiation, and convection under different air and wall temperatures. *(Redrawn by McCormick, 1976, after chart in E. A. Winslow and C. Herrington,* Temperature and Human Life. *Copyright 1949 © 1977 by Princeton University Press. Reprinted by permission.)*

proportions to thermal balance under different conditions of air and wall temperature [Winslow and Herrington, 35].

Note that with low temperatures, convection (contact with the air) and radiation are principal factors. With higher temperatures, heat loss through perspiration becomes a primary factor.

Relative Humidity

Evaporative heat loss through perspiration is severely limited by high relative humidity or moisture in the air. Figure 8-6 depicts the upper limits of tolerance in relation to temperature and humidity for working and resting nude males [Winslow et al., 36]. Temperature/humidities to the right of the curves could result in a heat stroke. Dry-bulb temperatures of over 100°F are tolerable when the relative humidity (RH) is less than 20 percent. However, at 90 percent relative humidity, a temperature of 90°F could be tolerated only with air movement to the body surfaces and a low level of activity.

Physiological Indices of Environmental Severity

We have seen that air temperature, humidity, air velocity, and radiation all affect the heat exchange process. Physiologists have long sought a single index, written as a combination of two or more factors, that would provide an accurate predictor of the strain imposed on the individual by these and other factors.

Table 8-4 summarizes some of the indexes that have been used, environmental factors to which the index is sensitive, constraints, and applications.

The American Society of Heating, Refrigerating, and Air-Conditioning

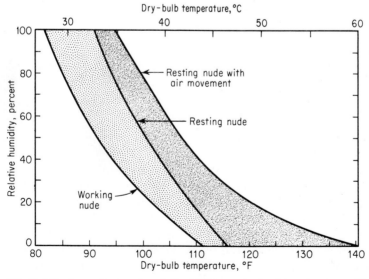

Figure 8-6 Approximate upper limit of tolerance for heat loss by evaporation. *(Winslow et al., 1942, as given in McCormick, 1976.)*

Table 8-4 Multifactor Indexes of Environment

Index	Abbreviation	Factors measured	Uses and constraints
Dry-bulb temperature	DB	Temperature only (thermometer)	Use with cold stress. Not sensitive to humidity, windspeed, or radiation.
Effective temperature	ET^X	Temperature, humidity, air movement	Comparative levels of skin "wettedness," thermal sensations, comfort zones. ASHRAE uses.
Wet/dry (Oxford)	WD	0.85 WB + 0.15 DB	Best use over 50% RH. Not sensitive to air move-ment or radiant load.
Heat-stress	HS	Determine the amount of perspiration to be evaporated for heat balance. Difference between this and maximum heat that can be lost defines load (BTU/h) which must be dissipated.	Hot-temperature index.
Predicted 4 hour sweat rate	P4SR	Sweat loss by acclimated young males at work. DB, WB, air movement, work rate, and clothing included.	Difficult to apply; very accurate under sweat conditions.
Globe temperature	GT	DB, radiation, wind effects. Thermometer in the center of a black-ened sphere.	Predicts over a wide range of environments.
Wet-bulb globe temperature	WBGT	0.7 WB + 0.2 GT + 0.1 DB. Composite of WB, dry-bulb, and GT appro-priately weighted.	Easy to compute Used by OSHA; applies indoors and out.

Source: Adapted from AFSC DH 1–3, DN3CL, p. 4.

Engineers [ASHRAE, 2] developed the Effective Temperature (ET) Index. The original index depicted combinations of dry-bulb temperature and humidity that produced the same sensations under experimental conditions. The ET index has been modified to show equivalent levels of skin "wettedness" [3] (Figure 8-7).

The wet-bulb globe temperature index (WBGT) represents a weighted combination of wet-bulb, dry-bulb, and globe-temperature measures [AFSC DH 1-3, 4]. This index is easy to determine and has been widely used in reporting research findings.

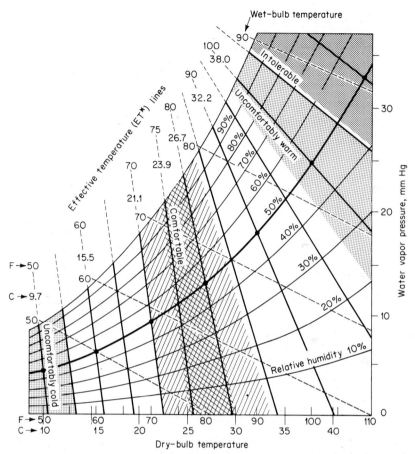

Figure 8-7 New effective temperature scale (ET^x). (ASHRAE Handbook, *and Product Directory. Fundamental Volume, 1977. Reprinted by permission. Also given in McCormick, 1976.*)

Acclimatization

The human adapts physiologically to some degree with habitual exposure to extreme environments. Lind and Bass [18] studied men working for 100 min at 300 kcal/h in extreme temperatures of 120°DB, 80°WB. Over a period of 9 days, they found a 2° drop in rectal temperature, a decrease in pulse rate by 35 pulses per min, and an increase in sweat loss. However, acclimatization was most pronounced on the first few days. Most acclimatization occurred within 4 to 7 days with virtually complete acclimatization within 2 weeks.

The United States Navy Medical Field Laboratory [Thomas, 32] was concerned with American ground forces during the Vietnam War. They studied young males at Camp Lejeune, N.C., who were exposed to 90°F and 74 percent RH. The experimental question was: For how many days and for how long each day should walking personnel be acclimated? Walk durations were 50, 80, and 100 minutes, with 10-minute breaks after 50 minutes for each duration. Measures taken were treadmill running time (cardiovascular efficiency), rectal temperature, heart rate, and sweat loss. Tests were conducted over 14 days. Conclusions were that between 60 and 90 min of daily exercise for 9 days were required for acclimatization to a hot, wet climate such as Vietnam.

Acclimatization to cold environments occurs to some degree within a week of exposure, although full acclimatization may take months or years [McCor-

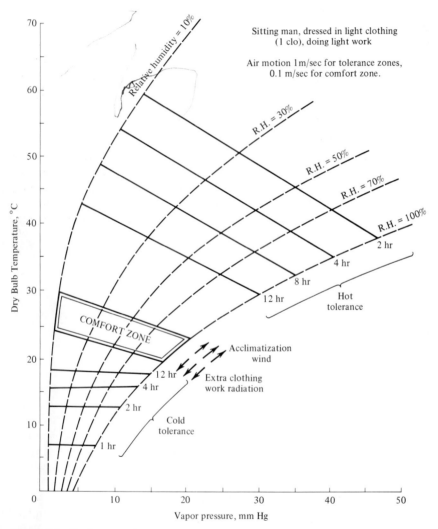

Figure 8-8 Environmental requirements for human comfort. F° = 1.8C° + 32. *(AFSC DH 1–3, 1977.)*

mick, 26]. Ability to tolerate extreme temperature after acclimatization does not fully protect the individual from the effects of extreme heat or cold.'

Comfort and Tolerance Zones

Thermal comfort refers to a condition in which the core temperature is normal and the rate of body heat storage is zero. The comfort zone, then, is a range of environmental conditions in which humans can achieve thermal comfort. It is affected by work rate, clothing, acclimatization, and so forth. It is more restricted than the long-term survival zone, which might be achieved by sweating or shivering.

Figure 8-8 defines the comfort zone for a specified set of conditions: minimal air movement and a radiant temperature of the surroundings equal to the dry-bulb temperature [AFSC DH 1-3, 4]. The arrows denote that certain conditions would extend the upper and lower limits of the zone. Also shown are the tolerance limits in hours for both hot and cold temperatures that are beyond the long-term comfort zone. The criteria apply to light work, but increasing the level of activity is a well-known technique to increase tolerance to cold.

Tolerance Limits for Heat

The maximum core temperature allowable is about 39°C (102°F) for a resting or light-working person and 40°C (104°F) for a person at hard labor. Maximum heat storage allowable is 1.5 kcal/kg of body weight and about 75 kcal/m² of body surface area. Body weight varies from 55 to 110 kg and surface area varies from 1.5 to 2.2 m². Tolerance times in minutes with respect to three different stress-index temperature scales are shown in Figure 8-9.

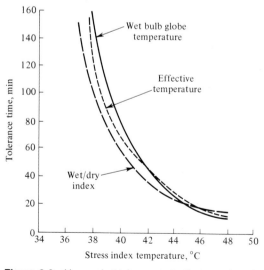

Figure 8-9 Human hot tolerances for three environmental indices. *(AFSC DH 1–3, 1977.)*

Tolerance Limits for Cold

The minimum core temperature allowable for cold is about 35°C (95°F). Although instances have been reported of the core dropping to 26°C and the body surviving, death typically results when attempts are made to rewarm the body [AFSC DH 1-3, 4]. Between core temperature of 86.0°F (30°C) and 89.6°F (32°C) there is a 50 percent survival of aircraft personnel lost at sea. Below 86.0°F, the personnel are unconscious.

Tolerance times for cold temperatures are shown in Figure 8-10.

These curves appear different from the heat limit curves. The temperature scale and tolerance time scale are inverted. Only dry-bulb temperature is shown since humidity is not a factor in tolerance to cold. The figure depicts tolerance times as a function of amount of clothing worn. The *clo* unit is a measure of thermal insulation specifically for a sitting, resting subject in a ventilated room at

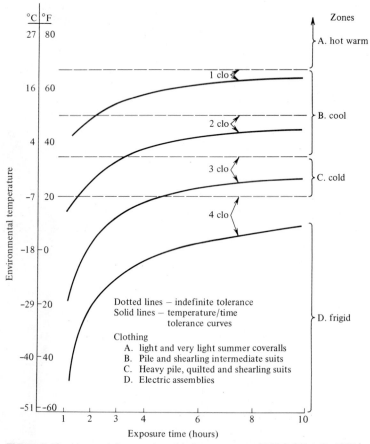

Figure 8-10 Human tolerance in cold air exposures. *(AFSC DH 1–3, 1977.)*

70°F, 50 percent RH. Most persons are comfortable in the nude at approximately 86°F. Typical work clothing is equivalent to 1 clo, the insulation necessary for comfort at 70°F. Thus, *1 clo is roughly the amount of insulation necessary to compensate for a drop of 16°F.* In Figure 8-10, 4 clo of insulation (64°F equivalent) is associated with the indefinite tolerance curve corresponding to approximately 20°F. Note also that for periods of an hour or two subzero temperatures are tolerable with 3- or 4-clo insulation.

Performance and Heat Stress

Studies have been conducted to determine the effects of heat stress on work, weight lifting, tracking, vigilance, and other tasks.

Figure 8-11 shows the relationship between workload in kilocalories per hour and rectal temperature [Lind, 17]. As room temperature was increased above 84° (ET), the rectal temperature rose very abruptly. For light work of 180 kcal/h, it rose from a core of 99.4°F at 80° (ET) to 100.7°F at 94° (ET). As workload was increased from 180 to 420 kcal/h, the rectal temperature rose from 99.4° to 100.3°F at all effective temperatures from 50° to near 80°. At about 80° (ET) the rectal temperature for each workload level increased abruptly. For 420-kcal/h workload, the upswing of rectal temperatures started at a slightly lower ET of 78°F, whereas for lighter workloads it began rising at about 82°F. The relationship between ET and dry-bulb temperature is given at the bottom of Figure 8-12, page 302.

The ability to lift a 15-lb weight repetitively was also shown to drop with ETs above 79°F (26.1°C). Figure 8-12 indicates a considerable variability in work done due to individual differences in lifting skill and use of incentives [Mackworth, 24]. However, the performance drop was more pronounced at 79°F and was higher for "good" (better than average) subjects than for average subjects. The pronounced drop is understandable since they were working at a higher performance level at 61° and 69°ET. Higher levels of heat stress caught up with even the most skilled and motivated subjects. The better subjects continued

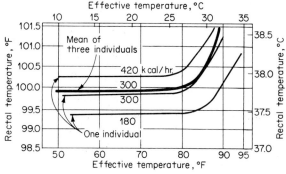

Figure 8-11   Rectal temperature as related to effective temperature (ET) for three levels of activity. *(Adapted by McCormick, 1976, from Lind, 1963.)*

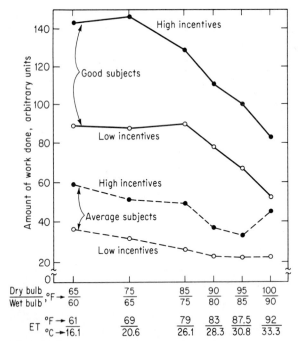

Figure 8-12   The relationship between effective temperature subject skill, incentives, and amount of work done. *(Mackworth, 1961 as given in McCormick, 1976.)*

to lift the weight even at 92°F (ET), but the margin of difference over average subjects was much less.

Azer et al. [6] studied the effects of heat stress and humidity upon tracking performance. A temperature of 95°F at 75 percent RH resulted in a significant decrement in performance (as compared with a control condition of 76° at 50 percent RH). However, the same temperature (95°F) at only 50 percent RH and 100° at 50 percent RH resulted in no difference from the control. Thus, the high humidity more so than the temperature seemed to be associated with tracking decrement. The high-humidity group also had a significant rise in core temperature while other groups did not. Thus, core temperature changes are related to performance decrement. In another study, performance decrement at a vigilance task was also associated with core temperature rises [Colquhoun and Goodman, 10].

Tichauer [31] reported the best performance in a job of picking in cotton weaving occurred in the range of 75° to 80°F (24° to 27°C) wet-bulb temperature. The study investigated temperatures from 60° to 95°F (17° to 35°C). It should be noted, however, that the optimum temperature range depends on a number of variables including level of workload. A lower temperature may be more comfortable for heavy workload tasks.

Slight seasonal differences in ambient temperature are also recommended

[AFSC DH 1-3, 4]. AFSC recommends 65 to 75°F (18.3 to 23.8°C) for summer comfort and 63 to 71°F (17.2 to 21.7°C) for winter comfort with relative humidities between 30 to 70 percent. Regional differences in ambient temperatures and humidities and other variables, such as workload, must be considered in setting indoor temperature levels.

Wind Chill and Temperature Effects

A strong wind in combination with a moderately cold temperature is known to feel much colder. These effects are not merely sensations. There is an actual cooling effect equivalent to that of the wind-chilled temperature.

The following table [Siple and Passel, 30] depicts the equivalent temperatures for a number of air temperatures in combination with a number of wind speeds.

Wind speed		Air temperature (degrees F) *					
mi/h	km/h	40	20	10	0	−10	−30
	calm	40	20	10	0	−10	−30
5	9	37	16	6	−5	−15	−26
10	16	28	4	−9	−21	−33	−46
20	32	18	−10	−25	−39	−53	−67
30	49	13	−18	−33	−48	−63	−79
40	64	10	−21	−37	−53	−69	−85

*C° = (F° − 32) × 5/9. *(Adapted by McCormick, 1976.)*

Should a pilot jump from 50,000 ft (15240 m) with loose-fitting summer personnel equipment, there is a danger of frostbite. Even at 35,000 feet the temperature is −65°F. To reduce exposure time, the pilot should free-fall to less than 20,000 ft before opening the parachute. Of course, wearing a pressure suit that covers the bare skin will reduce the hazard of frostbite [AFSC DH 1-3, 4].

Performance and Cold Stress

Hand-skin temperature (HST) is a critical factor in performing manual tasks in cold temperatures. Clark [9] cited evidence that a HST of at least 60°F is critical to manual performance, however, Lockhart [21] suggests that for certain tasks it should be higher.

Lockhart and Kiess [20] studied dexterity tasks at 0°F (−18°C) with and without infrared heaters. The time required to assemble parts on the Purdue Pegboard test was longer without the heater and increased abruptly during the 3 hr of testing. Assembly time without the heater was 41 s as compared to 25 s with the heater after 3 hours at 0°F.

Horvath and Freedman [15] studied men at −20°F for a period of 8 to 14 days. Scores on mental and visual tests did not deteriorate over time, but scores on a gear-assembly test did deteriorate.

Table 8-5   Techniques for Management of Heat and Cold Stress

Heat stress management

- Reduce relative humidity by dehumidifiers
- Increase air movement by fans or air conditioners
- Remove heavy clothing; permit loose-fitting white apparel
- Provide for lower energy expenditure levels
- Schedule frequent rest pauses; rotate personnel
- Schedule outside work so as to avoid high temperature periods
- Select personnel who can tolerate extreme heat
- Permit gradual acclimatization to outdoor heat (2 weeks)
- Maintain hydration by drinking water and taking salt tablets

Cold stress management

- Provide portable heating units (infrared)
- Increase body insulation in clo units appropriate to temperature
- Require moderate energy expenditure; avoid complete rest for long periods
- Avoid long exposure periods; rotate personnel
- Schedule work to avoid extreme cold temperature periods
- Provide protection from wind at extreme temperatures
- Select personnel who can tolerate the cold
- Permit gradual acclimatization to outdoor cold
- Provide warm liquids

Temperature Management Techniques

Table 8-5 summarizes techniques for dealing with situations where personnel must work in extreme temperatures. The objective of each technique is to maintain core temperature when the environment exceeds the body's natural thermoregulatory capabilities.

ATMOSPHERIC CONTROL

Air pressure and oxygen are environmental conditions that we normally take for granted, except under unusual environmental conditions when the air is contaminated, or at high altitude, or in deep water, where there is insufficient oxygen or pressure. Under these conditions there are physical and physiological changes that alter our efficiency and pose a health hazard. While these are primarily medical problems within the domain of the flight surgeon, aerospace physiologist, or industrial hygienist, they do affect performance and, hence, are of interest and concern also to the human factors specialist.

The industrial hygienist is concerned with air pollution and hazards associated with breathing smoke, exhaust fumes, toxic vapors and gases, insecticides, herbicides; exposure to ionizing radiation; and a variety of other atmospheric hazards. These hazards are well documented in Occupational Safety and Health Standards and are beyond the scope of this text. The interested reader is referred to OSHA Standards [11], the *Bioastronautics Data Book* [7], and Roth [28] for discussion and exposure limit data.

Atmospheric Content and Pressure

The earth's atmosphere consists primarily of a few gases, most significant of which are oxygen (21 percent), nitrogen (78 percent), and carbon dioxide (0.03 percent). Oxygen intake is essential to life. It is absorbed in the blood's hemoglobin with a diffusion rate proportional to the pressures exerted by the gases. Oxygen is carried to the tissues because of the pressure gradient between the bloods capillaries and the body tissue.

At sea level the atmospheric pressure is 14.7 lb per sq in (psi). Pressure is also expressed in millimeters of mercury, and at sea level it is 760 mmHg. Dalton's law states that the total pressure exerted by a gas mixture is equal to the sum of the partial pressures of the constituent gases. Thus the partial pressure of oxygen at sea level is $760 \times .21$, or 160 mmHg; nitrogen is $760 \times .78$, and so forth.

As one goes to higher altitudes, the total barometric pressure of air decreases exponentially and the volume occupied by a given amount of air increases. Boyle's law states that pressure times volume equals a constant.

Figure 8-13 illustrates the requirement for a larger percentage of oxygen as one goes to higher altitudes and pressure is reduced [*Flight Surgeons Manual*, 13]. With reduced pressure, the amount of oxygen the hemoglobin will absorb is reduced. To restore sea level conditions, oxygen must be increased. For

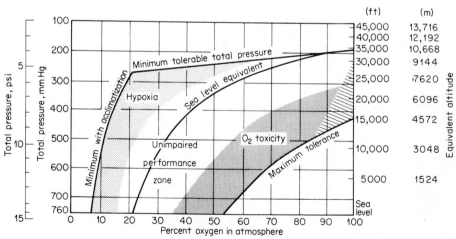

Figure 8-13 Physiological and unimpaired performance limits as a function of percent oxygen and total pressure. *(Adapted by McCormick, 1976, from Roth, 1968, based on data compiled by U. C. Luft and drawn by E. H. Green, Garrett Corp.)*

example, if the pressure were only 350 mmHg, to achieve the sea level equivalent, 160 mmHg, oxygen content would need to be increased to 46 percent ($350 \times .46 = 161$).*

Note that when the total pressure falls to about 160 mmHg, 100 percent oxygen would be required. At 42,000 ft (approximately 8 miles) life cannot be sustained even by breathing 100 percent oxygen through a mask. Pressurized compartments or pressure suits are therefore required at higher altitudes. Table 8-6 summarizes some of the physiological limits unless supplemental provisions are made [AFSC DH 1-3, 1].

At or near sea level, the red blood cells (hemoglobin) carry oxygen to body tissue at about 95-percent capacity. At 10,000 ft the hemoglobin is still 90 percent saturated with oxygen. At 18,000 ft the partial pressure of oxygen drops

*AFSC DH 1-3 recommends 149 inspired oxygen pressure as minimum rather than the exact sea level pressure of 160.

Table 8-6 Threshold Altitudes and Physiological Limitations

Altitude	Barometric pressure		
Feet	TORR	PSIA	Physiological limitations
5,000	632	12.32	Maximum for normal night vision without supplemental oxygen.
8,000	564	10.91	Maximum for prolonged flights without undue fatigue from mild hypoxia.
10,000	522	10.11	Threshold for increasingly severe hypoxia. Maximum for the pilot without supplemental oxygen.
20,000	307	5.94	Threshold for occasional symptoms of decompression sickness including abdominal gas pains.
25,000	282	5.54	Threshold for occasional severe manifestations of decompression sickness without proper denitrogenation or pressure cabin.
30,000	225	4.36	Critical threshold for high incidence of decompression sickness.
34,000	188	3.64	100% oxygen required for sea level equivalent.
40,000	141	2.72	Maximum for breathing pure oxygen without additional pressure (pressure breathing, pressure suit, or pressure cabin).
42,000	128	2.48	Maximum for reasonably prolonged emergency pressure breathing without pressure suit.
50,000	87	1.69	Maximum for brief emergency pressure breathing with immediate descent if not equipped with pressure suit.

Source: AFSC DH 1-3, 1.

to 40 mmHg or 70-percent saturation. At 63,000 ft the pressure is so low that the blood would boil unless environmental control measures were taken.

Types of Hypoxia

Figure 8-13 shows that there is a zone of unimpaired performance where increased percentage of oxygen is traded off against the lower pressure. If the oxygen supply is not increased, a state of oxygen deficiency exists at the cellular level. This condition is known as *hypoxia*. Mountain dwellers, such as natives of the Andes, have acclimated to the reduced pressures to some degree, but Figure 8-13 shows that there are limits to acclimatization.

Table 8-7 summarizes some common types of hypoxia. Note that high altitude is only one of the conditions that may result in a low partial pressure of oxygen.

Symptoms and Performance Effects of Hypoxia

There are marked individual differences in symptoms. Military aircraft personnel are required to periodically undergo a physiological training program that permits them to experience their own symptoms while in a chamber with reduced pressurization. Personnel work together in pairs, each alternating in removing the oxygen mask, with their buddy replacing it when the symptoms have been experienced.

Some of the early symptoms of decreased partial pressure of oxygen are euphoria, short breaths followed by long breaths, increased heart rate, hot flashes, headache, tingling, and general uneasiness. Impaired night vision is one of the earlier symptoms (5000 to 10,000 ft). More advanced symptoms are sleepiness, fatigue, blurred vision, tunnel vision, inability to divide one's attention among tasks, continuing to do whatever one was doing beforehand without apparent awareness of deficiencies in motor performance and memory, and a general lackadaisical attitude unconcerned with the hazard.

Table 8-7 Types of Hypoxia

Type	Causes
Hypoxic hypoxia	Low partial pressure of oxygen because of high altitude.
Anemic hypoxia	Normal oxygen content, but shortage of hemoglobin because of dietary factors.
Stagnant hypoxia	Normal oxygen content in blood, but it is not given off to tissue because of slow circulation. High Gs keep oxygen from brain. Symptom, blue fingernails.
Histotoxic hypoxia	Tissue cells poisoned by alcohol; unable to make use of oxygen properly.
Acute hypoxia	Short-period oxygen shortage.
Chronic hypoxia	Long-duration oxygen shortage.

The *Flight Surgeon's Manual* [13] indicates that 18,000 to 20,000 ft is the maximum altitude that is physiologically acceptable; visual performance is unacceptable above 13,000 ft. Mental processes, attention, and fatigue deteriorate seriously at about 15,000 ft.

Decompression Sickness

According to Boyle's law, the volume of gas within the body expands or contracts in proportion to the pressure applied to it. Thus, when the ambient pressure is reduced, gases inside the body expand. Gases are released through oral cavities in the body; however, when gases are trapped in the sinus or middle ear, the pressures can be very painful, even to the extent of bursting the eardrum. The *val salva* maneuver (holding the nostrils while exhaling with the mouth closed) is used to equalize pressures in the middle ear.

When the pressure is reduced suddenly, a state of rapid or *explosive decompression* exists. If the pressurized compartment of an aircraft were to be ruptured, the cabin would decompress rapidly and the pilot would have only a brief period of useful consciousness. The period varies with the altitude and the physical condition of the pilot. Rapid decompression from 8,000 to 40,000 ft allows only 18 s (average) of consciousness [AFSC DH 1-3, 1]. One must have quick access to an oxygen mask and begin breathing almost immediately to avoid transient hypoxia effects.

Hyperbaric Problems

Decompression sickness takes several forms and may occur underwater as well as at high altitudes. If a scuba diver should ascend from deep water too rapidly, nitrogen bubbles will form in the blood, body tissue, and joints. The painful condition associated with bubbles in the blood and tissue of the muscles and joints is termed the *bends*. Nitrogen bubbles in the lungs blocking transfer of gases is termed the *chokes,* symptomized by chest pains and coughing. *Parathesia* is a tingling around nerves, itching, and other skin irritation.

The scuba diver who comes to the surface too quickly must be replaced in the high-pressure environment and gradually brought back to the earth's pressure. A *decompression chamber* does essentially that. Divers are instructed to come up slowly and stay at prescribed depths for specified periods before coming to the surface, thereby allowing the nitrogen bubbles to dissolve in the blood. Decompression time also depends on how long the diver has been at a given depth.

Oxygen Toxicity and Nitrogen Narcosis

Referring back to Figure 8-13, it may be noted that it is also possible to have too much oxygen for a given pressure level. Forced breathing of oxygen can result in excessive oxygen dissolving in the blood cells and plasma. *Oxygen toxicity,* or poisoning, is characterized by nausea, twitching, dizziness, impaired vision, and numbness.

A hyperbaric (underwater) problem is *nitrogen narcosis* colloquially termed "rapture of the deep." This is a narcotic or anesthetic effect of nitrogen dissolving in the nerves. Symptoms are joviality and, at greater depths, drowsiness, weakness, and motor skill deficiency.

QUESTIONS AND PROBLEMS

Illumination

1 An illuminating engineer wishes to maintain a brightness (luminance) of 300 fL in an area. However, it is determined that the tasks vary in their percent reflectance as follows: drafting on linen (80 percent); general office tasks (60 percent); electronic assembly (20 percent); and inspection of dark fabrics (5 percent). Calculate the required illumination in footcandles for each task. What is the relationship between percent reflectance and illumination required?

2 An assembly operation was being installed in a new plant. It was found that the equivalent contrast for the task was 1.0 (10°). Reading from the VL8 curve in Figure 8-3, determine the background luminance in footlamberts. Express the answer as 10 to an integer power

3 Convert 10 fL to nits.

4 Given a luminance of 10 fL and a background reflectance of 25 percent, determine the illumination in footcandles required.

5 Convert your answer to question 4 to lux.

6 Given the intensity in lux required from question 5 and a luminaire placed 5 m over the assembly task, determine the required source intensity in candelas.

7 Given a task requiring 1000 fc refer to Table 8-2 and determine the maximum grade of assembly task that could be undertaken with the illumination provided.

8 A luminaire shining through a translucent surface with a luminance of 5000 fL is installed in an area where the background luminance is 100 fL. Determine the luminance ratio. Is the ratio within recommended limits?

9 Compute the brightness contrast ratio for the information given in question 8.

10 Assume that 5000 fL was a target luminance and 100 fL was the background luminance. What then would be the contrast ratio?

Temperature

1 Referring to Figure 8-8, a seated worker is in a bakery where the temperature is 38°C (100°F) and the RH is 30 percent. Would the person be able to tolerate the condition for an 8-h work shift?

2 Suppose in question 1 that the RH were increased to 70 percent at the same temperature. How long could the worker tolerate the condition?

3 Next, refer to Figure 8-7 (the effective temperature graph). Find the intolerable line and 70 percent RH. What is the hottest dry-bulb temperature recommended by ASHRAE at this humidity?

4 Referring to Figure 8-10, you were planning for 10 h of light work in a temperature of 50°F (10°C). How much clothing should you wear (in clo units)? If you were going to work only 1 h, how much clothing would be required?

Atmosphere

1 Compute the partial pressure of oxygen at 24,000 ft (300 mmHg).
2 Assuming a pilot were flying at 24,000 ft in an unpressurized aircraft, locate the data point in Figure 8-13 and indicate whether or not a physiological hazard exists and type of hazard.
3 Compute the percentage oxygen required at 24,000 ft to maintain a sea level equivalent partial pressure. Give the formula.
4 A balloonist at 2000 feet breathes a mixture of 70-percent oxygen for 8 h. What type of atmospheric problem is likely to be encountered?

REFERENCES

1 Air Force Systems Command, AFSC DH 1-3, DN 3A1, Section 3.6.3, p. 10, January 1, 1972.
2 *ASHRAE Handbook of Fundamentals,* ASHRAE, New York, 1967.
3 *ASHRAE Handbook of Fundamentals,* ASHRAE, New York, 1972.
4 Air Force Systems Command, AFSC DH 1-3, Section 3C, *Biothermal Aspects,* p. 4, January 1, 1977; *DH 1-6,* DN 6A5, p. 1.
5 American national standard practices for office lighting, *Journal of the Illuminating Engineering Society,* vol. 3, no. 1, 1973, pp. 3–27.
6 Azer, N. Z. et al: Effects of heat stress on performance, *Ergonomics,* vol. 15, no. 6, 1972, pp. 681–691.
7 *Bioastronautics Data Book,* 2d ed., NASA SP-3006, U.S. Government Printing Office, Washington, D.C., 1973.
8 Blackwell, H. R., Development and use of a quantitative method for specification of interior illumination levels on the basis of performance data, *Illuminating Engineering,* vol. 54, 1959, pp. 317–353.
9 Clark, R.E.: The limiting hand skin temperature for unaffected manual performance in the cold; USA Quartermaster Research and Engineering Center, TR EP-147, February 1961.
10 Colquhoun, W.P. and R.F. Goodman: Vigilance under induced hyperthermia, *Ergonomics,* vol. 15, no. 6, 1972, pp. 621–632.
11 Department of Labor, Occupational Safety and Health Standards, *Federal Register,* vol. 39, no. 125, June 27, 1974.
12 Faulkner, T.W. and T.J. Murphy: Lighting for difficult visual tasks, *Human Factors,* vol. 15, no. 2, 1973, pp. 149–162.
13 *Flight Surgeons Manual,* USAF Manual 160-5, July 1954.
14 Hopkinson, R.G. and J. Longmere: Attention and distraction in the lighting of work-places, *Ergonomics,* vol. 2, 1959, pp. 321–334.
15 Horvath, S.M. and A. Freedman: The Influence of cold upon the efficiency of man, *Journal of Aerospace Medicine,* vol. 13, no. 2, 1947, pp. 153–161.
16 *IES Lighting Handbook,* 5th ed., IES, New York, 1972.
17 Lind, A.R.: A physiological criterion for setting thermal environmental limits for everyday work, *Journal of Applied Physiology,* vol. 18, 1963, pp. 51–56.
18 Lind, A. R. and D. E. Bass: The optimal exposure time for the development of acclimitization to heat, *Federal Proceedings,* vol. 22, no. 3, 1963, pp. 704–708.
19 Lion, J.S., E. Richardson, and R.C. Browne: A study of the performance of

industrial inspectors under two kinds of lighting, *Ergonomics,* vol. 11, no. 1, 1968, pp. 23–34.

20 Lockhart, J. M. and H. O. Kiess: Auxilliary heating of the hands during cold exposure and manual performance, *Human Factors,* vol. 13, no. 6, 1971, pp. 457–465.

21 Lockhart, J.M.: Extreme Body cooling and psychomotor performance. *Ergonomics,* vol. 11, no. 3, 1968, pp. 249–260.

22 Logan, H. L. and E. Berger: Measurement of visual information cues, *Illuminating Engineering,* vol. 56, 1961, pp. 393–403.

23 Luckiesh, M. and F. K. Moss: "The new science of seeing," in *Interpreting the Science of Seeing into Lighting Practices,* vol. 1, 1927–1932, General Electric Co., Cleveland.

24 Mackworth, N. H.: Researches on the measurement of human performance, Medical Research Council (Great Britain) Special Report Series 268, 1950. Reprinted in H. W. Sanaiko (ed.), *Selected Papers on Human Factors in the Design of Control Systems,* Dover, New York, 1961.

25 McCormick, E.J.: *Human Factors in Engineering and Design,* New York: McGraw-Hill, 1976, p. 66.

26 McCormick, E.J.: *Human Factors in Engineering and Design,* New York: McGraw-Hill, 1976, p. 336.

27 Recommendations for quality and quantity of illumination and new footcandle tables, *Illuminating Engineering,* vol. 53, 1958, pp. 422–432.

28 Roth, E.M. (ed.): *Compendium of Human Responses to the Aerospace Environment,* NASA-CR-1205, vols. 1-4, November 1968.

29 Schuman, M.M., *Industrial Lighting, Industrial Health and Air Pollution Control,* vol. 17, Winter, 1971–72.

30 Siple, P.A. and C.F. Passel: Measurement of dry atmospheric cooling and subfreezing temperatures, *Proceedings of the American Philosophical Society,* vol. 89, 1945, pp. 177–199.

31 Tichauer, E. R.: The effects of climate on working efficiency, *Impetus,* Australia, vol. 1, no. 5, July 1962, pp. 24–31.

32 Thomas, R.E., Jr.: Optimum time of exposure for acclimitization to hot, wet environments in military operational situations. Unpublished research report, July 1971, citing U.S. Navy Medical Field Laboratory Report, vol. XV, no. 22, August 1965.

33 Van Cott, H. P. and R. G. Kinkade (eds.): *Human Engineering Guide to Equipment Design,* Washington: U.S. Government Printing Office, 1972, p. 49.

34 Visual comfort ratings for interior lighting: Report 2 (prepared by the Subcommittee on Direct Glare, Committee on Recommendations for Quality and Quantity of Illumination, IES) *Illuminating Engineering,* vol. 61, no. 10, 1966, pp. 643–666.

35 Winslow, C.E.A. and L.P. Herrington: *Temperature and Human Life,* Princeton University Press, Princeton, N.J., 1949.

36 Winslow, C.E.A. et al.: Physiological influence of atmospheric humidity, second report of the ASHVE Technical Advisory Committee on Physiological Reactions, *Transactions of ASHVE,* vol. 48, 1942, pp. 317–326.

Chapter 9

Design of Environment: Noise, Vibration, Acceleration

In the previous chapter the environments of illumination, temperature, and atmosphere were examined. In this chapter four additional environmental conditions will be explored: noise, vibration, acceleration, and weightlessness.

NOISE CONTROL

Although noises exist in nature, the ones that are a potential source for impaired hearing are the ones from technology—jet aircraft, weapon systems, industrial machinery and power tools, and so forth.

Exposure Standards

Noise levels exceeding 120 dB in the octave bands between 300 and 9600 Hz lead to a sensation of discomfort in a few seconds and 136 to 140 dB lead to a painful sensation. The United States Air Force (USAF) discusses the hazard of noise in terms of a requirement for ear protection [36].

Figure 9-1 depicts the recommended and mandatory ear protection criteria for various durations of exposure from seconds to 8 h. The slopes of the curves indicate that a 3 dB increase in SPL is permitted each time exposure duration is reduced by one half. However, protection is required above 135 dB regardless of the exposure time. Exposure to steady noise levels above 150 dB is prohibited regardless of protection [36].

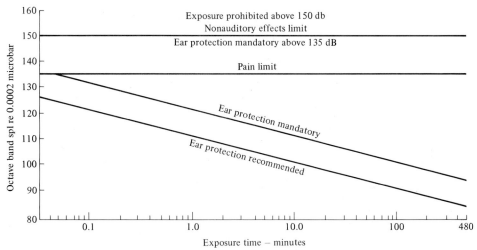

Figure 9-1   Short-term damage risk criteria. *(AFSC DH 1-3, 1977.)*

The short-term exposure limits, shown in Figure 9-1, are somewhat higher than the permissible levels if the unprotected ears are exposed continuously for 8 h a day over a duration of 25 years. Figure 9-2 shows the long-term exposure limits for USAF personnel.

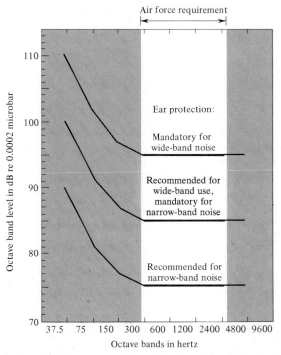

Figure 9-2   Long-term (8-hour) damage risk criteria. *(AFSC DH 1–3, 1977.)*

Table 9-1 Proposed OSHA Noise Exposure Standards

1 Exposure would be limited to an 8 h time-weighted average of 90 dBA with a 50% time reduction for each 5-dBA increase above 90.
2 Audiometric testing and a hearing conservation program would be initiated at continuous noise levels of 85 dBA and above.
3 Exposure to peak impulse noise up to 140 dB would be limited to 100 occurrences with a 10-fold increase in number for each 10-dB decrease in peak pressure.
4 Engineering and administrative controls would be required to the extent that they are feasible with hearing protection being used only as a supplemental measure.
5 Employers would be required to maintain employee audiograms during employment and for 5 years thereafter.
6 Employees would be permitted access to noise-monitoring records and audiometric data.
7 Workers would be notified when they are exposed beyond permissible levels.
8 Audiometric testing could be done only by certified audiometric technicians or personnel qualified by training or experience.

Source: Proposed standards of October 24, 1974, quoted by Emerson [11].

Wide-band noise refers to acoustical energy distributed throughout the spectrum, such as turbojet noise, while pure-tone noise refers to noise made up of pure frequencies within narrow bands, such as compressor whine, sirens, or propeller noise. Since most noise is a mixture of the two types of noise, the designer must decide which type is predominant by wide-band analysis, narrow-band analysis, and listening for tonal qualities, as discussed subsequently. Note that 85 dB is the mandatory long-term limit for narrow-band noise measured in four octave bands (500, 1000, 2000, and 4000 Hz).

The Occupational Safety and Health Administration (OSHA) [Emerson, 11] has proposed occupational noise exposure standards and required employer procedures for insuring observance of these standards (Table 9-1).

For an 8-hour work day the exposure limit is 90 dB on a sound level meter's A scale [*Federal Register*, 13]. Should the noise be 95 dBA, the permissible exposure time is halved to 4 h; for 100 dBA, 2 h; for 105 dBA, 1 h, and so on.

The exposure limit is actually a weighted average of decibel levels in several octave bands. When daily noise exposure is composed of two or more periods of noise exposure (T_N) at different levels, their combined effect should be considered.

Combined effect $= C_1/T_1 + C_2/T_2 \ldots C_n/T_N$

Where C_n = total time of exposure permitted at that level

This equation is especially applicable to supervisors who move about and are exposed to several levels [Hartman et al., 41].

Noise levels on the A scale are not directly equivalent to sound pressure levels. Figure 9-3 shows the dBA equivalents to sound pressure levels [13].

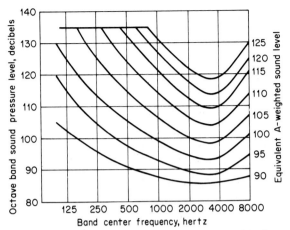

Figure 9-3 Equivalent sound-level contours used in determining the A-weighted sound level on the basis of octave-band sound analysis. (Federal Registrar, *1971*.)

The noise spectrum, derived from octave band analysis, is superimposed on the figure. The point of highest penetration on the spectrum defines the equivalent A-weighted sound level. Note that 100-dB noise at 125 Hz would meet the 90-dBA limit, but a 88-dB noise at 3000 Hz would exceed the 90-dBA limit. This method provides a rough approximation to dBA when the noise spectra are distributed in various frequencies.

Previously it was noted that the USAF limits for long-term narrow-band noise are 85 dB. The lower curve in Figure 9-3 shows that 85 dB is roughly equivalent to 90 dBA from 1000 to 8000 Hz.

Audiometric Measures

Table 9-1 indicated a requirement for measuring employees' hearing when they work in noisy environments of 85 dBA or more. Employees are measured before job placement and annually thereafter. They are also tested before termination and after long layoffs or sick leaves. Open records are maintained and employees are notified when exposed beyond permissible limits. Otological attention is given upon recommendation of a physician or audiologist.

There are simple hearing tests such as repeating a whispered message spoken at a specified distance and intensity. However, such tests are somewhat unstandardized and an audiometer is typically used instead. The tests may be given by a technician, or newer models permit the subject to control administration [Lipscomb and Taylor, 24].

The stimulus for an audiometer is typically a pure tone. The tone test, often used by speech and hearing clinics, involves listening over an earphone to tones of selected frequencies. Each tone is increased in intensity until reported as audible and decreased in intensity until no longer audible. Three up-down measurements (six crossings) are recommended [24]. The mean of the measure is the lowest intensity, which can just barely be heard. It is the absolute or audible threshold for the frequency. Measures are typically taken in the frequency range significant for hearing speech, for example, 250, 500, 1000, 2000, 4000, and 8000 Hz. Plotting these threshold dB levels yields an audiogram or minimum audible threshold curve.* Separate measurements are taken for each ear.

As the threshold level increases for a person over time, we speak of a threshold shift or hearing loss at certain frequencies. Figure 9-4 illustrates that there is an increasing hearing loss with age; the loss is greater in the higher frequencies than in the lower ones, and at any given age men typically have a larger threshold shift than do females, particularly at frequencies above 1000 Hz [Peterson and Gross, 26].

Nerve deafness, a condition of the nerve cells of the inner ears, may be related to aging but it may also be due to continuous exposures to high noise levels. It is more serious than *conductive deafness,* a condition resulting from defective transmission of sound by the middle and outer ear. Conductive hearing loss may be corrected by hearing aids or transmission of sound through the bone to the inner ear. Increasing the intensity may not help with nerve deafness.

Noise-Produced Hearing Loss

Hearing loss induced by noise may be temporary with recovery in a few hours or days, or it may be permanent. A noise-induced permanent threshold shift

*Graphic data requires filing a set of audiograms for the employee, one audiogram for each measurement data. The serial audiogram is tabular in format, requiring recording only the threshold dB level at each frequency for each ear. This requires only one line, and 10 measurements taken at different times may be filed on a single card.

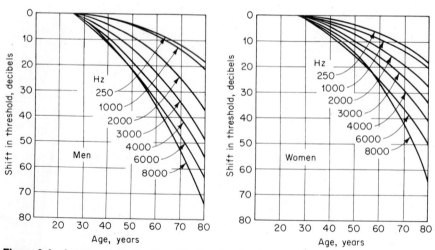

Figure 9-4 Average shift with age of the hearing threshold. *(Peterson and Gross, 1972.)*

(NIPTS) typically becomes progressively greater with subsequent exposures. Threshold shifts may be localized or generalized across frequencies, but typically the greatest loss is about 4000 Hz [Tomlinson, 34].

Continuous daily exposure increases the probability of a hearing impairment. A study of percent incidence of hearing impairment demonstrated that the percentage increased with exposure levels of 90 dBA and above and with age or years of exposure [*Industrial Noise Manual,* 21]. A longitudinal study was conducted of 200 workers with no previous history of exposure to intense noise. It was found that, over a period of from 2 to 44 years exposure to a single type of industrial noise, there was a progressive hearing loss with years of exposure and noise-level intensity. Also, losses at the frequency, 4000 Hz, were greater than at 2000 Hz and at 2000 Hz greater than at 1000 [ANSI, 29].

Intermittent Noise

Machinery noise may be continuous noise or it may be *intermittent noise,* such as periodic operation of a pneumatic drill. It may also be *impact* noise, such as a drop forge, or *impulsive* noise, such as a rifle fire. Although the various parameters involved make it more difficult to predict hearing loss, case studies of drop-forge operators and gunnery instructors indicate threshold shifts within a year or two [ANSI, 29; Peterson and Gross, 26]. With respect to intermittent noise, the longer the off-time in seconds, the higher the noise intensity that may be tolerated without a temporary threshold shift greater than 12 dB at 2000 Hz [Subcommittee on Noise, 19].

Table 9-2 [AFSC DH 1-3, 36] depicts the time off required each day for various sound pressure levels and exposure durations. In general, the longer the exposure and/or intensity, the longer the required time off for USAF personnel. For example, if a worker were exposed to 100 dB for 20 minutes, he or she should not be exposed again for at least 2 hours.

Table 9-2 Minimum Time in Minutes between Successive Noise Exposures

Duration of exposure (min)	Octave-band sound pressure level (dB)					
	90	95	100	105	110	115
5	0	2	3	7	18	200
10	2	3	7	40	*	*
15	2	5	20	*	*	*
20	2	6	120	*	*	*
25	3	11	*	*	*	*
30	3	20	*	*	*	*

*No further exposure until the next working day.
(Frequency range 300–9600 Hz.)
Source: AFSC DH 1–3 [36].

Physiological, Performance, and Annoyance Effects

Sudden noises may induce physiological reactions and emotional changes that return to normal after continued exposure to the noise. In addition to these, Jansen [22] has cited evidence of a pathological side effect of continuous exposure to noises of 95 dB or more. Cameron et al. [7] reported a greater incidence of physical illness among those exposed to considerable noise than among those who were not exposed to such noise.

The literature on the effects of noise on performance is somewhat conflicting, with some studies reporting performance degradation, others reporting no effect, and still others reporting enhanced performance. There is some evidence that noise is more degrading to vigilance tasks [Jerison, 23], complex mental tasks [Roth, 31], and tasks involving complex motor skills as opposed to routine tasks [Eschenbrenner, 12]. Noise, of course, may also interfere with communications (Chapters 4 and 12). Unexpected intermittent noises are more disruptive than continuous ones [12]. On the other hand, occasional noise can serve to arouse or increase attention. Warner [38] reported enhanced target detection with occasional 80- to 100-dB noise bursts. The attraction of discothèque music and drag races would suggest that loudness is welcomed under certain circumstances!

What about the dripping faucet or the cricket that delays our going to sleep at night? If noise is defined as unwanted sounds, then certainly these are instances of noise even though the decibel level is well below exposure limits. Traffic noises, low-flying aircraft, sirens, and trains rumbling are urban sounds that have been reported as sources of annoyance.

An indirect indicator of the annoying effects of noise comes from a study of time estimation by Stuart [40]. Three groups of subjects worked mathematics problems while listening over headsets to white noise of 85, 70, and 40 dB, respectively. It was found that the higher the noise level, the greater the tendency to overestimate the passage of time. Restriction to unpleasant surroundings would be expected to result in time appearing to pass more slowly. The findings confirmed those earlier reported by Loeb [39] for estimating 3- and 10-min intervals while working a jigsaw puzzle at 110 dB. Stuart [40] found significant group differences in short-term (20 sec) and long-term (23 min) time estimation. Performance was also poorer in the higher-noise groups.

Rating Annoyance in the Community

The International Organization for Standardization (ISO) has developed a procedure for predicting the public reaction to noise sources [28]. The procedure may be used prior to locating an industrial plant in a specific area provided sufficient information is available.

The procedure involves developing initially a spectrum of the noise intensity anticipated at the facility and superimposing the spectrum on Figure 9-5.

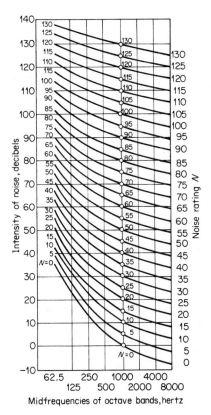

Figure 9-5 ISO noise-rating curves. (*ISO Acoustic Committee 43, as given in McCormick, 1976.*)

The next step is to determine the highest noise-rating curve (N) that the *maximum* intensity of the spectrum exceeds. Thus, a peak intensity of 80 dB at 125 Hz would exceed a N of 65, but the same intensity at 8000 Hz would exceed an N of 85. Clearly, the higher frequencies and intensities are more annoying.

There are some correction factors to be added or subtracted from the rating (see Table 9-3). The plus values are those that enhance the annoyance rating: pure tones, impulsive noise, rural neighborhood, and nighttime operations. Other factors are either zero or negative. Note that infrequently occurring noises merit large deductions from the rating. The following is the estimated public reaction to ranges of corrected N values:

Corrected N values	Estimated public reaction
Below 40	No observed reaction
40–50	Sporadic complaints
45–55	Widespread complaints
50–60	Threats of community action
Above 65	Vigorous community action

Table 9-3   Correction to Noise-Rating Number

Influencing factor	Possible conditions	Correction to uncorrected N
Noise spectrum character	Pure-tone component	+5
	Wide-band noise	0
Peak factor	Impulsive	+5
	Nonimpulsive	0
Repetitive character	Continuous (1 per min)	0
(30-sec noise duration)	10–60 exposures per hour	−5
	1–10 exposures per hour	−10
	4–20 exposures per day	−15
	1–4 exposures per day	−20
	1 exposure per day	−25
Adjustment to exposure	No previous conditioning	0
	Considerable previous conditioning	−5
	Extreme conditioning	−10
Time of day and season	Only during daytime	−5
	At night	+5
	Winter	−5
	Summer	0
Allowance for local conditions	Neighborhood:	
	Rural	+5
	Suburban	0
	Residential, urban	−5
	Urban near light industry	−10
	Industrial area, heavy industry	−15

Source: International Organization for Standardization [28], as given in McCormick, 1976.

Industrial Noise Measurement

Emerson [11] describes the first step in industrial noise control—deciding if there is a problem. A noise survey is conducted using a sound level meter and a floor plan of the plant area. Meter readings are taken and plotted on the floor plan. This approach will indicate areas where noise levels exceed 90 dBA at the moment. Noise levels may vary with time of day and closeness to the noise source. Overexposure of employees also depends upon total exposure time, as we have seen. The *audiodosimeter* measures total exposure time.

For workers moving from place to place, Hartman et al. [41] forecasted noise exposure via a computer simulation. The model employed known noise levels at the various work stations and times of exposure at each. Cumulative data at each noise level was calculated and expressed as a percentage of maximum permitted (OSHA) exposure at each level. The model permitted forecasting over 4500 working days, the cumulative daily exposure as a percentage of daily limit, for example, 367 percent without ear protection and 135 percent with protection.

Sound level meters have three scales: A, B, and C. Higher readings on the C scale than on the A scale indicate a low-frequency noise level (500 Hz or less). A difference between C and B scale may indicate a noise level below 250 Hz [Emerson, 11].

Octave band analysis involves placing filters over the output of a sound level meter and selectively listening to octave bands above and below 1000 Hz. Octave bands are centered above on 2000, 4000, and 8000 Hz and below on 500, 250, and 125 Hz. The levels will differ and the peaks indicate the predominant noise source. The output from an octave band filter set may be fed to a headphone or speaker and predominant sources may be identified by listening. Additional narrow-band analysis will reveal more jagged patterns with sharp peaks distinguishing individual noise sources. The highest peaks are the ones that should be attended to first in a noise source control program.

Noise-level measurements are also taken in transportation systems such as jet aircraft cockpits, commercial aircraft passenger compartments, and automobile interiors. Commercial applications are sometimes directed at providing a quiet ride suitable for conversations and comfort rather than meeting exposure limit criteria.

Techniques for Noise Control

Having determined the decibel level by octave band analysis and having determined that the level exceeds exposure limits, the next step is to select appropriate noise control techniques, apply them, and remeasure the noise spectrum to determine the extent of noise reduction. The acoustical engineer may apply several noise abatement measures before getting the noise spectrum down to acceptable limits. Ear protective devices should be only a supplemental device, according to OSHA, and the emphasis should be on reducing the causes of high noise levels.

As discussed in Chapter 6, environmental control of hazards may be applied to the source, path, or receiver.

Source Control   In industry, noise from machinery may be due to neglect, worn parts, or, occasionally, due to machines left running when not in use [Emerson, 11].

Sources of machinery noise are *vibration, impact, friction,* and *turbulence.* Vibrating machinery noise may be reduced by techniques such as balancing rotating parts, rubber mountings, surface damping, tightening, reducing speeds, and avoiding resonances. Impact noises should be eliminated, but may be reduced by using resilient materials and proper lubrication, enclosing an impact area, or reducing forces. Friction noise may also be reduced by lubrication and by providing smooth contact surfaces, rolling contact, precision gears, and so forth. Turbulence noise from pipes and ducts is reduced by streamlining, removing obstacles to flow, lining air ducts, proper sizing of valves, and reducing velocities.

Path Control   The transmitting medium may also be altered to reduce spreading noise. The solution may be as simple as increasing the distance between the source and listeners by effective plant layout, enclosing the source in a sealed, airtight compartment, or using intervening structures. Noise may also be channeled away by use of baffles, mufflers, and absorbing materials on walls, ceiling, and floors. Buildings in or near the flight path at airports require special acoustical treatment.

Receiver Control (Ear Protection)   The military jet aircraft industry has faced a challenge in meeting exposure limits in the cockpit. Personnel working around jet engine test stands are also subjected to these intense noise levels. No amount of acoustical treatment of the source or path can realistically reduce the noise to safe limits.

The highest quality ear plugs or earmuffs will reduce the noise level from 20 to 40 dB, and continued development by the military services may provide even greater attenuation. The use of both protective devices is recommended in very intense noise. The combined reduction by plugs and fluid-seal-type earmuffs will attenuate 35 to 40 dB in the frequencies below 2000 Hz and as much as 50 dB in the higher frequencies [AFSC DH 1-3, 36]. The pilot's helmet, if contoured to the skull, provides additional noise reduction.

Earmuffs are plastic domes that cover the ears and are connected with an adjustable spring band. Cushions are attached to the domes and may be filled with foam, air, or liquid. Muffs must be fitted to the contours of the skull for proper sealing. Muffs are easily monitored by safety personnel in industry, are long-lasting, and are quicker to install for brief exposures. However, they are more expensive than plugs, are bulky, hot, and uncomfortable, may not be effective with glasses or hard hats, and may lose attenuation capabilities.

Insert-type protectors of rubber, plastic, or wax-impregnated cotton fit directly into the ear canal. These plugs come in different shapes and sizes. They are less expensive, less cumbersome to wear or store, and are more comfortable in hot, humid spaces. However, the tight seal may cause discomfort, they are more easily lost, and they are harder to monitor by safety personnel. Custom-molded silicone inserts are also available.

VIBRATION CONTROL

Vehicles, as well as industrial and agricultural machinery, are among the common sources of mechanical vibration that interfere with comfort, working efficiency, and, in extreme instances, threaten health and safety.

The human may be exposed to vibrations transmitted simultaneously to the whole-body surfaces or to vibrations applied to particular parts of the body such as the head or limbs. Examples of the former are the vertical vibrations of surface vehicles; examples of the latter are vibrating headrests, hand-held power tools, and pedals.

Generally, we are concerned with vibrations transmitted through supporting surfaces such as the buttocks or feet. Vibrations could also come through a body immersed in a vibrating medium such as air or water and excited by high-intensity vibration. It is also possible for visual performance to be degraded by vibrating visual objects such as an instrument, even when the human body itself is not necessarily subjected to the vibration.

The subject of vibration is somewhat akin to the subjects of both noise and acceleration. Noise and vibration both involve waves set into motion, but the vibrating frequencies of greatest concern to us are those below the audible range, 1 to 100 Hz [AFSC DH 1-3, 36]. Motion sickness is the result of large-amplitude, low-frequency vibrations below 1 Hz. Frequencies above or below the 1 to 100 range are affected by individual factors and it is difficult to specify effects that are directly related to intensity, frequency, or duration of exposure [36].

The physical parameters of vibration are frequency (rate of oscillations, Hz); amplitude (maximum magnitude of cyclic displacement); and acceleration (second derivative of displacement, m/s^2).

Vibration intensity is sometimes shown in terms of the familiar decibel, although more often it is shown in acceleration notation (root-mean-square acceleration or RMS g in m/s^2). Some literature shows vibration limits values in terms of double amplitude (peak-to-peak distance from maximum negative to maximum positive displacement).

Directional Terminology

Like acceleration, the direction of linear motion is critical to human comfort and tolerances. Acceleration and vibration use similar terminology to differentiate directions of movement applied to the human body (see Table 9-4).

Sinusoidal vibrations may be expressed in terms of RMS acceleration, whereas nonsinusoidal or random vibrations are expressed in terms of peak or maximum acceleration.

Linear accelerations are most commonly applied to the human anatomy in the longitudinal axis regardless of the orientation or posture of the body. This type of directional acceleration (foot to head) is designated symbolically as $\pm g_z$ or $\pm a_z$. Accelerations applied in a forward-backward plane are designated $\pm g_x$ or $\pm a_x$, and those applied in a left-right or side-to-side direction, $\pm g_y$ or $\pm a_y$.

The USAF also speaks of foot-to-head accelerations as *vertical* vibrations and those applied across the body ($\pm a_x$ and $\pm a_y$) as *horizontal* vibrations. There are also *angular* vibrations, in rad/s^2, about a center of rotation; however, much less is known about exposure limits.

Exposure Limits

As with other environmental stresses, there are proficiency limits, comfort limits, and health and safety limits, sometimes discussed as exposure limits. The important physical factors determining human response to vibration are intensity, direction, frequency, and duration of exposure. Proficiency limits vary with exposure time only for certain types of tasks, as will be discussed.

Table 9-4 Acceleration and Vibration Terminology

	Acceleration			Vibration		
Direction of motion*	Heart motion toward . . .	Motion of eyeballs	Symbol	Heart motion	Other description	Symbol**
Forward	Spine	In	$+G_x$	Spine-sternum-spine	Fore-aft	$\pm g_x$
Backward	Sternum	Out	$-G_x$			
To right	Left	Left	$+G_y$	Left-right-left	Side-to-side	$\pm g_y$
To left	Right	Right	$-G_y$			
Headward	Feet	Down	$+G_z$	Head-feet-head	Head-tail	$\pm g_z$
Footward	Head	Up	$-G_z$			

*Other names used in literature for the physiological reaction are prone G (forward); supine G (backward); lateral G (right-left); positive G (headward); negative G (footward).

**USAF AFSC DH 1-3 uses the symbol "a" for vibration acceleration instead of the symbol "g."

Source: Adapted from *Bioastronautics Data Book* [20].

Figure 9-6 depicts the fatigue-decreased proficiency limits for vertical vibration as a function of exposure time and frequency. These limits were determined by the IOS and are presented in AFSC DH 1-3 [35]. Note that the horizontal lines demark 10-dB units. To determine exposure limits, the values shown are multiplied by 2, essentially raising each curve by 6 dB. The reduced comfort limits are determined by dividing the value by 3.15, essentially lowering the curves by 10 dB.

Figure 9-7 displays the same information for horizontal vibration [35]. Several important points may be gleaned from studying these figures. The most sensitive range for vertical vibration (4-8 Hz) is slightly higher than for horizontal vibration (less than 2 Hz). No reliable data is available for less than 1 Hz. Horizontal vibrations are more tolerable at lower frequencies but less tolerable at higher frequencies than vertical vibrations.

AFSC DH 1-3 also notes that the proficiency curves were based upon studies of aircraft pilots and vehicle drivers. Fatigue effects may differ slightly depending upon the nature of the task and its difficulty. Fine manual-skill tasks are more affected, whereas heavy manual work may be less sensitive to vibration. Modifying task factors are predicted to range from 1.4 to 0.25 times RMS acceleration limits. These correspond to +3 dB for the most sensitive tasks to -12 dB for the least sensitive.

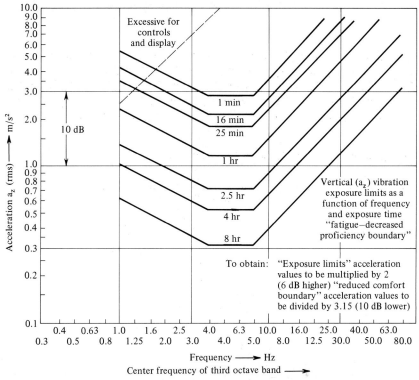

Figure 9-6 Vertical vibration limits/exposure time plot. *(AFSC DH 1–3, 1977.)*

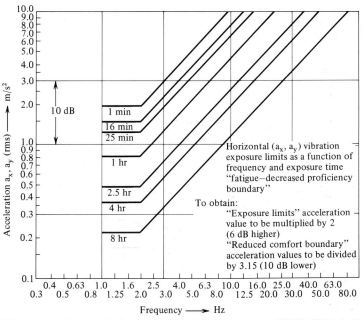

Figure 9-7 Horizontal vibration limits/exposure time plot. *(AFSC DH 1–3, 1977.)*

Combined Directional Guidelines   The user of these figures might also ask how to estimate limits when the vibration involves both a horizontal and a vertical component. The figures were based on discrete frequency vibrations applied to a sitting or a standing person in transport. However, should vibrations occur in more than one direction simultaneously, the corresponding limits apply separately to each component of the three axes. In other words, current research does not provide evidence that the combined effects result in either less tolerance or more tolerance than if the effect were considered singularly.

Intermittent Exposure Guidelines   In the previous discussion of noise, it was noted that there is some degree of recovery when the noise was intermittent. Thus, with longer off-times the tolerable limits could be prolonged. The question may be raised whether or not similar correction factors exist for vibration.

No reliable research data is available on this issue. AFSC DH 1-3 recommends that when exposure is divided into intervals, the total exposure limits should be based on the simple addition of the individual exposure times. Thus, if the vibration intensity in each work period is the same, the total daily exposure time limit may be used in evaluating permissible intensities.

Resonance and Transmission of Vibration

Every object has a natural resonant frequency. It is a well-known physical phenomenon that a vibrating system responds with maximum amplitude under the action of a harmonic force and that this occurs when the applied force is the same as the natural frequency of the vibrating body.

Rubber-tired vehicles generally have resonances in the 1- to 4-Hz range; tractors and trucks, 2 to 7 Hz, and so on [Radke, 27]. The human body also has a resonating frequency, as do each of the body members and organs. The human body vibrates when riding in a vehicle, and the effects are a consequence of the interaction of the frequency of the vibrating source and the resonant frequencies of the individual masses. Since body members and organs are not rigidly attached to the bone structure, they tend to vibrate at different frequencies rather than in unison. The result may be localized discomfort in the head, chest, abdomen, and testicles and general discomfort, although there are individual differences in the exact frequencies where the discomfort occurs.

The human body resonates as a whole at between 4 and 8 Hz. As already noted in Figure 9-6, this is the range of maximum discomfort. When the vibration frequency of the seat is in the range or slightly above the resonant frequency of the body or body part, the displacement of the mass is high and vibration is amplified. According to Radke [27], amplification occurs when the ratio of the two frequencies (seat/body) is less than 1.1414. When the ratio exceeds this value, there is attenuation or less displacement of the mass than the seat. In general, amplification is greatest when the seat vibrates at or near the frequency of the body or at a ratio of 1.0.

Another way of expressing the mechanical response of bodies is in terms of percent transmissibility. This is the ratio of output to input intensity times 100.

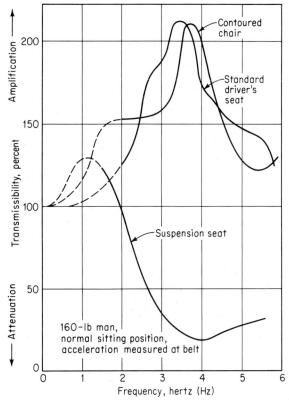

Figure 9-8   Mechanical response of the human body to vibrations when seated in different seats. *(Simons, Radke, and Oswald, 1956 and given in McCormick, 1976.)*

(Output here is the body or vibrated object; input is the shake table.) Values less than 100 percent indicate attenuation; values greater than 100 percent imply amplification. Figure 9-8 shows the transmissibility of three types of seats. The standard seat and contour chair resulted in over 200 percent amplification in the 3- to 4-Hz range, whereas the suspension seat resulted in substantial attenuation (20-30 percent transmission) in the 3- to 6-Hz range.

The difference between types of seats may be accounted for largely by damping techniques such as seat design, cushioning, and spring design. The buttocks may also damp the seated subject slightly. Studies of subjective reactions while standing and sitting show less annoyance at all frequencies to whole body vibration while standing. Bending and straightening the legs attenuates the vibrations as the race track jockey knows.

Performance Effects of Whole-Body Vibration

Ayoub and Ramsey [1] define vibration frequencies above 20 Hz as high frequency. They note that between 20 and 30 Hz, head resonance can be achieved with the head vibration exceeding the shoulders by a 3 to 1 ratio.

Grether [16] has noted that various studies of vibration indicate visual impairment is greatest in the 10- to 25-Hz range (image displacement on the retina causing blurring). Tracking performance is more degraded at 5 Hz or less. Other tasks requiring steadiness or precise muscular control are likely to be degraded. However, central neural processes, such as reaction time, monitoring, and pattern recognition, appear resistant to the effects of vibration [16]. These findings were based largely on laboratory studies on a shake table where disabling vibrations are not used.

Pathological Effects of Body-Part Vibration

Prolonged use of pneumatic jackhammers, drills, and riveters, particularly in the 100- to 250-Hz range, has been associated with a condition known as *Raynaud's disease* [AFSC DH 1-3, 35]. It is characterized by a numbness in the hands and feet, cramps in the fingers, loss of sensitivity to touch and pain, and increased sensitivity to cold. In the chronic condition, it seems irreversible and is characterized by lack of muscular control of the hands, such as inability to hold and manipulate. The disease is reversible if detected early.

Techniques for Vibration Measurement

Strain gauges are typically mounted at various locations on the human (head, neck, chest, abdomen, thigh). Subjects may be seated in a chair or suspension seat and may assume various postures, erect or relaxed, as dictated by the experimental design. The chair rests on a platform that is driven by a mechanical shake device. A displacement meter on the platform is used with a carrier amplifier to record table displacement on a recorder simultaneously with the strain recordings. Hence, the vibration of the table is used as a base of 100 percent and amplification or attenuation may be readily determined by comparing a shake table reading with strain gauge readings at different locations on the body.

Techniques for Vibration Control

Table 9-5 summarizes some of the techniques for reducing the vibration to the exposure limits.

One tempering comment—vibration is not always a noxious stimulus to be eliminated. Mild levels of vibration can be relaxing and soothing. There are vibrating beds, vibrating lounge chairs, scalp-massaging devices, oscillating shower attachments, sleep-induction electronic gadgets, and other machines, all designed to stimulate the body surface or to relax the tired person. Much less is known about the parameters of vibration that increase comfort.

ACCELERATION AND WEIGHTLESSNESS

We are held to the earth's surface by a gravitational force of 32.2 ft/sec², or 1 G. By definition, acceleration in G units is the ratio of acceleration to the acceleration of gravity. To illustrate, 161 ft/sec² is an acceleration of 161/32.2 or 5

Table 9-5 Techniques for Reducing the Effects of Vibration

Source control

- Reduce vibration intensity by techniques mentioned in relation to noise control (machine balancing, mounting, maintenance, speed reduction).
- Avoid operating frequencies that are in the range of body resonant frequencies.

Path control

- Limit exposure times whenever the frequency/acceleration levels exceed the fatigue-decreased proficiency limits shown in Figures 9-6 and 9-7. If practical, the design objective should be the reduced comfort limits.
- Rotate personnel to meet exposure time limits.
- Reduce transmission by improved cushions, suspension seats, and so forth.

Receiver control

- For certain industrial tasks, changing posture, particularly a standing posture, may be a practical solution.
- Provide damping apparel.
- Blurring due to vibrating visual objects could be compensated for, in part, by improved visibility techniques (piece enlargement, magnification, increased illumination and contrast) [Ayoub and Ramsey, 1].
- Vibrating effects of hand tools may be reduced by wearing thick, damping gloves as well as other techniques given above.

G. The effective weight of our bodies or body parts is proportional to the number of G units acting upon us. An aircraft pilot pulling up from a 3-G dive has three times his or her normal effective weight. An astronaut on the lunar surface, however, has only one-sixth of his or her normal effective weight and in deep space has no weight at all.

Humanity has long been concerned about the physiological and performance effects of deviation from a 1-G environment. In this section we shall examine the factors influencing acceleration tolerance and design solutions for better tolerance of these effects. One need not be in an aerospace environment to experience these effects. The force of an automobile impacting against a structure or a body falling to the ground from a building involves an acceleration in reverse that taxes if not exceeds our bodies' physiological limits.

Acceleration Terminology

There are three types of acceleration forces: linear, radial, and angular. With *linear* acceleration the rate of change of the velocity of mass is constant in a straight line. With *radial* acceleration the direction of motion continuously changes, as illustrated by a person tumbling at an increasing velocity or an aircraft turning. The axis of rotation is external to the body. *Angular* acceleration produces changes in both magnitude and direction of velocity, as illustrated by an ice skater or ballet dancer twirling rapidly on one toe. The axis of rotation passes through the longitudinal axis of the body. There are also combinations of the above as, for example, epicyclic tumbling and falling after ejection from an aircraft.

A distinction is also made between *abrupt* and *prolonged* acceleration. Abrupt acceleration is illustrated by an impact. The rate of change is less than 0.2 seconds and the total duration is less than 1 second. The effects on the human are limited to mechanical overloading (fractures); there is no time for fluid shifts. *Prolonged* acceleration refers to durations longer than 1 second. (Some authorities use a third category, *brief* acceleration, from 1-10 seconds). Hydraulic effects of fluid displacement are present as well as mechanical displacements and deformation of body structures.

This review will be limited principally to linear acceleration. The hydraulic effects of radial acceleration in tumbling are similar to those under linear acceleration. The further the center of rotation is from the head, the worse the physiological effects due to centrifugal forces. For example, rotation is more tolerable when the center of rotation is at heart level than it is when the center of rotation is at hip level. Later, some of the effects of angular accelerations will be discussed, those due to disturbances of the semicircular canals and equilibrium.

Techniques for Studying Acceleration Effects

Our information regarding the effects of abrupt acceleration come principally from animal experiments (hogs, chimpanzees, bears) on abrupt deceleration devices, a few human experiments on such devices with courageous volunteers such as Colonel John Stapp [33], and automobile impact studies with dummies and cadavers [Carpenter, 8]. Another data source is accident experience, where the Gs applied are calculated after the fact and the consequences are noted (tolerable, injurious, fatal). Prolonged acceleration effects at lower magnitudes have been studied on military centrifuge devices.

Exposure Limits

The major factors influencing acceleration tolerance are the *magnitude* and *duration* of the force; the *direction* of acceleration relative to the body axes, the *rate of onset,* and the type of *body restraint* and support provided.

Rate of onset and offset of acceleration have a definite effect; low rates are more tolerable. However, under impact conditions some very high rates have been experienced and tolerated. The area is not well enough understood to provide definite limit values.

Considerable research has been done on the effects of direction of acceleration and its relation to magnitude and duration of tolerance. In the section on vibration, the terminology used to describe direction of acceleration was introduced (Table 9-4). While this terminology is generally accepted, one may still encounter expressions to indicate the physiological reaction from the direction of motion, for example, positive Gs or tailward Gs for footward acceleration; spineward for backward acceleration; sternumward for forward acceleration. A binary classification of forces is vertical and transverse acceleration.

Any rapid change in velocity causes a physiological reactive force in the opposite direction. Since the internal organs, eyeballs, and tissue are not rigidly attached, they will lag behind the body's skeletal structure. Hence, the vernacular expressions, "eyeballs-in" for forward acceleration; "eyeballs-out" for backward accelerations, are sometimes used.

Figure 9-9 shows that there are substantial differences in the average magnitudes and durations of linear acceleration that are voluntarily tolerated when the direction of the Gs varies [Chambers, 10].

The implications of these findings are that the body should be oriented, if feasible, to provide the maximum tolerance. Our poorest tolerances are for accelerations through the longitudinal axis of our body, particularly for footward acceleration ($-G_z$). Headward acceleration ($+G_z$) is second poorest. With high footward acceleration, fluids are displaced into the head and eyes, causing pressures, confusion, pain, and sometimes eye hemorrhage or "red out." This type of G should be avoided at the higher magnitudes. High headward acceleration results in fluid displacement into the lower portions of the body, causing blackout. The *anti g suit* is most effective for headward acceleration. It consists of a system of inflatable bladders that provide pressures at critical body areas. This reduces the flow of blood from these areas, limits blood pooling, aids return of blood to the heart, and maintains arterial pressure.

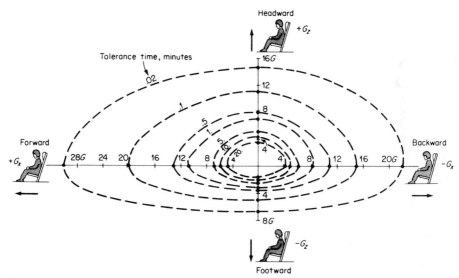

Figure 9-9 Average levels of linear acceleration voluntarily tolerated in different directions for specified durations. *(Adapted by McCormick, 1976, from Chambers, 1963.)*

Best tolerance is for forward acceleration ($+G_x$). Note in Figure 9-9 that over 28 G may be voluntarily withstood for .02 minutes, whereas 23 G may be tolerated for the same duration with backward acceleration ($-G_x$).

Protective Techniques

Since forward acceleration tolerance is slightly superior, aft-facing seats with full-length backs have been proposed for passenger protection in the event of a train or aircraft crash. While they have been used for military transport, public acceptance of riding facing backwards in commercial transport is an issue that has been raised.

Table 9-6 summarizes some of the technological advances in protection against the effects of acceleration, particularly energy absorption techniques for impact tolerance. Note that the roadway environment may also be redesigned for less hazard upon impact.

Table 9-6   Techniques for Reducing the Effects of Acceleration and Impact

Ground vehicles

- Energy-absorbing objects for gradual deceleration
    Padded dashboard
    Collapsible steering column with padded center
    Passive-restraint systems (inflatable air bags)
    Adjustable headrest

- Active-restraint system (seat belt and harness)

- Helmets for race drivers and motorcyclists

- Crashworthiness (reinforced doors and sidings, shock-absorbing bumpers, roll bars, and reinforced roofs)

Roadway devices

- Energy-absorbing or forgiving objects
    Breakaway signs and light posts (break at base on impact)
    Absorbing barriers (collapsible compression drums at forks)
    Concrete median barrier designs reduce effects of sideswipe
    Bridge protection devices (precluding impact with abutment)
    Roadside hazard structures eliminated, set back, or guarded

Aerospace vehicles

- Contour couches molded for astronauts ($+G_x$) and frontal support such as nylon netting ($-G_x$)

- Restraint system and helmet

- Anti g suit

- Water immersion (if feasible)

- Ejection seat or detachable escape capsule

We are all familiar with active restraint systems such as seat belts and shoulder harnesses (active in the sense that they must be connected to be useful). The problem, as we know, is getting drivers to use the active-restraint systems. Passive-restraint systems include the inflatable air bag in ground vehicles that activates upon impact without the driver doing anything (see Chapter 11).

The danger of whiplash from rear-end collisions is reduced by full back support with a properly adjusted headrest. Contoured couches molded to the individual's dimensions were an advancement in our space programs. Water immersion has been shown to increase G tolerances by equalizing forces over the body surface. Bondurant et al. [5] found that forward acceleration while immersed in water in a modified supine position provided greater tolerance than any other technique. Unfortunately, the weight penalty of water and operational effects are limitations to its practical application.

Performance Effects of G-Loading

Movement of the arms and legs is more difficult under acceleration. Figure 9-10 shows the effects of forward ($+G_x$) acceleration on gross body movements. The values shown are at the threshold of ability to perform, so movements under higher Gs would be impossible [Chambers and Brown, 9]. In aircraft or spacecraft, critical controls such as the control stick and ejection lever should be located near the position of maximum tolerance (25 G). Three-axis controllers for space vehicles are often located at the end of the right arm rest so that the astronaut need not lift an arm to reach it. Wrist action and thumbwheel adjustments are all that is required.

High acceleration also degrades reaction time, tracking performance, time estimation, visual acuity, and peripheral brightness sensitivity [Frazer, 14]. Targets must be larger at 7 G than at 1 G to be seen at the same brightness level. Increasing brightness may also offset the loss of visual function.

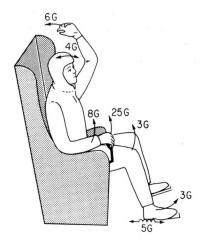

Figure 9-10 G forces that are near the threshold for various body movements. *(C. C. Clark and J. D. Hardy,* Preparing Man for Space Flight, Astronautics, February 1959, *as presented by Chambers and Brown, 1959. Copyright 1959 by American Psychological Association. Reprinted by permission.)*

A variety of illusions have been reported under certain types of accelerations. These illusions are sometimes discussed as spatial disorientation, or *vertigo*. For example, under continued constant rotation the pilot may cease to experience rotation because of the action of the semicircular canals in the inner ear. When the aircraft decelerates, the canal structure slows also, but the fluids in the canals continue moving a little longer because of inertia. The result is an experience of rotation in the opposite direction!

Another organ in the inner ear, the otoliths, is also subject to lagging behind the rest of the inner ear under G forces. The result is an illusion of tilting backward (nose-high attitude) when one is actually accelerating forward straight and level. An unsuspecting pilot may lower the aircraft nose to correct for the tilt and fly into the ground! The *coriolis phenomenon* is a loss of equilibrium when a pilot is rotating and turns the head perpendicular to the plane of rotation [Roth, 30]. There are many other types of equally perplexing and disturbing visual and proprioceptive illusions. The point is that our sense organs may be deceived under high acceleration. The solution seems to be to rely on one's flight instruments rather than sensations and to train pilots to be on the outlook for such illusions.

Weightlessness

Since the earliest planning for propelling the human into orbit or to the lunar surface and beyond, space scientists and medical experts had some misgivings about possible physiological effects of the weightless or reduced-weight state. Since our physiological processes had evolved in a 1-G environment and humanity had experienced no other environment, there were those who questioned the feasibility of such voyages. Particular concern was for muscle atrophy without gravitational forces to overcome it. Other concerns were for disorientation and oculoagravic illusions [Gerathewohl and Stallings, 15] associated with floating fluids in the inner ear. (The apparent upward displacement of images was largely an artifact of the technique for simulating weightlessness in aircraft.)

In terms of performance, the absence of gravity meant that concepts like up and down had no meaning except relative to the internal visual environment of the vehicle. There was concern that the tractionless state could result in biomechanical problems. When open forces were applied, particularly torquing, the unstabilized human body would react in the opposite direction, and without atmospheric pressures to slow down the movement, the human body was envisioned in uncontrolled tumbling or floating into surfaces. Further, it was known that walking or standing during intravehicular activities would be impossible without some form of foot stirrups or attachment to the bottom of the feet. Movement in a space compartment would be largely through pushing off, aided by manual assist with handholds and handrails. Problems associated with possible floating matter during drinking, eating, and personal hygiene were also anticipated.

Originally, the technology in pressure suit design for seated pilots did not allow the limb mobility necessary for performing semierect tasks such as walking on the lunar surface. There were a host of extravehicular activity (EVA) problems involving how to move along the space vehicle's external surface, propulsion and guidance through space, and reeling in long tethering lines.

Physiological and Physical Effects of Weightlessness

Most of us who have lived through the manned space programs learned that the physiological effects of zero-gravity and reduced-gravity states were not as debilitating as originally envisioned. With proper exercise and muscle tensing, the weightlessness effects were negligible. Berry (2) noted on various U.S. and Soviet space flights, certain consistent temporary effects such as changes in cardiac electrical activity, number of red and white blood cells, muscle tone, and loss of weight. To what degree these were a product of weightlessness or to other environmental and psychological stresses cannot be isolated.

A requirement for an artificial gravity (by rotating the space vehicle or by an on-board centrifuge) probably is not necessary in light of the negligible effects. Orbital missions of up to 60 days have led to the conclusion that weightlessness can be adapted to. Long-term or permanent space habitation may reopen this issue, but the expense of space colonization makes this issue still years away.

Bond et al. [4] reported an interesting finding regarding postural changes during the Skylab missions. The body assumes a sort of natural fetal posture, as shown in Figure 9-11. This finding has implications for the sizing of consoles and the heights of instruments on these consoles.

Brown [6] reports that in the absence of gravity the human body actually lengthens some 2 inches! A Skylab astronaut who was 68.1 in (173.0 cm) grew to 70.6 in (179.3 cm). An Apollo-Soyuz cosmonaut grew from 71.4 in (181.3 cm) to 73.4 in (186.4 cm) in only 9 days. Most of the growth occurred between days 6 and 9. The Skylab data taken from day 21 to day 82 indicated little growth after 20 days. Removal of G-loading apparently permits expansion of intervertebral discs. Return to preflight height occurs, but not immediately upon return to the 1-G environment. The finding has implications for pressure suit fitting and design of displays for eye height.

Performance Effects of Weightlessness

Technological planning and development during the 1960s and early 1970s led to onboard equipment that permitted the astronaut to adapt to the locomotion, force application, personal hygiene, and housekeeping problems associated with the absence of gravity. Advanced space suits were developed that provided the necessary limb mobility.

Stabilizing the body at the feet and the use of other restraint devices made the biomechanical problem nominal. Recognizing that everything had to be strapped down, including the astronaut while sleeping, adequate provisions were made.

Due to the abortion of a Gemini EVA mission, the ability of a human to

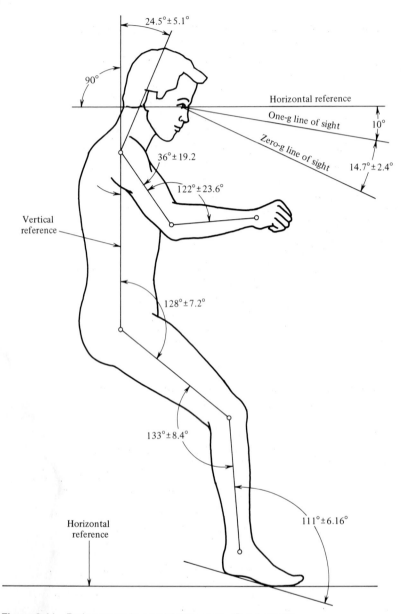

24.5°±5.1°

90°

Horizontal reference

One-g line of sight

10°

Zero-g line of sight

14.7°±2.4°

36°±19.2

122°±23.6°

Vertical
reference

128°±7.2°

133°±8.4°

Horizontal
reference

111°±6.16°

Figure 9-11 Body posture in a weightless state. *(Bond, 1975.)*

translate and maneuver in deep space with a backpack propulsion device remains untested. Self-stabilized astronaut maneuvering units (AMU) were developed for moving in various directions in space and for performing useful tasks with respect to hypothetical satellites and orbiting telescopes. A series of frustrating EVA incidents occurred prior to actually testing the unit and physiological indices were interpreted as evidence of high workload, although it is difficult to identify the exact cause. Thus, the feasibility of maneuvering in various directions has yet to be demonstrated.

Techniques for Simulating Zero-G and Reduced-G

There are several techniques for simulating zero-G [AFSC DH 1-6, 37], but there is really no adequate substitution short of actually being in orbit. Weightlessness can be achieved within the earth's gravitational field for a minute or less by flying an aircraft in a Keplerian trajectory or parabolic arc (Figure 9-12).

Astronauts in training may experience the effects while floating about in the

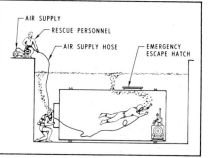

THE WATER IMMERSION TECHNIQUE CONSISTS OF COMPENSATING FOR THE EARTH'S GRAVITY BY SUSPENDING THE SUBJECT IN WATER TO ESTABLISH A CONDITION OF NEUTRAL BUOYANCY. WITH THE RIGHT PLACEMENT OF WEIGHT ON TORSO, ARMS, AND LEGS, A MAN SUBMERGED IN WATER EXPERIENCES NEUTRAL BUOYANCY SIMILAR TO THE WEIGHTLESS CONDITIONS ASTRONAUTS FIND IN SPACE.

THE DISADVANTAGE OF THE WATER IMMERSION TECHNIQUE IS THAT TESTS ARE RESTRICTED BY THE DAMPING EFFECTS OF THE WATER.

THE TEST SPECIMEN MUST BE SUPPLIED WITH AN EMERGENCY ESCAPE SYSTEM AND EMERGENCY BREATHING EQUIPMENT.

SUB-NOTE 2.1(2) Airbearing/ Frictionless Gimbal Platforms

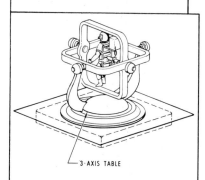

IN FRICTIONLESS GIMBAL SIMULATION, THE SIMULATOR IS INITIALLY BALANCED BY PLACING THE SUBJECT'S CENTER OF MASS AT THE INTERSECTION OF THE GIMBAL AXES.

THE DISADVANTAGE OF THE FRICTIONLESS GIMBAL SIMULATOR IS THAT IT PRODUCES UNWANTED ROTATIONS DEVELOPED BY SMALL DISPLACEMENTS OF THE SUBJECT'S CENTER OF MASS AS HE MOVES HIS APPENDAGES.

SUB-NOTE 2.1(3) Keplerian Trajectories/Zero-G Flight Pattern

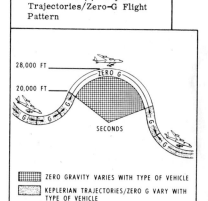

ZERO GRAVITY VARIES WITH TYPE OF VEHICLE

KEPLERIAN TRAJECTORIES/ZERO G VARY WITH TYPE OF VEHICLE

THE KEPLERIAN TECHNIQUE IS ACCOMPLISHED BY USING AIRCRAFT FLYING ALONG A KEPLERIAN TRAJECTORY TO PRODUCE A ZERO-G ENVIRONMENT.

THE KEPLERIAN TECHNIQUE IS LIMITED BY THE COST, TIME PER FLIGHT (20-30 SECONDS), AND THE PHYSICAL DIMENSIONS OF THE AIRCRAFT INTERIOR.

Figure 9-12 Techniques for simulating weightless effects. *(AFSC DH 1–6, 1974.)*

cargo compartment of a jet transport aircraft. However, weightlessness is then followed by high accelerations during the pull up from the ensuing dive, so the total physiological effects are mixed.

The frictionless aspects of space and reactive body movements to applied forces may be partially simulated by strapping an astronaut within a system of three gimbals on an air-bearing platform. Attempts to simulate the sixth degree of freedom by means of pulleys are expensive and generally not cost-effective for the training benefits. As indicated above, this is really no problem if adequate stabilization devices or translating aids are provided.

A third simulation technique involves underwater studies in tanks, swimming pools, or aquariums. Astronauts in pressure suits are appropriately weighted to achieve a neutrally buoyant state. This permits a gross simulation of EVA maneuvers such as erecting antennas or servicing an orbiting telescope. The problem, of course, is that there is a damping effect from movement in the water, which would not be the case in actual space.

To simulate walking at one-sixth G on the lunar surface, astronauts were suspended by cables at an angle that reduced the gravitational force accordingly. They were able to take large strides similar to what was later confirmed in the Apollo lunar expeditions.

Other Space Stresses

Weightlessness, of course, was only one of the many unusual stresses encountered in the manned space programs. There were the high accelerations of boost off and reentry; the low temperature problem, the atmospheric problems of a vacuum; visual problems in docking the lunar excursion module with the parent vehicle and the extreme contrasts of lunar surface illumination. Page limitations do not permit discussion of each of these problem areas. Technological achievements in conquering these alien environments simultaneously and developing lightweight equipment for guidance, communications, and data gathering may stand as one of the greatest achievements in the history of mankind.

COMBINED STRESS

Although most of the research has been confined to single stressors, it is obvious that in the real world there may be two or more potential stressors acting upon a person at the same time. For example, a pilot could be exposed to noise, acceleration, heat or cold, reduced atmospheric pressure, and personal factors such as loss of sleep or psychological stress. The question may be raised whether two or more stressors, each within acceptable limits, might combine to produce an effect that is comparable to a higher level of individual stress. Would it not be possible to specify recommended exposure limits for joint stressors similar to limits discussed previously for temperature and humidity or for pressure and oxygen content?

Figure 9-13 illustrates four theoretical effects of combined stress. Assume

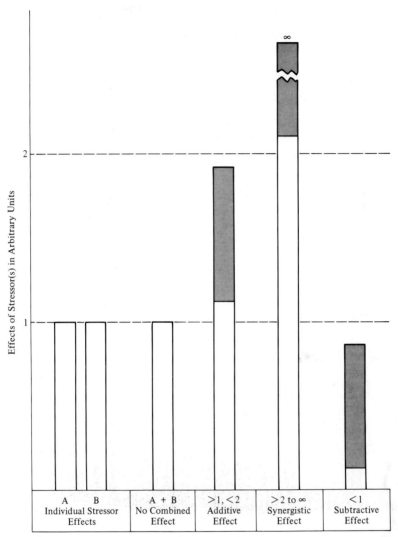

Figure 9-13 Theoretical effects for stress combinations.

there were two individual stressors (A and B), each with an effect equal to 1.0 in arbitrary units. The actual effects could be in terms of performance measures, physiological changes, or tolerance limits. Should the stress conditions occur in combination there are four categories of potential effect: (1) *no effect* greater than the individual stress conditions (1.0) or the greater of two stressors when their effects are unequal; (2) an *additive effect* greater than any single effect, but not greater than the addition of the effects of the single stressor conditions (2.0); (3) a *synergistic effect* greater than the addition of the single stressor effects; (4)

an *antagonistic* or *subtractive effect* in which the combination produces an effect less than the effects of the individual stressor conditions or less than the greater of two unequal stressor conditions.

Combined stress research is complex and time-consuming in terms of the number of treatment combinations required. Note that the simplest study usually involves two stressors, each under three levels—control (no significant stress), medium, and high levels. Such an experiment would require N^S or nine experimental groups where N equals number of levels and s equals number of stressors. If one wished to study two durations of each stress level, then the number of groups required would be 6^2 or 36 groups.

Combined stressors usually imply the stressors are applied simultaneously, but they could be applied sequentially and in different orders. They could also be applied simultaneously at times and sequentially at other times. Such complex temporal occurences may be realistic, but their study in the laboratory would further compound the experimental groups required. As with any stress study, one may wish to study the environmental factors under different situational factors (task loading, clothing, restraint, incentives) and under different host factors (age, sex, physical condition). A complex study of combined stressors would be represented by a three-dimensional matrix of environmental, situational, and host factors.

Research Findings   *The Bioastronautics Data Book* [3] summarizes a few studies that indicate additive effects, for example, heat decreases tolerance to $+g_z$ acceleration; hypoxia and cold each individually decrease $+g_z$ tolerance. Other two-factor studies reported deal with hypoxia and heat, cold, vibration, and radiation; radiation and cold; vibration and heat; weightlessness and acceleration, heat, and dehydration. The studies deal mainly with physiological changes and were conducted during the 1950s and 1960s with either humans or rats. Hypoxia and heat has also been reported as both a synergistic and an antagonistic effect by different investigators. Several of the findings appear contradictory.

In 1971 and 1972, Grether et al. [17, 18] reported two human studies dealing with the combined effects of vibration, noise, and heat. Heat was at 120°F (48.9°C); noise was at 105 dB for 35 min; vibration was at 5 Hz (z axis), 0.30 peak G for 35 min. Physiological measures were skin and rectal temperature, heart rate, and weight loss. Performance measures were tracking error, choice reaction time, mental arithmetic, repeating messages, visual acuity, and subjective rating. A somewhat surprising finding was that on all measures, excepting arithmetic and ratings, the changes or decrements for the combined stressors were slightly smaller than for the single greatest stressor. The authors concluded there was no additive stress interaction and, in fact, there was a slight antagonistic interaction. The second study essentially confirmed the findings of the first study. For example, tracking performance was less impaired by combined stresses than by vibration alone.

The authors allow for the possibility of increased motivation under combined stress. Subjects were necessarily aware of the number of stressors applied and might have worked harder to do well.

QUESTIONS AND PROBLEMS

Noise

1   A task to be performed by a USAF technician would involve exposure to a noise level of 110 dB continuously for about 30 min. Is it recommended or mandatory that the technician wear ear protection? (See Figure 9-1.)
2   Another USAF technician was scheduled to work in the same environment for only 5 min. Assuming she wore no ear protective devices and worked from 9:00 to 9:05 A.M., what is the earliest time she would be permitted to work in the same environment a second time? (See Table 9-2.)
3   Suppose it was determined that a 110-dB noise consisted primarily of pure tones in the 2000-Hz band. To meet long-term exposure criteria (Figure 9-2), how much reduction in noise level at the ear would be required? How much is recommended?
4   What is the total exposure duration each day that OSHA would allow the worker in question 3? (See text and Figure 9-3.)
5   If the technician in question 3 were wearing earmuffs that attenuated the noise level 30 dB at 2000 Hz, would the task meet long-term exposure criteria? (See Figure 9-2.)
6   In Chapter 3 it was stated that the human ear may be sensitive to a range from 20 to 20,000 Hz. Why do you suppose that SPL is measured at the octave bands discussed in this chapter? (See text and Figure 9-4.)
7   A factory is planning to move from its present location in a heavy industrial area to a suburban location. Due to the nature of certain machinery noise, management is concerned that there might be complaints from the community.

  The following information was submitted to you regarding the noise and other influencing factors. The plant machinery will begin operation in the summer and will operate 24-h per day. The peak noise is impulsive, consisting of 30-sec bursts approximately 15 times per hour. The noise levels in decibels are as follows:

250 Hz − 60	2000 Hz − 45
500 Hz − 60	4000 Hz − 40
1000 Hz − 50	8000 Hz − 40

  From Figure 9-5 and Table 9-3 calculate (1) the uncorrected N value; (2) the corrected N value; (3) the estimated initial community reaction to the factory noise (no previous conditioning). Use frequency with highest N value.
8   The management of the factory in question 7 decided to operate the noisy machinery only during the daytime and to reduce the noise bursts to 8 times per hour. After a period of considerable conditioning, what would be the corrected N value and the communities' estimated reaction?

Vibration

1   A vehicle driver is scheduled to work continuously (daily for 8 h) on an undamped, spring seat with a center frequency of 6 Hz. Measurements were taken to determine if the RMS acceleration exceeded recommended exposure limits. The reading was 0.03

m/s^2. Does the seat meet fatigue-decreased proficiency limits assuming no other information available? (See Figure 9.6.)

2   Management decided they wished to provide the driver in question 1 with a seat that would meet reduced comfort limits. What is the maximum vibration in m/s^2 permissible to meet this criteria?

3   A technician is scheduled to work in the back of a truck with a center frequency of 3 Hz for only 16 min. What is the highest vibration in m/s^2 he could take to meet proficiency limits?

4   Suppose it was learned that the technician's task involved doing some very precise manual tasks and that a modifying factor of 1.4 was required. Would you recommend that he be asked to perform the task at a vertical vibration level of 2.4 m/s^2? Why? What would you recommend?

5   The vehicle driver in question 1 had a split shift working from 8:00 A.M. until 12:00 noon and from 4:00 P.M. until 8:00 P.M. Assuming the same center frequency, 6 Hz, what is the maximum vibration in m/s^2 for fatigue-decreased proficiency limits?

6   Assume that a particular subject seated on a shake table resonates at 4 Hz. The table is then vibrated at a frequency of 5 Hz. According to Radke's ratio would you predict a transmissibility greater or less than 100 percent assuming no appreciable damping? Give the ratio and the percent transmissibility.

Acceleration

1   A jet pilot pulls up from a dive at 96.6 ft/sec^2. How many Gs were pulled?

2   According to Figure 9-9, how long would an astronaut be able to tolerate 8 Gs if the acceleration were: (a) headward; (b) footward; (c) backward; (d) forward?

3   If the astronaut in question 2 were required to pull an overhead control to eject, would the force of acceleration permit doing so? (See Figure 9-10.)

REFERENCES

1   Ayoub, M. M. and J. D. Ramsey: The hazards of vibration and lighting, *Industrial Engineering,* vol. 7, no. 11, November 1975.

2   Berry, C. A.: "Weightlessness," in *Bioastronautics Data Book,* 2d ed., National Aeronautics and Space Administration NASA SP-3006, U.S. Government Printing Office, Washington, D.C., 1973, chap. 8.

3   *Bioastronautics Data Book,* 2d ed., NASA SP-3006, U.S. Government Printing Office, Washington, D.C., 1973.

4   Bond, Robert et al.: "Neutral Body Posture in Zero-G," Skylab Experience Bulletin No. 17, Lyndon B. Johnson Space Center, Houston, Texas, July 1975.

5   Bondurant, S., N. P. Clark, W. G. Blanchard et al.: *Human tolerance to some accelerations anticipated in space flight,* WADC, TR 58-156, 1958.

6   Brown, J. W.: "Zero-G effects on crewman height," JSC Note 76-EW-3, JSC-11184, Lyndon B. Johnson Space Center, Houston, Texas, May 1976.

7   Cameron, P., D. Robertson, and J. Zaks: Sound pollution, noise pollution, and health: Community parameters, *Journal of Applied Psychology,* vol. 56, no. 1, 1972, pp. 67–74.

8   Carpenter, M. E.: "Human response simulation in automobile accident research," a literature review submitted to the author for course work, Texas A&M University, July 7, 1971.

9 Chambers, R. M. and J. L. Brown: *Acceleration,* paper presented at Symposium on Environmental Stress and Human Performance, American Psychological Association, September 1959.

10 Chambers, R. M.: "Operator performance in acceleration environments," in N. M. Burns, R. M. Chambers and E. Handler (eds.), *Unusual environments and human behavior,* The Free Press, New York, 1963, pp. 193–320.

11 Emerson, P. D.: Practical noise control, *Industrial Engineering,* vol. 7, no. 6, August 1975, pp. 24–28.

12 Eschenbrenner, A. J., Jr.: Effects of intermittent noise on performance of complex psychomotor tasks, *Human Factors,* vol. 13, no. 1, 1971, pp. 59–63.

13 *Federal Register,* vol. 36, no. 105, May 29, 1971.

14 Frazer, T. M.: "Sustained linear acceleration," in *Bioastronautics Data Book,* 2d ed., National Aeronautics and Space Administration, NASA SP-3006, U.S. Government Printing Office, Washington, D.C., 1973, chap. 4.

15 Gerathewohl, S. J. and H. D. Stallings, Jr.: *Experiments during weightlessness: a study of the oculo-agravic illusion,* School of Aviation Medicine, USAF, Randolph AFB, Texas 58-105, July 1958.

16 Grether, W. F.: Vibration and human performance, *Human Factors,* vol. 13, no. 3, 1971, pp. 203–216.

17 Grether, W. F., C. S. Harris, G. C. Mohr, C. W. Nixon, M. Ohlbaum, H. C. Sommer, V. H. Thaler, and J. H. Veghte: Effects of combined heat, noise and vibration stress on human performance and physiological functions, *Aerospace Medicine,* vol. 42, no. 10, October 1971.

18 Grether, W. F., C. S. Harris, M. Ohlbaum, P. A. Sampson, and J. C. Guignard: Further study of combined heat, noise and vibration stress, *Aerospace Medicine,* vol. 43, no. 6, June 1972.

19 *Guide for the conservation of hearing in noise,* prepared by the Subcommittee on Noise, American Academy of Opthalmology and Ontolarygology, rev. 1964.

20 Hornick, R. J.: "Vibration," in *Bioastronautics Data Book,* 2d ed., National Aeronautics and Space Administration, NASA SP-3006, U.S. Government Printing Office, Washington, 1973, chap. 7.

21 *Industrial Noise Manual,* 2d ed., American Industrial Hygiene Association, Detroit, 1966, p. 420.

22 Jansen, G.: "Effect of noise on physiological state," in W. D. Ward and J. E. Frick (eds.): *Noise as a public health hazard,* Washington, D.C., The American Speech and Hearing Association, ASHA Report 4, February 1969.

23 Jerison, H. J.: Effects of noise on human performance, *Journal of Applied Psychology,* vol. 43, 1959, pp. 96–101.

24 Lipscomb, D. M. and A. C. Taylor (eds.): *Noise Control Handbook of Principles and Practices,* New York, Van Nostrand Reinhold, 1978, p. 168.

25 Machle, W.: The effect of gun blast on hearing. *Archives of Ontolaryngology,* vol. 42, 1945, pp. 164–168.

26 Peterson, A. P. G., and E. E. Gross, Jr.: *Handbook of Noise Measurement,* 7th ed., General Radio Co., New Concord, Mass., 1972.

27 Radke, A. O.: Vehicle vibration: Man's new environment, ASME, paper 57-A-54, Dec. 3, 1957.

28 *Rating noise with respect to hearing conservation, speech communications, and annoyance,* International Organization for Standardization, Technical Committee 43, Acoustics, Secretariat-139, August 1961.

29 *The relation of hearing loss to noise exposure,* ANSI (formerly USASI), New York, 1954.

30 Roth, E. M. (ed.): *Compendium of human responses to the aerospace environment,* NASA CR-1205, vols. 2 and 3, November 1968, chap. 7.

31 Roth, E. M. (ed.): *Compendium of human responses to the aerospace environment,* NASA CR-1205 (5 vols.), November 1968.

32 Simons, A. K., A. O. Radke, and W. C. Oswald: A study of truck ride characteristics in military vehicles. Bostrom Research Laboratories, Milwaukee, Report 118, March 15, 1956.

33 Stapp, J. P.: Acceleration: How great the problem? *Astronautics,* vol. 4, no. 2, February 1959, pp. 38–39, 98–100.

34 Tomlinson, R. W.: Estimation and reduction of risk in hearing: The background and a case study, *Applied Ergonomics,* vol. 2, no. 2, 1971, pp. 112–119.

35 United States Air Force, Air Force Systems Command, AFSC DH 1-3, *Biodynamics,* Section 3E1, pp. 7–8, January 1, 1977.

36 United States Air Force, Air Force Systems Command, AFSC DH 1-3, *Bioacoustics,* Section 3F1, pp. 1-3, January 1, 1977.

37 United States Air Force, Air Force Systems Command, AFSC DH 1-6, DN 6A8, July 20, 1974, p. 5.

38 Warner, H. P.: Effects of intermittent noise on human target detection, *Human Factors,* vol. 11, no. 3, 1969, pp. 245–250.

39 Loeb, M.: The effects of intense stimulation on the perception of time, Report No. 269, Fort Knox, Ky.: U.S. Army Medical Research Laboratories, 1956.

40 Stuart, M.: The effects of white noise on time perception, task satisfaction, and performance. Master of Science thesis, Texas A&M University, December 1979.

41 Hartman, P., S. Rubinsky, and D. Shao: Simulating noise exposure, *Industrial Engineering,* vol. 8, no. 8, August 1976, pp. 22–25.

Part Four

Surface Transportation Systems

Chapter 10

Design of the Roadway Environment

As a driver of a vehicle in the roadway environment, the human brings to the situation the same capabilities and limitations as those discussed in Chapter 3. One has the same tracking skills, sensory and processing capabilities, and response capabilities as an operator in any other situation, but the roadway environment provides a unique set of circumstances to which one must adapt. The variability of the driving public also poses a problem in message design.

In considering the driving situation, there are four major subsystems: the environment, both human-made and natural; the vehicle and associated safety equipment; the driver; and the organizations responsible for the driver's activities, such as law enforcement agencies.

The scope of this text does not permit an in-depth study of all four subsystems. The vehicle subsystem will be discussed in Chapter 11. The law enforcement problem will be illustrated briefly as it relates to speed reduction strategies. In this chapter, driver behavior will be considered only to the degree that it can be modified by the roadway environment and, in particular, by traffic control devices such as signs, signal lights, and striping. Roadway design and operation is the responsibility of the highway engineer and the traffic engineer. By improving the process by which information is communicated to the driver, traffic accidents can be reduced, traffic flow can be enhanced, and more effective usage can be made of existing roadway facilities.

DRIVER EXPECTANCIES

One of the most important concepts introduced in this chapter is *driver expectancy*. This term is synonymous with "population stereotype" when applied to driver interpretations. Some writers speak of a "high degree of stimulus-response compatibility" in preference to "expectancy." The color red is said to be compatible with the action stop. Ellis [11] states that driver expectancy relates to those features of the roadway that prepare the driver to execute a pending roadway task and keep him or her prepared until the task is executed. The features prepare the driver to make a correct response to the roadway task.

From driving experiences, the driver has developed certain informational needs and expects to be provided certain types of information that is responsive to these needs. One also expects information to be displayed in a particular way so that it can be easily understood and expects that it will be available at precise times so that it can be acted upon. Whenever the information provided is in violation of these expectancies, the traffic system becomes less efficient and driver errors can eventuate into accidents.

Guidance and Navigation Tasks

King and Lunenfeld [25] have identified a hierarchy of driver tasks. *Positional* or control tasks are those associated with maintaining the vehicle on the roadway by steering and speed adjustments. *Situational* tasks are associated with interacting with traffic and maintaining a particular headway clearance with respect to other vehicles. Maintaining a safe path via positive guidance information regarding road and traffic conditions is essential [Alexander and Lunenfeld, 51]. *Navigational* tasks are those involved in route planning and maintaining a certain course so as to reach a destination.

It is assumed that the driving task hierarchy is in the order they were discussed. For example, when there is a conflict of tasks, the driver will *revert* to negotiating the more basic task. First priority is to keep from having an accident. Should one miss an exit ramp on a freeway, one will continue to maintain roadway and headway clearances and defer trying to accomplish the navigational task.

Recently interest has increased in ascertaining why certain roadway sections and sites have many accidents. Often maintaining a safe path on the roadway involves consideration of signing, roadway geometry, and drivers' expectations. Alexander and Lunenfeld [51] developed a user's guide designed to assist engineers in defining the nature of the problem at known hazardous locations and in formulating a design solution. Procedures included analyzing the driver's tasks, forecasting driver expectancies and visual obstructions, and identifying the information needed to negotiate the problem location safely. The analyses should lead to a redesign of the existing traffic control system to bring it into compliance with positive guidance criteria.

The authors have studied many urban intersections, freeways, and rural sites with high accident records. The user's guide provides human factors principles and procedures for engineers to improve hazardous sites. The emphasis is primarily directed at optimizing information handling for guidance level tasks, although navigational information is often involved in maintaining a safe path.

Recently there has emerged a body of research addressed to better ways of directing drivers to their destinations. This area of research, sponsored largely by the Federal Highway Administration (FHWA), had been long neglected. The driver desires advanced knowledge of roadway conditions ahead and the best course of action to avoid congestion. Had the driver known in advance there was unexpected traffic congestion along a planned route (due to an accident or maintenance work), he or she might well have selected an alternate route to the destination. This new area of research will be spotlighted in this chapter.

Modes of Driver Communication

Highway design engineers and traffic engineers communicate with drivers in several ways: static signs, traffic lights, painted markings on the roadway surface, more recently variable or changeable message signs (CMS), and highway advisory radio communications. A telephone call-in system for localized traffic information has also been employed [Huchingson and Dudek, 20].

Even the design of the roadway itself may be viewed as a form of communication. The geometry of the roadway includes lane and shoulder widths, horizontal and vertical curves, changes in the number of lanes, complex interchanges such as the multilevel diamond interchanges on freeways. The driver has certain expectancies about these roadway design features and any deviations from expectancies could result in confusion, erratic behavior, and potential accidents. Signs and markings may aid in anticipating unexpected roadway design, but the ultimate solution is an improved and standardized roadway geometry. Messer et al. [33] have recently studied this problem in a research program.

One of the more recent types of driver communication devices is the CMS. The driver's activities with respect to this type of informational display will be used to illustrate a model of the driver communication process. Figure 10-1 presents one type of CMS in which the words or characters are formed by a matrix of light bulbs. (The application was redirecting traffic to a special event.) Commercial advertising, scoreboards, bank marquees, and some service stations have used matrix-bulb displays for years, but the significant characteristic, as we shall see, is the real-time activation of the system.

The bulb-type display is only one type of matrix CMS. Another CMS system forms characters by rotating discs that have different colors on their surfaces. By electromagnetic actuation of appropriate discs, characters are formed in a manner similar to the card section at a college football game.

Other CMSs consist of rotating drums or scrolls, foldouts, or blankouts (on-off) that permit only limited changes of messages [Dorsey, 6; Dudek et al.,

Figure 10-1 Matrix bulb-type changeable message sign. *(Dudek et al., 1978.)*

8]. The technology of variable-message sign presentation also includes electrostatic vane matrix signs, electromechanical flap matrix signs, fiber optics, and trailer-mounted static and dynamic signs.

The messages to be displayed on a CMS are usually sent from a traffic control center that has surveillance of traffic conditions from police reports, closed circuit TV of the roadway (freeways), detectors embedded in the roadway, and so forth. Unlike static signs, the messages displayed may be altered at any moment as traffic conditions change. Messages are said to be in real time.

The following discussion will emphasize driver communication variables as they relate to the CMS. The reasons for this are two-fold: (1) the CMS is a new communication device only recently explored whereas much of the literature on static signs has already been documented in FHWA design standards; (2) the CMS represents a more complex communications problem. Message content, format, redundancy, and load have been issues in static signs for many years. However, static signs generally have briefer messages and their content is more often geographically linked, rather than varying over time as does traffic information.

A MODEL OF DRIVER COMMUNICATION PROCESS

Prior to a discussion of the variables in the driver communication process, it may be instructive to present a model of the driver's activities in sensing, processing, and responding to displayed information.

Figure 10-2 is a schematic of the communication process with respect to a CMS. The driver's activities will be discussed briefly in their sequence of occurrence. The issues raised will each be discussed further in later sections.

Detect and Recognize the Sign

The first driver activity must be to detect and recognize the sign as an informational source. The sign itself must attract attention in some manner.

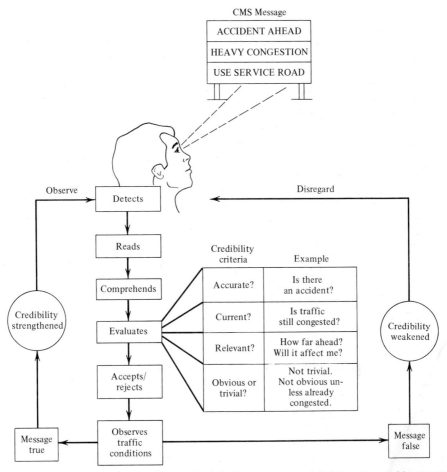

Figure 10-2 Schematic of the driver communication process in relation to a changeable message sign.

Flashing beacons are often used with static signs to attract attention to a railroad crossing, an unexpected intersection, or an icy bridge.

Changeable message signs of the bulb type are *dynamic* in character. The message may flash on and off or the sequences of messages may change often. Like commercial lighted signs on marquees, the signs are said to have *signal value,* or *conspicuity.*

Detection does not always imply recognition. A flashing railroad crossing signal upstream of a continuously flashing traffic light was erroneously interpreted as applying to the traffic intersection. The driver, who was hit by a train, saw the signal but failed to associate it with a railroad crossing. A distinctively coded signal is necessary in critical situations.

Many static signs we pass often on the roadway are ignored. We see the important ones like stop signs (involving accident risk or police apprehension), but we ignore those unrelated to our needs at the moment, such as parking restrictions. However, commuters may soon learn that dynamic roadway signs deal with current and relevant information, such as traffic conditions along their route. Thus, aside from its movement aspect, the CMS should attract attention. Weaver et al. [49] have demonstrated that a CMS (Figure 10-1) is highly effective in inducing drivers to take an alternate route to a special event.

Sometimes sign detection also involves a search task. The driver may be looking for a particular static sign, for example, a highway guide sign or route number that is embedded in an overhead sign with many other guide signs. Detection and discrimination may involve noting some unique symbolic shape or color.

Forbes et al. [13] studied the attention-getting characteristics of static signs in a series of studies. Advance warning is needed in low-attention areas such as rural freeways. Attention is increased by greater *brightness contrast* between the sign and the background and by a larger sign. No single *color* was best against all backgrounds, but a light green and yellow were seen best most frequently when paired with dark green trees, yellow-brown hills, gray-blue cliffs, and daytime-snow backgrounds.

Read the Message

The second driver activity is reading the message. The *legibility* of the CMS message depends upon many factors—the apparent size of the printed characters, the character style or font, the brightness contrast of the legend and background, the ambient lighting, the number of bulbs burned out, and so on. Factors affecting legibility of the message are discussed in sections on character factors and illumination factors.

Reading a message also depends upon *exposure time,* the amount of time the message will be available for the driver to read it. Exposure time depends on vehicle speed and how soon the driver first detects the sign. It is also affected by *restricted sight distances* (due to hills, curves, and roadway obstructions like trailer trucks) and by the competing demands of reading other signs and markings and maintaining headway clearances to other vehicles. The percent of available viewing time that is devoted to various activities has been studied by photographing driver eye movements [Rockwell et al., 41].

The duration of message exposure on the CMS is also controlled by the timing of the sequences. A sequence is a line or lines of information displayed at one time. The complete message may consist of two or more sequences.

All of these factors are constraints on available reading time and must be considered in message design. Long messages are not recommended because under traffic conditions the 85th-percentile driver may be limited to reading only about 10 words in matrix lights in a 10-sec exposure time [Dudek et al., 8]. A driver traveling at or near the speed limit, with many of the constraints on exposure time discussed above, may have 10 sec or less available viewing time.

When message length or load exceed the driver's available viewing time, we speak of *message overload*.

Comprehend the Message

Reading a book does not guarantee that we understand the material read. Neither does seeing a printed or symbolic message on a sign necessarily ensure comprehension. The issue of message understanding and designing *message content* and *format* to expedite comprehension is a complex new research area only recently investigated [Dudek et al., 8]. Printed word message guidelines and symbolic message design are discussed in a later section. There are several solutions to misunderstood signing, including message simplification, education, and repetition of the message.

Evaluate and Accept/Reject Message

Even if the driver completely understands the message, there is no guarantee that one will believe the message and follow the advice given. The issue of *message credibility* and the factors that weaken or strengthen drivers' confidence in the CMS system is a complex one only partially explored to date [Dudek et al., 7]. Traffic control centers may inadvertently weaken the credibility of the system by various mistakes in operation of the sign. In Figure 10-2, five criteria were given in terms of which the driver evaluates message credibility. One asks if the information is accurate, current, relevant, and not obvious, or trivial. Some examples of how the inappropriate use of messages may weaken message credibility are given next. In addition to these message content factors, the driver's inability to read or to understand a message may also weaken confidence in the system.

Factors Weakening Message Credibility   *Inaccuracies* in the message, such as an erroneous report of an accident ahead, may be later disproven. If a freeway driver is advised to exit and take a service road and later no accident or heavy congestion is observed on the freeway, the system's credibility is weakened. This is an example of the "cry wolf" effect.

It is also inaccurate if a system fails to give advice (even if there is an electronics or computer failure) when the traffic conditions ahead warrant giving advice. Drivers expect to be forewarned of unexpected congestion or delays.

Credibility may be weakened also by giving an overly precise quantitative message of traffic speed or traveling time, which is later disproven by reading a speedometer or watch. Any of these three inaccuracies may weaken credibility of the system.

Old information may not be detected as old initially, but if the same message appears each time the driver passes the CMS, one may question its currency and wonder if anyone is controlling it.

Relevancy is also critical to credibility. For example, if information is given about an accident 20 miles away or in regard to traffic on an intersecting freeway, the information may be of little interest to most drivers.

Information that is obvious or trivial is actually a subset of the relevancy issue. *Obvious information* is already known or easily deducible. A driver caught in a traffic jam may be amused if not offended by a display of "heavy congestion." Dudek et al. [10] found it is better to display the location of *a change in traffic condition,* for example, "Congestion begins—2 miles" or "Traffic clears—3 miles."

Traffic engineers seem to disagree on whether or not *trivial information,* unrelated to traffic conditions, should be displayed when there is no traffic problem. Some feel that a message should always be displayed—even time and temperature or safety slogans. Others feel that these uses may eventually result in disregarding the message. Some commercial displays to which drivers are repeatedly exposed are disregarded. These traffic engineers prefer to use the CMS only when some traffic response is desired from the driver. A series of dots or stars may be used to signify the sign is operating, but there is no news.

Observe Traffic Conditions

The credibility of some messages may be questioned the first time the message is seen. Other messages may seem plausible when first seen but when later compared with the actual traffic conditions, they lose credibility as discussed above.

Figure 10-2 should not be taken to imply that a single inaccuracy or other operational violation will destroy the driver's confidence in the system. We continue to read our newspapers even after numerous inaccuracies! But eventually the abused driver may learn to "turn off" signs perceptually, and an expensive traffic control system could lose its effectiveness.

DRIVER VISUAL COMMUNICATION VARIABLES

Much of early signing research dealt with issues related to static sign visibility and legibility: lettering styles and sizes, stroke widths, color combinations, and so forth. Design standards based on this research are now documented in the FHWA *Manual of Uniform Traffic Control Devices* [12]. You may have noted that there is a fairly standard lettering on signs on all United States highways, particularly the Interstate System (for example, use of lower-case letters for all names on guide signs). Certain background colors are standardized: white letters on a green background for new interstate signs, orange background for construction and maintenance signs, red background for stop signs, and so forth. The shape of the sign also has standardized meanings.

Lettering heights, and associated sign sizes, are based on the concept of "legibility distance." An early rule-of-thumb was to provide 1 in of lettering height for each 50 ft of viewing distance, but this rule has exceptions. There are standard letter series based on height-to-stroke-width ratios, and the legibility distance for letter series varies somewhat independently of letter height. Hofstetter [19] has reported that the major types of signs differ somewhat in their legibility distances.

The CMS is also being investigated [Dudek et al., 7] to determine visibility and legibility requirements as a function of type of display, lettering style, and ambient illumination.

In recent years, the focus of research attention has shifted also to other issues, such as the content and format of messages appearing on CMS [Mast and Ballas, 30]. In this section the major variables of a signing system will be examined and illustrated.

Message Content

Within very limited signing space, it may be necessary to communicate several pieces of information. The challenge to the CMS message designer is how to communicate in the fewest number of words. For example, how does one communicate on four lines of only 14 characters per line that there has been an accident ahead at a particular location and that certain traffic should exit the freeway and take an alternate route? (See *Message Load* for examples.)

With stringent word restrictions, it is necessary to establish some priorities with respect to what information is essential and what information is desirable. The most important information is *what the driver should do* and *one good reason why he or she should do it*. The advisory to "exit and use the service road" might be ignored if this were the only message. The good reason (accident ahead) might be sufficient additional information for the driver to act (unless he is a rubbernecker!).

The major message elements are *the problem* (accident, roadwork); the *effects* of the problem (congestion, delays, and lane blockage are desirable information); the *location* of the accident or congestion onset; and the *action* statement (advisory as to appropriate driving response). The accident location is desirable information in establishing relevance of the message for commuters who may be exiting at various locations. For facilities driven on largely by commuters, cross-street designations of location are understood, whereas on facilities for unfamiliar drivers, locations should be given in terms of miles ahead [Dudek et al., 10].

Dudek et al. [8, 10] have investigated CMS messages appropriate for many different types of traffic situations calling for rerouting traffic headed for certain destinations. Other CMS messages have been developed appropriate for displaying the condition of traffic (congestion, lane blockage, time delays, and time saved in taking another route). The messages were based upon both laboratory and field studies and the design recommendations have been documented in a design guide for traffic engineers [Dudek et al., 8] Mast and Ballas [30] conducted controlled field studies and determined that high-severity messages and time delay information were associated with a decision to take a bypass route.

Anchored display of current traffic condition: All possible states shown with one state lighted. Only extremes labeled for visitors.

Unanchored displays of the same condition: Code systems (1–5) and (A–E) depend upon drivers learning the code first. Visitors find the displays meaningless.

Figure 10-3   Anchored and unanchored displays.

Anchoring   An interesting finding of the research of Dudek et al. is that a coding system should be anchored. Figure 10-3 presents examples of anchored and unanchored displays. In presenting traffic condition information on an anchored display note that various possible traffic states are shown on a scale from light to very heavy or jammed. Only the current state is lighted. The extreme states are labeled so first-time viewers can get their frame of reference. In contrast, the unanchored display uses a coding system such as letter grades, number grades, or color codes. While these may be learned by commuters, they are often meaningless to the first-time viewer who does not understand the coding system.

Message Format

Format means different things depending upon the context in which it is used. In discussing word messages, format refers to the arrangement of message elements (words or lines of words) on a sign to form a total message. Figure 10-4 (A) illustrates three formats. The same message elements appear on each of the signs, but the order of the lines differs. The message was designed to advise drivers to avoid taking the interstate through the city (I-10) and to take a bypass route instead (I-610). The relative effectiveness of the formats has not been studied in the field by taking traffic measures of diversion; however, laboratory studies in which subjects constructed a preferred message for this situation support the first of these formats (see also *Message Redundancy* for further comment). Drivers also prefer a specific advisory as to what they should do rather than being required to make the decision themselves from reading only the two traffic state messages [Huchingson et al., 22].

Message Redundancy

Redundancy means several different things. Sometimes it refers to *repetition* of a complete message or the key elements of a message on consecutive signs or sequences of a CMS. An example of repeating a key element (the word "accident") is shown in Figure 10-4 (B).

     Redundancy is also used to imply unnecessary or low-priority information.

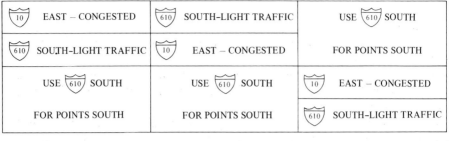

A

(A) Three different formats of the same message on a rotating drum CMS; (B) Two signs
that repeat the same key message: (C) Modification of the first message in (A) by deleting
a redundant message on line 2.

Figure 10-4   Examples of message format and redundancy.

The words "avenue" or "street" may be understood when used after the name
of an artèrial. Further study [Huchingson et al., 22] of the signs illustrated in
Figure 10-4 (A) resulted in the conclusion that traffic conditions on the bypass
route were somewhat redundant when the advisory is to take that route.
Therefore, a two-line message shown in Figure 10-4 (C) presents the required
information. Note also the change in format of the top line, presenting the
problem prior to the name of the facility.

A third usage of redundancy is in the context of coded information.
Consider, for example, the familiar interstate shield. It is coded in several
different ways—the unique shape, the red-white-and-blue color combination,
and the interstate route number. All three sources of information mean
interstate highway. In this context, redundancy provides *backup information*
such that understanding any one of the coding conventions would lead to the
conclusion that the sign referred to an interstate highway. Therefore, the
driver's processing of information is greatly aided by receiving the same
information in more than one way [Dewar, 4].

Redundancy in Degraded Words   In Chapter 3, it was noted that redundancy in the language enhances our anticipation of upcoming characters in words.
Similarly, redundancy in character formation permits reading printed material
that is partially blurred. Mounce et al. [52] studied the effects of loss of bulbs in a

CMS. Words varied in length from 4 to 10 characters. Most of the characters were composed from an array of 5 X 7 bulbs. The traffic-related words were projected one at a time on a screen for 3 seconds, after which the words were identified.

By removing the bulbs randomly from each character, the words were degraded in 10-percent increments from 10 percent to 50 percent of the bulbs. A "familiar" group initially saw the words with no bulbs missing and later saw them degraded progressively. The same list of 40 words in random order was presented five times. The task was one of recognition. An "unfamiliar" group initially saw the words degraded 50 percent and later saw them with progressively more bulbs in place. Piecing together the recognizable characters into meaningful words was somewhat more difficult.

Table 10-1 depicts the percentage of bulbs out, which was associated with 85 percent and 95 percent of subjects correctly identifying the words. Regardless of word length, 95 percent of the familiar group could recognize words when 28 percent of the bulbs were removed. The unfamiliar group met the 95 percent criteria with 8 percent removal. Word length did not matter for the familiar group, but longer (less common) words were slightly more difficult for the unfamiliar group. Four-character route numbers were alphanumeric (US-23, I-270). Performance was poorer for route numbers than for four-letter words (lane, exit, toll) for the unfamiliar group. Random sequences of numbers lack sequential dependencies.

Table 10-1 Bulb Loss Percentage Associated with Criterion Performances of 85% and 95% as a Function of Word Length and Familiarity

| Number of characters | Percent bulb loss | | | | | |
| | Familiar | | Unfamiliar | | Average | |
	85%	95%	85%	95%	85%	95%
4	45	28	23	11	31	17
5	44	31	21	12	32	21
6	43	25	20	8	31	17
7	49	31	21	10	30	20
8	41	25	20	6*	25	6*
9	46	23*	10*	8	16*	7
10	42	28	15	7	28	10
Route numerals	36*	31	18	8	26	17
Average	44%	28%	18%	8%	28%	14%

*Minimum bulb loss tolerable for criterion performance regardless of length.
Source: Mounce et al. [52].

Even though language redundancy permitted a high degree of word recognition with up to 50 percent of the elements missing, the authors recommended that bulbs be replaced when 10 percent had failed.

Abbreviations Reducing word length by abbreviating also capitalizes on message redundancy. Use of abbreviations will be required on matrix signs because of limitations on the number of characters that may be displayed on a line.

Table 10-2 lists abbreviations of traffic-related words that were given independently by 40 percent or more of a large sample [Dudek and Huchingson, 7]. Stereotyping refers to the degree to which the sample gave a common abbreviation. Only the modal abbreviations and their percentages are shown. Also, the table shows percentages of other samples who understood the abbreviation either by itself or in the context of a prompt word.

It was found that highly stereotyped abbreviations (for example, 50 percent

Table 10-2 Highly Stereotyped Abbreviations for Traffic-Related Words

Word	Abbreviation*	% Giving abbreviation	% Understanding alone	% Understanding in context
Road	Rd	94	88	100
Information	Info	83	92	96
Minute(s)	Min	78	72	88
Highway	Hwy	72	100	100
West	W	72	12	100
Route	Rt	66	32	86
Boulevard	Blvd	61	96	96
Moderate	Mod	56	32	76
Temporary	Temp	54	30	84
Lane	Ln	54	72	96
Mile(s)	Mi	51	72	100
Clears	Clrs	51	32	48
Heavy	Hvy	51	60	60
Construction	Const	50	76	92
Field	Fld	50	44	72
Roadwork	Rdwk	49	64	76
Level	Lvl	48	52	80
Blocked	Blkd	46	56	96
Condition	Cond	46	80	72
Freeway	Fwy	44	100	100
Major	Maj	41	72	100
Center	Cntr	41	92	96
Vehicle	Veh	41	84	96

*These abbreviations have not necessarily been approved for signing usage.
Source: Adapted from Dudek and Huchingson [7].

or more) were understood generally by at least 85 percent in context. However, for a list of 84 words the correlation between degree of stereotyping (modal percent giving an abbreviation) and degree of understanding in context was only +0.17. Many respondents could not think of a good abbreviation and small percentages selected a particular abbreviation. However, when these low-stereotyped abbreviations were viewed with another word, 85 percent or more understood many of the abbreviations.

The presence of a prompt word (for example, Freeway Blkd) greatly enhanced understanding in comparison with the abbreviation seen alone. Only 24 percent of abbreviated words met the 85-percent criterion by themselves, but 54 percent were understood with a prompt word.

Message Length and Load

The terms *length* and *load* are related, but not synonymous, concepts. *Length* refers to the number of words, or characters, that are displayed at once on one or more lines of a sign or sequence. There is some evidence that 8-word messages of 4 to 8 characters per word (excluding prepositions) may be approaching the limit of an average driver's processing capability [Messer et al., 34]. Hence, eight is approaching the maximum number of words that should be displayed at once. Message length is also limited by the driver's reading time within the available viewing time.

Load refers to the number of units of information displayed. To illustrate the meaning of a unit of information, the following message contains five units of information:

Message elements	Units	Information given
ACCIDENT	1	What happened
AT MILFORD STREET	1	Where it happened
HEAVY CONGESTION	1	What effect on traffic
STATE FAIR TRAFFIC	1	Who should be concerned
USE WILLIAMS STREET	1	What action should they take
	$\overline{5}$	

Each message element has a message load of one unit, even though some elements are longer than others. Normally, one unit of information appears on each line of a matrix-type CMS. Each unit provides an answer to a question that might be posed by the driver.

The five-unit message that was illustrated would be too long for two sequences of two lines each. The message designer would need to go to either a three-sequence message or else delete either line 2 or line 3 (which is desirable but not essential information). Two solutions for a two-line, two-sequence CMS are as follows:

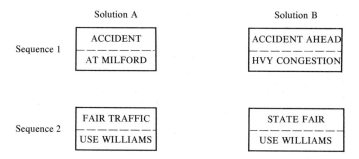

	Solution A	Solution B
Sequence 1	ACCIDENT / AT MILFORD	ACCIDENT AHEAD / HVY CONGESTION
Sequence 2	FAIR TRAFFIC / USE WILLIAMS	STATE FAIR / USE WILLIAMS

The capacity of this particular bulb-matrix sign was 14 characters per line, hence, the need for an abbreviation and omissions.

User Characteristics

The message designer's task would be simplified considerably if all drivers viewing the signs were alike. However, depending upon the location of the CMS, the drivers may be predominantly regular travelers or predominantly visitors who are passing through for the first time. Familiar drivers may have been exposed many times to the roadway, the area surrounding the roadway, the cross streets and guide signs along the roadway. In general, they will require less information to understand a message that directs them to take an exit and follow an alternate route. Because the area is highly familiar, parallel avenues may already be known. Unfamiliar drivers may require very specific instructions. This should not be taken to mean that familiar drivers will accept and obey the message more readily than visitors. Acceptance depends upon previous operations of the signs and their credibility, plus knowledge of alternate routes and their desirability at that time of day.

Local drivers and visitors also differ in the names they will understand to describe a facility. Local drivers may know a facility by the name given to the freeway while the visitor will know the facility only in terms of its interstate route number as given on a map.

In addition to differences in familiarity, there are also *regional* differences in words. The word "loop" is understood in some sections of the country while "beltway" or "belt" may be used in other sections. The road that runs parallel to a freeway or interstate may be called a frontage road, service road, feeder road, or access road [Huchingson et al., 22].

Not only does the driver expect information to be given in familiar terms and local usages, but also expectancies have been developed regarding the types of facilities that are implied by the words used in a message. For example, the particular name given to an alternate route to which traffic is diverted may imply that it is a controlled-access facility, a two-lane, two-way street, or a four-lane undivided facility. Research [22] revealed that the name "temporary bypass" implied that the driver would be returned eventually to the freeway on which he or she was then traveling (with almost as much implication as the word "detour"). However, it did not imply that the facility was a controlled access facility.

Testing for the connotations of new words used in signing is important because the driver must not be deceived by the words used. A signing system using words that promise a better facility than is provided could lose credibility. On the other hand, words that promise less than is provided could result in some drivers' not following the advice to divert.

Dynamic Display Characteristics

Descriptions and examples of five types of dynamic displays follow:

Type	Examples
Flashing	Static signs with two beacons alternately flashing; a CMS with certain key words flashing or entire message flashing.
Sequencing	Total message is divided into parts and one part at a time is displayed as a sequence. Often used in movies to list cast and contributors at the beginning.
Run-on (traveling)	One-line message continuously moving *horizontally* from right to left. Used for special bulletins on TV and for building-top news bulletins or commercials.
Rolling	Lines of messages move continuously upward. Used for listing actors and their character roles at the end of a movie.
Write-on	Individual words on a line appear one at a time in reading sequence. All words remain while successive lines of words appear. Used on TV continuous news stations where network programming is blanked out.

Each of these displays has a unique manner in which messages are changed, and each is characterized by different apparent movement. The run-on display permits showing a longer message on a single, short line, but it takes more time to read it than a sequencing display [Messer et al., 34]. A sequencing display has received the most research attention as a practical display mode for roadway communications.

Sequencing Time   An important design question is how long a particular sequence should be displayed. The rate of message change depends somewhat on message length. Consider a message consisting of eight words or two phrases of four words each. Each phrase will be displayed as a sequence on two lines of two words each. Preliminary recommendations are to allow approximately 4 sec exposure time for each sequence or 2 sec per line as a minimum. The total exposure time would be about 8 sec [Dudek et al., 8]. Research continues on the feasibility of briefer exposure times and required blanking time between sequences and messages [Dudek and Huchingson, 7].

Dividing Sequenced Messages   Sequenced displays are typically divided into either two or three sequences for roadway application. Longer sequences usually exceed the available reading time.

The two-line display is recommended in preference to the one- or three-line displays because most message phrases (or complete thoughts) seem to fit neatly into two-line phrases. For effective communications it is important that a phrase or thought *not* be divided such that part appears on one sequence and part in another sequence.

The following illustrates a three-sequence message which has been properly divided and one which has a phrase divided improperly on two sequences.

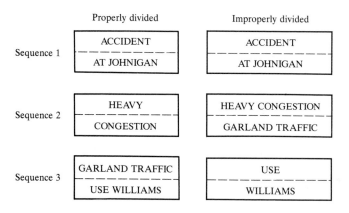

Remember that in traffic, drivers may read any of the sequences first. The message "Use Williams" could be misleading since only a particular destination group is advised to do this. It is also important that the information makes sense. The second sequence on the right does not make sense by itself. Messages should be divided, or chunked, for self-contained intelligibility of each sequence.

Character Factors

Characters refer to the material displayed, usually letters but occasionally numbers or common symbols. The apparent size or visual angle that should be subtended by characters depends largely on the legibility distance. However, when matrix bulbs are used there are some options on the height-to-width ratio (matrix size) of the typical character. Figure 10-5 (A) illustrates a word in matrix lights with most of the letters formed by a 5 × 7 array of bulbs. Do you think it is more legible than the 4 × 7 array? (Figure 10-5 (B). The array made up of four columns of bulbs is more efficient in allowing the placement of more characters on a line. (Obviously, some characters such as N, T, or I will deviate from the four-bulb width specification.)

Spacing between characters of a word depends upon whether a continuous or a modular matrix array is used. With the modular unit, the character occupies the same line space regardless of the number of bulbs needed to form the character's width. Thus, there would be more space before and after an I than

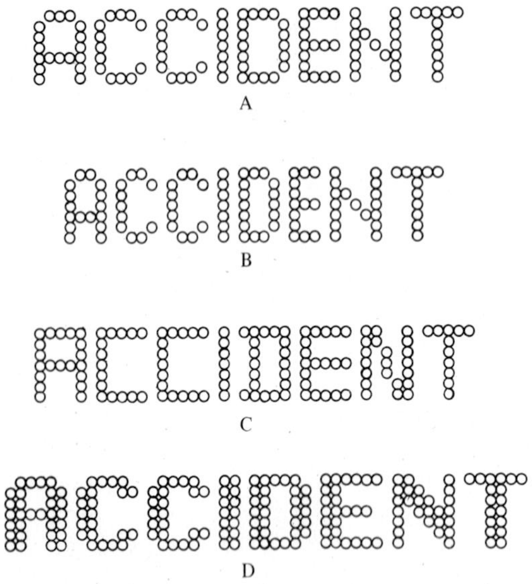

A

B

C

D

(A) rounded character, 5 x 7 (B) rounded character, 4 x 7
(C) square character, 5 x 7 (D) rounded character in double
stroke or thick-thin stroke.

Figure 10-5 Examples of character factors for a changeable message display.

after an N. With the continuous matrix array, a constant spacing is maintained
between characters, regardless of the character's width. The continuous
technique permits slightly more characters per line, which is important with
messages composed of long words.

There are several options in the *style,* or *font,* of the characters. The words
are typically made of all capital letters when used on a bulb-type CMS.
Obviously, they should be printed words rather than script. The characters may
be either square or rounded. Letters such as C, O, and D, which are partially or
completely arced, would seem to be more discriminable if the bulb in the corners
were not lighted, thereby partially arcing the character. A study by Maddox et
al. [50] using matrix dots on a cathode-ray tube found that squared letters
employing a maximum number of dots are read more accurately than rounded
letters. Recent research [Dudek and Huchingson, 7] tends to support the
standard round character for most alphanumeric characters. Figure 10-5 (A) and
(B) display a word in rounded pattern and (C) in square pattern.

It is also technically feasible to *slant* the characters slightly. It is not known
whether this improves legibility, but it limits slightly the number of characters
per line. Characters may also be constructed of thick-thin or *double-stroke* width
(two columns of bulbs). This character style also greatly limits words per line.
The technique has been used to accentuate a given word, although the
comparative legibility of the double-stroke words for an entire message has not
been investigated. Figure 10-5 (D) illustrates a word in double-stroke characters.

The technique of employing red or green *colored lights* for characters, instead of the traditional white lights, is common on modern scoreboards and stock exchange displays. Colors may be used to accentuate different types of information displayed on complex displays. However, caution must be used not to employ colors that may sacrifice legibility.

Illumination Factors

Each character in matrix bulbs is typically housed in an egg-crate-type divider so that light from one character does not *irradiate* or spill over onto another character, thereby increasing the blur. A dull black background also absorbs light and improves distinctness of characters.

Matrix bulb displays must also contrast with the ambient background illumination. An acceptable intensity in darkness would be too dim when viewed on a bright, sunny day or at dawn or dusk when the sun is either behind or radiating directly into the display. Also, the displays must be lighted such that if they are located adjacent to bright commercial light displays or nightclub marquees, they are still conspicuous. Finally, rain, fog, and haze may result in degraded visibility. The intensity of the sign must be regulated to provide adequate brightness contrast under various ambient lighting conditions. Decreasing the display luminance greatly reduces accuracy in reading dot-matrix displays [Snyder and Taylor, 53].

SPECIAL APPLICATIONS

In this section, message design techniques applicable to static road signs, particularly symbolic messages and urban area guide signs, are discussed. Other modes of communication include traffic lights, flashing beacons, and highway markings. Nighttime driving, particularly in fog or rain, reduces visibility. Roadway illumination and other design techniques are necessary to enhance visibility for signs, markings, and objects on the roadway. Current research in several of these areas will be presented.

Symbolic Messages

Bulb-matrix signs lend themselves better to display of word messages than symbolic messages. It is difficult, if not impossible, to display complex symbols such as the interstate shield on the more economical bulb-matrix displays of 5 × 7 arrays. However, symbolic signs are becoming increasingly common on static road signs. *The Manual of Uniform Traffic Control Devices* (MUTCD), a Federal Highway Administration handbook for highway engineers [12], requires the use of certain symbolic signs, while the International Road Sign System proposes the use of still other symbols. In addition, roadway markings, such as the no-passing yellow line, are symbolic in nature.

Figure 10-6 illustrates some common types of symbolic signs: pictorial silhouettes, diagrammatics, and geometric shapes (some of which are used in

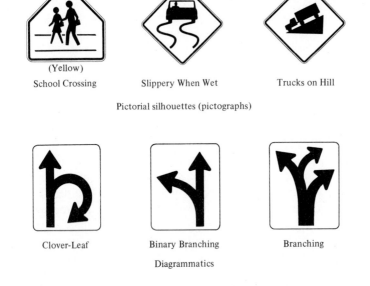

(Yellow)

School Crossing   Slippery When Wet   Trucks on Hill

Pictorial silhouettes (pictographs)

Clover-Leaf   Binary Branching   Branching

Diagrammatics

(Red)
No Right Turn   No Passing Zone   Yield   Trailblazer

Geometric shapes and colors

Figure 10-6   Examples of symbolic signs. *(Some from* Manual of Uniform Traffic Control Devices, *1971.)*

combination with word messages). Geometric shapes have been used as a code for certain types of information and have been used on *trailblazers*. Trailblazers may be a series of signs marking a route to some destination, such as a historical site or other traffic generator.

Symbolic sign studies are somewhat divided in their support for their usage, but generally, symbolic signs are thought to be more quickly detected and comprehended than word messages [King and Tierney, 27]. They conserve sign space and have been widely used in Europe because they do not depend upon understanding the language.

Prior to adopting symbolic messages, it is necessary to conduct studies to establish that the messages are understood. Research by Gordon [15] on roadway markings and by Koppa and Guseman [28] on signs and markings suggests that many symbolics in current usage may not be completely understood. Table 10-3 illustrates some misunderstandings. In each instance, one

Table 10-3 Common Misunderstandings of Symbolic Signs

Sign	Intended meaning	Percentage misunderstanding	Common misunderstandings
	Slippery when wet	23	Roadway winds or curves several times
	Left turn permitted from two lanes	34	Can only turn left from left lane
	Left lane turns left only	20	Can proceed directly ahead from left lane
	Do not turn right	9	2% thought traffic was all headed right
	Merge of a minor roadway from the right	21	Thought merging roadway was a major roadway
	Advanced and on-site railroad crossings	50	Did not distinguish the two types of signs
	Advanced and on-site school crossing signs	61	Did not distinguish the two types of signs
	45 degree left curve and 90 degree left turn	21	Did not distinguish the two types of signs
	Left lane ends and right lane ends	40	Did not distinguish the two types of signs

Source: Adapted from Koppa and Guseman [28].

should consider the impact of the error in a driving situation. The findings suggest a need for additional public education and the use of word-message panels under the symbolic signs for awhile after the symbolic sign is first installed on the roadway.

Diagrammatic Signs Diagrammatics provide advanced information to alert drivers to be in the correct lane for turning and freeway exit. Diagrammatics have been studied in the field [Mast and Kolsrud, 31; Roberts et al., 38] for diverse applications such as clover-leaf interchanges, single left exits at forks, right and left exits in combination, and lane drops.

Mast and Kolsrud [31] have reported success with the usage of diagrammatics when the situation depicted is not too complex. The graphic component must be simple. Complex graphics increase driver interpretation time as compared to conventional signs [31]. However, more consistent patterns of driver behavior and fewer accidents have been reported after the installation of diagrammatic signs on a beltway exit [Roberts et al., 38].

Roberts and Klipple [39] found that for lane drops a word panel displaying "must exit" or "exit only" were most helpful in forming correct interpretations.

Geometric Shapes The prohibitive symbolic sign for "no U-turn" or "no left or right turn" has been the subject of some controversy. Dewar [4] has been concerned that it may take longer to process information on prohibitive turn control signs than permissive signs that indicate acceptable turning movements. Dewar reported that the red slash tends to obscure the legibility of the symbol, and he recommended a partial slash that did not cover the symbol. Early research reported that many drivers thought they were permitted to perform the prohibited turn. However, research with a large sample in Texas in 1978 by Koppa and Guseman [28] found that only 2 percent made this type of error with respect to the circle/slash no-turn sign.

Urban Area Guide Signing and Driver Expectancies

Driver expectancies also exist with respect to the signing system used on city streets and arterials within a city. King and Lunenfeld [26] surveyed a large sample of "strangers" and "local strangers" to an area and found that over 50 percent reported they had at some time during a recent trip "felt lost." Of these, half actually did get lost in a city. Half of the problems reported dealt with navigating urban streets and arteries. Freeway entry and route following was much less of a problem.

The authors noted that the most important problem in urban guidance is violation of driver expectancy, that is, the signs do not provide the expected information.

The following are some examples of things that drivers expect of guide sign messages:

We expect ....

- The names of streets will stay the same (names won't change across the city).

- The names given on street signs will match names given on maps.

- Advance notice will be given whenever drivers must make a decision to change lanes upstream of intersections and lane drops.

- The location of advance signs upstream of intersections, exits, and forks will allow sufficient leadtime to read the message and make lane-changing maneuvers in traffic.

- There will be continuity between signs throughout a highway section (the same signing conventions and ways of denoting destinations and exits).

- When there is a fork in the roadway, destinations to the right will be reached by taking the right fork; left destinations, the left fork.

These are but a few illustrations. Most existing signs and markings could be said to exist to satisfy drivers' expectations. However, it is the obvious deficiencies in signing—those which have contributed to our becoming lost—that we best remember.

When driver expectancies are violated, there are worse things that may happen than becoming lost or having difficulty finding a destination. Some drivers may make a late decision to correct the mistake. They may switch lanes abruptly and hazardously; they may engage in other hazardous maneuvers such as braking or abruptly decelerating, crossing over the exit gore area, driving off the roadway to check a map, or executing an illegal U-turn. These activities are obvious contributors to accidents.

Markowitz et al. [29] have studied the formatting of static guide signs in which there were three destination names, each with a directional arrow. Subjects searched for a destination and gave the associated direction of travel. They found that name positions in the middle of the sign gave better performance than names at the top or bottom. They also found that there should be no more than three or four destinations on one guide sign.

Traffic Signals

Signs are only one of the major techniques of driver communications. Signal lights, flashing beacons, and roadway markings are other familiar visual techniques. Traffic signals have undergone changes in design and operations. In 1978, Koppa and Guseman [28] found in Texas considerable misunderstanding of the "protected left turn" sign in reference to the green arrow; the flashing amber left-turn arrow recently introduced; and flashing amber lights for nonoperational traffic lights. Fortunately, most of the misunderstandings were in the direction of leading to greater caution than required. However, they could impede traffic flow and frustrate other motorists. Public education was encouraged.

Signal phasing and sequencing is principally a traffic engineering problem, but a human factors problem arises when there are unstandardized turning movement sequences at various intersections along the same arterial (for example, left turn after through movements, left turn before through movements, and simultaneous left turn and through movements, all existing along a route, may create some false starts).

Also of interest are techniques for designing the signal mast or housing so that the light is only visible to traffic that is controlled by the signal. This is particularly a problem when two arterials intersect at an acute angle.

A right-turn-on-red (RTOR) law has been adopted in many states after extensive research indicating that the law expedited traffic flow, saved gasoline, reduced auto emissions, and did not increase accidents [McGee et al., 32]. Right turns after stopping to check cross traffic are permitted at both signalized and unsignalized intersections. Drivers must, of course, yield to pedestrians crossing in front of them. Blind pedestrians with seeing-eye dogs have had some difficulty adapting to the new law [Washington Star-News, 47]. Prohibiting RTOR is necessary at certain intersections where there is insufficient distance to see cross-street traffic, conflicting signal phasing, and where there are more than four intersecting approaches.

Railroad Warning Devices

The well-publicized failure of drivers, even school bus drivers, to notice flashing red signals at railroad grade-level crossings (or to see a train crossing the roadway at night) has stimulated FHWA-sponsored research on active warning devices that could be added to the current system [Ruden et al., 44]. Two add-on modifications for improved conspicuity have been researched in a low-visibility laboratory capable of simulating day, dark, and fog conditions. Certain add-ons have been field-tested on rural highways. The modifications were a horizontal array of three 8-inch white strobe lights added to the conventional beacon unit and red, white, and blue strobe lights mounted on the gate arm that is lowered at crossings.

Among the findings were the information that flash rates between 70 to 90 flashes per minute provided better conspicuity than slower or faster rates, but these findings were applicable to alternately flashing incandescent lights. The current beacon flash rate is typically 35 to 55. For strobe lights, rates of 100 flashes per minute or more and irregular patterns add to conspicuity. The field-tested strobes used 120 flashes/min alternately for the two outside strobes and 240 flashes/min for the center strobe.

Eight in (20.3 cm) and 12 in (30.5 cm) lenses increased conspicuity under all lighting conditions better than did increasing the intensity of smaller lens. The two best strobe positions were overhead (17 ft-high cantilevered) and roadside (9 ft high). The three gate-arm strobes flashing in irregular patterns improved daytime conspicuity. Clear (xenon) offers better conspicuity than red or blue. Red or blue require greater intensity for comparable conspicuity; however, the color red is associated with warning devices. Field studies are continuing prior to firm design recommendations in this area.

Drivers often cross railroad tracks even with lights and bells operating. No moving train is visible and there is ambiguity as to arrival time of the train. Innovative active warning devices are needed that provide a positive indication of arrival time, train distance, or risk involved in crossing.

Speed Control

The issue of speeding as related to driver and vehicular characteristics is discussed in Chapter 11. Traffic engineers and law enforcement agencies have sought roadway design techniques that would increase motorists' likelihood of reducing speeds to safe limits. A series of research studies have been conducted applicable to speed control in specific situations: on rural curves, in school zones, during wet weather (especially at high-skid potential sites), and, of course, on the highways in general since the fuel crisis.

In London, automatic signs displaying "You are speeding" have been successful in reducing speeds 24 h a day without traffic enforcement [Police Research Service Branch, 37]. The CMS was actuated by vehicles passing over detectors in the roadway surface 80 yards upstream of the sign. As previously noted, drivers are more sensitive to real-time signing and, particularly, individualized speeding information. The sight of a patrol car on a highway also has the effect of stimulating speed reduction, but the effect is somewhat localized and transient.

The flashing beacon in conjunction with a static sign has been found to be effective in reducing speeds in many situations. This is a form of real-time signing since the beacons operate only at certain times generally. Sometimes the word message itself flashes, such as the word "icy" in the message "Bridge icy ahead." Hanscom [17] conducted a field study of the effects of an activated (flashing) sign and static signs at a bridge that warned of icing conditions. Sign activation at the bridge itself had a greater impact on motorist speed reduction than activation 1000 ft (305 m) upstream of the bridge when displayed only during hazardous periods. Figure 10-7 illustrates also the effects of various configurations of signs with an activated message as compared with a single static sign.

Flashing beacons were researched on a high-speed, two-lane highway at a rural school zone [Rosenbaum et al., 43]. The beacons indicated periods when a 15 mi/h (24 km/h) speed limit was in effect. Although the reduction was only to 34 mi/h (55 km/h), static signs without beacons produced no significant reduction in speed.

Flashing beacons have been successful in reducing speeds of the upper 25 percent of speeders when employed in conjunction with symbolic "slippery when wet" signs on wet pavement sections with a potential skidding hazard [Hanscom, 18]. The credibility of the message is, of course, screened by the driver's observations and knowledge: accident history of the site, weather and pavement appearance, curvature or superelevated structure ahead. However, static signs without real-time beacons were not effective in speed reduction.

Special signing and marking techniques have been employed to reduce

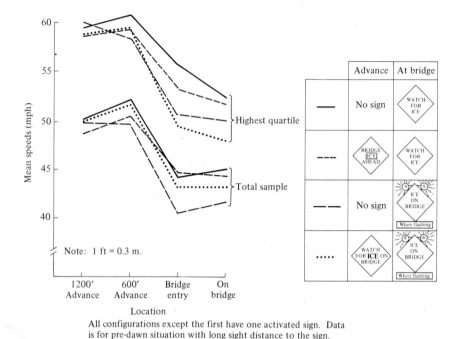

Figure 10-7 Examples of mean speed data reported to four icy bridge signing configurations *(Hanscom, 1976).*

speeds on sharp curves in rural areas. Marking techniques explored include transverse striping, widening the edge markings and making the roadway appear narrower at the curves [Rockwell et al., 42]. Speed reductions were largely transient (gone after 30 days). Those using the highway repeatedly learn the vehicular speed that the curvature will allow safely, and static signs and markings have little effect for them. Rumble strips laid across highways upstream of construction sites have been especially effective at night in notifying drivers of a reduced speed zone.

Both design techniques and other strategies have attracted the attention of law enforcement agencies responsible for speed reduction. Warning signs of speed check zones ahead have been field tested with and without a patrol car present [Hunter and Bundy, 24]. Lower speeds occurred only at the car site, that is, the halo effect of the sign did not reduce speeds downstream of the sign, whereas the car's presence did have a local effect.

The presence of a highway patrol car on a highway has been reported to reduce the average speed of traffic approximately three miles upstream and downstream of its location [Brackett, 1]. However, it is not practical to station a patrol car every six miles along highways. To attempt to reduce speeds over a wider area, another patrol car strategy has been to have a moving vehicle, but this approach has met with limited success.

Brackett [1] borrowed the concept of *intermittent reinforcement* from the literature on human learning and retention and applied it to the speed control strategy situation. In lay terms, if the driver did not know exactly *where* or *when* a police vehicle would be encountered (having recently seen it on the highway), then the drivers might reduce their speeds over a wider range. The strategy involved 2 weeks of *continuous reinforcement,* that is, the vehicle was present every day of the week. However, the location of the vehicle was varied from mile 4 to mile 14 over a 17-mile section of highway. Later, the vehicle appeared only on 2 or 3 days per week on a random basis. The research findings were that the technique of intermittent reinforcement resulted in a significant reduction in speeds throughout the entire section of highway.

No Passing Markings and Signs

Gordon [15] conducted an extensive study of road-marking codes to determine driver understanding. Details cannot be reviewed here but, in general, many roadway markings are not well understood by motorists. The double-yellow stripe on two-lane roads is understood by nearly all drivers although Koppa and Guseman [28] found that 14 percent thought it could not be crossed to turn into businesses or driveways.

The single yellow stripe on undivided two-lane highways to signify a no-passing zone (NPZ) is also well understood. However, the stripe is sometimes encountered quickly in a succession of hills and curves, and motorists cross the stripe returning to their lane after passing. Some states extend the stripe on their highways to allow for the fact that drivers will do this.

Innovative techniques are being explored to communicate to drivers that a no-passing zone is upcoming. Weaver et al. [48] explored the feasibility of using a series of *advanced dotted markings* in yellow extending upstream from the solid yellow stripe. The dotted markings were to convey to the drivers in the act of passing that they must return to their lane before reaching an upcoming solid stripe.

A survey conducted in several regions of the United States found that 68 percent of the drivers understood the markings without prior explanation. An additional sign erected at the beginning of the dotted markings increased initial understanding to 92 percent. This was a symbolic warning sign showing a planned view of center line dashes and a parallel stripe beginning halfway up. A highly visible pennant (Figure 10-6) on the *left* side of the roadway at the beginning of the NPZ also increased understanding of the dotted markings a comparable degree.

A regulatory sign that would tell the driver there is insufficient sight distance in which to begin passing is also being explored. This sign may leave understood that a NPZ is ahead (for example, Do not begin passing) or may mention the NPZ and leave understood the passing restriction (No passing zone ahead).

At the time of the study (1977), the use of the symbolic circle and red slash in lieu of "do not" was disliked by 75 percent of drivers in the context of passing.

Nighttime and Wet-Weather Visibility

The introduction of high-mast luminaires (sodium, xenon, and mercury vapor lamps) on freeways and interchanges has greatly improved nighttime visibility. Roadway luminaires must provide sufficient contrast to detect objects. They may also introduce a glare depending upon the reflective characteristics of the surface materials. A major goal of lighting installation engineers has been to reduce disability glare so that nighttime detection is satisfactory.

The benefits of low-pressure sodium vapor lamps inside underpasses and tunnels has been demonstrated by field studies of brake applications and more stable vehicle speeds leading to smoother and safer traffic operations.

Nighttime visibility of overhead signs is technically feasible without external light sources by employing a particular type of reflective sheeting material as a background for lettering on signs [Robertson and Shelor, 40].

Another nighttime visibility issue of concern to safety programs is the high frequency of wrong-way entries onto divided highways. The driver approaches a divided highway intersection with either two-way or four-way stop signs and then turns on to the wrong side of the median. The driver may not know the intersecting highway is divided and may not see the median upon turning.

Vaswani [46] analyzed specific intersections with a history of wrong-way entries and concluded that signs and markings should be designed for nighttime visibility since, under low beams, the limits of peripheral roadside vision are greatly restricted. Design recommendations included extending the nose of the median to the edge of the crossroad, reflective paint on the median concrete, delineators, moving the cross-traffic stop near to the intersection, painting a line across the far side of the crossroad (which must not be entered), and a diagrammatic sign depicting a divided highway intersection ahead.

Rainfall simulators have been used [Morris et al., 35] to produce artificial rain on a moving vehicle and thereby determine the effects of rain, windshield, and wiper characteristics on visual performance. It was found that the film of water on the windshield itself (rather than distant visual obstruction) was the primary factor in reduced visual acuity. Rain rate was a significant factor in daytime with the wiper on. At night, smaller drop sizes degrade vision more than rain rate. Wiper speeds above 50 cycles per minute (cpm) did not improve visual performance.

Other Areas of Signing and Marking

The foregoing discussion relates only to selected application areas. The FHWA is interested in improved and standardized traffic control devices in many areas. In addition to the above, papers presented to the Transportation Research Board annual meeting [45] include topics such as the signing and marking of reserved special-usage lanes and bus service priority lanes (busways). The familiar, overhead red X and green arrows have been employed successfully on reversible lanes (which change direction from A.M. to P.M. rush hours).

However, the design of printed and symbolic messages for signs that indicate restrictions of use to certain hours is a challenging research area. Painted words and symbols on the pavement of certain reserved lanes are also being explored.

Other topics include roadside guide signs at international airports, signing and marking of bicycle lanes (bikeways), and pedestrian signs and sign 's, including the use of symbolics for "Walk" and "Don't Walk."

DRIVERS' AUDITORY COMMUNICATION VARIABLES

The conventional usage of the word *signing* presumes a visual display. The FHWA has also used the expression "auditory signing" to refer to the presentation of information to the ears. Traffic information may be received by commercial radio, citizens band radio, a telephone call-in system, or by short-wave radio transmission. A Highway Advisory Radio (HAR) System has been planned for many years, and its feasibility has been demonstrated [Brizell and Veale, 2]. This short-range roadside transmission system provides drivers with local traffic conditions rather than city-wide information, as is typically given over commercial radio. Although it requires that the driver be tuned to a particular radio frequency for information, it has the advantages of being in real-time and, unlike visual signs, it may reach drivers over a wider range without the erection of many signs at different locations.

To ensure that drivers entering a radio broadcast zone are tuned to a particular frequency, it has been proposed that there be located on the highway upstream of the broadcast area a sign such as:

"Radio Traffic Alert—Tune to 1066" (the frequency in Hz)

This may be amplified by "Broadcast area begins—½ mile." One-half mile or 800 m provides about 32 sec to locate the frequency and this is adequate tuning time [Brizell and Veale, 2; Gatling, 14]. A second sign may be installed at the beginning of the broadcast area.

The descriptor "radio traffic alert" has been reported as implying greater urgency than other descriptors such as "radio traffic information" or "radio traffic advisory" [Huchingson et al., 21]. The word "alert" should be used only when there is an urgent situation, such as an accident requiring the traffic to divert to another route.

In addition to the roadway sign, there is a need for an audio alert signal on the radio broadcast to indicate the beginning and end of a complete message.

The variables investigated for radio messages are similiar to those for visual messages, but the findings for message design are somewhat different.

Language Style

Audio messages are not limited to the brief language style of visual signs. The nature of the media permits the construction of messages in complete sentence form. Prior to extensive research, it was surmised that a conversational language style might be preferred by drivers and might result in better retention of the messages. However, the results of several studies [Huchingson et al., 21] indicated that it was better to present traffic information in short or even very brief language style. Examples of conversational and very brief language styles are illustrated below:

CONVERSATIONAL-STYLE MESSAGE	VERY BRIEF-STYLE MESSAGE
• ATTENTION TRAFFIC ON THE NORTH-BOUND CENTRAL FREEWAY	• ATTENTION NORTHBOUND CENTRAL FREEWAY TRAFFIC
• THERE HAS BEEN AN ACCIDENT ON CENTRAL FREEWAY AT ROWLAND AVENUE	• ACCIDENT AT ROWLAND AVENUE
• CONGESTION IN THE AREA IS CURRENTLY HEAVY	• HEAVY CONGESTION
• YOU ARE ADVISED TO EXIT, USE THE SERVICE ROAD, AND REENTER THE FREEWAY AT THE RAMP NORTH OF CARTER CREEK AVENUE	• USE THE SERVICE ROAD TO CARTER CREEK

Surveys in three regions of the United States found the very brief language style was consistently preferred to the conversational style. The highly redundant conversational style did not improve retention of the key information; in fact, the brief style resulted in significantly better recall. Another study of drivers negotiating a diversion route, having previously been given audio route instructions in the two styles, failed to show a difference in success in route following [Dudek et al., 9]. Since the listener is within the broadcast range for a limited time only, it would be advisable to present the brief message several times rather than the longer, more wordy message only once or twice.

Message Content and Format

The major types of information and their order of appearance were illustrated in the messages above. As with visual signing on a CMS, they include the problem (accident), the location, an effect statement, and an action or advisory message. However, the audio message must always begin with an attention statement that addresses a particular destination group. An attention statement would be redundant on certain visual signs. Should the radio message illustrated above be displayed on a CMS, only northbound Central Freeway traffic would see the CMS; hence, an attention statement would be unnecessary. However, the audio message could be heard by drivers headed in either direction or by drivers on the service roads or other arterials in the area. Therefore, a need exists to always begin with the attention statement.

When the action statement applies only to a selected destination group, a second attention statement is given immediately before the action statement, as was required for visual signing. For example, "Downtown traffic, use Carson Street."

Message Redundancy

It is difficult to retain auditory information, especially when route directions are included. The message should be repeated at least twice. Another type of redundancy has been termed "internal redundancy" [Huchingson et al., 21]. In the present context, this refers to *repeating the names* of streets immediately after their first mention. An example of an internally redundant message is as follows:

"Turn left on Broadway and follow Broadway to Northeast Highway; turn right on Northeast Highway. . . ." Best results in following route instructions will likely be achieved through both types of redundancy, complete repetition and internal redundancy.

Message Load

The issue of the maximum amount of audio information that may be recalled is unsettled because investigators have employed different approaches to presenting and measuring retention. This discussion will be limited to directional or route-following messages. The complete message will include several types of information, discussed above, but it is the *action statement* that must be recalled because it contains the directions for following the diversion route. Failure to remember any part of the directions could result in failure to negotiate the route successfully.

Gatling [14] suggested that 5.5 units of information is about the limit of human processing when the subject hears a route-following message twice and is later required to recognize the names of the streets mentioned in the message.

In a study reported by Huchingson et al. [21], Banning found successful recall of up to eight units of information when the information consisted of only street names and turns in a logical diversion pattern. In Banning's study, the subjects actually drove the vehicle along routes requiring a total of four turning movements at intersections. The fictitious street names were presented on displays in the car and were presented at the same time an actual street sign would appear. A correct turning movement at the correct street intersection was counted as recall of two units of information.

Banning found that 80 percent of his subjects, who were previously unfamiliar with the street names or the diversion route, were able to successfully follow a route consisting of four turns and four street names. The message was presented twice using internally redundant messages. However, for routes requiring five or six turns (10 and 12 units of information, respectively), it was found that route following was less successful. For such complex routes, it was recommended that trailblazer signs be erected and that the action message should be to follow the symbol which appeared on every trailblazed sign.

Few of us could successfully recall eight different types of information given on a tape recording if we were asked to repeat the message. But driving a route successfully is a different task. First, the driver must only *recognize* the name of a street given previously. He need not reproduce the name nor necessarily recall the order in which it appeared. Second, drivers are *oriented*. They know previously the direction they wish to go in and the direction in which they are headed initially. The turning movements given are usually simple ones consisting of a movement (either left or right) *away* from the freeway, then *parallel* to the freeway in the direction one was headed on the freeway, and finally *back* to the freeway. In essence, this is a C-shaped pattern or reversed C pattern.

Drivers would appear to have certain expectancies as to the direction they should turn at each turning intersection. (Being oriented, they would not likely turn back in the direction from which they came!) Hence, the route-following task is much simpler than recalling a sequence of names and turns that have no logical pattern.

Route Descriptor Idioms

Although we know something about designing radio messages to communicate with drivers, research is continuing into the idiomatic ways that we communicate with one another [Huchingson et al., 21]. One source of information on how we communicate in our society is the systematic study of how drivers give instructions or directions to others when asked to describe a particular route.

For example, how would you describe to a visitor in your city the route from a distant business district to the college? Or how would you describe an alternate route through the city one might take if the business bypass route were blocked by an accident? Your instructions should be sufficiently complete that the person does not become lost.

The message you gave could be analyzed in various ways. For example, how did you describe turns—by left/right movement or by cardinal directions (north, south, east, west)? How did you describe the place where the driver should turn? Did you give the street name; did you mention the traffic light; did you describe a landmark (like a service station) at the turning intersection? Did you give the distance traveled before reaching the turning intersection? If so, did you estimate it in miles or fractions thereof; did you state the number of traffic lights passed; or did you include landmarks passed along the route?

Verbal route-following messages must be stated in terms that are familiar to the driver if the messages are to be understood. It is true that visual signs (trailblazers) would be much easier for an unfamiliar driver to follow than audio messages if the route were a detour planned in advance of maintenance. But an accident could occur anywhere along a route and providing a system of trailblazers along various potential bypass routes throughout the length of the freeway could be expensive and clutter the roadside. The feasibility of audio guidance through short-range radio transmission is being considered as an alternative as well as a complementary system to visual signing.

TECHNIQUES FOR RESEARCHING DRIVER COMMUNICATIONS

Let us suppose an investigator has a funded research contract to investigate fully a signing area. For example, a research objective could be to develop effective messages for display on a CMS that will influence traffic to divert from a freeway to a temporary bypass route. This example will serve to illustrate some techniques typical of a sponsored research program.

A research program is divided into a series of phases: a planning phase, a laboratory phase, a controlled field study phase, and a field validation phase. Table 10-4 summarizes research techniques employed in signing evaluation. Several of the laboratory and field techniques merit explanation.

Table 10-4 Research Techniques for Evaluating Signs and Traffic Control Devices

Phase	Research technique
Planning	• Technical literature review • Site visits and correspondence with traffic agencies • Driver interviews at rest stops along highway • Questionnaires given to groups of potential users • Develop research objectives and experimental designs
Laboratory studies	• Slide or movie presentation of signs • Drivers build sign messages by selecting words from a deck of word cards (content and format choice) • Reaction time and glance legibility studies • Eye-scan and dwell-time studies of search and attention • Secondary loading via tracking while sign reading • Closed-loop simulations of lane-change decisions
Controlled field studies	• Proving-ground studies. (Vehicle driven on a closed roadway with signs, markings, lights installed. Human performance and vehicle behavior measured.) • In situ instrumented vehicle studies. (Vehicle driven by subjects on actual roadways. Success in route following and vehicle responses such as braking, speeds, and steering wheel reversals are measured in real time.) • In situ studies with slides of signs projected on windshield screen.
Field validation studies	• Traffic engineering measures, for example, percent of traffic that followed a particular route; traffic speeds and volumes. • Recording license plate numbers to trace groups of drivers taking certain routes. Follow-up questionnaires request drivers' reasons for actions taken. • Closed-circuit TV and videotaping of traffic behavior (brake lights, stops, reversals, lane changes, and hazardous erratic behavior). • May study traffic behavior before and after a traffic control device was installed or may select matched highways to study signing variables at approximately the same time.

Laboratory Studies   A set of experiments are defined to investigate the effects of variables on message understanding, simulated traffic behavior, relative attention value of signing elements, legibility, driver opinion, or preference. The research technique selected depends upon study objectives, but the following techniques are illustrative.

Slide Presentations   This experimental technique could consist of a movie presentation of the roadway ahead taken from the driver's view. At appropriate locations where a sign would appear, artists' renderings of sign messages may be displayed on 35-mm slides. The task may be to respond as one imagines he or she would respond to the message in the real-world situation or the task may be simply to indicate one's interpretation of the meaning. Simplified studies may present only the slides without the film.

Card Sorting   When the experimental question deals only with interpretation or meaning of a message, alternative words may be administered on a deck of cards. One technique, termed "build-a-sign," requires subjects to construct a complete sign message using a deck of cards with various alternative words on each card. Both content and format preferences may be studied by this technique [Dudek et al., 10]. Preferred designs should always be followed up by studies of how well drivers understood the preferred messages.

Reaction Time and Glance Legibility   In highly controlled studies, measurements of reaction time or interpretation time are often taken. Two major ways to measure the time variable are: (1) Present a slide with instructions to press a switch when, for example, one can read and understand the message displayed on the slide. Switch pressing removes the slide and the respondent quickly gives an answer. (2) Control the duration of sign exposure in microseconds by means of a shutter-type tachistoscope (T-scope). A picture of the sign is flashed on the screen for a fraction of a second. Measures of errors in interpretation are taken. Conceptually simple signs are assumed to be associated with correct interpretation at a brief exposure time. This method is said to measure *glance legibility* (GL). Dewar et al. [5], compared an original set of signs and two subsequent modifications of them in terms of percentage correct by glance legibility and in terms of reaction time in milliseconds. They found correlations between 0.55 and 0.69 between reaction time and GL measurements. Sometimes the subject's *decision reaction time* is measured by his or her pressing one of several keys, each representing a different course of action.

Eye Scan and Dwell Time Studies   Sometimes the researcher's interest is in documenting the pattern of movement of the eye's pupil under traffic-loading conditions. From temporal and graphic eye-scan data, it may be inferred precisely when a sign was first noticed (target value), how frequently or how long the eyes dwelled on it (complexity or interest value), and other temporal measures.

Rockwell, Bhise, and Safford [41] have employed an eye-marker camera that monitors the driver's eye fixation point and superimposes the positions on a film strip of the visual scene as observed by the driver. The technique has been widely used in aircraft cockpit research and advertising research. The very small visual angle between a distant road sign and the distant roadway itself presents a problem in its use in certain field situations. However, it is feasible to make inferences regarding attention when the signs are closer to the driver (for example, overhead versus roadside signs). There is considerable interest in exploring potential applications of the technique.

The tachistoscopic method has also been adapted to eye search and scan situations. Pain and Knapp [36] studied various types of barricade stripes by randomly assigning a tiny test configuration to a position on one of four simultaneously presented color pictures of background visual noise. The subject's task was to scan the four busy pictures and tell which picture contained the small test configuration. By employing a brief exposure time, the relative target value of several test configurations was ascertained.

An alternative technique for measuring duration of eye fixation on a sign is to measure performance on a secondary loading task, for example, tracking success. With instructions to devote only spare time to the secondary task, success in tracking provides an indirect measure of the time required to scan, read, and interpret signs of varying content, format, or load.

Laboratory Simulations   Simple closed-loop simulations have also been employed in signing research. Case, Hulbert, and Wojeik [3] had drivers perform a tracking task with a moving roll of paper on which lanes and signs had been drawn. This technique, modified to video or film applications, may be used to study being in the correct lane for turning movements and diagrammatic signing decisions. Controlled field studies accomplish much the same thing with higher fidelity but at added expense.

Controlled Field Studies

The transition between the laboratory and the field is often bridged by another research technique that offers much of the real-world fidelity of field studies, but at the same time provides the experimental control of the laboratory. These techniques are termed "controlled field studies."

Proving Ground Studies   A real-world driving environment may be simulated in an area restricted from public use, for example, the aircraft runway of a former Air Force base provides a stretch of concrete suitable for simulating a roadway. Appropriate static signs may be installed, the pavement may be marked, and a CMS may be installed on a trailer. Subjects in research vehicles may drive the course and respond according to instructions.

The proving grounds are desirable whenever questions of visibility or legibility are an issue (for example, ambient lighting, angle of view, visual obstructions, and effects of changing distances). Driver behavior may also be measured. Simulation of traffic is difficult and expensive; however, headway clearances to a vehicle ahead may be simulated.

In Situ Instrumented Vehicle Studies   Vehicles may be instrumented to measure vehicular responses such as braking, speeds, acceleration, and steering wheel reversal. As in the laboratory, the subject is given instructions and behaviors and verbal responses may be recorded. The instrumented vehicle may be employed both at the proving grounds and in roadway driving studies.

In situ means that the driver/subject will be controlling the vehicle in the real-world roadway situation. Sometimes the subject responds to real-world signing and other forms of communications. However, many experimental sign messages may not have been studied sufficiently to merit their exposure to public viewing. View of the sign may be restricted to the driver only by projecting slides of the signs on a screen on the right-center side of the windshield or where the inside rear-view mirror would be normally (Figure 10-8). The onset of simulated signs is controlled by the experimenter. Slides appear at the same times and locations that a real sign would appear. Response time is measured by the driver activating a switch on the steering column which also turns off the sign display.

An advantage of having subjects drive in traffic is that the traffic provides the distractions that are missing in laboratory studies. Attending to distractions affects time remaining for sign reading. However, in situ studies are still laboratory studies because experimental control is exercised over the subjects and verbal and driving responses are recorded individually. In field studies the individual drivers are generally unknown and they are not aware that they are being measured.

In situ studies permit the investigation of variables such as driver learning and short-term recall. These variables are difficult to study in traffic behavior where "follow-the-leader" behavior is a confounding variable. For example, in the traffic situation many drivers may not have seen or learned a message given on a sign or over the radio. However, they may still correctly obey the displayed advisory message by copying the behavior of other traffic.

If the measure of interest is maximum or *best performance*, laboratory

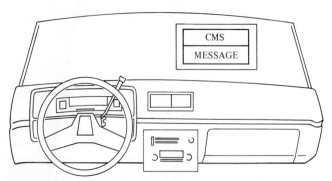

Figure 10-8   In-car display of signs in a research vehicle.

techniques are excellent (this would also apply to best interpretation of the meaning of signs). However, if the measure of interest is *typical behavior* (what people will do in a situation), then the field technique has an advantage since the drivers are unaware their performance is being recorded. Human relation studies have shown that there is a tendency for laboratory subjects who know they are being observed to respond in a manner that will please the experimenter. With in situ traffic studies they may give a socially acceptable response in accordance with traffic laws. Typical behavior is recorded most accurately when subjects are "caught in the act of being themselves." Such behavior is better studied by hidden camera or traffic engineering methods.

Field Validation Studies

The investigator who initially had many different candidate messages for influencing drivers to divert from a freeway will have narrowed the messages to only a few after the in situ and laboratory studies. The final proof of the effectiveness of the messages can only come from observing and verifying that they succeeded in doing to traffic what they were supposed to do (for example, a designated percentage of drivers voluntarily diverted as advised by the message).

Field studies are no place for experimenting with questionable messages. The city or agency that has permitted the investigators to install the signing system does not want an adverse public reaction. Usually, field studies investigate only the most promising concepts and *validate* their effectiveness.

Traffic Measures Field evaluations may involve taking measures of traffic volumes at various locations—on the freeway, ramps, service roads, and diversion routes. An investigator may be interested in knowing the *percentage of traffic* that diverted from the freeway and successfully negotiated the bypass route. Obviously, there will be some traffic exiting to their destinations rather than to the sign message, and there will be others on the bypass route who were not even on the freeway. To trace the traffic patterns of particular vehicles, *input-output license plate studies* have been used. License plate numbers are observed and recorded on tapes at various locations, for example, at the exit ramps and at a point on the bypass route where it reenters the freeway. The license plate numbers are matched at the locations to determine vehicular movement patterns.

Sometimes the drivers are contacted by mail (with the cooperation of the state licensing agency) and a few questions are asked about their reasons for responding as they did. This approach is often more practical than roadside interviews that require stopping traffic.

Closed-circuit TV observations, videotaping, and photography of traffic are other useful techniques. Traffic may be photographed slowing down upon approaching a CMS. (Brake light applications are especially visible at night.)

Vehicles may also exhibit erratic maneuvers (abrupt lane changes, weaving over the exit gore area, driving too slowly). As discussed previously, such behavior may signify driver confusion or violations of expectancies. In studying the effects of new guide signs at an international airport, Dewar et al. [5] analyzed tapes on a VTR monitor and recorded volumes and the number of vehicles that stopped, reversed directions, or changed to a lane going in another direction.

Before-and-After Studies Traffic studies, like all behavioral research studies, must have a control condition. We must be confident that the traffic responses observed are a result of the variable introduced rather than being due to some unknown factor. Measurements may be taken *before* the experimental messages were introduced and then taken again several times *after* the signs have been in operation. The before measures are the control condition. Any changes thereafter are assumed to be due to the sign variables' being studied.

One problem is that if the control group measures were taken several months earlier, it is possible other changes may have taken place besides the presence of the sign. For example, if the before measures were taken in winter and the after measures taken in late spring, there will be difference in daylight and darkness during peak traffic periods; there may be difference in weather; driver composition may include more visitors in the spring, and so forth. The researcher must be alert for such *confounding variables* which could bias the findings.

Matched Group Studies This research strategy is an attempt to select two situations (for example, two sections of a highway or freeway) that are essentially identical with respect to important variables such as number of lanes, traffic volumes, speeds, and roadway geometry. In theory, the approach is similar to using identical twins in psychological studies of the effects of heredity and environment. In practice, it is very difficult to find two highway sections that are identical. It is necessary to take a large number of measures to randomize sources of variation. When two sign variables are studied, the procedure sometimes is to *alternate conditions* (for example, placing one variable on highway A one week and on highway B the next week; the other variable being switched to highway A).

Researchers must be continuously vigilant for *carry-over effects* whenever more than one signing variable is introduced to the same driving population. Drivers do remember past experiences and those experiences may have either positive or negative transfer effects in their understanding and behavior with respect to the second signing variable. From the standpoint of unbiased results, it would be ideal for one driving population to see *only* one sign and another identical driving population to see *only the other* sign. In practice, the problem is one of finding identical populations. Sometimes the differences between presumably matched groups are a more significant variable than the signing variable. The solution seems to be exercising caution in selecting populations and repeating the study several times in different locations to increase confidence in the findings.

Novelty Effect   Any new sign may attract attention when it is first installed. Only after it has been in operation for a while can its effectiveness be established. It is important to take measures over a period of several months after the novelty effect has worn off.

QUESTIONS AND PROBLEMS

1   Suppose you were driving on a freeway and you observed a CMS displaying one of the following messages. Indicate for each message a possible violation of driver credibility and tell why it might violate one's expectancy.
     Message 1—"17 minutes to the Garden State Expressway"
     Message 2—"Light traffic"
     Message 3—"Drive courteously"
     Message 4—"Truck overturned ahead" (No accident later observed.)
2   The shape of static signs is said to have standardized meanings on all signs. You may have learned these in a driver's education course, but are you still aware of them? Let's test your knowledge: What does an octagon mean? (Stop, obviously.) An equilateral triangle? (Yield.) But what do these shapes mean: a diamond, a circle, a pennant, a cross buck, a pentagon, a horizontal rectangle, a vertical rectangle, and a trapezoid? The highway department has gone to expense to communicate meanings through shapes, and it is assumed the public is responding. Look for these shapes while driving around your community. You may need to drive on the highways to see the pennant and trapezoid.
3   If there are freeways or expressways in your home city, think about a place where you have entered a particular freeway and later exited it. Now, try naming the major cross streets or exits along this route. How successful were you? Do you think if a message stated that an accident were at or near one of these cross streets, this would be more informative than giving the distance in tenths of a mile? Discuss.
4   A message on a CMS advised you to get off of a freeway and take another specified route. You noticed some of the traffic continued on the freeway. Would you be likely to take the advice? Please list any additional information that you would require before deciding whether or not to divert.
5   You are driving on an interstate highway approaching a large city in which there is a through route (I-10) and a bypass route (I-610). You notice a CMS that displays the following: "I-10 congested; I-610 congested." In terms of a driver's needs, what is wrong with this display? Discuss.
6   In presenting sequenced displays on a CMS, it was recommended that each sequence of two lines be presented for 4 sec with two sequences requiring 8 sec. A traffic engineer estimated that a driver's total viewing time would be only about 8 sec. It was decided it would be better to display the entire message *twice* in 8 sec, thus providing redundancy. Comment on the advisability of this course of action.
7   A traffic engineer wished to display the following message: "Accident Ahead—15-minute delay—Use Service Road—Next Exit." There is a CMS capable of displaying 14 characters per line including spaces. It can display two lines per sequence and up to three sequences in the available viewing time. Divide the message in the most appropriate manner for display.
8   A traffic engineer received the following message: "There has been a bad accident on Northbound Gulf Freeway at Ledbetter Avenue and traffic is backed up. You had

better advise all traffic headed west on I-10 to take I-610 Westbound." The traffic engineer is told to compose a very brief message that can be presented over the Highway Advisory Radio. Construct a brief message using the important information.

9   A visitor to your city telephones you from a local shopping center. He wants to meet you on campus, but he has no idea how to get to the college from where he is now. Prepare a written message that you would read to him on how to get to the campus. Be sufficiently complete in your instructions that he does not get lost.

10 Think of the last time you were lost when traveling in a large or unfamiliar city. What information that was *not* presented on signs do you think would have provided the necessary information so you would not have overshot the correct exit or turn intersection and would have insured that you found your way to your destination?

11 You are conducting research on radio messages that might be effective in describing to motorists a diversion route which they should take through a large city. The message involves making six turns at intersections named in the message. Let us presume that a subject actually heard the message over an operational HAR system. Driving behind him/her in an unmarked car, you discover that he/she was able to negotiate the complex diversion route without error. What conclusions would you make from his/her performance?

12 A passenger vehicle is driving on a state highway entering a small city. The highway is sufficiently wide for two lanes of traffic in each direction, but there are no lane separation markings. The speed limit is 45 mph and the vehicle is traveling approximately 45 mph and is in the left lane. The front-seat passenger points to the right and the vehicle abruptly switches to the right lane and slows up to make a right turn on to an intersecting city street. A pickup truck, traveling in the same direction in the left lane, also switches to the right lane and accelerates around another vehicle in the left lane. Seeing the first vehicle, the pickup driver brakes, but the pickup collides with the rear end of the first vehicle. Who is at fault? Discuss contributory factors.

REFERENCES

1   Brackett, R. Q.: *Comparative Evaluation of Speed Control Strategies,* Ph.D. dissertation, Texas A&M University, December 1977.

2   Brizell, E. G., III and N. L. Veale: *Highway Advisory Radio in the Philadelphia Area,* FHWA-RD-78-77, April 1978.

3   Case, H. W., S. F. Hulbert, and C. K. Wojeik: Development of an expeditious method for off-site testing of freeway sign formats (sign-tester), Final Report. UCLA Institute of Transportation and Traffic Engineering, September 1965 (PB169862).

4   Dewar, R. E.: *Psychological Factors in Perception of Traffic Signs,* Road and Motor Vehicle Traffic Safety Report, Ministry of Transport, Canada, February 1973.

5   Dewar, R. E., J. G. Ells, and P. J. Cooper: Evaluation of Roadway Guide Signs at a Large Airport, *Transportation Engineering,* June 1977.

6   Dorsey, W.: *Variable Message Signing for Traffic Surveillance and Control: A State-of-the-Art Report,* Federal Highway Administration, FHWA-RD-77-98, January 1977.

7   Dudek, C. L. and R. D. Huchingson: *Human Factors Design of Dynamic Visual and Auditory Displays for Metropolitan Traffic Management,* FHWA Contract DOT-FH-11-9459, August 1978.

8 Dudek, C. L. et. al.: Design Guide, vol 1 of *Human Factors Requirements for Real-Time Motorist Information Displays,* Federal Highway Administration, FHWA-RD-78-5, September 1978.

9 Dudek, C. L. et. al.: *Highway Advisory Radio Studies,* Progress Report of In-Situ Field Studies, Human Factors Design of Dynamic Visual and Auditory Displays for Metropolitan Traffic Management, DOT-FH-11-9459, January 1980.

10 Dudek, C. L. et. al.: Human Factors Evaluation of Traffic State Descriptor Variables, vol 10, *Human Factors Requirements for Real-Time Motorist Information Displays,* FHWA-RD-78-19, 1978.

11 Ellis, N. C.: *Driver Expectancy Checklist,* Project HPR-2(108), Contract No. FH-11-7031, research contract sponsored by the FHWA and 18 participating states, July 1971.

12 Federal Highway Administration: *Manual of Uniform Traffic Control Devices for Streets and Highways,* 1971.

13 Forbes, T. W. et. al.: Color and brightness factors in simulated and full scale traffic sign visibility, *Highway Research Board,* vol. 216, 1968, pp. 55–65.

14 Gatling, F. P.: *Auditory Message Studies for Route Diversion,* FHWA-RD-75-73, June 1975.

15 Gordon, D. A.: *Studies of Road Marking Code,* Federal Highway Administration, Office of Research and Development, FHWA-RD-76-59, April 1976.

16 Hanscom, F. R.: *Evaluation of Diagrammatic Signing at Capital Beltway Exit No. 1,* Virginia Highway Research Council Report 71-r6, HRIS No. 54-226099, September 1971.

17 Hanscom, F. R.: An evaluation of signing to warn of potential icy bridges, *Transportation Research Record,* vol. 531, 1975, pp. 18–35.

18 Hanscom, F. R.: Evaluation of signing to warn of wet weather skidding hazard, *Transportation Research Record,* vol. 600, 1976, HRIS No. 54-153129.

19 Hofstetter, H. W.: Computed distances of legibility of standard traffic control signs, *Journal of the American Optometric Association,* vol. 38, 1967, pp. 381–385.

20 Huchingson, R. D. and C. L. Dudek: Development of a Dial-In Telephone System Based on Opinions of Urban Freeway Motorists, *Transportation Research Board,* vol. 536, 1975, pp. 11–18.

21 Huchingson, R. D. et. al.: Human Factors Evaluation of Audio and Mixed Modal Variables, vol. 13, *Human Factors Requirements for Real-time Motorist Information Displays,* FHWA-RD-78-19, 1979.

22 Huchingson, R. D. et al.: Human Factors Evaluation of Route Diversion and Guidance Variables, vol. 12, *Human Factors Requirements for Real-Time Motorist Information Displays,* FHWA-RD-78-19, 1978.

23 Huchingson, R. D., R. W. McNees, and C. L. Dudek: Survey of Motorist Route Selection Criteria, *Transportation Research Record,* vol. 643, 1977.

24 Hunter, W. W. and H. L. Bundy: *A Study of the Effect of the Speed Zone Concept,* North Carolina University Highway Safety Research Center, June 1975, HRIS No. 51-145112.

25 King, G. F. and H. Lunenfeld: Development of Informational Requirements and Transmission Techniques for Highway Users, NCHRP Report No. 123, 1971.

26 King, G. F. and H. Lunenfeld: *Urban Area Highway Guide Signing,* NCHRP Project 3-12, Summaries of Unpublished Reports, NCHRP Summary of Progress, 1973.

27 King, L. E. and W. J. Tierney: *Glance Legibility: Symbols versus Word Highway Signs,* West Virginia University, Highway Research Information Service (HRIS), No. 54-225961, 1970.

28 Koppa, R. J. and P. K. Guseman: *Public Understanding of Traffic Control Devices in Texas,* FHWATX78-2321F. November 1978.

29 Markowitz, J., C. W. Deitrich, W. J. Lees, and M. Farman: *An Investigation of Design and Performance of Traffic Control Devices,* Bolt, Beranek, and Newman, Report No. 1726, Contract No. CPR-11-5955, 1968.

30 Mast, T. M. and J. A. Ballas: Diversionary Signing Content and Driver Behavior, *Transportation Research Record,* vol. 600, 1976, pp. 14–19.

31 Mast, T. and G. Kolsrud: *Diagrammatic Guide Signs for Use on Controlled Access Highways,* vol. 1, FHWA-RD-73-21, Washington D.C., U.S. Department of Transportation, Federal Highway Administration, 1972.

32 McGee, H. W. et al.: *Right-Turn-on-Red,* vol. 1, Voorhees and Assoc., for Federal Highway Administration, FHWA-RD-76-89, May 1976.

33 Messer, C., J. M. Mounce, and R. Q. Brackett: *Highway Geometric Design Related to Driver Expectancy,* vol. 2, FHWA-RD-79-35, May 1979.

34 Messer, C. et al.: A Study of the Physical Design Requirements for Motorist Information Matrix Displays, vol. 9, *Human Factors Requirements for Real-time Motorist Information Displays,* FHWA-RD-78-19, 1978.

35 Morris, R. S., J. M. Mounce, J. W. Button, and N. E. Walton: Visual Performance of Drivers During Rainfall, *Transportation Research Record,* vol. 628, 1977.

36 Pain, R. F. and B. G. Knapp: "Experimental Evaluation of Markings for Barricades and Channelizing Devices," a paper presented to TRB Committee A3C04, August 1978.

37 Police Research Service Branch, London, England: *Police Research Bulletin,* no. 28, 1976, pp. 9–13.

38 Roberts, A. W., E. F. Reilly, and M. V. Jagannath: Freeway diagrammatic signs in New Jersey, *Transportation Research Record,* vol. 531, 1975, pp. 36–47.

39 Roberts, K. M. and A. G. Klipple: Driver expectations at freeway lane drops, *Public Roads,* vol. 40, no. 1, June 1976, pp. 32–35.

40 Robertson, R. N. and J. D. Shelor: Using Encapsulated-Lens Reflective Sheeting on Overhead Highway Signs, *Transportation Research Record,* vol. 628, 1977.

41 Rockwell, T. H., V. D. Bhise, and R. R. Safford: *Development of a Methodology for Evaluating Road Signs,* Systems Research Group, Ohio State University Interim Report No. EE5315B, June 1970.

42 Rockwell, T. H., J. Malecki, and D. Shinar: *Improving Driver Performance on Rural Curves Through Perceptual Change - Phase III,* Ohio-DOT-08-75, March 1975, HRIS No. 52-145112.

43 Rosenbaum, M. J., P. Young, S. Byington, and W. Basham: Speed control in rural speed zones, *Transportation Research Record,* vol. 541, 1975, pp. 12–25.

44 Ruden, R. J., C. F. Wasser, S. F. Hulbert, and A. Burg: *Motorists' Requirements for Active Grade Crossing Warning Devices,* FHWA-RD-77-169, DOT-FH-11-8846, October 1977.

45 Transportation Research Board, *Fifty-Sixth Annual Meeting Program,* Washington, D.C., Jan. 24-28, 1977.

46 Vaswani, N. K.: Poor visibility under low-beam headlights: A common cause of wrong way driving, *Transportation Research Record,* vol. 628, 1977.

47 Washington Star-News: "Traffic light plan alarms blind," November 6, 1974, Evening Star Newspaper Company, Washington, D.C.

48 Weaver, G. D. et. al.: *Passing and No-Passing Zones: Signs, Markings, and Warrants,* FHWA-RD-79-5, September 1978.

49 Weaver, G. D., S. H. Richards, D. R. Hatcher, and C. L. Dudek: Point Diversion for Special Events Field Studies, vol. 15 in *Human Factors Requirements for Real-time Motorist Information Displays,* Report No. FHWA-RD-78-18, August 1978.

50 Maddox, M. E., J. T. Burnette, and J. C. Guttman: Font comparisons for 5 X 7 dot matrix characters, *Human Factors,* vol. 19, no. 1, February 1977.

51 Alexander, G. J. and H. Lunenfeld: A user's guide to positive guidance in highway control, *Proceedings of the Human Factors Society,* 23rd Annual Meeting, Boston, Mass., 1979.

52 Mounce, J., C. Messer, R. Huchingson, and C. Dudek: Bulb-loss effects on message readability of motorist-information matrix signs, *Transportation Research Board,* vol. 643, 1977.

53 Snyder, H. and G. Taylor: The sensitivity of response measures of alphanumeric legibility to variations in dot matrix display parameters, *Human Factors,* vol. 21, no. 4, 1979, pp. 457–571.

Chapter 11

Design of Surface Vehicles

Surface vehicles may be broadly classified as private and public. Privately owned vehicles include those used by the individual for recreational or home usage: motor boats, bicycles and mopeds, snow mobiles, lawn mowers, and so forth. There are other privately owned vehicles used in one's occupation, such as agricultural tractors, cranes, lift trucks, and other materials-handling vehicles.

The scope of this chapter will be limited mainly to motor vehicles used on roadways, particularly the automobile. Small trucks, vans, recreational vehicles (RVs), and motorcycles will be treated in certain areas and the agricultural tractor will be briefly discussed. From a design standpoint these vehicles share many common human factors requirements although they impose some unique ones, of course. Detailed discussion of the myriad of private vehicles would be a book in itself, so the principal focus will be on the private-passenger road vehicles.

Public surface vehicles include mainly bus and rail rapid transit systems. Rail systems may also interface with airports. The topic of terminal or station design merits some discussion from the standpoint of communications and efficiency.

The fuel shortage and increased usage of private vehicles has resulted in an increased government interest in public transit systems and public requirements for design and services. Recognizing that conventional transportation modes may not be meeting the public needs, we will briefly discuss advanced concepts and intermodal transportation concepts.

PRIVATE VEHICLES

The design of the motor vehicle is one of many factors contributing to highway traffic safety. Among the design characteristics are handling qualities, visibility, easily located controls, appropriate display of information, and a design of seats and interior compatible with human body dimensions. Safety engineering has also made headway in design to increase the chances of the motorist's escaping uninjured in the event of a major accident.

Reduction of traffic accidents has been a major goal of both federal and state legislation. Agencies such as the National Highway Traffic Safety Administration (NHTSA) have sponsored extensive research and have developed national programs directed at this goal on all fronts. Forbes [10] and Shinar [41] have summarized research on driver performance and characteristics. Human factors, in its broader sense, extends to the pedestrian, driver education, licensing and rehabilitation, identification of the unsafe driver, and contributory factors to accidents, such as fatigue, sleep loss, use of alcohol and drugs, and social and demographic factors.

The perfectly designed vehicle cannot be expected to be a panacea for reduction of many types of accidents, but the development of this chapter will indicate ways in which it can be expected to aid in doing so. The intoxicated driver, a contributing factor in over one-half of the fatal traffic accidents [Haight, 14], will still be on the roadway. However, even in this area techniques have been proposed for making it more difficult for drunk drivers to start the engine. Also, an in-car breath analyzer on the steering column would transmit this information to specially coded, exterior lights that would notify other drivers and enforcement authorities. While many of these schemes still have technical problems before being feasible, the point here is that future development in automotive design may well tackle the more directly contributing factors to highway accidents.

The passenger vehicle may be considered in terms of (1) controls and displays; (2) seat design; (3) interior dimensions; (4) visibility, (5) handling characteristics; and (6) special safety equipment. There are other factors such as aesthetics, comfort, ride qualities, and performance, which are included in discussion of the listed factors.

The automobile manufacturer considers many variables in establishing the design of its new models. Human factors engineering is only one consideration and responsibility, for incorporating effective design is shared by several design groups rather than being centralized under the direction of a human factors engineering function. Automotive manufacturers are, however, attentive to human factors considerations, the Society of Automotive Engineers' (SAE) recommended practices, and Federal Safety Standards. The corporate package design, both external and internal, is governed also by previous corporate design practices, the practices of competitors, and by innovative styling to attract the eye of the buying public.

The automobile is often viewed as an extension of the individual's personality. An older, successful person may purchase an oversized car that is luxurious, comfortable, and replete with work-saving features. The younger buyer may demand a vehicle with semi-sports car features such as bucket seats and race-car instrumentation, one which emphasizes performance, controllability, and compactness.

Today, rather than purchasing the ideal vehicle, the average buyer may consider cost and fuel economy as major criteria. Foreign imports and slower, battery-powered vehicles for short-distance commuting are becoming more popular. Federal standards for minimum miles per gallon have resulted in American manufacturers' developing smaller and lighter vehicles. The impact of the compact and subcompact will be emphasized in this chapter.

Controls and Displays

Controls may be classified as primary and secondary. Primary controls are those essential for steering and power management: the steering wheel, accelerator pedal, and brake pedals. Some writers [Mortimer, 25] also include the transmission selector lever. Secondary controls are essentially every other control inside the vehicle. Some are standard features (ignition switch, washer/wipers, lights, and parking brake). Other controls are optional (cruise control, radio, air conditioning, electric windows and door locks), and some are available only on certain models.

Primary Controls Power assist has greatly simplified the problem of designing controls for the weaker drivers. However, special control devices are needed for the handicapped (Chapter 13). As noted in the Appendix to Chapter 5, the pedals should be located such that the angle at the ankle is approximately 90 degrees. For very short drivers, pedal extension units may be added at low cost to bring the pedal up to 2.75 in (7 cm) closer [AAA, 22]. A few models permit adjusting the brake and accelerator linkages to the driver's height. Seat adjustments, steering column adjustment, and other techniques will be discussed subsequently.

The accelerator pedal typically rotates about the heel of the foot with displacement at the ball of 1.5 to 2.0 in (4-5 cm) [Chaillet, 6]. If the displacement is too small, accurate speed regulation will be more difficult. As the profile of the vehicle has been lowered the angle of the pedal has become slightly more horizontal. Accelerator dimensions are typically 5 in (13 cm) $\times$ 2 to 3 in (5-8 cm). The brake is about 6 in (15 cm) $\times$ 2.5 in (6 cm) on automatic transmission vehicles [Hall, 15].

The steering wheel has become smaller in recent years, and less torquing moment is required. The wheel diameter of a semi-sports car is slightly less than that of a conventional car and the rim is slightly wider. On two 1978 models

[Road and Track, 33] the diameters were 14.75 in (37.5 cm) and 15.4 in (39.1 cm) and the rims were 1.12 in (2.85 cm) and 0.85 in (2.16 cm), respectively. With the emphasis on maneuverability the sports version may have a padded cover to enhance grip. However, steering wheel styling largely reflects the driver's taste, more so than functional requirements.

Major changes in the steering column emphasize safety and visibility: an optional detent adjustment of the angle of the column for variations in sitting height; a recessed hub and padded hub and bars; and design of the bars for improved visibility of the instrumentation. Although models differ widely in styling, the upper hemisphere is open (Figure 11-1).

Secondary Controls In this section several secondary controls will be discussed in terms of human factors design and desirable new features currently available on luxury models.

The *gear selector* lever is mounted on the right side of the column on most bench-seat models and on the center console on the semi-sport, bucket-seat models. To preclude inadvertant movement, the column-mounted lever is detented and the console-mounted lever typically has a push-button lock release.

The optional *cruise control* is typically activated by an alternate-action push button at the end of the turn-signal lever on the left side of the column. Although convenient for resetting after brake applications, the location may not be apparent to first-time users. Luxury models have a three-position switch on the dashboard with an auto position that permits the vehicle to return to the preset speed after brake application.

Climate controls are typically two-selector levers operating in a horizontal plane. One is for mode selection and each position must be labeled. The other is for temperature range selection and only extreme positions require identification [Motor Vehicle Safety Standard 101, 26]. The fan speed control is also on the panel. Designers exercise considerable freedom in this panel design. Luxury models have an auto selector position and associated thumbwheel for thermo-static control. This relieves the driver of manual regulation when there is frequent door opening.

The pull-on knob *light switch* is fairly standardized in its mode of activation. The *high-beam/dimmer switch* is being incorporated onto the turn-signal arm. This presents no problem provided the driver knows the switch is there and steering movements can be easily negotiated with one hand. As noted in the next section, the floor dimmer switch has been difficult for some drivers to locate. Luxury models have electronic, light-sensitive sensors that dim the high-beam automatically when oncoming traffic lights are sensed. Sensitivity is adjustable by a rheostat. Another feature for the forgetful is lights that shut off automatically when the engine has been turned off for a certain amount of time.

Windshield wiper/washer controls with two-speed wipers are standard, but a desirable optional feature is intermittent wiper action (pulsing about every 6 sec) for light sprinkles or misting conditions. The design of the wiper/washer control

Figure 11-1 Illustration of instrumentation for luxury bench-seat vehicle (above) and semi-sports bucket-seat vehicle (1978).

is not standardized. Some recent models have the control mounted on the column, left or right, for easier access.

External mirror adjustment from a door panel lever has long been offered so that the driver need not roll down the window. Some models also provide the driver the capability for adjusting a passenger-side mirror via a dashboard control.

Other optional features include a radio antenna molded into the windshield glass to preclude vandalism, rear-window wipers and defogger, electrically operated windows and door locks controlled by the driver as well as the passenger. There are many work-saving and visibility-improving devices that are desirable. The middle-class consumer is naturally concerned with the issues of reliability, extra cost, and cost of repair. Also, this question should be raised: Could failure at any time introduce a greater hazard than a manual capability?

Driver Expectancies for Control Locations   The general location of primary controls has been standardized by anthropometric considerations and SAE practices [Motor Vehicle Safety Standard 101, 27]. The location of secondary controls is largely unstandardized even on American-made automobiles and especially between foreign-made and American-made automobiles.

Three common methods of inferring that location expectancies of drivers are being violated by control layout design are (1) to ask drivers to report incidents of control confusion; (2) to measure the exact location where they would expect a control to be installed and to compare high-percentage, expected locations with actual locations on particular models; (3) to measure how long it takes to locate various controls and how frequently controls are incorrectly identified. McGrath [23] has employed all three methods.

In 1973, McGrath conducted field interviews of problems reported by drivers in locating and operating controls on their own vehicles. Drivers interviewed at rest stops reported difficulties encountered on the present trip. The same information was requested from first-time rental car users at an international airport.

As expected there were substantial differences between the familiar driver and the unfamiliar driver. Rental car drivers had more difficulty in locating or operating the vent and horn controls. Nine percent had trouble locating the parking brakes, dimmer switch, and cigarette lighter, while familiar drivers had no such difficulty except for the dimmer switch, which was then typically located on the floor. Both groups had great difficulty (21-25 percent) locating and operating climate controls. The windshield washer control was more difficult to locate than the wiper control due to more diversified locations and less definitive labeling. Six percent of the rental car drivers had difficulty finding the ignition switch although it was almost always located on the right side of the steering column or on the lower right instrument panel. Five percent of the rental-car drivers could not locate door handles under the arm rest. All other problem incident rates were less than 5 percent.

An interesting footnote was that the manager of a rental car agency reported that many drivers apparently could not locate an ignition key release switch in certain cars. They walked away with the key in the ignition switch, which led to a major increase in rental car thefts. Release switches have been largely replaced by the buzzer (see *Displays*).

McGrath [23] conducted another survey in 1975 in which 1708 drivers were asked to mark on a drawing where they would expect to find 14 common secondary controls. The responses were to a mail-in questionnaire administered by the Department of Motor Vehicles in four southern California cities. Drivers were asked the types of vehicles they were currently or had recently driven and responses were classified into four categories: (1) late-model, American-made, full-sized sedan; (2) compact sedan; (3) light truck or van; (4) late-model, small, foreign-made vehicle. All had automatic transmission except the foreign-made car.

Over 300 data points were obtained for each of the five models.[1] The dot-density distributions were then summarized in frequencies within 2 × 2 in (5 × 5 cm) squares. To simplify discussion, McGrath reported the data in six general regions. Table 11-1 presents the expectancy percentage data. Although McGrath gave all percentages, the summary table reports only a single region when there was very high agreement or two or more regions when there was less agreement.

In general, it was found that the radio, climate controls, ashtray, and lighter were expected to be on the right panel; the headlight switch, wiper/washer, and hood release on the left panel; the parking brake and release was generally on or below the left panel, except on foreign cars with bucket seats, where it was between the two seats. The vent control could be on either side.

The locations generally reflect the interior packaging designs of motor vehicles in the early 1970s. If the study had been conducted today one would expect a different distribution—for example, the climate controls are more often on the left and the ignition switch, dimmer switch, and hazard flasher are commonly located on the steering column.

Although expectancy percentages reflect recent design practices, this in no way lessens their importance. When a substantial percentage of the population has come to expect the control in one location and that location is changed, there will be a transition period when many drivers are confused. One might ask: How serious are such confusions? Delay in activation can be serious in some situations. For a driver attempting to find a hazard flasher switch after one's car had broken down on a highway at night, it would be quite serious. Similarly, a windshield wiper switch that could not be readily located during a sudden thunderstorm or hood release activation which was delayed when the engine was on fire could be hazardous.

McGrath [23] conducted further studies of the time to locate controls on a

---

[1]The full-sized sedan was divided into those with circular and those with rectangular instrumentation, but the data was later combined.

Table 11-1 Percentage of Motorists Expecting Secondary Controls in Six Regions

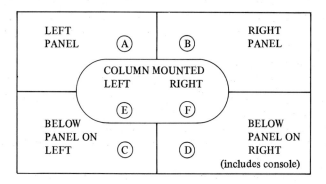

Control	Region	Full-Sized	Compact	Truck/van	Small foreign
Headlight switch	A	86.4	87.0	82.9	81.4
Radio	B	98.8	97.2	98.3	94.4
Defroster	B	78.5	75.3	81.9	75.1
	A	20.4	18.8	17.2	16.9
Cigarette lighter	B	97.4	92.0	98.0	90.3
Wiper/washer	A	70.5	73.9	71.1	60.5
	B	27.0	22.0	26.1	33.1
Heater	B	80.4	78.1	85.7	75.8
	A	17.5	14.5	11.8	(C) 14.0
Vent control	A	53.1	49.2	49.7	48.4
	B	39.4	36.7	31.4	31.7
Ashtray	B	98.4	87.4	97.2	84.0
Hazard flasher switch	F	48.5	46.7	49.1	41.5
	A	16.0	20.3	19.4	21.5
	B	17.0	16.3	15.6	22.1
	E	17.9	15.0	15.0	12.1
Parking brake	C	54.8	70.1	76.5	44.5
	A	38.1	13.5	17.4	(D) 40.6
Hood release	A	79.2	73.4	72.8	70.9
	B	11.4	12.3	(C) 15.9	(D) 13.5
Ignition	B	48.3	50.0	60.1	60.2
	F	44.8	41.1	30.7	33.9
Parking brake release	A	76.6	50.8	55.6	34.8
	C	16.8	34.7	36.9	(D) 38.2
Hi-beam/dimmer	C	83.6	88.1	86.3	73.7
	E	11.3	7.7	8.2	20.0

Source: Adapted from McGrath [23].

1973 LTD and a 1969 Toyota with 261 drivers tested in each model. Response time was found to be correlated with the distance from expected to actual control location. Error rates and response time were also correlated. For example, on these particular vehicles, the vent control, hazard flasher switch, and cigarette lighter took longer to locate than other controls and the same three controls had the highest error rates (17 to 24 percent) for both the LTD and Toyota (error rates mean confusing the control with any other control). The highest particular confusions, such as reaching for the wiper and touching the headlights, were less than 3 percent.

The SAE has developed recommended practices [36] regarding locating automotive controls (SP407), although standardization is still largely limited to primary control locations. There is also a need for international standards, since many households now own both an American-made and a foreign-made automobile, and drivers must remember the standards for whichever vehicle they are operating.

Labeling and Symbolic Coding Location coding is probably the most important type of coding for drivers, since the eyes should be scanning the roadway rather than searching for labels located on or near controls. However, labels are useful in familiarization and even while driving, labels that are read quickly are better than trial-and-error methods.

Foreign-made vehicles employ a pictorial coding system for secondary controls. In 1973, the International Standards Organization [19] recommended standard symbols for upper and lower beam lights, turn signals, ventilating fan, windshield washer and wiper, and hazard warning. Heard [17] has recommended additional symbols for other controls and displays.

In the United States there has been caution in adopting a requirement for symbols for motor vehicle controls. Table 11-2, from Motor Vehicle Safety Standard 101 [26], specifies acceptable labels and symbols for passenger cars, trucks, and buses manufactured after September 1, 1972. Note that only five symbols are permissible. (The turn-signal arrows have been used as a display for many years.)

Most labels for secondary controls, except those foot-operated or on the steering column, are to be illuminated when the headlights are turned on. Heating and air conditioning labels need not be illuminated unless the air jet is on the windshield.

Regarding symbology, the trend toward increased usage has extended to agricultural equipment, especially the tractor. Some 53 symbols have been recommended for use on farm machinery [*Agricultural Engineers Yearbook*, 1]. Although many symbols may appear quite logical to those developing the system, they may not be so apparent to others. Green and Pew [12] studied the ability of American subjects to correctly interpret 19 automotive symbols, and subjects also rated the communicativeness of new pictographic designs. Improvements in symbology continue under the sponsorship of SAE.

Table 11-2   Control Identification and Illumination Standard

Column 1	Column 2	Column 3	Column 4
Motor vehicle equipment control	Word or abbreviation	Permissible symbol	Illumination
Engine start	Engine Start[1]	None	
Engine stop	Engine Stop[1]	None	Yes[1]
Manual choke	Choke	None	
Hand throttle	Throttle	None	
Automatic vehicle speed control		None	Yes
Headlamps and taillamps	Lights[2]		
Vehicular hazard warning signal	Hazard		Yes
Clearance lamps	Clearance Lamps[3] or CL LPS		Yes
Identification lamps	Identification Lamps or ID LPS	None	Yes
Windshield wiping system	Wiper or Wipe		Yes
Windshield washing system	Washer or Wash		Yes
Windshield defrosting and defogging system	Defrost or Def	None	Yes
Heating and air conditioning system		None	Yes

[1] Use when engine control is separate from the key locking system.

[2] Use also when clearance, identification lamps, and/or side marker lamps are controlled with the headlamp switch.

[3] Use also when clearance lamps, identification lamps, and/or side marker lamps are controlled with one switch other than the headlamp switch.

Source: Motor Vehicle Safety Standard 101 [27].

Control Accessibility   Federal Standard 101, paragraph S4.1 [27], "Control Location," defines accessibility requirements for 11 controls on passenger cars, multipurpose passenger vehicles, trucks, and buses manufactured on or after September 1, 1972. The applicable controls are listed as steering wheel, horn control, transmission shift lever, ignition switch, headlamp switch, turn-signal control, illumination intensity control, windshield washer and wiper controls, manual choke, and driver's sun visor.

Paragraphs S4.1 and S5 state the controls shall be operable by a person seated at the controls with a nonextending pelvic restraint (lap belt). S5.2 further defines restraint as "nonextending upper torso and pelvic restraints fastened so that the upper torso restraint can be moved 4 inches away from the sternum and there is no slack between the lap belt and pelvis." Convertible passenger cars and certain buses are excluded from the shoulder harness requirement.

Although the standard is specific regarding restraint requirements, it is ambiguous in not defining "person," since functional arm reach varies consid... ably between the smallest user and the average user. A design change that improves reach accessibility is moving the frequently used secondary controls from the panel to the steering column. However, visual feedback may be sacrificed by the location under the wheel, and the possibility of error accompanies combining many functions on a single control on the column.

Displays   The automobile driver, unlike the pilot flying on instruments, receives a vast majority of information through the windows and mirrors. While driving, the principal automobile instruments are the speedometer and fuel gage, which are scanned only occasionally. Mourant and Rockwell [28] found that experienced drivers use the speedometer less than novice drivers.

Semi-sports cars have a circular tachometer, oil pressure, voltmeter, and water temperature gauge. Conventional cars have a series of backlighted word messages that inform the driver of engine problems, brake failure, unlocked seat belt, and so on. Sports car enthusiasts and car magazine writers feel the engine gauges have functional value over the "idiot lights" in that they permit anticipation of hazardous conditions in time to seek help. No studies are known of the degree to which semi-sports car drivers regularly use the tachometer and other instruments, but cockpit instrumentation is preferred.

Luxury models provide warning lights for low fuel, a desirable feature on all automobiles. Backlighted messages are also available for low window-washer fluid, door ajar, and unlocked trunk. Presumably lights could be provided at added expense for almost any contingency. Indicator lights without words are required for high beam and turn directional information.

There are also audio cues required. A buzzer sounds when the key is in the ignition, the engine is off, and the door is open. This is obviously to discourage careless drivers from leaving the key and thereby increasing theft. Older models required locking the door with the ignition key to discourage the key in the ignition, but this approach presumes drivers will lock their vehicles. Buzzers, of course, also signal failure to fasten safety equipment, and there are backup audio cues for turn signals.

Returning to instrument displays, the gear-lever position indicator is typically a rectangular display below the speedometer on vehicles with column-mounted gear shifts. Gear positions are shown on the console or on the knob itself on some semi-sports cars. This position requires removing the eyes from the roadway. Other models employ backlighted letters for the gear positions integrated into a circular speedometer.

The speedometer on conventional American-made models has a white-on-black linear scale with units of speed in both miles per hour and kilometers per hour. With the national speed law, some vehicles do not display the full capability of the vehicle (for example, 85-mi/h maximum is displayed on a vehicle with 109-mi/h capability). The position of the pointer relative to its position when vertical may be a qualitative cue to subjective speeding. If so, a vertical pointer position of 50 to 55 mi/h or even less is desirable. Semi-sports cars often display up to 130 mi/h with the vertical position at 65 mph (see Figure 11-1).

The mileage counter (odometer) is typically located under the speedometer. A trip odometer is an optional feature that provides essential information for rental car and expense account users. There is a trend toward adding more and more information to the speedometer so that some are extremely cluttered, and information is in such small letters and numbers that it is difficult to read while driving.

A fuel-economy display (marked with red and green zones and labeled power/economy or min/max) is included on some semi-sports cars. An interesting omission on some luxury models is the clock. In an era when most drivers have wrist watches, the often unreliable clock may become an option.

Seat Design

The dimensions of the automobile seat and its adjustment capability are critical to the functional design of the vehicle's interior. The seat must interface with the vehicle interior for proper egress/ingress, and it must provide reach capability, knee and leg clearances, and external and instrument panel visibility.

Seat Dimensions   The minimum seat elevation will define the 95th-percentile male eye reference point that, in turn, limits his maximum overhead visibility through the windshield. The maximum seat elevation will define the 10th-percentile[2] female eye reference point and her downward vision through the windshield. Van Cott and Kinkade [38] recommended a minimum adjustment range of 4 in (10 cm) vertical in 1-in increments to accommodate the extremes. Few vehicles provide this range of vertical adjustment.

[2]Automotive industry uses 10th, 50th, and 95th percentiles of design purposes.

The seat's longitudinal position is also important. The 10th-percentile female must be within comfortable reach of all controls, while the 95th-percentile male must be provided thigh support and, of course, knee clearances with respect to the steering wheel and panel equipment. The seat should be adjustable fore and aft through a range of at least 6 in (15 cm), preferably in 1-in increments [38].

Table 11-3 defines recommended dimensions and angles for vehicular seats. Note that the seat back, cushion excluded, should be no closer than 29 in (78 cm) from the nearest panel control or accessory. The front of the cushion should be no closer than 15 in (38 cm) from the base of the steering wheel. The nearest position should insure that the driver's eye is not less than 20 in (51 cm) from the sloping windshield and the front of the seat is at least 12.25 in (31 cm) from the back of the accelerator. For adequate knee clearance for the taller driver, the distance from the back of a foot control to the base of the steering wheel should be a minimum of 25.5 in (65 cm).

To provide the required range of seat adjustment, a control is typically located on or near the floor on the driver's side. Reliability and ease of operation without vision are paramount.

The recommended angle from pan to seat back is in the range of 105 to 115 degrees. Back angles are slightly less on buses, trucks, vans, and recreational vehicles than on automobiles. Passenger seats fully recline on some models. Also, bucket seats may rotate for ease of ingress and egress.

Seat Comfort   Rebiffé [31] has recommended a set of comfort limits for inclination of various joints of the body. Viewing the body from the side as a stick figure, the ankle angle should be 90 to 110 degrees; the knee angle, 95 to

Table 11-3   Recommended Vehicular Seat Dimensions and Angles

Dimension or angle	Inches	Centimeters	Degrees
Pan width	18–21	46–55	
Pan height	10–15	25–38	
Pan depth	15–17	38–43	
Pan angle from horizontal			6–8
Pan angle to seat back			105–115
Back height*	18–22	46–53	
Back** to panel controls	29 min	78 min	
Back-cushion steering wheel	15 min	38 min	
Seat-front accelerator	12.25	31	
Foot-control steering wheel	25.5 min	65 min	
Seat base** to ceiling	41 min	104 min	

*Does not include adjustable headrest or high-back seat required to prevent whiplash during rear-end collision.
**Seat cushion excluded
Source: Adapted from Van Cott and Kinkade [38].

135 degrees; the hip joint angle[3] should be 95 to 120 degrees; the upper arms within 20 to 30 degrees from the torso line and 20 to 45 degrees from vertical. The steering wheel should not be so high or distant that the elbow angle exceeds 120 degrees.

Comfort limits expressed in angular terms provide a basis for understanding some of the minimum distances discussed previously. Interior designers work with two-dimensional manikins or drafting templates hinged at the joints to assess the effects of workspace design on joint angles. SAE J826b [35] defines the use of a three-dimensional H-point machine for checking conformance of seating compartments with specifications.

Dutch [9] investigated various seat heights relative to steering wheel heights while subjects rotated the wheel 180 degrees. Minimum and maximum seat heights for comfort were reported. Little is known on exactly how the driving population grasps the steering wheel. The elbow angle may be greater in turning a corner than in making smaller adjustments on a relatively straight highway. This variable (and waist-line depth) must be considered in setting steering wheel heights relative to seat heights.

Wachsler and Learner [39] found that ratings of seat comfort after 5 min were as reliable as those found after 4 or more h. This does not imply that one will not fatigue, but rather that a particular seat design will maintain its same comfort rating relative to other seat designs independently of its duration of use. Rieck [32] found that seat comfort judgments were not correlated with the number of movements made by a person per unit time, a finding that seems to contradict the common sense observation of fidgeting.

Another aspect of comfort deals with ride qualities associated with vibration of the vehicle. The seat is the primary point of contact although the floor and control surfaces are also involved. Vibrations are damped by the suspension system and by cushioning. Vibration was discussed in Chapter 9, and conventional seat cushioning in Chapter 7. Major advancements have been made in this area, as dramatized on television by the diamond cutter making a perfect strike while seated in a vehicle traveling over rough terrain.

The cover of the cushion may be either leather or a synthetic product. Relative comfort of surface materials is more in the realm of aesthetics than improved ride comfort. An important consideration when adequate temperature control is not available is providing for contact point ventilation so the driver or passenger does not perspire and stick to the surface.

Bucket seats are standard in small cars and optional in American semi-sport and midsized cars. Bench seats, which permit up to six passengers, are used in larger American cars. Some feel that the bucket seats provide better body stabilization during cornering, while the bench seat allows for greater change in posture on long trips.

---

[3]Hip joint angle is referenced to the H-point, the pivot center of the torso and thigh, in both two- and three-dimensional representations.

From the standpoint of safety, SAE-recommended practice J879B [34] requires certain tests to ensure that the seat does not separate from its attachment points upon impact. The forward loads are generally 20 times the weight of the seat and rearward static moments with a simulated occupant should withstand 3300 in lb, about the H-point for each passenger.

Interior Dimensions

With high gasoline prices and federal standards for required mileage per gallon, Americans are beginning to adapt as drivers and passengers to compacts and subcompacts. One of the concerns of the taller and heavier person was the adequacy of the interior design for comfort. One manufacturer of a 1971 American-made subcompact compared its dimensions with those of a popular German-made subcompact [Olsen, 30]. The following is illustrative of the dimensions taken into account. All data were given in inches.

	Dimensions	1971 Pinto	1970 VW	Pinto +/– VW
Front:	Maximum effective leg room	41.0	39.8	+1.2
	Foot entry room	13.5	10.4	+3.1
	Effective head room	37.8	39.1	– 1.3
	Shoulder room	52.5	46.0	+6.5
	Hip room	51.8	49.0	+2.8
Rear:	Minimum effective leg room	31.4	31.2	+0.2
	Couple distance	30.0	26.4	+3.6
	Foot entry room	9.0	5.1	+3.9
	Effective head room	36.3	36.2	+0.1
	Shoulder room	51.6	50.7	+0.9

The roof of the American-made vehicle was 7.7 in lower than its foreign counterpart, but it had comparable head room in the back seat and only 1.3 in less in the front seat by lowering the seats with the familiar hump over the driveshaft and differential.

Head room data reported for various compacts and subcompacts are comparable to the tabled data: front head room of 37 to 38 in and rear head room of 36 to 37 in. Although the 95th-percentile male sitting height is 38.0 in seated erect and vertical, the more relevant dimension is slumped sitting height (36.6 in for 95th-percentile male). Slightly reclining seats lower the head. An argument could be made for reporting the head room dimensions in terms of the head clearance of the 95th-percentile male, that is, distance from the top of the head to the interior roof when seated. This is what the user really wishes to know.

The shoulder and hip room dimensions refer to wall-to-wall dimensions at certain locations. Shoulder room in subcompacts is typically a few inches wider than hip room, but it varies widely from 50 to 60 in. As noted in Chapter 3, the 95th-percentile male is 20 to 21 in in shoulder breadth, so two such males seated side-by-side would have 10 to 20 in of space between them.

Leg room dimensions strongly favor the front seat (typically, 41-44 in as compared with 30-37 in for the rear seat). Since the 95th-percentile male buttock-knee dimension is 26 in and, as noted earlier, 29 in from the back of the cushion is recommended, these values would meet minimums assuming that the leg room measurements were taken at knee level with respect to a reclining front seat.

Entry to and egress from the rear seat in a two-door vehicle is expedited in some models by use of a foot pedal on the side of the front passenger seat to enable tilting the seat forward. Shoulder harness extensions hinder the process of entry and egress. Rear passenger hand grips are also provided in some models to assist in getting up. The two-door vehicle typically has a larger door for ease of back-seat entry/egress. Although desirable, when such vehicles are parked closely in parallel, one cannot open a larger door quite as wide, and extra door weight has also been noted.

Visibility

Problems of driver visibility may be broadly classified in two categories: (1) external visibility through the windshield, other windows, and rear-view mirrors; (2) the design of headlights and rear lights for improved daytime and nighttime visibility.

Window Visibility   In planning the visibility of the occupant, designers refer to an *eyelipse,* which pinpoints the range of eye positions. Automobile designers have long been concerned with obstructions to outside visibility. A single wide-angle windshield and elimination of the vent window were efforts to improve visibility. Although it cannot be stated that 360 degrees of clear vision would significantly reduce accidents, there is still concern that windshield pillars, interior mirrors, and decals may obstruct vision. The hood of the vehicle, a potential visual obstruction, is tapered downward slightly in most models.

Increasing use of multilane facilities has also increased reliance of the driver on rear-view mirrors for detecting vehicles on either side that may be overtaking one's vehicle. Large pillars to the left and right of the rear window block some of the driver's rear vision. According to Mortimer [25], Federal Safety Standard 111, "Rear View Mirrors" calls for an inside mirror which provides a horizontal field of not less than 20 degrees and an outside mirror which provides at least 10 degrees (SAE J-834, 1967). Even with both mirrors, blind areas still exist for vehicles that are on the left or right almost level with the vehicle itself (Figure 11-2). Kelley and Prosin [20] studied driver eye fixations on a wide-angle mirror and concluded that 100 degrees of rear visibility is needed. Rear view visibility may be increased by using convex mirrors, increasing mirror size, and locating the mirror closer to the driver's eye [Mortimer, 25].

Rear window visibility has been compromised somewhat by streamlined styling. Slanted windows may offer less vertical viewing distance and possibly allow more snow and sleet to accumulate than the more vertical, classical window in some current models. Frost and steam may be removed by either

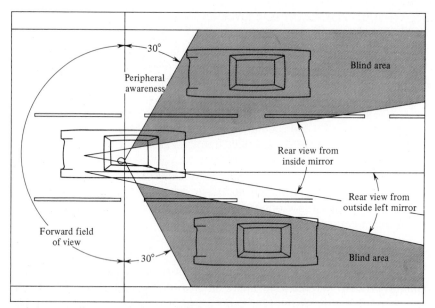

Figure 11-2 Blind spots in rear visibility. *(Mortimer, 1972.)*

electric wire defrosters or forced air defrosters. Rear window wipers are also available.

Another facet of the windshield visibility problem relates to the characteristics of the windshield itself or materials that may be placed on it. Streamlined styling has resulted in increased inclination of the windshield from vertical. This increases refractive errors and slightly reduces light transmission, while also increasing reflections from inside the vehicle at night [25]. Tinted glass is excellent for reducing daytime glare, but it also decreases nighttime visibility slightly [Doane and Rassweiler, 8]. In 1979, United States safety standards were proposed governing the maximum reflectivity for glazing materials and/or products applied to windows as well as for materials that decrease the transmission of light beyond acceptable limits. No percentage change is permitted for the windshield and front side windows, while nominal changes are permitted for other windows.

Vehicle Lighting

A knob light switch typically may be rotated to increase instrument panel intensity. Variable control is necessary, of course, to accommodate ambient lighting variability and dark adaptation. As noted previously, certain secondary controls are also illuminated concurrently with the headlights.

Almost half of all accidents involve two vehicles traveling in the same direction. Many of these accidents occur at night. Rapid and visible communications between drivers of intentions to stop and/or turn are essential. Colbourn et al. [7] found the headway maintained in clear weather is approximately 2 sec, irrespective of speed or instructed probability of the lead vehicle's stopping. Under poor visibility, reaction time would be longer, plus many drivers are unaccustomed to rapid braking.

It has been suggested that a different colored taillight be used for vehicle presence than is used for vehicle stopping. A following driver could then tell when a vehicle was braking, whereas with only one color the driver must distinguish between intensities of red to infer braking.

Mortimer [25] investigated various rear lighting configurations with two, four, and six separate lamps. He identified three different vehicle functions (presence, stop, and turn) and studied the effects of partial and complete separation of these functions by pairs of lights. He also studied green-blue as a potential "presence" light color and, in one configuration, amber as a turn light color. Measures included time-shared reaction time in the vehicle following and ratings of effectiveness. It was concluded that color coding reduced reaction time to turn and stop signals as compared with flash coding and intensity coding alone. The best configuration by both measures was the six-light configuration with the three light functions displayed separately by the three colors. However, he noted, amber can be confused with red, even at close range. Green-blue was recommended for presence.

Extending the coding scheme, velocity and deceleration rates could be displayed by rear light coding such as frequency modulation. Red light intensification when the brake is actuated is a common cue to drivers in stop-and-go or slow traffic. A distinctive cue that the vehicle ahead is decelerating very rapidly rather than merely slowing up may be helpful in avoiding rear-end collisions, although Mortimer [25] has reported that deceleration should not be effected by release of the accelerator without braking.

It is not known to what degree misinterpretation of function has contributed to rear-end collisions. Probably more often tailgating (maintaining unsafe headway clearances) is due to driver factors, although inadequate visibility is sometimes a factor. Recent model vehicles have employed enlarged bar configurations and brighter taillights to enhance visibility under degraded visual conditions. The concept of coding high vehicular velocity has some merit in the domain of enforcing speed limits.

Turn signals flash at 1 to 2 Hz and are distinguished from hazard flashers by being unidirectional. An uninvestigated area is the effect on accidents of malfunctioning turn signals, particularly failure of turn signals to go off automatically after a turn has been made. Many drivers assume that a flashing right-turn signal, for example, on a vehicle approaching an unsignalized intersection, is a declaration of intent to turn right. A vehicle traveling behind a slower signaling vehicle may pass in an otherwise unsafe situation. A vehicle waiting on a side street (on either side) may even move out into the intersection. The driver assumes incorrectly that the vehicle will turn right at the intersection and, hence, moving into the intersection will be safe. Faulty turn signals that must be manually reset have sometimes managed to pass annual inspection.

Continuing headlight research has been concerned with the obvious problem of a blinding glare when an oncoming vehicle failed to use the low beam or when the low beam was misaligned. State inspection procedures are designed to detect beam misalignment. Drivers also lose their acuity for targets in their own lane when facing a high-intensity headlight.

The vehicle-lighting industry has developed a low-beam headlight that gradually decreases intensity above the horizontal axis of the lamp. This provides longer distance vision for the driver, but it may introduce greater glare for the oncoming vehicle than do sharp cutoff lamps [Mortimer, 25]. Research and development in polarized and adaptive headlights is continuing to come up with a low-beam headlight that provides adequate distance visibility for stopping at high speeds without also introducing disability glare to oncoming traffic. There is some evidence that yellow fog lights do not actually penetrate better, and they reduce headlight output by 20 percent [25].

Many drivers use their headlights for up to an hour before dusk or after dawn. The lights are not needed for road vision; they are used principally to insure detection by oncoming traffic. If there are no traffic laws governing the use of low beams during these periods, some drivers will not use them. Attwood [2] found that unlit oncoming vehicles tended to be visually masked by the veiling brightness of other oncoming vehicles in a convoy with low-beam lights on. This could lead to unsafe passing maneuvers on two-lane roadways. He recommended a lights-on law for Canada extending from 30 minutes before sunset to 30 minutes after sunrise.

Handling Characteristics and Speed Control

In Chapter 5 the discussion of design of control systems dealt with the general problem of vehicular handling qualities. The decision on the type of vehicle to purchase rests sometimes on the consumer's belief and expectations regarding the vehicle's longitudinal and lateral handling characteristics—to negotiate curves at higher speeds, to maintain stability during quick turning maneuvers, to accelerate and brake rapidly and safely.

Vehicle handling response is affected by steering wheel torque, suspension system, wide wheel base, low center of gravity, tires, and ambient driving conditions. High-performance driving schools are being engaged to teach emergency vehicle drivers to maintain vehicle control during slalom-type maneuvers around a sequence of traffic cones at controlled test centers. A driving school at Texas A&M University also teaches techniques for avoidance of accidents at traffic intersections where the driver may need to abruptly change lanes.

From a design standpoint there are wide differences in vehicle controllability during slalom maneuvers and evasive action. These differences have an obvious impact on safety and, to the degree that vehicle design provides feel and "seat-of-pants" cues that aid the driver and minimize training time, these differences are also human factors engineering problems. For ease of handling in parking and city street maneuvering, a small vehicle with a smaller steering radius is at an obvious advantage.

Wet-weather accidents on highways are a problem not only for the highway designer, but also for the tire manufacturer. The popular extra-wide tires on semi-sports cars actually increase the probability of hydroplaning on wet surfaces. The driver must decelerate or risk losing vehicular control.

A vast majority of drivers exercise caution during icy roadway conditions. Monthly statistics on motor vehicle fatalities indicate they are highest in the summer months and lowest during January and February [National Highway Traffic Safety Administration, 29]. The relationship between speeding and fatal accidents has become common knowledge through safety campaigns and education.

Eye motion photography has shown that experienced drivers do not rely heavily on their speedometers to gauge speed [Mourant and Rockwell, 28]. Extensive psychological research has addressed the role of vehicle characteristics in drivers' estimation of speed (with the speedometer itself covered). Variables investigated or considered were vehicle size, suspension system, engine noise and soundproofing, and peripheral visual field through windows. There are also driver factors such as adaptation to high speeds, comfortable driving speed, and experience and condition of the driver. Also important are the trip length, prevailing speeds of other traffic, roadway design, and degree and type of speed enforcement.

The complex issue of why drivers maintain excessive speed is beyond the scope of this chapter, although it is a major objective of highway safety research. Small cars have various sensory cues that enhance the sensation of speed at a lower actual speed. Large luxury vehicles are typically driven faster. However, it has not been established whether this is due to ignorance of speed because of insulation from speed sensations of noise, vibration, and buffeting or whether the luxury car driver chooses to drive faster for other reasons such as confidence in the vehicle, trip length, and time factors.

If it is true that speeding is due to underestimation of the actual vehicle speed because of design characteristics, then the increasing use of compacts and subcompacts should be accompanied by a decrease in mean driving speed. Structurally, the small car offers less protection upon collision with trucks and larger vehicles, so even with speed reduction we cannot be too hopeful of a substantial reduction in fatalities.

Safety Provisions

In the discussion of deceleration in Chapter 9, various current techniques were introduced for restraining the driver during impact. The reader is familiar with collision research in which test vehicles are driven into rigid barriers to determine the effects on a simulated human of secondary collision with the stationary steering wheel, instrument panel, or windshield. To stop a 30 mph vehicle in 30 ft (9.14 m) would impose 1 G deceleration (but few vehicles can brake that quickly). If the sheet metal on the front of a vehicle crushes a total of 1 ft (30 cm), the passenger compartment would decelerate 30 Gs. If an unrestrained occupant traveling at 30 mph hits his head on the vehicle interior and is stopped in 3 in (7.6 cm) by materials, the laws of physics tell us the driver would sustain 120 Gs, which of course, is not survivable [Carpenter, 5].

Motor vehicle manufacturers and government-sponsored agencies conduct research on restraint systems at test centers with sophisticated anthropometric dummies that simulate fairly well the kinematics of the human body on impact. Computer models, validated against dummy impact studies, are also used to evaluate new restraint systems and interior modifications without going to the cost and delay of barrier tests [Carpenter, 5].

Less than 50 percent of drivers currently use the active restraint devices. The air bag passive restraint system offers the hope of absorbing energy and saving many lives upon impact. Deceleration occurs over a longer distance. The system should be reliable and not subject to activation on minor impacts with bumpers. It should be easily replaceable and, desirably, it should meet noise level standards.

Recently, child restraint safety standard 213 has been revised to improve crashworthiness of special seating and bed systems for infants and small children [Melvin 24; National Highway Traffic Safety Administration, 29]. Essentially, the systems employ tether belts and special lap belts for attachment. Guaranteed use is not assured, because some states allow holding children in the arms in lieu of restraint equipment.

An 80 percent increase in light trucks and vans in the last decade and a higher increase in fatalities per billion miles than automobile fatalities, has prompted stricter federal safety standards regarding instrument panels, seat backs, sun visors, and arm rests. Steering assemblies must cushion the impact and have a rearward movement no more than 5 in (12.6 cm) on 30 mph barrier impacts [29].

The use of protective helmets by adult motorcyclists has been a touchy issue. Many cyclists did not like required wearing of helmets and spearheaded a movement that repealed the helmet law in 23 states (as of 1979). However, safety agencies have noted a significant rise in fatalities due to head injuries in states without helmet laws [Koehler, 21]. Some cyclists have claimed the helmet reduces peripheral vision and makes it more difficult to hear significant sounds. After testing, safety scientists have found nominal visual and auditory losses because of the helmet [Hames and Petrucelli, 16]. The issue of motorcycle helmets is not unlike that of the use of personal safety equipment in industry, where many workers will reject anything that is inconvenient or less comfortable on the grounds that the accident in question has never happened to them in years of working without the safety equipment and the equipment is, therefore, unnecessary. Cyclists are also encouraged to drive with headlamps on since motorists in accidents often claim the cycle was not seen.

The Agricultural Tractor

Although the scope of this text does not permit discussion of each type of private vehicle, mention should be made of a vehicle that is presently receiving considerable attention in human factors engineering—the design of the operator platform of the agricultural tractor. For those who still visualize a tractor as an

Figure 11-3 Modern agricultural tractor. *(Courtesy of Deere and Co., Moline, Ill.)*

automobile-sized vehicle with the operator seated in the open on a C-frame metal seat, it may come as a surprise to see or board a modern tractor (Figure 11-3).

Many cabs are fully temperature-controlled with the accent on 360-degree visibility and downward visibility for attachment of implements and function monitoring. Conveniences include AM radio, tape deck, and ice chest in the tool box (portable refrigerators are an option).

Many tractor seats are planned for all-day usage: contoured with densely padded cushions, torsion bar suspension, a swivel seat that locks ahead, flip-up arm rests, and three-position adjustment of the high back. Restraint systems are standard.

The tractor has many hydraulic and transmission levers. Some manufacturers employ shape and color coding of the lever handles. Like automobiles, the control designs feature different styling concepts, but the American Society of Agricultural Engineering (ASAE) standards insure that control design is somewhat standardized as to location and mode of operation [1].

Since platform height may range from 48 to 85 in (122-216 cm), ladders and handrails are required for entry. Some enter from the rear and others from the side. Tractor design also emphasizes better stability and adaptation to its various functional requirements.

PUBLIC VEHICLES

Although it would appear that a majority of the public prefers to drive alone in his or her own vehicle, there is a duplication of fuel consumption in separately transporting one or two persons to a common destination. Wasted fuel and the traffic congestion problem have increased the urgency for improved public transportation systems that a larger percentage of the public will use. The price of gasoline has altered private vehicle modes but has yet to induce most of the public to leave the driving to someone else.

One inducement to ride city buses would be significantly reduced travel time. As will be discussed, commuters dislike waiting and taking longer to get to their destinations than by private means. Express buses from the suburbs are sometimes allowed to take special usage lanes on freeways. These lanes are reserved for buses, taxis, emergency vehicles, and van pools. Although improving public service, they necessarily increase the demand on other lanes and increase the private transportation problem.

Many larger American cities are spread out in all directions from the central business district (CBD). Rail service lacks flexibility in rerouting, but it would be impractical for even bus service to come within convenient walking distance of many users. A partial solution is for suburban commuters to drive to a local parking area (for example, an outdoor drive-in theater), park their cars, and board a scheduled express bus. This concept is termed "park-and-ride." Sometimes local taxis or jitneys transport the commuter to the boarding location.

This solution will not affect many private vehicle drivers. Many industrial districts are not centrally located nor easily accessible except by transfer to another bus. Also, many drivers regularly use their vehicles during the work day. With the increased use of private vehicles, public service is not scheduled as frequently as it was during the 1930s and 1940s, when a majority of urban workers regularly used public transportation. Large buses or mass transit seldom operate at a profit except at the peak demand periods. New modes of transportation better suited to changing conditions and user requirements may be needed.

User Requirements and Preferences

Government agencies and manufacturers of rapid transit public transport systems have been concerned with what it would take to convince the public to switch from private to public transportation or to switch from one mode of public transportation to another. Golob et al. [11] classified characteristics of public transportation systems into three categories: (1) levels of service; (2) convenience factors; (3) vehicle design characteristics. Although primary interest may be in factors of vehicle design and on-board conveniences, the overriding consideration in a decision to change transportation modes may well be operational or service factors.

In a General Motors-sponsored study, Golob et al. administered 1603 questionnaires to 1260 households with 786 individuals responding. The potential users were given 168 pairs of items and were asked to select one of two items. For example, would "making a trip without changing vehicles" be preferable to "easier entry and exit from the vehicle." The paired-comparison method requires that each item (system characteristic) be compared with each of the other items. In this study comparisons were made of up to 32 items within each of nine blocks. Respondents' choices were then averaged and converted to a scale value from 0.0 to 1.9. Although the technique of scaling within blocks may introduce some distortion, the findings are still very enlightening.

Table 11-4 lists the characteristics in descending scale value. To simplify discussion they have been grouped into categories of scale value ranges. The findings indicate that service (speedy trip, brief wait, no transfer, long service hours) are among the major considerations. Other than a guaranteed seat, on-board conveniences are much less important. Social factors, other than no crowding, were rated comparatively low in importance.

Table 11-4 User Preferences for Characteristics of Public Transportation

Scale value ranges	System characteristic in order of scale value
1.5 to 1.85	Arriving when planned Having a seat No transfer trip
1.2 to 1.5	Calling without delay Shelters at pick-up Less waiting time Choose pick-up time Lower fares Longer service hours Shorter walk to pick-up Shorter travel time and direct route
0.5 to 1.0	Easy fare paying Easy entry/exit Dependable travel times No crowding on vehicle Space for packages Adjustable air, light, and sound More phones in public places Adjustable seats Ability to meet friends on vehicle Vehicle/neighborhood compatibility Room for baby stroller, wheelchairs Riding in privacy Forming talking groups while riding Asking questions from systems representative Avoid annoying individuals
0.0 to 0.45	More pleasant route Ride with different kinds of people Chance to meet more people Coffee, newspaper, etc. on board Stylish vehicle exterior

Source: Adapted from Golob et al. [11].

The preferences represent the requirements of the average respondent. An elderly or handicapped person might rate entry/egress and wheelchair provisions much higher. Also, such preferences implicitly represent evaluations of currently provided facilities. Thus, if intense noise, vibration, temperature variation, and air circulation had not been a problem on previous trips, the evaluator would not likely rate these factors as high as otherwise. Confidence in the safety of the vehicle was not a rated item, but a recent disaster with many casualties could have a major effect on mode selection.

Length of the trip is also a variable. Food, beverage, and on-board bathroom facilities would be expected to be more important on a 3-h or longer trip than on a 30-min commuter trip. Many airlines provide movies, magazines, and headsets to pass the time on longer trips. The controversial issue of public smoking also needs to be raised.

A technique for assessing the importance of systems characteristics is to include a statement of how much extra fare one would be willing to pay for a service or convenience item. Another question should be: What is the likelihood of your using the public vehicle if it included the (x) most important characteristics you have selected? Many public transportation surveys receive enthusiastic support by respondents, yet they are speaking for what would be desirable for the community rather than their personal needs.

Design for the Extreme Users

The design of facilities for the physically handicapped in wheelchairs and the blind is discussed in Chapter 13. However, public vehicles also accommodate a large percentage of anthropometrically deviant persons who are ambulatory, yet require special design interfaces for safety and efficiency. *Travel Barriers* [U.S. Department of Transportation, 37] discusses certain design aids with particular reference to buses. The following discussion includes but is not limited to the items discussed.

Bus seating should be limited. Having a seat is mandatory for certain users. Smaller buses and more frequent service would also reduce waiting time at pick-up areas. Entry and exit from high-platform buses often requires lifting the legs far above (or below) recommended step maximums. Mechanically extendable steps or terminal ramps with gradual incline would reduce effort and expedite boarding.

Rapid transit systems typically have externally controlled fare payment systems. The coin-receiving mechanism should require less precise depositing than coin slots. Users prefer the use of cash or change to tokens, tickets, and other exchange modes [Gustavson et al., 13]. Turnstiles could be widened and push bars replaced with automatic doors opened by pressure pads after coin deposit.

Within the vehicle, multiple floor-to-ceiling stanchions provide better stability than straps or hand-holds while walking or standing on a moving vehicle. Aisles should be wide enough for two to pass sideways without disturbing seated passengers. Floors and interior surfaces should be padded in the event of falls and to help mask ambient noise. Rear seats on buses should be damped to preclude nauseating vibrations.

Seats on public vehicles should be designed in width and leg room to accommodate the anthropometric extremes. Seats could vary in size with assignments based on obvious body dimensional differences. Properly designed, the overall interior space requirement might be no greater than the current multipurpose seat design. Seat restraint should offer the safety of private passenger vehicles.

As previously noted, the trip length is an interfacing design variable. Obviously, commuter transit does not require the same comfort standards as a cross-country transit system. Buses as well as other transportation modes with trips in excess of 2 hours should be equipped with aircraft-type bathrooms (otherwise, time is lost with frequent rest stops). Regulations governing smoking make longer trips unbearable for those addicted to the habit. A design solution may be specially ventilated compartments (at extra fare) that separate the interior atmospheres of the smoking and nonsmoking travelers.

Terminal Design

A discussion of the many different configurations of railroad, bus, and aircraft terminals is beyond the scope of this text. However, two areas where significant advancements at the human-machine interface are being made are in passenger communications and building layout to avoid major waiting problems.

Passenger Communications An obvious area of improvement has been in the increasing use of international pictographic symbols for directing passengers to luggage claim, telephones, rest rooms, and so forth. Second, some airports use low-power radio systems for directing traffic in the parking lots. Terminals are designed to reduce walking distances from the parking lot to the terminal building.

Instead of all airlines being housed in a single terminal, each major airline may have its own terminal and these may be separated by considerable distance. Rather than requiring transferring passengers to carry heavy baggage from one terminal to another, an economic rail transportation service is provided between terminals. This may consist of a series of streetcar-like vehicles that move at frequent intervals in a counterclockwise direction between terminals.

The AIRTRANS system at the Dallas-Fort Worth International Airport is an example of such a system. The vehicles are automated and computer-controlled with position monitoring, speed control, and route alteration to meet passenger demand. There are five separate routes differing somewhat in the terminals where they stop. Some also go to remote parking lots, car rental, and a hotel. Each route is assigned a color code as an aid to service.

Bateman [3] conducted a systems analysis of users informational requirements in using such rail shuttle systems. The important consideration is users being given the appropriate information when it is needed in a form that is readily understood. Passengers who are not given sufficient information become confused and ask other passengers since there is no operator and often no station attendant. Examples of required information are as follows: (1) The assignment of airlines to terminal buildings as shown on an airport map or signs. Smaller airlines may share a terminal with a major airline. The airline to which one is transferring could be in the same building as the arriving airline, hence, the shuttle is unnecessary. (2) The fact that the rail shuttle is the only transportation system (except taxi). Walking is not an option. (3) Trailblazed directions for getting to the rail shuttle on a lower level. (4) Most important is a succession of static or dynamic information boards (or telephone computerized messages) that tell the passenger what is needed. For example, the passenger first needs to consult his or her airline ticket for connecting flight airline and flight number. Conventional flight data displays give arrival/departure times and gate numbers for boarding. However, the complexity of communications comes from the fact that each terminal has several shuttle stations that must be matched to the appropriate boarding gate and certain routes service only certain airlines. Figure 11-4 illustrates a modified display board recommended by Bateman [3].

Since the shuttles are computer-controlled and routes vary with demand, destinations are not shown on the vehicles themselves. Instead, airlines serviced by a given shuttle are shown on a large display at the boarding station and a backlighted color signals the route of the shuttle arriving (for example, red, green, or yellow route). Figure 11-5 illustrates a proposed display at each boarding station.

You are leaving TERMINAL 2E (Frontier, Ozark and Texas International)
    American and Braniff passengers: Consult TV display
    determine the gate number of your flight.

TO REACH	RIDE	TO
Air Canada	Yellow or Green	Braniff B
American Gates 1–7	Yellow	American A
American Gates 8–16	Yellow	American B
Braniff Gates 1–8	Yellow or Green	Braniff A
Braniff Gates 9–16	Yellow or Green	Braniff B
Braniff Gates 17–24	Yellow or Green	Braniff C
Continental	Green	Continental
Delta	Green	Delta
Eastern	Yellow	American B
Great Plains	Yellow	American B
Metro	Yellow	American B
Mexicana	Yellow	American A
Rio	Yellow or Green	Braniff A
Auto Rental	Red	Auto Rental
Hotel	Yellow	Hotel
North Parking	Red	North Parking
South Parking	Yellow	Hotel: Transfer to Blue

Figure 11-4 Proposed station information board for shuttle selection. *(Bateman, 1979.)*

YELLOW	GREEN	RED
Braniff C	Braniff C	Auto Rental
Braniff B	Braniff B	North Parking
Braniff A	Braniff A	
Hotel	Delta	
American B	Continental	
American A	Texas Int'l.	
Texas Int'l.		

Figure 11-5 Proposed markings over shuttle door. *(Bateman, 1979.)*

Regular users may have little difficulty with the directional displays but the first-time user may be confused unless the required information is available at the appropriate time. Irate passengers might even avoid a particular airport in the future if they missed a flight because of unnecessary delays.

Terminal Layout

Passengers (either local enplaning or transferring) should have 30 min or more from arrival at the terminal until boarding time. An early arriving passenger wishes first to check-in (to be assured of a seat on the plane and to check baggage if necessary). If he or she is required to wait until a given time, a long queue could develop. A second potential source of a queue is the security check of carry-on baggage. These obstacles passed, the passenger may wish to browse magazine racks or stores, or to have a drink or snack.

The layout of some terminals (for example, Washington Dulles) permits the passenger to attend to check-in and security check whenever he or she arrives. Other airports are laid out and/or follow operating procedures which require that all passengers wait in two lines. Upon early arrival at a check-in station, the passenger is not allowed to check-in until a specified time. Or if he or she is allowed to do so, the passenger must be seated in an airline anteroom, without conveniences, until boarding time. With either operating plan the passenger may decide to attend to other affairs before checking in. Upon returning he or she is faced with a long line of passengers and is denied a preferred reserved seat on the plane, which would have been an option for early arrival.

Finally, the security check comes after announcement that the flight is ready for boarding. All passengers in the anteroom, sometimes in excess of 200, must converge and vie for a place in the second line.

Efficient planning of an airline terminal will greatly reduce the duration of waiting in lines by allowing passengers flexibility in when they attend to these routine operations.

New Concepts in Local Public Transportation

Canty and Sobey [4] have summarized several newer concepts proposed for local urban transportation. Certain concepts are more suitable for transporting small numbers within the CBD. Others apply to rapid transit service from the

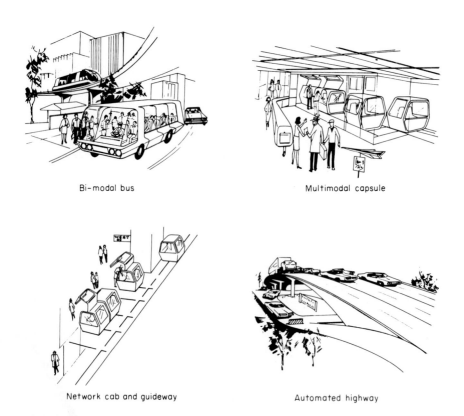

Figure 11-6   Sketches of conceptual urban transportation systems. *(Canty and Sobey, 1969, as given in McCormick, 1976.)*

residential suburbs to the CBD. Also included in the following discussion is the tram system, moving sidewalks, and intermodal transportation systems (Figure 11-6).

An advanced concept for transportation within the CBD is the *bimodal bus*. This is a modern bus capable of running on a rail (much like the airport shuttle) or converting to a conventional bus with a driver. Another concept, the *network cab*, is similar to the elevated cabs found at major amusement parks that accommodate two to four passengers. These individual cabs suspended from moving cables have replaced the bus-like monorail system at one state fairgrounds possibly because they accommodate small groups and provide almost continuous service (albeit periodically delayed by other cab boardings).

The *tram system* employs tractor-drawn wagons with passengers seated sideways and open to the elements except for a sunroof. The tram has been used at amusement parks to transport patrons to and from parking lots and on industrial plant lots with widely separated work facilities. In comparison with the bus, it offers efficiency in boarding time and variable transport size by adding or removing passenger wagons. Its limitations are that it lacks all-weather protection, and limited enforcement of boarding and exiting could be unsafe except at slow speeds.

Moving sidewalks are another energy-saving device applicable to short-distance CBD movement at low speeds. Many pedestrians are not content with the speed and attempt to walk on the moving track. Innovative concepts are needed to provide a trade-off between efficient speeds and safety.

The *automated highway* is a technique proposed for moving passengers from the suburbs to the CBD. The private vehicle is simply driven onto a moving track and, like the moving sidewalk, it is propelled to a distant location where the vehicle is driven off. Although conceptually simple and a gasoline-saving device for motorists, the development of moving highways capable of high-speed transport of heavy vehicles may be some years away. Driving on and off a moving track safely is also a developmental area.

New Transportation Concepts between Cities

Driving long distances over monotonous interstates is not necessarily enjoyable and many drivers would welcome automating the function if one's vehicle were available to drive away at the end of the trip. *Intermodal* concepts offer a practical solution to the long-distance problem. The reader may have noted semitrailers being transported on rail freight cars. The same concept, the *autotrain*, has application to motor vehicle transport except that passengers would ride in comfortable rail cars. Travel time would need to be competitive with private vehicle time.

Recently there has been a reduction in the number of routes offered by the government-subsidized AMTRAK passenger train system. It may be that modern passenger trains do not meet the cross-country user's needs. However, there are heavily populated regions of the United States such as the Atlantic seaboard from Washington, D.C. to Boston, where high-speed rapid transit rail service would be a practical trade-off timewise to aircraft shuttle flights.

Aircraft shuttle flights between cities 100 to 500 miles apart have been a popular transportation mode. However, there has been a trend for new airports to be located many miles from the CBDs. The additional travel time for passengers via courier car, taxi, or other modes to and from the CBDs has resulted in a total trip time comparable to what could be provided by high-speed express trains that travel directly between major CBDs of cities.

Current concepts generally employ conventional railroad tracks. However, experimental rapid transit systems employing air-bearing principles are being tested; they would travel on special guiderails at speeds of 300 to 500 mph. Operated as express trains, high-speed rapid transit offers both competitive travel time and all-weather dependability.

There is also a potential market for rapid-transit systems between the suburbs and the CBD and to-and-from international airports. The computer-controlled Bay Area Rapid Transit System (BART) is an example of a successful intermediate-speed rail system.

In summary, quality of service looms heavy in selling public transportation and perhaps explains the reluctance of the private vehicle driver to voluntarily switch to public transportation. But as the price of gasoline continues to multiply and public highways and airways become saturated the practicality of alternative transportation concepts may be enhanced.

QUESTIONS AND PROBLEMS

1   Providing interior designs that accommodate the extreme body dimensions is in some ways like buying a wardrobe suitable for all sizes. Comment on the desirability and practicality of automobiles being designed specifically for the 20th-, 50th-, and 80th-percentile driver with an adjustment capability of 15 percentile plus and minus.

2   Classify secondary controls in the car you drive into the six regions in Table 11-1, and compare the location with the expectancy data. On which controls would you disagree with the majority response?

3   The McGrath studies of driver expectancies identified certain locations expected for secondary controls and the consequences of deviations in terms of response time and error rates. Suppose a new model was designed that deviated radically from the expected locations. Design a study that would indicate the seriousness of the new layout for driver operations.

4   Will a standardized pictographic symbology for automobile controls and extensive public education on their meaning solve the problem of unstandardized locations of the controls? Comment.

5   Luxury models have backlighted word messages that inform drivers of various failures. Do you feel it is desirable to have a panel of such lights for various functions traditionally checked by a service attendant so that the driver at self-service stations does not need to open the hood? Comment on why it is or is not desirable.

6   A student research project demonstrated that a digital speedometer could be read more accurately and slightly quicker than the moving pointer speedometer in current use. Would you recommend a digital speedometer? Discuss the pros and cons of this change.

7   During the 1920s and 1930s a one-seat coupe was a popular vehicle. Comment on the desirability of the return of this vehicle to mass production. Why do you suppose the rumble seat and running board were phased out?

8   The automotive industry has introduced many work-saving devices for luxury automobiles (at extra cost). Think of a situation in which one or more of the automated functions discussed could result in a more hazardous situation than a manual system. Can you think of other functions that should be automated?

9   It was suggested that taillights could be coded to indicate excessive speeding. What obstacle do you see to such a suggestion?

10   List in order of importance at least three requirements you would demand of public transportion for you to use the bus or other service when going to a business district or to work in a large city.

11   Do you feel that the American public will give up their vehicles and take public transportation, or will they demand intermodal transportation for the following trips?
   a   Within the CBD
   b   From the suburbs to the CBD
   c   From CBD to CBD of cities less than 500 miles apart

REFERENCES

1 *Agricultural Engineers Yearbook,* Section 4, Universal Symbols for Operator Controls, 1975.
2 Attwood, D. A.: The effect of headlight glare on vehicle detection at dawn and dusk, *Human Factors,* vol. 2, no. 1, 1979, pp. 35–45.
3 Bateman, R. P.: Design evaluation of an interface between passengers and an automated ground transportation system, *Proceedings of the Human Factors Society,* 1979. Figures from unpublished Texas A & M report.
4 Canty, E. T. and A. J. Sobey: *Case studies of seven new systems of urban transportation,* General Motors Corporation, Research Laboratories, Research Publication GMR-1047, Warren, Michigan, January 1971.
5 Carpenter, M. E.: *Human Response Simulation in Automobile Accident Research,* paper presented to Industrial Engineering 631, Texas A&M University, based on research as a General Motors test engineer, July 1971.
6 Chaillet, R. F.: *Human Factors Engineering Design Standards for Wheeled Vehicles,* Human Engineering Laboratory, Aberdeen Proving Grounds, Report AD-646681, 1966.
7 Colbourn, C. J., I. D. Brown, and A. K. Copeman: Drivers' Judgments of Safe Distances in Vehicle Following, *Human Factors,* vol. 20, no. 1, 1978, pp. 1–11.
8 Doane, H. C. and G. M. Rassweiler: "Corporate Road Tests of Night Visibility Through Heat-Absorbing Glass," *Highway Research Board,* vol. 127, 1955, pp. 23–44.
9 Dutch, W. G.: Interior dimensions of small cars determined by the method of fitting trials, M.Sc. Dissertation, University of Manchester, 1965.
10 Forbes, T. W. (ed.): *Human Factors in Highway Traffic Safety Research,* Wiley-Interscience, Wiley and Sons, New York, 1972.
11 Golob, T. F., E. T. Canty, R. L. Gustafson, and J. E. Vett: Research Laboratories, General Motors Corporation, Research Publication GMR-1037, Warren, Michigan, October 26, 1970.
12 Green, P. and R. W. Pew: Evaluating Pictographic Symbols: An Automotive Application, *Human Factors,* vol. 20, no. 1, 1978, pp. 103–114.
13 Gustavson, R. L., H. V. Curd, and T. F. Golob: *Use preferences for a demand responsive transportation system: a case study,* General Motors Corporation, Research Laboratories, Research Publication GMR-1047, Warren, Michigan, January 1971.
14 Haight, F. A.: A traffic safety table, *Journal of Safety Research,* vol. 5, no. 4, December 1973.
15 Hall, J.: "Evaluation and Comparison of Design Features of American Luxury Touring and Grand Touring Cars," Texas A&M University Report for Industrial Engineering 631, May 1979.
16 Hames, L. and E. Petrucelli: "What the experts think about motorcycle safety," *Traffic Safety,* September 1977.
17 Heard, E. A.: Symbols study-1972. Society of Automotive Engineers Paper No. 740304, February 1974.
18 *Highway Safety Facts,* National Center for Statistics and Analysis, National Highway Traffic Safety Administration, April 1979.
19 International Standards Organization, Road vehicles - symbols for controls, indicators, and tell-tales-Part I. Geneva, Switzerland: ISO Standard 2575/1-73(E), 1973.

20 Kelley, C. R. and D. J. Prosin: *Motor Vehicle Rear Vision,* Final Report, Contract FH-11-6951, U.S. Department of Transportation, Dunlap and Assoc., Inc., 1969.

21 Koehler, M.: *Evaluation of Motorcycle Safety Helmet Usage Law,* Texas Traffic Safety Program Contract 1AC 78-08-36-A-1-AA, December 1978.

22 *Making Travel Safe Catalog,* American Automobile Association, Traffic Engineering and Safety Department, Falls Church, Va., May 30–November 30, 1975.

23 McGrath, J. J.: *Driver Expectancy and Performance in Locating Automotive Controls,* Vehicle Research Institute Report no. 14.1, June 1975.

24 Melvin, J. W.: Child Restraint Systems and Public Policy, *The HSRI Research Review,* University of Michigan Highway Safety Research Institute, vol. 9, no. 3, 1978.

25 Mortimer, R.: "Human Factors in Vehicle Design," Chapter IX in T. W. Forbes (ed.): *Human Factors in Highway Traffic Safety Research,* Wiley-Interscience, Wiley and Sons, New York, 1972.

26 *Motor Vehicle Safety Standard 101:* "Control Location, Identification, and Illumination—Passenger Cars, Multipurpose Passenger Vehicles, Trucks, and Buses," effective: January 1, 1972; revised: August 9, 1973.

27 *Motor Vehicle Safety Standard 101* (S 101-2, Part 571): revised August 9, 1973.

28 Mourant, R. R. and T. H. Rockwell: Strategies of visual search by novice and experienced drivers, *Human Factors,* vol. 14, 1972, pp. 325–335.

29 National Highway Traffic Safety Administration; *National Traffic Safety Newsletter,* April 1979, pp. 9–12.

30 Olsen, F. G.: *Engineering the Pinto,* Society of Automotive Engineers, Detroit, Mich., Automotive Engineering Congress (710149), Jan. 11–15, 1971.

31 Rebiffé, R.: An ergonomic study of the arrangement of driving position in motor cars, *Proceedings of the Symposium of the Institute of Mechanical Engineers* (London), 1966, pp. 26–33.

32 Rieck, A. von: Uber die Messung des Sitzkomforts von Autositzen, *Ergonomics,* vol. 12, no. 2, 1969, pp. 202–211.

33 Road Test of the 1978 Cadillac Seville and 1978 Camaro Z-28, *Road & Track,* October 1978, pp. 63–66, 72–76.

34 SAE Recommended Practice (SAE J879b): Motor vehicle seating systems, Body Engineering and Automotive Safety Committee, revised July 1968.

35 SAE Standard (SAE J826b): Devices for use in defining and measuring vehicle seat accommodations, Body Engineering Committee, November 1962, revised by Human Factors Engineering Committee, January 1974.

36 Society of Automotive Engineering (SAE) Practices SP407, "Driver Expectancy and Performance in Locating Automotive Controls," 1976.

37 *Travel Barriers,* PB187-237, U.S. Department of Transportation, National Information Service, 1970.

38 Van Cott, H. P. and R. G. Kinkade (eds.): Design of Individual Workplaces, in *Human Engineering Guide to Equipment Design,* Washington, D.C., U.S. Government Printing Office, 1972, chap. 9, p. 398.

39 Wachsler, R. A. and D. B. Learner: An analysis of some factors influencing seat comfort, Research Laboratories, General Motors Corporation, Report GMR-327, 1961.

40 Kizzia, T.: New trains are reviving America's romance with the rails, *Popular Mechanics,* Hearst Corp., New York, October 1975.

41 Shinar, D.: *Psychology of the road - the human factors of traffic safety,* Wiley, New York, 1978.

Part Five

Communications and Data Processing Systems

Chapter 12

Design for Speech Communications and Training

During the 1940s, 1950s, and 1960s, much of the research and development reported in the human factors literature on speech communications dealt with two topics—the evaluation of speech intelligibility in a noise field and techniques for modifying various systems components to enhance speech intelligibility.

In the 1960s, and especially in the late 1970s, research and development shifted toward voice synthesizers and speech recognition devices. These devices have a multitude of applications to industry, transportation, telephone communications, computers, and devices for the handicapped. Small speaking machines were developed to provide verbal feedback to children in the course of learning to spell, and in general, provided voice output in the area of computer-assisted instruction.

Because of the newness of the devices, the human factors literature in the area is still somewhat limited, but the potential problems at the human-machine interface merit discussion.

Voice applications to person-computer interaction are discussed in Chapter 14. However, basic to interactive systems is a body of research regarding how two people communicate with each other in solving problems. Speech is a major mode of communications when technology permits acceptance of verbal commands.

The popularity of long-distance telephone conversations stimulated teleconferencing as an alternative to face-to-face communications, but the ease of use of the telephone also introduced certain problems in protection of the user.

This chapter is divided into four major headings: (1) speech intelligibility research and evaluation; (2) speech synthesis, recognition, and computer processing; (3) telecommunications; and (4) training devices. The latter area will be briefly introduced and will spotlight the interfaces with calculators and childrens' learning aids.

SPEECH INTELLIGIBILITY

Communications engineers are interested in the development of communication systems suitable for transmission of intelligible speech. This speech can be heard in an ambient noise field or over headphones with static-type interference or other voices.

Three approaches are typically taken to enhance and evaluate intelligibility:

1 Measuring and evaluating the effectiveness of speech transmission in a system by intelligibility-testing methods or by short-cut estimation methods
2 Modifying the transmission system by electronic techniques such as peak clipping, filtering, and automatic gain control and by techniques at the speaker or earphones, such as noise shields on the microphone and ear protective devices
3 Modifying the message characteristics with software improvements, developing operating procedures, and training speakers and listeners

Each of these topics will be briefly discussed subsequently.

Characteristics of Speech

Speech may be viewed as a wave form depicting speech pressure levels over time as measured 1 meter from the speaker. The speech spectrum may also be analyzed into a series of octave bands and speech pressure levels may be determined for each band using band-pass filters. Overall speech level is a measure of the unfiltered speech wave over the entire audio-frequency spectrum. Spectral level is the pressure level per cycle, that is, the root-mean-square (RMS) pressure in each band divided by the bandwidth in hertz. Like noise, speech levels are expressed in decibels (dB).

The pitch of the human voice corresponds to its dominant frequency, and the loudness of the voice is a subjective sensation related to its RMS pressure level. In addition, the harmonic composition of wave forms determines the timbre. Timbre and resonating qualities permit distinguishing individual voices.

Phonemes   The fundamental speech sound is termed a *phoneme* or, more commonly, a vowel or consonant sound. Languages differ in their uses of particular phonemes. The fundamental speech sounds in the English language consist basically of 16 vowels and 22 consonants, although counting finer differences there are considerably more.

Phonemes are produced by the articulators, mainly the tongue, teeth, lips, and roof of the mouth (palate). These interact to constrict the breath stream. They do this in various ways such as stopping air passage in *plosives* (*p* in stop); forming a narrow slit for air passage in *fricatives* (*th* in their); closing the midline of the mouth in *laterals* (*l* in let); rapidly vibrating an articulator in *trills* (the rolled *r* in European languages) and unobstructed air passage for vowels [McCormick, 27].

Electronic engineers have recently become interested in exactly how the vocal tract produces sounds that travel from the vocal cords to the lips. They are interested in a model for the synthetic production of speech using filters (this topic will be introduced later).

The sound pressure level of phonemes differs considerably. Fletcher [16] measured the level in decibels of the average talker at a normal level of effort (Table 12-1). Note that the eleven phonemes with the highest pressure levels are all vowel sounds. This finding will have implications for the topic of peak clipping.

Speech Spectrum Levels   The sound pressure level of speech differs across the frequency spectrum. For example, for a representative sample of speakers with an overall speech level of 65 dB, the long-time RMS pressure level is in the range of 32 to 38 dB at frequencies below 700 Hz, but it drops sharply at higher frequencies (for example, 15 dB at 2000 Hz). These are average values. Peak instantaneous pressures by the 99th-percentile voice may exceed 50 dB at 500 Hz whereas the 20th-percentile voice may be only 20 to 25 dB in this same frequency range.

Table 12-1   Typical RMS Pressure Levels of Phonemes

Key word	Sound*	Pressure level (dB)	Key word	Sound*	Pressure level (dB)
talk	o'	28.2	chat	ch	16.2
top	a	27.8	me	m	15.5
ton	o	27.0	jot	j	13.6
tap	a'	26.9	azure	zh	13.0
tone	o	26.7	zip	z	12.0
took	u	26.6	sit	s	12.0
tape	a	25.7	tap	t	11.7
ten	e	25.4	get	g	11.7
tool	u	25.0	kit	k	11.1
tip	i	24.1	vat	v	10.8
team	e	23.4	that	th	10.4
err	r	23.2	bat	b	8.0
let	l	20.0	dot	d	8.0
shot	sh	19.0	pat	p	7.7
ring	ng	18.6	for	f	7.0
me	m	17.2	thin	th	0

*Spoken by an average talker at a normal level of effort.
Source: Fletcher [16].

Dynamic Range Fletcher [16] also found that telephone speech levels ranged from about 50 to 75 decibels with the median speaker talking at about 63 to 66 dB.

Table 12-2 illustrates sound pressure levels for a talker 1 meter from the measuring device [Kryter, 22]. Although whispering and shouting introduce extreme variations in pressure levels, note that the minimum and maximums for normal speech range from 39 to 99 dB.

In designing a communication system one might like to transmit the full range of speech power; however, practical constraints sometimes restrict the dynamic range. *Dynamic range* is defined by Kryter [22] as "the difference in decibels between the pressure level of noise in the system and the pressure level at which overload occurs." The lower level is the masked threshold and the upper level approaches the threshold of discomfort in the ear as discussed in Chapter 4.

Only a very high-quality communications system would require a dynamic range of 60 dB. Most commercial broadcasts have only 40 to 45 dB and practiced listeners and talkers can communicate effectively with a range of only 20 dB. On military systems microphones used with amplifiers should admit variations in signal input of at least 50 dB [MIL STD 1472B, 12].

Evaluating Speech Intelligibility

One approach to evaluating a system's suitability for speech is to administer speech intelligibility tests. A trained speaker (on tape) might read a passage and the listener would then repeat the passage. Certain key words are scored or the listener might answer questions that would depend upon having heard the key word. For example, "What character comes before e?" The answer is obvious if the letter e were heard clearly.

There are many types of intelligibility test material. The *Modified Rhyme Test* (MRT) involves the listener's deciding which of several words on a checklist was heard in the passage. The candidate words differ only in a single character, usually the first or last consonant. The *phonetically balanced* (PB) word list consists of carefully selected words that have speech sounds in proportion to the use of these sounds in everyday speech. Hence, the test score is representative of a real-world listening task. Testing with one-syllable PB words is recommended for military systems where high sensitivity and accuracy is required [MIL STD

Table 12-2 Sound Pressure Levels of Speech 1 M from the Talker

Measure of sound pressure	Whisper (dB)	Normal level (dB)			Shout (dB)
		Minimum	Average	Maximum	
Peak instantaneous pressures	70	79	89	99	110
Speech peaks	58	67	79	87	98
Long-time RMS pressures	46	55	65	75	86
Speech minima	30	39	49	59	70

Source: Kryter [22].

1472B, 12]. *Nonsense syllables* such as gaf, faz, and zuhg are also sometimes used. They are more difficult to understand than words, so small amounts of noise may interfere with intelligibility.

Each listener is then scored in terms of percentage of total key words correctly heard (percent word intelligibility) or percentage of sentences in which the essence or the key word was given correctly [Kryter, 22].

Articulation Index   Intelligibility testing, like most behavioral research, is very time-consuming and requires controlled conditions, many subjects, and a skilled administrator. Communications engineers sought an alternative method for predicting intelligibility of a speech system without testing subjects. The articulation index (AI) method is one simple technique for estimating intelligibility.

The AI concept can best be explained by illustrating its derivation. One technique for derivation, the 20-band method, involves dividing the audible speech spectrum (200-6100 Hz) into a series of octave bands, each selected so that the band contributes equally to speech intelligibility. Spacing between mid-frequencies of the bands will not be at a constant interval because bands between 1100 to 3500 Hz contribute proportionally more to understanding speech than do bands higher or lower. Another technique, the one-third octave band method, accomplishes much the same thing by assigning higher weights to those bands most critical to speech intelligibility.

The steady-state noise spectrum is measured and may then be plotted on a worksheet along with the spectrum of speech peaks at the ear. Next, one calculates the difference between speech and noise levels at the mid-frequency of each octave band. If the difference is zero or negative (noise exceeding speech level), a value of 0 is assigned. If the difference is 30 dB or more, a value of 30 is assigned (the maximum contribution of any of the 20 bands).

The 20 values are then totaled and divided by 600. The resulting articulation index will necessarily range from 0 to + 1.0. An AI of 1.0 would mean that the speech spectrum exceeded the noise spectrum by 30 dB or more in every band. This would be an excellent system. AI values above 0.7 are recommended for

Table 12-3   Intelligibility Criteria for Voice Communication Systems

Communication requirements	Score		
	PB words	MRT	AI
Exceptionally high intelligibility; separate syllables understood.	90%	97%	0.7
Normally acceptable intelligibility; about 98% of sentences correctly heard; single digits understood.	75%	91%	0.5
Minimally acceptable intelligibility; limited standardized phrases understood; about 90% of sentences correctly heard (not acceptable for operational equipment).	43%	75%	0.3

Source: MIL-STD-1472B [12].

communications systems operated under stress. Commercial communications require an AI of 0.5. Values below 0.3 have poor intelligibility. To understand speech with a communication system with less than 0.3 would require special vocabularies and radio-telephone voice procedures [Beranek, 1]. Table 12-3 provides intelligibility criteria for three types of measures.

Figure 12-1 illustrates the calculation of the AI by the one-third octave band method using variable weights. Products are totaled to yield the AI. The

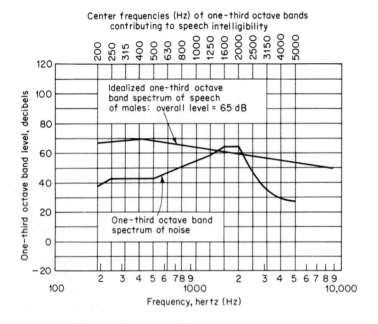

1. Band	2. Speech peaks minus noise, dB	3. Weight	4. Column 2 x 3
200	30	0.0004	0.0120
250	26	0.0010	0.0260
315	27	0.0010	0.0270
400	28	0.0014	0.0392
500	26	0.0014	0.0364
630	22	0.0020	0.0440
800	16	0.0020	0.0320
1000	8	0.0024	0.0192
1250	3	0.0030	0.0090
1600	0	0.0037	0.0000
2000	0	0.0038	0.0000
2500	12	0.0034	0.0408
3150	22	0.0034	0.0758
4000	26	0.0024	0.0624
5000	25	0.0020	0.0500
		AI =	0.4738

Figure 12-1   Calculation of the articulation index by the one-third octave band method. *(Adapted by McCormick, 1976, from Kryter in Van Cott and Kinkade, 1972.)*

articulation index is a widely used measure for reporting the degree of intelligibility of particular systems. In graphic displays of research findings it would be the independent variable.

Speech-to-Noise Ratio   Another index for expressing speech intelligibility is the speech-to-noise (S/N) ratio, a concept analogous to the signal-to-noise ratio (Chapter 4). For any indicated frequency a S/N ratio is simply the plus-or-minus difference between the speech and noise level. Negative values indicate that the noise level exceeds the speech level. Even in such a high noise field a surprisingly large number of words can be understood.

Figure 12-2 illustrates that visual cues from reading the lips of the speaker also significantly enhance the intelligibility of speech.

Speech Interference Level   Another common index for expressing speech intelligibility is the speech interference level (SIL) index. It is applicable to face-to-face communications in a continuous noise spectrum. The SIL is simply the maximum noise in three octave bands that will permit reception of 75 percent of a set of phonetically balanced words or 98 percent of words in sentences [Kryter, 22]. Some experts have employed octave bands of 600 to 1200, 1200 to 2400, and 2400 to 4800 Hz (22). Others have used the centers of octave bands at 500, 1000, and 2000 Hz [Peterson and Gross, 31].

The use of ambient noise levels expressed in terms of SIL is illustrated by a study of the voice level that would be required for reasonable speech intelligibility for various combinations of SIL and distance from the person speaking [Webster, 41]. Figure 12-3 depicts SIL values where it would be possible, difficult, or impossible to understand a speaker who was at various distances and speaking at various voice intensities. For example, for an SIL of 67

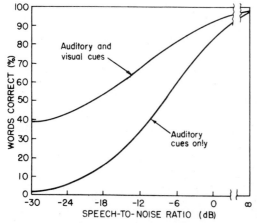

Figure 12-2   Intelligibility of words with and without visual cues from observing the talker. *(Sumby and Pollack, 1954, and in Van Cott and Kinkade, 1972.)*

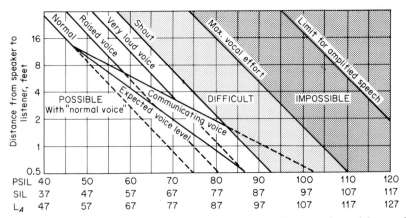

Figure 12-3 Voice level and distance between talker and listener for satisfactory face-to-face communications expressed in SIL values. *(Webster, 1969, as given in McCormick, 1976.)*

a person 8 ft away who was shouting could be heard with difficulty; with an SIL of 57 the same speaker could be heard if he or she spoke with a raised voice.

Peterson and Gross [31] recommend for satisfactory long-distance telephone use an SIL of less than 60. SILs of 60 to 75 permit hearing with difficulty, but above 80 hearing is virtually impossible. It was recommended that 5 dB be added to these criteria values for local phone calls. With improved communications since the criteria were reported in 1972, the latter values may be more generally applicable.

An extension of the SIL theme is the development of acoustical noise criteria (NC) curves. These series of curves show maximum permissible noise levels in each of eight octave bands. Measured noise levels in a facility should not exceed the NC curve used as a standard. For example, for a quiet room suitable for telephone usage, noise levels should not exceed the 35- to 40-NC curves. If noise levels reached the 80-NC curve, shouting would be required and telephone usage would be unsatisfactory. NC curves have been widely used to relate measured background noise spectra to ability to communicate effectively at various distances.

Modifying the Transmission System

Electronically the transmission system may be modified by selectively passing certain frequencies (filtering), by cutting off the peak amplitudes and passing only the center of the speech wave (peak clipping), by automatically controlling the gain, and other techniques.

Filtering Narrow band filtering permits eliminating certain low or high frequencies and still achieving 80 percent intelligibility of PB words. A low-pass filter, of course, gradually eliminates all frequencies above some cutoff frequency. A high-pass filter eliminates frequencies below the cutoff. French and Steinberg [17] demonstrated that understanding speech in quiet conditions is not

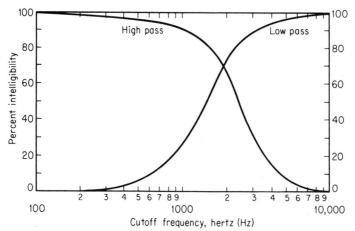

Figure 12-4 Effect on intelligibility of the use of high- and low-band pass filters. *(French and Steinberg, 1947, as given in McCormick, 1976.)*

normally dependent on any particular frequency range within the audible spectrum. Note in Figure 12-4 that eliminating either all frequencies above 1900 Hz or eliminating all frequencies below 1900 Hz gave about 67 percent intelligibility. As noted earlier, the range of about 1000 to 3500 Hz affects intelligibility the most. Frequencies above 4000 Hz or below 600 Hz may be filtered without much effect. However, certain phonemes such as the *s* sound are dependent upon the 4000 Hz or higher frequencies, and a few short vowels depend heavily on frequencies below 1000 Hz.

Peak Clipping   It was shown in Table 12-1 that the speech pressure level of vowel sounds is much higher than that of consonant sounds. Fortunately, understanding speech is heavily dependent upon hearing the consonants. Much of the power of the vowels in conversational speech is for emphasis and not essential to intelligibility. Therefore, by electronically clipping off the ends of speech waves (top and bottom), intelligibility of speech is not sacrificed.

Peak clipping may make the speech sounds appear somewhat harsh or distorted. Distortion is actually more obvious in quiet conditions than in noisy ones, and filtering techniques may be used to reduce the harshness [Kryter, 22]. Consonants may appear louder in relation to vowel sounds than in ordinary speech, which is no cause for alarm.

Licklider and Miller [24] found that percent intelligibility remained very high even after 18 to 30 dB had been clipped. In contrast, when the *center* of the speech wave was clipped only 6 dB, the words were almost totally unintelligible. Center clipping eliminates discrimination of the low-powered consonants.

Communications engineers are able to make use of this reduction in amplitude of vowels and consonants to the same level in peak clipping. Communications systems have finite limits on power transmission. By clipping

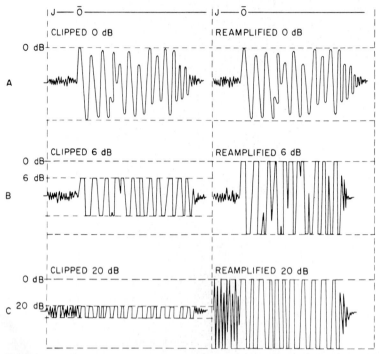

Figure 12-5   Illustrations of undistorted speech, 6 dB and 12 dB peak clipping with reamplification of the word, "Joe." *(Licklider, 1948. Copyright 1948, by University of Illinois Press. Reprinted by permission.)*

the speech and then reamplifying the clipped signal so the peak amplitude of the remnant is the same as the original wave, the intensity of the weak consonants becomes greater than before clipping without additional power in the system. Figure 12-5 illustrates two levels of peak clipping and reamplification [22]. Peak clipping of 12 to 20 dB may be employed on most military systems where the S/N ratio is less than 15 dB [MIL STD 1472B, 12].

   Speech Transmission and Reception Equipment   Figure 12-6 illustrates some of the other equipment that is included in a speech communication system for use in an extremely intense noise field [22]. In addition to peak clipping and low-pass filtering, there are amplifiers; an automatic gain control (AGC) that adjusts the amplifier to some average signal strength over a period of time; a compressor or peak limiter in the receiver; a noise shield that fits tightly against the face of the speaker; noise-cancelling microphones and contact microphones that are placed directly in contact with the throat, jaw, or surface of the head.

   Other equipment includes loudspeakers when communicating with a large group and individual headphones when communicating with fairly stationary individuals. Binaural headphones should be provided whenever the ambient

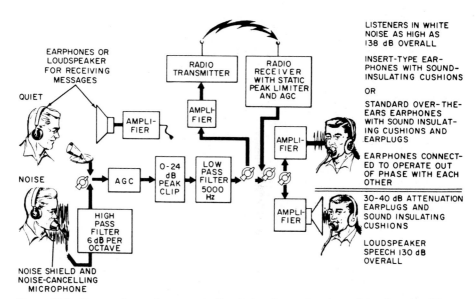

Figure 12-6 Proposed speech communication system for use in extreme-intensity noise. *(Kryter, 1958, and in Van Cott and Kinkade, 1972.)*

noise is 85 dBA or greater [12]. Headphones and other protective devices will normally limit the ambient noise level to less than 85 dBA. See Chapter 9. For military systems [12] headphones and speakers should provide for reception in the range of 200 to 6100 Hz (250-4000 Hz is minimum range). Multiple speakers must respond uniformly ± 5 dB in the 100- to 4800-Hz range. For multichannel monitoring, loudspeakers should be not less than 10 degrees apart radially with respect to a central operator position so that sources can be discriminated.

Voice communications controls should include the following: a *volume* control with a minimum value that is still audible; a *power* switch (often integrated with volume on commercial equipment, but preferably separated on military equipment); a *squelch* control to suppress channel noise during no-signal periods; and a *speaker/side tone* circuitry that permits hearing one's own voice unmodified. Foot-operated talk-listen controls are recommended for operators using both hands; however, backup hand-operated controls are required for emergency use and when the operator moves to another position [12].

Binaural Intelligibility Enhancement Finally, the transmission system may be modified by providing for dual-channel listening over headphones. At a crowded cocktail party, how is one able to follow the voice of one person with so many competing background voices, some even louder than the person's of interest? One explanation is in terms of binaural listening capabilities. Looking directly at the person, we see the lips moving and the target voice arrives at each ear at the same approximate time, while other voices arrive at the two ears at different times.

Rappaport [33] investigated listening over headphones to taped messages with one, three, five, and seven different voices speaking simultaneously. In each instance the first voice was *diotic* (presented by dual channels to each earphone simultaneously). The other two to six voices were *dichotic* (presented in one earphone only; half the voices in each earphone).

Rather than a confusing babbling of voices, Rappaport found an almost constant 94 percent intelligibility for the diotic voice even with seven voices talking at once! A control condition with all voices presented in each earphone (all diotic) resulted in less than 40 percent intelligibility with three voices and less than 20 percent intelligibility with seven voices.

Spatial localization of the diotic or stereophonic voice was the explanation offered. The diotic voice appears localized in the center of the head while the dichotic voices are perceived as off to one side or the other. Rappaport discounted the possibility of binaural summation (increased loudness of the diotic voice) or voice quality differences as major contributors to the improved intelligibility.

There are several practical applications of the dual-channel method. An air traffic controller listening diotically would be aware of, but not be interfered by, a second voice intruding over the headphone. In many applications the critical information could be reserved for diotic messages, thus insuring their priority. Enemy eavesdroppers listening monaurally to the multiple voices would hear only a babbling of unintelligible voices. During enemy attempts at jamming voice communications, the diotic voice should be more highly correlated than the noise, noted Rappaport. Speech enhancement, like signal enhancement, could be significantly improved by binaural methods if it were electronically possible to separate the noise from the speech.

Modifying the Message

Systems designers usually have control of the design of the messages transmitted by voice over the communication system. Attention to the selection of words and their phonetic composition may greatly enhance the listeners' understanding of the message.

At least five language factors influence speech intelligibility: word familiarity, word length, sentence structure, vocabulary size, and phonetic composition of words (see also Chapters 3 and 10).

Word Familiarity Thorndike and Lorge [40] have documented the frequency of use of 30,000 words in the English language. Howes [19] found that words frequently used in everyday language are more intelligible in a high-noise environment than infrequently used words.

A legal secretary listening over a dictaphone may have little difficulty in understanding the jargon, whereas a novice could well be confused by poorly enunciated legal terminology. Similarly, operators who use technical language in their work are more likely to interpret correctly technical words. Frequency count data is not available in most professions or trades, but surveys may be taken to determine word familiarity.

Kryter [22] also noted that a priori knowledge of situational constraints enhances intelligibility. A pilot approaching a control tower anticipates hearing landing instructions and already knows the arrangement of the air field, wind conditions, and time of day. As discussed in Chapter 10, regarding route following instructions, the human also filters the information to take in only certain key information.

Word Length Although common words are typically shorter words, Howes [19] found that longer words are more intelligible in high-noise fields (Figure 12-7). Recall that negative S/N ratios mean better intelligibility, so longer words and frequently used words are more intelligible in intense noise.

This apparent contradiction is clarified by considering language redundancy. A short word may be distinguishable from other short words by only a single consonant, as noted for the Modified Rhyme Test. Longer words may be intelligible even if a particular syllable is not completely intelligible. In military operations, the words "affirmative" and "negative" are used instead of "yes" and "no." This is critical binary information that must be transmitted.

Sentence Structure Sometimes a single word (heard or seen) may not be intelligible (or legible), but the same word in the context of a sentence or phrase may be understood. The language is highly redundant, and we fill in missing information.

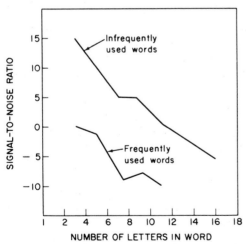

Figure 12-7 The relation between frequency of word use, word length, and speech-to-noise ratio for 50 percent intelligibility. *(Howes, 1957, and in Van Cott and Kinkade, 1972.)*

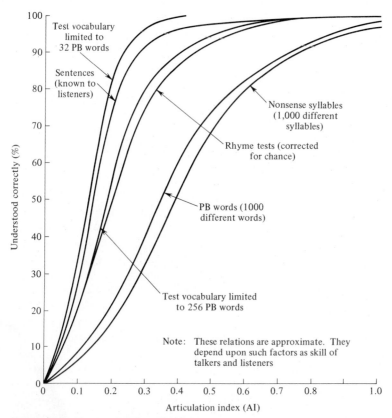

Figure 12-8 The intelligibility of various types of test material expressed in terms of articulation index values. *(Kryter, 1966, and in Van Cott and Kinkade, 1972.)*

Figure 12-8 illustrates this effect. Note, for example, that in listening in a speech system with an AI of only 0.2, 75 percent intelligibility was achieved for sentences, whereas less than 50 percent intelligibility was achieved for lists of words at the same AI value.

Vocabulary Size In general, the fewer the number of words likely to appear in a message, the greater the probability of high intelligibility. Miller, Heise, and Lichten [29] studied vocabularies of 2, 4, 8, 16, 32, and 256 words in S/N ratios ranging from +9 dB to −18 dB. There was an inverse relationship between percent of words understood and vocabulary size in all S/N ratios. Intelligibility was, of course, much poorer in negative S/N values and did not exceed chance probability when there were only two word possibilities at −18 S/N. When speech recognition devices are discussed subsequently, we shall see that limiting the vocabulary is also important for machines to discriminate words and phonemes.

Parenthetically, Miller et al. [29] also investigated unselected monosyllables and found they yielded the poorest performance of all in a noise field. This would be expected from the discussion of word length earlier. Also, nonsense syllables and unpatterned numerals are difficult to discriminate because predictability based on sequential dependencies is lacking.

In operational settings the same limited set of words should be used (rather than employing synonyms). Also, the sentence structure and language style of the message should be consistent.

Phonetic Composition   Miller and Nicely [30] studied the intelligibility of each phoneme when masked in random noise at progressively lower S/N ratios down to −18 dB. At −18 dB S/N ratio, all consonants were confused. At −12-dB S/N the voiced consonants were discriminable as a group from the unvoiced consonants, but they could not be distinguished within each group. Voiced consonants are m, n, d, g, b, v, z, and ʒ (ʒ is the sound *zh* as in "azure"). Unvoiced consonants are t, k, p, s, f, and Θ (Θ is the sound *th* as in "thin").

As the S/N ratios were increased to positive values, the consonants became progressively discriminable from one another until at +12-dB S/N ratio, all consonants could be discriminated from each other. However, it was noted in discussion of the AI that +30 was desirable for excellent transmission.

The development of such a "tree of confusion" (with a trunk of complete confusion and branches of successive consonants being discriminable) has application to message design. First, if feasible, one should avoid the use of words discriminable by only a single weak consonant. For example, among the last consonants to become discriminable (at positive S/N ratios) are *b* and *v*, *d* and *g*, *f* and Θ. Second, it may be necessary to spell out the word, character by character, using the International Word-spelling Alphabet (Alpha, Bravo, Charlie, and so on.) The words in this alphabet have been carefully chosen such that no two words sound alike.

Message and Operational Design Criteria

Table 12-4 summarizes techniques for message design and also lists a few operational procedures to enhance speech intelligibility in noise.

For military systems where very critical information is being transmitted, a priority of messages should be established in advance. Critical messages should override those of lower priority, and remaining messages should continue to follow in order of priority [MIL-STD-1472B, 12]. Messages should be repeated with no more than a 3-second pause between cycles. An initial (nonverbal) alerting signal is recommended to attract operator attention and prepare him or her to listen. Standard codes such as "Mayday" are employed. Emergency vehicle operators and citizen-band radio operators have also developed standard languages for communicating with one another. Other characteristics of effective verbal messages were discussed in Chapter 10.

Table 12-4   Techniques for Increasing Message Intelligibility in High Noise

Language factors

- Use words familiar to the user in the operational context.
- Employ a brief, standardized vocabulary.
- Embed critical words in phrases and sentences. Use the same sentence format so that words can be anticipated.
- Where applicable, use longer words that are understood.
- Avoid similar sounding words if practical.
- Use the International Word-Spelling Alphabet.

Operating procedure

- Repeat the message several times until acknowledged.
- Ask the listener to repeat the message and correct any errors.
- Select trained speakers without dialect who enunciate distinctly, stressing or increasing the intensity of weak consonants. Speakers should modulate their voices and talk in a mature, formal, impersonal, and calm manner.
- Train listeners in the vocabulary and sentence structure of messages and in operating procedures.

SPEECH SYNTHESIS, RECOGNITION, AND COMPUTER PROCESSING

Modern society is in the market for machines one can talk to (and which can talk back) to replace the artificial, inflexible computer language and input keyboard. Voice communications are also more efficient. Chapanis [6] and colleagues have shown that when two people work together to solve a problem, they work twice as fast when communicating by speech as when communicating by other means such as typing, handwriting, or visual signals. Hence, speech as a control input would be useful. Modern society is also in the market for a device capable of speaking complete sentences not previously recorded in sentence structure. From keyboard inputs, the device would speak any message desired rather than producing a printed message.

There are, then, two major aspects of speech processing systems: voice synthesis and voice recognition. Voice synthesizers are devices in which voice tracks may be generated from operator inputs and later be used for a variety of applications. Voice recognition devices permit the human to communicate directly with machines using the voice as a control input source. The human voice replaces the keyboard or other control device.

A variety of specific applications will be discussed subsequently. Speech recognition is technically the more difficult problem. Ultimately, the two processing systems may be combined so that the human can talk to the machine and the machine can talk back.

Voice Synthesizers—Machines that Speak

Voice synthesizers are not simply reproductions of prerecorded speech. If so, their capacity would be limited. Synthesizers actually generate speech by combining phonemes that make up the spoken language.

Voice synthesizers vary from large black boxes to small portable units that resemble hand-held calculators. The user builds voice messages by entering a series of commands from the device's keyboard. Digit combinations correspond to words produced by the machine. The commands are stored until the talk button is pressed. The commands are then fed to a phoneme synthesizer, an electronic analog of the human vocal system, which then articulates the sound through a loudspeaker.

The synthesizer has an almost unlimited vocabulary since it stores all the phonemes used in making words in the language. Some systems reduce the vocabulary slightly for economy by eliminating phonemes not in the English language and some intonation patterns.

An example of a voice synthesizer is the Phonic Mirror Handivoice (*Electronics*, 14). It not only stores synthesizer commands necessary to pronounce 45 phonemes, but also its memory is programmed with coded commands for 893 common words, all 26 letters of the alphabet, 13 word prefixes and suffixes, and 16 short phrases. Thus, the user does not need to start from scratch in building commands.

Applications of Voice Synthesizers   A potential application of small portable units is for those vocally impaired with cerebral palsy, multiple sclerosis, nervous disorders, or those who are mute. The hand-held unit produces up to four words at a time via three-digit codes. A larger lap-sized unit has 128 touch-sensitive keypads corresponding to specific words or graphic symbols. For those without any use of their hands, breath- and muscle-actuated switches are available [14].

The voice synthesizer was originally developed for industrial applications such as inventory control, personnel training, and voice-output computer systems. Although relieving the eyes of time-delaying scanning in such tasks, the voice output also has an obvious application for those who cannot see well or cannot see at all.

Since many books are not in Braille, a useful invention would be a reading machine that could scan printed material and either spell the words out by character or, preferably, pronounce the words directly. The Kurswell Reading Machine [Robinson, 34] actually pronounces words in proper sentence format from printed text. This and other devices for the blind are discussed in Chapter 13.

There are voice synthesizers on the market today that may be attached to computer terminals and provide an integrated voice track. The terminal keyboard is used to build voice messages. This capability has an application to computer-assisted instruction, which will be discussed subsequently. Wiggins estimated that by the mid-1980s every manufactured computer would have the capability to speak [42].

Children's Learning Aids   Speak and Spell was a child's learning aid introduced by Texas Instruments as a 1978 Christmas toy. It received the attention of the microelectronic community because it offered at a retail price of $50 a simple speech synthesizer. The device appeared to be a portable cassette-tape recorder that asked the child in a natural sounding voice to spell a specific word. The child spelled the word using a keyboard of letters and the machine voice congratulated the speller for a correct answer or encouraged another try after an incorrect answer [Robinson, 35].

The voice was not simply a playback of a previously taped voice, as with traditional talking dolls. Phonemes comprising the vocabulary were, of course, generated from high-quality tape recordings, and these recordings were subsequently digitized at an 8-kHz sample rate. Computer programs then analyzed the pitch and energy contours of the original speech and found the vocal tract parameters that matched the spectral shape of synthetic speech to the original. Each parameter was then coded, processed, and the voice output was hand-edited by listeners [Robinson, 35]. A microprocessor controlled the selection of words and determined the correctness of the answer.

The intriguing aspect of Speak and Spell was that two tiny memory chips, employing a technique called "linear predictive coding" (LPC), permitted the storage of much more speech than a digitized version. Up to 16 chips (TMC-0350) may be used in a single system. This would store 2 million bits that at 1200 bits per sec would offer about 30 min of speech and a vocabulary of over 2500 words. The speech signal-processing circuitry used in the learning aid was similar to that used in more sophisticated processing devices [35].

The upshot of miniaturization was that a single semiconductor chip used in the Speak and Spell and ultradense computer memory chips could store tens of thousands of binary bits which previously required a roomful of electronics. The result was a synthesizer within the means of the buying public.

The teaching of spelling is only one of many potential applications. Talking learning aids may ask a variety of questions in geography and history, employing key phrases such as "What is the capital of . . . ?" "When was the . . . ?" Computer-aided instruction is an application of the technology. Other applications are verbal warning devices on aircraft and automobiles and, as previously noted, aids to the linguistic and visually impaired, manufacturing, entertainment, and toys [Shafer, 37].

Vocoders   Digital electronics is developing new ways to compress voice signals for efficiency in telephone line transmission. A microelectronic circuit manufacturer has developed a device called "codec," which will convert telephone signals (analog speech) into digital form much like the vocoder developed by Bell Laboratories in the 1950s. The vocoder also compressed the speech, permitting the transmission of more binary bits per second when a message was sent. This permitted the same transmission line to carry more messages [Robinson, 35].

Speech Recognition Devices—Machines That Listen

A need has long existed for a device that could recognize acoustical wave patterns as being specific words in the language. The spoken commands could then serve as a system input in the same fashion as the many controls discussed in Chapter 4. Certain applications would increase systems efficiency by eliminating unnecessary manual activities. Other applications are to situations where the hands are not available or useful.

Applications of Speech Recognition Devices   The potential market for such devices is staggering. An application mentioned earlier was the replacement of the keyboard terminal or other input devices to computers. Home appliances could also be voice-actuated. Typewriters could receive inputs directly from the human voice. Voice-actuated environmental control systems and telephone dialers are also potential applications.

Speech recognition devices have application to sorting and inspection tasks, such as at bulk mail distribution centers. Already in operation is a device for control of access to restricted areas or central computer facilities [35]. The computer determines the validity of the number spoken and then compares the vocal pattern with a stored voice pattern of the speaker (much like inspection of fingerprints or photographs of the face).

Applications to telephone communications are obvious. Telephone directory assistance could be automated. Financial transactions could be given over the telephone again after verifying the voice of the speaker.

Applications in the domain of surface transportation are being pursued. Voice-actuated wheelchairs, sensitive only to the voice of the user, are currently in use. Automobile controls using a limited vocabulary could also be voice-actuated [Workshop on Voice Technology, 32]. Up to five words in a series could be recognized and converted to a signal to actuate or adjust a control. For example, "Increase speed to 5-5." However, inadvertent control actuation could be a serious problem.

Combining voice recognition and voice synthesis is an obvious next step. One could verbally interrogate a computer and receive feedback on the status of engine instruments or any other stored data on a vehicle [Wiggins, 42].

There are several applications to industry today. Voice programming of numerical control devices reduces error since commands are displayed for verification before initiation [Martin, 25]. In quality control, color television faceplates are inspected in the Owens-Illinois Company and voice inputs (measurements) are compared with established specifications to decide if the product should be accepted or rejected. Tecumseh Products Company uses direct data entry via speech at a receiving inspection station, thereby reducing errors in product writeup and response time [Martin, 25]. Voice response has also been used to instruct wiring in electronic assembly and telephone installation wiring [Flanagan, 15].

In December 1977, a workshop was held at NASA Ames Research Center, sponsored jointly by NASA, Naval Training Equipment Center (NTEC), and Naval Air Development Center (NADC). The topic was "Voice Technology for Interactive Real-Time Command System Applications" [32]. Breaux [32] emphasized the need for an automated training system for ground control approach (GCA) controllers of aircraft since two instructors are currently required for each trainee. Individualized instruction employing speech recognition devices was recommended to conserve manpower in training. Hence, air traffic and training simulators are application areas.

Another major application area in voice-interactive systems technology is in situations where voice entry would be an attractive alternative to keyboards or other control devices in aeronautical flight management. The cockpit is reaching a saturation point so far as reserving panel space for each parameter of information, and some information is needed only occasionally. Information could be shared on a computer-terminal display. Rather than keyboard or other techniques for inputing the desired information, voice-actuation is a possibility.

Another voice application is to situations where controls are inaccessible because of seat orientation. Under high G forces the seat of a new combat fighter could be tilted back 60 degrees, but this would make panel controls inaccessible to the pilot. A voice recognition system would permit voice activation of controls up to extremely high G forces before voice quality degrades [Curran, 10].

Constraints to Speech Recognition Devices   Speech recognition by machines is a formidable task only partially conquered by 1980. For at least 25 years scientists have been studying spectrograms of human speech (energy is speech waves visually displayed in terms of frequency, intensity, and time). It would seem plausible that each word should have a unique acoustic wave pattern and, if so, word recognition should be a simple matter of the machine's scanning the pattern, comparing the sample pattern with a data bank of reference voice patterns, and deciding which word was spoken. Once recognized, the data could input any number of systems.

Unfortunately, human variability messes up this simplistic approach. Word patterns are stable only over periods of about 10 milliseconds [Robinson, 35]. Frequency and amplitude of the voice pattern vary constantly. The sequence of patterns depends upon where the word appears in a sentence and the sounds in the following and previous words. Imagine a machine trying to decide if the message were "gray tie is" or "great eye is"! [35].

There are also differences in how people pronounce and enunciate words, and even the individual's speech will differ when one has a head cold or is in an emotional state. Finally, there are tens of thousands of words in the language (and only 40 or 50 phonemes), so the computer memory would need to be vast to match the phoneme sound patterns to words in an unlimited vocabulary.

Isolated Word-Recognition Devices   Despite these problems a rudimentary technology of word recognition exists and is in use today. Recognizing individual words is a less formidable task than recognizing a string of sounds representing a series of words in sentences. Sentences require that the computer be programmed to understand the basic rules of grammar, syntax, and semantics. Linguists and psychologists working in the area of *artificial intelligence* are tackling the problem of incorporating this knowledge into computers with reportedly somewhat limited success [Robinson, 35]. We know that well-defined pauses between words assist the machine in recognizing individual words.

Isolated word-recognition machines are on the market today, but the more accurate ones are still beyond the means of most of us. The major computer manufacturers in the United States are working on word-recognition equipment as is Japan's largest electronic company, Nippon Electronic Company (NEC) [Robinson, 35].

Rather than trying to recognize word patterns point for point (which is also confounded by differences in the duration of spoken words), the technique employed in word-recognition machines is *statistical pattern recognition* between sets of parameters from a sample and the reference speech pattern. A technique invented by Bell Laboratories and called linear predictive coding (LPC) employs statistical pattern recognition. It is based upon a model of the human vocal tract and includes fundamental speech frequencies, intensities, and numbers specifying a cross-sectional area of the human speech-producing tube. Each 10 milliseconds of speech sample is analyzed by several complex techniques.

By limiting the vocabulary to 100 words, an identification accuracy of 98 to 99 percent has been achieved in the laboratory, but only 50 percent in the field [Robinson, 35]. The machine asks for a repeat of the message when it cannot make an identification. Other factors interfering with identification are background noise, inconsistent microphone placement, insufficient training, inconsistent speaking style, and lack of user cooperation.

"Training" in this context refers to the person repeating each word in the vocabulary 5 to 10 times so the machine can generate a reference pattern. The user must speak the same way each time. Workers who distrust a word-recognition device may later inadvertently change their way of speaking and claim the machine could not understand them.

Devices for Public Use   Before the public in general could use such a device, additional research is needed to find universal speech characteristics. Once trained with one or a few speakers, ideally the word recognizer should be able to recognize everyone. *Speaker-independent* machines have application to automated telephone directory assistance, hence, the continuing interest by Bell Laboratories. Fifty men and 50 women were classified into a set of 6 to 12 groups. Persons within each group had sufficiently similar speech patterns so that the word recognizer could identify speech without having previously been given samples of the individual's voice for reference [Robinson, 35]. So some progress is being made in developing a device for the general public. However, at present the person asking for telephone directory assistance must spell out the person's name character by character.

Continuous Word Recognition in Natural Speech   The big challenge ahead lies in the recognition of continuous or connected speech, even without extensive use of artifical intelligence-related techniques. If each word must be spoken in a rigid, exacting manner or spelled out by character, the efficiency of the system over keyboard entry is reduced.

The Japanese NEC has introduced in the United States a continuous speech-recognition system suitable for a vocabulary of up to 120 words. Ninety-eight percent accuracy is claimed after only one training pass (two passes for those pesky digits 0 through 9). Any passage of five vocabulary words not exceeding 2.5 seconds may be processed in a fraction of a second. The cost of the machine in 1979 was $67,000 to $78,000 [35]. However, there is a potential market for continuous speech devices in processing mail at postal distribution centers.

A major problem noted previously is that in talking naturally, people tend to run words together without pauses. Rather than demanding an unnatural speech from the public, another approach is to use dynamic programming techniques to seek the boundaries of words. No pause between individual words would then be required. The computational process is complex, but with limited vocabularies continuous speech-recognition devices will become practical. Some feel that the greatest drawback to real-time voice recognition is the limited vocabulary size. There is also an interest in spotting key words that may appear in unrestricted, continuous speech.

TELECOMMUNICATIONS AND OTHER VOICE COMMUNICATIONS

The telephone introduces a number of human factors issues. The keyboard is discussed in Chapter 14 with other data entry devices. Recently, teleconferences have become more popular. Long-distance communications also incur a problem of user protection that will be discussed in terms of ways of preventing unsuspected financial losses. Voice communications is also one of several modes of communication with a computer, as we have seen, and research in the area of effective ways of working with a partner in solving problems has revealed some interesting data.

Teleconferences

It is feasible for a group of people to be connected by telephone conference lines and for video of the participants to be included if desired. With such capabilities one might ask why it would be necessary for salespeople or business executives to take the additional time to fly across the continent for face-to-face communications.

In 1975 there were certain reservations regarding teleconferencing as a complete substitute for personal contact. A survey [Christie and Hollaway, 9] found that telephones were regarded by users as better for asking questions, discussion, and problem solving, but travel was still much preferred for bargaining and negotiating. Travel was used three times as often as the telephone with strangers, but the telephone was used equally often with acquaintances. Although there is a hardcore group who would not change their travel habits regardless of comparative costs, in general, most people surveyed tended to use telephones more often as travel time increased from one-half hour to 4 hours [9]. Duncanson and Williams [13] found 90 percent of the users of a video conference facility stated they would use it rather than travel 50 miles or 1½ hours.

Klemmer [21] summarized the value of teleconferences with video cameras in four conclusions:

1 Seeing the other person is of real but limited value, that is, many *wanted* to see the other, but it was of little practical use.
2 If video is used the resolution should be able to handle printed material.
3 Hard copy may be desirable.
4 Color, stereo, and hi-fi are not important to the users.

These statements were made in 1973 and may be subject to changing viewpoints. However, electronic conferencing requires a change in attitude from the traditional, and the side-benefits of the boondoggle must be considered in addition to the technical benefits of face-to-face communications.

User Protection

Long-distance telephone communications are both faster and cheaper than comparable transportation modes, and certainly real-time information is essential for business activities, stock market transactions, and private emergency calls. A major technical limitation has been that the dialer's identity is unknown to the receiver, the phone company, and the person who signed an agreement to pay the service charges (hereafter called the purchaser).

From the receiver's standpoint, there is the danger of harrassment, obscenities, and repeated calls with no message leading the receiver to an unlisted number or taking the phone off the hook.

From the purchaser's standpoint, financial liability for any long distance calls placed from the number can result in a major setback for those of modest means. It is quite possible for a teenager from an extension line to place numerous calls during a month to a friend now living a great distance away and to talk for over an hour each time. The purchaser, an unsuspecting parent, may be liable for a bill of several thousands of dollars. One telephone company reported it was not permitted to notify the purchaser until the end of the month and, actually, the bill may not be received until the middle of the following month. During the 6-week period 100 or more calls could have been placed from the confines of a minor's private room.

To protect the purchaser, a system of feedback is necessary. One would unlikely sign a credit card purchase for thousands of dollars, yet the purchaser may be totally unaware of the extent of the indebtedness until long after the services have been rendered. Children may be disciplined, but only after the financial loss is known.

What human factors steps could be taken to protect the purchaser (short of disconnecting the phone, which may be necessary for other reasons)?:

1   To ensure that the purchaser wishes for the call to be placed, an identity card could be inserted in the unit, much like the system used to check credit cards for installment purchases. Only adult users would be issued the cards so that children with their own telephones would be unable to make long-distance calls without access to the card. (A company record of the code number of the dialer would also aid in curbing crank calls.)

2   A stopgap solution would be an automatic recording that interrupted the conversation whenever the call exceeded some dollar cost and announced: "Your call cost is now ten dollars." Reading the toll charges in a telephone directory is insufficient since many do not bother to do this, or even if they do, they may be unaware of the length of their conversation.

3   Whenever a phone bill, cumulated each month in real-time, exceeded previous monthly phone bills from the number by two or three times, the local phone company would have this information and would call the purchaser for verification. With prior purchaser consent they would disallow further long-distance calls pending verification. This solution would be applicable to a large number of calls, each of nominal cost.

4   The purchasers could sign an agreement when the phone was installed that they would not be responsible for any long-distance calls exceeding X minutes or Y dollars. The company would then be responsible for monitoring the cost to a purchaser of long-distance calls.

Until positive safeguards are developed and implemented, the purchaser will remain liable, which may result in embarrassing debts and poor public relations between the company and their customers.

Interactive Communications and Problem Solving

A discussion of person-computer interaction will be presented in Chapter 14. Interaction, in this context, refers to the quality of on-line person-computer systems wherein the partners cooperate in solving problems by each reinforcing and extending the immediately preceding actions of the other. Voice is an important mode of interactive communications.

Chapanis [7, 8] and colleagues at Johns Hopkins University have conducted a series of studies on interactive communications. People are beginning to communicate with computers in natural language, but little research had previously addressed issues such as the most efficient modes of communications (voice, typewriter) or how people communicate in solving problems. Ultimately, the objective would be design specifications for efficient communication methods with a source of information such as a computer. In the interactive studies there is a *seeker*, a person designated the task of solving problems, and a *source*, a person in an adjacent, soundproofed room who has a folio of information (much like a computer). Collectively, the two have the information necessary to solve the problem.

The series of studies dealt with variables affecting the effectiveness of the partners in solving the problems. Some problems were cooperative, such as how to wire a digital logic panel or how to schedule four college courses with certain constraints. Other problems were conflictive; the two persons would argue and discuss issues such as ranking national issues or deciding how to cut the university's athletic budget.

The early studies dealt with comparisons of time to solve problems when using communications such as typewriting, handwriting, and voice. Not only were the problems solved significantly faster with a voice channel, but also conditions with voice in combination with typing, handwriting, and TV communications were all significantly faster than other combinations that did not include voice [Chapanis et al, 8].

Other interesting findings were:

1 Subjects could arrive at a concensus agreement as quickly when communicating by voice only as they could with voice and face-to-face communications.

2 Skill in typing did not significantly decrease problem-solving time. Only one-third of total task time was spent in sending; the other two-thirds was involved with receiving, searching, and waiting.

3 Voice communications involved use of more words than handwriting or typing. Face-to-face communications were wordier still than voice only.

4 When the seeker had a voice channel, he or she employed more words than when typing; when only the source had a voice channel, he or she was more verbose. Number of words used depended on the availability of a voice channel rather than whether one was a seeker or a source.

What if the communicators have the freedom to interrupt their partner? The subjects sent significantly more messages, but the messages tended to be more concise than when they were restricted from interrupting until the partner had finished talking. Communicators were more likely to press a button seeking control of the system when a voice channel was available, as opposed to typing or other modes.

The type of task also influences the percent of time spent communicating. When the task involved argumentation or opinion exchange, as much as 75 percent of total time was spent communicating (as opposed to taking notes or searching for information). When the task involved exchange of factual information only, about 50 percent of the time was spent communicating. Regardless of whether high school or college educated, the subjects spent about the same proportion of time with various activities.

TRAINING DEVICES

Human factors, in its broader sense, is concerned with education and training of systems personnel. It is beyond the scope of this design-oriented text to attempt to do justice to a discussion of the conditions enhancing learning or transfer of training or to techniques for evaluating training effectiveness. However, a brief discussion of the design of training devices would be in scope.

Training devices may be broadly classified into training aids and training equipment [Kinkade and Wheaton, 20]. Training aids include films, slides, TV, graphic material (flow charts), and well-organized written material for lectures and demonstrations. Training equipment consists of part-task trainers, whole-task trainers, and simulators.

The type of training device that is appropriate depends largely on the stage of training. During initial *indoctrination,* training aids and static mockups are usually sufficient. *Procedural training* teaches systems nomenclature and step-by-step activities. Functional mockups, photographs, and drawings are generally used. For the next stage, *familiarization training,* the equipment should be functional; part-task trainers are necessary for practice. Finally, for *skill training,* it is important to have closed-loop control dynamics. Aircraft simulators, driver trainers, and radar-tracking simulators are examples of devices. On-the-job training is employed in industry with employees working in the actual job situation with supervision.

Fidelity of Simulation

One of the objectives of the series of training devices is to cut down on the total training time and expense of employing a skills trainer or the real system. In driver education, as with more complex system training, it is not generally safe to start with controlling the real vehicle. Originally it was thought that a high-fidelity simulator was essential for practice and to sustain motivation. However, practice in lower-fidelity flight trainers has resulted in a 50 percent savings in flight hours [Kinkade and Wheaton, 20].

Kinkade and Wheaton distinguish between equipment fidelity, environmental fidelity, and psychological fidelity. *Equipment* fidelity refers to the degree to which the simulator dynamics duplicate the appearance and feel of the operational equipment. A driver simulator with equipment fidelity would be an automobile cab with steering wheel feedback dynamics, moving instrumentation, and so forth. *Environmental* fidelity refers to the degree the system simulates sensory stimulation outside, for example, a 3-D display of the roadway, sky, and trees moving by. *Psychological* fidelity refers to the degree that the equipment is perceived by the trainee as duplicating operational equipment and the task situation. Trainees may overlook minor deviations from the actual equipment. Hence, high psychological fidelity may be achieved with fairly low environmental fidelity.

Buckout et al. [3] found that simulated motion during the learning of high-speed, low-altitude aircraft flight training contributed significantly to learning tracking skills, but contributed little to learning procedural tasks. Equipment and environmental fidelity are much more important in skill training than procedural training or familiarization. Providing high fidelity (such as motion cues) may double or even triple the total cost of the device and the training system manager should consider the trade-off between the added expense and the benefit in terms of transfer of training to the operational task.

Adaptive Training

Adaptive training refers to a range of training situations in which the training material is varied depending upon the trainee's current state of knowledge or skill, training goals, or background. School children receive more individualized instruction by attending learning centers where they work on material at their own pace, rather than being held to the classroom norms.

Programmed instruction and teaching machines are self-instructional techniques that are based upon adaptive training principles. Training objectives are defined in advance and are implemented in the design of the material. (These are knowledges and skills needed on the particular job.) The trainee proceeds at his or her own pace so the task is neither too difficult nor too easy. The trainee is actively responding to questions, and errors are identified immediately so that the correct response is made and reinforced. The trainee gradually progresses, in graded steps, from simple to more difficult material.

Programmed instruction may involve using a text or booklet. Branching programs are included in the booklet so that the trainees may proceed through the material along different routes, again based on their individual ability and rates of learning. Additional training is directed in topic areas for which one has limited knowledge, whereas the trainee who demonstrates knowledge of the material may proceed to more advanced material. Programmed instruction in industry has been estimated to reduce total training time by one-third [Ross, 36].

Most of us are familiar with the teaching machines popularized by B. F. Skinner [38], which are based on the same principles outlined above for programmed instruction. The trainee views a series of frames, makes an active response by a control movement, and receives immediate feedback of the correctness of the answer. Like the programmed text, branching to other frames is provided for those who have not mastered the material.

Computed-assisted instruction (CAI) allows the digital computer program to handle the reinforcement and branching activities. The trainee sits at a terminal and inputs answers to displayed questions. Again, the computer assigns additional material based on the quality of answers. CAI is expensive and can be no more effective than the instructional strategies programmed into it.

In summary, adaptive instruction principles may be applied to various training techniques varying from programmed text booklets, to individualized instruction on conventional training systems or teaching machines, to sophisticated computer-assisted devices (see Chapter 14).

Adaptive training procedures have also been applied to closed-loop tracking simulators. An objective is to adjust the systems control dynamics to the trainee's level of skill, that is, to simplify the systems dynamics to a level that an errorless performance is achieved and to progressively increase the difficulty of systems dynamics as proficiency improves.

Hand Calculators

Hundreds of studies have been conducted on the uses of hand-held, four-function, and programmable calculators for students at all educational levels [Calculator Information Center, 4]. The studies deal almost exclusively with the effectiveness of the devices as compared with paper and pencil, slide rule, and other methods. Educators are concerned with the effect of calculator use on improvements in computational skills, promoting achievement, and improving attitudes toward mathematics and academic work. Disadvantages alleged are that the calculator, as a substitute for conventional computations, may encourage laziness and emphasize answers rather than operations. Also, it may not be available to all students and may possibly encourage copying answers. Most research [4] has found little or no detrimental effects in terms of adverse attitudes or retarding the learning of math. Understanding concepts is more important than performing calculations. The calculator exists and will be used later so its proper use should be taught in schools.

Despite the immense amount of literature on the pros and cons of using calculators and on developing workbooks and self-instructional material for calculators, very little human factors research has been conducted on the design of the keyboard, displays, and instructional material except by the manufacturer's in-house and often proprietary research.

For the blind user, there are talking calculators, keyboards with braille, and cassette instructional manuals [Champion, 5].

Children's Mathematical Learning Aids

Several mathematical learning aids have come on the market in recent years, among them Quiz Kid, Monkey See, Little Professor, and Dataman. These hand-held devices may at first glimpse appear to be small calculators, since they have a keyboard of numbers, four functions, and other push buttons. Actually, they are learning aids like electronic flash cards or an ever-present teacher. They are not conventional calculators because they do not initially provide a display of the answer to the equation fed in on the keyboard. Rather they are designed to provide feedback to the user regarding the correctness of an answer given by the user. Learning aids vary considerably in cost and functional capability, but a high correlation between cost and enjoyment was not evident [Mason, 26].

The Quiz Kid and Monkey See are very similar in function and are shaped like a facsimile of an owl or a monkey. Green lights in the eyes signal a correct answer while red flashing eyes signify an error. The child performs six steps: keying a number, a function, another number, an equal sign, an answer, and a question mark. After the light feedback, the Clear button is pressed. The child is not given the answer, but rather he or she must perform the calculation in the head or on paper. Also, as pointed out by Mason [26] there is no feedback that

Figure 12-9 Children's learning aids. *(Courtesy of Texas Instruments, Inc.)*

the intended control buttons were actuated correctly. Mason recommended the addition of a display readout; however, she also noted that the devices were designed for economy, and they are popular with the children.

Mason also recommended a slight rearrangement of the keyboard with the Clear, ?, and = control buttons on the bottom row coded by the color blue, and the function buttons, which are in the right-hand column, coded in yellow to distinguish them from the numbers. Shape coding was another option. Mason also raised the issue of whether the 3 X 3 numeric keyboard should be inverted (as is traditional on calculators) or should be arrayed with the 1 - 2 - 3 on the top row, as is current practice on telephone keyboards and other devices. Research in this area will be discussed in Chapter 14.

Mason also recommended that the zero and decimal point be on the top row. By tradition, the zero has been on the bottom row; however, she noted that children are taught that the zero precedes the one, and with a top to bottom numeric keyboard arrangement, the zero should go at the top. Finally, the on/off switch should be moved to the top center of the device (above the eyes), where it is out of the way. Instructional material could be clarified with an example of the sequence of operations using shape-coded circles, squares, and hexagons corresponding to the three types of functions. However, she noted that fourth-grade children enjoyed playing the various games provided in the book and had little trouble operating the aid.

The Little Professor provides an additional capability of four levels of problems (10 problems per level). One may select the function and level. When the go button is pressed, a sequence of 10 problems are given and again, the child provides the answer to each. A major difference from less expensive aids is that there is a horizontal readout display at top which displays both numbers and function (for example, 10 X 3 =). If the answer given is incorrect, a series of three Es is displayed. If an incorrect answer is given three times, the correct answer is displayed.

Mason [26] noted that in school we are taught in addition, subtraction, and multiplication to place the equation in a vertical orientation. She recommended that the upright readout be arrayed vertically on the left-hand side of the box. The function (+, −, or ×) should be on the same row as the second number and a line should be below it.[1] Also, we are taught to enter the right-hand digit first, and entry of the answer should follow this algorithm.

According to Mason, the control buttons (on, set, level, and go) should be located in a row in the sequence of use. The display readout should not be so deep in the cutout that simultaneous vision of the display is difficult for an adult or other children using the device to play games.

Dataman is similar to the Little Professor except that it permits the child to feed in any equation and, in addition, it has a memory bank to store problems that have given difficulty and to play them back for practice. Another major feature is a series of five mathematical games that are fun for one or several children. A readout may provide the number of right answers, the number of problems tried, and the total times taken to complete them. The user is given two tries to get the right answer. Game buttons are coded by shape, as a class, and by both legend and symbolic codes on the buttons. Mason recommended that games for one player and those for more than one player be on separate rows. Several other arrangement recommendations were made based on sequence of use and recommendations for color and shape coding of classes of operations.

Dataman is intended for users as young as 7 years old, and it is important that the instruction manual (intended for the child to read) be appropriately illustrated and written for understanding by this age group. An alternative recommendation was that the parent work with the child in learning operations. Instruction booklets can be lost, so a shortened version could be provided on a flip-out cover or on the back of the device.

Sets of preplanned problems for various levels are desirable, based upon the adaptive learning principle of progression in graded steps. Another desirable feature is a flexibility for programming one's own problems or going over only the problems missed. A capability for conversion to a regular calculator also would be desirable.

The design recommendations of Mason were based upon extensive observations of and interviews with children using the devices. The design recommenda-

---

[1]The format of division creates an additional design problem.

tions have not been implemented on prototypes, nor have they been subjected to testing at this time. It is important that the human-machine interfaces be investigated and hopefully standardized for both learning aids and hand-calculators to which children will eventually transfer.

QUESTIONS AND PROBLEMS

1 From your familiarity with various spoken languages, can you recall particular phonemes that are in the English language but not in some other language?
2 Calculate the articulation index for the following data using the one-third octave band method (Figure 12-1). Evaluate in words the acceptability of a speech system with the AI value (Table 12-3).

Center freq.	Speech–Noise	Cntr. freq.	S–N	Cntr. freq.	S–N
200	0	630	32	2000	26
250	4	800	40	2500	18
315	10	1000	38	3150	12
400	18	1250	31	4000	6
500	24	1600	28	5000	2

3 Referring to Figure 12-3, indicate for a listener 16 ft away the voice level required for the following SIL values: 45, 52, 57, 67. Which SIL value would you recommend for workers communicating frequently all day?
4 Did the Rappaport study of binaural listening indicate that a diotic presentation of a group of voices over earphones enhances intelligibility of a particular target voice? Discuss.
5 Howes found that longer words were more intelligible than shorter words in a noise field. However, in the study reported in Chapter 10 for visually displayed words in matrix lights, it was found that longer words with more bulbs out were more often not recognized than shorter words when administered to unfamiliar drivers. How would you explain these apparently conflicting findings?
6 Thomas Edison was said to have invented the "talking machine," which led to the phonograph, high-fi, and tape deck. What capability does a voice synthesizer offer that is different from a synchronized taped voice track incorporated into other devices?
7 Why is it more difficult to develop machines that can translate spoken passages over the telephone from an anonymous caller than it is to recognize individual words from a limited vocabulary?
8 Recap briefly at least five different application areas for a speech recognition device. Think of a different application which would be useful, but which is not mentioned in the text.
9 List five characteristics or principles of programmed instruction or teaching machines. Do not include branching operations or specific techniques employed.
10 What would be one advantage and one disadvantage of designing numeric keyboards for calculators and learning aids with the digits 1 through 9 arrayed in three rows of three numbers top to bottom rather than bottom to top?

REFERENCES

1 Beranek, L. L.: *Acoustic Measurement,* Wiley, New York, 1949.
2 Beranek, L. L. and R. B. Newman: Speech interference levels as criteria for rating background noise in offices, *Journal of the Acoustical Society of America,* vol. 22, 1950, p. 671.
3 Buckout, R., H. Sherman, C. T. Goldsmith, and P. T. Vitale, The effect of variation in motion fidelity during training on simulated low-altitude flight, WADD-TDR-63-108, 1963, Wright Air Development Center, WPAFB, Ohio.
4 Calculator Information Center, Bulletins 7 through 22, 1977-78. 1200 Chambers Road, Columbus, Ohio (contracted with National Institute for Education, Department of Health, Education, and Welfare).
5 Champion, R. R.: Talking calculator used with blind youth, *Education of the visually handicapped,* vol. 8, Winter 1976-77, pp. 102–106.
6 Chapanis, A.: Interactive Human Communications, *Scientific American,* vol. 232, March 1975, pp. 36–42.
7 Chapanis, A.: Interactive Human Communications: Some Lessons Learned from Laboratory Experiments, Johns Hopkins University Technical Report 5, ONR Contract No. N00014-75-C-0131, September 1976.
8 Chapanis, A., R. Ochman, R. Parrish, and G. D. Weeks: Studies in interactive communications, I. The effects of four communications modes on the behavior of teams during cooperative problem solving, *Human Factors,* vol. 14, 1972, pp. 487–509.
9 Christie, B. and S. Hollaway: Factors affecting the use of telecommunications by management, *Journal of Occupational Psychology,* vol. 48, 1975, pp. 3–9.
10 Curran, M.: Voice Integrated Systems. *Proceedings of Voice Technology for Interactive Real-Time Command/Control Systems Applications,* 1977, pp. 123–140.
11 Deatherage, B.: Auditory and Other Forms of Sensory Information Presentation, in H. P. Van Cott and R. G. Kinkade (eds.), *Human Engineering Guide to Equipment Design,* Washington, D.C., U.S. Government Printing Office, 1972, chap. 4.
12 Department of Defense: Mil-Standard-1472B, *Human Engineering Design Criteria for Military Systems, Equipment, and Facilities,* December 1974.
13 Duncanson, J. P. and A. D. Williams: Video conferencing: Reactions of users, *Human Factors,* vol. 15, 1973, pp. 471–485.
14 Electronic voice system generates messages for vocally handicapped, *Electronics,* vol. 50, no. 23, Nov. 10, 1977, pp. 32–35.
15 Flanagan, J. L.: Computers that talk and listen: Man-machine communications by voice, *Proceedings of the IEEE,* vol. 64, 1976, pp. 405–415.
16 Fletcher, H.: *Speech and Hearing in Communications,* D. Van Nostrand Co., New York, 1953.
17 French, N. R. and J. C. Steinberg: Factors governing the intelligibility of speech sounds, *Journal of the Acoustical Society of America,* vol. 19, 1947, pp. 90–119.
18 Hottman, S. B.: Computer speech generation and recognition: Implementations and applications, a report to Industrial Engineering 635, Texas A&M University, May 1979.
19 Howes, D. H.: On the relation between intelligibility and frequency of occurrence of English words, *Journal of the Acoustical Society of America,* 1957, vol. 29, p. 296.

20 Kinkade, R. G. and G. R. Wheaton: "Training Device Design," in H. P. Van Cott and R. G. Kinkade (eds.), *Human Engineering Guide to Equipment Design,* Washington D.C., U.S. Government Printing Office, 1972, chap. 14.

21 Klemmer, E. T.: Interpersonal communication systems: Relevance, credibility, impact, Presidential Address to Division 21, American Psychological Association, Montreal, 1973.

22 Kryter, K. D.: "Speech Communications," in H. P. Van Cott and R. G. Kinkade (eds.), *Human Engineering Guide to Equipment Design,* Washington, D.C., U.S. Government Printing Office, 1972, Chap. 5.

23 Licklider, J. C. R. et al.: The intelligibility of rectangular speech waves, *American Journal of Psychology,* 1948, vol. 61, p. 1.

24 Licklider, J. C. R. and G. A. Miller: "The Perception of Speech," in S. S. Stevens (ed.), *Handbook of Experimental Psychology,* John Wiley, New York, 1951, chap. 26.

25 Martin. T. B.: Practical applications of voice inputs to machines, *Proceedings of the IEEE,* vol. 64, 1976, pp. 487–501.

26 Mason, P.: "Human factors considerations in the design of childrens' mathematical learning aids," a report to Industrial Engineering 631, Texas A&M University, 1979.

27 McCormick, E. J.: *Human Factors in Engineering and Design,* McGraw-Hill, New York, 1976.

28 Miller, G. A.: *Language and Communication,* McGraw-Hill, New York, 1951.

29 Miller, G. A., G. A. Heise, and W. Lichten: The intelligibility of speech as a function of the content of the test materials, *Journal of Experimental Psychology,* vol. 41, 1951, pp. 329–335.

30 Miller, G. A. and P. E. Nicely: An analysis of perceptual confusions among some English consonants, *Journal of the Acoustical Society of America,* vol. 27, 1955, p. 338.

31 Peterson, A. P. G. and E. E. Gross, Jr.: *Handbook of Noise Measurement,* 7th ed., General Radio Co., New Concord, Mass., 1972, p. 38.

32 *Proceedings of a Workshop on Voice Technology for Interactive Real-Time Command/Control Applications,* December 6-8, 1977, Ames Research Center, Moffett Air Force Base, available from R. Breaux, Code N-71, NAVTRAEQUIPCEN, Orlando, Fla. 32813.

33 Rappaport, M.: Increasing voice communication channels using man's binaural listening capacity, *Human Factors,* vol. 7, no. 1, 1965.

34 Robinson, A. L.: Communicating with computers by voice, *Science,* vol. 203, 1979, pp. 734–736.

35 Robinson, A. L.: More people are talking to computers as speech recognition enters the real world, *Science,* vol. 203, Feb. 16, 1979, pp. 634–638.

36 Ross, W. L., Jr.: The industrial market for programmed instruction, in S. Margulies and L. D. Eigen (eds.) *Applied Programmed Instruction,* Wiley, New York, 1961.

37 Shafer, R. W.: "Overview of speech synthesis technology," a paper presented to *Speech Recognition Synthesis,* a 1978 MidCon Professional Program, Dallas, Texas, Dec. 12–14, 1978.

38 Skinner, B. F.: *The Technology of Teaching,* Appleton-Century Crofts, New York, 1968.

39 Sumby, W. H. and I. Pollack: Visual contribution to speech intelligibility in noise, *Journal of the Acoustical Society of America,* vol. 26, 1954, pp. 212–215.

40 Thorndike, E. L. and I. Lorge: *Teachers Word Book of 30,000 Words,* Teachers College, Columbia University, New York, 1944.

41 Webster, J. C.: *Effect of noise on speech intelligibility,* American Speech and Hearing Association, Washington, D.C., ASHA Report No. 4, 1969, pp. 49–73.

42 Wiggins, R. H.: "Low cost speech synthesis," a paper presented to *Speech Recognition Synthesis,* a 1978 MidCon Professional Program, Dallas, Texas, Dec. 12-14, 1978.

Chapter 13

Design
for the Handicapped

We are all handicapped in one way or another. Some of us are too big or too small for an environment designed for the average body. Some are left-handed and are given scissors, classroom desks, and a variety of equipment designed for right-handed people. Some lack the sensory-motor skills to adapt to activities in which they wish to participate.

The topics of this chapter are people who are severely handicapped in a particular way and the human factors technological advancements that reduce the constraining effects of the handicap. Rehabilitation through design and engineering augmentation is much more than a humanitarian goal. By becoming more self-sufficient, the severely handicapped are able to contribute to the nation's productivity and reduce the expense of welfare and individual care.

Some prefer not to use the word "handicap," referring instead to "disability," "impairment," "functional limitation," or "deficiency," or referring to the group as "special" or "exceptional." A person may say "I am blind, but I am not handicapped." There is truth to the statement because the degree of handicap is based largely upon the compensatory ability of the person and the willingness of society to provide alternative capabilities through rehabilitation engineering, facility design, and training.

A classic example of compensation is Helen Keller, a rare combination of blind and deaf in infancy, yet possessing a brilliant mind and indomitable courage to overcome the handicap. Another example is a person born without arms who developed dexterity with the toes, even to being able to type. The pairing of people with different handicaps is another technique for overcoming the constraining effects. A physically handicapped man and a strong blind man successfully navigated very treacherous rapids in a canoe. The blind man provided the oar strength and the quadriplegic provided the verbal guidance information regarding boulders in the pathway.

Handicaps are often classified into four areas:

1 Physical or motor handicaps—being without use of one or more limbs. This area includes those in wheelchairs and semiambulatory persons with crutches and braces, impaired motor coordination, or cardiopulmonary problems;
2 Sensory handicaps—impaired vision or hearing;
3 Intellectual handicaps—being mentally retarded;
4 Emotional handicaps—being psychologically disturbed.

The emphasis will be on the first two areas because the largest body of design-related research has been in those areas.

The intellectual requirements for certain industrial tasks may have been set too high. Wade and Gold [50] reported that mentally retarded were able to learn to perform a fairly complex assembly task involving a 24-piece bicycle brake, when the task was broken down into a sequence of manageable subtasks.

A conservative estimate of the handicapped population of the United States is 13 million [Urban Mass Transportation System, 47]. With advances in medicine leading to increased longevity, and with a declining birth rate, we should expect in the future a larger percentage of the population classified as handicapped.

The Rehabilitation Act of 1973 prohibited discrimination in employment solely by reason of handicap where federal assistance was involved in the program. The Rehabilitation Act of 1974 extended coverage to all areas of civil rights, including education and training, effective April 1978. The Education for All Handicapped Children Act of 1975 affirmed the right for a "free appropriate public education" for all handicapped people effective September 1978. The Equal Employment Opportunity for the Handicapped Act of 1979 (sec. 446), introduced to Congress at this writing, would extend the Civil Rights Act of 1964 to disabled persons whether or not the employer received federal assistance.

Of the 10,000 members of the Paralyzed Veterans of America (PVA), 82 percent were unemployed in 1979, while 90 percent had been employed prior to their injury [Dudley, 12]. Fund raising has promoted an image of hopelessness and pathos leading to a stereotyped concept in the minds of business management. Before many of the severely handicapped are likely to return to the work force in other than entry-level jobs, concepts of their vocational ability and potential must be altered.

The Architectural Barriers Act of 1968 required that buildings designed, constructed, altered, or leased after that date using federal funds be accessible to handicapped persons. The Architectural and Transportation Barriers Compliance Board was created in 1973 to enforce compliance and provide guidelines. In this chapter, facility design requirements such as ramps, curb cutouts, and wheelchair-accessible workspaces will be discussed.

The cost of removing architectural barriers or providing communication aids for the sensory handicapped in federally funded programs is a major concern of some. However, the solution need not involve redesigned facilities exclusively for the handicapped. Holden [22] points out that providing a water fountain for the wheelchaired person does not necessarily mean lowering the height of the faucet. An inexpensive solution would be providing a paper cup holder next to the fountain.

In this chapter, illustrative examples of technological solutions for aiding the handicapped will be presented—notably, technology for the blind, the deaf, and the mobility-impaired persons. Considerations will include communications, individual mobility, and interfaces as a driver of a vehicle as applicable.

Bioengineering and medical developments in the areas of prosthetics (for substitution of missing limbs), artificial sensory organs, organ transplants, and microsurgery are generally beyond the scope of this chapter. The emphasis will be on how technology may supplement rather than directly restore the handicapped person's capability. Techniques include devices employing other sensory and motor abilities not impaired and orthotic devices that augment the movement of inadequately functioning limbs.

DESIGN FOR THE PHYSICALLY HANDICAPPED

According to a 1974 report of the National Academy of Sciences [33], there are at least 4.5 million Americans who are physically handicapped. The origin of the disability may be spinal lesions, amputation, diseases such as cerebral palsy, polio, multiple sclerosis, muscular dystrophy, and arthritis, or there may be congenital deformations. Special attention will be given to the spinal cord injured (SCI) because it presents one of the most challenging design areas.

Types of Handicaps

The medical classification of the spinal cord injured is often defined by where the lesion took place. The spinal cord (Figure 13-1) extends downward from the neck through the cervical (C), thoracic (T), lumbar (L), and sacral (S) regions. If the break occurs lower on the cord (in the thoracic region), the person has no use of chest, abdominal, and leg muscles but retains full use of the upper limbs and is classified as a paraplegic. However, if the lesion occurs very high on the cord (in the cervical region), the person may be either totally disabled or lose control of the arms as well as the legs. These persons are classified as quadriplegics. Lesions at C-3 or above are usually fatal. Some survive using a respirator.

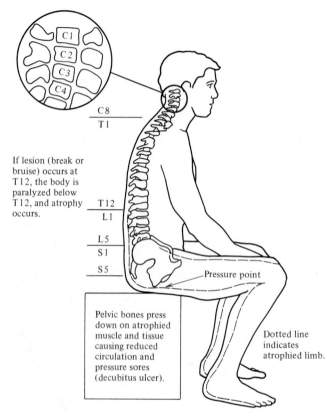

If lesion (break or bruise) occurs at T12, the body is paralyzed below T12, and atrophy occurs.

C1
C2
C3
C4

C8
T1

T12
L1

L5
S1

S5

Pressure point

Pelvic bones press down on atrophied muscle and tissue causing reduced circulation and pressure sores (decubitus ulcer).

Dotted line indicates atrophied limb.

Figure 13-1   Diagram of the spinal cord. *(Adapted from Jones, 1978.)*

As indicated in Figure 13-2, the exact location of the lesion has implications for the degree of use of the upper limbs. It is common practice to describe the quadriplegic further as a "C-6," "C-5," and so on, to indicate the region of the lesion. "T-1," the highest thoracic vertebrae, marks the crossover region from paraplegia to quadriplegia.

The Paraplegic

Paraplegics have their lesion in the thoracic region. Persons with lesions below T-6 can attain a very high degree of physical and psychological independence [Koppa, 28]. They have good trunk stability and many develop great muscular strength in the arms and upper body. They participate recreationally in wheelchair basketball, and some are even able to stabilize themselves well enough to use crutches. Former Governor Wallace of Alabama is a well-known T-6 [28]. Paraplegics with lesions above T-6 have some problems with trunk stability and require the use of orthoses such as corsets, chair harnesses, and braces.

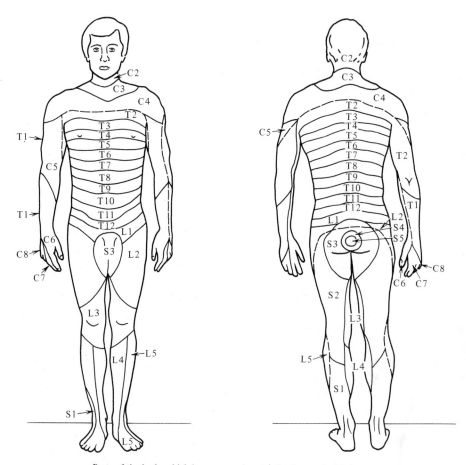

Parts of the body which become paralyzed following a spinal lesion.

Fracture–dislocation of particular spinal cord segments affects various parts of the body. By and large, paralysis occurs below the lesion, though it need not be total. The following gives an indication of the parts of the body affected by a lesion at a particular segment.

Lesion at C4 affects the diaphragm
Lesion at C5 affects the biceps, arms
Lesion at C6 affects the wrist flexion and extension
Lesion at C7 affects the triceps
Lesion at C8 affects the hand

Lesion at T2–T7 affects the chest muscles
Lesion at T9–T12 affects the abdominal muscles
Lesion at L1–L5 affects the leg muscles
Lesion at S2 affects the bowel and bladder

The person with a complete fracture–dislocation at the level of C3 or above usually will not survive.

Figure 13-2 Physical problems associated with lesions. *(Adapted from Jones, 1978.)*

The Quadriplegic

Quadriplegics, or quads, as they call themselves, typically sustained their injury as a young adult in an automobile or motorcycle accident or in a sporting event such as football or diving. There are at least 50,000 such persons in the United States [National Academy of Sciences, 33]. Many are capable of productive jobs given proper job design, access, and transportation to the workplace.

Designing for quads provides a challenge to bioengineers and human factors specialists. Much of the voluntary movement of their arms is missing, but they can move their arms somewhat. Chest and back muscles are paralyzed, and wheelchair sitting is somewhat unstable. The C-4 or C-5 quad is the highest level of spinal lesion for which out-patient maintenance is practical.

Hoist devices are provided to move the person from a bed to a chair or tub. Eating utensils or a pencil may be wedged between two digits if the hand is drawn up into a fist. Writing, when attempted, resembles the markings of a preschool-aged child.

Despite these inconveniences many quads are quite capable of sitting in wheelchairs or other motor vehicles. A quad at Texas A&M operated an electric-powered motorized wheelchair by means of a small lever controlling speed and direction of travel. He was able to peck out on a typewriter his exam papers and term papers and ultimately earned a Masters Degree in Industrial Engineering.

It is important to remember that there has been no damage to the brain or vocal tract of a quadriplegic. With adequate motivation augmented by engineering and facility design, many quads have professional educational and employment opportunities.

The Amputee

Another large group of physically handicapped are those who lost one or more limbs in industrial or traffic accidents or military service. Those who lost both lower limbs are functionally similar to some paraplegics, and design recommendations offered subsequently regarding wheelchair interface are applicable.

Those who are missing one or both upper limbs were traditionally fitted with a functional grasping device. Recent advancements in prosthesis have led to the construction of arms and hands that have the appearance of a human limb and, hence, distract from the disability. As noted earlier, the technology of prosthetics is beyond the scope of this text, but environmental interfaces with the amputee are in scope. For example, manual door openers can be designed so that grasping and twisting is not required simultaneously.

The Coordination-Impaired

Those with cerebral palsy, multiple sclerosis, Parkinson's disease, and many elderly persons are characterized sometimes by trembling that makes it difficult to perform tasks requiring dexterity, such as inserting coins in slots and activating switches. The loss of balance may also require the use of handrails on ramps and elevating equipment. There are also persons with arthritis and pulmonary and cardiac diseases who are handicapped in their ability to move without assistance.

Workplace Design for the Physically Handicapped

With the increasing entry of the physically handicapped into the workplace, design of work stations for compatibility with their handicaps will become a major area of interest. Although it is true that computer-telecommunications technology may eventually bring many jobs to the handicapped [Overby et al., 38], there may be psychological disadvantages to working at home alone rather than at the workplace with others. Moreover, many jobs cannot be contracted out since they are somewhat dependent upon an interchange of activity with other workers.

A systems approach to developing design criteria for the physically handicapped involves initially ascertaining the physical work requirements of occupations for which the handicapped might qualify. The University of Michigan [45] has a mobile occupational assessment laboratory housed in a truck-drawn trailer that permits moving the measurement equipment to the worksite. Surveys are taken of physical work requirements of both able-bodied and physically handicapped.

A job analysis is first conducted of various tasks and task elements. Associated human attributes are then determined. Each task element is assessed or measured in terms of a set of job attributes: duration, frequency, energy expenditure, dexterity required, reach distances, maximum forces exerted, potential job hazards. Techniques for measuring certain attributes were discussed in Chapters 3 and 6. Vocational rehabilitation counselors are taught these techniques.

The ultimate goal of this type of occupational research is the acquisition of job design criteria for certain handicapped persons so that occupations may be screened for their suitability and workspace design can be restructured to accommodate the skills of the handicapped. Thus, the worker in a wheelchair may be hired and assigned a job with confidence that the task elements are not beyond a reasonable expectation of successful accomplishment.

One aspect of vocational rehabilitation involves designing the workspace envelope and all components within easy reach of the wheelchair worker. Dreyfuss [10] conducted extensive research on the anthropometrics of the paraplegic in a wheelchair as well as others on crutches and canes. The findings have been widely circulated on a data wheel (a 3^d Humanscale) with cutout windows displaying data such as maximum reach in various directions for various body sizes [Diffrient et al., 11]. Figure 13-3 from General Services Administration [18] summarizes ranges of reach dimensions from a wheelchair.

The data are useful in designing for certain paraplegics and others confined to a wheelchair. (In the next section the entire question of wheelchair interfaces with facilities will be discussed). However, the data imply normal movement of the arms and upper body and are not applicable to those with muscular

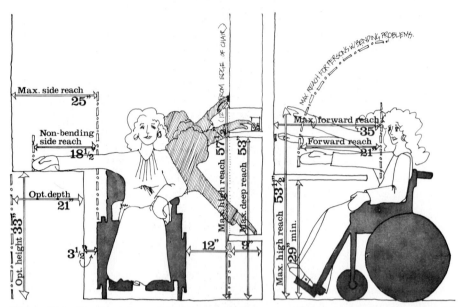

Figure 13-3 Range of forward and lateral reach from a wheelchair. *(General Services Administration, 1978.)*

dystrophy or spinal injury. Those who lack trunk balance must be strapped to the chair; some have restricted head movement. Children, of course, have a shorter reach.

Goebel [19] investigated the grasping reach envelopes of 15 persons with functional impairments of the upper extremities employing the Kennedy device discussed in Chapter 3 (Figure 13-4). Since trunk stability was largely nonexistent, reach distances were taken with the back rigidly against the seatback. Grasping implied principally one-time functional movement like operating a control requiring essentially only a "paw." Although the quad does fatigue easily, all subjects were able to complete the series of measurements in all directions and heights in a single sitting. (Order of measurements were counterbalanced across subjects.)

As noted by Koppa [28], whose research with adaptive controls for vehicles is reported subsequently, the reach envelopes do not necessarily imply a force capability at the limit values similar to what is reported for those not disabled. Quads require arm-steadying, orthotic aids to hold the hand in place while performing useful work with an extended arm. (In the extreme case, functional orthotics involves mechanical power systems to move the arm; however, these persons are not as likely to be at the workplace.)

Fitting the work station to the wheelchaired worker involves essentially applying the principles given in Chapters 6 and 7 to the unique anthropometric and functional capabilities of the handicapped person. Specific jobs must employ tools adapted to specific functional limitations and should include provisions for retrieving, without assistance from others, tools or material dropped. Work

Figure 13-4 Quadriplegic performing maximum grasping reach. *(Goebel, 1978.)*

tasks vary and the degree and nature of the disability varies so it is difficult to prescribe universal design criteria. The work station designer must use knowledge of the functional disability and his or her own ingenuity as a guide to adapting the work station to the physically handicapped.

Facility Design for the Physically Handicapped

Since the passage of architectural barriers legislation, there have been published several excellent design guides for improving accessibility, which emphasize environmental design for the wheelchair-bound person and to a lesser degree for the blind, deaf, and persons on crutches and braces. The General Services Administration's *Design Criteria: New Public Building Accessibility* (PBS [PCD]: DG5) is the federal standard prepared in response to Section 2 of Public Law 90-480, which authorized the General Services Administration (GSA) to insure wherever possible accessibility and use of buildings by the physically handicapped [18]. Several states such as North Carolina [31] and Illinois [24] have excellent illustrated standards. Olson and Meredith [37] have a pictorial guide for design of homes and appliances. Cotler and DeGraff [7] have prepared a guide for college campus facilities. Illustrative data is presented in this section.

Wheelchair Characteristics

The dimensions of the wheelchair, its functional characteristics, and human anthropometrics place constraints on the functional capabilities of the user. Figure 13-5 illustrates certain wheelchair dimensions [Jones, 24]. The most

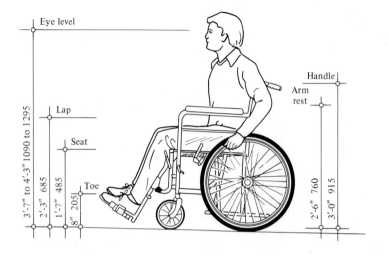

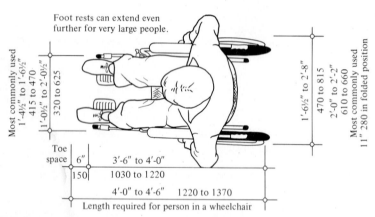

Figure 13-5 Dimensions of an adult wheelchair. *(Adapted from Jones, 1978.)*

obvious difference from an ambulatory person is that the eye level of an adult is only 43 to 51 in above floor level (109-129 cm) and reach capabilities are limited.

The most common wheelchair is approximately 43 in (109.2 cm) in length and 24 to 26 in (60.9-66.0 cm) in width. Including the toes of the shoe on the foot rest, the total length may extend to 48 to 52 in (122-137 cm) for an adult male. Some wheelchairs are as wide as 32 in (81.5 cm), but this dimension does not include the arms and elbows of the paraplegic during manual movement. These data have implications for clearances. The lap level of the person is about 27 in (68.7 cm) and the arm rests are 29 to 30 in (73-76 cm). These dimensions have implications for the underside of desks, benches, lavatories, and so forth (see *Residential Design*).

The length of the wheelchair, of course, is a deterrent to the person's forward reach to door openers, faucets, and other controls. The person turns the chair to one side to increase accessibility. This requirement also has certain implications for floor space design, as we shall see. The front wheels pivot, permitting an excellent turning radius, but still the minimum turning space is about 63 × 63 in (170 × 170 cm). Most guides recommend an area of 6 × 6 ft (183 × 183 cm) for a turn of 180 degrees.

Paralysis below the waist means that wheelchair users are insensitive there to touch and temperature. They may be burned by hot water pipes below the lavatory without knowing it. Insulation or a maximum temperature of 105°F is specified. Persons confined to wheelchairs often suffer from pressure sores or decubitus ulcers on the thighs and buttocks, so proper support is paramount. Foam, gel, and flotation pads are available to distribute the weight over the entire buttocks and to reduce pressure, pinching, and rising temperature.

Outside Building Design and Doors

A building site must provide, of course, sidewalks and walkway approaches to the door where the wheelchair will enter. An important dimension is the slope of the walkway. Mace [31] noted that a slope or ramp must not exceed 8.33 percent or 1 in (2.5 cm) rise per 12-in (30.5 cm) run, even with handrails. Without handrails 5 percent or 1 in rise per 20-in (50.8 cm) run is the maximum slope. This also applies to curb cutouts.

A reserved parking space, appropriately marked, should be at least 13.0 ft (396 cm) wide or 4 ft (122 cm) wider than a standard space (see *Wheelchair Lifting Aids*). Curb cuts should be directly ahead of where the handicapped driver exits the car. Curb cuts or ramps should be textured and should also be located at all crosswalks.

Many new buildings are designed with one entrance at near grade level. The location of the door should take prevailing winds into consideration since many handicapped have reduced pulling strength.

If the entrance is elevated, a ramp or sloping walkway must be provided. To meet the maximum rise standards, these ramps may be quite lengthy. Intermediate platforms (level areas of 3-6 ft) are required at least every 30 ft as rest areas [Mace, 31; Cotler and DeGraff, 7]. Dropoffs must be railed.

Consider a wheelchair user reaching for a door knob or opener on a door that opens outward. With the opener on the right side of the door, he or she reaches with the left hand so the opening door will clear the chair. This means the chair itself must extend farther to the right—at least 1 ft (30 cm). Authorities disagree on how much level space is required in front of the door. Cotler and DeGraff recommended a 6 × 6 foot (183 × 183 cm) level area with 3 ft (92 cm) to the right of the door. Olson and Meridith recommended 1 ft (30 cm) on either side of the outward swinging door [37].

To prevent the foot rest from bumping into a glass door, different authorities recommend 7.5- to 14-in (19-36 cm) kickplates at the door bottoms. Doorways must be at least 34 in (86 cm) wide [Mace, 31] and some recommend 38 in (97 cm) for outside entrances [37]. The threshold of a doorway (or doormats and other transitions) should not be elevated over 0.5 in (1.27 cm).

Bathrooms   Extensive research has been given to the design of different types of bathrooms, latrines, and showers. At least one toilet stall accessible to the handicapped must be provided on each floor (or 2 percent of total fixtures). Mace [31] recommended a 6-ft (163 cm) stall for floor-mounted water closets and a 5-ft (152 cm) stall for wall-mounted stalls (again the footrest is a constraining factor). Horizontal rails or grab bars at a height of 33 in (84 cm) are necessary (see Figure 13-6). In general, 40 in (102 cm) is the maximum height for towel dispensers and waste disposal. Mirror bottoms should be at 30 in (76 cm). Lavatory faucets should not be farther than 18 in (46 cm) from the front edge.

Elevators   Wheelchair users need elevators in multifloor public buildings since there is seldom sufficient interior space for switch-back ramps meeting incline standards. Mace [31] recommended a minimum cab of 5 × 5 ft (152 × 152 cm) or slightly different but equivalent rectangular space. This space will allow several other passengers. A slightly smaller cab is possible if only the handicapped is transported and he or she backs in or backs out.

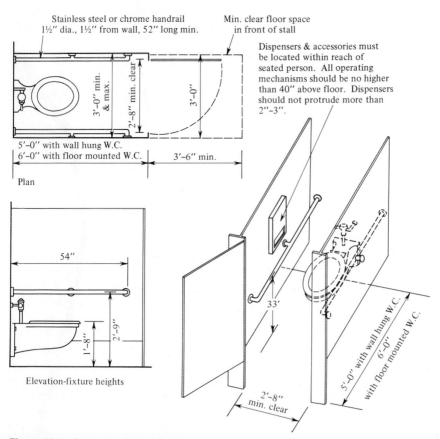

Figure 13-6   Dimensions of a toilet stall for wheelchair interface. *(Mace, 1974.)*

Authorities disagree on the maximum height of the inside call buttons listing standards from 3.5 to 5 ft (102-152 cm) for the top row. However, the emergency call box or telephone should never be more than 4 ft (122 cm) high, and typically it is located under the call buttons. (The 4-ft standard applies to public telephones as well.)

Very low outside call buttons are inconvenient for tall ambulatory users and a 48-inch (122 cm) maximum is a reasonable compromise height.

Auditoriums   The steep slopes in some assembly seating areas offset the center of gravity for wheelchair users, causing discomfort. The wheelchair should be on a level area—either at the front, back, or on a midway cross-aisle. A two-row flat space on the aisle would allow for the 43-in (109 cm) wheelchair plus ingress/egress room. Seating on a cross-aisle would take less row space provided the aisle were sufficiently wide for the 16-in (41 cm) projection into the aisle. Persons with leg braces require 24 in (61 cm) in front of the seat.

Aisle Clearances   From the earlier discussion of the width of wheelchairs, certain clearance requirements emerge. For two wheelchairs to pass, a 6-ft (183 cm) aisle is recommended. Five feet (132 cm) is the minimum for passage [GSA, 18]. For a wheelchair user seated at a table, an aisle at least 42 in wide (102 cm) is required behind. The space between two fixed tables with back-to-back occupants should be at least 65 in (165 cm) for wheelchair passage between them.

The General Service Administration recommends 36 in (91.5 cm) for one-way passage [18]. Cafeteria line rails must be at least 34 in (86 cm) wide. Aisles in fixed library stacks require a minimum of 32 in (85 cm) for accessibility by the handicapped; 42 in (102 cm) is strongly recommended for another person to stand sideways, permitting the wheelchair to pass. A large person on crutches will also require 32.5 in (85.5 cm) minimum for the proper spacing of the crutches, and Jones [24] recommended 36 in (91.5 cm).

Residential Design

The real estate market is catering to wheelchair users by providing homes and apartments that have workspace accessible to the handicapped. Regarding control heights, this means lowering to 30 to 40 in (76-102 cm) wall controls such as light switches, thermostats, fuse boxes, window latches, and drapery cords. A short person in a chair is much like a small child when reaching for objects. Burners on the stove should be staggered to prevent burning the arm while reaching for containers on the back burner. A mirror for checking food cooking on a back burner is desirable. Of course, cabinet and refrigerator shelves must be accessible. The oven door must not be so low that it does not clear the wheelchair arm. Side-opening doors are preferable.

Figure 13-7 shows the knee space required for working at a counter. The space must be 30 in wide (76 cm); 29 in high (73 cm), and 24 in deep (61 cm)

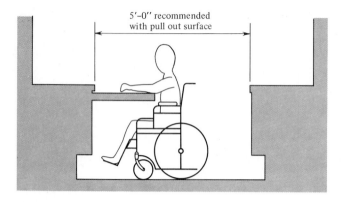

Pull out or built in work surface with knee space

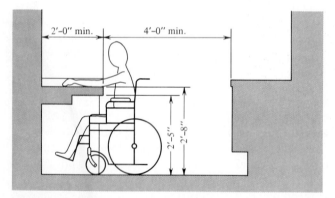

Figure 13-7   Dimensions of a counter for wheelchair interface. *(Mace, 1974.)*

[Olson and Meredith, 37]. Counter toe space must be 9 in (23 cm) high and 6 in (15 cm) deep.

Closets should have sliding doors. Spacing between furniture, beds, and walls must be planned for passage of the wheelchair. In short, the entire workspace must be rescaled and evaluated for compatibility with the wheelchair dimensions and users' constraints.

The Outlook for Barrier Removal   Equal opportunity legislation is making more and more public facilities accessible to the handicapped. In most instances the design solution has been to add additional equipment that could also be used by the nonhandicapped, so the added expense is nominal. In a few instances a required lowering of handled objects (for example, at a grocery market) would constitute a major problem for the owner. Also, if a single control for everyone is placed very low, it may present a problem for very tall persons who may not notice it or who have difficulty reaching it without stooping.

Despite the strides that have been made in adapting the human-made environment to the constraints imposed by wheelchair design, there are finite limits to its feasibility. Wheelchair clearances are a necessity, but there are some older structures and facilities which cannot be made completely accessible, and there are undeveloped natural areas which are equally constrained.

A major area for development should be improving the design of the wheelchair itself to provide the user greater accessibility in unmodified areas. If a higher reach is the major constraint there are two approaches: (1) extension arms held by the person, which would have mating clamps which interface with certain equipment for grasping and manipulating; (2) stable extendable tripod lifts on the wheelchair itself with bases adaptable to slightly uneven terrains. Conceivably, the chair could be designed to remain horizontal on slightly uneven surfaces such as walks, auditoriums, or ramps. Additional power could be provided for safe movement up somewhat steeper inclines. Better restraint systems could be provided so the person may not fall or slide out on forward tipping.

These comments should not be construed as relaxing architectural barrier enforcement. Rather, they are aimed at extending the handicapped person's range of accessibility to facilities that would otherwise not be practical. Designing a completely accessible environment is beyond the capability of government or industry, and accessibility to certain areas will remain restricted until the wheelchair system itself is redesigned. The new device may not even resemble the present-day wheelchair, as will be discussed in the next section.

Mobility Aids for the Physically Handicapped

A physical handicap is principally a constraint on body movement. A goal of the handicapped is greater independence in mobility and ultimately moving about when and where one chooses without assistance from others. Technological advancements are making this goal increasingly realistic.

Today, there is a burgeoning industry of adaptive equipment for those with lower disabilities, such as arthritics and amputees. A popular item is the three-wheeled electric scooter providing vehicular control, but bearing no resemblance to the wheelchair (Figure 13-8).

The Norman wheelchair [36] is actually a small footstool on four wheels; the front wheels swivel. It takes up less space than a chair and permits passage through narrow spaces such as check-out aisles, turnstiles, and revolving doors. Without arm rests or back, it is suitable for tasks like gardening, filing at a cabinet, or transitioning easily to a desk chair, workbench, or tub. Also, it collapses for front-seat stowage in a motor vehicle.

Wheelchair-lifting aids Transitioning to and from a wheelchair poses a major problem for older or heavier wheelchair users. They may travel in surface vehicles with others who lack the strength to assist them into a vehicle. For the

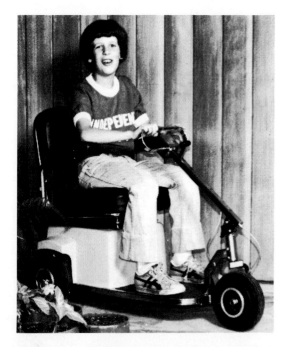

Figure 13-8 New mobility aids. *(Tricycle courtesy of Palmer Industries, Endicott, N.Y.; scooter courtesy of Voyagers, Inc., South Bend, Ind.)*

more severely handicapped, a hydraulic hoist may be attached to the top of an automobile for lifting the person in a sling out of the wheelchair and onto a car seat. Afterward the wheelchair is folded and stowed. The Veterans Administration provides design and test criteria for safety and quality of automotive lifts [52].

Many severely handicapped persons would prefer to remain in the wheelchair while being transported, thus avoiding the inconvenience of transitioning. The modern van has made this anthropometrically possible with certain conversions. A 1979 edition of the *Paraplegia News* [48], a monthly magazine, lists 16 different vendors of electric or electromechanical wheelchairs with lifting devices that are either adaptable to a side-door van or are a standard feature of a modified van converted for wheelchair use. Figure 13-9 (A) and (C) illustrate van lifting devices.

The wheelchair may be backed onto one type of lift or the chair may be lifted while front-facing (facing in the same direction as the vehicle) or rear-facing on other lifts. One system advertises a rotary lift with the chair initially front-facing, then rotating the chair backward into the van. The boarding ramp is raised and wheels locked to prevent roll-off during the lift. Grasping bars across the front or side are also provided. Some vans have a raised or bubble top and a higher door for clearance of the person's head without inconvenience.

The side-door entrance offers certain advantages over the traditional rear-door entrance. There are both parallel and curb parking advantages. There is a shorter travel distance inside, and rear storage is possible. However, if the chair is lifted while facing either backward or forward into a side-door van, boarding the lift requires an extrawide parallel-parking space. One advertisement speaks of possibly being "trapped outside the van" by another vehicle parked parallel to the van. A front-facing or rear-facing lift takes less side space (approximately 38 in or 97 cm). Some vans are equipped with sliding doors that take less parking space than conventional, outward swinging doors.

The lift should have the capability of adjusting speed of lift and stopping at either curb or street level. It should be lightweight, should fold away to take a minimum of storage space, and should interface with the van and different types of wheelchairs.

If a person is to operate the van alone, there must be accessible control switches both inside and outside. The outside switches for lifting and retraction should be conveniently located for the person while in the wheelchair. They could be remotely actuated; however, for traditional manual actuation an advantage of the front-facing or rear-facing lift is that the controls are inside the van and actuated with either the left or right hand. (A person whose back is to the van cannot reach interior controls and one facing the van would have a long and awkward reach, often not feasible.)

Many current van lift designs imply that someone else will be present during boarding and exiting. The lift is principally a physical aid to ingress/egress. If someone else is present to push the wheelchair, an economical alternative to a lift is a fold-down, rear-entry ramp. This is commercially available also. To meet safety requirements the ramp treadway must be rather long, posing a space problem for both side or rear entry.

Other types of wheelchair lifts include stairway elevators for the home that raise or lower the person directly over the staircase Figure 13-9 (D); a device for hoisting the person into a bathtub; and a lift feature to the wheelchair base that gradually raises the paraplegic to a standing posture. (Another device is

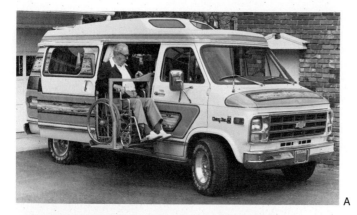

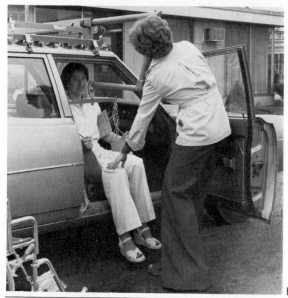

Figure 13-9 Wheelchair lifting devices for vans, automobiles, and stairways. *(Courtesy of the following: (A) ABC Enterprises, Mentor Ohio; (B) Ted Hoyer and Co., Oshkosh, Wis.; (C) Gresham Driving Aids, Inc., Wixom, Mich.; (D) Earl's Stairway Lift Co., Cedar Falls, Iowa.)*

available to lift the person out of the chair with the lifting unit mounted on a heavy-duty podium structure). If the paraplegic has sufficient upper body strength, she may simply pull herself up to a portable frame for standing support. Physiologically, there are certain advantages to standing even if one cannot walk.

In summary, there are many ingenious lifting devices, but there are few unbiased human factors tradeoff studies or evaluations regarding the comparative merits of lift devices being offered commercially to the handicapped.

Driving Aids for Paraplegics For total independence the handicapped person desires to drive alone. Hand controls are commercially available for

C

D

those lacking only use of their legs. These controls operate the accelerator and brake pedals through a series of links and rods mounted to the steering column, as shown in Figure 13-10.

A 4:1 mechanical advantage is attainable with these levers over the corresponding force required for foot pedals. Some vendors advertise that the linkages do not interfere with use of the foot pedals by another driver.

There are also available modifications to make turning the steering-wheel easier and improve accessibility of controls for a person in a wheelchair. There are steering-wheel spinner grips, joy stick steering controls to replace the wheel, extensions for the steering column, column-mounted secondary controls, electric parking brakes, and left-foot accelerators for amputees. The Veterans Administration [49] and the Human Resources Center [29] have manuals that summarize equipment available for prescription by rehabilitation agencies.

There are other wheelchair interfaces in addition to control operation and

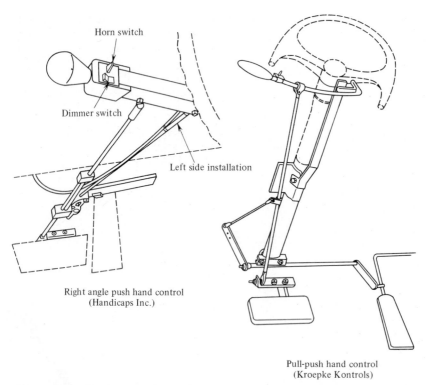

Horn switch

Dimmer switch

Left side installation

Right angle push hand control
(Handicaps Inc.)

Pull-push hand control
(Kroepke Kontrols)

Figure 13-10   Hand controls for accelerator and brake. *(Koppa, 1978.)*

accessibility. A front-seat floor section may be lowered several inches (or the roof raised) so that the eye level is at least below the top of the windshield. The wheelchair restraint system is a major problem. The wheels are, of course, locked, mounted in wheel wells, and tied down at several points, but it is questionable that any tie-down technique meets safety standards for passenger seats discussed in Chapter 11.

The wheelchair van is becoming popular whether or not the person drives. Taxi service in a wheelchair van is being offered in some cities. However, before purchasing an expensive van the patient may wish to be sure that he or she can be licensed to drive. Advanced hospitals have a driver rehabilitation section, often within occupational therapy. Therapists conduct tests and make recommendations regarding driving capability. Specially equipped vehicles are available for driver training. Zuniga [51] reported that 90 percent of the patients at the Texas Institute for Rehabilitation and Research, including quads, who were recommended for driver training were successful in getting a license.

Driving Aids for the Quadriplegic

Designing vehicle controls for the quad represents a much greater challenge than designing for other types of wheelchair drivers because of their limited handgrasp and reduced arm strength. Prior to designing controls or stability aids, it would first be desirable to know the levels of force application that could be expected of the quad.

Force Requirements for Hand Controls   Koppa [28] tested 24 quads from the Texas Institute for Rehabilitation and Research (TIRR) in Houston, employing a device called the A&M Driver Control Operability Measurement System (ADCOMS). Several static strength measurements were taken on a simulated lever in the up, down, fore, and aft directions. Torque readings were taken also on the rim of a steering wheel, with patients turning it at least two turns left and two turns right with each hand, using a grip device if necessary.

Table 13-1 summarizes the input force data for three levels of handicap: (1)

Table 13-1   Comparative Static Strength of Three Levels of Quadriparesis

Input type, direction and arm	C-6/C-7 Mean	SD	C-6 Mean	SD	C-5/6+ Mean	SD
Steer						
Left turn	7.4*	4.0	5.3	3.2	2.4	2.9
Left arm	(32.9)**	(17.8)	(23.6)	(14.2)	(10.7)	(12.9)
Left turn	7.8	3.2	6.0	3.7	2.3	2.9
Right arm	(34.7)	(14.2)	(26.7)	(16.5)	(10.2)	(12.9)
Right turn	8.1	3.8	7.4	3.6	3.4	3.8
Left arm	(36.0)	(16.9)	(32.9)	(16.0)	(15.1)	(16.9)
Right turn	7.7	2.7	7.8	4.5	3.8	5.4
Right arm	(34.3)	(12.1)	(34.7)	(20.0)	(16.9)	(24.0)
Lever						
Forward	23.9	11.6	16.0	9.9	9.4	6.2
Left arm	(106.3)	(51.6)	(71.2)	(44.0)	(41.8)	(27.6)
Forward	21.4	9.7	15.4	5.7	10.0	9.4
Right arm	(95.2)	(43.1)	(68.5)	(25.4)	(44.5)	(41.8)
Aft	22.0	12.3	13.8	8.0	8.9	5.3
Left arm	(97.9)	(54.7)	(61.4)	(35.6)	(39.6)	(23.6)
Aft	18.6	11.4	15.4	6.6	6.3	5.6
Right arm	(82.7)	(50.7)	(68.5)	(29.4)	(28.0)	(24.9)
Up	14.8	6.5	13.3	6.8	9.3	8.1
Left arm	(65.8)	(28.9)	(59.2)	(30.2)	(41.4)	(36.0)
Up	14.1	7.3	14.6	8.2	9.4	8.8
Right arm	(62.7)	(32.5)	(65.0)	(36.5)	(41.4)	(39.2)
Down	15.7	9.4	13.1	6.2	5.4	2.3
Left arm	(69.8)	(41.8)	(58.3)	(27.6)	(24.0)	(10.2)
Down	16.1	10.3	15.5	8.4	6.7	4.5
Right arm	(71.6)	(45.8)	(69.0)	(37.4)	(29.8)	(20.0)

*Pounds.
**nt = newtons.
Source: Adapted from Koppa [28].

C-6 to C-7 (the least handicapped); (2) C-6; and (3) "higher than C-6" (the most severely handicapped). All differences in force between the three groups were significantly different from one another except two groups (right-arm, right-turn, and pull-up measures between groups 1 and 2). It was concluded the higher the lesion, the less force capability available. The most-severe and least-severe handicapped differed the most on tasks involving fore and aft movements which used the triceps.

Patients who had been relicensed to drive were also compared with those who had not been relicensed. Differences were significant at at least the 0.1 level for all conditions excepting two. In general, strength is a useful discriminator between those successfully completing the program and those not doing so.

In Chapter 3 data similar to Table 13-1 were presented for military males. Other than predictable group differences in strength, another observation was that the military group had between 10- and 20-lb (44.5-90.0 nt) difference between their left hand and their right hand (about 15 percent), whereas the severely handicapped did not differ significantly in their arm strength. Koppa concluded that the quads' lack of handedness with respect to force means that an adaptive control designer may be able to configure the driver control layout for operation by either hand.

Koppa also cautioned that the data reported were for maximum forces rather than for continuous forces, such as those often required during steering and throttle control. Standard power-steering systems often require 1 to 4 lb of force (4.5-17.8 nt), although steady, small, driving corrections require much less force. Data for the able-bodied [NASA, 34] suggest that a long-term comfortable amount of input that an operator can exert is from 15 to 33 percent of maximum. Therefore, Koppa recommended using 15 to 25 percent of the force data shown in Table 13-1 as an appropriate design value.

An implication was that if the resulting value was less than 1 lb (4.5 nt), there may be a problem in using a standard power steering. Moreover, throttle control input must be higher than steering input because it must be sustained and precisely controlled throughout driving.

Primary Control Design

A cruise control, although desirable, could not be used efficiently in many low-speed, stop-and-go situations. The need may well be for systems requiring drastically reduced effort (advertised as *zero effort steering*). Koppa [28] evaluated three adaptive control configurations: low-effort power steering and power brakes; servo throttle/brake with low-effort power steering; and integrated pedestal throttle/brake with low-effort, high-gain power steering. A joy stick control is an attractive alternative to a rotating control, but this device was not available for testing.

Vehicles equipped with these modifications were driven by quads on various driver-education type maneuvers (parking, braking, turning, obstacle avoidance, and cone-marked courses) in a closed test area.

There are commercially available various types of spinner grips that may be

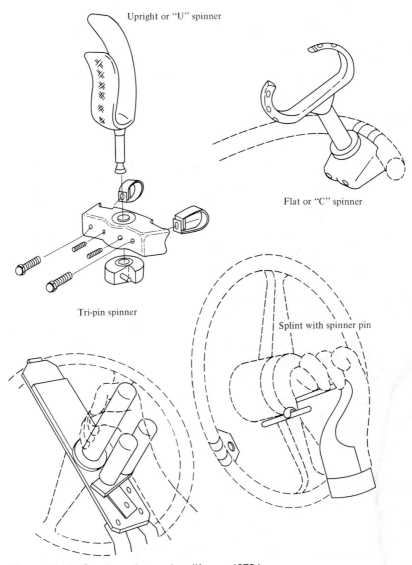

Upright or "U" spinner

Flat or "C" spinner

Tri-pin spinner

Splint with spinner pin

Figure 13-11 Steering spinner grips. *(Koppa, 1978.)*

attached to the steering wheel of quads. The C-6 and above have very little grasping capability so the tri-pin spinner (Figure 13-11, lower left) is often used because it requires a minimum wrist action and no grasping. The hand is simply slid into the grip and turning forces may be applied without the hand slipping out.

The hand designated for steering is unavailable for other control actions so the other hand (usually the left) must manage throttle, braking, and secondary control functions. Koppa [28] has evaluated certain innovative hand controls for

Figure 13-12 Tri-pin approach for a servo hand control interface. *(Koppa, 1978.)*

the quad. The throttle-brake was a single fore-and-aft lever extending from the left side of the steering column with the wrist supported by a tri-pin (Figure 13-12).

Secondary Control Design

Quads have reported difficulty operating conventional column-mounted devices like wiper/washers, lights, and dimmer switches. Since both hands are fully occupied, neither may be removed to perform any of these other driving activities. Either the vehicle would have to be stopped first or some alternate capability would have to be provided by design.

Koppa [28] investigated several secondary control designs involving selectors mounted on the left-door surface. They were activated with the side of the left hand without removing the hand from the throttle/brake control. The challenge was to find controls, or a single control, permitting each function to be activated independently without risking inadvertent actuation. Although no best design was forthcoming, a single joy stick was generally preferable to separate modified toggles or a momentary in-out, up-down lever. Secondary control activation is an obvious area for eventual speech-control systems.

DESIGN FOR THE BLIND AND VISUALLY HANDICAPPED

Many of us are visually impaired to the extent of needing prescriptive lenses (eyeglasses) for reading or for distant viewing. Others are weak at color discrimination, speed of focusing on objects at different distances, adapting to the dark or bright lights, reading details on moving objects, or perceiving depth when approaching an object. The impact of some of these disabilities will be considered later with respect to driving. However, the primary focus will be on design aids for the persons who are totally or functionally blind. In the United States, there are approximately 315,000 people with severe visual impairment [Shingledecker and Foulke, 42].

Design Aids for Communication

Braille print consists of a 2×3 array of raised dots. Various combinations of the dot patterns represent each letter and numeral. The blind person moves his or her fingers across the Braille print and is tactually able to discriminate the letters and words by position of dots, distances between dots, and size of dots. According to Allen [1], with practice skilled readers can read up to 200 words per minute with Grade II Braille. The major drawback is that it is expensive to transcribe books, journals, and other reading material into Braille. An entire library in Braille is generally prohibitive.

Tactile Devices

Another approach to tactile representation of printed material was the optical-to-tactile convertor (Optacon). This was a small portable device consisting of a hand-held optical pickup camera that scanned the page while the fingers of the other hand were stimulated by a vibrating tactile stimulator [Linvill, 30]. The device converted a matrix of 144 photo-transistor outputs to a spatially corresponding array of vibrating tactile reeds or pins. It took about 160 hours of training to learn to read 50 words per minute—much slower than Braille—but it was applicable to conventional printed material [McCormick, 32].

Another device, the Tactile Vision Substitution System, converted visual objects in the environment to tactile stimulation [Collins and Bachy-y-Rita, 5]. Images were sensed on special eyeglasses and transmitted by fiber optics to a lightweight television camera that converted the visual image to corresponding patterns of electronic impulses. The array of electrodes were sensed by the fingers. With extensive training the person could integrate (decode) the transmitted impulses into information patterns. The device was experimental, but it offered a potential for sensing pictorial information.

Allen [1] termed the Optacon and other such systems "direct translation devices." He concluded that no direct translation device can achieve the desired reading speed of 200 words per minute. The devices are fatiguing to use over long durations, and they require extensive training. Since 65 percent of the registered blind are over 65-years old, this group would prefer a device less physically demanding and more easily learned.

Allen maintained that a practical design solution must come from either the use of actual speech (for example, "talking books") or synthetic speech of high quality. He concluded that useful "reading machines" will shortly be available at low cost. Reading machines are more aptly termed text-to-speech conversion devices.

Text-To-Speech Conversion Devices The process of converting printed text to natural sounding synthetic speech is a formidable task. Essentially, it consists of developing an extensive set of algorithms that will reveal the linguistic structure of speech and then modeling the speech production process based on these structures.

The linguistic structure necessary to specify waveforms comes from two processes: lexical analysis and parsing. *Lexical analysis* involves breaking down speech into a sequence of elements (morphs), each having a pronunciation symbol and a part of speech. Knowing the part of speech is important for proper speech sound translation. *Parsing* involves marking certain semantic features that indicate the need for emphatic stress when spoken. By parsing sentences the listener can recognize quickly phrasal units (for example, noun and verb phrases) in the synthetic speech, and by other techniques one can recognize syntactical structure.

In learning to speak we were given certain letter-to-sound rules, but later we learned that they did not always work (such as *have* and *behave*). A sequence of two consonants in different syllables is not always pronounced the same way as when in one syllable, for example, the "th" in "three" versus that in "hothouse." It is essential that the machine be taught these exceptions, otherwise it would pronounce words as a person unskilled in the spoken language does on occasions.

Timing and pitch control are important also for synthetic speech to sound natural. Timing involves such things as the proper duration of a vowel sound, which can be affected by following consonants and syntactical boundaries. Pitch contours vary with the grammatical mood of the sentence (declaration, question, command). Knowing which words to stress is important to correct interpretation.

Finally, phonetic speech synthesis involves applying these rules and selecting vocal tract model control parameters that specify the phonemes making up the sentence. (See Chapter 12.)

The potential advantages for the blind of having a text-to-speech device are substantial. Spoken speech is readily understood without training; listening is not particularly fatiguing; a sighted person is not required; and the blind could read any material in a library. Advancements in electronic technology will soon reduce costs to make personal devices practical.

One may ask: What are the human factors engineering problems with reading machines? Allen [1] identified two major areas: first, the evaluation of speech intelligibility for naturalness, pitch, and timing control using the techniques described in Chapter 12. Second, the optical character recognition device (OCR) has a number of user problems. It is possible to use either a hand-held camera or an automatic scanner. There are problems in providing controls for camera or scanner positioning. For example, a capability for rapid scanning and backup may be required. A long delay between the position of the scanning camera in the text and current speech readout may be a problem. If the speech is not clearly translated, the scanner may need to back up, repeat, or even spell out difficult text. Thus, there are still many potential problems at the human-machine interface when the OCR is applied to a variety of material, font styles, and so forth. Visual pattern recognition, such as figures in a textbook, is an even more challenging area for translation to effective speech interpretation for the blind.

Design Aids for Pedestrian Mobility

There are two major ways for improving the mobility of the blind to walk from place to place quickly, smoothly, and safely without undue psychological stress. First, the blind may be provided with personal mobility aids that provide for sensing remote as well as local cues. Second, the environment may be modified to enhance sensing and to remove hazards that may not be detected with current sensor technology. Finally, there are certain policy barriers that restrict the blind's manner of functioning, for example, on public transportation.

Personal Design Aids   The blind pedestrian traveling alone is typically either accompanied by a guide dog or carries a long, white cane to detect obstacles.

Several electronic sensory aids have been developed for the blind. These devices convert ultrasonic energy or coherent light into auditory or tactual signals suitable for the blind to receive. One device is the laser cane. It resembles the long cane typically used by the blind; however, it detects obstacles without actual contact by the cane, hence extending somewhat the distance of sensitivity. Shingledecker and Foulke [42] provide an extensive review of studies evaluating the blind while walking test courses using several types of canes. However, for methodological reasons, definitive answers on their relative merits as compared with the conventional cane are not reported.

Another device called the "Sonicguide" presents binary auditory signals to the blind pedestrian from objects in the vicinity. For centuries it has been known that the blind have an uncanny ability to detect objects nearby, but it remained for Cotzin and Dallenbach [8] to demonstrate in a controlled experiment that the blind's knowledge of distances and obstacles was actually based on subtle auditory cues they received from reflections of incidental or deliberately produced sounds. Kohler [27] later verified the findings and described the role of guiding sounds and sound shadows in detecting objects by "echolocation." From the standpoint of environmental design, it is important that the blind not be deprived of these remote cues by unwittingly removing reflecting surfaces.

In the course of walking around their environment, the blind have also learned spatial orientation skills. Juurmaa [25] found that both congenitally blind and the adventitiously blind subjects did much better than blindfolded sighted subjects in conceptually organizing space. This was measured by having individuals from each group guided over a complicated path by the experimenter and then having each retrace the path without help. Other tasks involved taking the shortest distance to the starting point and estimating distances traveled.

The blind pedestrian also uses cues such as the wind, the sun, and most important, the feel of the surface underfoot. The tactual and kinesthetic cues may be from natural surfaces, but the environmental designer may modify the texture of surfaces to capitalize on this sensitivity. Cratty [9] investigated the blind's ability to walk a straight line for a distance of about 34 yards (30.5 m) without auditory, tactual, or kinesthetic cues. He documented a deviation of about 1.3 in (3.2 cm) per stride. Uphill changes in slope were slightly more difficult to detect than were downhill changes in slope.

In discussing research with the blind, Shingledecker and Foulke [42] emphasized the importance of valid measures and a theory regarding informational processing by the blind pedestrian. Safety was operationally defined by frequency of unintended bodily contacts with objects, unintended departures from paths, and time spent crossing a street in excess of necessary time. The objective should be the same as with sighted persons: moving quickly, smoothly, and safely without undue psychological stress. A long stride length was found to be more highly related to a minimum of reported psychological stress than was measured heart rate.

As already noted, the blind are often dependent upon auditory reference. Auditory cues are less accurate than visual ones in ascertaining distances and locations of sources. There are also extraneous auditory sounds that mask the sounds providing useful information. The sighted person has a preview of the circumstances to which he or she must eventually respond. On an unfamiliar route, the blind is unable to "work ahead" of his or her immediate spatial position and must either reduce walking speed or risk safety.

Shingledecker and Foulke [42] noted that walking situations pose varying degrees of difficulty depending upon the immediate need for spatial information. They recommended the use of the secondary loading technique (Chapter 2) to measure the demands of a situation on the channel capacity of the blind pedestrian. A situation with reduced demands (that is, being able to anticipate objects) would be evident by improved performance on a secondary loading task.

Barrier-Free Design for the Blind

From the foregoing discussion it is evident that the human-made environment may be better designed for communications and to reduce hazards both inside and outside of buildings. Some of the more obvious design solutions are the elimination of low-hanging objects along a walkway (or protruding objects not on the ground, such as the rear of a truck); railing or barricading drop-offs, and eliminating curbs or slight changes in elevation that could be a tripping hazard. The cane user could wedge the tip of the cane in cracks or large floor gratings.

From a communications standpoint, it is important that necessary information be provided. Since the blind respond to echoes, the work environment should not eliminate this source of information. Braille strips are often installed on signs and elevators. However, many persons who are blind or visually handicapped do not read Braille, so use of large raised letters on existing signs is better. The letters should be at least 5/8 in high, 1/32 in raised, and be light letters on a dark background for those who can partially see. Door knobs leading into hazardous work areas could be coded with tactual cues such as deep knurling.

Tactile cueing features may be built into the pedestrian environment. Texture strips may be sensed through the cane and a change in texture may be used to communicate that the person is approaching some walkway hazard such as tree trunks, posts, or benches. For those with poor vision, potential hazardous areas may be denoted by a marked change in the color of the walkway.

Auditory cueing may be provided in situations normally communicated by lights. For example, when an elevator is going up there should be one chime ring, and when the car is going down there should be two rings. Much more could be done to provide auditory cues and speech-synthesizer information at the workplace.

On passenger aircraft, the blind are allowed to bring their guide dogs aboard (according to Civil Aeronautics Board rules), but airlines often require that the blind sit in the bulkhead area where there is more space for the dog. Some guide dogs are quite small and could fit under normal aisle seats according to Kloner and Weber [26]. During takeoff and landing, disabled persons are not allowed to have canes or crutches at their seats. The authors argued that these aids are important in the event of an emergency and a simple design solution would be a strap or sprocket device to prevent them from flying about. There are also folding canes and crutches that consume less space and could be stowed nearby.

Driving Aids for the Visually Impaired

Obviously, the blind do not drive motor vehicles, but those with severe visual impairment would still like to drive a vehicle if there were design aids that could restore their functional vision. According to Booher [4], individuals with 20/200 static visual acuity as measured on a Snellen Chart, have been able to pass the acuity test in some states by wearing telescopic spectacles. The bioptic telescope attached to the lens resulted in 300 visual patients [Hayes, 20] being licensed to drive.

Two miniature Galilean telescopes (Figure 13-13) are mounted in the upper portion of each carrier lens. The lenses have the patient's normal refractive correction. For general vision the person lifts the head to look through her own carrier lens. However, when she needs to read signs or spot detailed objects in the environment, she lowers her head to the telescopic lens for focusing.

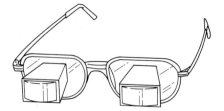

Figure 13-13 Bioptic telescopic specta-cles. *(Booher, 4. From* Human Factors, *1978, vol. 20, no. 3. Copyright 1978 by The Human Factors Society, Inc. and repro-duced by permission.)*

The question raised in licensing is whether the person can drive without posing a hazard to himself or others. Accident data for such drivers indicate substantially fewer accidents than for the general population, although number of miles driven and driving conditions for those using the bioptic lens were not known. Fonda [16] has opposed licensing with the use of telescopic lenses, citing potential highway safety hazards from reduced central fields, a ring scotoma (absent or depressed vision) at the juncture of the telescope and carrier lenses, and so on. However, no evidence has been cited that such phenomena interfered with driving performace.

Actually, there are several visual functions considered to be as important to safe driving as static visual acuity measured by most licensing agencies. Henderson and Burg [21] noted that color vision and stereopsis are being needlessly measured in some states, while other more important visual skills are not measured. Accident studies cite deficiencies in dynamic visual acuity, peripheral angular movement, and central movement in depth as important correlates of accidents per miles driven [21, 4]. Authorities disagree on the importance of peripheral vision—some feel that 70 degrees left and 70 degrees right should be a minimum [Allen, 2] while others argue that a much smaller visual field is satisfactory with the use of mirrors and head and eye movement [Richards, 40].

In summary, the decision whether a person with poor static visual acuity should be allowed to drive with bioptic telescoptic lenses depends upon his or her other visual capabilities as well as maturity, intelligence, and motivation. Finebloom actually found only 300 of some 10,000 visual patients rehabilitated with the lenses for other purposes, who could drive well enough with them for licensing. Certainly, the approval of a visual-care practioner should be required before licensing.

DESIGN FOR THE DEAF AND HEARING-IMPAIRED

In Chapter 9 the measurement of hearing loss was discussed in relation to noise exposure. Hearing loss may be congenital or associated with aging (presbycusis), disease, toxic drugs, head injury, or exposure. About 13.4 million Americans have hearing-impairment, although only 300 to 600 thousand are totally deaf [Eliott, 13].

Design Aids for Communication

For the person who is hard-of-hearing, the design solution may be increased volume or amplification of sounds over the telephone, public address, radio, television, and personal communications. Loud voices may be annoying to others, and personal hearing aids are preferable.

Amplification

Electronic hearing aids were introduced commercially in the 1930s. Modern developments include amplitude compression (limiting or reducing the intensity when the acoustic input exceeds some level), reduced distortion, and directional microphones. Cosmetically, the miniaturization of hearing aids has increased their acceptability. The individual tailoring of the amplification system to the individual's audiogram or pattern of hearing loss also increases discrimination test scores.

Artificial Organs

The largest amount of research and development has been in the area of enhancing the understanding of speech by the totally deaf. In the area of auditory prosthesis, 17 persons were fitted surgically with a single electrode auditory implant [House and Urban, 23]. The implant users could not understand speech by means of prosthetic stimulation alone; however, their scores on a lip-reading test were significantly higher than the scores of those reading lips without the implant. Apparently the perceived sounds did aid in speech recognition in some way [Bilger, 3]. Implants were more effective for those who used them throughout the day and for those who had lost their hearing, as opposed to the congenital deaf. According to Elliott [13] a multichannel electrode may be necessary before this experimental device becomes practical for speech understanding.

Design Aids for Communicating with Deaf Children

Deaf children as a group are as intelligent as children who can hear, yet many are diagnosed as functionally retarded because they have a language deficiency associated with their inability to hear or speak. Children learn the deaf sign language (finger positioning), and this serves as a communications medium between deaf persons or between the deaf and their teachers or the few others who understand it. However, the deaf person who can communicate only by sign language is relatively isolated in a society composed largely of hearing persons who communicate through speech.

The author once worked briefly for a deaf person who communicated his wishes entirely through beautiful handwriting. Technology now permits faster and more remote techniques, as discussed in the next section.

In terms of receiving information, lip reading greatly aids the understanding of speech provided, of course, the deaf person is sufficiently close to look at the speaker's lips. The Upton eyeglass [46] was designed to augment lip reading. A minute prism was mounted on one of the eyeglass lenses and the deaf person received binary signals in the visual field near the talker's mouth. The signals were in regard to fricatives, stops, and nasal speech sounds. As noted in Chapter 12, certain consonants are more difficult to interpret correctly, so the Upton eyeglass aided lip reading by visually clarifying the articulation of speech sounds.

Therapists have been largely concerned with teaching deaf children to understand the language, to communicate through sign language; and to read lips. The congenitally deaf are also functionally mute, so a real challenge comes in teaching one to articulate words without auditory feedback. Helen Keller learned to speak, but proper voice intonation, which the hearing child has learned through imitation, is difficult to communicate to the deaf.

Design Aids for Communicating with the Deaf Adult

Most persons who are deaf are not also visually impaired, so a logical media for communication has been through the visual-speech interactive technology. Another communication medium is through the tactile sense discussed previously in relation to the blind. Vibrotactile and electrotactile devices [Elliott, 13] have been developed. The Optacon could be used with extensive practice to teach discrimination of words and printed sentences through fingertip stimulation.

In terms of remote communications the interactive display technology has much to offer. The adult deaf person who has learned to read and write should not be required to view a speaker directly to receive information, nor should the person receiving the message be required to view the deaf person. Regarding the latter, Texas Instruments, Inc. [43] has developed a teletype device that permits communications by the deaf over the telephone. For example, a deaf worker who will miss a day's work may call in over the telephone via a teletypewriter, and the coded message is then converted to a printed output. This type of device may soon be required in large organizations employing several deaf workers. With the development of the voice synthesizer (Chapter 12), the printed message could be readily converted to a synthetic voice output.

As noted in Chapter 12, the voice synthesizer quite literally gives the mute person, or the deaf person with poor voice intonation, the ability to communicate via data entry over the keyboard. The quality of the speech is much more understandable than that produced by the congenitally deaf. It is also possible that a speech recognition device could be trained to recognize a deaf person's voice, which could then be converted to high-quality speech via a voice synthesizer. A miniature synthesizer could be portable.

Another speech recognition device currently being perfected is the automatic typewriter that is inputed directly from a vocal input. Such a direct-output dictation machine has an application to the business environment, but as a receiver of information, the deaf would be greatly aided. Visualize a deaf person attending a lecture in a large auditorium. An interpreter using sign language may be practical only when there are several deaf persons; also, the deaf must be close enough to see the hand movements. With the automatic typewriter technology, the voice output could be inputed to a computer terminal display providing a real-time readout of the speech in printed format.

Live television programs now provide closed captions similar to the translations (subtitles) of foreign films. Thus, if adult deaf persons can read printed material fairly rapidly, it may soon be technically feasible for them to receive remotely a visual speech output. Real-time voice information could be received in print without distracting others with sign language via intermediaries near the speaker.

Driving Aids for the Deaf

Studies of accident and violation statistics are somewhat divided on whether being totally deaf has resulted in unsafe driving practices. Some studies indicate that the deaf have fewer violations [Finesilver, 15; Fox, 17]. In a study with deaf and nondeaf matched on relevant variables including annual mileage, no difference was found for female drivers, but a higher frequency of accidents and violations was found for the deaf male [Coppin and Peck, 6]. Another study found deaf drivers over the age of 50 had more accidents than average drivers, while deaf drivers under 50 had fewer accidents than average drivers. [Roydhouse, 41].

In speculating on the importance of auditory information for driving purposes, the items commonly listed are train whistles, railroad crossing bells, emergency vehicle sirens, engine noises signifying problems with one's own vehicle, and horns from other vehicles. Henderson and Burg [21] found that with vehicle windows closed, persons with normal hearing hear outside horns and sirens very poorly. The sounds were largely masked by engine noises, and the masking effect was equivalent to that of a person with severe hearing loss. Since people drive with tape recorders, radio, air conditioning, talking, and other internal masking sources, it is unknown under these conditions to what degree outside signals can be heard by anyone.

Often the guidelines for licensing drivers who are found to be hard of hearing on a voice recognition test are that they should be required to have two outside mirrors and an inside rear-view mirror, and usually they are required to take a special deaf driver's course [Booher, 4]. Deaf drivers generally compensate with increased visual vigilance. However, commercial truck drivers, who may need to hear the voices of children over the sound of their engines, may require better hearing [4]. In Quebec, bus drivers and taxi drivers cannot have a severe hearing loss (40- to 60-dB loss) and be licensed, but they may drive public vehicles without passengers when deaf in one ear only [Quebec Ministry of Transport, 39].

No state in the United States prohibits the deaf from driving passenger cars [Booher, 4]. Some deaf do have difficulty with drivers' education and licensing exams. Special drivers education courses are available for the deaf with captioned visual information. The deaf are encouraged not to drive alone over unfamiliar routes, to check often for mechanical problems, and to use outside mirrors. Basically, information is lacking on what auditory requirements are necessary for safe driving, so it is difficult to prescribe alternatives for the deaf.

In-car displays could probably be developed that would inform the deaf of engine noise problems. Special sensors could be developed that would sense certain types of external sounds and these could be displayed by instrument lights. Conventional buzzer sounds in vehicles could also be displayed visually.

QUESTIONS AND PROBLEMS

1 The constraining effects of a disability may be overcome in what three ways?
2 What changes would be required in a typical classroom for compatibility with the requirements for a wheelchair student?
3 Using the facility design criteria provided in the chapter as a checklist, evaluate the accessibility of a college building that was constructed 20 or more years ago. Have any changes been made to meet accessibility standards? What changes would need to be made to remove architectural barriers?
4 In what respects does a quadriplegic differ from a paraplegic?
5 Why would a quad have difficulty with conventional hand controls for acceleration and braking or with a conventional steering knob on the wheel? Should hand controls be on the left or right of the wheel for a quad?
6 What are three modifications necessary to a van for a paraplegic to drive it from a wheelchair without any assistance from others?
7 Considering the design recommendations for controls given in Chapter 5, what violation do you see in a combined throttle-brake lever?
8 Briefly, why is it difficult to design a reading machine that can speak as intelligibly as the average person?
9 Why would a blind person walking on the surface of the moon be unable to sense the presence of a boulder a short distance ahead?
10 Could a blind student with a cane find his or her way to your classroom without being led (assuming the room number was known)?
11 What are two devices that would permit the deaf to interpret spoken speech without seeing the speaker and permit the mute to communicate orally?

REFERENCES

1 Allen, J.: An approach to reading machine design, *Human Factors,* vol. 20, no. 3, 1978, pp. 287–293.
2 Allen, M. J.: Vision and driving, *Traffic Safety,* vol. 69, no. 9, 1969, pp. 8–10.
3 Bilger, R. C.: Evaluation of subjects presently fitted with implanted auditory protheses, *Annals of Otology, Rhinology, and Laryngology,* vol. 86, suppl. 38, 1977.
4 Booher, H. R.: Effects of visual and auditory impairment in driving performance, *Human Factors,* vol. 20, no. 3, 1978, pp. 307–320.
5 Collins, C. C. and P. Bachy-y-Rita: Transmission of pictorial information through the skin, *Advances in Biological and Medical Physics,* vol. 14, 1978, pp. 285–315.
6 Coppin, R. S. and R. C. Peck: "The totally deaf driver in California: Part II" Sacramento, Calif, California Department of Motor Vehicles Report No. 16, December 1964.

7 Cotler, S. R. and A. H. DeGraff: *Architectural Accessibility for the Disabled of College Campuses,* New York State University and State University Construction Fund, Albany, N.Y., October 1976.

8 Cotzin, M. and K. M. Dallenbach: Facial vision: the role of pitch and loudness in the perception of obstacles by the blind, *American Journal of Psychology,* 1950, vol. 63, no. 4, pp. 485–515.

9 Cratty, B. J.: The perception of gradient and the veering tendency while walking without vision. *American Foundation for the Blind Research Bulletin,* 1967, vol. 14, pp. 31–51.

10 Dreyfuss, H.: *The Measurement of Man, Human Factors in Design,* 2d ed., Whitney Library of Design, New York, 1967.

11 Diffrient, N., A. R. Tilley, and J. C. Bardagjy: Humanscale 1/2/3, Cambridge, M.I.T. Press, 1978.

12 Dudley, B. R., Jr.: New protection for the employment rights of disabled citizens, *Paraplegia News,* vol. 32, no. 8, August 1979.

13 Elliott, L. L.: Development of communication aids for the deaf, *Human Factors,* vol. 20, no. 3, June 1978, pp. 295–306.

14 Engelman, S. and R. Rosov: Tactual hearing experiment with deaf and hearing subjects, *Exceptional Children,* vol. 41, 1975, pp. 243–253.

15 Finesilver, S. C.: "A study on driving records, licensing requirements, and insurability of physically impaired drivers," Denver, Colorado: Denver University, Final Report, Grant No. SRS-RD-2283-G, Social Rehabilitation Service, Dept. of Health, Education, and Welfare, 1970.

16 Fonda, G.: Bioptic telescopic spectacles for driving a motor vehicle, *Archives of Ophthalmology,* vol. 92, no. 4, 1974, pp. 348–249.

17 Fox, H. G.: Silent but skilled, *Police Chief,* vol. 36, no. 1, 1969.

18 General Services Administration: *Design Criteria: New Public Building Accessibility,* PBS(PCB):DG5, GSA Public Buildings Service, May 1977.

19 Goebel, L. A.: *Maximum grasping reach of operators possessing functional impairments of the upper extremities,* Master's Thesis, Department of Industrial Engineering, Texas A & M University, December 1978.

20 Hayes, L. B.: "Telescopic lens system and driver licensing," Conference of Safety Management Institute, Bethesda, Md., 1975.

21 Henderson, R. L. and A. Burg: "Vision and audition in driving," Santa Monica, Calif: System Development Corp., Final Report No. DOT-HS-801265, 1974.

22 Holden, C.: The handicapped: HEW moving on civil rights in higher education, *Science,* vol. 194, 1976, pp. 1399–1402.

23 House, W. F. and J. Urban: Long-term results of electrode implantation and electronic stimulation of the cochlea in man, *Annals of Otology,* 1973, pp. 504–517.

24 Jones, M. A.: *Accessibility Standards Illustrated,* Capital Development Board, State of Illinois, June 1978.

25 Juurmaa, J.: Transportation in mental spatial manipulation: A theoretical analysis, *American Foundation for the Blind Research Bulletin,* vol. 26, 1973, pp. 87–134.

26 Kloner, W. and E. Weber: New rules on airline accessibility, in "Breaking Down Barriers," C. J. Sabitier, Jr., *Paraplegia News,* vol. 32, no. 8, August 1978.

27 Kohler, I.: Orientation by aural clues, *American Foundation for the Blind Research Bulletin,* vol. 4, 1964, pp. 14–53.

28 Koppa, R. J.: *Adaptive Control Requirements for the Quadriparetic Driver,* Ph.D. dissertation in Industrial Engineering, Texas A & M University, May 1979.

29 Less, M., E. C. Colverd, J. Dillon, and J. Young: *Hand controls and assistive devices for the physically disabled driver,* Human Resources Center, Adaptive Driver Education, Atherton, N.Y., 1977.

30 Linvill, J. G.: "Research and development of tactile facsimile reading aids for the blind (the Optacon)," Stanford Electronics Laboratories, Stanford University, Stanford, Calif., March 1973.

31 Mace, R. I.: *An Illustrated Handbook of the Handicapped Section of the North Carolina State Building Code,* North Carolina Building Code Council, Raleigh, N.C., 1974.

32 McCormick, E. J.: *Human Factors in Engineering and Design,* McGraw-Hill, New York, 1976, pp. 137–138.

33 National Academy of Sciences. *Mobility for spinal cord impaired people,* workshop report, Feb. 22–24, 1974.

34 National Aeronautics and Space Administration: *Bioastronautics Data Book,* NASA SP-3006, sec. 14, 1964.

35 Nickerson, R. S.: Human factors and the handicapped, *Human Factors,* vol. 20, no. 3, June 1978, pp. 259–272.

36 The "Norman" Wheelchair, an exciting new breakthrough for thousands of restricted wheelchair confinees, brochure by Falkenberg, Inc. Portland, Oregon, 1979.

37 Olson, S. C. and D. K. Meredith: *Wheelchair Interiors,* National Easter Seal Society for Crippled Children and Adults, Chicago, Illinois, October 1973.

38 Overby, C. M., T. M. Myer, J. Hutchison, R. Wiercinski: Some human factors and related socio-technical issues in bringing jobs to disabled persons via computer-telecommunications technology, *Human Factors,* vol. 20, no. 3, June 1978.

39 Quebec Ministry of Transport, *Medical guide to determine ability to drive a motor vehicle,* Department of Transport, Quebec, Canada, July 1973.

40 Richards, O. W.: Visual needs and the possibilities for night vision: Part 3, *The Optician,* Dec. 1, 1967.

41 Roydhouse, N.: Deafness and driving, *New Zealand Medical Journal,* vol. 66, 1967, pp. 878–881.

42 Shingledecker, C. A. and E. Foulke: A human factors approach to the assessment of the mobility of blind pedestrians, *Human Factors,* vol. 20, no. 3, 1978, pp. 273–286.

43 Texas Instruments (TI) News Bulletin No. 769, New Communications Service Available to Hearing-Impaired TIers, January 9, 1979.

44 *UM Recorder,* News of the University of Michigan Rehabilitation Engineering Center, vol. 1, no. 1, February 1979.

45 University of Michigan and State of Michigan Department of Education Bureau of Rehabilitation: "Assessment of jobs and workers for accomodation of the physically handicapped—A description of project activities," a brochure from the Ergonomics Laboratory, Department of Industrial and Operations Engineering, University of Michigan, 1979.

46 Upton, H.: Wearable eyeglass speech reading aid, *American Annals of the Deaf,* vol. 113, 1968, pp. 222–229.

47 Urban Mass Transportation Administration and Transportation Systems Center, *The handicapped and elderly market for urban mass transit,* U.S. Department of Transportation, Washington, D.C., 1975.

48 *Paraplegia News,* vol. 32, no. 8, August 1979.

49 Veterans Administration: Program guide: Add-on automotive adaptive equipment for passenger automobiles, VA Prosthetics and Sensory Aids Service, March 31, 1978.

50 Wade, M. G. and M. W. Gold: Removing some of the limitations of mentally retarded workers by improving job design, *Human Factors,* vol. 20, no. 3, 1978, pp. 339–349.

51 Zuniga, E. N.: Personal communication on driver training at the Texas Institute for Rehabilitation and Research, 1976, as reported by R. J. Koppa [28].

52 Veterans Administration: VA standard design and test criteria for safety and quality of automobile wheelchair lift systems for passenger motor vehicles," Veterans Administration Prosthetic Center, VAPC-A-7708-8-3, May 1978.

Chapter 14

Human Factors in
Expanding Technology:
Data Processing
and Consumer Products

As we begin the final chapter, there are still a number of application areas that merit discussion. In an era when it seems that every transaction is becoming computer-based, the topic of person-computer interaction is essential. Microcomputers are becoming standard job aids for industrial engineers and scientists.

The electronic typewriter of the 1980s combines many of the features of a conventional typewriter and a computer. Word processors are equipped with hard copy or CRT display readouts (CRT accessories) and offer the capability of text editing, automatic alphabetizing of listings, and computing numeric data.

Since data entry devices provide a media for communicating with computers, they could be classified as a subcategory of equipment within the topic of person-computer interfaces. However, there are many data entry devices (for example, the conventional typewriter) that have a direct, hard-copy output without necessarily communicating directly with a computer. Therefore, data entry and person-computer interaction will be considered separately.

Seibel [31] has defined data entry as "man to machine communication." Such a broad definition would encompass the various controls discussed in Chapter 4—switches, levers, cranks, and so forth. It is true that a variety of controls could be employed to enter data, but more commonly, data entry is associated with keyboards or other inputing techniques such as voice actuation (Chapter 12), graphic input devices, and handprinting.

Person-computer interaction in time-shared systems involves a two-way communication or dialogue. In this chapter, the emphasis will be on user problems in trying to communicate with a computer that can only understand what the user said literally, not what he or she meant to say. Types of errors often made and design recommendations for reducing errors in query systems will be spotlighted.

Later in the chapter, we will shift gears and discuss briefly consumer products and the impact of the Consumer Product Safety Act [9] on the manufacturer's responsibilities. The reader is challenged to apply the principles and criteria introduced in this text to a host of consumer products. These products surround us in our homes and each has an obvious human factors interface, yet research in this area is less well documented than are human factors interfaces in the larger closed-loop systems. There is no question that the consumer industry has lagged behind the military and industrial systems in recognizing the need for human factors data, but the potential for design-related errors is fully as great.

DATA ENTRY SYSTEMS

Historically, organizations were assigned responsibility for training large numbers of operators on devices such as typewriters, keypunch machines, and mail-sorting machines. It was evident to training organizations that entry speeds and error limits of the operators were in large measure a function of the design of the keyboard provided to the operators. We shall see later that even in the early 1930s people were thinking of ways to redesign the alphanumeric keyboard to improve operator performance.

The typewriter employs a single-press, alphanumeric keyboard. Numeric keyboards are employed in keypunch operations, calculators, and touch-tone telephone dialing. But the keys do not need to be struck one at a time in rapid sequence and, in fact, pressing several keys at once can increase the speed of data entry for a trained operator. Multipress or chord keyboards are used on the stenotype machine and have been employed on manual mail-sorting machines.

There are also graphic and analogue devices, for example, the light pen used for graphic design inputs and the "mouse," joy stick, or conventional step keys used in text-editing applications. These and other devices will be discussed in the next section.

Single Key Press Devices

The most popular input device is the single key press device. Gould [17] has discussed four classes of single keying devices and the advantages and disadvantages of each (Table 14-1). In general, these devices increase in order of complexity and with complexity, special training and recall of procedures is required. However, the last two devices provide more flexibility in the types of problems they can address.

The simplest device (one-to-one mapping) is illustrated by the sales

Table 14-1   Advantages and Disadvantages of Classes of Keying Devices

Class	Examples	Advantages	Disadvantages	When to use
Mapping one function to one key	• Fast-food hamburger point-of-sale terminals • Function keys on the IBM MCST	• Recognition rather than a recall task • Functions are always visible • Easy to learn; fast to execute • May take advantage of people's place memory • May code groups of functions	• May require a huge keyboard • Special-purpose applications are expensive • Generally not suited to a powerful system • Not easily extendible	• When repetitive, frequent use of functions is required • For rapid access to often-used macros • When functions cannot be easily factored • Little training time and high turnover of employees
Mapping a few functions to one key	• Dial telephone • Hand-held calculators • Alternate coding on typewriter keyboard	• Requires fewer keys than one-to-one mapping • Recognition rather than recall task • Visible functions • Easy to learn • Easily incremented • Can use standard keyboard	• Probably more error-prone than one-to-one mapping • User needs to press more than one key • Cannot optimize layout for all levels • One may forget which mode one is in	• When there is already a well-learned subset of functions
Mapping many functions to one key	• Menu selection in a library information system (prompting and selection) • Command language and computer-aided instruction via Touchtone telephone buttons (no prompting)	• Telephone buttons are readily available • Can use with a simple inexpensive terminal • Can use with unmarked keys or with overlays • Software (rather than hardware) organization leads to flexibility	• Hard to learn and, historically, hard to implement • Initially, without prompting it requires user to attend to more than one thing • Recall rather than recognition task (without display guidance) • Functions are not visible (unless overlays, displays, etc.) • Abstract language rather than button press	• When people are willing to be trained • When universal access is required • When many rapid sequences of button presses (functions) not required • When functions factor easily (for example, hierarchical functions) • When prompting, a display and excellent feedback are available • With well-structured hierarchical applications

Table 14-1 *(Continued)*

Class	Examples	Advantages	Disadvantages	When to use
Mapping many functions to many keys (spelled or typed-out functions where a function is a combination of command and variables)	• Computer command languages (CP, CMS, TSS, TSO, MULTICS) • Computer-based editors • Computerized text editors	• Very powerful and flexible • Easily extendible and modifiable • Command and variables are entered in the same manner	• Harder to learn • Recall rather than recognition task • Users may use only a subset of the language • Error-prone • Slower to type a command than to push a single button • Disadvantageous for nontypists	• When the number of functions is greater than 50 • When the number of operands is very large (each command could be a single button, however) • When user can type and is above average intelligence • When applications undergo frequent modifications • When the terminal is used for several similar applications • When a typewriter is required to enter both functions and text

Source: Adapted from Gould [17].

terminal at fast-food hamburger businesses. The machine requires little learning. The salesperson takes an order and presses the button corresponding to the item selected. Since each item has a location on the keyboard, the items are quickly identified with unique places. The computer has stored prices and does all the arithmetic in the transaction.

Calculators, telephones, and conventional typewriter keyboards illustrate the second class, mapping a *few* functions into one key. Of course, each key has a separately identified place, but it is the combination of keys that produces meaningful sequences which are inputted. The possibilities for error are greater than for one-to-one mapping. Letters may be transposed or we may forget the last part of a message while typing or dialing the first part. Seibel [31] reviews the literature on ways of arraying data so that the user is less likely to make errors and is able to work faster.

Menu selection and computer-aided instruction are examples of mapping *many* functions into one key. In systems involving person-computer dialogue, the user makes choices in the identification of specific information needed and the computer, in turn, provides feedback to enhance the communication

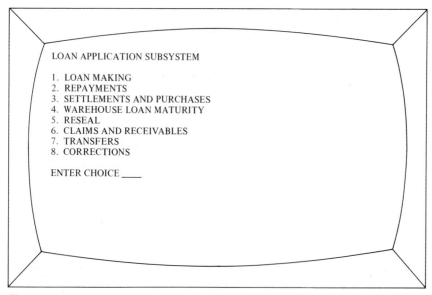

LOAN APPLICATION SUBSYSTEM

1. LOAN MAKING
2. REPAYMENTS
3. SETTLEMENTS AND PURCHASES
4. WAREHOUSE LOAN MATURITY
5. RESEAL
6. CLAIMS AND RECEIVABLES
7. TRANSFERS
8. CORRECTIONS

ENTER CHOICE ____

Figure 14-1 Menu selection frame format. *(Pew, 1979.)*

process. Menu selection is becoming common in automated library systems. Figure 14-1 illustrates a menu-choice text for a loan application [Pew, 28]. The user in this system positions the cursor on the choice entry line of the menu frame and then types in the appropriate digit. This number designates the next frame according to a predetermined sequence or hierarchy of branching functions.

The last class of single key-pressing device listed in Table 14-1 involves mapping many functions to many keys via computer programming. As most of the readers know, the possibilities for error increase markedly with computer languages and inputting programs requires extensive training. An obvious advantage is that the program can be modified or extended as the information needs changes.

Multipress or Chord Keyboards

Table 14-2 lists advantages and disadvantages of special types of input devices; the first discussed is the multipress or chord keyboard. The basic premise of the chord keyboard is that the decision time required to make two simultaneous presses with two hands is relatively small compared to the time required to make corresponding sequential presses with the fingers of one hand. We know from playing chords on a piano that people are capable of pressing multiple keys almost simultaneously (within 0.3 sec). As early as 1959, Lockhead and Klemmer [22] studied an eight-key chord keyboard system for data entry. One or two keys per chord were used for entering alphanumeric characters. Chords employing three to seven keys pressed simultaneously by the fingers were used to

Table 14-2 Advantages and Disadvantages of Special Types of Input Devices

Class	Examples	Advantages	Disadvantages	When to use
Chord devices	• Piano • Stenotype • Mail-sorting • Modified typewriter	• Potentially faster keying rates	• Difficult to learn and interpret • Error-prone	• For highest keying rates • In routine, repetitive classifications • Perhaps, on highly technical, frequently typed material
Electro-mechanical pointing or writing devices on computer-controlled graphic displays	• Light pen • "Mouse" • Joy stick	• Can quickly locate a target on a display • Excellent selection device for large numbers of potentially selectable alternatives • However, standard keyboards can be modified to provide the same analogue functions	• Presently clumsy when used simultaneously with a keyboard • Slow for data entry • Expensive	• Text-editing applications • Graphic applications • When switching to another input device is not cumbersome
Direct human input	• Constrained or unconstrained handwriting • Speech • Finger pointing • Eye pointing	• Natural • Possibly little learning required	• Most input devices do not require much learning • Not much faster than keying • Presently expensive, generally unreliable, and limited in scope • Requires verification feedback	• Perhaps less error-prone than pushing keys • Voice can be used with personalized discrete vocabularies

Source: Adapted from Gould [17].

generate common words. Chording is the principle underlying the Stenowriter stenotype machine [Galli, 16] and the word-writing machine [Ayres, 3]. Performance claims of 200 to 300 wpm have been made, which is obviously much faster than a typist using a conventional, single-press typewriter keyboard.

Ratz and Ritchie [29] and Seibel [33] have studied the choice reaction time associated with each of 31 possible one-hand chords (produced by combinations of the five fingers of one hand). Single-key presses were slightly faster, but the other patterns did not differ much (.306 to .352 msec). They concluded that entry speed was determined by motor constraints and not by decision time.

Seibel [32] has demonstrated also that keying reaction time is not dependent on the number of alternative responses (he studied 1023 different chords instead of 31 and found only a 25-ms difference in reaction time).

Learning an all-new-chord typewriter could involve extensive retraining. However, Seibel [30] demonstrated the feasibility of a chord keystroke on a modified standard typewriter with two extra key shifts. Chord strokes stood for commonly occurring words, phrases, prefixes, and suffixes. He claimed that learning the expanded vocabulary does not interfere with one's training and productivity on a standard typewriter, and that the payoff is an entry rate of one and one-half the standard typing rate.

Another application area for persons who are not already typists is mail sorting. Mail clerks have been trained to use various chord keystroke machines, one of which is illustrated in Figure 14-2.

Letters may be sorted into one of 144 possible destinations by simultaneously pressing two keys, one for each hand. Conrad and Longman [8] studied mail clerks trained on a standard typewriter and a matched group on the chord keyboard. The chord typists were initially faster, and after 7 weeks they maintained the advantage in entry speed. The standard typists were slightly more accurate, but this was attributed to the fact that they had visual feedback of what they had keyed, whereas the chord typists did not.

From a design standpoint, Alden et al. [2] concluded that the fastest keying may be achieved with chord keyboards that minimize the number of finger movements and the distance between finger reaches. Some chords are obviously more difficult to strike than others, for example, pressing with the fore, big, and little finger without use of the ring finger was one of the highest in response time and error percentage [Seibel, 33].

The Biomechanics of Keyboard Design

Most of us have accepted as a necessity that a typewriter keyboard be located in stairstep fashion on the control unit with the array of keys highly visible. Experienced typists seldom look at the key labels. The single keyboard design was likely based upon the traditional mechanics of how the keys struck the paper.

Kroemer [20] examined the keyboard from a biomechanical standpoint and

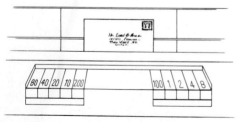

(a) Design of keys   (b) Keyboard in use

Figure 14-2 Burroughs chord keyboard. *(Courtesy of the Burroughs Corporation, 1980.)*

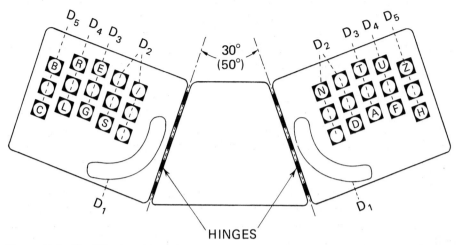

Figure 14-3 The K-keyboard based upon biomechanical considerations *(Kroemer, 1972. From Human Factors, 1972, vol. 14, no. 1. Copyright 1972, by The Human Factors Society, Inc., and reproduced by permission.)*

recommended his own K-keyboard, which was a radical departure from the traditional design. Those who type a good deal know that it can become somewhat tiresome holding the lower arms horizontal and also holding the palms horizontal and prone. The forearm muscles are kept in tension, introducing fatigue.

Kroemer developed a keyboard (Figure 14-3) that was divided into two sections, with one section assigned to one hand. Note that the sections were tilted laterally. He measured various declination angles and measured error rates, muscular strain, and subjective ratings after an endurance time of 19 min of typing. He also compared performance with his experimental K-keyboard at 45-degrees declination and with a standard keyboard. Of all angles investigated, the horizontal orientation was the worst on all counts. Angles from 44 to 66 degrees were preferred, while a perfectly horizontal or vertical keyboard was least preferred. In general, the K-keyboard, which keeps the wrists straight, was superior to the standard keyboard.

Other Design Requirements for Keyboards

Alden et al. [2], have reviewed the literature on design standards for keyboards. They concluded there are few definitive findings on which to base design standards, but they abstracted the following general design considerations:

Key dimensions: Diameter—0.5 in (1.27 cm) Center-to-center spacing— 0.75 in (1.81 cm)

Force and displacement: Force—0.9–5.3 oz (25.5–150.3 G) Displacement—0.05 to 0.25 in (0.13–0.64 cm)

Feedback: High force and low displacement were disliked and difficult to type on. Feedback is important during training; has little effect with experienced typists.

Keyboard size: A miniaturized keyboard for touch operation degrades performance, but size itself has little effect on self-paced or sequential activities.

Keyboard inclination: 10–35 degrees preferred (IBM Selectric permits adjustments in this range). No evidence that performance is degraded for tilts outside the range, but 0- and 90-degree angles are probably the worst conditions.

Numeric cluster: The 10-key touchtone telephone format is superior to the adding machine format [Conrad and Hull, 7]. (This topic is discussed later.)

Operator preferences: Preferences in various studies did not correlate highly with measured performance.

Entry method: Chord entry is faster than sequential entry for special tasks such as mail sorting.

Older keyboards employed circular keys with flat surfaces, but modern keyboards use square or rectangular keys with rounded corners to prevent slipping between keys. Concave surfaces also help to center the fingers.

It is difficult to conduct keyboard research on single parameters. Most studies tend to evaluate product lines where several variables other than the one of experimental interest are varied simultaneously. Parametric studies of the relation between individual keyboard design variables and operator performance have seldom been reported.

Layout of Alphanumeric Keyboards

No discussion of keyboards would be complete without mention of the standard "QWERTY" typewriter layout. Seibel [31] noted that at least 10 million typewriters in the United States have keys arranged in the traditional way developed a century ago. This estimate may not include other data entry devices using typewriter-like keyboard layouts such as computer terminals.

In 1936, Dvorak et al. [15] criticized the standard QWERTY typewriter layout because it assigned most of the work to the left hand and had unbalanced finger loads. Many high-frequency keys were on the top row rather than on the home row, and common typing sequences required more difficult finger patterns. Dvorak developed his own keyboard (Figure 14-4) in which the more common letters were on the home row. Note that numbers were still on the top row, but the odd ones are on the left and the even ones are on the right. The keyboard was said to take into account differences in finger strength and reaction time. It also permitted alternating between the hands for common digrams (two-letter sequences).

In the 1950s, Strong [35] conducted a study in which 10 QWERTY typists were retrained on the Dvorak keyboard. After 28 days they presumably regained their previous speed but not necessarily the same accuracy. Given a 5-minute speed test, this group was found to be slightly inferior in speed and accuracy to a control group that had not been trained on the Dvorak. Strong concluded there was no justification for adopting the Dvorak for government use. However, a

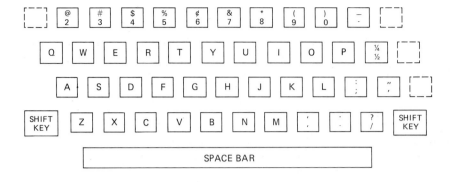

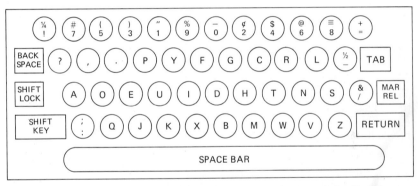

Figure 14-4 Standard electric typewriter arrangement, above, and the Dvorak arrangement, below *(Upper figure from Seible in Van Cott and Kinkade; lower figure from Dvorak, 1936.)*

relevant issue is how groups without previous training on either keyboard would compare in performance. In 1971 Dunn [14] and McCauley and Parkinson [23] reopened the issue by reporting some impressive results with children and adult computer programmers using the Dvorak keyboard.

Kinkead [19] studied keying speeds for the Dvorak, QWERTY, and an optimal keyboard specifically designed to improve keying speed. He noted that there were 135 digrams which account for 85 percent of the digrams in English (the others occur less than 0.2 percent of the time). An "optimal" keyboard was laid out such that almost all of these digrams were actuated by alternating finger action from one hand to the other. Finger loads were based upon functional considerations, with the least frequent letters assigned to the little and ring fingers on the bottom row. Kinkead measured keying times per digram, and given the frequency of digrams' occurrence in English, he estimated the keying time for the three keyboard layouts.

It was found that keying times for the QWERTY and Dvorak layouts were the same (125 ms) for the 135 digrams analyzed. From further analysis he concluded that the total time savings for the Dvorak compared with the QWERTY was only 2.6 percent and even the optimal design was only 7.6 percent faster than the standard.

The controversy may well continue as to whether the Dvorak or perhaps some other functionally conceived layout is superior in terms of typing speed and error reduction. There is a question whether a vowel or certain frequently occurring consonants should ever be assigned to the little and ring fingers (in Chapter 3 we learned the other fingers are faster). However, a major constraint to layout change is the economics of retraining a population of typists, modifying or outdating the millions of existing typewriters, and introducing a negative transfer-of-training problem for several generations.

The alphanumeric layout of the QWERTY typewriter has now become standard for all electric and manual typewriters and for teleprinter keyboards [34]. However, there are still differences between models in other function keys and characters with respect to location, labeling, and type of control. These differences lead to initial confusion in using new machines and transitioning between machines. Table 14-3 illustrates some of the differences.

There is a need for standardization of these other keys. For better or for

Table 14-3 Differences in Location, Labeling, and Type of Control for Four Common Data Entry Keyboards

Function or character	Model A	Model B	Model C	Model D
Break	"Attn" Left side	"Break" Right side	"Break" Right side	None
Carriage return	⟵⏋ Right side vertical bar	RETURN Right side horizontal bar	RETURN Right side horizontal bar	⟵⏋ Right side square key
Enter	Same as above	Same as above	Same as above	"Enter" Bottom right side (separate function)
Numerics	Conventional typewriter (across top)	Conventional typewriter	Three types: conventional, keypunch, and 10 keys on right side (separately)	Conventional key-punch or 10-key type
On-off	Right front rocker switch	Right rear rocker switch	Left rear rocker switch	Right front push-pull control
Clear	None	Right side	Hit "Cntrl" and "L" at same time	Hit "Alt func" and "Clear" at same time
!	Right of "P" (lower case)	Above "1" (upper case)	Above 1 (upper case)	Above 1 (upper case)
:	Right of "L" (upper case)	Right of "0" (lower case)	Right of ; (lower case)	Right of L (upper case)

worse, the basic arrangement of the alphanumerics appears to be unlikely to change.

Layout of the 10-key Keyboards

The digits 0 through 9 may be laid out in several different ways, and the merits of each of these layouts in terms of keying time and error rates have been the subject of several studies. When the touchtone telephone sets were being developed, the question arose as to how the keys should be arrayed. Should they be arrayed in the conventional dial-telephone manner, in two columns of five digits, in two rows of five digits, in a clockwise circular array like a speedometer, or like a calculator keyboard in reverse (as discussed in Chapter 12)? The following is a summary of the findings of Deininger [12]:

Measure	Reversed calculator	Two horizontal rows	Two vertical columns	Telephone	Speedometer
Keying time (sec)	6.0	6.17	6.12	5.90	5.97
Percent error	2.5	2.3	1.3	2.0	3.0
Votes for (ranked)	3rd	1st	5th	2nd	4th
Votes against (ranked)	2nd	4th	1st	5th	3rd

The data are far from conclusive. The conventional dial arrangement had slightly better combined ratings and performance scores (perhaps because we are accustomed to finding phone numbers in those locations). The layout in two horizontal rows was most preferred. The layout in two vertical columns was least preferred, although it showed the fewest errors. (Incidentally, the digits were arrayed horizontally with 1, 2 on the top row, 3, 4 in the second row, and so on, rather than having column one, 1 through 5, and column two, 6 through 0.)

The decision to go with the reversed calculator layout was likely based upon other considerations such as compactness. Although the performance data did not support its superiority, the total distance traveled in keying random telephone numbers would be shorter and, hence, with training, performance scores should favor this array.

A question was raised in Chapter 12: Why do calculators and telephones employ a reversed arrangement of digits? The population stereotype favors the telephone arrangement. This arrangement has also been used for television channel selection and many appliances. But there is little empirical evidence that one is better than the other for two groups, each working with only one keyboard arrangement. Conrad and Hull [7] compared the two formats with two groups of housewives and found that keying time (number of 8-digit entries per min) slightly favored the telephone (7.8 versus 7.4 entries per min). There were also fewer errors (6.4 to 8.2 for the calculator). However, the calculator arrangement was established by tradition and has been employed on almost every electronic calculator keyboard in existence. It would be difficult to change for reasons cited for the typewriter keyboard. A problem is likely to arise primarily for persons using both machines often and, perhaps simultaneously.

Certain computer terminals have the 10 keys patterned in three rows on the right half of the alphanumeric keyboard. Pressing a "NUM" key converts the output of the J, K, L, U, I, and O to the numbers 1 through 6. The numbers 7 through 0 are still on the top row. Keypunch machines also have this configuration, except it is lowered one row since there is no top row conventionally used for numbers.

Both typists and experienced users of 10-key calculators have a transfer-of-training problem in using this numerical keyboard. The numbers are arrayed in a *diagonal* pattern, and the zero is on the top rather than the bottom row. More search time and errors have been reported. A separate 10-key numeric pad to the right of the keyboard is recommended.

Older adding machine keyboards employed a 10 × 10 matrix of digits with a separate row for each number in a sequence. Data entry times were no faster and error percentages slightly higher than the compact, 10-key keyboard [Minor and Revesman, 26]. Apparently, whatever advantage it had in terms of place memory (a separate location for each number in a sequence) was offset by the disadvantage of longer distances of movement and potential errors in hitting a number in the wrong column.

Graphic and Analogue Input Devices

Up to this point, the focus has been on discrete entry keyboards. There are also multistate input devices for graphic and analogue entry. One of the earliest

Figure 14-5   The RAND Tablet and associated CRT. *(Courtesy of the Rand Corp., 1980.)*

examples was the light pen. The light pen involved a photoelectric and optical lens system and associated logic. It was designed to point out alphanumeric or pictorial data on a CRT and to graphically enter data by writing on the surface of the CRT. There were several technical and human factors problems in its use, but it offered the advantages of naturalness, giving positional information without further scanning, and requiring less formidable programming than other devices [DeGreene, 11].

Another special graphic-input device is the RAND tablet (Figure 14-5). The user writes with a stylus on a copper plate while monitoring the CRT. The spot on the CRT follows the relative position of the stylus on the plate, thus freehand writing is recorded. With the Grail (Graphic Input Language) system, the computer recognizes certain markings as symbols and normalizes the symbol for display. It also recognizes upper-case Roman numerals, Arabic numerals, and flowchart figures. The approach is suited for automated design of automobiles, bridges, complex computer programs, and mathematical models [11].

Card et al. [5] studied the relative efficiency of four devices for text editing: the "mouse," an isometric rate-controlled joy stick, and conventional keys such as the step keys and text keys on teleprinters (see Figure 14-6). The mouse is a small box that is moved by the operator on a table-like surface to transmit the

Figure 14-6 Four text-editing menu devices. *(Card, English, and Burr, 1977.)*

Table 14-4   Movement Times and Error Rates for Text-Editing Devices

Device	Movement time for non-error trials (sec)						Error rate	
	Homing time		Positioning time		Total time			
	M	SD	M	SD	M	SD	M	SD
Mouse	.36	.13	1.29	.42	1.66	.48	5%	22%
Joy stick	.26	.11	1.57	.54	1.83	.57	11%	31%
Step keys	.21	.30	2.31	1.52	2.51	1.64	13%	33%
Text keys	.32	.61	1.95	1.30	2.26	1.70	9%	28%

Source: Card, English, and Burr [5].

X-Y coordinates for the cursor. The findings, shown in Table 14-4, suggest the mouse was slightly faster and less subject to errors.

Card et al. [6], have also been interested in models for predicting the time required to perform text-editing tasks. Text-editing time involves text acquisition time (a reading and planning task) and text execution time. The model for text execution was defined as a summation of keystroke time, pointing time, homing time, mental preparation time, and systems response time. The benchmark reduced to 0.49 Nk (number of keys) plus systems response time. The model was found to predict well for the mouse.

Direct Human Input

The final category for data input deals with various techniques for directly entering data without any control devices. In Chapter 12, voice entry was discussed at some length. Devoe and Graham [13] explored the use of constrained handprinting of input data (a constrained sequence of strokes and shapes and all capital letters). For on-line printing, rates were 30 characters per min with 3 percent error rates. Seibel [31] recommended that a typewriter-like keyboard be used if the volume of data entry is at all heavy, since a majority of professional people today are able to use typewriters. However, he maintained there is still a place for handprinted data entry where entries are relatively infrequent and are a small part of the total task being performed. Another advantage is that printing is a one-hand task and some operators will require use of the other hand.

The feasibility of handprinted numeric inputs (without the delays due to key punching) has come about by the development of automatic off-line handprinted character recognition devices. The optical character reader (OCR) was discussed in Chapter 13 in its application to reading machines. According to Seibel [31], OCRs exist that have 99 percent accuracy for printed numbers and they are replacing keypunch operations in some systems.

Reading handprinted words is another matter since the opportunities for error are greater for letter recognition than for number recognition. The OCR is better suited for reading straight typed copy with a single type of font (Chapter 13). If handprinting is subject to human variability, handwriting is likely to be even more variable, and OCR applications are largely experimental. Gould [17], whose comments were earlier abstracted in Table 14-2, was not convinced that handwriting is that much faster than keying, and keying is easy to learn. He did not feel that the state of technology in character recognition made it practical in 1980. However, the state of technology is rapidly changing and recognition of constrained draft-quality printing, at least, may soon be a reality.

PERSON-COMPUTER INTERACTION

The computer-related field is changing, perhaps faster than any other technological field with a heavy demand from the business, military, scientific, and engineering communities. Numerous documents have been written on the role of high-speed computers in modern life and their effects on our life styles. In 1960 Licklider [21] anticipated a "man-machine symbiosis" or close cooperation between the two components in which the human set the goals, formulated hypotheses and models, asked questions, defined criteria and procedures, and the computer tested models against data, answered questions, carried out procedures, and displayed results. Licklider identified five obstacles to symbiosis, of which language problems was considered to be the most serious.

Human factors research has been encouraged in the areas of how to effectively communicate with computers and how to arrange information (in hierarchies or otherwise) so the information is most meaningful to a user at any given time. DeGreene [11] has emphasized the need for human factors research data on what people do in computerized systems, how they perform, how they make errors and specifically which errors they make, how they detect errors, and so forth. In Chapter 12, the work of Chapanis and others on how two people work together to solve problems was discussed. In a later section, specific errors noted in one type of computer system will be discussed.

There are presently few design handbooks for designing computer software similar to those discussed earlier for controls, displays, and work stations. However, design criteria are needed and will eventually emerge. A major software issue is design of user languages so as to avoid a breakdown in communications with the computer. Certain types of feedback are necessary to close the loop in the communication process. Gould [17] has discussed some of these issues. Pew [28] has developed some general principles and detailed recommendations for design and formatting information on a menu-type terminal display. Nickerson et al. [27] have discussed some of the broader issues, such as restrictions to accessibility of a computer and the need for users to be informed regarding how long a delay there will be so he or she may attend to secondary tasks. This section will be largely limited to specific design considerations, although a minimum of computer systems description will be required for the less familiar reader.

Time-Sharing Systems

Conventional batch processing involved long delays at the computer center after a problem was submitted. Programming errors were common and several cycles of program submittals were necessary before the program was completely debugged. Time-sharing systems permitted the person to interact continuously with the computer by running the program, obtaining immediate feedback on errors, and making on-the-spot corrections. Person-computer interaction may be viewed as a dialogue or two-way communication with instructions and data coming from the user, and results of performing operations, error messages, and other pertinent information coming from the computer. Some systems permit a more natural dialogue where the person and computer may each ask questions for clarification.

Today, not only is the computer time-shared locally through remote terminals, but also a network of time-sharing systems are formed by connecting telephone-quality data lines. Various users working independently operate on-line with the computer via remote teletype, graphics, or similar terminals. The time-sharing capability led to user-oriented programming languages, a package of editing and debugging tools, and a set of executive commands that gave the user access to various systems and services located elsewhere.

Since the users today may be scientists, engineers, or others not trained in computer technology, it is most important that the system be human engineered at the person-computer interface.

Selection of User Languages

There are three major classes of user languages: the single-frame interaction; the preplanned sequence of interaction; and the free-form user-generated interactive sequences [Gould, 17]. The advantages and disadvantages of each will be briefly considered, followed by a discussion of some typical errors reported. Ideally, the system should cooperate with the user in identifying mistakes in use of the language, although currently the solution is more often training the user.

Single-Frame Interaction   *Single-frame interaction* involves generation of variables and an implied command: for example, "enter" or "display." Simple data entry with verification and simple, single-frame query systems are illustrative. The system is fast, easy to learn, and can be easily modified. However, it is not as powerful as other systems and may require the user to provide extra input. It is used for systems requiring little interaction and for simple data entry and retrieval.

Preplanned Sequences   *Preplanned sequences* imply that the user either generates or selects variables, as with prompted entries. "Prompting," in this context, is illustrated by filling in the blanks or selecting from a menu list. Prompting is an effective aid for infrequent users or novices. Menu selection, illustrated previously in Figure 14-1, is a recognition task rather than a more difficult task requiring information recall. The task is *structured,* thereby reducing the likelihood of user inefficiencies such as inappropriate but acceptable commands.

A disadvantage of filling in the blanks is that it does require recall and, thus, it is more subject to errors like misspellings and wrong alternatives. The user must know the vocabulary of acceptable words—words that are not ambiguous to the system. It is much slower than free-form interaction, which is discussed next. With branching techniques (involving progressive disclosure of information) the user does not always know how to arrive at the desired answer through successive questioning.

Preplanned sequences are recommended for infrequent users—when the applications are stable and understood (for example, loan information); when the number of alternatives at each node is less than 10; and where the applications factor nicely into a hierarchy or successive branching operation.

Free-form Sequences *Free-form* language implies that the user generates the interactive sequences—both command and variables. Examples are information retrieval by formal queries using either a special retrieval language or a natural language. (There are also information creation applications such as computer-based text editors.)

Free-form languages are powerful in their applications, extendible, and potentially faster. They also allow the user to do unanticipated things. The disadvantages are difficulty in initial learning and a wide range of individual differences in successful usage. Free-form languages should be used when there are many choices for functions at each node, for example, the names of all medical doctors in New York City who speak fluent German. In other words, the free form is used when a sequence of interactions could not be easily specified in the initial programming of the system.

Generation or free-form languages are used by experienced users because they can be expanded easily and can handle exceptions easier (such as synonyms). Gould [17] concluded that although they may appear formidable because there are no prompts, people are able to learn the arbitrary codes. By contrast, *selection* (menu and fill-in) is based on a series of prompting messages usually in a hierarchical or branching arrangement. Selection is slower than free form for experienced users. Audio, hard-copy systems, and/or a fast-response display system (CRT terminal display) are output accessories for selection.

Vocabulary Size in Two-Person Dialogue

The introduction of natural language and the intriguing possibilities of the human operator in dialogue with a computer has stimulated research in the area of interactive human communications was already introduced in Chapter 12. Employing the two-person team approach and communicating via teletype, Kelly [18] found that the size of the vocabulary employed did not significantly affect the efficiency with which humans communicated in solving problems. The restricted vocabulary group was allowed only 300 different words; a slightly restricted group was allowed only 500 different words; while the unrestricted group could use any words. The significance of the findings for a free-form natural language system is that it is feasible to restrict the vocabulary slightly and still communicate equally well.

Michaelis et al. [25] conducted further studies of the number and types of words that subjects used within the constraints of a restricted vocabulary. Surprisingly, the words selected did not have much in common with high-frequency words in two well-known word lists (Kucera and Francis's written English; Howe's spoken English). Also, there was considerable subject variability in the words used even in the restricted vocabulary. However, a major conclusion was that small vocabularies may be used provided they are tailored to specific applications. In Chapters 10 and 12 the recommendations regarding message design are consistent with these findings.

Errors in Query Systems

When the natural language was first introduced, it was thought to be the ultimate in usefulness because the user would not need to know a formal programming language. In fact, however, the user is constrained to being highly specific when requesting information. The ambiguities we employ in conversational English tend to confuse the query system and yield either wrong answers or no answers. Gould [17] has studied the types of errors commonly made by persons seeking information from a computer data source. The following are examples:

Disjunctive ("or") queries can be error-prone. The intent may be for the computer to give a listing of all persons in either of two classifications, for example, doctors and nurses. However, should the system be asked to give doctors *or* nurses it will literally give only those in one classification.

Negative queries are sometimes stated in an ambiguous manner. For example, "Give me the names of people who do not own a car and ride a bicycle." The system would assume the negative applied to both cars and bicycles when this was not the user's intent.

Another type of error relates to *explicit conditional branching constructs.* In conversational usage, we may state, "If the lights are on, leave them on." The statement does not tell the computer to turn them on if they are off, although this may be implied by the user. It is necessary to have an "or else" statement when there is conditional branching.

Other errors include *context ambiguities.* Obviously, "move over there" is meaningless to a computer. Users also leave off qualifiers necessary to pinpoint a particular subset of desired information. In the English language certain words are both nouns and verbs. We distinguish them from grammatical context, but often commands are abbreviated to the point that an intended noun or verb usage is not clear. Examples of such words are "space," "switch," "place," "update" (status).

The computer may not accept certain synonyms, such as "case" for "item," or it may not distinguish past and future tenses, and so forth.

In summary, the simplicity of a natural language such as conversational English is complicated by the ambiguities introduced by the careless or unsuspecting user. Certainly training will help. However, a system should be error forgiving. If we do not understand a friend we ask for a restatement of the request in more specific terms. If the message is still misunderstood, we may attempt an answer and ask if this was what the person wanted to know.

Interactive computer systems must not merely read out answers that erroneously lead the user to believe the answer given was to the question the user intended to ask. At best, the computer should cooperate in assuring a correct interpretation of intent. At least, the computer should qualify the answer by stating it is the answer to a particular question that the user may then check for accuracy.

In the next section various types of feedback from a computer are discussed. Most of these are currently provided although clarification of ambiguities and feedback regarding ways of preventing serious errors are areas where further research is needed.

Types of Feedback in Interactive Systems

There are at least eight types of feedback [Gould, 17] needed or desired by the user of an interactive system in the course of dialogue.

- *Input verification*   Knowledge that the system is working and that the user's input was correctly typed. On touchtone telephones there is a beep for each key press and on other keyboards a tick or other auditory cue. The terminal display reads out the user's input so that typing errors may be determined.
- *Process completion verification*   The user needs to know the data was sent, received, and filed. The user's next action will depend upon the system's completion of a previous action. If the system has for some reason not accepted the last input, the user needs to know this. When an exception occurs, there should be a flashing light, changing tone, or other cue.
- *Request for stored data*   The user needs information displayed regarding the next frame of a menu item, requested part numbers, a file to be edited, and other stored data.
- *State of the system*   When there are delays greater than those normally encountered, the user may wish clarifying information on questions such as: Is the last input being processed? What mode is it in? What is the expected processing time? Are others time-sharing the data?
- *Tutorial feedback*   Examples of requests for help are: "Let's see my profile" or "How do I do this?" The computer provides a documented output.
- *Clarification of ambiguities*   Whenever the system cannot understand the input, it must provide feedback to that effect. As noted previously, this is a problem with natural languages and an area for further research and development. Speech or pointer inputs may also be misunderstood.
- *Feedback to prevent likely serious errors*   This form of communication would be desirable but is not presently provided on most systems.
- *Feedback on the history of the interactive system*   Often the user would simply like a recap of what has been done thus far, a summary of data input, or an answer to "What did I do previously in a particular situation?"

Dialogue Specification Principles

Pew and Rollins [28] reported their experiences with revising and expanding a set of specifications prepared for a complex government system into a set of recommended practices for dialogue design to be used in subsequent dialogue development. The case study dealt with a menu-selection interactive system. The following is a list of general principles based on the recommendations of Pew and Rollins for producing good dialogue from the user's perspective.

- *Know the user population*   It may be an objective to create dialogues for users who have limited understanding of computers, but who are knowledgeable with respect to the programs the computer will manage.
- *Respond consistently and clearly*   The user should be made to feel in control of the system by providing a sensible next step at every point. Dialogue frames should never dead-end with no further action available to the user. Inappropriate entries should be indicated by an error message (perhaps with a reference paragraph to a users manual that would clarify the type of error committed). Explicit options on what to do next should be given. This requires a system designed to anticipate possible states in which the user could find himself or herself and appropriate options to take.

    Error messages should be simple, direct, and unambiguous. The system should not be referred to as a person. An example of correct usage: "Loan search produced no output; check loan #." Poor usage: "Try again, I cannot find that loan in my files."

    Do not imply that the user was at fault; offer information useful in correcting the error. Example: "Loan number should have four characters." Poor usage: "You entered the wrong number of characters."
- *Carry forward a representation of the user's knowledge base*   The system should remember choices and data already entered so that at a later point in the transaction, the user is not required to do these things again.
- *Adapt wordiness to users' needs*   Since the user may be highly familiar with the particular application system, relatively brief messages and standardized terminology and abbreviations are recommended. However, brevity should not compromise clarity.
- *Provide the user with every opportunity to correct the error*   Provide immediate feedback about data entered and the integrity and consistency of new data as compared with existing data.
- *Promote the personal worth of the individual user*   Respect the user's intelligence. One way is an open-ended design which provides a minimum task requirement, but which permits the more knowledgeable user to go beyond the minimum and take initiative in solving problem cases or seeking further data sources. For example, the novice may examine each menu in a branching structure and refer to previous data, whereas the experienced user may employ a menu bypass feature to move directly to an advanced frame, thereby saving time and effort.

Frame Specifications

Pew and Rollins [28] have developed detailed recommendations for frame design, layout, sequencing, and prompting for menu-type applications. The recommendations were based on the above principles and field experience in connection with a Department of Agriculture project. They were based on the authors' background and limited interviews with Department of Agriculture system analysts. Table 14-5 provides examples of frame specifications. Table 14-6

Table 14-5   Examples of Frame Specifications

- All frame lines, except where noted below, should be left justified.

- Every frame has a title on a line by itself.

- The last four lines of every page are reserved for error messages, communication links, or system status messages.

- Every nonmenu frame should have an abbreviated reference to an operating manual and paragraph number (on same line as the title).

- When an output frame contains more than one page, the notation "page __ of __" should appear right justified on line 20.

- Use only approved abbreviations. Pretest abbreviations on a user sample.

- If the full 20 lines are not needed, develop a frame layout that is balanced and uncluttered on the screen.

- On menu frames when the list of items exceeds 15–20, consider reorganizing the list into two separate frames.

- Menu items should be listed in logical order and in accordance with expected frequency of use.

- The sequence of menu frames should be dictated by the logical flow of the user's analysis of the transaction.

- Menu choices should always be expressed in terms of specific alternatives.

- When an input frame is completed and a substantive action is to be performed by the central computer as a result, the user should be prompted as to the specific function that will be performed when he presses the enter key. Example: "Press enter to start loan calculation."

Source: Adapted from Pew and Rollins [28].

Table 14-6   Examples of Error Checks and Error Recovery Procedures

- Error messages should communicate the location of each error, the nature of the error, and a suitable recovery procedure.

- Location of the error may be indicated by placing the cursor at the first position at which the error was detected. This will cause a video inversion of the field (white characters on black becoming black characters on white). The nature of error and recovery procedure are given in the text on lines 21–24.

- Error messages should be as specific as possible. For example, the statements, "Alphabetic characters required" or "Numbers required" are preferred to the statement, "Field in error." If boundaries of a data field are exceeded, the acceptable number of characters should be indicated. If entry of certain variables is required to complete a transaction, the message, "This field required," may be used.

- When a restricted set of function keys is appropriate to a particular point in a dialog, other function keys shall be made inactive. Depressing the wrong function key should produce prompts concerning acceptable actions, such as, "Press enter to complete loan; press default to create a suspense file."

- For some errors corrective actions cannot be anticipated. In such cases the error message should be as specific as possible, such as "Search for loan #6354 produced no output."

Source: From Pew and Rollins, [28].

provides additional examples illustrating how error messages may be composed to aid in communicating specifically why a message was not accepted, how the user may correct the message, and how the user will know if the message has been accepted.

Much of what is known today in the area of person-computer systems design is based upon field studies and generalizations from principles developed elsewhere. Much remains to be done in laboratory research wherein specific design changes are systematically introduced and measures of error and time are taken to acquire a correct answer. Laboratory studies will provide a measure of the operational value of specific design recommendations.

CONSUMER PRODUCTS

There are many products that we purchase as individuals, each of which have human factors interfaces. Some of these, such as the family dwelling, the automobile, the telephone, and the typewriter, have already been discussed. One could readily list other household belongings—appliances, books, furniture, recreational equipment, and so forth. Space does not permit a detailed discussion of each item, so the reader must take the initiative in applying the design principles and criteria discussed previously to these consumer products. The issue of product safety has received the greatest attention and will be discussed first.

Product Safety

With the passage of the Consumer Product Safety Act in 1972 [9], the designers of consumer products in the United States became liable for faulty designs that contributed to accidents. Increasingly, the injured plaintiff (or the surviving heirs) are suing the manufacturer of products not safely designed. Certain attorneys are now specializing in product liability cases and employing the services of human factors and safety specialists who are qualified to determine the extent to which the product was unsafe.

Consumer product safety is clearly a safety engineering design issue. However, we have already seen that certain cases clearly fall within the purview of the human factors specialty, for example, when the user is required to read instructions or displays, hear messages, or execute control tasks in an environment where design-related errors may jeopardize safety.

Many safety issues do not involve human factors issues, of course. A product that fails to meet quality control standards may jeopardize user safety, but the design solution may be improved materials and quality testing. A human factors interface would be whether the person could be expected to perform effectively under various environmental stresses associated with poor design or product failure.

What are some examples of human factors errors in the design of consumer products? An obvious one is failure to warn the operator that he or she may inadvertently perform a hazardous act in using the product (or, in some instances, even in touching the product). A large outdoor-crane operator failed to judge correctly the distance to high-strung electrical wires, and he was electrocuted upon contact of the crane arm. Since it is very difficult to judge the distance of hanging wires, the operator should have been warned of the potential hazard of using the crane in close proximity of wires. One could argue that this was an employer (contractor) duty, but often the contractor is not as acquainted with operational characteristics of equipment as is the manufacturer.

Severe burns have been incurred in handling equipment in which there was improper guarding and labeling of hazardous equipment. For example, an electric transformer box was installed at ground level in the back yard of a residence, and the box was not properly secured. A small child was able to open it and severely burn himself. The reader is familiar with the movement to prevent children from getting into medicine bottles and other dangerous consumables by displaying the green "Mr. Yuk" symbol and by requiring that the cap be lined up in a certain way so that a small child would have greater difficulty opening it. Warning systems understandable by those who do not read well, that is, children or language handicapped, are becoming more common on all hazardous products.

Any flagrant violation of a human factors criteria resulting in an accident could be the subject of a litigation. For example, a vehicle was hit by a train locomotive at a grade-level crossing that did not have an active warning system. It was demonstrated in court that the driver could not have heard the train whistle under the particular circumstances in time to avoid his vehicle's being hit by or hitting the train. Sometimes boxcars are parked on a series of parallel tracks and they are so close to a grade-level roadway crossing that the motorist's line-of-sight is obstructed for an approaching train on a distal track. This is an error in operation more so than an error in design but nevertheless, human error is a directly contributing causal factor in the vehicle being hit.

In Chapter 6 safety engineering design guidelines were given for the workplace, for example, designing machinery so that injury is less likely to occur through careless operation. The emphasis there was on protecting the worker. However, it is clear that these same design deficiencies may also become booby traps for the user of products, and the user requires a similar measure of protection.

Ideally, there should be an agency to which consumer product manufacturers could take their prototype product and receive a "stamp of safety approval" prior to its release to the consumer. Assuming that sufficient knowledge exists regarding conditions that lead to risk of injury, such data should be made available to specialists who could accept or reject the product, much like a building inspector.

A problem with this simplistic solution is that there is such a variety of new products. Potential errors are often inherent in the unique ways the product is to be used, which may not be immediately apparent from product inspection. In other words, the product may be safe for many conditions of use and for a majority of users but unsafe under other conditions. The design solution may be highly dependent on contemplated conditions of use and could involve warnings to consumers or operating agencies regarding restrictions in use.[1]

Although it may not be currently feasible to guarantee the manufacturers of new products that their product will not sometime be the subject of litigation, a convenient stop-gap measure would be a document listing by product all court cases in the United States involving the product of interest and the court's decision. Product designers would at least have the benefit of reviewing precedent cases so as to be alert for potential design errors for which they might be liable. Small manufacturers should not be required to enlist the services of specialists to research court cases involving the product.

One final note relates to the proverb: "Do not throw the baby out with the bath water." There exists the danger that an increasing number of product liability cases involving large monetary awards to the plaintiff may ultimately result in corporations' refusal to manufacture worthwhile products for fear of being sued. (A familiar analogy is the indiscriminate offering of services by physicians who have been victims of malpractice suits.) In the previous chapter there was a discussion of devices and modifications for the handicapped driver. Should a small manufacturer of such devices be sued and charged because of a single accident, the manufacturer might immediately cease production to avoid further financial loss. The point is simply that not every accident is necessarily design-related, and the courts must exercise due caution in separating those seeking monetary gain by shifting the blame to a product from those who have indeed been the victims of negligent design of a product.

Consumer Product Evaluation

Consider the multitude of items involving human factors interfaces that one might find around the home, especially a middle-class home with young, active individuals. Table 14-7 summarizes a few items. Each of the items has human factors interfaces: controls, displays, workspace restrictions, noise, vibration, and safety interfaces, maintainability problems, and instructions for operation and safety in use.

Advertisements, brochures, and sales talks highlight the strong features of particular models, particularly the capabilities of the model. The manufacturer may or may not have attended to human factors interfaces aside from styling and product appeal. Space does not permit a discussion of the current state of technology in each area, much less a critique of human factors interfaces.

In a graduate course in human factors in design the author has assigned projects to students in an area of interest to them. Topics need not be limited to products around the home. Some students were encouraged to tackle larger operational systems, for example, a service station, market check-out counter,

---

[1]There is an injury information clearinghouse that disseminates information related to causes and prevention of product-related injuries. The law also permits prescribing the form and content of labels permanently affixed to the product.

Table 14-7   Common Household Items Involving Human Factors Interfaces

Entertainment

Television—controls, displays, cabinet interfaces
Video recorders
Stereo receiver display/control panel
Home-movie projectors and accessories
Digital clock radio
Musical instruments, cases, and attachments
Home computers, electronic toys and games
Telephone unit designs and location interfaces
Books, magazines, newspapers, and other reading material

Power tools and equipment

Power lawnmowers and edgers
Hedge and grass trimmers
Chain saws, woodworking and metalworking tools
Automobile tools and test equipment

Appliances

Range, microwave oven, refrigerator, dishwasher, compactor, disposal, blender, can opener, washer/
dryer, coffee maker, freezer

Other household items

Table and desk lamps, lighting fixtures
Household safety and security (door locks, alarms, smoke detectors, fire extinguishers, protective
weapons)
Individual heating and cooling units (fans, electric heaters, bathroom units, fireplace equipment)
Plumbing fixtures (faucets, drains, water closet, outside cutoff)

Recreational and athletic equipment

Riding units (motorcycles, mopeds, bicycles, snowmobiles, skis, motor boats, sail boats, roller and
ice skates, recreational vehicles, campers, dune buggies, sky gliders)
Mobility accessories (scuba diving gear, sky diving gear, horseback riding gear, jogging, dancing,
gymnastics accessories)
Competitive athletic equipment (team sports—baseball, football, basketball, bowling, soccer, volley-
ball; small-group sports—tennis, pool, handball, weightlifting, frisbee, fencing)
Outdoor supplies (camping equipment, firearms, fishing gear, hiking, exploring, mountain climbing gear)

Maintainability design

Maintainability design issues related to motor vehicles, televisions, air conditioning units, plumbing banking loan department, motel check-in and check-out desk, design of a room of the home (the kitchen is a favorite), or specific military systems. Systems and industrial engineering techniques were incorporated in defining requirements. But the focus in the course was always on optimizing the human interfaces with specific equipment.

Students were encouraged to review whatever human factors literature was available, but the major objective was to get the student out into the field to critically observe particular technology around him or her. Having selected a product—sports cars, microwave ovens, washer/dryers, stereos, lamps, or whatever—the student was expected to study the human factors interfaces on at least three models in that area and next, to compare the models point to point and decide which had the better design. No single model would be expected to be best on all criteria and, in fact, none might be optimal. Models selected should be in the same price range. If not, superior features would be expected of the more costly.

The final task would be to make recommendations to the class regarding a "well-human-factored" product and to defend the design to classmates who might have some other ideas. Students would prepare their own checklists based upon the principles and design criteria learned in the course. Those selecting a vehicle might take measurements of dimensions and compare them with anthropometric data. Controls, displays, environment, and safety aspects would be critically examined.

As an example, consider a ride lawnmower or garden tractor. There are safety standards for outdoor power equipment [American National Standard Institute, 1]. Table 14-8 presents certain provisions of the standards including vehicular stability, shielding and guarding, and prompt manual shut-off. Thus, a minimum requirement for a mower model would be indications that the vehicle appeared to meet these safety standards. In addition, functional human factors requirements would be considered: What is the turning radius? How close can the vehicle cut to tree trunks? How easy is it to shift gears and regulate power? How quickly can the cutting height be changed or a grass catcher or other attachment be mounted? How do seat cushions and suspension systems compare?

The critical student may ask other questions involving the trade-off with a walking power mower, in terms of criteria such as speed of cutting yards of various sizes, safety, fuel consumption, and human energy expenditure. If the mower were to be transported in the back of a motor vehicle, what are the logistics problems of a small manual mower and a larger mower that one rides? Other systems criteria could be considered, such as reliability in starting, operation in high grass, maintenance requirements, evenness of cut, and all-weather usage effects on the yard.

From the above it is evident that an effective evaluation would include not only comparisons of three models in terms of human factors and safety interfaces, but also an evaluation of the functional acceptability of the ride mower in comparison with a walking power mower. There are some document-

Table 14-8   American National Standard for Outdoor Power Equipment

1   **Starting arrangement**
Must be positioned so operator need not stand within the angle of discharge opening.

2   **Safety interlock system**
Gear shift must be in neutral, mower clutch in neutral or disengaged, and ignition key must be unlocked before engine can be started.

3   **Stability**
Longitudinal stability must be achieved up to a 30-degree slope and lateral stability up to a 20-degree slope without lifting off the ground.

4   **Enclosed deck**
Shielding on under side of blade with openings for grass tips to make contact with blade. Prevents large objects from making contact with blade. Towed rotary mower attachments must not have front openings in the blade enclosure.

5   **Shields and guards**
Permanently attached shields and guards must be provided to eliminate accidental contact by the operator during starting, mounting, and operating.

6   **Safety discharge chute**
An extension of the normal mower deck opening. Acts as a guide and deflector, causing particles to be thrown away and downward from operator.

7   **Braking system**
A brake pedal to be operated by the right foot and a parking brake must be provided. Latter must hold when mower is parked on a 16.7-degree slope.

8   **Blade speed, enclosure and stopping time**
Blade speed must not exceed 19,000 feet per min. Mower deck must extend at least $\frac{1}{8}''$ below blade. Blade must stop within 7 sec after operator shuts off power drive or declutches.

9   **Foot pedal materials**
All foot pedal material must be slip resistant.

10   **Uniformity of controls**
There must be logical standardization of controls so that each particular type of control is activated and reactivated in the same manner.

11   **Steering**
Steering mechanism must not lock in operating position. A steering stop is required to prevent excessive turning angle that might cause tipping. Tiller bar steering is not permitted.

12   **Shut-off control**
Units must have a shut-off control, for example, a key switch.

13   **Sound levels**
The sound level must not exceed 95 dB when a test microphone is located 10 in to the right and left of the centerline of the operator's position, 30 in above the seat and 4 in forward of the seat back rest, when mower attachment is mounted.

Source: American National Standards Institute, Inc. [1].

ed data sources: writing the manufacturers, examining consumer magazines such as *Consumers Reports* [10], which compares new models on various criteria, and reviewing brochures and user manuals. But again, the objective is to get the student to collect unbiased and unedited first-hand data. One should actually ride the three models of mower with a sensitive eye for differences. Second, regular users (owners or gardeners) could be interviewed, preferably those with a perspective of driving several different models.

The final recommendations are expected to incorporate the best features of each model. If there are no functional differences, the student should not force a choice. Remember that the objective of a human factors design evaluation is not necessarily to define the optimal, but to screen for features that would invite error and hazards to the user. Conceivably, two models might be equally good and the third substantially poorer. Identifying the lemon may be more useful than trying to split hairs between two equally acceptable designs!

CONCLUDING REMARKS

This text has not attempted to summarize all aspects of human factors as a systems science. From Chapter 4 on, we have concentrated on only one major aspect—the design of equipment, facilities, and environments emphasizing the human capabilities and limitations that constrain and define design criteria for technology and the workplace. Numerous examples of applications have been cited, although the intent has not been to provide a reference guide for modern-day technology.

The design criteria given clearly cut across conventional academic disciplines. They are not the unique concern of any academic department because the human being is so multifaceted. Thus, the experimental psychologist may tend to focus on the human as a sensing, perceiving, information-processing, learning, affective, and responding organism. The engineering anthropologist and biomechanics specialist may tend to view the human as a unique combination of bones, joints, muscles, and levers that constrain body reach and movement, work methods, loads that may be lifted, forces applied, and susceptibility of the body to fatigue and injury. The work physiologist may tend to focus on the human's physiological indicators of strains imposed by work and environment and the metabolic, homeostatic, and adaptive processes going on in association with work. Finally, there are industrial and other engineers who are interested in specific design and procedural questions and who may employ the research techniques developed in their own and in other disciplines to answering these applied questions. Human factors research borrows from many disciplines in seeking design solutions to practical problems.

Human factors research is synergistic in the sense that the subject is not the human in isolation (or in relation to generalized stimuli), but rather the human in relation to specific equipment and environments. In closed-loop systems the human output is only a part of the total systems output. It is difficult to isolate the two outputs and, in fact, we are often not interested in doing so because the applied question may be couched in terms of the adequacy of the system output.

However, human factors design interests are not limited to closed-loop person-machine systems. It is not necessary that there be a direct feedback loop wherein the operator's output modifies the system's input (as described in

Chapter 2). There are those principally interested in complex, closed-loop systems, such as vehicles and other tracking devices. Traditionally the focus was on those types of systems. However, a poorly designed sign, a book, building, door lock, or clothing may well degrade the user's performance whether or not the user's performance directly influences the behavior of the device in closed-loop fashion. The scope of human factors technology is broadening to address design issues wherein the human is not necessarily an element in a control loop system.

Although it is useful to view the human as a part of a larger system, contributing or degrading performance as do other elements, this is not to imply that the specialty of human factors skirts the issue of human value systems. Even in complex research where many objective performance measures are taken, the subject is often asked questions of preference among treatment variables. It has been emphasized that technology is simply a tool that mankind has developed to reduce its own drudgery. The human is the master. The specialty of human factors comes to grips with questions of how to marry the human with technology to enhance the productivity, safety, welfare, and enjoyment of the human being.

The methods of human factors researchers are the methods of both the scientist and the engineer. The literature reviewed in this text clearly implies the use of scientific rigor in experimentation and testing and the demand for reliable data. Yet the methods are patterned after engineering in being iterative, creative, and evaluative and modifying the research objective until the findings will be directly applicable to the answering of problems needing answers.

Above all, human factors data are useful. Some view with disdain a science or technology geared to applied questions pointing out the unsuspected spin-offs of basic research. To this objection Meister [24] has noted that even mathematics began as an effort to assist the Egyptian farmers to measure their farm lands. The spin-offs of the United States space program are further evidence of the value of specific applied research to applications not apparent at the time the research was conducted.

In this text, certain application areas have been addressed for which there is presently limited research data. The text could have simply summarized the research findings that are documented and ignored areas where data was sparse. The author has chosen not to allow the paucity of hard data to restrict subject matter. The problems exist whether or not the economic resources and management incentives have been marshalled to solving the problems. It is hoped that an outgrowth of *New Horizons for Human Factors in Design* will be to stimulate others to research in these areas. Whereas human factors design criteria are fairly well documented in government-sponsored systems, there is still a major void in criteria related to products developed by private resources (consumer products). As the educated public increasingly recognizes the importance of functional, human factors criteria, commercial producers may be more inclined to advertise their in-house research efforts leading to human-engineered products and systems.

It is recognized that few readers will ever be practicing ergonomists or human factors specialists. It has not been the objective of this introductory text to educate the reader to the level of a consulting practitioner. The tutorial goal will have been reached if the reader has become sensitized enough to human factors thinking to scrutinize equipment and environment critically for human errors and discomfort associated with design and say: "There must be a better way than this." Recognition that there is a person-machine problem and a systematic approach for solving it is half of the battle.

QUESTIONS

1   If it is easier to learn to use a one-to-one mapping device, why do most single-key press devices map several functions into one key?
2   Why haven't chord typewriters replaced the standard QWERTY keyboard?
3   Since the QWERTY keyboard was not well planned in terms of assigning frequently used characters to the fastest fingers and providing alternate hand use for common digrams, why has the keyboard layout been adopted as a standard? Couldn't a new generation of typists be trained on a more efficiently laid-out keyboard?
4   In what sense does a time-sharing interactive system involve more efficient dialog with a computer than a batch-processing system? Explain.
5   Although a natural language negates the need for learning a formal programming language, what is the major problem in its wide usage by the untrained public?
6   What type of feedback is often not provided in most computer programming?
7   What type of research is needed in person-computer interaction?
8   Give an example of a litigation case which involves consumer product safety at the human factors interface and one which does not.
9   Does the developer of a new product currently have a governmental agency that could approve the safety of the product prior to it being offered to the public. If so, which agency? If not, why not? How can the developer reduce the chances of being involved in a litigation over the product?
10 Select one of the items listed in Table 14-7; examine three models of the item available in the marketplace; point out model differences using sketches; and tell which model is best and worst from a human factors standpoint. The study may examine controls, displays, workspace, and safety interfaces on the three models.

REFERENCES

1   American National Standards Institute, Inc.: American National Standard Safety Specifications for Power Lawn Mowers, Lawn and Garden Tractors, and Lawn Tractors, ANSI B71.1-1972, March 31, 1972.
2   Alden, D. G., R. Daniels, and A. Kanarick: Keyboard design and operation: a review of major issues, *Human Factors*, vol. 14, no. 4, 1972, pp. 275–293.
3   Ayres, A.: Word-writing machine producing closed-up printing in response to simultaneous actuation of keys, Patent specification 3,225,883, patented December 28, 1965.
4   Barmack, J. C. and H. W. Sanaiko: *Human Factors in Computer-Generated Graphic Displays,* Institute for Defense Analyses, Arlington, Virginia, Study 234 (AD 636 170), April 1966.

5 Card, S. K., W. K. English, and B. Burr: *Evaluation of Mouse, Rate-Controlled Isometric Joy Stick, Step Keys, and Text Keys for Selection on a CRT,* Xerox Research Report, SSL-77-1, Palo Alto, California, 1977.

6 Card, S. K., T. P. Moran, and A. Newell: *The Keystroke-Level Model for User Performance Time with Interactive Systems,* Xerox Research Report, SSL-79-1, Palo Alto, California, 1979.

7 Conrad, R. and A. Hull: The preferred layout for numeric data-entry keysets, *Ergonomics,* vol. 11, 1968, pp. 165–173.

8 Conrad, R. and D. J. Longman: Standard typewriter versus chord keyboard—an experimental comparison, *Ergonomics,* vol. 8, 1965, pp. 77–88.

9 *Consumer Product Safety Act,* Public Law 92-573, 92d Congress, S. 3419, Oct. 27, 1972.

10 *Consumer Reports,* Mount Vernon, N.Y., Consumers Union of the United States, Inc., vol. 43, no. 11, November 1978.

11 DeGreene, K. B.: Man-computer interrelationships, *Systems Psychology,* McGraw-Hill, New York, 1970, chap. 10.

12 Deininger, R. L.: Human factors engineering studies of the design and use of pushbutton telephone sets, *Bell Systems Technical Journal,* vol. 39, no. 4, July 1960, pp. 995–1012.

13 Devoe, D. B. and D. N. Graham: Evaluation of hand-printed character recognition techniques, Final Report Contract AF30 (602)-4385, Project 4594 (Sylvania Project 171), Sylvania Electric Products, Inc., Waltham, Massachusetts, January 1968.

14 Dunn, A. G.: Engineering the typewriter from a human factors viewpoint, *Computers and Automation,* February 1971, pp. 32–33.

15 Dvorak, A., N. Marrick, W. Dealey, and G. Ford: *Typewriting Behavior: Psychology Applied to Teaching and Learning Typewriter,* American Book Co., New York, 1936.

16 Galli, E. J.: The stenowriting machine (abridged), Report No. RC-308, IBM Research Lab, Yorktown Heights, N.Y., July 5, 1960.

17 Gould, J. D.: Man-computer interfaces for informational systems, lecture to human engineering short course, University of Michigan, 1979.

18 Kelly, M. J.: Limited vocabulary natural dialogue, *Proceedings of the Human Factors Society,* 19th Annual Meeting, Dallas, Texas, 1975.

19 Kinkead, R.: Typing speed, keying rates, and optimal keyboard layout, *Proceedings of the Human Factors Society,* Dallas, Texas, Oct. 14-16, 1975.

20 Kroemer, K. H. E.: Human-engineering the keyboard, *Human Factors,* vol. 14, no. 1, 1972, pp. 51–63.

21 Licklider, J. C. R.: Man-computer symbiosis, *IRE Transactions on Human Factors in Electronics,* HFE-1,4-11, March 1960.

22 Lockhead, G. R. and E. T. Klemmer: An evaluation of an 8-key wordwriting typewriter, IBM Research Report, RC-180, IBM Research Center, Yorktown Heights, New York, November 1959.

23 McCauley, R. and R. Parkinson: The new popularity of the Dvorak simplified keyboard, *Computers and Automation,* February 1971, pp. 31–32.

24 Meister, D.: *Heresies: Brief Essays on Human Factors,* Navy Personnel Research and Development Center, San Diego, California, March 1977.

25 Michaelis, P. R., A. Chapanis, G. D. Weeks, and M. J. Kelly: Word usage in interactive dialog with restricted and unrestricted vocabularies, *IEEE Transactions of Professional Communication,* vol. PC-20, no. 4, December 1977.

26 Minor, F. J. and S. L. Revesman: Evaluation of input devices for a data setting task, *Journal of Applied Psychology,* vol. 46, 1962, pp. 332–336.

27 Nickerson, R. S., J. I. Elkinds, and J. R. Carbonnel: Human factors and the design of time-sharing computer systems, *Human Factors,* vol. 10, 1968, pp. 127–134.

28 Pew, R. W. and A. M. Rollins: Dialog Specification Procedures: rev. ed., Bolt, Beranek, and Newman, Inc., Report No. 3129, September 1975.

29 Ratz, H. C. and D. K. Ritchie: Operator performance on a chord keyboard, *Journal of Applied Psychology,* vol. 45, 1961, pp. 303–308.

30 Seibel, R.: A feasibility demonstration of the rapid-type data entry station, Research Report No. RC-845, Thomas J. Watson Research Center, Yorktown Heights, N.Y., December 1962.

31 Seibel, R.: Data entry devices and procedures, *Human Engineering Guide to Equipment Design,* chapter 7, H. P. Van Cott and R. G. Kinkade (eds.), U.S. Government Printing Office, Washington, D.C., 1972.

32 Seibel, R.: Discrimination reaction time for a 1,023-alternative task, *Journal of Experimental Psychology,* vol. 66, 1963, pp. 215–226.

33 Seibel, R.: Performance on a five-finger chord keyboard, *Journal of Applied Psychology,* vol. 46, 1962, pp. 165–169.

34 Standards, proposed USA standard general purpose alphanumeric keyboard arrangement for informational interchange. *Communications of the ACM,* vol. 11, no. 2, 1968, pp. 130–131.

35 Strong, E. P.: A comparative experiment in simplified keyboard retraining and standard keyboard supplemental training, General Services Administration, Washington, D.C., 1956.

Appendix

Additional Tables

Table A Other Selected Body Dimensions (inches)

Body part	5th Percentile Ground troops	Aviators	Women	95th Percentile Ground troops	Aviators	Women
Hand length	6.85	6.98	6.32	8.13	8.14	7.89
Palm length	3.77	3.92	3.56	4.61	4.69	4.24
Hand breadth	3.20	3.22	2.72	3.83	3.80	3.33
Foot length	9.65	9.62	8.74	11.41	11.42	10.42
Foot breadth	3.53	3.54	3.16	4.29	4.58	3.84
Head length	7.19	7.32	6.80	8.14	8.27	7.80
Head breadth	5.59	5.67	5.33	6.40	6.50	6.12
Interpupillary breadth	2.01	2.10	2.00	2.67	2.75	2.57
Ear length	2.17	2.31	1.77	2.72	2.88	2.34
	Army Aviators (*)	USAF (**)	USAF	Army Aviators	USAF	USAF
Interscye (maximum back breadth)	19.8	22.3	–	24.3	26.2	–
Waist–front length	14.0	14.1	12.0	17.1	17.4	16.3
Waist–back length	16.7	16.7	14.4	20.0	20.0	17.9
Shoulder length (neck/acromial)	5.3	5.7	5.1	6.9	7.4	6.5
Sleeve length (wrist/spine)	32.5	33.5	29.2	37.3	38.1	33.5
Sleeve inseam length (wrist/armpits)	17.4	–	–	20.9	–	–
Elbow rest height (from seat)	–	8.2	7.4	–	11.6	10.6
Arm span	–	65.9	–	–	75.6	–

Table A *(Continued)* **Other Selected Body Dimensions (centimeters)**

Body part	5th Percentile			95th Percentile		
	Ground troops	Aviators	Women	Ground troops	Aviators	Women
Hand length	17.4	17.7	16.1	20.7	20.7	20.0
Palm length	9.6	10.0	9.0	11.7	11.9	10.8
Hand breadth	8.1	8.2	6.9	9.7	9.7	8.5
Foot length	24.5	24.4	22.2	29.0	29.0	26.5
Foot breadth	9.0	9.0	8.0	10.9	11.6	9.8
Head length	18.2	18.6	17.3	20.7	21.0	19.8
Head breadth	14.2	14.4	13.5	16.3	16.5	15.6
Interpupillary breadth	5.1	5.3	5.1	6.8	7.0	6.5
Ear length	5.5	5.9	4.5	6.9	7.3	6.0
	Army Aviators (*)	USAF (**)	USAF	Army Aviators	USAF	USAF
Interscye (maximum back breadth)	50.3	56.6	–	61.7	66.5	–
Waist–front length	35.7	35.7	30.5	43.4	44.2	41.4
Waist–back length	42.4	42.4	36.7	50.9	50.9	45.4
Shoulder length (neck/acromial)	13.6	14.6	13.0	17.5	18.7	16.4
Sleeve length (wrist/spine)	82.6	85.2	74.2	94.8	96.8	85.1
Sleeve inseam length (wrist/armpits)	44.3	–	–	53.2	–	–
Elbow rest height (from seat)	–	20.9	18.7	–	29.5	26.9
Arm span	–	167.4	–	–	192.0	–

*MIL-HDBK-759 [20].
**AFSC DH 1–3 [1].
Source: Adapted from MIL-STD-1472B, notice 2, except as noted [21 in Chap. 3].

Table B Circumferences of the Human Body (inches)

Body part	5th Percentile			95th Percentile		
	Ground troops	Aviators	Women	Ground troops	Aviators	Women
Head (hat brim)	20.94	21.18	20.57	23.16	23.59	22.73
Neck	13.5	13.6	11.8	16.1	16.4	14.4
Chest	33.0	34.4	30.8	41.7	43.3	39.5
Waist	26.9	28.9	23.4	37.8	40.0	32.9
Hips	33.5	34.3	33.7	42.1	42.7	41.8
Hips (sitting)	–	38.2	34.5	–	47.0	43.6
Upper thigh	18.9	19.5	19.2	25.1	26.3	25.4
Calf	12.4	13.1	12.0	16.2	16.3	15.4
Heel/ankle	12.32	12.08	11.21	14.57	14.30	13.11
Ankle	7.6	7.9	7.4	9.9	9.7	9.2
Foot (ball)	8.9	8.9	8.2	10.8	11.0	9.6
Biceps (flexed)	10.6	11.0	9.1	14.6	14.5	12.1
Elbow	–	11.2	9.2	–	13.5	11.8
Forearm	10.3	10.4	8.7	13.0	13.0	10.8
Wrist	6.2	6.0	5.4	7.3	7.6	6.4
Hand	7.68	7.71	6.62	9.28	9.11	7.82
Trunk (shoulder/ crotch)	59.3	61.6	56.0	70.3	71.6	65.5
Arm scye (shoulder/armpit)	15.6	15.7	13.2	19.8	20.9	16.4

Table B Circumferences of the Human Body (centimeters)

Body part	5th Percentile			95th Percentile		
	Ground troops	Aviators	Women	Ground troops	Aviators	Women
Head (hat brim)	53.2	53.8	52.2	58.8	59.9	57.7
Neck	34.2	34.6	29.9	41.0	41.6	36.5
Chest	83.8	87.5	78.4	105.9	109.9	100.2
Waist	68.4	73.5	59.5	95.9	101.7	83.2
Hips	85.1	87.1	85.5	106.9	108.4	106.1
Hips (sitting)	–	97.0	87.7	–	119.3	110.8
Upper thigh	48.1	49.6	48.7	63.9	66.9	64.5
Calf	31.6	33.3	30.6	41.2	41.3	39.2
Heel/ankle	31.3	30.7	28.5	37.0	36.3	33.3
Ankle	19.3	20.0	18.7	25.2	24.8	23.3
Foot (ball)	22.5	22.6	20.8	27.4	27.0	24.5
Biceps (flexed)	27.0	27.8	23.2	37.0	36.9	30.8
Elbow	–	28.5	23.5	–	34.2	30.0
Forearm	26.1	26.3	22.2	33.1	33.1	27.5
Wrist	15.7	15.3	13.6	18.6	19.2	16.2
Hand	19.5	19.6	16.8	23.6	23.1	19.9
Trunk (shoulder/ crotch)	150.6	156.3	142.2	178.6	181.9	166.3
Arm scye (shoulder/armpit)	39.6	39.9	33.6	50.3	53.0	41.7

Source: Adapted from MIL-STD-1472B, notice 2 [21 in Chap. 3].

Table C   Detail Design of Discrete Linear Controls

Manual push button (PB)

Use in high-frequency-of-use situations, often in keyboards.

May be operated by one finger, in either a random or sequential manner, or may be operated by different fingers as data entry devices.

Surface is concave (indented) to fit finger or may have friction surface where indenting is not feasible.

Provide positive indication of activation (snap feel, click, or integral light). Touch-sensitive PBs have other feedback.

Channel or cover guard when must not be accidentally activated. May be flush-mounted, especially with audio feedback.

When adequate spacing between PBs not feasible, may provide barriers or mechanical interlocks.

Square or rectangular buttons are better for labeling.

Foot push button

Use only when hands occupied or for noncritical operations such as press-to-talk.

Actuate by toe or ball of feet (not heel); use a friction surface.

May use a pedal to aid in locating the control; positive feedback of actuation is necessary.

Keyboard

Use same as push buttons; when operated with alternate fingers, should be square to prevent slipping between buttons.

Standard arrangement of PBs for data entry. Numeric information in $3 \times 3 + 1$ matrix with zero on separate bottom row.

See MIL-STD-1280 (28) for combined alphanumeric keyboard. May have numeric keyboard to right of standard keyboard (as on word processor keyboards).

Slope should be between 15 and 25 degrees (16–17 recommended).

Table C *(Continued)*

Toggle

Use: Select two or three settings when space is limited. Excellent for check reading. Three-position toggle is suitable only when a rotary or legend switch is not feasible or when center position is off.

Orient vertically with down switched "off" unless horizontal required for functional compatibility. Snap action provides feedback.

Rocker switches and tab keys are push switches suitable for check-reading when vertically mounted.

Legend switch (backlighted push button)

Use: Same as push buttons. Function is highly visible by integral lights. Lights on and color coding provide check-reading information.

Must be legible with or without internal lighting.

A maximum of three lines of lettering is permitted.

Lamps must be replaceable from the front.

Push-pull controls

Use: Automotive hand brakes, headlight switches, vents, and similar ON/OFF functions. Because of pull-on requirement, not used for vehicle control functions, where forward is an increasing function.

Variations of the flat knob are the T-handle, modified T-handle with rounded ends, stirrup-handle, and L-handle (turn to unlock).

Table D   Detail Design of Continuous Linear Controls

Lever

Use: When a large force or displacement is involved. However, a smaller lever resembling a toggle or pencil may be used for slewing electronic equipment, on air-conditioning systems, and so forth.

Coding handles or knobs is recommended when several levers controlling different functions are grouped together. Standard aircraft control shapes exist.

Label as to function and direction of movement.

Provide limb support for making fine or continuous adjustments: wrist support for finger movements; forearm support for small hand movements; elbow support for large movements.

Lever length varies with the mechanical advantage needed. Location of control may be varied for greater force application in certain planes and directions (see Chapter Three).

Separation between two controls varies 1 in with whether they are operated in a slot with one hand or with two hands.

The joy stick is a special type of lever for multidimensional control movement. Spring-loaded displacement controls permit seeing or feeling the location. Rigid pressure controls save space since they do not displace. Displacement controls are most effective within a 90° arc.

Pedal

Use: When a large displacement or force is necessary for the legs; precision or speed is less important.

Pedal must return to null position when force removed.

Provide heel support when pedal angle is greater than 20 degrees above horizontal. A recessed heel section will aid in locating pedal and preventing foot from slipping off.

Use nonslip surface material. The surface should be at least 3 in wide and 2 in long (11–12 in for continuous usage).

Pedals operated by standing operators (if necessary) should be operable by either foot.

Maximum pedal resistance should not exceed the pressure exertible by the weakest user. It varies with whether ankle-operated or leg-operated and whether foot is resting on the pedal.

Minimum pedal travel should be increased by at least 0.5 in when heavy footgear is worn, since it is difficult to gauge pedal travel.

Maximum pedal travel is usually 2–4 in but depends upon type of action and the particular function. Minimum separation of pedals is 4.5 in (random usage).

When leg action is involved, the angle of the pedal with respect to vertical permits maximum force at about 30 degrees. When operated by ankle action, the optimum angle varies with control location. However, the foot-leg angle should never be less than 90 nor more than 130 degrees. The pedal surface should not form an angle greater than 60 degrees with the floor.

Table E   Detail Design of Discrete Rotary Controls

Rotary selector switch

Used to select 3 to 24 detented positions.

Bar-shaped knob recommended, but shape coding permitted when used in a group for different functions.

Limit to 12 positions when used without visual reference.

Numbers on scale should not be opposite one another to reduce confusion as to which end is the pointer.

Provide stops at ends of control positions, snap-action stops at positions.

Provide reference lines at each position with at least 50% contrast.

May provide key to prevent unauthorized use.

Detent thumbwheel

Used only as a compact digital control/input device (10 positions). Several thumbwheels may be used to set in numbers such as radio frequencies. Number may be on a separate counter or on the thumbwheel itself.

Use concave surfaces and/or friction area between positions.

Detent thumbwheels snap into position.

Desirable to have adjacent numbers visible to indicate direction of increase or decrease (when numbers are on the thumbwheel).

Internal illumination of counter required if display brightness less than 1 fL (3.4 cd/m^2).

Table F   Detail Design of Continuous Rotary Controls

Knob

Use: Precise adjustment of continuous variables with little force.

Moving knob on a fixed scale preferred.

No pointer on multirevolution knobs; may have lift-up handle for cranking or twirling the knob.

Pointer or dot on single-revolution knob; skirt is recommended.

May be color-, shape-, or size-coded.

Certain specific knob shapes and colors are reserved for multiturn functions; others for single-turn functions when position is not important. Those from the first group may be used for the second group, but not the reverse. When mixing shapes from two groups, certain shapes may not be used.

MS 91528 establishes shapes and colors for electronic equipment knobs but AFSC DN 1–3, subnote 3.2.1 indicates certain reservations.

Use no more than three concentric ganged knobs; use size coding when absolute tactual discrimination is needed. (1, 2, 3¼ in or 25.4, 50.8, 82.55 mm.) Larger knob controls major functions, smaller knob controls minor or low-gain functions.

Continuous thumbwheel

Use: Precise adjustment of gain or attitude control.

Pitch and roll thumbwheels are oriented in correspondence to the axis of rotation of the vehicle; yaw may be controlled by a ball-shaped thumbwheel. Forward or up movement of pitch thumbwheel causes vehicle to pitch down.

Thumbwheels may be operated with one or two hands (close together with one-hand operation).

Surfaces should be friction-coated, preferably knurled or fluted.

May be coded by location, labels, or color.

Table F *(Continued)*

Handwheel

Use: When two-hand operations required by operational forces.

May code by color, size, location, or label.

Displacement without removing hands should not exceed ±60 degrees. When maximum displacement is 120 degrees or less only the two sections of the wheel that are grasped need be provided (yoke). With larger rapid displacements, a spinner handle may be attached.

Contour molding on underside of rim aids holding; resistance varies with function.

Except for valves, the direction of movement is conventional.

Crank

Use: Multirevolutions with high rates. Larger cranks for larger forces. Permits unlimited range; may be used for precise or gross adjustments. May be used with knobs or handwheels for rapid slewing.

May be coded by location, label, or color.

Crank handles must be comfortable to grasp, must minimize slipping, and must turn freely in the shaft.

Resistance varies with size and precision requirements.

For most rapid rotation of large cranks, they should be mounted on the side of the pedestal in a vertical plane (with axis of rotation parallel to the frontal plane of the operator).

For most rapid rotation of small cranks (light loads), the cranks should be front-mounted with their axis of rotation perpendicular to (60 to 90 degrees from) the frontal plane of the operator.

When two cranks are used simultaneously, the right crank is mounted on the side and the left crank on the front (axis parallel to and perpendicular to the frontal plane of the operator respectively).

Name Index

Subject Index

548